Andean Ecology and Civilization

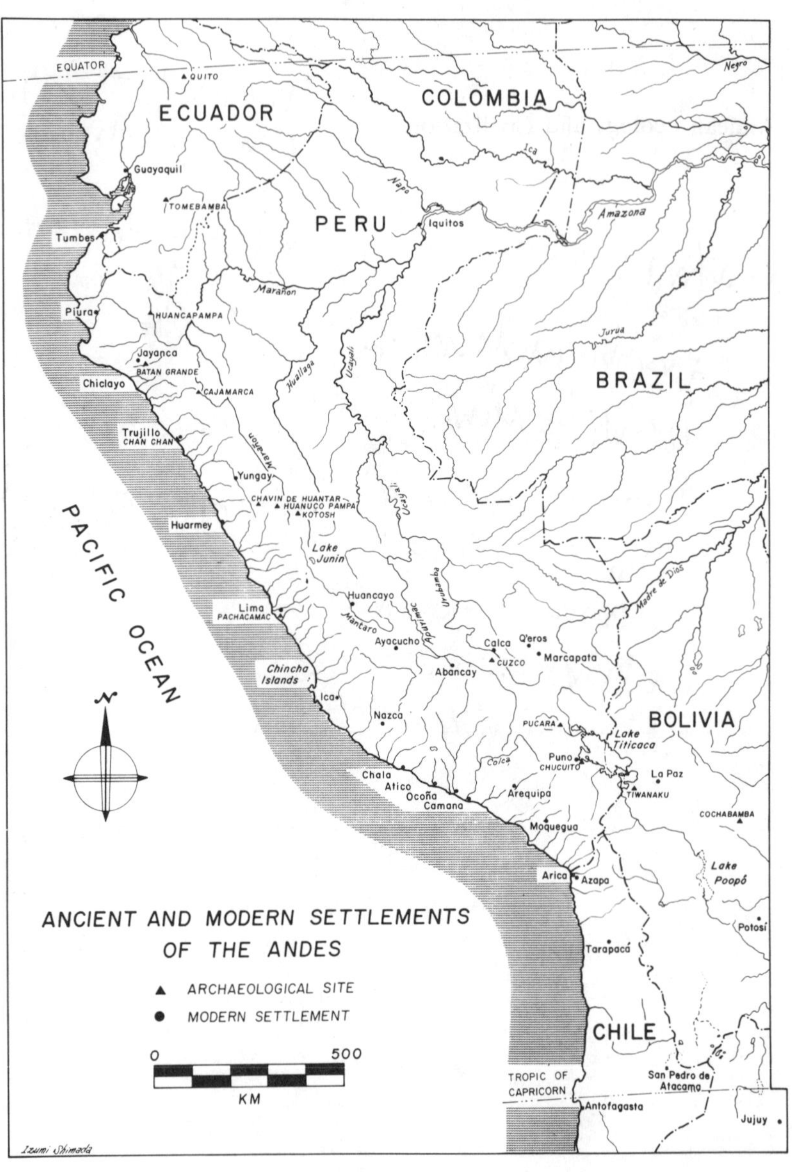
EQUATOR
QUITO
ECUADOR
COLOMBIA
Negro
Ica
Napo
Guayaquil
TOMEBAMBA
PERU
Iquitos
Amazona
Tumbes
Marañon
Piura
HUANCAPAMPA
Jurua
Jayanca
BATAN GRANDE
Chiclayo
CAJAMARCA
Huallaga
Ucayali
BRAZIL
Trujillo
CHAN CHAN
Marañon
Yungay
CHAVIN DE HUANTAR
HUANUCO PAMPA
KOTOSH
Ucayali
Huarmey
PACIFIC OCEAN
Lake Junin
Urubamba
Madre de Dios
Huancayo
Apurimac
Lima
PACHACAMAC
Mantaro
Ayacucho
Calca
Q'eros
CUZCO
Marcapata
Abancay
Chincha Islands
Ica
Nazca
PUCARA
BOLIVIA
Lake Titicaca
Puno
CHUCUITO
Colca
La Paz
Chala
Atico
Ocoña
Camana
Arequipa
TIWANAKU
COCHABAMBA
Moquegua
Lake Poopó
Arica
Azapa
Potosí
Tarapacá
ANCIENT AND MODERN SETTLEMENTS
OF THE ANDES
ARCHAEOLOGICAL SITE
MODERN SETTLEMENT
0
500
KM
CHILE
San Pedro de Atacama
TROPIC OF CAPRICORN
Antofagasta
Jujuy
Izumi Shimada

Papers from Wenner-Gren Foundation for Anthropological Research Symposium No. 91

Andean Ecology and Civilization

An Interdisciplinary Perspective on Andean Ecological Complementarity

Edited by Shozo Masuda, Izumi Shimada, and Craig Morris

UNIVERSITY OF TOKYO PRESS

Publication of this volume was assisted by a grant-in-aid for the publication of scientific research results from the Ministry of Education, Science and Culture (Japan).

ISBN 0–86008–372–1
ISBN (Japan) 4–13–066094–2 / UTP 66945

Printed in Japan

Contents

Preface

The idea for a major interdisciplinary symposium on lowland-highland interaction in the Andes was proposed during an informal meeting at the American Museum of Natural History in January of 1979 and took over four years to bring to fruition. The Taniguchi Foundation symposium held in Japan (December 19–26, 1980) dealt with a substantially similar theme and helped to bring into clearer focus various specific and general issues that we subsequently addressed in our week-long conference, Wenner-Gren Foundation for Anthropological Research Symposium No. 91: An Interdisciplinary Perspective on Andean Ecological Complementarity, held in Cedar Cove, Florida, May 18–25, 1983.

Clearly, realization of a symposium that brought together 23 scholars from five nations required careful planning, coordination and the generous support of various granting institutions. Our special gratitude to the Wenner-Gren Foundation for Anthropological Research of New York City and the Kashima Foundation of Tokyo for their grants that made this conference possible. We also thank the Ethnological Foundation of Japan, Tokyo, for their support in coordination of the participation of Japanese scholars. Their travel expenses were covered by Scientific Research Grants from the Ministry of Education of the Japanese government. We are grateful to the symposium participants for their valuable advice and assistance before and during the conference. We are particularly indebted to Ms. Lita Osmundsen, Director of Research of the Wenner-Gren Foundation, for her unfailing support and advice. The faultless logistical arrangements she made together with Nina Watson-Newhouse and Mima Jonides of the Foundation, the Merritt family of the Cedar Cove Conference Center, and others, allowed the symposium participants to maximize their time together.

This publication of the proceedings of the conference was made possible by generous grants from the Ministry of Education, Science and Culture (Publication Subvention Grant) of the Japanese government and from the Wenner-Gren Foundation. Additional support was provided by the Ethnological Foundation of Japan. In editing and, particularly, translating the manuscripts the editors were assisted by the following colleagues: Melody Shimada, Enrique Mayer, Mariana Mould de Pease, John Hyslop, Hiroe Nishizawa, Yoshio Onuki, Freda Wolf de Romero, Raffael Cavallaro, and Elizabeth Hart. During final editing in Lima, the Centro Cultural Peruano-Japonés and the Museo Amano kindly provided facilities for our use. It should be clearly noted that Mariana Mould de Pease and Ana María Soldi served as rapporteurs, and their transcription of the discussion during the conference proved valuable in subsequent revision of manuscripts and preparation of the Introduction contained in this volume. They also provided many helpful comments during the conference and editing process. Lastly, our sincere thanks to Kazuhiko Kurata and the staff of the University of Tokyo Press for their patience and efforts in the preparation of this volume.

The Editors

List of Contributors

Alan K. Craig
Department of Geography, Florida Atlantic University, Boca Raton, Florida, U.S.A. 33431
Jorge Flores Ochoa
Departamento de Antropología, Universidad Nacional de San Antonio Abad, Cuzco, Perú; Casilla 582, Cuzco, Perú
Tatsuhiko Fujii
Research Division, National Museum of Ethnology, Senri Expo Park, Suita, Osaka, Japan 565
Olivia Harris
Department of Anthropology, Goldsmiths' College, University of London, New Cross, London, U.K., SE14 6NW
Jorge Hidalgo Lehuede
Instituto de Antropología, Universidad de Tarapacá, Arica, Chile
Catherine J. Julien
Institute of Andean Studies, P.O. Box 9307–0307, Berkeley, California, U.S.A. 94709
Hideo Kimura
Department of International Relations, Asia University, Sakai, Tokyo, Japan 180
Shozo Masuda
Department of Latin American Studies, University of Tokyo, Komaba, Meguro-ku, Tokyo, Japan 153
Enrique Mayer
Department of Anthropology, University of Illinois, Urbana, Illinois, U.S.A. 61801
Craig Morris
Department of Anthropology, American Museum of Natural History, Central Park West at 79th Street, New York City, New York, U.S.A. 10024

Elías J. Mujica
Instituto Andino de Estudios Arqueológicos, Apartado 11279, Lima 14, Perú
John V. Murra
Department of Anthropology, Cornell University, Ithaca, New York, U.S.A. 14853
Yoshio Onuki
Department of Cultural Anthropology, University of Tokyo, Hongo, Bunkyo-ku, Tokyo, Japan 151
Franklin Pease G. Y.
Departamento de Letras y Ciencias, Pontificia Universidad Católica del Perú, Lima 21, Perú
Susan Ramírez
Department of History, DePaul University, 2323 North Seminary Avenue, Chicago, Illinois, U.S.A. 60614
María Rostworowski de Diez Canseco
Instituto de Estudios Peruanos, Horacio Urteaga 694, Lima 11, Perú
Frank Salomon
Department of Anthropology, University of Wisconsin, Madison, Wisconsin, U.S.A. 53706
Richard P. Schaedel
Department of Anthropology, University of Texas, Austin, Texas, U.S.A. 78712
Izumi Shimada
Department of Anthropology, Harvard University, Cambridge, Massachusetts, U.S.A. 02138
Hiroyasu Tomoeda
Research Division, National Museum of Ethnology, Senri Expo Park, Suita, Osaka, Japan 565
Norio Yamamoto
Research Division, National Museum of Ethnology, Senri Expo Park, Suita, Osaka, Japan 565

Introduction

Izumi Shimada

General Considerations

Central Andean civilization as a whole represents the culmination of complex and continuous interplay, a *creative dynamism*, of natural and cultural factors and processes that, taken together, are without parallel. The horizontally condensed, extreme altitudinal differences created by geological peculiarities and activities, in turn, give rise to impressive environmental diversity and complexity. In addition, the climatic and economic importance of the nearby Pacific and the multi-functional character of the native camelids add up to a unique set of natural conditions (Masuda 1981: v-vi). Against the above background, the Central Andes saw the emergence of such notable cultural developments as the Inca empire or *Tawantinsuyu*, the largest native political system ever to appear in the New World, with its practice of large-scale population transplantation that significantly altered the pre-Incaic cultural landscape. The Spanish conquest of the empire and the subsequent exploitation of human and natural resources altered the course and character of the creative dynamism between man and environment in the Central Andes.

Understandably, there has been a long history of scientific research on the nature and consequences of man-environment interplay and interregional interaction in the Andes. The geographer C. Troll (1935, 1958), for example, illustrated the close association among "life zones," regional cultures, and latitudinal and longitudinal ecological variation. Many anthropological investigators were long influenced by the "Culture Area" approach and premises which were heuristically useful, but at the same time tended to impose artificial spatial boundaries and a static picture of interregional interaction. The often-heard description, the Three Worlds of the Central Andes—coast, highlands, and Amazonian jungle—oversimplifies and even misrepresents Andean Man's perception of his world, as well as his behavior in space, which is commonly much more complex and often crosscuts the boundaries of the Three Worlds.

Over the last 15 years, J. V. Murra (1968, 1972, 1975) has been instrumental in instilling a dynamic and interzonal perspective among students of Andean civilization largely through ethnohistorical studies of late prehispanic societies, such as those of the Inca and Lupaqa, which established economic and political control crosscutting major ecological zones. His work, particularly the *archipiélago vertical* explanation (see his retrospective account in the section, "Conceptual Base and Framework"), has stimulated field and archival research into lowland-highland articulation among his students and colleagues. The emerging results of these investigations have been presented at various international conferences (e.g., The Proceedings of the XLII International Congress of Americanists 1978; Collier et al. 1982; Millones and Tomoeda 1982; Murra and Wachtel 1978). Continuing research by both Andean and foreign scholars merits regularly scheduled forums where scholars can evaluate their respective and collective data and interpretations for judicious charting of future research directions, priorities, and methodologies.

Issues, Aims, and Organization of the Symposium and This Volume

Wenner-Gren Foundation Symposium No. 91, "An Interdisciplinary Perspective on Andean Ecological Complementarity," organized by the editors of these proceedings, largely focused upon geographical areas and research issues and methodologies shown to be in need of further exploration and testing in previous conferences, particularly those held in Paris and Senri, Japan.

The Wenner-Gren symposium was distinguished by its attempt to be truly (1) *diachronic*, (2) *interregional*, and (3) *interdisciplinary*. The comprehensive title of the volume reflects this intent. The conference brought together 23 Andeanists (archaeologists, ethnographers, ethnohistorians, an ecologist, and an ethnobotanist) from Chile, Great Britain, Japan, Peru, and the United States. Together they covered prehispanic to modern eras and various lowland and highland regions from Ecuador to northern Chile and from the Pacific coast to the Amazonian jungle. The basic subject matter of the symposium was a comprehensive understanding of the character, evolution, and effects of the creative dynamism between man and environment in the Central Andes (see Mayer in the section, "Ecology and Cultural Ecology"). We felt it essential that the disciplines of ecology and ethnobotany be represented (see Craig and Yamamoto in the section, "Ecology and Cultural Ecology") in addition to a broadly conceived group of anthropologists. However, in distinguishing multidisciplinary and interdisciplinary research, we emphasize the need to integrate various disciplines in all stages of their collaborative research, from formulation to implementation of research to analyses of the results. Although most of the contributions in the volume are not, strictly speaking, interdisciplinary in character, the *conference was seen as a setting for in-depth discussion of the feasibility and implementation (and for some, mid-stage assessment) of such an integrated approach.*

The area coverage reflected our basic underlying design for the conference. Nearly half of the participants represented the South-Central Andes, the circum-Lake Titicaca *altiplano* and immediately adjoining lowlands to the east and west, reflecting the data and geographic base for Murra's work and a constellation of related studies, including the continuing Japanese ethnological mission led by S. Masuda.

Anthropological studies concerned to various degrees with the organizational exigencies of the South-Central Andean ecology proliferated during the 1970s (largely stimulated by Murra's research). Consequently, we saw the divergence and over-extension of earlier concepts and explanations from their original intent and scope (Murra in this volume), as well as new productive avenues of research. For example, the *verticality* theme was explicitly or implicitly incorporated into many studies to describe, analyze, or explain an ecological reality, a subsistence strategy, historic pattern, or model of cosmological or social organization. Others, working in areas where the modern market economy and entrepreneurial opportunities have made significant inroads, have found verticality to be of a limited value as a descriptive, analytical or explanatory tool. These cases are likely to represent, however, destructured, pale reflections of earlier situations. Murra (in this volume) has been concerned with the culminating achievements of Andean civilization, late prehispanic state-level societies and their articulation with the environment.

The term *verticality*—which has been over-used (Mujica in this volume) and presents a polarized, rigid view of the environment and its management—is minimized in this volume in favor of the more comprehensive and flexible phrase "ecological complementarity." Just as there is a diverse range of ecological tiers along the vertical dimension, a similar range of variation may be found horizontally. The latter phrase subsumes simultaneous control or access by a single ethnic group of horizontally and/or vertically dispersed ecological and production zones. Given the complexity and diversity of the Andean ecology, there is a very wide range of complementary permutations in time and space for ethnic groups with different organizational capabilities. *Our task is to identify those permutations that have been exploited and the associated institutions, as well as explain the natural and cultural factors that gave rise to those particular choices.* In his 1972 publication, Murra provided some answers and directions to follow in dealing with the above task.

By taking advantage of recent concentrated research efforts in the South-Central Andes, *we aim at further testing and elaboration of Murra's archipiélago vertical, as well as a comprehensive treatment of the task defined above.* More specifically, we are interested in documentation of the cultural (including ideological) and natural conditions associated with specific forms of ecological complementarity. Also, detailed case studies of internal structures and dynamics within the *islas* of the vertical archipelago (including native-colonist relationships) are necessary (see Hidalgo, Julien, Morris, Pease). An additional concern is the transformation and continuing viability of the vertical archipelago (the system as a whole and individual components such as *kurakas*) during the Incaic, Colonial, Republican, and modern eras (see Flores, Harris, Hidalgo, Julien, Masuda, Morris, Pease). What have been the most enduring aspects of traditional forms of ecological complementarity? What can be said of the past and future of present-day situations? What resources have been the subjects of prehistoric and historic ecological complementarity? These questions and issues, some of which were already raised by Murra in his article "Limits and Limitations of the Vertical Archipelago in the Andes" (reprinted here) underlie contributions in the "Ecological Complementarity in the South-Central and Southern Andes" section.

The "Limits and Limitations" article already alluded to the questionable applicability of the vertical archipelago in North Peru. Murra closed this article with the observation that "the characteristics and regional variations, the limits and limitations of the vertical archipelago model are open for discussion." In fact, recent ethnohistorical studies (Oberem 1978; Salomon 1978) in Ecuador have defined the northern limits. In addition, archaeological and ethnohistorical research on the North and Central Coasts (Dillehay 1979; Netherly 1978; Rostworowski 1970, 1975, 1977; Shimada 1982) point to the presence of other forms of ecological complementarity, such as "resource sharing," "horizontal archipelago," and "long-distance maritime exchange," that deserve further attention. Thus, the five papers presented in the section "Variations in the North: Comparative Perspectives," reflect another basic aim of the conference and the book: *testing of the applicability of the vertical archipelago model and documentation of other forms of ecological complementarity and their underlying cultural and ecological conditions in and outside of the South-Central Andes.*

With prevalence of an "extended" vertical ecology in north Peru (Brush 1976), what sort of structural modifications to the vertical archipelago do we see—if, indeed, it existed (see Onuki, Rostworowski, Schaedel)? Together with extended verticality, what sort of effects did the impressive demographic and economic growth that characterized the fertile, large North Coastal valleys have on coast-highland interaction (see Ramírez, Rostworowski, Schaedel, Shimada)? What resources were sought on the coast and highlands (Onuki, Shimada)? These questions and those already described earlier form the basis of the papers and attendant discussion in this section.

Contributions by H. Kimura and C. Morris, though not readily subsumed within the geographical organization of the conference and book, have topical relevance to numerous papers.[1] From the vantage of Amazonian ethnographies and alliance theory, Kimura presents a broad analysis of Andean exchange. Morris explores how the structure and organization of the Inca empire may have been shaped by the principle of ecological complementarity and the developmental implications that arise from this. His paper has direct bearing on another basic theoretical interest of the conference and volume: *the relationship between the degree and nature of sociopolitical organization and the character of the associated forms of ecological complementarity*, an issue discussed by Flores, Mayer, Mujica, Murra, Salomon, Schaedel, and Shimada, among others.

The final two papers by R. P. Schaedel and F. Salomon critically assess the varied forms and causes of ecological complementarity presented at the conference and *elucidate future research tasks and directions*, the latter being the last basic aim of the symposium. Salomon presents a cogent picture of interrelationships among the contributed papers and identifies various common themes and concerns, some of which diverge from our basic questions and aims. These differences are not unexpected when 23 scholars with different intellectual backgrounds and spatial, temporal, and topical interests are brought together.

The remaining portion of this introduction characterizes the basic problematical issues, consensus, and achievements (intended or unintended) that are represented in this volume.[2]

Achievements, Consensus, and Problematical Issues

We should first note the difficulty and debate surrounding the relative merits and correspondence between native and imposed (Spanish and scientific) terms and classifications (see Craig and Pease in this volume; also Ramírez 1981, 1982). The *Ocho Regiones Naturales* that are said to closely correspond to indigenous geographical divisions (Pulgar n.d.: 14–15) are widely employed in this book (e.g., Flores, Harris, Onuki, Yamamoto). Yet, the divisions are too often presented or treated as *spatially and temporally invariable*, in spite of increasing documentation of the flexible nature of their boundaries (Mayer) and the dynamic nature of the environment (e.g., gradual post-glacial desiccation, sand-dune movement, coastal uplift, El Niño and associated rains and floods) and long-term impacts of human activities (field burning, overgrazing, deforestation; see Craig, Shimada, Yamamoto; also Rostworowski 1981). Expansion (e.g., following the 1983 El Niño) and shrinkage of chapparal or herbaceous/shrubby type *lomas* (e.g., caused by droughts) have long-term effects not only on coastal inhabitants but also on highlanders coming down to the coast with their llamas (Masuda). We must think of ecology and cultural ecology in terms of process and not as a mere label.

The same designations, such as *yunga* and *quechua* used for certain areas of the western and eastern slopes of the Andes as far south as Bolivia and as far north as northernmost Peru, seem to belie the considerable ecological variability that exists in reality among the designated zones. The differences in views and data on *yunga* and *quechua* utilization in dispersed regions of the eastern and western slopes presented by Flores, Harris, Mayer, Onuki, Yamamoto, and others suggest the suspected variability indeed has corresponding variability in cultural uses and perceptions. Clearly, the nature and degree of correspondence between emic and etic perception and description of Andean ecology and environment deserves further refinement. In general, the critical review of ecological and geographical literature by Craig makes us aware of the tenuous and limited nature of our knowledge of Andean ecology and environment. The need for improved communication and collaboration between anthropologists and historians, on the one hand, and environmental scientists, on the other, is apparent. Masuda's study of marine algae (*cochayuyo*) collectors from the *altiplano*, for example, has greatly benefited from the input of marine biologists and botanists investigating algae and *lomas* (Craig). One wonders whether activities such as guano and *cochayuyo* collection involving llama caravans down to the coast might have been combined. If not, one still needs to explore why the activities were carried out independently.

At the same time, the volume contains a number of papers that present what Shimada calls a "holistic" perspective of the key resources of Andean civilization, i.e., comprehensive understanding of the cultural and natural features of the resources, including their physical locations, intrinsic and prescribed qualities (cultural perception and value), procurement strategies, processing or manufacturing technologies, and consumption or use patterns. Julien, Masuda, and Shimada offer such a perspective on guano, *cochayuyo*, and arsenical copper, respectively. As Morris notes, archaeology, perhaps more than any other discipline represented in the symposium, has the potential and task of pursuing this perspective. Together with various articles contained in *La Tecnología en el Mundo Andino* (Lechtman and Soldi 1981), we now have a relatively complete picture of a respectable number of key Andean resources. It is apparent that investigation of productive organizations (whether household, village [Mayer], or state level [Morris and Murra]) must go hand in hand with a holistic perspective of key resources. Only with advances on both fronts can we expect to achieve a satisfactory understanding of Andean ecological complementarity. It is encouraging to see that some participants in the symposium have independently or in concert examined different aspects of certain key resources to produce a relatively complete picture. Consider, for example, the case of guano discussed by Craig and Julien. Masuda's discussion of *cochayuyo* is effectively complemented by Flores' observations on its use and value in areas near Cuzco.

In theory, however, a holistic approach encompasses both ecological/environmental and organizational dimensions of a given ecological complementarity. An important advantage of this approach is that, because of its processual character, it forces us to define the nature of articulation between the social and economic components of a given pattern of ecological complementarity and those of the "home base." Clearly, such an approach is possible only with sustained research with a primary focus on ecological complementarity (Morris, Shimada).

In general, discussion of resources still lacks the necessary specificity (subsistence vs. nonsubsistence, raw materials vs. processed goods, seasonal vs. year-round, necessary vs. luxury goods, manpower vs. material goods, etc.). Future testing of Mujica's evolutionary model of varied forms of ecological complementarity requires such details and clarification of "sufficiency" in regard to varied types and facets of "resources." It should also be noted that *non-subsistence resources* have received little attention (see Shimada's and Schaedel's comments).

Morris emphasizes the need to closely monitor the production, distribution, and consumption of non-subsistence goods of special value such as woolen textiles, feathers, precious metals, *Spondylus* shells, coca, and *chicha* in understanding the Inca political economy and elaboration of the principles of ecological complementarity.

Similarly, Masuda reminds us of the *continuing* significance of *marine resources.* Together with Julien, who focuses on guano, Masuda reiterates the fact that Andean perception of resources extends to the Pacific and offshore islands. He laments that, although the significance of marine resources is intensely debated and researched in respect to pre-agricultural cultural developments on the coast, such interest and concern rapidly dissipate following the establishment of an agrarian life style, despite the fact that marine resources continue to this day to be an integral part of not only coastal but also highland subsistence and lifestyles. It is curious, however, that in the south *cochayuyo* is collected primarily by *altiplano* peoples. The cultural and historical factors underlying the areal extent of consumption of different marine algae deserve future attention, as their areas of use may reflect the extent of major prehistoric cultures such as the Chavín, Mochica and Chimu, in the case of northern algae, and the Tiwanaku and Wari, for the southern counterparts.

At the same time, refinement of *our* environmental perceptions and emphasis on the creative dynamism between man and environment are indicated by a multitude of terms such as production (Mayer), growing (Julien), and resource (Shimada) zones. Production and growing zones clearly refer to specific, temporally variable agricultural areas, while resource zones are more comprehensive in subsuming areas with both subsistence and non-subsistence related resources which are variably perceived and exploited by different groups. Unlike the invariable, vertically differentiated folk ecological divisions, the above terms are useful because of their flexible, dynamic, and specific character. Mayer shows that with appropriate technology and extra investment of time and energy, production of particular crops can be extended well beyond the traditional folk divisions. Similarly, in his discussion of the *Yunga* Tradition in Andean prehistory, Onuki argues that the *chala* zone on the coast has the potential to be an extension of the *yunga* zone in cultivating essentially *yunga* crops. In this context, Onuki is speaking of the *yunga* zone as a macro-Production Zone. It is important to emphasize that the papers by Mayer, Onuki, Yamamoto, and Shimada, among others, focus on *productive* techniques and organization rather than the exchange behavior and relationships that have dominated recent literature on Andean economy.

Flores reminds us that in the Peruvian Andes, it is not latitude but altitude that exercises the major influence on production activities. However, the mosaic nature of Andean cultural and natural landscapes has been largely ignored due to overwhelming emphasis on vertical zonation, and these terms may help rectify this imbalance. These designations are also applicable to situations that may vary according to the season of the year, nature and degree of labor and time investments, organizational capabilities, and cultural needs and perceptions.

Overall, however, there is much more awareness of the complexity and extent of temporal and spatial variability (including that caused by human activities) in Andean ecology and environment. There is also heightened awareness of the need for more interdisciplinary research on man-environment interplay in the Andes.

Similar interregional and temporal variability and problematical emic-etic correspondence has been noted (particularly by Pease and Ramírez) in regard to designations such as *kurakas*, *caciques*, *provincias*, *valles*, and *forasteros* that commonly appear in ethnohistorical sources. In translating various articles that were originally presented in Spanish, these problematical terms were left in their original language with a brief explanation attached whenever possible (also see the Glossary at the end of the book). Early writers were influenced by what they first encountered in northern Peru during their march toward Cuzco, and situations in the south were often viewed from this perspective. They rarely explained their usages and typically lacked adequate knowledge of the relevant situations, such as "discontinuous" or "discontiguous" territoriality or *dominio salpicado*. In fact, a detailed analysis of Andean vs. Spanish views of "discontinuous territoriality" by Ramírez provides important insights. In general, the ethnohistorical contributions in this book seem to embody healthy skepticism and caution pertaining to etic-emic relationships and terminological confusion.

The basic issue of the Andean perception and utilization of their ecology and environment also encompasses the aforementioned phenomenon of "discontinuous territoriality." This is one of the fundamental features of Murra's vertical archipelago, and a better understanding of the associated institutions and ecological features has direct bearing on the basic aims of the symposium. It is discussed to varying degrees by Harris, Hidalgo, Julien, Morris, Ramírez, and Rostworowski, among others. Discontinuous territoriality now appears to have been pervasive and to have had considerable antiquity throughout the Central and South-Central Andes (Rostworowski). It has been emphasized by ethnohistorians working primarily in the South-Central

Andes (e.g., Cock 1976; Cook 1976) but Ramírez and Rostworowski now show similar phenomena existed in North Peru during the late prehispanic and Colonial eras. Rostworowski analyzes patronyms and legends found in ethnohistorical documents and argues for pre-Incaic, dispersed, permanent populations of North Coastal (*Yunga*) and southern (*Llacuaz*) origins in the North Highlands. She argues that this phenomenon of "discontiguous territoriality" apparent in the *Visita* to Cajamarca is not a feature of a "vertical archipelago" and associated colonies. Murra (1972) posited the possibility of coastal colonies in the North Highlands during Chimu domination of the North Coast. However, Rostworowski sees these totally assimiliated foreigners installing and forming a *guaranga* within the sociopolitical system of the Cajamarca region. Did they retain their original social linkages with their "homes"? How long were they there? Could they have been the descendants of ancient colonists who established their autonomy when the coastal polity that originally established them collapsed? What functions did the discontiguous territoriality serve? Although it remains for archaeologists to verify her hypotheses on the origin, cause, and timing of the arrival of these settlers, it will be a long and difficult task (see Morris' comments). Available archaeological evidence suggests the possible presence of North Coastal population(s) from around A.D. 900–1000 (see Schaedel and Shimada; also Shimada 1982). What the archaeological evidence does suggest, on the other hand, is that North Highland population(s) concurrently established their own colonies on the North Coast (Shimada).

Ramírez effectively complements Rostworowski in providing details of pre-Incaic horizontally (and to a lesser extent, vertically) dispersed resource control patterns by regional lords or *kurakas* and their transformation under the Inca (see Julien and Pease for South-Central Andean situations) and, later, Colonial domination (Hidalgo, Julien, and Pease). Her work reinforces the point that ecological complementarity encompasses both horizontal and vertical dimensions. Ramírez also adds an important dimension to the general discussion of "discontinuous territoriality," which, she argues, was more "resource sharing" (Dillehay 1979) or "share cropping" and embodied the distinction of *dominio directo* (absolute control over the lands or some resources) and *dominio útil* (actual use or the right to sublet the lands). She suggests that non-local Indians working in a given resource zone delivered products to the proprietary lord of the zone in return for use, but did not consider themselves his subjects. Thus, she recommends the use of the term *dominio salpicado* rather than "discontinuous territoriality" as the latter implies one lord "owning," rather than "using" the resource zones of others. Determination of whether resource sharing/share cropping arrangements (as opposed to absolute control) also apply to various forms of ecological complementarity in the southern and eastern portions of the Andes remains a major future task. Also, we must ask whether Ramírez and Rostworowski are dealing with the same or different phenomena. Harris, speaking of the ethnographic situation in Northern Potosí on the eastern slopes of the Bolivian highlands, emphasizes how well embedded the discontinuous pattern of land use and occupation is in Andean social organization. She cautions at attempting to explain ". . . every case of an island inserted into the territory of a different group as diversification of resources.' "

The preceding discussion has particular importance for archaeology. Lorandi (1980) has already pointed out the possible developmental significance of conflict and tension inherent in a system of dispersed, multi-ethnic "islands" in the emergence of pan-Andean horizons (see Morris and Murra). Conversely, it seems archaeologists are too willing to assume continuous territoriality or too hasty in defining the territorial boundaries of a given state or empire on the basis of widely dispersed settlements or artifact clusters. Given the antiquity and pervasiveness of "discontinuous territoriality" or *dominio salpicado* in the Andes, the widespread tendency among archaeologists to readily demarcate a continuous territory for a given polity must be scrutinized.

On a more general level, Morris and Mujica discuss difficulties in identifying or distinguishing material expressions of various forms of ecological complementarity. Julien reminds us of the critical importance of tight chronological control, together with detailed knowledge of the structure of political authority, in reconstructing synchronous patterns of resource control. All the ethnohistorical studies (particularly Julien and Ramírez) in this volume face the difficult task of simultaneously analyzing continuities and changes among pre-Inca, Inca, and Colonial eras, a span of less than 100 years in many areas. Difficulties in differentiating superimposed changes are addressed or seen in some of the ethnohistorical contributions. Julien, for example, takes exception to the idea that organizations documented for the 1560s–70s reflect the pre-Inca past and projects a picture of pre-Inca political organization quite different from the Lupaqa view which she suspects is more of a reflection of Inca provincial structure of the circum-Lake Titicaca region (also see Julien 1982). She questions the assumption that the political organization of 1567 is a reflection of the pre-Inca past. The 1567 document from Arequipa which she scrutinizes seems to be biased toward Lupaqa and *kuraka* (regional ethnic lord) views. As a consequence, we see some significant divergences among ethnohistorians working in Arequipa (Murra 1968, 1972; Pease 1978, in this volume). This reassessment of the Lupaqa situation as the "base line" in regional reconstruction has direct bearing on one of the basic aims of the symposium, the elaboration and verification of Murra's model.

At the same time, these studies, together with a recently published valuable index of documents available in Arequipa (Masuda 1984), reveal many important documents and directions for their analysis.

The contributions dealing with the South-Central Andes make significant inroads toward delineating the southern limits of the vertical archipelago and identifying other patterns of ecological complementarity. Focusing upon archaeological data for the Pukara and Tiwanaku cultures that emerged on the northern and southern shores of Lake Titicaca, respectively, Mujica discusses the ecological and cultural conditions underlying the evolution of "indirect" and "direct" ecological complementarity, meaning exchange and direct control through permanent colonies, respectively. The former is believed to have operated during the Pukara era, while the latter that covered both eastern and western slopes of the Bolivian *altiplano* corresponds to the resource control pattern of the Tiwanaku culture. He hypothesizes that the evolution from indirect to direct complementarity stems from the interplay of a set of "permitting" and "encouraging" factors such as demographic growth, political unification of the circum-Lake Titicaca *altiplano* and associated control of the full range of the local resources, and emergence of coersive organizations. Like Julien, he emphasizes various uncontrollable natural limitations on agriculture in the *altiplano*, such as frost, flood, and drought. However, we need more detailed assessment of various agricultural intensification techniques such as ridged fields, *qochas*, and associated irrigation. The need to clarify the nature of relevant resources has already been mentioned and Schaedel also comments on the problematical political status of Pukara and its "control" of resources.

The situations described by Hidalgo, Julien, and Pease, on the other hand, represent the "vestiges" of late prehispanic large scale vertical archipelagos. Hidalgo shows that there were remnants of a system of simultaneous control of multiple resource zones, much like that described by Murra during the sixteenth to eighteenth century, at least as far south as Atacama, north Chile. His study serves as a fine jumping off point for defining the southern limits of the vertical archipelago and we may find that the limits correspond to the southern extremes of the Tiwanaku culture. Hidalgo's study also has relevance to the structural limitations of the vertical archipelago (Murra, Mayer, and Morris). The process of population dispersion and eventual severance of social ties that Hidalgo describes seems partially related to the prolonged isolation of distant colonies. This observation may also apply to the situation described by Rostworowski for *yunga* settlers in the North Highlands. In addition, the adaptability of the *kurakas* in a rapidly changing world is echoed by Julien, Pease, and Ramírez. Pease shows various strategies adopted by *kurakas* in Arequipa to retain and maximize their traditional rights, as well as grasp new opportunities of the Colonial era, and in the process reveals variability in vertical resource control patterns.

Complementing discussion of various patterns of ecological complementarity on the western slopes of the South-Central Andes is Harris's ethnographic description of ethnic territorial divisions in northern Potosí. These are vertical strips of more or less equal width but variable or indeterminate length (some extending 150 km). In theory, the altitudinal zonation found in this "extended verticality" allows each group working within the strip access to a similar or identical range of production zones and products. However, settlement and ethnic group distribution, as well as patterns of product acquisition, in some cases do not correlate well with the ecological reality. This deviation seems to be related to the uneven nature of the sociopolitical organization within each strip (unified or patchwork of *ayllus*). Here, the *kurakas*, unlike those cases discussed by Hidalgo, Julien, Pease, and Ramírez, have lost much of their traditional importance, perhaps as part of the general organizational decay since Inca times. Harris argues that the observed spatial organization, nonetheless, reflects the traditional duality of lifestyles adapted to the *puna-suni* (wool, *ch'arki*, potatoes, *chuñu*) and the valley or *likina* (maize, wood, beans, peaches, etc.) on both sides of the *taypi* (concept of mediating line or intermediate position), which corresponds to the ecotones described by Craig. Here, then, is a situation where the ecology is effectively synthesized in cognitive/ideological domain. Harris's work effectively complements the duality of *yunga* (maize-yuca) and *puna* (potato-camelids) complexes delineated by Onuki for the northern cis-Andean region (cf. Yamamoto). Their works are also complementary in terms of temporal dimensions. Both conclude that modern situations are largely decentralized or destructured versions of earlier patterns. What is needed, however, are detailed ethnohistorical studies of ecological complementarity on the eastern slopes. Wachtel's (1982) study of Inca state-sponsored large-scale maize production in Cochabamba effectively illustrates the necessity and productivity of such studies. Lastly, Harris and Onuki reiterate the importance of the intermediate zone in vertical resource control, an observation made by Mayer and Rostworowski (1977).

Earlier discussion on the contributions by Ramírez and Rostworowski, comparing with situations in the South-Central Andes, provided a glimpse of the divergence in ecological complementarity that developed in North Peru. On the basis of her ethnohistorical research, Netherly (1977) has argued that a wide variety of mechanisms of resource exploitation and control developed and were concurrently used on the late prehispanic (Chimu) North Coast. The five papers representing North Peru similarly argue for a wide range of ecological complementarity patterns. Schaedel, employing archaeological, ethnohistorical, ethnographic, and linguistic data, offers a long-term reconstruction of North Peruvian ethnic groups and their interrelationships, concluding that "we are dealing with peoples who have been in proximity for millennia with fluctuating patterns of accommodation, but with rather sharply distinct cultural traditions that belie a shared pattern of past ecological complementarity." The perspective and conclusions of Onuki, largely derived from analysis of ecological potential and limitations, show some important agreements and discrepancies with those of Schaedel. Schaedel postulates the presence of ethnic groups controlling transitional zones between coast and highland regions and perhaps playing an intermediary role between the ethnic groups of these two regions. This hypothesis deserves verification, particularly the conditions under which such groups were subsumed by either highland- or coast-based polities whose struggles to gain control over as much of the *yunga* zone as possible is seen by Onuki to have been a major developmental force in Andean prehistory. In fact, Onuki offers an important new model on the emergence of Andean plant domestication and the Formative period. Unlike other models that are bound to one of the major environmental zones of the Three Worlds of the Andes in which the particular proponents have carried out fieldwork, the *yunga* model is conceptually and geographically more fiexible and takes into account both eastern and western *yungas*. Here, the root of creative dynamism underlying plant domestication and the Chavín culture is seen in the struggle to gain access to or control as much of the *yunga* zones as possible, and not so much in the inherent qualities of any given major environmental zone.

Shimada presents a cautious discussion of an extensive Ecuadorian-Peruvian coastal maritime exchange network employing a standardized medium of exchange (*naipes* or arsenical copper sheet artifacts resembling "axe money") whose production and distribution is seen to have been under Middle Sicán state control. The ethnohistorically documented late prehispanic network linking the Ecuadorian and Peruvian

Coasts and Chincha *mercaderes* (Rostworowski 1970; Salomon 1980) are thus believed to have antecedents in the Lambayeque region. Pease's cautionary note and suggestion that the network primarily involved elite ritual exchange is reasonable in light of the differential accumulation of exotic goods and *naipes* that Shimada reports. Given the ethnohistorical indications of close and long-established North Highlands-North Coast ecological complementary as discussed earlier, the inferred participation of North Highland population(s) in a maritime exchange network is reasonable. Much like ongoing research in the Chincha region of the South Coast that is expected to shed new light on the probable involvement of *altiplano* population(s) in a maritime exchange network, the North Peruvian counterpart deserves further attention. We may find the spatial extent of Andean ecological complementarity to have been much greater than anticipated. In fact, we may have a good example of a horizontally oriented (maritime, coastwide) pattern of resource control articulating with and complementing a vertical pattern to form macro-ecological complementarity.

Overall, the North Peruvian contributions offer an internally quite coherent picture that serves as a good point of comparison. In addition, these papers fill the major gap in our knowledge left by the emphasis on ecological complementarity developed by *puna*-based societies south of Cajamarca (see Murra), on the one hand, and recent studies in the Ecuadorian highlands, on the other. In the latter area, where the *paramo* predominates, Oberem (1978) and Salomon (1980) have shown the northern limits of the vertical archipelago. We now have some understanding of the situation in the *puna-paramo* transition.

In addition, these papers seem to support the thesis that the spatial parameters, complexity, and nature of ecological complementarity are closely linked with the degree of sociopolitical integration of the populations involved and the nature of resources being sought (Shimada 1982: 183–85). Schaedel, in his "Discussion" offers a more detailed assessment of the advances and consensus (or lack of) achieved on the above issue during the symposium. Mayer also focuses his attention on the organizational forms and capacities associated with production zones. He argues that, of the various key facets of Murra's model, the political variables embodied in the phrase "maximal control" have not received the attention they deserve. He examines the internal dynamics among the three nested sociopolitical organizations of household, village, and *señorío*, or supra-village ethnic polity. The basic underlying belief here is that there is a specific Andean collective form of productive organization that is at the core of the creative dynamism between man and environment. He shows cooperation and conflict between the diverse interests of households and community to have creative effects on overall production and vertical expansion of the production zones (Lorandi 1980). Further, he argues that Andean village organization and associated production zones can accommodate the requirements of residence as well as affiliations of diverse interest groups, thus accounting for the multi-ethnicity of the "islands" described by Murra in his model. In general, Mayer elucidates the sociopolitical dimensions of Murra's model as well as elaborates Murra's "ecological tiers" by superimposing production zones on them.

Flores' study of three regions near Cuzco that are situated at different elevations and represent three levels of sociopolitical integration and assimilation into the modern urban-centered monetary/market economy effectively complements the work of Mayer. He emphasizes continuities in the traditional Andean mentality and behavior of exchange and interaction among communities located at different elevations. Flores argues that changes since the Spanish Conquest "... have modified more the form than the base of the diverse relation of interaction and vertical control among [highland] peasant communities" and that participation in modern markets is a roundabout way of getting to goods that cannot be obtained today in local barter. He asserts that the market system is "... secondary and even peripheral to the peasant economy." Data on exchange rates of varied goods presented by Flores should be compared with those of Tomoeda in determining the Andean perception of resources and the extent to which the monetary/market system has variously affected different regions.

The crucial interrelationships between sociopolitical organizations and patterns of ecological complementarity are also examined for the prehistoric situation. Shimada reconstructs the organizational requirements of metallurgical production and suggests the involvement of different levels of sociopolitical organizations for different phases and activities. Morris is concerned with the organizational exigencies associated with elaborating the principle of ecological complementarity to the level of the Inca empire.

Just as Mayer and Schaedel (in his "Discussion") emphasizes the need to examine in more depth what is meant by "control" of resources, the North Peruvian papers suggest considerable variability in its meaning. A similar range of variability in areas to the south is suggested by other papers.

The significance of llama caravans in various patterns of ecological complementarity in the South-Central Andes has been noted by various workers (e.g., Browman 1974; Inamura 1981; Lynch 1983; Masuda and Mujica in this volume) but was not adequately discussed in this symposium. Llama caravans may have had similar importance for the ecological complementarity of late prehispanic polities on the Peruvian North Coast (Shimada and Shimada, in press).

Little can be said of the situation on the eastern slopes of North Peru. Did the coastal polities have outposts on the eastern slopes? Consider Balsas de Marañon mentioned by Rostworowski. We need more long-term transect studies of the sort being carried out by Mayer and Fonseca.

Another issue that requires further discussion is the cognitive and ideological dimensions of lowland-highland interaction and ecological complementarity. Schaedel's observation that "the perceptions of how the coastal people regard themselves and their relationships with highlands and highlanders and vice versa is essential to a full discussion of the theme of this symposium" is a point well taken. We need to ask what are the basic features of the ideological superstructure that has reinforced the verticality through time, and how participants perceive functions of vertically oriented exchange.

Like Schaedel, Tomoeda argues that a full understanding of how simultaneous control of multiple niches is maintained requires that the total configuration (ecological-economic, social, and ideological dimensions) of relationships among *punaruna* (pastoralists) and *llaqtaruna* (agriculturalists of Apurímac in south Peruvian highlands) be examined. Rituals and attendant songs, as well as marriage patterns (Tomoeda and Fujii) reflect the *punaruna's* conception of the *llaqtaruna*. The herders are seen by both groups to be of lower socio-economic status and it is this mutually perceived inequality that largely sustains a "disproportionate exchange rate" in favor of the herders. The agriculturalists with their superior status are expected to be generous. The essential qualities of agricultural products such as maize and coca in herders' rituals are apparent not only in items used and consumed during the rituals but in the analogy with llamas. Tomoeda finds the *llaqtaruna* and *punaruna* share a common cosmology. Tomoeda's discussion effectively complements the paper by Yamamoto as the latter is concerned primarily with the economic-ecological dimensions of the mixed agro-pastoral society in Marcapata. It should be kept in mind that the latter is dealing with a basically self-sufficient group with control over much of the eastern slopes where communal control of land use and management is still pervasive. Perhaps more comparable is the decentralized exchange situation described by Harris. She shows some symbolic linkage between aesthetic principles found in textiles, on the one hand, and the economic and social organization of subsistence, on the other, and wonders if there are more as yet unrecognized connections. Certainly this is a line of inquiry that deserves our attention. Similarly, relationships between such dichotomized groups as *llaqtaruna* and *punaruna* or *huari* and *llacuaz* (Duviols 1973) require further investigation. In regard to the latter dichotomy, Rostworowski offers a diachronic perspective and discussion of their possible origin, as well as their perception of each other. In all these cases, we touch upon difficult issues of emic and etic perceptions and cultural understanding beyond what is possible from economic/ecological approaches.

In respect to the preceding, Kimura notes the pervasiveness and varied functions of endogamy in Andean societies. Data from the study of Tomoeda and Fujii (also Harris) that show the strong tradition of endogamy among *puna* and valley inhabitants seem to support Kimura's contention that "the economically self-sufficient social unit may make its boundaries more solid by endogamy." There are, however, sharing of and mutual respect for cosmology between *puna* herders and valley agriculturalists.

Most of the ethnohistorical and ethnographic papers in this volume take the vertical archipelago of state-level societies that formed the principal concern of Murra as the point of departure or comparison. Thus, they tend to perceive their respective situations as "destructured," "decomposed," or pale reflections of the former, highly organized system. Yet, as Morris and Murra note, the principle of ecological complementarity was being transformed under the Inca. We are fundamentally interested in the rationale of Andean Man over time and space, and what is significant and deserves our continuing attention are the internal structures and dynamics of given ecological complementarities and their overall transformation over time. Given the dynamic nature of the Andean cultural and natural landscapes, we must pause and reconsider our research priorities, particularly for the historical and modern eras. Rather than continuing to emphasize the vestigial status of earlier systems of complementarity, the creative dynamism of recent eras should be assessed on its own terms.

One major achievement of the symposium was the suggestion and documentation of the varied forms and respective components of ecological complementarity that have emerged over time and space. In this volume alone, we see the agro-pastoralism of condensed verticality on the eastern slopes (Yamamoto), contemporaneous *yunga* (maize-yuca complex) and *puna-suni* (camelids-potato complex) traditions (Harris, Onuki, Tomoeda; also Mayer, Yamamoto) possibly applicable to both eastern and western slopes, horizontal and vertical resource sharing of the cis-Andean region (Ramírez, Shimada), a long-distance maritime exchange network (Shimada), vertical movement for direct, short-term exploitation of specific resources combined with home base exchange (Masuda), and vertical archipelagos (Hidalgo, Julien, Morris, Murra, Pease), among other forms. Although almost infinite permutations of ecologically complementary patterns can be generated out of the diverse Andean ecology, only a small number of them are actually "realized." If we are speaking of economically self-sufficient ecological complementarity, the aforementioned list will be even shorter.

Complementing the above accomplishment is the in-depth understanding we have achieved of certain key Andean resources, some of which (e.g., coca, *cochayuyo*, *naipes*), in spite of localized occurrence or production, were widely distributed over time and space and may have served as a sort of standardized media of exchange.

Significant advances were also made in regard to the specification of the associated organizations and resources. Many of these forms, however, are described or inferred only in outline and still lack the details of internal dynamics. Similarly we lack sufficient understanding of the complementarity of different coterminous forms of ecological complementarity. At the same time, the emergent picture of the multiplicity of systems of ecological complementarity over time and space provides a broad context in which Murra's vertical archipelago can be properly appreciated.

Another general observation is the encouraging sign of various long-term studies, often interdisciplinary in character, that are exclusively concerned with Andean ecological complementarity, in contrast to let us say 15 years ago when much of the relevant data came out of research that was only coincidentally or partially concerned with the subjcct. The inter-regional transect study by Mayer and Fonseca is a fine example of the sort of research we need. Their data base and diachronic interests have resulted in various generalizations that are relevant and worth elaborating by related specialists working in other areas and time periods. Overall, in this volume we find more research tasks and directions defined by the symposium participants directed toward the archaeologist. Unfortunately, we do not see the converse to be the case, at least for the moment. This asymmetry may be related to the biases in current research priorities described earlier.

Clearly, we are not seeking a single best approach to the subject of ecological complementarity. During the course of the symposium, we felt a new spirit of interdisciplinary collaboration emerging. As we hope this symposium will serve as the starting point for regularly scheduled meetings on the subject, the significance of this interdisciplinary symposium can be judged in several years.

NOTES

1. The original design of the symposium included a Mesoamerican specialist for an "outsider's" perspective; other commitments of the scholars invited precluded this.

2. Some of the significant observations made by the symposium participants in the course of day-to-day discussion recorded by the rapporteurs have been incorporated into this Introduction.

REFERENCES CITED

Browman, David L.
1974 Pastoral Nomadism in the Andes. Current Anthropology 15:188–96.

Brush, Stephen
1976 Man's Use of an Andean Ecosystem. Human Ecology 4(2):147–66.

Cock, Guillermo
1976 Los Kurakas de los Collaguas: Poder Político y Poder Económico. Historia y Cultura 10: 95–118.

Collier, George A., Renato I. Rosaldo, and J. D. Wirth, eds.
1982 The Inca and Aztec States, 1400–1800: Anthropology and History. New York: Academic Press.

Cook, David N.
1976 La Visita de los Conchucos por Cristóbal Ponce de León, 1543. Historia y Cultura 10:23–45.

Dillehay, Tom
1979 Prehispanic Resource Sharing in the Central Andes. Science, 204: 24–31.

Duviols, Pierre
1973 Huari y Llacuaz. Revista del Museo Nacional, 39:153–91. Lima.

Inamura, Tetsuya
1981 Adaptación Ambiental de los Pastores Altoandinos en el Sur del Perú. *In* Estudios Etnográficos del Perú Meridional. S. Masuda, ed. pp. 65–83. Tokyo: University of Tokyo.

International Congress of Americanists
1978 Actes du XLII Congrès International des Américanistes. Paris.

Julien, Catherine J.
1982 Inca Decimal Administration in the Lake Titicaca Region. *In* The Inca and Aztec States, 1400–1800: Anthropology and History. G. A. Collier, R. I. Rosaldo, and J. D. Wirth, eds. pp. 119–51. New York: Academic Press.

Lechtman, Heather N. and Ana María Soldi, eds.
1981 Runakunap Kawsayninkupaq Rurusqankunaqa: La Tecnología en el Mundo Andino. Mexico City: Universidad Nacional Autónoma.

Lorandi, Ana María
1980 Arqueología y Economía: Hacia una Visión Totalizadora del Mundo Andino. Obra del Centenario 2:27–50. La Plata, Argentina: Museo de La Plata.

Lynch, Thomas
1983 Camelid Pastoralism and the Emergence of Tiwanaku Civilization in the South-Central Andes. World Archaeology 15:1–14.

Masuda, Shozo
1981 Introducción. *In* Estudios Etnográficos del Perú Meridional. S. Masuda, ed. pp. v-viii. Tokyo: University of Tokyo.

Masuda, Shozo, ed.
1984 Contribuciones a los Estudios de los Andes Centrales. Tokyo: University of Tokyo.

Millones, Luis and Hiroyasu Tomoeda, eds.
1982 El Hombre y su Ambiente en los Andes Centrales. Senri Ethnological Studies 10. Senri: National Museum of Ethnology.

Murra, John V.
1968 An Aymara Kingdom in 1567. Ethnohistory 15:115–51.
1972 El Control Vertical de un Máximo de Pisos Ecológicos en la Economía de de las Sociedades Andinas. *In* Iñigo Ortiz de Zúñiga, Visita de la Provincia de León de Huánuco en 1562. Tomo 2, J. V. Murra, ed. pp. 429–76. Huánuco, Perú: Universidad Nacional Hermilio Valdizán.
1975 Formaciones Económicas y Políticas del Mundo Andino. Lima: Instituto de Estudios Peruanos.

Murra, John V. and Nathan Wachtel
1978 Anthropologie Historique des Sociétés Andines. A special issue of Annales 33 (5–6): 889–94.

Netherly, Patricia
1977 Local Level Lords on the North Coast of Peru. Ann Arbor: University Microfilms International.

Oberem, Udo
1978 El Acceso a Recursos Naturales de Diferentes Ecologías en la Sierra Ecuatoriana. Actes du XLII Congrès International des Américanistes 4: 51–64. Paris.

Pease G.Y., Franklin
1978 Del Tawantinsuyu a la Historia del Perú. Lima: Instituto de Estudios Peruanos.

Pulgar Vidal, Javier
n.d. Las Ocho Regiones Naturales del Perú. Lima: Editorial Universo.

Ramírez, Susan
1981 La Organización Económica de la Costa Norte: Un Análisis Pre-

liminar del Período Prehispánico Tardío. *In* Ethnohistoría y Antropología Andina. Amalia Castelli, M. Koth de Paredes, and M. Mould de Pease, eds. pp. 281–97. Lima: Museo Nacional de Historia.

1982 Retainers of the Lords or Merchants: A Case of Mistaken Identity. *In* El Hombre y su Ambiente en los Andes Centrales. L. Millones and H. Tomoeda, eds. pp. 123–36. Senri Ethnological Studies 10. Senri: National Museum of Ethnology.

Rostworowski, María

1970 Mercaderes del Valle de Chincha en la Época Prehispánica: Un Documento y Unos Comentarios. Revista Española de Antropología Americana 5:135–78.

1975 Pescadores, Artesanos y Mercaderes Costeños en el Perú Prehispánico. Revista del Museo Nacional 41:311–49.

1977 Etnía y Sociedad: Costa Peruana Prehispánica. Lima: Instituto de Estudios Peruanos.

1981 Recursos Naturales Renovables y Pesca, Siglos XVI y XVII. Lima: Instituto de Estudios Peruanos.

Salomon, Frank

1980 Los Señores Etnicos de Quito en la Época de los Incas. Otavalo, Ecuador: Instituto Otavaleño de Antropología.

Shimada, Izumi

1982 Horizontal Archipelago and Coast-Highland Interaction in North Peru: Archaeological Models. *In* El Hombre y su Ambiente en los Andes Centrales. L. Millones and H. Tomoeda, eds. pp. 137–210. Senri Ethnological Studies 10. Senri: National Museum of Ethnology.

Shimada, Melody and Izumi Shimada

In press Prehistoric Llama Breeding and Herding on the North Coast of Peru. American Antiquity 50.

Troll, Carl

1935 Los Fundamentos Geográficos de las Civilizaciones Andinas y del Imperio Incaico. Revista de la Universidad de Arequipa 9:129–82.

1958 Las Culturas Superiores Andinas y el Medio Geográfico. Revista del Instituto Geográfico 5:3–48.

Wachtel, Nathan

1982 The *Mitimas* of the Cochabamba Valley: The Colonization Policy of Huayna Capac. *In* The Inca and Aztec States, 1400–1800: Anthropology and History. G. A. Collier, R. I. Rosaldo, and J. D. Wirth, eds. pp. 199–235. New York: Academic Press.

I

Conceptual Base and Framework

The first two papers by J. V. Murra together offer a helpful retrospective as well as prospective view of research on Andean ecological complementarity that owes so much to his "vertical archipelago" explanation. The first is retrospective in two senses: it briefly traces Murra's *personal* effort to elucidate various dimensions of Andean ecological complementarity, as a cultural "ideal," a major *organizational achievement*, and a set of interwoven *productive mechanisms*; second, it offers a critical evaluation of the achievements (or lack of) and directions of recent studies on the same subject.

In regard to the first point, more explicit statements began appearing in print in the 1960s. The first paper also outlines his own research approach, priorities, and tasks, such as an in-depth examination of the "fate of ecological complementarity" under *Tawantinsuyu.* In this regard, C. Morris in this volume presents some complementary observations. Murra continues to emphasize research on the *culminating achievements* of Central Andean *puna*-based societies and polities before the Spanish conquest. His temporal framework, otherwise, is not clearly specified. He assesses the relevance of many ethnographic and ethnological studies in terms of documentation of the "moraines" of old archipelagos and other indications of the durability and functioning of traditional Andean patterns.

In regard to the second point, Murra offers a mixed assessment of recent research efforts. Relatively few studies are seen to have followed Murra's basic intent and interests, which are clarified in his papers that follow. On the other hand, the divergence of many recent studies (particularly those by archaeologists) from his expectations may also reflect the complexity and variability of Andean ecological complementarity over time and space and the still inadequate data base and field methodologies. Many of the papers contained in this volume, in fact, manifest this divergence and/or testify to these difficulties.

1

"El Archipiélago Vertical" Revisited

John V. Murra

I

Ecological complementarity, the simultaneous control by a single ethnic group of several geographically dispersed ecological tiers, was an attempt to explain the achievements of the pre-1532 Andean world.

With the passing of time it became the kind of suggestion which seems obvious and in the public domain. In the 12 years since I offered this explanation, its origins and antecedents have come under close scrutiny while other students have attempted to apply it to colonial societies and even to contemporary ones. While continuities in the Andean world are so pervasive as to make such applications attractive, I would like to take advantage of this meeting to re-state my original intention: given the scattered geographical distribution of Andean polities, how does one explain that for centuries and perhaps millennia, the seat of power and the highest demographic density in the pre-European Andes are found at altitudes above 3,400 meters?

Some characteristics of these very high ecological floors must have seemed attractive early in Andean history—to herding polities, for example (Flores 1968, 1977). Another consideration would be the efficient defensibility of human settlements in the *cordilleras* during periods of *awqa runa*, described by Waman Puma as times of continuous warfare ([1615], 1980: 63–65; Hyslop 1979). I do, however, think that such rational deductions pale when confronted with the central phenomenon which originally attracted our attention: in pre-industrial societies, dense populations are always an indication of success, but how can such density be achieved in *puna* conditions? This puzzled the original European observers and remains unexplained for their modern descendants, even when they apply the most modern technical know-how.

The answers seem to lie in the high productivity of Andean economies and not of any single region or zone. Still, the *puna* does have advantages invisible to the European eye: here, very early, the inhabitants "domesticated" the cold, thus enabling them to process the many varieties of *ch'uñu* and *ch'arki* which allowed massive storage of such food for macroeconomic and not merely peasant uses.

It would be difficult to exaggerate the significance of storage as the key aspect of highland economies in the Andes, particularly if we recall that, unlike Meso-America (Katz 1972), here we do not have an oral tradition of famines in historical times. In more recent but still pre-European times storage as high state policy (Morris 1981) is, it seems to me, intimately linked to the absence in the Andes of marketplaces or *pochteca*-like merchants (Sahagún [1547–77, 1956]: book ix). Neither was there tribute-in-kind. The task before us is to describe these "absences" in other than negative terms: if there was no tribute in archipelagic economies, what did the revenues of the authorities consist of? And if there were no market places, nor traders, how were exchanges made?

For many observers, such linking of ecological complementarity to the questions above is neither evident, nor indispensable. Twelve years later, I must admit that research has not followed the path that seemed to me to be the most promising. There has been more interest in delimiting the reach of complementarity, an endeavor in which I myself participated. Already in 1973, in a working paper read in Arica (Murra 1976, 1978), I indicated that there were regions considered Andean today but where before 1532 we do not find long-distance archipelagos and where exchanges were indeed in the hands of professionals (Oberem 1978; Salomon 1980). It has also been claimed that societies with coastal nuclei such as those analyzed in cases 2 and 4 of the 1972 article, would have rather different forms of organization (Rostworowski 1977, 1978). Additional geographical limits and structural limitations have also been suggested by research undertaken during these twelve years. I imagine that such efforts will continue as we become more familiar with the range of ethnic formations and the varied conditions of their development.

A recent thesis argues that only coercion kept people at that altitude: force prevented Andean peoples from getting their own share of coca leaf, hot peppers, or salt by putting them at the mercy of their lords, who, it is claimed (Bradby 1982), monopolized the traffic to the lowlands. The author does not take into account the rest of the products which were obtained through complementarity (timber, maize, meat, *wanu*, *qochayuyu*, fish, fruit), nor the fact that for centuries before the emergence of lords, Andean groups such as those at Chavín, had already achieved complementary access.

The research tactic which I personally would like to pursue would be to concentrate on the culminating achievement of the Andean world: the *puna* societies south of Cajamarca and north of Jujuy where before 1532 there flourished Chavín and Wari, Cusco and Tiwanaku, the Lupaqa and the Yaru, the Charka and the Chanka. Ethnic groups and polities emerged in this region in whose success complementary access played a decisive role.

II

Given such a task, I think it is useful to recall that the greater part of information regarding productive activities and exchange which had to be joined to suggest Andean ecological complementarity were already in hand before 1972, when I prepared and published the now-familiar essay. I wrote it for a six-week seminar brought together by Angel Palerm to compare Andean and Meso-American civilizations.

Already in 1923–24 Hermann Trimborn and, in 1928, Louis Baudin had at their fingertips most of the same data (although most of the administrative inspections of the 1560s had not yet been published). Both scholars were aware that controlled exchanges took place between diverse geographical regions. In fact, one of them refers to "vertical trade." Such a characterization is not an error of fact, but rather of interpretation. It was commonplace at that time in the history of anthropology to confuse the many kinds of exchange which are not commercial with trade (see the book honoring Sir Moses Finley, 1983).

Beyond Trimborn and Baudin, I can think of at least one other, independent analysis which prior to 1972 took into consideration the existence and importance of complementarity in the Andes, that of Ramiro Condarco Morales in his *El escenario andino y el hombre* (La Paz 1970–71). In the last chapter Condarco speaks of *grandes zonas simbióticas* which permit macro-adaptations. The complementarity is achieved by way of physical occupations:

> . . . las zonas simbióticas estructuradas desde la altiplanicie o desde los valles microtérmicos con zonas de ocupación situadas a ambos lados de los Andes, es decir: en la costa y la montaña. . . fueron las más importantes de todas, puesto que crearon "zonas transversales de complementación" primariamente aisladas, en orden de sucesión longitudinal, pero contínuamente extendidas unas tras otras a lo

largo de los Andes Centrales. . . En los factores de solidaridad creados por tales procesos de interrelación, radica en gran parte la base de la total unificación social centroandina.

Así, a la macroadaptación predominante a lo largo de las zonas transversas de complementación, fiscalizadas desde las tierras altas. . . sobrevino a la postre, un proceso de sobre-macroadaptación. . . en sentido de las longitudes, proceso que tuvo la virtud de unir las zonas simbióticas transversas relativamente aisladas en un todo socio-político unificado, donde las bases ecológicas y económicas. . . . fueron la base o el secreto de la constitución de las grandes estructuras políticas, especialmente encarnadas por Tiwanaku o el Imperio Incaico. (1970–71: p. 554; 1978: p. 69)

Alas, I discovered this work only in 1975, when I was doing research in the Archivo Nacional of Sucre. Neither had Condarco Morales seen the inspection protocol of Garci Diez de San Miguel ([1967] 1964), which would have provided him with excellent evidence.

III

I now return to the chronicle of my own efforts. In 1964, while evaluating the *visita* of the Lupaqa, I referred to their simultaneous use of diverse and dispersed ecological tiers. A more formal effort, in English, was published in the journal *Ethnohistory*, in 1968. But only in 1972 when preparing for the comparative seminar organized by Angel Palerm, did I decide that the moment had come to put down on paper my intuitions in certain detail. I realized that in Mexico I could receive the double benefit of commentaries by the Meso-American participants as well as of colleagues coming from the Andean republics. Among these I would like to mention Jorge Flores Ochoa, Jorge Hidalgo, Luis G. Lumbreras, Agustín Llagostera, Udo Oberem, Franklin Pease, María Rostworowski, and Nathan Wachtel.

When I arrived in Mexico, the essay was lacking only the final part—that which dealt with the fate of the archipelago under Cusco rule. During the remaining days before the seminar began, I tried to enumerate the structural changes imposed by Cusco during the period immediately preceding the cataclysm of 1532. If we consider the importance of this theme (see chapter 8 of Murra [1955] 1980), this last part of the essay remained brief and inadequate. In the version I am preparing for publication by the Instituto de Estudios Peruanos I intend to devote a much larger and more detailed analysis to the fate of ecological complementarity when Tawantinsuyu eroded its significance for its own state purposes.

Perhaps a final observation, part of this historical account. The essay I wrote in 1972 in Spanish was meant for an Andean audience familiar with the geography and with previous efforts to understand the achievements of Andean man. My main aim was to offer a contribution to the ongoing debate about the Andean past. I published it for the first time in the second volume of the administrative *visita* of Iñigo Ortiz ([1562] 1967, 1972). There was no English version of this essay until Gabriel and Chavín Escobar translated it in 1981, which version has remained unpublished.

IV

Among the elaborations which have been offered since 1972, some seem closer to my original aim; for example, the analysis offered by Ana María Lorandi (1980) in her "Arqueología y etnohistoria: hacia una visión totalizadora del mundo andino." In it she went beyond where I had dared to tread in 1972. She suggests that the tensions and conflicts over hegemony inherent to a system of dispersed, multi-ethnic "islands" such as I had described "could have been at the root of the emergence of pan-Andean horizons" (p. 29). I feel that the elaborate way in which she has expanded mere hints in the 1972 text and how she linked the discussion to Wendell C. Bennett's "co-tradition" deserve the attention of the archaeologists.

In January 1983, during a symposium dedicated to the archaeology of the Atacama region organized by Agustín Llagostera and Lautaro Núñez, scholars from all five of the Andean republics could take for granted the existence of "archipelagos" linking Qollasuyu with the coast and with the eastern lowlands. Much attention at this meeting was devoted to specifying the indicators which would allow the archaeologist to distinguish outlying "islands" settled on a permanent basis by Aymara polities from other kinds of highland manifestations. For example, in the high oases (at 2,400 meters), where our meeting took place, there are Formative, Tiwanaku, and Inka remains everywhere. But in that region, south of the Tropic of Capricorn, the relations between the *altiplano* and the oases were not necessarily that of "archipelagos."

We dedicated several days to efforts of clarification: how to recognize the archaeological differences between the several kinds of articulation and their indicators. Listening to the debate, I learned a lot about the kinds of written sources we must try to provide to facilitate the work of archaeologists. The historical references for Lipes and Jujuy which they were asking for are scarcer than those for the Q'ara-q'ara or for the Killaka further north, but they do exist. I find comfort in the fact that in 1983 archaeologists were willing to contemplate research which they had rejected in 1973 (see Murra 1979).

Finally, the hypothesis of the archipelago permits us to return to the fruitful question of Gerardo Reichel-Dolmatoff, formulated in 1959 at México. There Reichel asked himself why there were no kingdoms in the Northern Andes such as had arisen in the Central and Southern Andes. Contrasting the *señoríos* of the *páramo* with those of the *puna*, Reichel says:

> . . . the social units conducting warfare were based on local ecologies and techniques. This strengthened the regional character of small chiefdoms whose political power was constantly threatened. . . .
>
> Although there was a notable cultural advance over the centuries . . . population pressure did not force them into a more intensified agricultural system, nor did it propel them towards more far-reaching political controls as happened in the Andean cultures. What happened here were migrations and local but highly destructive wars. . . .
>
> Although some [of the *páramo* inhabitants] created local cultures of a rather complex kind, the discontinuities in such factors as settlements, population density, the location of favorable geographic environments . . . inhibited greater advances . . . . (1961: pp. 88–89)

In this context, perhaps it would be useful to consider once more the comments of Troll (1931) who, in studying the history of highland societies south of Panama, warned us that there was a profound difference between *puna* and *páramo* conditions. The endemic wars, the "discontinuities" of which Reichel speaks, were inhibitory factors common to both zones. To clarify the differences between the two we have to realize that what was "inhibitory" in one highland situation could be perceived as just its opposite in another: the multiplicity of contrasting environments, relatively close to the *puna*, became an advantage, a potential source of wealth, rather than an inhibitory factor. The decisive fact was the opportunities provided by the *puna* (*ch'uñu*, *ch'arki*, long-term state storage) which remained unavailable on the *páramos*.

V

I would not want to close these retrospective observations without commenting on the great effort made by ethnologists to check the moraines of the archipelago in our time.

It is remarkable that, in spite of the pressures exercised against everything Andean and those who created them during the 450 years of colonial and republican regimes, we still encounter among highland peasants a preference for locating their fields in complementary fashion, on several different ecological tiers, sometimes located several days' walk from the center of population. There is well-documented, contemporary evidence of sizeable groups who have managed to maintain their ethnic self-awareness, along with access to their outliers in the lowlands.

It could be psychologically reassuring to catalogue the places and populations where the colonial and republican efforts to create *reducciones* and *comunidades* have been unsuccessful. The agrarian reform act of 1953 in Bolivia declared lowland outliers still in the hands of highland peasants to be "estates", thus liable to confiscation and alienation under the law. However, as Harris (1978) and Platt (1982) have shown, there are regions where *altiplano* polities have continued to practice *doble domicilio* throughout the nineteenth century and continued to defend their rights to live thus until today. Harris has shown that certain age groups are more likely to exercise their traditional rights to faraway fields. Platt has collected evidence to document the tax and legal maneuvers which the inhabitants of northern Potosí have used in order to protect their *valladas*.

What we perceive as progress in this field is probably tied to various factors, but one of them is, without a doubt, better ethnographic work. It is commonplace now to expect the ethnographer to have mastered one of the Andean languages. His presence and participation in the field are renewed over a decade or more; the respect for a diachronic dimension in Andean life and for the archival search for the past, are now customary (Núñez del Prado 1957, 1984; Fonseca Martel 1973; Platt 1978, 1982; Harris 1978 and in the present volume).

VI

The ethnological task has been facilitated by the fact that we no longer have to leap across the gap between 1532 and contemporary Andean life. The historical space between the two dates is slowly being filled in. The promise of an Andean history (Pease 1978, 1980) beyond that which we temporarily called ethnohistory, represents real progress. The effects of the *encomienda* and later of the *reducciones*; of the early appearance of the *hacienda* in the coca-leaf growing *yungas*; and of the Bolivian legislation aimed toward the commercialization of land—all have received monographic attention.

Such historical research verifies a gradual but continuous erosion of the sources of specifically Andean wealth. For four and a half centuries the pattern of multiple, simultaneous settlements controlled from the *puna* has been whittled away to the point where in many regions it has disappeared or its remnants can be barely discerned in a legal *reconocimiento*.

However, it is noteworthy that frequently modern exchanges follow the old caravan routes connecting parts of bygone archipelagos. César Fonseca has documented the trips of highlanders from Cauri at 3,900 meters on the Upper Marañón, who annually cross the *cordillera* to a valley called Chaupi Waranga. There, at a settlement called Yacan, the Caurinos used to control their own maize fields as recently as the beginning of this century. Even though they have lost direct control, the exchanges they engage in now are guided by *unay*-prices and remain virtually outside the money economy.

VII

Ecological complementarity continues to be an Andean ideal, in the sense that highland ethnic groups are aware of its usefulness and desirability even where they can no longer share in it. They recognize as do we, how strong the opposition to ecological complementarity being a full-fledged reality still is and has been: threatened by Tawantinsuyu, by the European colonial regimes, by the nineteenth century republics and, finally, in our time, by the laws of agrarian reform.

There is no doubt in my mind that cyclical complementarities in Andean agriculture, of the kind described by Golte (1980), had much to do with its original emergence many thousands of years ago. Archaeology has documented transhumance long before there was any agriculture in the Andes; when cultivation made its appearance, the calendrical cycle allowed the pooling and redistribution of distinct and geographically separate resources. However, as permanently inhabited outliers became the norm, the seasonal cycle could be ignored. When European institutions made permanently settled archipelagos impossible, the cultivating cycle reasserted itself, a wan, rudimentary attempt to hold on to traces of what had constituted the sources of Andean wealth.

Viewed dispassionately, ecological complementarity can be seen as a series of mechanisms which prevailed in Andean agriculture at those times when there were no marketplaces but many state-operated warehouses. The rise and fall of ecological complementarity can be plotted by archaeologists and historians. Its functioning immediately before the Late Horizon can be documented from the written sources; its modifications and re-utilization by the Cusco state are in the process of becoming an object of investigation. We understand the process of its erosion and destruction much better than its florescence.

However, we also have available to us another perception: ecological complementarity was a major human achievement, forged by Andean civilizations to handle a multiple environment, vast populations, and hence high productivity. It helps us understand the unique place of the Andean achievement in the repertory of human histories; it may even point to future possibilities.

(Translated by Freda Wolf de Romero)

REFERENCES CITED

Albó, Xavier
1979 Khitipxtansa: ¿ quienes somos ?, América Indígena 39 (3): 477–528.

Baudin, Louis
1928 L'Empire socialiste des Inkas. Paris.

Bradby, Barbara
1982 Plan, Market, and Money: A Study of Circulation in Peru. Thesis, University of Sussex.

Condarco Morales, Ramiro
1970–71 El escenario andino y el hombre. La Paz. (Early mimeo version, Oruro).
1978 Reflecciones acerca del eco-sistema vertical andino. Avances 1: 65–74.

Diez de San Miguel, Garci
[1567] 1967 Visita hecha a la provincia de Chucuito por Garci Diez de San Míguel en el año 1567. Lima: Casa de la Cultura del Peru.

Finley, Sir Moses
1983 Trade in the Ancient Economy. P. Gamsey, K. Hopkins, and C. R. Whittaker, eds. London.

Flores Ochoa, Jorge

1968 Los pastores de Paratía. Mexico: Instituto Indigenista Interamericano.

1977 Uywamichiq punarunakuna; Pastores de puna. Lima: Instituto de Estudios Peruanos.

Fonseca Martel, César

1973 Sistemas económicos andinos. Lima.

Golte, Jürgen

1980 La racionalidad de la organización andina. Lima: Instituto de Estudios Peruanos.

Harris, Olivia

1978 El parentesco y la economía vertical en el ayllu Laymi (Norte de Potosí). Avances 1: 51–64.

Hyslop, John

1979 El área Lupaca bajo el dominio incaico. Un reconocimiento arqueológico. Histórica 3 (1): 53-80.

Katz, Friedrich

1972 Pre-Columbian Civilizations. London: Weidenfeld & Nicolson.

Lorandi, Ana María

1980 Arqueología y etnohistoria: hacia una visión totalizadora del mundo andino. Obra del Centenario, t. II, pp. 27–50. Museo de La Plata, Argentina.

Morris, Craig

1981 Tecnología y organización inca del almacenamiento de víveres en la sierra. *In* Runakunap Kawsayninkupaq Rurasqankunaqa, t. I. Heather Lechtman and Ana María Soldi, eds. pp. 327–75. UNAM, México.

Murra, John V.

1964 Una apreciación etnológica de la visita. *In* Diez de San Miguel [1567], 1964: 419–44.

1968 An Aymara Kingdom in 1567. Ethnohistory 15 (2): 115–51.

1975 Formaciones económicas y politícas en el mundo andino. Lima: Instituto de Estudios Peruanos.

[1973], 1976 Los límites y las limitaciones del 'archipiélago vertical' en los Andes. *In* Homenaje a Gustavo Le Paige. pp. 141–46. Antofagasta: Universidad del Norte.

1978 Los límites y limitaciones del 'archipiélago vertical' en los Andes. Avances 1: 75–80.

1979 Los olleros del Inka: hacia una historia y arqueología del Qollasuyu. *In* Historia: problema y promesa, homenaje a Jorge Basadre, Lima.

[1955], 1980 The Economic Organization of the Inka State. Greenwich, Conn: JAI Press.

Murra, John V. and Nathan Wachtel

1978 Anthropologie Historique des Sociétés Andines, a special issue of Annales 33 (5–6): 889–94.

Núñez del Prado, Oscar

1957 El hombre y la familia: su matrimonio y organización político-social en Q'ero. Cusco.
1984 Libro homenaje al trabajo de Núñez del Prado. In Q'ero. Preparado por Jorge Flores Ochoa. Cusco.

Oberem, Udo
1978 El acceso a recursos naturales de diferentes ecologías en la sierra ecuatoriana. Actes, XLII Congrès International des Américanistes IV: 51–64.

Ortiz de Zúñiga, Iñigo
[1567] 1967 & 1972 Visita de la provincia de León de Huánuco en 1562, 2 tomos. Huánuco: Universidad Nacional Hermilio Valdizán.

Pease G. Y., Franklin
1978 Del Tawantinsuyu a la historia del Perú. Lima: Instituto de Estudios Peruanos.
1980 Relaciones entre los grupos étncios de la sierra sur y la costa: continuidades y cambios. *In* Senri Ethnological Studies, No. 10. pp. 107–22. Senri.

Platt, Tristan
1978 Symetries en mirroir. Le concept de *yanantin* chez les Macha de Bolivie. Annales 33 (5–6): 1081–107.
1982 El estado boliviano y el ayllu andino. Lima: Instituto de Estudios Peruanos.

Reichel-Dolmatoff, Gerardo
1961 Agricultural basis of the sub-Andean chiefdoms of Colombia. *In* The Evolution of Horticultural Systems in Native South America, J. Wilbert. Caracas: Sociedad de Ciencios Naturales La Salle.

Rostworowski, María
1977 Etnía y sociedad: Costa peruana prehispánica. Lima: Instituto de Estudios Peruanos.
1978 Señorios indígenas de Lima y Canta. Lima: Instituto de Estudios Peruanos.

Sahagún, Bernardino de
[1547–77] 1956 Historia General de las Cosas de Nueva España. 4 vols. México: Editorial Porrua.

Salomon, Frank
1980 Los señores étnicos de Quito en la época de los Incas. Colección Pendoneros. Otavalo: Instituto Otavaleño de Antropologia.

Trimborn, Hermann
1923–24 Der Kollektivismus der Inka. Anthropos 18–20: 579–606, 978–1000.

Troll, Carl
1931 Die geographische Grundlagen der Andinen Kulturen und des Inkareiches. Ibero-Amerikanisches Archiv 5: 258–94.

Waman Puma de Ayala, Felipe
[1615], 1980 Nueua Coronica y Buen Gobierno. México: Siglo Veinteuno.

2

The Limits and Limitations of the "Vertical Archipelago" in the Andes

John V. Murra

When the Andean civilizations are compared with those of Meso-America,[1] a group of differences appear that can be summed up as follows:

1. In the Meso-American civilizations, the incomes of the kings and the state were based (although not exclusively) on tribute extorted from the conquered ethnic groups; parallel to this, a flourishing commerce existed, moving the resources of one ecological level to others; fairs and gigantic market places facilitated exchange and macro-economic integration; a guild of professional merchants, the *pochteca*, not only organized interzonal traffic but also served the political ends of the state apparatus.

2. In contrast, there was no tribute in the Andean kingdoms; political authorities received their incomes in the form of human energy invested in the cultivation of state *papakancha*, the expansion of irrigation works, or the colonization of new environmental niches. The utilization of such energies was regulated through periodic *mit'a*, tied to demographic possibilities and a system of dual division by moieties (*saya*) and by lineages.

Although there was, no doubt, occasional trade of high mountain and low valley products, the traffic of Andean resources from one ecological tier to another was realized not through commerce but through mechanisms maximizing the reciprocal use of human energies. The pre-Columbian *mit'a* and other mechanisms of this nature merit detailed study, not only in the library or laboratory, but also in the intensive field work of archaeologists, ethnologists, and historians.

This article was first read in 1973 and published in 1976 as "Los limites y las limitaciones del 'archipiélago vertical' en los Andes" in *Homenaje al R. P. Gustavo Le Paige, S. J.*, pp. 141–46. Antofagasta, Chile. The article was translated into English by P. Dillon and first appeared in *Andean Perspective Newsletter* 2:14–19, 1978.

I

Beginning in 1964 with the description of the Lupaqa kingdom on the shores of Lake Titicaca[2] I have tried in various publications to analyze and understand the ecological aspects of Andean economic organization, to verify its presence in diverse regions of the Andean world, and to define the geographical and temporal limits beyond which such a mode of production was replaced or will eventually be substituted by others. I have offered the results of my investigation up to June 1972 in an article,[3] included in the second volume of the *visita* of Huánuco, an essay that some of you have been able to consult.

Summarizing here the "vertical archipelago" model, I will say that its essential characteristics were:

1. Each ethnic group made an effort to control a maximum of floors and ecological niches in order to take advantage of resources that, in the Andean conditions, were found only there. The largest ethnic groups like the Lupaqa could maintain possession not only of oases in Ilo, Moquegua, or Lluta,[4] but also of coca leaf plantations in the *yungas* of La Paz which were many days walk from the center of power, pasture, and the production of staples, situated on the shores of the lake.

2. Although the bulk of the population was on the *altiplano*, the ethnic authority maintained permanent colonies situated in the periphery in order to control distant resources. These ethnic "islands," separated physically from their center yet maintaining continuous social contact and trade with it, formed an archipelago, a typically Andean pattern of settlement. This trade, which permitted simultaneous access by the same population to resources very distant between them, has been called "commerce," using models from other latitudes. It has also been confused with seasonal migrations and transhumance. In fact, in the present day, in many diverse parts of the Andean world, the colonial economy, and later the capitalist, have reduced vertical archipelagos to limited relations of ritual barter or seasonal exchanges.

3. The relations existing between the center and the peripheral islands were those that are called reciprocity and redistribution in economic anthropology. This means that the domestic units devoted exclusively to the herding of camelids in the *puna*, to the cultivation of maize or the gathering of *wanu* on the coast, to timber or the harvest of coca in the *yungas* did not lose their rights to tuber and *quinua* producing lands in the center. Such rights were claimed and exercised through kinship ties maintained and periodically reaffirmed ceremonially in the settlements of origin. Although they were living

and working far from the lake, the inhabitants of the peripheral islands formed part of the same universe as those from the center, sharing a single social and economic organization.

4. One more unexpected characteristic of the peripheral islands: they were frequently shared by various *altiplano* groups. Not that there was not competition, struggle, and temporary hegemonies in order to control the entire tier. But in many situations, diverse centers found themselves sharing the resources of a valley, a coca field, or an "island" during truces, in tense but real coexistence.

5. To the extent that kingdoms grew and contained more and more numerous populations, there occurred, at least, two notable phenomena of structural change.

5a. The peripheral islands were established in more and more distant zones. Whereas the Lupaca maintained colonies in the coast and the *yungas*, *Tawantinsuyu* began to move members of these ethnic groups to much greater distances. According to Cutinbo, lord of all the Lupaca between 1550 and 1565, there were:

> Many *mitimae* Indians who were subjects of this province and were now in Cuzco, Ayaviri, Copacabana, and Chuquiabo and in many other parts even in Quito which is more than three hundred leagues from this province and in Chile because the Inca had put them [there] as *mitimaes*. (Diez de San Miguel [1564] 1964: 1700).

At such distances from the center, how could rights be maintained to *papakancha*, herds, and other strategic resources? I believe that the difficulties of exercising such rights imposed limitations or, better said, a structural modification of the model. The new relations between center and distant periphery seem more difficult to maintain through ties of kinship. It is plausible that within the mechanisms of reciprocity and redistribution, there now appeared elements of asymmetry and exploitation.

Such an assumption may suffer from ethnocentrism, given that as anthropologists we have never been able to delimit the elasticity of kinship ties. Every year the ethnology of precapitalist societies offers us new data and dimensions to document the versatility, poly-valence, and syncretic capacity of kinship tiers.

5b. The peripheral colonies are not only located at greater distances, but they also change functions: whereas small societies like the Chupaychu of Huánuco controlled productive islands producing *ch'uñu*, coca, cotton, *maiz*, and wool, such colonies could exercise other functions when the ethnic group was larger. For example, in addition to the clearly ecological "islands," the Lupaqa had others: in Cupi resided the potters of both Maasaa as well as those of Alasaa for all of the Lupaca; in Sunicaya resided the metallurgists from both moieties, repeating the multi-ethnic pattern already observed in (4). *Tawansinsuyu* used peripheral colonies for military and strategic ends as described in the *visita* of Iñigo Ortiz.

II

In the 1972 essay I mentioned many times the need for testing the limits of the "vertical archipelago" model, in order to understand its capacity and functions.

In (5a) above, we saw one of these limits: Upon the expansion of the population which it controlled, the growth of the power of the authorities, the increasing difficulty of exercising effective control over rights maintained at the center by the inhabitants settled in the "islands," the archipelago changes structurally. Contradictions appear between the interest of the lords and the *mitmaqkuna*; the relations of reciprocity and redistribution are weakened.

Others of these limits and limitations consist in the amputation of productive niches for the benefit of *encomenderos* in the early Colonial period, and the *haciendas*. The loss of rich but distant, and therefore difficult to control zones is frequent. In the last decades, the agencies for agrarian reform of the various republics with Andean populations have continued the process of breaking up the archipelagos and impoverishing their inhabitants, since they still have not realized the existence of Andean patterns of settlement of simultaneous exploitation of various ecological "stories" by one and the same population.

In spite of the losses of functions suffered during the last four centuries there still remain enough to suggest that their present study in the field, ethnologically, deserves high priority not only because it will allow us to comprehend the earlier mode of production, but also because it can suggest solutions for the future of Andean agriculture, a system of cultivation and uses of human energy without parallel in other latitudes.

There is another historical limit of the model: When did the archipelagos come into existence and under what circumstances? Only archaeological investigation can offer us answers. Lynch's investigation in the Callejón de Huaylas (1971) and those of T. C. Patterson and R. S. MacNeish (pers. com.) suggest that thousands of years ago transhumance and other seasonal migrations may have preceded the formation of groups such as those described in the article of 1972.

Since the aforementioned studies were undertaken in the central Andean zone, it is desirable that such inquiries be amplified, as much towards the south where the *altiplano* and *puna* form an important part of the archipelago as towards the north where *paramo* and not *puna* is found at high altitudes.

Finally, we have to face the possibility that there were conditions in the Andes that favored the formation of the vertical archipelagos and others that inhibited it. It is obvious that the lacustrine kingdoms of Titicaca could extend their islands toward the Pacific since neither in the coast nor the intermediate territories was there a nucleus of dominant opposing power. On the other hand, the Wanka kingdom of the Mantaro Valley, with a demographic density and military might comparable yet superior to that of the Lupaqa (Espinoza 1972) controlled oases on the coast, although they did have them on the edge of the forest.

In the 1972 article (pp. 444, 449, and 152–154) I made reference to María Rostworowski de Diez Canseco's doubts; she suggests that in different zones of the Central Andean coast, the model of vertical control was introduced by conquerors from the highlands (Huari or earlier), who imposed their norm. According to Rostworowski, the ethnic groups between Piura and Ica could supply themselves not only with their minimal needs but much more, by taking advantage of the rich resources of the sea and irrigation agriculture and obtaining the ceremonial and exotic products that they lacked by means of trade with the eastern jungle, the *sierra*, and other populations on the same coast. Given such a contingency, the presence of the inevitable garrisons at the intakes of the irrigation canals neither aids nor weakens our argument.

The characteristics and regional variations, and the limits and the limitations of the vertical archipelago model were open for discussion in 1973.

NOTES

1. Among the works which offer a serious comparison of this disposition I will mention Frederick Katz's recent book (1972). In July of 1971, Ecuadorian colleagues organized un Simposio de Correlaciones Antropológicas Andino-Mesoamericanas. In July and August of 1972, under the initiative of Mexican colleagues, a six week long comparative symposium on the same theme was organized at the Universidad Ibero-Americana.

2. Diez de San Miguel [1567] 1964. See also Murra 1964, 1968.

3. "El 'control vertical' de un máximo de pisos ecológicos en la economía de las sociedades andinas," in Ortiz de Zuniga [1562] II: 1972: 429–76.

4. According to Romulo Cuneo Vidal: "We see the people of Chucuito going down to the lands of Moquegua, Azapa, and Camarones, those of Acora toward Tacna, Lluta, and Codpa, and those of Pomata toward Tarata, Putina, and Sama; and, finally, those of Ilave toward Ilabaya, Ilo, and Islay." (Cited from p. 139 of the unpublished book, *History of Ancient Hereditary Cacicazgos of Southern Peru, 1535–1825*. In the possession of Mrs. Enriqueta Cuneo de Santisteban.) The seven *parcialidades* of the Lupaqa kingdom were: Chucuito, Acora, Ilave, Juli, Pomata, Yunguyo, and Zepita.

REFERENCES CITED

Espinoza Soriano, Waldemar

1972 Los Huancas, Aliados de la Conquista: Tres Informaciones Inéditas sobre la Participación Indígena en la Conquista del Perú, 1558–1560–1561. Anales Científicos 1:5–407. Huancayo: Universidad Nacional del Centro del Perú.

Katz, Friedrich

1972 Ancient American Civilizations. London: Weidenfeld & Nicolson.

Lynch, Thomas F.

1971 Preceramic Transhumance in the Callejón de Huaylas, Peru. American Antiquity 36:139–48.

Murra, John V.

1964 Una Apreciación Etnológica de la Visita. *In* Visita Hecha a La Provincia por Garci Diez de San Miguel en el Año 1567. Waldemar Espinoza Soriano, ed. pp. 419–42. Lima: Casa de la Cultura del Perú.

1968 An Aymara Kingdom in 1567. Ethnohistory 15: 115–51.

1972 El Control "Vertical" de un Máximo de Pisos Ecológicos en la Economía de las Sociedades Andinas. *In* Visita de la Provincia de León de Huánuco en 1562, Vol. 2. J. V. Murra, ed. pp. 429–76. Huánuco: Universidad Nacional Hermilio Valdizán.

II

Ecology and Cultural Ecology

This section brings together contributions from an ecologist (Craig), an ethnobotanist (Yamamoto), and an ethnographer (Mayer) who complement each other by examining Central Andean ecology and cultural ecology from different geographic bases and scales, and analytical levels. Unlike most of the remaining papers in this volume, which are restricted in data base, time period, and geographical area involved, these three articles are concerned with widespread and long-lasting cultural and/or natural features. The papers are ordered from general to specific.

Craig presents a broad characterization of the dynamic and complex Central Andean geology and ecology over the last 15,000 years, as well as a critical review of various ecological classificatory schemes in use. He provides a basis for understanding the nature and degree of correspondence between folk and scientific perceptions and descriptions of Andean ecology and environment.

Mayer's paper is based on a long-term study of Andean productive organizations found in a transect spanning the eastern and western slopes of the Andes. He is concerned with clarification of the processes and organization of "control" and "maximization" in the "expansive" or "vertical" vision of Andean peoples, a significant issue that binds together symposium participants representing varied disciplines.

Although his data base is regional and synchronic in nature, Yamamoto is concerned with the internal workings of the widespread agropastoralism that integrates the uniquely Andean components of potatoes and llamas and alpacas into a long-lasting cultural ecological system.

3

Cis-Andean Environmental Transects: Late Quaternary Ecology of Northern and Southern Peru

Alan K. Craig

Scientific interest in Andean environmental zonation began with the work of Von Humboldt (1807) who first observed distinct vegetational changes related to temperature and altitude. For the next century little progress was made despite the prodigious efforts of the Italian naturalist Antonio Raimondi (1874–1913). Peruvian and foreign botanists continued to catalog species, but it was the peripatetic Weberbauer (1911) who made the first significant move toward an ecological classification system. He inspired Herrera (1921) and other Peruvians and culminated his life's work with the well-known *El Mundo Vegetal de los Andes Peruanos* (1945). Meanwhile, MacBride (1936–1960) provided the taxonomic base for further development.

An important and innovative study of ecologic zonation was empirically designed by Holdridge (1964) who influenced his student Tosi (1960) to apply it to Peru in the form of "Life Zones." The Holdridge classification of life zones is based on long-term measurements of temperature and effective precipitation as expressed by vegetation arranged altitudinally (see Fig. 3.1; Holdridge 1964). The terminology is systematic, dominantly botanical, and applicable worldwide. Other environmentally oriented classification systems produced by Drewes and Drewes (1966) and Troll (1968) have been used in Peru but have not gained wide acceptance. Perhaps the most promising of the truly ecologic studies in Peru were those made by Hans-Wilhelm and Maria Koepcke (1951, 1952, 1953, 1954) whose brilliant careers were unfortunately cut short by tragedy.

As a result, we do not have any ecological zonation of Peru based on the biota; Holdridge's "Life Zones" are actually distinguished solely on the basis of their more easily observable representative vegetation. In other words, wildlife is missing from all these botanically oriented schemes and it is therefore incorrect to refer to them as ecological systems. Hopefully, we may someday arrive at a genuinely representa-

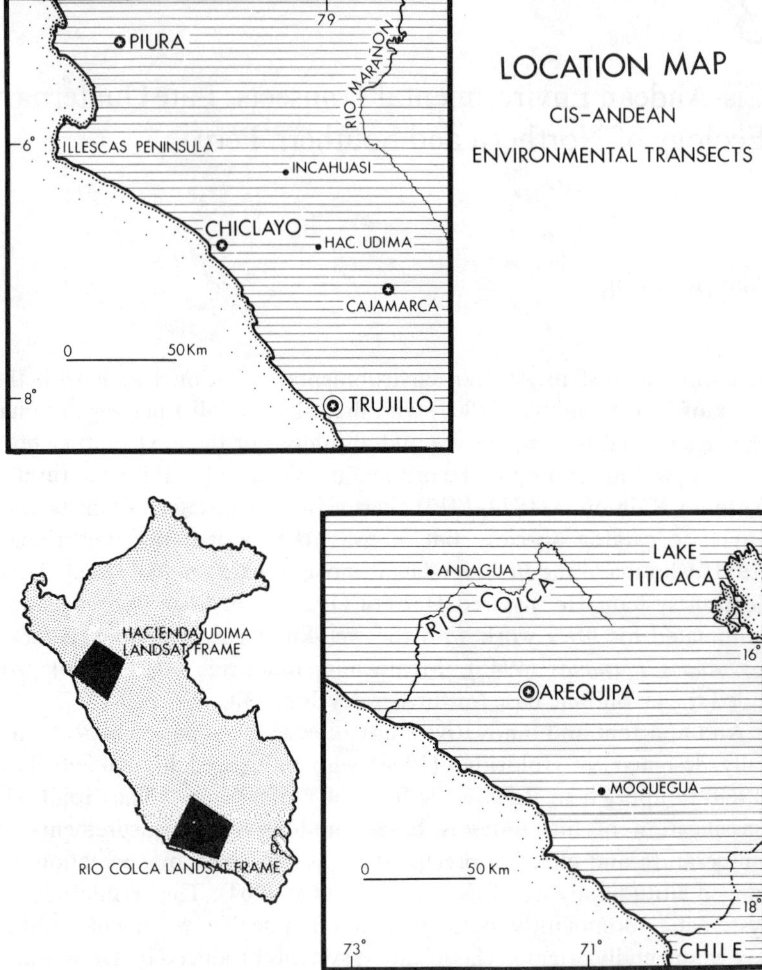

Fig. 3.1. Location map of study areas.

tive system that incorporates meaningful zoogeographic data as well. Promising examples of this genre can be found in the spectacled bear study of Peyton (1980) and the camelid summary of Franklin (1982).

Quite apart from the antecedents just described, the Peruvian geographer Pulgar Vidal (1946) has codified the ancient, folk-recognized environmental terminology favored by ethnographers and historians and in turn has become well-established in archaeological literature. However, it should be remembered that this ethnocentric approach will certainly fail to be appreciated beyond the political boundaries of Peru and will make future comparative studies difficult.

Late Quaternary Landscapes and Bioindicators

Andean archaeologists, and especially those studying Paleoindians, have attempted in recent years to construct generalized paleoenvironmental models suitable for the continent of South America and more detailed reconstructions of their own study areas. Predictably these efforts are disappointing. This should not be surprising when we consider there is as yet no clear consensus for the much more intensely studied Northern Hemisphere where correlations between Old and New World stades and interstades are no longer as easily made as they once were.

Nevertheless, Patterson and Lanning (1967) have given us a commendable pioneer "broad brush" paleoclimatic model for South America even though their data base was necessarily limited. Since that time, considerable progress has been made in climatic and geomorphological research (Craig 1980) tending to complicate what was formerly considered to be a comparatively straightforward Andean glacial history. Nogami (in press) used isotopic dating to prove glaciation in the Bolivian *altiplano* began more than three million years ago. Stades there do not correlate well with those in southern Chile or in neighboring parts of Peru. Sifting through this confusing evidence, I conclude that (Craig, in press) the Late Pleistocene of the Andes cannot easily be internally correlated along its length, much less so inter-continentally. Evidently local conditions were dominant factors in alpine glaciation and we must not anticipate that Late Pleistocene-Holocene landscapes of southern Peru had exact duplicates in northern Peru.

Recent field work in the Incahuasi area of northern Peru (Fig. 3.1) (Craig, unpublished data) discloses ample geomorphic evidence of alpine glaciation descending to 3,800 meters. The comparatively unweathered appearance of roches moutonnées, erratics, tarns, and other glacially induced features indicates they were formed during the last Late Pleistocene stade. During this period (16,000–14,000 B.P.?), increased precipitation caused profound biotal changes in northern Peru that are still discernable today.

Vegetation is of course the most obvious bioindicator of microclimatic environments. In the relict tropical rainforest habitat found near Hacienda Udima in the upper Zaña Valley, we have an outstanding example. It represents the remnant of a "life zone" that was formerly much more extensive along the cis-Andean foothills when it became established during pluvial intervals of the Late Pleistocene. Now flourishing at about 2,600 m, we must recognize that this forest was somewhat lower and laterally more extensive at the beginning of the Holocene. The presence of a piedmont tropical rainforest resource niche (Netherly 1977) is important because it makes some trans-Andean trade contacts unnecessary during development of the complex coastal societies (Shimada 1982).

Both above and below the band of tropical rainforest, there were extensive montane scrub and forest zones on slopes having a somewhat drier, more temperate environment. Today, disjunct land snail populations survive in remnants of these environments that have been spared the widespread practice of fire-clearing crop fields and pastures (Plate 3.1a).

Above these Late Pleistocene-Holocene woodlands, steppe-like grasslands must have been extensive as evidenced by the evolutionary proliferation of the large Pleistocene herbivores whose remains have been found there (Cardich 1964; Rick 1980). With domestication of the two camelids (ca. 4,000–3,000 B.C.) we may be certain that as herds increased, cultural manipulation caused an expansion of grasslands at the expense of forest cover, particularly in southern Peru where the

Plate 3.1a. Top of the relict snail forest at 2185 m on trail to Incahuasi. Arrow indicates snail hunter searching *Talla* trees in a quebrada with fire-cleared fields and maguey plants on adjacent hillslopes.

prehistoric lamoid population numbered in the millions (Franklin 1982). This deforestation had a profound effect on soil moisture (and the microhabitat in general) by enhancing the long-term xeric tendency created by pre-existing factors causing deglaciation.

However, post-glacial desiccation could not have had any significant effect on the essentially steady-state conditions of the maritime desert where bioindicators show us hyperarid conditions have been in place throughout most of the Late Pleistocene to the historic period. Uninterrupted sequences of guano located along the coast between 6° and 23° south latitude and attaining a maximum thickness of 150 m indicate these highly soluble beds of bird excrement have never experienced substantial rain. This assessment of coastal climatic conditions is reinforced by morphology of the *Tillandsias* and other fog *lomas* plants that display highly evolved mechanisms for survival in a desert regime. While precipitation in the higher elevations of the Andes was undoubtedly being reduced, this merely decreased seasonal flow of meltwater entering those quebradas crossing the desert to reach the sea. Below 1,000 m, the coastal interfluves remained as dry as they had been for hundreds of millenia.

At the end of the last glacial stade, *puna* vegetation became more extensive, especially upward with shrinking of the nival zone. As deglaciation progressed, the montane woodlands became compressed between the high and low arid barriers. These forests narrowed appreciably in vertical extent from northern to southern Peru until they virtually disappeared on approaching the epicenter of Atacaman hyperaridity in northern Chile where their role as a resource niche was negligible. Geologic evidence obtained from deep cores drilled in the desert *salares* indicates hyperarid conditions were dominant throughout all of the Tertiary and perhaps even to the Jurassic period.

While these slow climatic changes and environmental adjustments were taking place, Paleoindians suddenly appeared in the highlands and began to exploit the abundant cervid and lamid game resources. Other Pleistocene megafauna disappeared quickly from the study area and most were extinct by the beginning of the Holocene period. In any event, Paleoindian hunting activities involving mastodons and ground sloths do not appear to have had any discernable impact on this Andean landscape. Remains of these animals so far have been found exclusively in cis-Andean river floodplains.

During the 5,000 to 7,000 year interval between extinction of megafauna in Peru and the domestication of the llama and alpaca, a very extensive guanaco population became the principal target species of Early Man, although the vicuña may have been equally important, especially in the southern Peruvian highlands. The guanaco is notoriously far-ranging and adaptable in its habitat preferences, but the llama, and especially the alpaca, have specific grazing requirements. Domestication is believed to have occurred near Lake Titicaca and the Pampas de Junín (Franklin 1982). Some proto-lamoid species—as yet unidentified—must have evolved very rapidly during the Late Pleistocene to provide genetic stock for these closely related domesticates. Habitat preference of this ancestral animal probably was intermediate between those of the guanaco and the llama-alpaca. This *Paleolama* stock may have been present in the so-called short-necked llama of coastal northern Peru, and in the diminutive *wiquinche* domesticate of forest Indians in central Chile. These two animals have not survived, but the present day camelid population as a whole is believed to be numerically equivalent to prehistoric levels and thus constitutes the single most important animal resource of the aboriginal landscape (Franklin 1982).

The Lomas Resource

Efforts to clarify the exact composition, distribution, and useful resource components of the Peruvian lomas vegetation have been smothered in problems. Ecologists, archaeologists, and geographers have each used this term in idiosyncratic ways (Koecpke 1954; Péfaur 1981; Péfaur, *et al.* 1981; Engle 1973; Lanning 1963; Craig and Psuty 1968). Usually the word *lomas* refers to coastal vegetation supported entirely by winter fog (*garúa-camanchaca*) moisture. However, the word also means *slope* in Spanish so it is often applied to the desert scrub found in the lowest Andean foothills some distance inland. In addition, it has been applied to quebrada floodplain vegetation and the ephemeral bloom created by cyclical desert rains that occur in northern Peru. This semantic confusion and loose application of nomenclature for entirely distinct environmental niches is the basis of widespread misunderstandings and polemics. For an even-handed review of the "lomas problem" specialists should refer to Kautz (1976).

To meet the objectives of this symposium, it is necessary to define lomas vegetation and assess its role as an ecologic niche and natural resource in the "vertical archipelago" of resource exploitation posited by Murra. In this discussion, I confine my use of the term *lomas* to those depauperate maritime vegetational communities dominated by *Tillandsia* species and other xerophytics dependent upon fog-derived moisture (Plate 3.1b). Such communities can be found from the seaward

Plate 3.1b. Unreported *Tillandisa* dominated lomas community at crest of Cerro Reque, lat. 6°30′S, near Chiclayo; elevation 580 m.

face of the Illescas Peninsula (Anon. 1967) southward (Péfaur 1982) to Sala near the Chilean border. In Chile an even more rachitic community dominated by the cactus *Eulychnia* occupies this coastal niche (Rundel and Mahu 1976).

Apart from its importance as a bioindicator, lomas was singled out by Patterson and Lanning (1967) as a key food source for specialized hunters and gatherers during the Early Formative period on the Peruvian coast. In 1971 he identified guanaco and wild potato as the principal food items in this environment. While there are some modern anecdotal reports of grazing by guanacos in lomas (as defined above), the only hard evidence comes from the summit of Morro Moreno (Mann, *et al.* 1953) in northern Chile where an animal that had been feeding on cactus spine epiphytes was killed by biologists. I interpret most accounts of seasonal migration of guanacos into the lomas habitat to be instances where the somewhat more varied inland *lomas* or slope communities are involved. Guanacos are grazers rather than browsers (Franklin 1982) and consequently prefer to seek grasses. Until they have been documented browsing on *T. straminea*, it seems premature to include them in the coastal lomas resources. Similarly, areas of coastal lomas, including some mapped by Engle (pers. com.), commonly are developed on naked rock outcrops that tend to be extensive between Ica and Ocucaje. In such cases the presence of wild potato (*Solanum* species) is impossible although I am willing to concede these plants have been found in lomas elsewhere, especially in the Amancaes and Lachay *lomas* (Ochoa 1962) which are in reality a chapparal community.

From another point of view it should be noted that few, if any, herbal medicines derived from coastal fog lomas have been identified in the pharmacopea of modern *curanderos* or in ethnographic reports with which I am familiar (e.g., Towle 1961). However we evaluate coastal fog lomas, it was, and is, poor in terms of available food. The argument has been made that it represented an important source of fuel (Pozorski 1982) but I maintain that if this was the *raison d'etre* for the juxtaposition of Archaic settlements, they must have soon exterminated the very slow-growing *T. straminea* while ignoring the readily available combustible marine algae. If, in fact, there were herds of deer and guanaco to be found in coastal lomas, stalking them in cover only a few centimeters high must have been a most tedious task unless they were run down by dogs and pursued on foot in the Patagonian manner.

In all probability, we have yet to identify the most commonly exploited resources of coastal fog lomas.

LANDSAT Comparison of "Pisos Ecológicos"

Murra's seminal concepts regarding verticality and *pisos ecológicos* have stimulated considerable research and obviously constitute the reason for our present meeting. Prior to the recent detailed studies of Japanese scholars (Onuki 1980, 1981; Fujii and Tomoeda 1981; Inamura 1981; Yamamoto 1981; Shimada 1982; Masuda 1981, 1982) we have few extensive reports with exact data on *pisos ecológicos* with the notable exception of Rivera Palomino's (1971) application of the Holdridge system to the Department of Ayacucho. No matter what nomenclature has been used, it remains difficult to demonstrate comparatively the ranking of these zones in terms of hectarage between northern and southern Peru using data reinforced by field studies. Using contour intervals on existing topographic maps is clearly not a reliable methodology as can be seen from analysis of satellite imagery.

A comparison of prehistoric vs. contemporary agricultural land use using *andenes* and ridged-fields as the principal indicators would be an important support to Murra's underlying thesis of former population densities and agricultural productivity (1983) on the *puna* and *altiplano* supported by ethnic outliers constituting an archipelago. Needless to say, approaching such a study empirically is a herculean task. The

Peruvian Andes are simply too extensive, inaccessible, and complex to make a ground-based physical inventory practical.

Fortunately, we can overcome most of the difficulties by using remote sensing. Good to excellent quality multispectral (MSS) LANDSAT imagery now exists for much of Peru and perhaps 30% of the Andean highlands are covered by conventional aerial photography at various scales. With satellite photographs, very large areas (maximum about 30,000 km^2) can be studied non-stereoscopically at relatively small cost. As of this writing, no LANDSAT-4 frames are available. Consequently, this study was made from sensors incapable of recording objects less than 80 meters in width. In effect, this prohibits the identification of *andenes* until the larger scale, higher resolution images are received.

LANDSAT images are ordered from computer lists produced by a point search request. I chose four cis-Andean points where field data and/or substantial published information was available, identifying each point by latitude and longitude. The request also established parameters such as the spectral band, maximum permissable cloud cover, season, date, time of day, etc. From 18 frames meeting these basic requirements, only the comparatively large scale (1:250,000) Río Colca frame was suitable. Further searches did not produce an equivalent image for northern Peru, so a frame at a much smaller scale (1:3,363,000) of the Hacienda-Udima area was chosen where considerable "ground truth" (i.e., recorded field observations) was available from previous work on the Bátan Grande–Río La Leche Project directed by Shimada located nearby.

Interpretation of the Udima Image

Hacienda Udima Plate 3.2 was chosen for the computer point search of available imagery because it was known to be located in a highly unusual remnant of cis-Andean montane rainforest having numerous prehistoric sites of interest to archaeologists (see *Willay* 10:5). Frame 8137914521500 was the only image reported back as available; all four spectral bands were designated to be good quality and cloud cover estimated at 30%. When ordered, the print proved disappointing in band 5 (generally considered to be best for maximizing environmental data) and cloud cover to the east of Cajamarca toward the Río Marañon was especially frustrating. Additionally, the small scale (1:3,369, 000) as compared to the Río Colca frame, does not permit the same degree of detail to be extracted regarding topographic features and

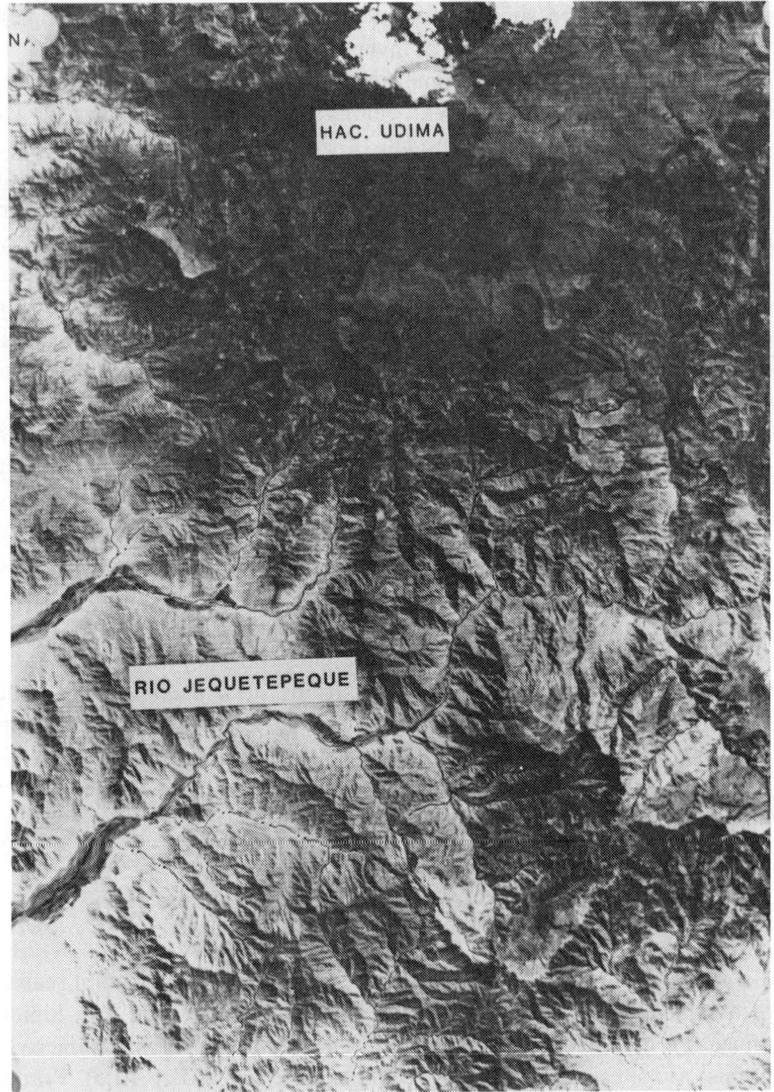

Plate 3.2. LANDSAT image of the Udima area, northern Peru.

makes boundaries of the natural regions less accurate.

In spite of these difficulties, some useful results have been obtained, largely due to ground truth collected during 1979 in the headwaters of the Río de La Leche (Incahuasi area). Observations made there are applicable to much of the northern portions of the Udima image. The

Udima frame is dominated by the east-west trending valley of the Río Jequetepeque which provides a natural corridor from the irrigated plains of the coastal desert directly inland to the important prehistoric population center located in the Cajamarca basin. The upper half of its course flows through rugged terrain with strong, geologic control created by a thick sequence of sedimentary beds of varying lithology striking more or less parallel to the course of the river. The flood plain and tributary headwaters are extensively cultivated, especially on the northward facing dipslopes. This same pattern is found along the Río Chicama to the south and the Ríos Nanchoc, Zaña, Chancay, and de La Leche to the north. Río Marañon flows through a deeply incised cañon across the northeast corner of this frame but has virtually no floodplain and does not reflect substantial agricultural land use.

The single most important ecotone (conspicuous environmental change) is the lower boundary of the wet *puna* (*paramo*) which coincides rather closely with the 3600-m interval (see Fig. 3.2 for a comparison of classification systems). Crop fields and habitations are conspicuously lacking about 3700–3800 m although it is extensively utilized for livestock pasturage. This *paramo* lifezone has developed upon an old (Mesozoic) erosion surface now thickly blanketed with volcanic ash and bombs from eruptive centers no longer readily identifiable. Late Tertiary-Pleistocene uplift has created a very active drainage network which has destroyed most of this surface. Important remnants are found to the north in the Incahuasi area and to the south toward the Hualgayoc-Cajamarca sector.

Remnants of igneous peaks (e.g., Choicopico, Mishahuanga, San Cirilo, Chinchín) pierce this *paramo* surface, rising about 4000 m and showing evidence of recent (ca. 28,000 B.P.) alpine glaciation (Plates 3.3a, b). Many form classic horns with small bounding cirques, tarns, and weakly developed moraines. So far, no geomorphic indications of an earlier glacial stade have been detected for this study area. Nevertheless, lakes, ponds, and boggy areas are common on this surface which receives very substantial rainfall.

Lifezone boundaries immediately below the *paramo* are difficult to map because they are "stacked" due to the steep ramparts and cliffs usually developed by rapid headward erosion.

The peculiar montane rainforest in the Udima area is clearly not as extensive as suggested by Robinson's generalization (1964) of Weberbauer's (1923) phytogeographic map. There is no readily apparent explanation for the survival of this forest in this particular area. Further field studies may reveal the microclimatological factors responsible for this interesting preservation.

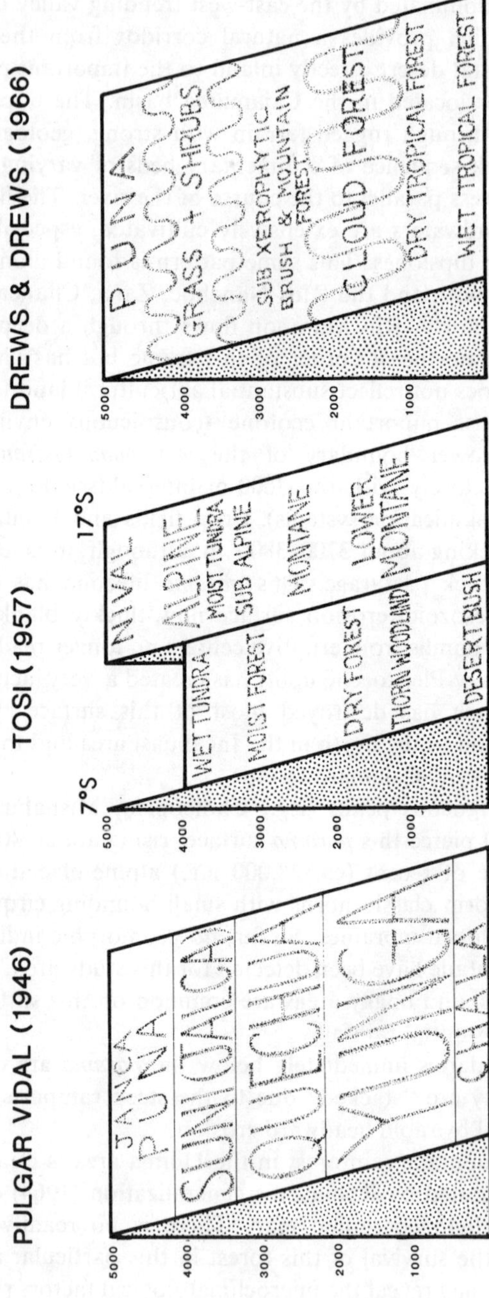

Fig. 3.2 Comparison of Peruvian ecological zonation systems.

Plate 3.3a. Cirque headwall on northern face of Cerro Choicopico near Laguna de Minas, Incahuasi area. Typical wet *puna* (moist tunda-Tosi) at 3580 m.

Plate 3.3b. Andesite glacial erratics on *puna* surface at 3530 m below cirque (A). Tussock grass (*ichu*) in foreground supports cattle grazing.

Poor edaphic conditions (soil parameters) as much as lack of rainfall may account for the comparative underutilization of the lower *suni-quechua* zone. Outcrops of quartzites, sandstones, and metamorphics produce poor soils under xeric conditions as do the rapidly exfoliating granodiorites near the *chala* boundary. However, in the final analysis, much of the present day land-use patterns are more culturally determined than caused by physical extremes. The ethnic origins of the subsistence agriculturists determine whether they attempt dry farming of European cultigens, or concentrate on indigenous crops suited to the highland environments.

Interpretation of the Río Colca LANDSAT Frame

Because the quality of Bands 5 and 7 is outstanding, the Río Colca frame (Plate 3.4) offers an opportunity to carry LANDSAT imagery interpretation to a much higher level than is possible with the poor quality Udima frame. Considerable published ground truth is available for the southern area, especially the serendipitous Colca Valley observations of Shippee (1932) and Cook (1982) and the microclimatological data of Richter (1981) and Schröder (1981). These studies permit some meaningful observations to be made on the matter of land use patterns and the general validity of verticality in this sector. Nevertheless, the final interpretive effort is certainly flawed by the lack of personal field experience in precisely those remote areas where agricultural patterns are dispersed and most difficult to detect.

What emerges is a pattern of land use (or exploitation of *pisos ecológicos*) rather different from the general impression created by the ethnographic case studies from other areas in central and southern Peru. Here we see the *chala* and the *jalca* combine to clearly dominate the study area. The *yunga* is utilized only in two of the five major transmontane valley systems and substantially so only in the Majes. The *puna* is extensive and virtually devoid of population centers; it is an unusually high *puna*, broken up by numerous volcanic *nevados*, explosion calderas, eroded cinder cones, lava flows, and tephra deposits that make travel and communications arduous (the Shippee expedition required three days to move 20 horizontal kilometers from the Río Colca gorge across to the tributary Andagua Valley by means of a 5,600-m pass because it was impossible to follow the Río Andagua upstream (see also Weibel and Fejér 1981). It is evident that aboriginal population density was greatest in the Upper Colca Valley above a conspicuous *knickpunkt* where the gradient of the Río Colca changes abruptly to form the deep gorge of its lower course. The estimated 1570s tribute-paying population of 30,700 (Shippee 1932:575) was decimated by 1931 and several sizable, abandoned *reducciones* were photographed from the air. Whatever the causes of depopulation, LANDSAT offers nothing to suggest this trend has reversed.

Many tributary valleys in the *quechua-suni* zone show no evidence

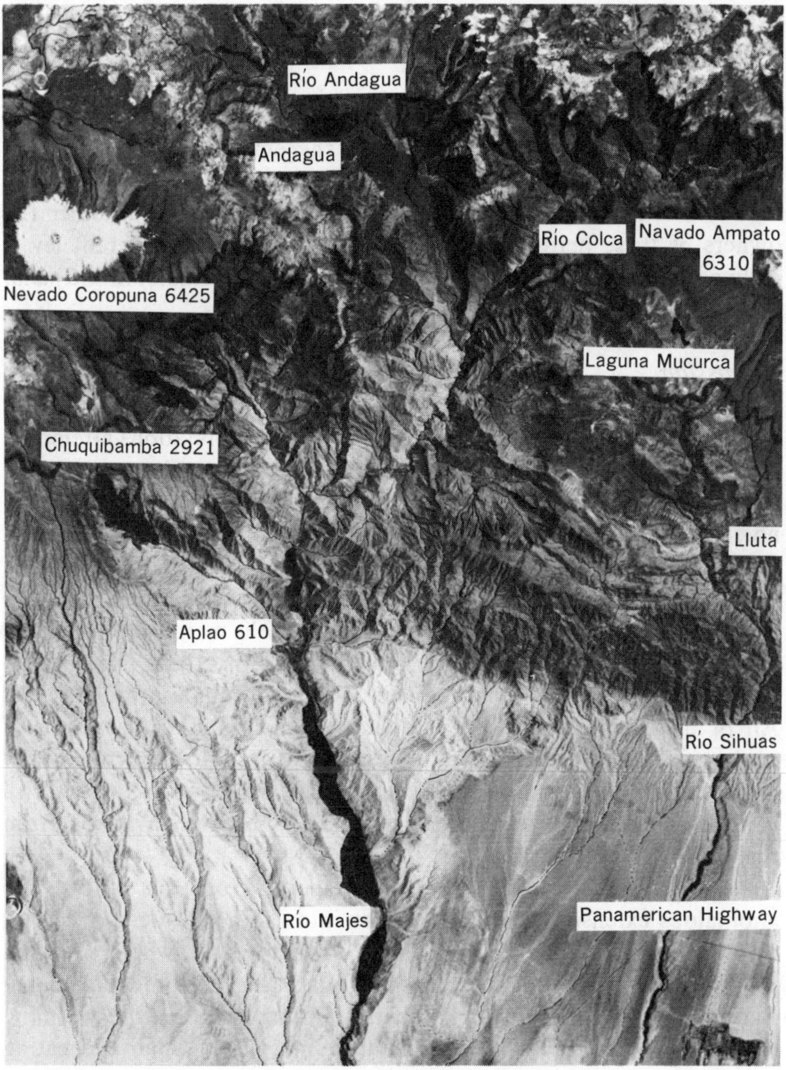

Plate 3.4. LANDSAT image of the Río Colca area, southern Peru.

of any previous field patterns dense enough to be discernable at the 1:250,000 scale. I attribute this to unfavorable precipitation conditions brought about by a combination of katabatic heating and rainshadow effects caused by the extremely rugged terrain. Where crops are grown, andenes predominate, apparently irrigated largely by meltwaters. However, these vacant areas are known to be used in part for European livestock grazing. Failure to utilize this normally important *piso* is predictable as xeric conditions increase southward toward the Atacaman center of hyperaridity.

The high *puna* of the Río Colca headwaters has long been an important center for lamoid husbandry; the emphasis on alpaca suggesting that moist *bofedales* (fresh water grassy marsh) are common. From the limited descriptions available, it is not clear whether the owners of these herds maintain multiple domiciles at different levels or live permanently in a dispersed pattern (not detectable) in the *puna.*

Discussion

Given the many constraints that apply to the interpretations attempted in this study, it is further necessary to point out that the two satellite images used are not necessarily representative of typical areas of northern and southern Peru. The degree of detail is grossly different between the two frames because the scales are not equivalent. Neither is there an approximate topographic equivalency between the two areas—altitudes in the south reach nearly 6,700 m vs. 4000+ in the north. Cloud cover is especially irksome in the northern frame; published ground truth is much greater for the Arequipa area, etc., etc. All of these factors make a comparative analysis and discussion of environmental transects regrettably imprecise in a first approximation using remote sensing. But it is evident this will soon be a powerful method when high quality, large-scale imagery becomes available from the LANDSAT-4 series.

Nevertheless, certain facts quickly emerge from this study. The anomalous extension of tropicality far into the headwaters of certain cis-Andean valleys, as in the case of Jequetepeque, where so-called *chaupi-yunga* growing conditions are found nearly to the Cajamarca Basin, may well be due to katabatic reinforcement of the warming caused by the normal winter temperature inversion. Katabatic heating occurs when local topographic configuration funnels cold air from the sierra into the narrow valleys where it descends with increasing velocity, becomes compressed, and consequently warmer under the greater weight of the atmospheric column. Similar conditions are well-known in some alpine areas of Europe and North America where *föehn* and chinook winds are common.

We see at once that in the Río Colca frame the most extensive areas under cultivation are not in the *yunga-quechua* regions, as the literature would lead us to believe, but rather in the *chala* or *desierto subtropical.* Of course, this is a contemporary cultural artifact caused by exploitation of the desert piedmont soils using irrigation wells sunk in the broad alluvial fan. Similarly, in the Udima frame, cultivation is not distributed in the expected pattern; wet *paramos* occur above 3,600 m and most cultivation is compressed into the upper *quechua-suni* belt, but with apparent slope preferences.

Both frames give the impression that the "carrying capacity" of the *oikumene* (inhabitable area) has not been reached. Numerous examples of terrain apparently suitable but not under cultivation can be identified. Careful field work in these areas may reveal evidence of prehistoric utilization or (more likely) microenvironmental detriments not observable at the present limits of image resolution.

As Tosi (1960) points out, the ecological zonation of Peru is unusually complex. His "Mapa Ecológico del Perú" was created in 1957 under considerable difficulties. The intricate Holdridge system depends upon detailed meteorologic data; at that time Peru maintained only 48 meteorological stations in the entire nation—half were located along the desert coast, and many others were patently unreliable. Tosi bravely applied these sparse data to the unreliable 1:1,000,000 scale 1952 national base map and simply extended the Holdridge vegetational classification inland from areas of field observation, using the elevational boundaries provided by crudely controlled contour lines. The results appear comparatively detailed and convey an impression of reliability, but we must remember they are essentially hypothetical and do not, for example, take into account localized climatic factors.

Consequently, the Tosi Ecological Maps do not correlate well with the reality of the satellite images, particularly in northern Peru. This is especially noticeable with regard to the extent of his pmh-SA (*paramo muy húmedo-Subalpino*) and distribution of bh-M (*bosque húmedo-Montaño*). The Udima frame shows the former to be much more extensive and the latter considerably reduced. Descriptions of the Udima biota reported to me (W. Alva, pers. com.) suggest it is a relict bmh-M or even bp-M equivalent. Tosi's map does in fact indicate bmh-M in the Zaña headwaters but only as part of an extensive altitudinal zonation applied in the manner indicated above. Both lifezones are now totally transformed in the headwaters of the Río de La Leche where field observations confirm profound ecologic changes have occurred as a result of seasonal burning to prepare crop fields. This cultural landscape bears no resemblance to the *pisos ecológicos* it has replaced.

Conclusions

Existing satellite imagery with resolution greater than 80 m can be successfully used to interpret land use patterns and most of the *pisos ecológicos* of the Peruvian Andes. Vastly improved resolution in the LANDSAT-4 system will soon make this method outstanding assuming large-scale (>1:250,000) images become available. To match the increased accuracy of this remote sensing technique, equivalent progress must be made in the environmental-ecological classification system used in order to make quantification and comparative analyses more precise. The Pulgar system is too generalized and highly ethnocentric; the Holdridge-Tosi system is too complex for most anthropological studies and must be plotted on photogrammetrically-based topographic maps in order to be realistic. Consolidation of the Holdridge nomenclature—possibly incorporating significant animal, or other natural resource indicators—is to be recommended.

This study generally substantiates Onuki's contention that the Peruvian *pays* (folk-recognized regions) have ecologic significance and exist in dynamic relation to the environment. Changes, both artificial and natural, are evident throughout both frames studied in detail.

The considerable habitat differences noted between cis-Andean transects in the Udima-Río Colca areas do not conflict with the mainstream of Murra's ethnological hypotheses. Yet they do suggest that a single, rigid cultural approach to agricultural subsistence would not have been successful in both sectors. The natives of the southern archipelagos would not have adapted easily to the forests of Udima.

REFERENCES CITED

Anon.

1967 Derrotero de la Costa del Perú. Lima: Ministerio de Marina, Direccion de Hidrografía y Faros.

Cardich, Augusto

1964 Lauricocha: Fundamentos para una Prehistoria de los Andes Centrales. Buenos Aires: Centro Argentino de Estudios Prehistóricos.

Cook, Nobel David

1982 The People of the Colca Valley: A Population Study. Dellplain Latin American Studies No. 9, Boulder, Colorado: Westview Press.

Craig, Alan K.

1980 Geomorphologic Research in Western South America: The Surprising Seventies. *In* Benchmark 1980. Proceedings 10th Annual

Conference Latin Americanist Geographers (CLAG), pp. 272–86.
in press On the Persistence of Error in Paleoenvironmental Studies of Western South America. *In* Simposio Atacameño, San Pedro de Atacama: Museo Regional "R. P. Gustavo Le Paige."

Craig, Alan K. and Norbert P. Psuty
1968 The Paracas Papers, Vol. 1, No. 2, Reconnaissance Report, Boca Raton: Florida Atlantic Univ., Dept. of Geography, Occasional Publications No. 1.

Drewes, Wolfram U. and Arlene T. Drewes
1966 Clima y Fenómenos Relacionados de las Laderas Orientales Andinas del Perú Central. Lima: Univ. Nacional Federico Villareal, Facultad de Educación y Ciencias Humanas. Serie Traducciones No. 6.

Engle, Frederic
1973 New Facts about Pre-Columbian Life in the Andean Lomas. Current Anthropology 14:271–80.

Franklin, William L.
1982 Biology, Ecology, and the Relationship to Man of the South American Camelids. *In* Mammalian Biology of South America, Michael A. Mares and Hugh H. Genoways, eds., Vol. 6, Special Publication Series, Pymatuning Laboratory of Ecology, Univ. of Pittsburgh, pp. 457–89.

Fujii, Tatsuhiko and Hiroyasu Tomoeda
1981 Chacra, Laime y Auquénidos—Explotación Ambiental de una Comunidad Andina. *In* Estudios Etnográficos del Perú Meridional, Shozo Masuda, ed. pp. 33–64. Univ. of Tokyo.

Herrera, Fortunato L.
1921 Contribución a la Flora del Departamento del Cuzco. 2nd. ed. 1 Parte. Cuzco: Imprenta de "El Trabajo."

Holdridge, L. R.
1964 Life Zone Ecology. Provisional Edition. San Jose, Costa Rica: Tropical Science Center.

Humboldt, A. Von
1807 Ideen zu einem Geographie der Pflanzen nebst einem Naturgemalde der Tropenländer. Tubingen.

Inamura, Tetsuya
1981 Adaptacion Ambiental de los Pastores Altoandinos en el Sur del Perú. *In* Estudios Etnográficos del Perú Meridional, Shozo Masuda, ed. pp. 65–84. Univ. of Tokyo.

Kautz, Robert R.
1976 Late Pleistocene Paleoclimates and Human Adaptations on the Western Flank of the Peruvian Andes. Unpublished Ph.D. dissertation. Dept. of Anthropology, Univ. of California, Davis.

Koepcke, Hans-Wilhelm
1951 Trascendencia de los Estudios Ecológicos en el Perú. Pesca y Caza 2:57–60.

1952 Division Ecológica de la Costa Peruana. Pesca y Caza 3:3–23.

Koepcke, Hans-Wilhelm and Maria Koepcke

1953 Die Warmen Feuchtluftwusten Perus. Bonner Zoologische Beitrage 1–2(4):79–143.

Koepcke, María

1954 Corte Ecológico Transversal en los Andes del Perú Central con Especial Consideración de las Aves. *In* Memorias del Museo de Historia Natural "Javier Prado," No. 3. Lima: Univ. Nacional Mayor de San Marcos.

Lanning, Edward P.

1963 A Pre-agricultural Occupation on the Central Coast of Peru. American Antiquity 28:360–71.

Lynch, Thomas F.

1981 Zonal Complementarity in the Andes: A History of the Concept. *In* Networks of the Past: Regional Integration in Archaeology, P. D. Francis, F. J. Kense, and P. G. Duke, eds., Proc. 12th Ann. Confer. Arch. Assoc. Univ. Calgary, pp. 221–31.

MacBride, James F.

1936–1960 Flora of Peru. Chicago: Field Museum of Natural History, Botanical Series. 13 Vols.

Mann, Guillermo F., Hilde Zapfe, Rubén Martínez, and Gerardo Melcher

1953 Colonias de Guanacos—*Llama guanicoe*—en el Desierto Septentrional de Chile. Investigaciones Zoológicas Chilenas, 1(10):11–13.

Masuda, Shozo

1981 Cochayuyo, Macha, Camarón e Higos Charqueados. *In* Estudios Etnográficos del Perú Meridional, Shozo Masuda, ed. pp. 173–92. Univ. of Tokyo.

1982 Dinamismo Inter-regional en los Andes Centrales. *In* El Hombre y su Ambiente en los Andes Centrales. Luis Millones and Hiroyasu Tomoeda, eds. pp. 93–106. Senri Ethnological Studies No. 10.

Matos, Ramiro M.

1975 Prehistoria y Ecología Humana en Las Punas de Junín. Lima: Revista del Museo Nacional, 41:37–74.

Netherly, Patricia

1977 Local Level Lords on the North Coast of Peru. Ph.D. dissertation, Cornell University. Ann Arbor: University Microfilms.

Nogami, Michio (et al.)

in press Quaternary Chronology of the Altiplano near La Paz, Bolivia. Tokyo: Proceedings of the XXIV International Geographical Union Congress.

Ochoa, Carlos M.

1962 Los *Solanum* Tuberíferos Silvestres del Perú (Secc. *Tuberarium*, Sub-secc. *Hyperbasarthrum*.) Lima. n.p.

Onuki, Yoshio

1981 Aprovechamiento del Medio Ambiente en la Vertiente Occidental de los Andes en la Región Meridional del Perú. *In* Estudios

Etnográficos del Perú Meridional, Shozo Masuda, ed., University of Tokyo, pp. 1–32.

1982 Una Perspectiva Prehistórica de la Utilización Ambiental en la Sierra Nor-Central de los Andes Centrales. *In* El Hombre y su Ambiente en los Andes Centrales, Luis Millones and Hiroyasu Tomoeda, eds. pp. 211–28. Senri Ethnological Studies No.10.

Patterson, Thomas C. and Edward P. Lanning

1967 Los Medios Ambientes Glacial Tardío y Postglacial de Sudamérica. Boletin de la Soc. Geográfica de Lima, LXXXVI:1–19.

Pearson, O. P. and C. P. Ralph

1978 The Diversity and Abundance of Vertebrates Along an Altitudinal Gradient in Peru. Lima: Memorias del Museo de Historia Natural "Javier Prado," 18:1–97.

Péfaur, Jaime E.

1981 Composition and Phenology of Epigeic Animal Communities in the Lomas of Southern Peru. Journal of Arid Environments, 4: 31–42.

1982 Dynamics of Plant Communities in the Lomas of Southern Peru. Vegetatio, 49:163–71.

Péfaur, Jaime V. (sic), Evaristo López T., and Jose Davila Flores

1981 Ecología de las Biocenosis de Lomas en Arequipa. Boletín de Lima, 16–18:1–10.

Peyton, Bernard

1980 Ecology, Distribution, and Food Habits of Spectacled Bears, *Tremarctos ornatus*, in Peru. Journal of Mammalogy, 61:639–52.

Pozorski, Sheila G.

1982 Subsistence Systems in the Chimu State. *In* Chan Chan: Andean Desert City, Michael E. Moseley and Kent C. Day, eds. Albuquerque: Univ. of New Mexico Press, pp. 177–96.

Pulgar Vidal, Javier

1946 Historia y Geografía del Perú. Lima: Univ. Nac. San Marcos. n.p.

Raimondi, Antonio

1874–1913 El Perú. Lima: Imprenta del Estado, 5 vols.

Richter, Michael

1981 Klimagegensätze in Sud Peru und Ihre Auswirkungen auf die Vegatation. Erdkunde, 35(1–4):12–30.

Rick, John W.

1978 The Preceramic Cultural Ecology of the Central Peruvian Puna: High Altitude Hunters. Ph.D. dissertation, Dept. of Anthropology, Univ. of Michigan.

1980 Prehistoric Hunters of the High Andes. New York: Academic Press.

Rivera Palomino, Jaime

1971 Geografía General de Ayacucho. Univ. Nacional San Cristóbal de Huamanga.

Robinson, David A.
1964 Peru in Four Dimensions. Lima: American Studies Press.
Rundel, P. W. and M. Mahu
1976 Community Structure and Diversity in a Coastal Fog Desert in Northern Chile. Flora, 165:493–505.
Schröder, Rudolph
1981 Niederschlagsverhältnisse und Agrarmeteorologische Bedingungen für die Landwirtschaft im Einzugsgebeit des Titicacasees. Erdkunde, 35(1–4):30–42.
Shimada, Izumi
1982 Horizontal Archipelago and Coast-Highland Interaction in Northern Peru: Archaeological Models. *In* El Hombre y Su Ambiente en los Andes Centrales, Luis Millones and Hiroyasu Tomoeda, eds. pp. 137–210. Senri Ethnological Studies No.10.
Shippee, Robert
1932 Lost Valleys of Peru: Results of the Shippee-Johnson Peruvian Expedition. Geographical Review, XXII(4):562–81.
Tosi, Joseph A., Jr.
1960 Zonas de Vida Natural en el Perú: Memoria Explicativa Sobre el Mapa Ecológica del Perú. Boletín Técnico No. 5 Instituto Interamericano de Ciencias Agrícolas de la OEA, Zona Andina, Lima.
Towle, Margaret A.
1961 The Ethnobotany of Pre-Columbian Peru. Viking Fund Publications in Anthropology No.30.
Troll, Carl, ed.
1968 Geo-ecology of the Mountain Regions of the Tropical Americas. Proceedings of the UNESCO Mexico Symposium, 1966—Colloquium Geographicum, Vol. 9, Geographisches Institut der Universität, Bonn.
Weberbauer, August
1911 Die Pflanzenwelt der Peruanischen Anden. Leipzig: Wilhelm Engleman.
1923 Mapa Fitogeográfico de los Andes Peruanos Entre 5 y 17 Grados de Latitud S. Lima.
1945 El Mundo Vegetal de los Andes Peruanos. Lima: Ministerio de Agricultura. Lima.
Weibel, Max, and Zsolt Fejér
1981 El Cañon de Colca, la Cisura de Erosión más Profunda de los Andes. Boletin de Lima 13:3–7.
Yamamoto, Norio
1981 Investigacion Preliminar Sobre las Actividades Agropastoriles en el Distrito de Marcapata, Departamento del Cuzco, Perú. *In* Estudios Etnográficos del Perú Meridional. Shozo Masuda, ed. pp. 85–137. University of Tokyo.

4

Production Zones

Enrique Mayer

Introduction

> En ese tiempo los pueblos yuncas tenían, para regar sus tierras, un acueducto muy pequeño que salía de una quebrada que se llamaba Cocochalla y que estaba un poco arriba de San Lorenzo. Pariacaca convirtió ese acueducto en una acequia ancha, con mucha agua, y la hizo llegar hasta las chacras de los hombres de Huracupara. Los pumas, los zorros, las serpientes, los pájaros de toda clase, barrieron el piso del acueducto, lo hicieron ellos. Y para hacer el trabajo, todos los animales se organizaron: "¿ Quién va a guiar la faena, quién va a ir por delante?," dijeron. Y todos quisieron ser los guías. "Yo, antes de todos," "Yo," "Yo" reclamaban. Ganó el zorro. "Yo soy el curaca; yo voy a ir por delante," dijo. Y comenzó el trabajo, encabezando a los otros animales. El zorro guiaba la obra, los otros le seguían. Y cuando iba avanzando el trabajo, por encima de San Lorenzo, en un cerro, de repente se echó a volar una perdiz. Saltó: "Psic, psic!" gritando. El zorro quedó aturdido; "Huac!" diciendo, se cayó; rodó hacia abajo. Los otros animales se enfurecieron e hicieron subir a la serpiente. Dicen que si el zorro no se hubiera caído, el acueducto hubiera seguido por una ruta más alta; ahora pasa un poco por debajo. Y aún se ve muy claro dónde cayó el zorro; el agua baja por allí mismo.
>
> Dioses y Hombres de Huarochirí
> Cap. 6 (Traducción J. M. Arguedas)

The work of John V. Murra on Andean production systems certainly has stimulated new research ideas and interpretations. One can trace the intellectual origins of his thinking on "verticality" to his thesis in 1956 in which, in the chapter on rites and crops, he draws a clear distinction between two kinds of agriculture simultaneoulsy practiced in the Inca state to produce the more delicate but prestigious maize as well as the lowly but crucial subsistence Andean tubers and grains. On a more regional scale, discussing the evidence for or against the existence of trade in the Inca state, we find the following speculation (Murra 1956:238):

> One aspect of Andean trade which may or may not be Pre-Incaic is the tendency for highland people to stabilize the bartering situation between climatic zones by transplanting colonies of their own kin at the other end of the exchange. . . .Thus the *coca* and *uchu* growing settlements "subject" to Xauxa Valley dwellers sound from the description like village or most likely tribally sponsored projects.

Subsequent archival and field work in Huánuco and in the *altiplano* generated a clearer and more precise formulation of how the mechanisms of verticality actually could work in terms of an articulation of productive capacities between different climatic zones. This system allowed not only for the satisfaction of subsistence needs or the fulfillment of caloric minima, but also, in his vision, for the enhancement and growth of autonomous and ever more expansionist *señoríos*, or ethnic polities (Murra 1968, 1972). In this paper I discuss three main points concerning subsequent interpretations of Murra's work. First, in his 1972 article, Murra uses four key words—*control*, *máximo*, *vertical*, and *pisos ecológicos*—and it seems to me that we have tended to focus our attention on the latter two, to the detriment of the others. The concept of control is derived from the domain of politics and thus is not an "ecological" but a political variable. Power, "geopolitics," and organizational capacities are central to Murra's (1972) thinking on verticality. It follows that *máximo* is dependent on the capacity to control and implies that the more powerful the group, the more *pisos* can be controlled and also the further apart these can be from each other. Distant colonies can produce valuable goods and revenues that further enhance the political and economic possibilities of the controllers. The control and exploitation of colonies is a mechanism of accumulation, both political and economic, and it underwrites the political economies of these *señoríos*. Murra's early suggestion, quoted above, that these were tribal projects is sustained and expanded in the later formulations.

Another question I address in this paper deals with a more precise formulation of what is actually a *piso ecológico*. I propose that we superimpose the concept of *production zone* as a man-made thing on top of the natural variations of the environment. When we think of production zones as man-made things, rather than as "adaptations" to the natural environment, our attention is directed to how they are created, managed, and maintained. Then the importance of the political aspects of control by human beings over each other in relation to how they are to use a portion of their natural environment will again come to the fore.

A final consideration concerns the distinction between different levels of organization. A close look at the historical evidence used by Murra reveals that we have to consider at least three distinct levels of social organization, all of them neatly nested in each other but nevertheless conceptually and practically distinct. The first level is the domain of the agricultural productive "peasant" household. The second level concerns the locally aggregated group of households in a given place and exploiting a common set of resources. (In the sixteenth-century *Visitas* these latter are called *pueblos*, or villages, and are located in specific places, with dwellings near their *chácaras* as their most obvious indicators.) The third level of social organization concerns the larger kinds of units capable of mobilizing local groups as well as individual households. Murra terms these ethnic groups, or *señoríos*. Despite the diversity between them, these ethnic groups shared some common characteristics as yet not completely understood. For example, we used to assume that these ethnic groups, like other "tribes" in the ethnographic record, defended clearly demarcated territories, but this assumption has become infinitely more complex once we realize the implications of vertical control.

Under the verticality regime each household was clearly affiliated with an ethnic group. It also seems that the villages and hamlets were also *sujetos* (subject) to particular ethnic polities. At the same time, the hamlet could contain within it people who were active members and beneficiaries of village organization but were affiliated to different ethnic groups. In this paper I suggest that we still know too little about village organization to understand the full implications of verticality. This may seem surprising because more of Andean local village organization has survived into the present, despite the destructuring and restructuring actions imposed by the Spanish colonial administration which interacted with the internal dynamics of villages to produce present configurations. The lack of adequate understanding of the village level organization is also surprising since it has been extensively studied by ethnologists in the last decades. What has been lacking is the framework that allows us to integrate this level into the larger ethnic or *señorío* level.

I am particularly concerned here with the interaction between the household and the village—or community-level—of productive organization. Without an understanding of local village organization, the complexities of the verticality model cannot be completely understood. It is my contention that the household alone cannot by itself deal with all the technical and organizational problems of production in a given zone; it needs the concurrence of other instances of "supra-household" (Guillet 1978:89–105) organization, which perforce must be locally organized regardless of the ethnic affiliation of its members.

Since my work is with contemporary Andean peoples, the household and village levels are far more in evidence today. The third, ethnic, level is elusive because it has largely been repressed and destroyed during 450 years of colonial rule. Even at these two levels, many aspects of the Andean productive system are still operative, though they are only part of the expansive vision of a system that has served the Andean people so well.

Organization of Production Zones

Given the enormous diversity of microclimatic and ecological conditions, the technological task for Andean peoples is to create conditions for stability and security of production. This implies a process of simplification of nature's diversity (Brush 1977:9). The real technological challenge in the Andes lies in the effort to adapt the needed staple and desired luxury crops to as many of the varied microenvironmental conditions as possible. I argue that there is a specific Andean collective form of organization of production that, under varying and changing social and ecological conditions, will constantly generate technological solutions that bridge the gap between desired crops and the local environmental conditions that favor, limit, or impede production (e.g., Julien in this volume). The understanding of the features of this productive organization can only be achieved by a comparison of how various crops are grown along an ecological gradient.

César Fonseca and I began such a task in 1974 as part of a long-term project that transects the Andes from the coast to intramontane valleys and down again to the lowlands where highland colonization stops. To date we have been able to survey and map the production zones in the Cañete Valley (Fonseca and Mayer 1978; Fonseca 1978; Mayer 1977, 1978; Mayer and Fonseca 1979; De la Cadena 1977, 1980). A second (but incomplete) survey of the transect was done by me in the Mantaro Valley (Mayer 1979). Fonseca has worked since then in his own native Llata with Robert McK. Bird. The next stage of research to the lowlands is currently in the planning stage. The aim of all this is to look for and study the basic patterns of Andean productive organization to see if common Andean organizational principles can be elucidated. We are nowhere near a satisfactory solution, but we have begun to organize data collection in certain ways that seem promising.

The first step was to clarify the concept of *piso ecológico.* What we are really dealing with is a contrast between human concepts, on the one hand, and manufactured things, on the other—the latter we call *production zones.* Various criteria have been used to conceptualize zones on a continuous ecological gradient as stress factors make conditions for biological life more and more difficult (Odum 1971). Steep environmental gradients such as in the Andes favor a zonal approach since the gradients are characterized by more discontinuous plant communities, not only because of abrupt changes in the physical environment but because the boundaries are sharpened by competition and coevolutionary processes between interacting and interdependent species (Odum 1971:145). The recognition, description, and utilization of these natural clusters, or *ecotypes* (Troll 1968), takes many different forms, depending on the criteria by which they are judged, the internal characteristics that make one zone distinct from another, and the way that boundaries are determined.

Previous ecological zonations in the Andes have not always been explicit in specifying the criteria used to define them. In general, three kinds of conceptual zonations exist. The first use Western scientific criteria (see Craig in this volume) or, for example, those zonations that follow the guidelines of Holdridge (1967) and the careful work of Tosi (1960) on the *Zonas de Vida Natural en el Perú* (reissued by ONERN in 1978). Tosi's zones are descriptions of natural plant communities related to three climatic variables expressed in 1000 m altitudinal belts (theoretically at their climax stage in ecological succession). As an attempt to describe the natural environment Tosi's scheme therefore does not take into account the profound modifications caused by human activities. Attempts to refine the Tosi classification for ethnographic purposes have been made by Brush (1977), Mitchell (1976b), Custred (1977), Winterhalder and Thomas (1978), and Gade (1967:109–198), among many others.

The second kind of zonations that have been used are those made by the local Andean people and thus describe what their "subjective" (Valée 1971) criteria of relevance and importance are. Pulgar Vidal's *Ocho Regiones Naturales del Perú* (n.d.) is an extrapolation of such Andean concepts with geographical, climatological, vegetational, landscape, and other criteria added to a varying degree. Fonseca (1972a: 318–24; 1981) has pointed out that Andean thinking about the natural environment is much more gradient-like in its approach, in that Andean people use terms such as *jalka/kichwa/yunga* in relation to each other with reference to a mid-point or line (*chaupi* or *taypi* [Harris in this volume]), rather than as absolute descriptions of particular environmental regions. It is the contrasts (which really interest *campesinos*) that can be applied to geographical areas, things, people, food, music, or whatever, in various orders of magnitude from very large areas such as the whole of the *puna* (which would be *jalka*) in contrast to the valley of Chaupiwaranga (which would be *kichwa*). Within the valley there would be further *jalka/kichwa* distinctions, on down to such small contrasts as when two *tuna* (prickly pear) plants growing near each other are compared, the lower one being the *kichwa tuna* while the upper one is the *jalka tuna*.

Another set of zonations has emerged from government offices which seek to delimit areas of influence into "recommendation domains": "A group of roughly homogeneous farmers with similar circumstances for whom we can make more or less the same recommendation" (Shaner, Philipp, and Schmehl 1981:44). I used this type of zone in the Mantaro Valley study for the International Potato Center; I called these zones "agro-life zones" and "subzones" (Mayer 1979:35–55).

In contrast to these conceptual schemes, there are real production zones, which are where farmers grow their particular crops in specific ways. In each community these zones are clearly identifiable, with precise boundaries (in some cases even communal fences) and, by and large, a characteristic type of field that adjusts slope to the requirements of the plant (e.g., the way it receives its moisture, the needs of the grazing animals that are to use it). Examples of these fields would be slope terraces, irrigated terraces, meadows, and orchards. These distinct field types have the advantage of forming easily recognizable patterns for mapping from aerial photos, and this technique has been used to map all the production zones in the Cañete Valley (Mayer and Fonseca 1979: map 1). Smith, Denevan, and Hamilton (1982:25–50) have identified abandoned raised fields in the Titicaca Basin in the same way. Since one type of field occupies a specific territory, production zones form bounded ecosystems that permit rigorous ecological study. We must recognize, however, that these microenvironments are modified by human action. For each production zone there is a specific form of social organization among people who have access to it that permits the production of crops.

A formal definition of *production zones* is as follows: a communally managed set of specific productive resources in which crops are grown in distinctive ways. It includes infra-structural features, a particular system of rationing resources (such as irrigation water and natural grasses), and the existence of rule-making mechanisms that regulate how these resources are to be used. Complementary to the management of these resources, individual production units (such as households) hold access rights to specific portions of these resources. They have full rights to all products obtained by them from their labor and they have the right to transmit them to others.

Despite the natural diversity in the Cañete Valley, production zones are fairly uniform. In our land-use map (Mayer and Fonseca 1979) we identify only ten distinct types.[1] Descriptions of these zones, the crop assemblages in each one, the rotation systems, mechanisms of water distribution, and how crops are grown in them can be found in our several publications mentioned above.

Our map allows us to estimate that the total cultivable hectarage of the Cañete Valley is twice as large as that estimated previously by ONERN: 68,000 ha. versus 34,000 ha. (Mayer and Fonseca 1979:8). The difference arises because ONERN had largely ignored *sierra* agriculture, a reflection of the low esteem government agencies have of this important group of farmers. Our survey also shows a massive conversion of ancient maize terraces to a new type of alfalfa meadow on which cows graze to produce cheese for the Lima market, and an incredibly dynamic expansion of the agricultural front into highland desert land to open areas for the cultivation of commercial fruit. These shifts, in favor of the national economy and in certain ways detrimental to *campesino* interests, demonstrate nevertheless the creative dynamism of these farmers who by hand are hewing out of rocks and boulders new productive areas, intensifying production, and converting their resources to fit changed outside circumstances.[2] This kind of expansion can only be achieved with a great deal of internal organization.

The social organization that characterizes the management of a production zone is presented in a schematic form in figure 4.1. It is a dual decision-making system. At one level the household is the actual unit producing the crops, while at a higher level the community manages and administers the territory through the control it exercises over the households. Ideally, this body controls a vast and heterogeneous territory. A complex organization of authority delegates control so that different hierarchical positions are in charge of a local specialized segment of territory. Decisions about land management are both centrally coordinated and locally decentralized. The ecologically specialized production zones are depicted at the center of the diagram; on

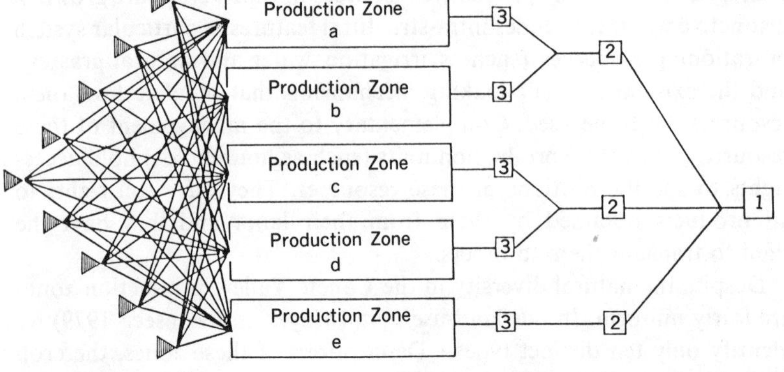

Fig. 4.1. Land management under peasant agricultural systems.

the right is a schematic representation of the levels of authority that administer and manage the territory. Each production zone is under the management of a local set of authorities (3) who make decisions throughout the growing season and see that the rules are enforced by fining infractors and reporting problems to higher levels (2) and (1). The left side of the diagram represents individual units such as households that have access to land in each production zone, but for whom the conditions for working the land are laid down by the authorities. It follows that in each production zone the rules will differ according to the agronomic requirements of what is grown there. This does not imply that there is blind conformity or no room for individual interpretations of these rules. Ultimately, households can influence the conditions of land-use through assemblies and political pressure on the authorities. Land-use patterns in this system specialize production in zones, but the production units are diversified. Farmers thus can have the time, freedom, and ability to simultaneously cultivate land in other production zones, whether these be within the overall administrative domain of the local authorities or in other distant areas.

There is a dynamic, symbiotic, and conflict-ridden relationship between the constituent households at one level and the community at another. The households are autonomous production and consumption units, and the community is the association of households in a territory administered by them as a unit. This dynamic relationship manifests itself in a constant tension between the interests of the households, which push for as much autonomy and independence as possible, and the communal side of their own collective selves, which imposes restrictions and controls. At certain times and in certain production zones we can see a total absence of communal controls; at other times and places there are strict controls enforced. This tension, this constant debate, this push and pull generates individual technological solutions for each production zone and generalizes them as innovations for all.

Dynamics in Production Zones

Let us observe, by means of some examples, how this individual, collective dialectic works in terms of the organization of production zones.

1. *Crop selection versus zonation.* New crops are introduced and domesticated and varieties are selected for use in production zones by individual households. Experimentation and adaptation is constant (Johnson 1972) and belies all the talk about unthinking traditionalism. New plants are sown in kitchen gardens (Fonseca 1972a:319) out of curiosity and are only paid serious attention if, in addition to a crop, the plants also produce viable seeds. Another important feature of the agricultural system within the domain of households is the maintenance of genetic diversity by careful management of the family's stock of seeds (Brush, Carney, and Huamán 1981). There may be a period of experimentation in actual *chacras* by intercropping the new crop in an existing production zone. Some farmers may have enough faith in the new crop to grow it as a full field crop in a given production zone, ignoring existing rules and practices as well as skeptical neighborly comments.

If this kind of experimentation produces successful results, a process of persuasion and convincing of the collective group must take place in order to assign a portion of the territory for the introduction of this crop. Zoning and rezoning of community territory occurs frequently. For instance, the Putinzanos, the first apple growers in the Cañete Valley, once convinced of the agronomic and economic viability of apples, decided to convert all but one of their maize zones into apple orchards (Mayer and Fonseca 1979:32). In Laraos, grazing rights are clearly zoned according to animal type: sheep are permanently grazed in the high *puna*; cows alternate between special cow pastures in the lower *puna* and in the *maizal* after the harvest, which means that only the cobs can be harvested since the *chala* (the stalks) are a communal resource; horses and donkeys are allowed on the fallowing sectors of the sectorial system; goats and other smaller ruminants are restricted to the lower uncultivated mountain slopes (Mayer 1977:61; Fonseca and Mayer 1978:32). Comparative analysis in the valley has revealed considerable variation in these rules, showing again how the dialectic individual/community works out its particular solutions in each case.

The factors that ultimately determine the collective decision as to what and where to produce depend on: (1) what the people want to consume and sell; (2) what is being produced in adjacent production zones; and (3) ecological limitations to particular varieties and species. Because maize is the more delicate crop, in any one community, it always gets the priority of lower zones even though potatoes and Andean tubers would bring better yields if they were planted in the lower zone. Thus, the decision to reserve one zone for maize also determines where the potato zone will be. Within a regional framework we note a tendency to domesticate upward—for as new crops are introduced they displace the existing ones to higher production zones. What also can happen is that one crop displaces another altogether and the latter is not shifted to a different production zone.

Gade (1967:154) has distinguished between the "absolute" and the "effective" limits of crops. The extremes of invested effort to which farmers are willing to go to raise the effective limits of crops can be shown by the example of maize. People in the Cañete once considered having their own maize so important that they extended the effective limit of the crop as high as possible (3600 m). Because of that they had to invest in irrigation to extend the supply of moisture beyond the rainy season (since plant growth is slowed down by altitude and lack of insolation in these narrow canyons, it takes ten months for the crop to mature at these altitudes). This decision in turn implied the need for the construction of very elaborate terracing and irrigation systems. Other crops, equally or better adapted to these altitudes would not have needed such heavy investments.

2. *Expansion, contraction, and segmentation of production zones*. The above process, considered over a longer period of time, produces the expansion or contraction of production zones in response to demand. There is reason to believe that the myriad of terraces and irrigation canals in the upper part of the Cañete was a response to increased demand for maize, which we know was an Inca concern but not necessarily a Colonial one. Current reduction of demand in maize has produced the outright abandonment of maize terraces (in areas where irrigation water has diminished) and the conversion of the majority of the remaining terraces into alfalfa meadows. Concomitant changes are the practically complete disappearance of *chicha* as a ceremonial drink and the substitution of bottled beer, which in turn has triggered the incredible expansion of barley growing throughout the Andes. Yet all communities have preserved at least one maize zone for their *cholco*

(corn on the cob), *cancha* (toasted corn), and *mote* (hominy) consumption.

Expansion of production zones implies the physical construction of needed infrastructure for a particular kind of crop. The kind of infrastructure built depends on the needs of the plant that is going to grow there. Thus, field type, fences and canals, etc., like any capital investment, respond to the inherent functions this machine is built to perform.

In the Cañete Valley, expansion and opening of agricultural land in the *desierto semi-árido subtropical* (1000–2000 m) implies the cyclopean task of making the desert bloom. Community and individual interact. The main irrigation canals are built by communal labor, and anyone wishing to have land allotted in this new area must work on the construction of the canal. Individuals then clear their own land, construct access canals and private stone walls and begin the process of soil formation and planting. It is probably not strictly necessary to be a member of the community in which this expansion is taking place to be permitted to work in the *faena* of canal construction. Once land is allotted, one becomes a member of the community and of the irrigation association of that particular canal. In all of the canals, membership is mixed, with individuals from all *barrios* and kinship groups. Heads of household have land in all, or practically all, canals of the communal system, as long as they or their ancestors participated in the construction of the main canal.[3] In terms of the myth collected from the same area, quoted above, the *zorro*, the *puma*, *serpiente*, and bird *ayllus* (if I may interpret) would all have rights to cultivate maize in Huracupara. It would not matter that these *ayllus* have their "home bases" in other communities. The community of Catahuasi is made up of members who are from other places in the valley as well as outside of it.

Individual participation in production zone membership is not that difficult to achieve, regardless of origin or affiliation, though considerable variation both regionally and over time can be expected. More problematic is the establishment of a communal land claim over an area. Such claims are fiercely disputed and lead to the kinds of land disputes with which we are familiar: between communities, between communities and *haciendas*, and between communities and individual defensive associations of unaffiliated small property owners all of whom claim rights to occupy particular pieces of territory.

Segmentation of production zones can take several forms in response to the process of intensification, which implies a progressive fine-tuning of increased technological and labor inputs. This process may result in the subdivision of a previously larger production zone into smaller ones covering the same area, where the upper zone is now worked as extensively as before and the new lower production zone is worked more intensively than the whole. In the Mantaro Valley this process has reduced production zones to very small areas. As one moves down the eastern slope, fallow is progressively reduced, so that in higher areas one sees three crop years and four fallow, while lower down on the same slope one sees four crop years (potatoes/Andean tubers/grain/grain) with three fallow years individually—rather than communally—rotated. Yet in some badly eroded hilly areas at the same altitude, individual rotations with two crop years (potato/grain or Andean tuber/grain) and two years of fallow exist in response to poorer soil conditions (Mayer 1979:70).

3. *Disintegration of production zones.* Unlike abandonment, the process of disintegration implies a progressive dismantling of communal controls and the triumph of individualism in agricultural decision-making. In figure 4.2, I show the progressive dismantling that the sectorial fallow system has undergone in the Mantaro Valley, caused, among other things, by increased pressure on the land that led to an overall shortening of the fallow system. The distintegration took various forms and occurred in several successive stages (Mayer 1979:67–71). In situation (1), in response to community pressure on land, the size of each sector under cultivation was increased, eliminating several sectors and thus diminishing fallow years. An alternative would have been to lengthen the crop cycle without changing the size of the sectors, not alloting more land, but just having more cropping years, some repeated in the rotation sequence. Land is cultivated longer at the expense of fallow years. This is situation (2) in figure 4.2

In situation (3), both processes combine to create a larger sector, although the community no longer decrees how, where, or what should be rotated. Only two sectors remain (one in crops, the other in fallow and allowing grazing rights). In this situation each family must have a great number of plots in each sector, since all the crops must be produced in one sector only. When the community gives up regulation of land use and the whole territory is parceled out, we have situation (4). Here families privately decide rotation patterns and the years of fallow according to their resources, their needs and the residual soil fertility of their plots. The unshaded parcels in situation (4) are those that have been left fallow. Progressively, fallowing is abandoned between one rotation cycle and the next, depicted as situation (5).

This sequence of disintegration, based on historical process, also provides a geographical representation of the present-day situation, since the communities in the lower zones began the process of disman-

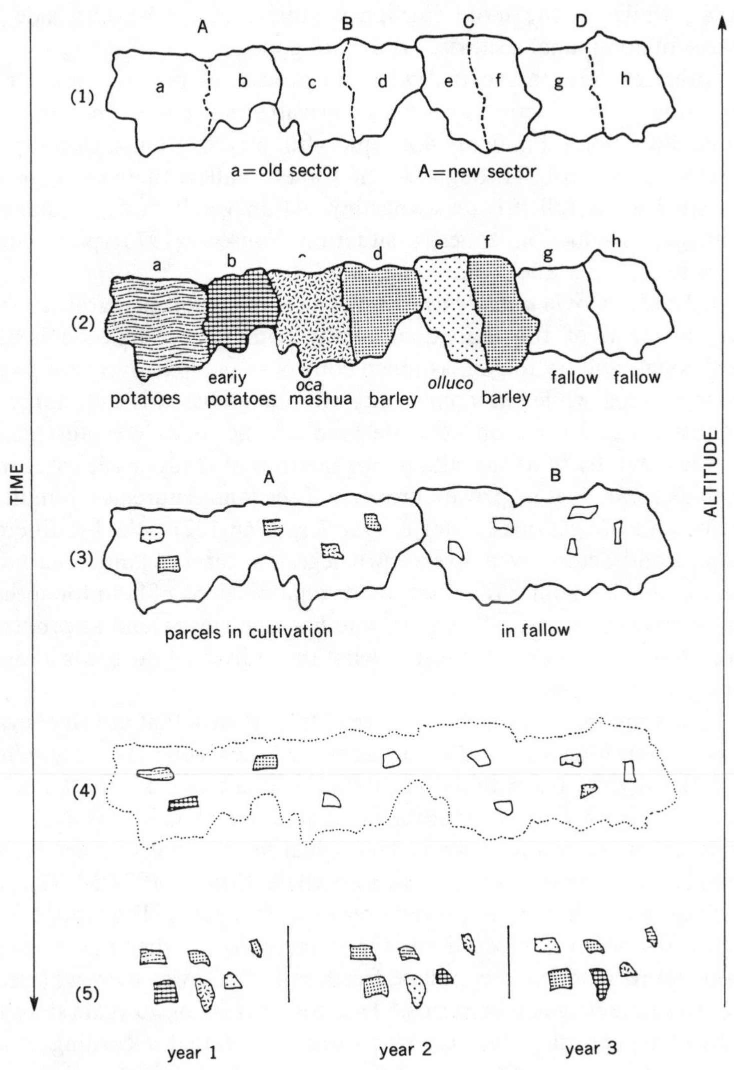

Fig. 4.2. Disintegration of sectorial fallow/rotation systems.

tling their sectors earlier than those in the intermediate and high zones. In higher-lying areas, fallow still seems to be a necessary biological process not substitutable by fertilization, since longer fallow characterizes all higher agriculture in the Mantaro Valley. What is interesting is that the more tuber-oriented communities on the eastern side of the valley still maintain more of the sectorial fallow system in higher areas, while on the more European grain-oriented western side, all traces of communal sectorial fallow are gone.

Although often associated with the process of privatization, disintegration of production zones and privatization should not be confused. Situation (5) in figure 4.2 depicts full privatization with complete individual control. Throughout the Cañete Valley, there exists in the irrigated areas full private ownership within viable and communally managed production zones, a situation Fonseca (1975: pers. com.) likes to call "parallel land ownership."

4. *Land tenure in production zones.* The implication of parallel property in terms of the individual versus community dialectic is that individuals will try to gain as much control as possible over how to use their parcels, while the community will encumber this autonomy by imposing restrictions on how the land can be used. We must define tenure carefully to avoid falling into the trap of ready-made categories such as communal or private property. I see land tenure as a bundle of rights and obligations (*Notes & Queries*, 1966:122) held by different groups and actors over diverse privileges concerning land. The focus here is to ask who has the right *to use* what portions of land for specific productive purposes, rather than who has rights over land as property. We must pay careful attention to what the individual farmer is allowed to do by the community.

Following this approach, it can readily be shown that use rights vary production zone by production zone. In each zone the community imposes diverse restrictions on how individuals can use the land, depending not only on the conditions required by the cultigens in specific production zones but also on other social factors that impinge on the productive process. I have shown elswhere (Mayer 1977:59–72) how use rights vary in the five production zones in Laraos. They range from many restrictions imposed by the community in the higher *moyas* (sectors) to practically complete freedom in the lower *potreros* (meadows) and the irrigated orchards.[4] In a time period of 70 years since the turn of the century, the imposed rules have varied according to the particular interests of the group in power during a given period of the village's history. From 1900 to about 1950 (the period when the *Libre Pensadores* were in power), restrictions on land and water tenure were considerably eased so that individuals gained much more control over their productive decisions in all production zones. This in turn led to a reaction by a younger group of *comuneros* (*La Quinta Internacional*) who, when they gained power in the community, reinstituted many, though not all, of the communal controls in three of the five production zones.

Is it possible at this stage to generalize about land and water tenure in the Andes? One widespread system, the sectorial fallow system,[5] is associated in many communities with higher lands (between 3400 m and 4000 m), no irrigation, the cultivation of tubers and hardy European grains, the use of the *chaquitaclla* (footplow) (Gade and Rios 1976) as the main tool to break the ground, and the creation of communal controls described above. There are some areas where the sectorial fallow system is absent at the appropriate altitudinal level—as, for example in Uchucmarca (Brush 1977)—associated probably with particular climatic conditions, and in the Mantaro Valley where the system has been dismantled. Many areas that once used to belong to communities but had been taken over by *haciendas*, became pasture zones after displacing the local agricultural population. Since the agrarian reform restored land to the communities, people are beginning to re-establish sectorial fallow systems in these areas.

We can make tentative generalizations about the tenure arrangements in the sectorial fallow system, the production zone in which there are the greatest number of communal controls. The community intervenes decisively in terms of what, when, and where the farmer can cultivate. Because the community retains grazing rights on the sectors that are in fallow as well as, in many cases, the stubble grazing rights in recently harvested sectors, it also regulates the agricultural calendar by dictating the harvest date, and scheduling the animal and plant cycles appropriately (Cornick and Kirby 1981). The community also acts as a court to settle disputes between farmers, a function that arises out of having to set up a court system to punish individual farmers who are in contravention of the rules of use imposed by the community.

A system of authority is specifically assigned to the supervision of the production zones. In Laraos, the village officials in charge of the sectorial fallow system are called *meseros* and serve their *cargo* for one year. Isbell (1978:89–93) describes three interlocking *varayoq* (staff holder) systems, each one associated with one production zone. Because one of the *cargo* systems was too much under the control of the local priests, the Chuschinos abolished it and replaced it with a new system which was supported by the government; thus they used agrarian reform to recuperate Church lands. In Tangor (Mayer 1974: 235–53), the *vara* system's primary function is to manage the *muyuy* system and to settle disputes arising from its operation. In some communities, such as Miraflores in Cañete, land is still distributed annually by the authorities, while in most communities farmers return to their own family plots after the fallow years.

A careful look at the symbolic statements made during the *fiestas* associated with these *varas* shows that the rituals also are associated with different production zones (Isbell 1978:139–145; Mayer 1974: 40–45). It therefore follows that a calendrical *fiesta* associated with agriculture will reveal which of the production zones is considered the most important for that community. Care must be taken, however, since in the Laraos irrigation canal cleaning *fiesta* much stress is placed on their *maizal*, while it is actually the *puna* lands that are economically the most important. A case can be made for ideological manipulation. Parallels also exist between the communal and individual levels mirrored in the ceremonial cycle. Household-level *fiestas* organized to sow maize (Mayer 1974:149–153; Fonseca 1974:99–104; Ossio 1976: pers. com.) or the famous *marca del ganado* rituals reported in *Allpanchis* (1971) and by Tomoeda in this volume, clearly are individually organized concerns that bring family members together, in contrast with communally organized land distribution ceremonies (Fonseca 1972b; Mayer 1972) or communal irrigation canal *fiestas*.

Individual farmers hold a different bundle of rights over the productive process. They can decide how much land they are going to work (which is different from the amount of land they own, since they always have recourse to internal exchange arrangements between *comuneros*) and how this land is going to be worked. The kind of plowing, furrowing, drainage system, and so on, are also the farmer's to determine, as are the kinds of seeds, manure, insecticides (if any), and other plant care. Finally, it is the autonomous decision of the farmer to recruit his own labor (Mayer 1974:85–138). He can, within the limits set by the community, decide on the crucially important issues of early-middle-or late-season planting (Camino, Recharte, and Bidegaray 1981).

Individual households have complete rights to the products that are the fruits of their labor and they have the right to transmit rights of access to their heirs. They can buy, sell, and give away individual pieces of land to other parties, though there are kinship, communal controls as well as legal restrictions as to who the buyers can be. There are very few communities remaining that periodically redistribute land, though the tendency still is visible. An official survey claims that 44 percent of the communities still redistribute land (*Comunidades Campesinas* 1980:27). In general, today's rules reserve access rights to people who are members of communities, to their heirs, and to relatives. Total strangers have a more difficult time becoming established in a community, though their presence is not that rare. We must assume that in the past the right to assign land within production zones was not always within the sole domain of local communities.

It would be tempting to find in this sectorial fallow system the ideal model of prehispanic land tenure systems and to relegate all deviations to postconquest phenomena of Colonial interference and to privatization. However, our research has shown that the more intensively land can be worked (i.e., the longer it can be cultivated in a more permanent way), the more independence farmers want to have over productive decisions. Thus, the degree of communal control varies with the ecological gradient, since lower lands can be worked more intensively, and vice versa. For example, in the *altiplano* in Bolivia, land in more favorable niches is allocated in more "private" ways as *sayañas,* in contrast to the more collectively managed *aynoqa* (Carter 1974). In Marcapata, Peru, the contrast is between the *banda* and *kita chacra,* the latter being worked more independently than the former (Yamamoto 1981:107). The upper part of the *banda chacra* is under the sectorial fallow system while the lower parts are more permanently in maize (Yamamoto 1981:106). Fujii and Tomoeda's (1981:44) study of Cayrabamamba similarly reveals a more intensive cultivation of maize and potatoes in lower zones which they call the *complejo chacra,* in contrast to the *laymis* higher up. Because of the more restricted rotation patterns, and the nonexistent fallowing in these *chacras,* individual controls are much greater than in the higher zones. In some cases these *chacras* are even considered absolute private property precisely because of the absence of communal restrictions.

5. *Distribution of irrigation water.* On the western slopes of the Andes another factor becomes crucial: the control by the community of irrigation water. By rationing water in certain ways, the community determines the crops that can be grown in the various production zones. Thus, the distribution of water, a limiting factor, becomes the crucial factor in communal control as one moves from the *sierra* to the drier coastal areas in the irrigated zones of the Cañete. Many of the features described above for the sectorial fallow system are also applicable to irrigation systems under communal control.

Access rights to particular portions within an irrigated production zone are gained by having worked on the construction of the communal infrastructural features, such as the main canals. These rights are maintained by regularly attending the *faenas* (obligatory work projects) that keep the canals in working order, which goes together with serving as *cargo* holders in the associated *fiestas.* Water is allocated differently in each production zone, depending on the requirements of the main crops growing there. For example, in Laraos, *papas mahuay* (early maturing potatoes) require irrigation every two weeks in the dry season; maize can grow even if it is only irrigated three times during the growing season, and this again differs from the requirements of alfalfa meadows which need water every week, or orchards, which have very complex irrigation schedules arranged in such a way so as to produce a crop of fruit when the market price of the apples is highest.

In general, water-rationing systems are worked out as a result of individual interests that coalesce into pressure groups. The conflicting interests are resolved democratically in assemblies to allocate different amounts of water in different ways in each production zone. As in any democracy, the interests of more powerful groups may better be served than those of the general majority. These rules then become the givens that determine a great deal of the agricultural practices for the individual farmers. Mitchell (1976a) shows how irrigation water is zoned in Quinua, Ayacucho, to extend the supply of moisture beyond the rainy season because crops need additional water in the upper zone. In the lower zone, water is needed because there is an absolute shortage of moisture throughout the growing season.

In Putinza, the supply of water is also very short, and water must be rationed very carefully. Water sources depend on underground filtrations, with maximum availability reaching a peak during the rainy season. This permits water to be simultaneously distributed along the four canals and it is therefore the season when the greatest area of land can be irrigated. If the sources of water seem to be particularly abundant in a given year, water is sent to a special production zone where plots are cultivated in maize intercropped with beans and cucurbits. These crops can grow with little water; and when the amount available diminishes, water to this production zone is cut off altogether in favor of the more delicate, valued, and revenue-producing apple orchards. Later in the season, as the flow continues to diminish, all the water flows along one canal by *turnos* (turns) rather than in all simultaneously. In years when the community decides that there is not going to be enough water, a collective decision is made not to cultivate in the maize sector at all (Mayer and Fonseca 1979:34).

Systems of water distribution also vary by production zones and according to communities. Free water is *toma libre*; individuals may take as much water as they wish, when they want to. Controlled water can vary from fairly free to very restricted ways of distribution. A less constrained distribution system is when the farmer who wants water pays his fee to the *repartidor* (official in charge of distribution), who then assigns it among those who came to ask during a particular week. More stringent communal controls are usually termed *mitas de agua. Mitas* can be assigned to individuals or groups of individuals, who then have water during the whole day to irrigate all of their fields scattered throughout the production zone along several of the canals. Or *mitas* can be assigned to the canals, in which case the order of irrigation can be from the last field at the end of the canal to the first, or from the first to the last, or some other variation, each one with particular advantages and disadvantages to individual farmers or groups. The actual solutions worked out in each production zone and community vary as local concerns are thoroughly hashed out by the most interested parties. Disputes about water take place frequently, and there is also a court system to settle water disputes that is analogous to the court system to settle crop disputes in the sectorial fallow system. The threat of fines is far less of a compulsory mechanism than is the threat to cut off the water supply of the offending farmer.

One new element that becomes cleary visible when one looks at water distribution is the question of priority and hierarchy. In Huantán, as recently as thirty years ago, water was allocated to groups of four or five farmers along a canal, who became the *patrones* of that day. Other *comuneros* helped the *patrones* in the agricultural tasks during those days, and this help was returned on the day when the *comuneros* became the *patrones* (Fonseca 1978). The order in which these groups of farmers were assigned their water allotments implied that the rest of the agricultural cycle was also fairly well predetermined; those privileged by early water distribution could harvest sooner than farmers at the end of the roster. In Auco, also in the Cañete Valley, there is an annual ceremony called *la asentada de la mita de agua* (the assignment of water turns) (Fonseca 1978:6–7). The authorities provide a big feast for all *comuneros*, because they receive the best choices and priorities for water distribution during their tenure, a privilege that is rotated among the *comuneros*. The amounts, periodicities, and groups of farmers who are to irrigate on a given day are decided on that day. The distribution of water privileges accurately reflects social hierarchies.

Thus, where irrigation is necessary, communal controls do not weaken despite the possibility of working production zones more intensively (Netting 1976), but communal controls shift from land to water.

What are the main elements that characterize communal management of production zones in the Andes? Guillet (1978), defining the "suprahousehold sphere of production," specifies the following agronomic productive functions: (1) factor proportionality; (2) creation and enforcement of production rules; (3) scheduling and coordination; and (4) labor recruitment to maintain production zones. In addition, he stresses the important fact of collective defense of land, not directly associated with production per se but nevertheless a very necessary precondition. To these productive considerations we must now add more social specifications. Community controls are usually concerned with matters of common interest: to protect the rights of other farmers (though not always in an egalitarian way) and to consider the long-range maintenance and use of natural resources. In addition, communal organization must deal with matters of priority and hierarchy: who has access to the production zone and under what criteria, who gets the choice pieces of land, who gets the water first. Individuals have rights and are concerned about agricultural inputs, the product of their effort, and the transmission of the rights of access to production zones to their heirs, though I suspect that in the past this issue was handled more stringently through such matters as kinship and *ayllu* membership. Individual interests tend towards autonomy of decision-making, seeking the reduction of demands that the community can impose on them.

A tentative generalization concerning all production zones which would have validity over time and thus would allow us to pose questions for historical and archaeological research should include the following features: (1) recognition that production zones are communal creations which allow individual access; (2) acknowledgement that the rights to access are controlled by the community in part, and that the concomitant obligations to these rights include the giving of labor and participation in the rule-making, rule-breaking, and rule-enforcing mechanisms of the local community; (3) communal and extracommunal control over the rationing process, setting up priorities and hierarchies of privilege; (4) control of the agricultural calendar, not only to ensure the proper scheduling activities which are important in multi-zone exploitations (Golte 1980) but also as a mechanism to enhance the controls the community can exercise over individuals; (5) agricultural ceremonies, associated with ritually ensuring a balance of appropriate climatic conditions; and (6) the ritual validation of hierarchies and privileges that justify them in terms of appeals to higher ideological principles (such as, for example, appeals to the good of all) and the functions of ritual in recruiting labor, ensuring compliance, and achieving a greater degree of solidarity.

All of these communal controls also create the conditions for greater and more controlled labor exactions, which go beyond the maintenance or expansion of production zones. For example, this mechanism is crucial in ensuring that the *Kuraka's*, the Inca state's, and the *Huaca's* claims on land and labor get assigned and worked first (in the sense that these have priority) in a given production zone, before individual commoners are allowed to work their own plots. State and *Kuraka* plots must have been located within the locally created and managed production zones.[6] There is also the communal right to distribute and redistribute access rights, though these last are not always completely within communal control, but are affected by land distribution policies of higher level entities like the *señoríos* and the state.

The Limitations of Village-based Verticality

So far, we have restricted the discussion to considerations of how production is organized. We must now deal with other aspects that interdigitate with the organization of production zones. How can surplus be generated from existing production zones? How can "supra-village" social groups gain control of the communal level of organization and reorient its productive capacities to its own social, political, and economic ends? How do production zones fit in with verticality? In this section I discuss the inherent limitations affecting the expansion of localized villages into many production zones.

1. *Aggregation of production zones.* The process of aggregation refers to the efforts made by villages as units to create and control as many production zones as possible. It is a different process than that implied when individuals from one village have access to production zones in other villages. There are many factors that affect the capacity of a local group of people to control a maximum number of production zones. One of these is distance. The number of production zones that can be simultaneously managed by all households within a village depends on how far these zones are from each other. Distance in any case, should be conceived by the villagers' own criteria of near or far. It is determined by the steepness of the gradient allowing either greater ease or difficulty of movement between one zone and the next, features largely determined by the local and regional topography. Gade's (1967) and Brush's (1976a:161–165) classification of "compressed," "extended," and "archipielago" models are examples of the application of this concept of distance. Distance per se is not so useful as a measure. It must be combined with intensity of labor requirements, since production in some zones requires few labor inputs that are sporadically applied, while in other zones—such as herding areas—constant attention is needed by only a few people. Still other production zones require a great deal of labor inputs that are unevenly distributed throughout the year. Golte (1980) calculates that labor requirements in each production zone are not enough to occupy household labor full-time; and because productivity in each zone is low, several production zones must be combined in order to produce enough for subsistence needs.

The number of production zones that a community can actually create and control further depends on the size of the village population. But more importantly, it also depends on the size and complexity of the social organization of the locally productive households. The larger the farming unit (the more members it has), the greater the possibility of dividing the tasks among a larger number of production zones. A family that can permanently assign people to take care of herding animals in the *puna*, as well as have the necessary manpower to cultivate in different production zones, is more capable of exploiting all the resource possibilities in a community than a family that is short of the necessary productive labor composition (Webster 1980; Custred 1980). This is not only a matter of demographics or of the domestic cycle (Goody 1966; Lambert 1977), but also of kinship and social organization. Progressive nuclearization of families as a result of European and Christian pressures is one important factor in the de-structuring of the Andean political economy.

We must also consider whether there are tendencies toward specialization and division of labor within a village. We have tended to assume that every family would desire access to all production zones, but an equally valid alternative is a possible specialization of tasks within a village whereby some groups are more concerned with the exploitation of certain specialized resources in particular zones than in others. Village organization ensures maximum control over all the production zones, with internal specialization and differentiation. Goat herders and cheese makers in Laroas are specialized groups, separate from the group that combines agriculture with wage work in the nearby mines. Specialization within villages permits the presence of people from other villages and zones to reside within it and yet have access to the production zones they are interested in from the perspective of the interests of their home villages. Coordinating all these special interests is one of the functions of community organization.

Another indicator of multiproduction zone management is the location of the village: it will be located closer to those production zones that require the most intense care. Given today's limitations of village organization, two common patterns emerge: those of primarily agricultural villages located at the boundaries between potato and maize zones (Fonseca 1972a, Brush 1977), and pastoral villages located between the limits of agriculture and their pasture lands (Custred 1977). José Portugal has compiled this information in a useful survey of communities in Peru (*Comunidades Campesinas* 1980:28) which shows that nearly half (46 percent) of the communities control only two zones, and in this group the combination of pasture with agriculture is by far the most frequent (41 percent). Communities with three systems (irrigation, rain-fed agriculture [*secano*] and pastures) account for 22 percent. The remaining 20 percent are communities with only one system, either irrigation (two percent), or *secano* (nine percent) or pastures (nine percent) only. However, we must assume that within each one of these official categories there are further production zones differentiated in these villages.

Shifts in emphasis in production zones are also associated with changes in location of the villages themselves. In the Cañete Valley, there are new settlements in the lower fruit-growing areas while the older and higher villages are suffering a marked decline in population (De la Cadena 1977). In the famous case of Huayopampa in the Chancay Valley, the whole village moved to a new site (Fuenzalida, et al. 1968; 1982). In many communities prehispanic settlements are located higher than the contemporary residences. Archaeolgical and archival research that pays close attention to a chronology of settlement patterns in relation to production zones should reveal great historical shifts of villages up and down the slopes depending on the particular productive emphasis in each historical period.

Within this framework we must also consider the relationship between the villages and the process of creating *anexos*, or satellite villages, as ways in which a village can expand control over different and more distant production zones. These *anexos* are often situated in places where a different mix of production zones are available. *Puna anexos* are associated with many agricultural communities in Central Peru.[7] In the Cañete Valley there is also a tendency to create *anexos* lower down to begin the process of orchard expansion; Putinza and Catahuasi started off as *anexos*. Portugal's survey shows that 25 percent of all communities have *anexos* with greater frequency in the northern departments where the Andes are much more broken (*Comunidades Campesinas* 1980:14).

The social relationships between *anexo* and mother community are often characterized as political dependence and domination. Fuenzalida (1970:36–49) describes the relationships between the *mistis* of Moya in Huancavelica and their *chuto* (Indian) herders in the *anexos* as violent and exploitative. In contrast, Inamura (1981) characterizes the relationship of agricultural *ayllus*, each one with their *anexos* in the *puna* in the district of La Puica, Arequipa, as "symbiosis" rather than domination with close collaboration between *puna* and valley people through kinship, *compadrazgo*, barter, and complementary mutual aid such as using llamas for transporting agricultural produce.

Even if the *puna* and valley villages are not in a relationship of *anexo* to *comunidad madre*, indirect control by a group of villagers over other, more distant villages has larger historical significance. Here the general relationships between agriculturalists and herders becomes important.[8] In the contemporary central Andes, agricultural villages are in control of the *puna* lands, which are worked by a distinct group of people, usually somewhat despised by the agriculturalists—who are nevertheless dependent on the herders whose animals are herded alongside their own. The herders' dependence on agricultural products as well as on political representation explains their submission. Fujii and Tomoeda (1981:51) describe relationships in Caraybamba in this way: "The high *puna* is exploited by the *punaruna* through a system of pastoralism, these people being indirectly controlled by the *llaqtarunas* (townspeople)." In contrast, historical examples from the *altiplano* reveal at least partial control by the herders over the agriculturalists (Saignes 1978:1166).[9] In any case, the massive data on barter and privileged exchange relationships (Flores 1968; Casaverde 1977; Caro 1978; Fonseca 1972b; Mayer 1971) show the interdependence between the two groups in many ways and lead us to view with skepticism the relations of domination and submission.

Given the inherent limitations of local village organization, it is a mistake to confuse the possibilities of vertical control that a local village is capable of mobilizing with the potentialities of vertical control as organized by a *señorío*. Village organization is not a pale reflection (Murra in this volume) of verticality but a component of the whole system concerned with the local exploitation of resources. We cannot confuse a component of the whole with the system itself.

2. *Independization of production zones.* This process refers to the severing of the links between one or more production zones from the whole. Today, the overwhelming tendency is toward the separation of production zones from each other, but this process probably took place in other historical periods as well. The *puna* lands in the Cañete Valley are breaking away from their *comunidades madre*. The issues are complex and concern a three-pronged fight over the control of *puna* lands which are now the most valued resource. On the one hand, there are the dependent herders (the *pastores*) who are severing their ties with the agriculturalists by refusing to herd the latter's sheep in order to expand their own herds. On the other hand, there are the old *libre pensadores* who were able to amass huge private *haciendas* within community territory as *comuneros*, but whose right to do so is now being challenged by the next generation of agriculture and mining *comuneros*. The reaction of the *libre pensadores* is to try to become an independent

community by means of an alliance with the rebellious *pastores*. The third party in this dispute are the *haciendas* (now, SAIS Cooperatives), who want to expand their borders throughout the *puna*. It is easier to swallow up small and specialized purely *puna* groups while it is more strategic to lead the battle against *hacienda* encroachment in alliance with the old *comunidad madre* since it is this latter which has the original titles and greater capacity to mobilize opposition (Fonseca and Mayer 1978; Mayer 1977, Mayer and Fonseca 1979).

A similar process is taking place in the lower parts of the Cañete Valley. The new fruit-growing production zones, once *anexos* of a larger community, are cutting themselves off from their old communities and seeking the status of separate communities. Putinza and Catahuasi are examples; they once were *anexos* of Pampas and Tupe but broke off from them because they found the labor exactions and other controls imposed by their mother communities too onerous while they were building and expanding their apple orchards. Further fieldwork will help us to understand how these newly independent communities have settled the water rights among themselves and their old villages, since irrigation water comes from land within the old communities.

In the Mantaro Valley, the process of independization has been brought almost to its possible ecological limits. Alberti and Sánchez (1974: 49–58) describe the historical process by which Mito, once a Colonial *reducción* that had lands from the banks of the Mantaro River all the way to the *puna*, progressively lost territory until it had shrunk to its present minute size. The process was accompanied by the concomitant settlement of new areas, their becoming villages, and their final elevation to official status as *comunidades* of nine small villages and two large *puna haciendas* within a time span of one century. One way in which individual farmers have tried to reconstruct access to multiple production zones, apart from trade links, is by owning land in several villages, which is possible given the advanced degree of privatization in the valley.

The government has played an important part in this process of political fragmentation to single production zone communities, since it readily elevated *anexos* to district status and even more easily provided any group that wanted it with papers recognizing them as *comunidades de indígenas*. Privatization of land, intensification of agriculture, the breakdown of sectorial fallow systems, and a growth of commercialism were the consequences of this process, as was the multiplication of a number of microcommunities which no longer control much land at all. Thus, the current tendency is to destroy village-based verticality by breaking up the multiple production zone management characteristic of Andean villages.

The Toledan *reducciones* profoundly modified village composition, location, functions, and integration into larger political territorial units. From the very beginning the Spanish were concerned about the dispersion and what to them seemed to be a confusion in village organization, so much so that they soon started arguing about the need to *reducirlos*. It is our task to make sense of what to European eyes seemed so confusing and disorganized. The first simple question concerns village size and location in relation to production zones over time. Other questions include: Were villages much smaller but closer to their respective production zones in pre-*reducción* times? Was there a greater degree of single production zone specialization with local residences nearby, while what was then considered to be a village was a more dispersed unit? What shifts over time can we see in terms of creation and intensification of production zones by studying village locations and settlement patterns? What was the internal composition of villages in terms of ethnic, state, and local population components?

Individual Interest Groups in Villages

We now turn to an examination of individual interest groups and their concerns over how to use production zones. To be effective, an interest group must be capable of exerting pressure on the communal level so that its particular interests have a bearing on the outcome in the communal decision-making process. What one actually observes in a given production zone is the outcome of the power struggle between the different interest groups represented in the village. If one group clearly dominates, their interests will be reflected in the way that land is worked. When power is more evenly distributed, then the way a production zone is being used will reflect the outcome of all kinds of negotiations and compromises, as well as shifts of power among groups within the villages. This approach takes for granted that the internal composition of villages is heterogeneous.

It also follows that we need not necessarily think only of families when we consider the individual level. Institutions and organizations can have access rights to land within a given production zone, for example, *yupanakuy* (communal) lands belonging to the different *barrios* in Yacan (Fonseca 1972b) or *cofradía* lands in Laraos, expropriated by the *libre pensadores* at the turn of the century. Such institutions have their representatives at the local level to ensure that the institution's claims and interests are not forgotten. These representatives are the people who actually mobilize the work on the land for these organizations. The power local representatives can exercise within the village does not only derive from the one vote of its representative but much more importantly from outside the village, as is the case with the *cofradía* lands whose expropriation by the municipality of Laraos was bitterly opposed by the Church hierarchy. Although numerically inferior, such an institution can represent a strong and powerful influence on the way a production zone is to be used.

When we analyze these interest groups, we must distinguish between two factors that influence their decisions over how to use production zones: *direct influences* have to do with how a particular interest group wants to use a production zone, with what technology, and in what ways; and *indirect influences* which are also concerned with production decisions, although the reasons for favoring a particular choice over another come not from production concerns themselves but from other demands and obligations that impinge on that particular individual interest group and *indirectly* influence the way they want to use a production zone. These latter factors are often termed "constraints" in the modern, agriculturally related social science literature (ICRISAT 1979). For example, in today's *campesino* world, one group of *comuneros* wants to use land as intensively as possible to produce the cash crop that brings the highest returns. Another group that earns most of its cash income from outside the community would oppose such a move and favor a more extensive, less labor-intensive use of the same land to obtain subsistence crops. The second group's interests in how to use the land is indirectly constrained by their interests in the cash nexus.

Individual interests thus are torn between two kinds of demands. On the one hand there are those demands inherent in being participant members of production zones. Communal labor demands in production zone maintenance, the scheduling of their tasks according to the established rules, serving *cargos,* and so on, are locally emanating demands. Let us call these demands the demands arising out of *residence requirements* following Saignes (1978). The other kinds of demands on an individual come from his membership in larger groups which may or may not transcend the local village; these latter demands arise out of an individual's *affiliation.* The demands placed on the miners in contemporary Laraos, for example, include compliance with a 24-hour work-shift schedule, which can interfere with agricultural tasks, support for the miners union, and the feasting of the *ingenieros* (managers) from the mine with lavish *pachamancas* in order to ensure that patronage relations continue to provide employment opportunities and other privileges for Laraoinos. Thus, the miners' concerns over their time, money, and resources affect the way they perceive and want to use their production zones. In my observation, miners are the most traditional agriculturalists of the Cañete Valley because they see in their agriculture a complement to their income; they produce food rather than cash crops, and this food includes the best local *choclos* necessary for the *pachamancas*.

In historical and prehispanic times an important requirement placed on the individual was the compliance of tribute (*corvée*) labor obligations. Part of these demands could be discharged on the local production zone on state parcels, and these demands thus became part of the residence requirements for individuals. But affiliation requirements also imply *mit'a* labor contributions in other places or even work at home in textile production (Murra 1956). The amount of labor time taken off for these purposes influences how a production zone is worked and in how many zones a family can work.[10] Absorbing 30–40 percent of labor time on nonagricultural tasks is another way in which the unused labor capacity that Golte (1980) mentions can be utilized. Tribute labor and multiple-zone exploitation can become contradictory demands if not carefully administered by competent authorities. The *racionalidad colonial* behind *reducciones* was to reduce family access to many production zones beyond those required for minimum subsistence levels, in order to be able to expand available labor time for tribute.

I propose that we think of villages as arenas where diverse interest groups interact and coalesce. Diversity of interests may equally arise out of local internal situations and from extra-village linkages that impinge on the village. They can affect land-use interests either directly or indirectly by imposing constraints on different groups and their labor times. The function of local community organization is to arrive at a consensus between diverse interests and to determine those rules and conditions in which production zones are going to be worked. The ultimate outcome of which decisions are implemented depends on local-level politicking and does not exclude the clout that external groups can bring to bear on the situation.

My argument, however, is that outside groups need not necessarily control a whole village and its production zones to achieve the desired multiple vertical control in several production zones. I think that today, as well as in the past, the structure of village organization permits the participation of members of very diverse social groups in local production zones. Because village structure can accommodate the requirements of residence as well as affiliation of diverse interest groups, Murra's model of inter-ethnic sharing of resources comes to rest in the particular characteristics of Andean village organization and its production zones.

In technological terms, we can observe the communal level of organization selecting from a whole range of technological choices, enhanced by the diverse provenience of its members, who each can bring a particular cultural tradition with them. These are, in turn, adapted to local climatic and ecological conditions. Technology thus needs to be considered as a means-end schema, as well as a cultural tradition in which desired ends are made compatible with existing choices of means. Village organization is an institution that creates appropriate technology within a given economic, political, and environmental context. It also follows that technology is constantly changing and adjusting itself according to the demands placed on it by the human beings who are managing this complex machine that I have called production zones.

Some brief examples of local productive organization with multiple affiliation of its individuals are instructive. Throughout the Cañete Valley, outsiders who have lands along specific community-controlled irrigation canals participate actively in the *faenas* of irrigation canal maintenance, as well as in the membership-validating *fiestas* that go with the maintenance work (Fonseca and Mayer 1978: 35). In 1969 there were several immigrant families trying to establish themselves in Tangor, and they were even more punctilious in complying with the *cargo* system than the local Tangorinos (Mayer 1974: 260–61). Platt (1982) and Harris (1978) note the phenomenon of *doble domicilio* (double residence) in the Potosí area of Bolivia which assures the Machas and Laymis continued access to lowland areas in modern times. This phenomenon is also common in Peruvian communities but, because it is illegal, is not a strategic datum often revealed to inquisitive anthropologists. Silvia Rivera (1976: pers. com.) reports that in *hacienda* times in Pacajes, the *hacendado's parecelas* rotated along with the *campesino's* lands in the *aynoka,* which was managed in common between the *hacendado* and the *hilacata* (village leader) of *hacienda* people.

Thiery Saignes describes how the people living in the *yungas* of Ambaná in the seventeenth century, who were affiliated with the *puna kurakas* and paid tribute to them, nevertheless being co-resident with the local *yunga* people, were, as everyone else, required to comply with their residence requirements. To the tribute obligations must be added:

. . .the supplementary obligations that are implied in their member-

> ship in the social milieu of the valley:*corvées* on the *haciendas,* services to the *corregidor,* to the church, or at the *tambo,* the priest's salary, participation in the *fiestas* (*cargos*) within the organizations of the town's religious sodalities. This part of the obligations resulted from the neighborhood solidarities and reactivated the rights to lands in the valley. (1978:1168; my translation)

María Rostoworowski's contribution in this volume shows how the *pachacas* in Cajamarca are distributed amongst practically all the *pueblos,* so that with the exception of the *pueblos principales,* each *pueblo* is composed of representatives of several *pachacas* in the Diego de Velazques de Acuna *Visita* of Cajamarca in 1571–72. Murra (1975) gives us an example of how at least three ethnic groups shared *unos cuantos surcos de coca* (a few furrows of coca) in Quivi. This arrangement was such that to the former slave Rodrigo, they appeared to be *revueltos los unos con los otros* (all mixed up with each other) (Murra 1975:93). This *compartido* (shared) production zone was carefully *deslindado* (delimited) so that each of the ethnic groups' representatives knew which furrows, terraces, and canals were assigned to whom. Together they even collaborated in damming up lagoons in the distant *puna* in order to assure themselves of enough irrigation water.

Conclusions

It would be a lengthy and complex task to elucidate the internal organization of villages through time in order to understand how the double requirements of affiliation and residence can suitably be managed through local village organization. Antoinette Fioravanti's (1978:1187–91) study of contemporary Ambaná shows that the organization into moieties, as well as between *vecinos, comuneros,* and *obreros* are at once territorial organizations that coordinate access to diverse ecological areas as well as endogamous organizations that perpetuate the three groups. This kind of organization permits the double requirements of residence and affiliation to interact, even though today the connections between the highlands and the *yungas* are very different from the past reported by Saignes (1978). I would also like to call attention to the symposium on *Ayllu, Parcialidad y Etnía* (Castelli, Koth de Paredes, and Mould de Pease 1981) in which several excellent case studies are presented on the issues of kinship, ethnic, and territorial affiliation of various groups with a historical perspective. Fonseca's

(1981:168–88) contribution is particularly suggestive since he posits that the same principles that underly the organization of production are also present in terms of the social organization of the groups that share these productive tasks without losing their distinctiveness. He concludes:

> The pre-Columbian criteria of social organization seem to be the same as those that characterize the organization of production that are still operative in traditional communities of the country. The classificatory elements of Upper/Lower, Left/Right were used to classify and to locate the *ayllus* within a larger unit which could have been the ethnic group as a totality. In the same manner, when the *ayllus* were reduced into *pueblos* during the Colonial period, the new *comuneros* used these same criteria to communally create production zones. (Fonseca 1981: 186; my translation)

Production zones need not necessarily be restricted to agriculture. Palacios (1977) describes how specially inundated pasture lands for seasonal grazing of alpacas are created by irrigation in the high *puna*. Some communities in the Mantaro Valley have created a *cargo* for the purpose of controlling trout fishing. *Comuneros* are allowed to fish for free, but outsiders must pay the community a fee every time they want to fish. For historical times, Ortiz de Zevallos and del Río de Calmell (1978) report on salt-water lagoons near the coast, built and maintained by the communities of Coayllo, Chilca, and Calango, which were "owned" by the *kuraka* of Mala. Ana María Soldi (1982) reports on how sunken gardens in the desert used low water tables to agricultural advantage. Further research will undoubtedly reveal the variety and magnitude of production zones in which resources are exploited in this way, both in the past and now.

According to our definition, however, not all phenomena of zonation that we can detect are production zones. Some zones arise naturally out of the discontinous way the environmental resources are distributed; and, if man exploits them without the social organizational features described above, they cannot really be called production zones. Furthermore, differential working of agricultural land, from more intensive to more extensive as distance from a market center increases, generates clear agricultural zones on a flat plain with uniform resource distribution without any communal or supra-household intervention, as von Thünen (1826) showed many years ago. Boserup's (1965:85) schematic description of the process of intensification also implies the creation of different zones along an extensive/intensive diachronic axis. A decisive intervention by the participating units that are exploiting the resources is required in our definition of production zones. In the 1950s the *hacendados* of the agro-industrial part of the Cañete Valley had been overusing pesticides, and this resulted in resistant stains of insects that were cotton-disease vectors, necessitating an integrated pest control program. Each *hacienda* contributed a certain amount of money and with it an experiment station was set up to monitor insect activity. This station issued and enforced stringent rules on how cotton was to be planted, when and with what, and how it should be sprayed (Boza Barducci 1972). We can talk here of a production zone since there was a supra-*hacienda* sphere of production decisively intervening in certain aspects of the production process.

The existence of production zones as a form of production is not uniquely Andean. Rhoades and Thompson (1975), Brush (1976b) and Guillet (1983) point out that many features of communal control of the productive process are also characteristic of villages in other mountain environments, such as the Alps and the Himalayas. Nor is the fact that villages communally manage resources uncommon elsewhere in the world. However, in all these cases the features in common reduce themselves to the village level, which has inherent structural limitations to expand multi-zonal agricultural production.

What is unique in Andean production zone and village organization is that Andean social organization has been able to break through the limitations of village-based verticality. The village is organized so as to be able to include in its communal and solidary organization peoples and institutions from various and different *señoríos*—each one with distinct interests and aims, yet capable of cooperating with each other on a day-to-day basis in the coordination, creation, and exploitation of communally managed production zones. In this breakthrough in organization we find the dynamic, expansive, and transformational capacities of verticality that underly the political economies of *señoríos* and the prehispanic state. The careful study of this organizational capacity at the local level in historical times has been neglected because of the initial enthusiasm which led us to search for the appliability of the verticality model in the Andes at all levels and throughout time.

My aim has been to show that some, but not all, of the very dynamic aspects of Andean social organization are still operative at the village level. Today we hear much about the low potential of *sierra* agriculture and its inability to sustain development despite the fairly radical agrarian reform process that has begun to take place in the Andes. In Peru this process is not complete, since only the "top down" phase has been implemented. In the future we will surely see progressively more and more actual control by the Andean people of their productive resources. Contrary to the opinion of a high agrarian reform official who once accused this kind of "Murrista" research of being "an exquisite flight into folkloric academicism," this paper has shown that the search to understand how the Andean people organize production is of crucial importance.

NOTES

1. The ten types of production zones are: two types for rain-fed agriculture, *secano* or *aisha* (sectorial fallow system and individual fallow rotation systems). Irrigation agriculture, which is the dominant system in the Cañete, resulted in five open field crop zones and three kinds of permanent orchards. The five types of open field crop zones are: (1) *Andenes de maíz*; (2) *Andenes o potreros con sementera anual y rotación de cultivos Andinos y alfalfa;* (3) *Potreros de alfalfa;* (4) *Parcela con sementera anual y rotación de cultivos costeños;* and (5) *Campos Agroindustriales*. We distinguished the orchards on the basis of the dominant fruit crop growing in them (apple orchards, vineyards, and citrus groves).

2. See also Fuenzalida et al. 1968, 1982, Fioravanti Molinié 1978, and *Boletín* 1975 for descriptions of similar processes in other western flank valleys.

3. See also Espinoza 1971, who describes a water-rights dispute between three communities in the seventeenth century in the nearby Mala Valley. One contention was that the construction of the canal confers rights to the water to those who worked on it.

4. See also Brush 1976b:130, Netting 1976, and Rhoades and Thompson 1975 for descriptions of similar processes in other mountain areas of the world.

5. It has been studied by Matos (1964:19–27) in Taquile, where it is called the *suyu* system; by Carter (1973) for the Aymara-speaking *altiplano* areas, where it is called the *aynoca;* in Cuyo Cuyo on the eastern slopes of the Andes of Puno, where it is known as the *manta* system (Camino 1980; and Camino, Recharte, and Bidegaray 1981), and in Marcapata where it is the *banda chacra* (Yamamoto 1981). Custred (1973) reports that in the highlands of Cuzco it is called the *laymi,* as it is in Apurimac (Fujii and Tomoeda 1981). In the Mantaro, in Tangor, and in Chaupiwaranga, they are *turnos* (in Spanish) or *muyuys* in Quechua (Mayer 1974, 1979), while in neighboring Yacan they are the *chacras de manay* (Fonseca 1974:33). In the Cañete they are called *moyas de aisa* (Mayer and Fonseca 1979).

6. Mitchell (1980:139–154) interprets "first" in a different way and comes to the conclusion that ecological reasons make it impossible to cultivate state

and church lands first. He therefore interprets this requirement, frequently reported by the chroniclers, as another aspect of state-sponsored ideological manipulation.

7. In Chaupiwaranga, the community of Paucar strategically infiltrated the *puna* haciendas and when there were enough *wacchilleros*, they became an *anexo* of Paucar as soon as the political context became propitious. In this way they recuperated the *puna* lands.

8. Duviols (1973:153–192) has suggested that there is an ancient ecological/economic and social specialization and symbiosis between herders *qua* ethnic groups (*Huaris*) and agriculturalists (*Llacuaces*).

9. Historical data for Caure in Chaupiwaranga (Yacha) territory also show pastoralists with access to maize lands with the locus of authority of one *parcialidad* of the Yacha in the *puna*. Access to maize lands was lost at the beginning of this century (Fonseca 1972a).

10. In 1562 one such individual in Tancor claimed that all the combined tribute requirements he owed the *encomendero* came to five months per annum (Murra ed., 1972:82–83). I have tried to assess whether Agostín Luna Capcha's statement is reasonable by adding the times required to comply with all the tasks, and such a calculation does tally with his claims (Mayer 1984).

REFERENCES CITED

Alberti, Giorgio and Rodrigo Sánchez

1974 Poder y Conflicto Social en el Valle del Mantaro (1900–1974). Lima: IEP.

Allpanchis

1971 Ritos Agrícolas y Ganaderos del Sur Andino. Cusco: Revista del Instituto de Pastoral Andina, No. 3.

Arguedas, José María

1966 Dioses y Hombres de Huarochirí. México: Siglo 21.

Boletín del Instituto Francés de Estudios Andinos

1975 Número especial dedicado a la comunidad de San Juan de Huascoy. Tomo 4, Nos. 1–2, 3–4. Lima.

Boserup, Esther

1965 The Conditions of Agricultural Growth. Chicago: Aldine.

Boza Barducci, Teodoro

1972 Ecological Consequences of Pesticides Used for the Control of Cotton Insects in Cañete Valley, Peru. *In* The Careless Technology: Ecology and International Development. M. T. Farvar and J.P. Milton, eds. pp. 423–38. Garden City, N. Y.: Natural History Press.

Brush, Stephen B.

1976a Man's Use of an Andean Ecosystem. *In* Human Ecology 4(2): 147–66.

1976b Introduction to Cultural Adaptations to Mountain Ecosystems. Human Ecology 4 (2):125–34.

1977 Mountain, Field, and Family: The Economy and Human Ecology of an Andean Village. Philadelphia: University of Pennsylvania Press.

Brush, Stephen B., Heath J. Carney, and Zósimo Huamán
1981 Dynamics of Andean Potato Agriculture. Economic Botany 35 (1) 70–85.

Camino, Alejandro
1980 Tiempo y Espacio en la Estrategia de Subsistencia Andina: Un caso de las Vertientes Orientales Sud-Peruanas. Senri Ethnological Studies, No. 10. El Hombre y Su Ambiente en los Andes Centrales. pp. 11–38. Senri: National Museum of Ethnology.

Camino, Alejandro, Jorge Recharte, and Pedro Bidegaray
1981 Flexibilidad Calendárica en la Agricultura Tradicional de las Vertientes Orientales de los Andes. *In* La Tecnología en el Mundo Andino: Runakunap Kawsayninkupaq Rurasqan Kunanqa. Heather Lechtman and Ana María Soldi, eds. pp. 169–94. México: UNAM.

Caro, Deborah A.
1978 *Review of* Alpacas, Sheep and Men, by Benjamin Orlove. Annales: Ecónomies, Sociétés, Civilizations, 33e Anneé, No. 5–6:1214–17.

Carter, William
1973 Comunidades Aymaras y Reforma Agraria en Bolivia. México: Instituto Indigenísta Interamericano.
1974 Land in a Traditional Aymara Community. Paper read at the Symposium on the Community and the Hacienda Reconsidered. 1973 Annual Meeting of the AAA. México: ms.

Casaverde, Juvenal
1977 El Trueque en la Economía Pastoril. *In* Pastores de Puna. J. Flores Ochoa, ed. pp. 171–91. Lima: IEP.

Castelli, Amalia, Marcia Koth de Paredes, and Mariana Mould de Pease, eds.
1981 Etnohistoria y Antropología Andina: Ayllu, Parcialidad y Etnía. Lima: Segunda Jornada del Museo Nacional de Historia.

Comunidades Campesinas
1980 Comunidades Campesinas del Perú, Información Básica. Lima: Ministerio de Agricultura, Dirección de Comunidades Campesinas y Nativas.

Cornick, Tully, and Roger A. Kirby
1981 Interactions of Crops and Livestock Production in the Generation of Technology in Sloped Areas. Cornell International Agriculture Mimeograph 90. Ithaca, N. Y.: Cornell University.

Custred, Glynn
1977 Las Punas de los Andes Centrales. *In* Pastores de Puna. Jorge Flores Ochoa, ed. pp. 55–86. Lima: IEP.
1980 Parentesco, Subsistencia y Economía en zonas de Puna. *In* Parentesco y Matrimonio en los Andes. E. Mayer and R. Bolton, eds. pp. 539–68. Lima: PUC.

De la Cadena, María Soledad
1977 Hombres y Tierras: Población y Estructura Agraria en la Cuenca del Río Cañete. Memoria de Bachiller. Lima: PUC.
1980 Economía Campesina: Familia y Comunidad en Yauyos. Tesis de Licenciatura. Lima: PUC.

Duviols, Pierre
1973 Huari y Llacuaz, Agricultores y Pastores: Un Dualismo Prehispánico de oposición y complementaridad. Revista del Muséo Nacional 39: 153–92. Lima.

Espinoza Soriano, Waldemr
1971 Agua y Riego en tres Ayllus de Huarochirí. Siglos 15 y 16. Revista del Muséo Nacional 38: 147–66. Lima.

Fioravanti Molinié, Antoinette
1978 La communauté aujourd'hui. Annales: Economies, Sociétés, Civilizations, 33e Anneé, No. 5–6. pp. 1182–96.

Flores Ochoa, Jorge
1968 Pastores de Paratía. México: Instituto Indigenista Interamericano.

Fonseca Martel, César
1972a La Economía "Vertical" y la Economía de Mercado en las Comunidades Alteñas del Peru. *In* Visita de la Provincia de León de Huánuco en 1562, Iñigo Ortíz de Zúñiga, Visitador. John Murra, ed. pp. 315–38. Huánuco: Universidad Nacional Hermilio Valdizán.
1972b Systemas Económicos en las Comunidades Campesinas del Perú. Tésis Doctoral. Universidad Nacional Mayor de San Marcos, Lima.
1974 Modalidades de la Minka. *In* Reciprodicad e Intercambio en los Andes Peruanos. Giorgio Alberti and Enrique Mayer, eds. pp. 86–109. Lima: IEP.
1978 Proceso de Cambio de Cultivos en una Comunidad Campesina de los Andes. Discusión Antropológica. Lima: Departamento de Ciencias Histórico-Sociales, Universidad Nacional Mayor de San Marcos.
1981 Los Ayllus las Marcas de Chaupiwaranga. *In* Etnohistoria y Antropología Andina: Segunda Jornada del Museo Nacional de Historia. Amalia Castelli, Marcia Koth de Paredes, and Mariana Mould de Pease, eds. pp. 167–88. Lima.

Fonseca Martel, César and Enrique Mayer
1978 Sistemas Agrarios y Ecología en la Cuenca del Río Cañete. Debates en Antropología 2:25–51.

Fuenzalida, Fernando
1970 Poder, Raza y Etnia en el Perú Contemporáneo. *In* El Indio y el Poder. Lima: IEP.

Fuenzalida, Fernando, José Villarán, Jürgen Golte, and Teresa Valiente
1968 Estructuras Tradicionales y Economía de Mercado: La comunidad de Indígenas de Huayopampa. Lima: IEP.

Fuenzalida, Fernando, Teresa Valiente, Jose Villarán, Jürgen Golte, Carlos I. Degregori, and Juvenal Casaverde

1982 El Desafío de Huayopampa: Comuneros y Empresarios (edicion aumentada). Lima: IEP.

Fujii, Tatsuhiko and Hiroyasu Tomoeda

1981 Chacra, Layme y Auquénidos: Explotación Ambiental en una Comunidad Andina. *In* Estudios Etnográficos del Perú Meridional. Shozo Masuda, ed. pp. 33–64. Tokyo: University of Tokyo.

Gade, Daniel

1967 Plant Use and Folk Agriculture in the Vilcanota Valley of Peru: A Cultural-Historical Geography of Plant Resources. Ph.D. Dissertation, University of Wisconsin.

Gade, Daniel and Roberto Ríos

1976 La Chaquitaclla: Herramienta Indígena Sudamericana. América Indígena, 36 (2):359–74.

Golte, Jürgen

1980 La Racionalidad de la Organización Andina. Lima: IEP.

Goody, Jack, ed.

1966 The Developmental Cycle in Domestic Groups. Cambridge: Cambridge University Press.

Guillet, David

1978 The Supra-Household Sphere of Production in the Andean Peasant Economy. Actes du XLII Congrès International des Américanistes, Paris, 2–9 Sept. 1976. pp. 89–105.

1983 Toward a Cultural Ecology of Mountains: The Andes and the Himalayas Compared. Current Anthropology 24 (5):561–74.

Harris, Olivia

1978 El Parentesco y la Economía Vertical del Ayllu Laymi (Norte de Potosí). Avances 1:51–64.

Holdridge, L. R.

1967 Life Zone Ecology. San José, Costa Rica: Tropical Science Center.

ICRISAT

1979 Socioeconomic Constraints to Development of Semi-tropical Agriculture. India: Hyderabad.

Inamura, Tetsuya

1981 Adaptación Ambiental de los Pastores Altoandinos del Sur del Perú: Simbiosis Económico-social con los Agricultores. *In* Estudios Etnógraficos del Perú Meridional. Shozo Masuda, ed. pp. 65–84. Tokyo: University of Tokyo.

Isbell, Billie Jean

1978 To Defend Ourselves: Ecology and Ritual in an Andean Village. Austin: University of Texas Press.

Johnson, Allen W.

1972 Individuality and Experimentation in Traditional Agriculture. Human Ecology 1(2):149–60.

Lambert, Berndt
1977 Bilaterality in the Andes. *In* Andean Kinship and Marriage. R. Bolton and E. Mayer, eds. pp. 1–27. American Anthropological Association Monographs, No. 7. Washington, D. C.

Matos Mar, José
1964 La Propiedad en la Isla de Taquile. *In* Estudios Sobre la Cultura Actual en el Perú. Lima: UNSM.

Mayer, Enrique
1971 Un Carnero por un Saco de Papas: Aspectos del Trueque en la zona de Chaupiwaranga (Pasco). *In* Actas Memorias del XXXIX Congreso Internacional de Americanistas, Lima. Tomo 3, pp. 184–96.
1972 Censos Insensatos: Evaluación de los Censos Campesinos en la Historia de Tangor. *In* Visita de la Provincia de León de Huánuco en 1562, Iñigo Ortíz de Zúñiga, Visitador. John Murra, ed. pp. 341–65. Huánuco: Universidad Nacional Hermilio Validzán.
1974 Reciprocity, Self-sufficiency, and Market Relations in a Contemporary Community in the Central Andes of Peru. Latin American Studies Program Dissertation Series No. 72, Cornell University, Ithaca, N.Y.
1977 Tenencia y Control Comunal de la Tierra: Caso de Laraos (Yauyos). Cuadernos del CONUP 24–25:59–72.
1978 Aspectos Colectivos en la Agricultura Andina. Primer Congreso Internacional de Cultivos Andinos (Ayacucho, 1977). IICA, Serie Informes y Conferencias. La Paz.
1979 Land Use in the Andes: Ecology and Agriculture in the Mantaro Valley of Peru, with Special Reference to Potatoes. Lima: Centro International de la Papa, Social Science Unit Publication.
1984 A Tribute to the Household: Domestic Economy and the Encomienda in Colonial Peru. *In* Kinship Idcology and Practice in Latin America. Raymond T. Smith, ed. Chapel Hill: University of North Carolina Press.

Mayer, Enrique and César Fonseca
1979 Sistemas Agrarios en la Cuenca del Río Canete (Depto de Lima). Lima: ONERN.

Mitchell, William P.
1976a Irrigation and Community in the Central Peruvian Highlands. American Anthropologist 78 (1):25–44.
1976b Social Adaptation to the Mountain Environment of an Andean Village. *In* Hill Lands: Proceedings of an International Symposium. J. Luchop, et al., eds. pp. 187–98. Morgantown: University of West Virginia Press.
1980 Local Ecology and the State: Implications of Contemporary Quechua Land Use for the Inca Sequence of Agricultural Work. *In* Beyond the Myths of Culture. Eric B. Ross, ed. pp. 139–54. New York: Academic Press.

Murra, John V.

1956 The Economic Organization of the Inca State. Ph.D. thesis, University of Chicago.

1968 An Aymara Kingdom in 1567. Ethnohistory 6 (2):115–51.

1972 El "Control Vertical" de un Máximo de Pisos Ecológicos en la Economía de las Sociedades Andinas. *In* Visita de la Provincia de Léon de Huánuco en 1562, Iñigo Ortiz de Zúñiga, Visitador. John Murra, ed. Tomo II. Huánuco: Universidad Nacional Hermilio Valdizán.

1975 Formaciones Económicas y Políticas del Mundo Andino. Lima: IEP.

1985 "El Archipiélago Vertical" Revisited. (In this volume.)

Murra, John V., ed.

1972 Visita a la Provincia de León de Huánuco en 1562, Iñigo Ortíz de Zúñiga, Visitador. Tomo II. Huánuco: Universidad Nacional Hermilio Valdizán.

Netting, Robert McC.

1976 What Alpine Peasants Have in Common: Observations on Communal Land Tenure in a Swiss Village. Human Ecology 4 (2):135–46.

Notes and Queries in Anthropology

1966 Guía de Campo del Investigador Social. (Union Panamericana) Manuales Técnicos XII, Washington D. C.

Odum, Eugene

1971 Fundamentals in Ecology. Philadelphia: W. B. Saunders Co.

ONERN

1970 Inventorio, Evaluación y Uso Racional de los Recursos Naturales de la Costa: La Cuenca del Río Cañete. Lima: ONERN.

1978 Mapa Ecológico del Perú. Lima: ONERN.

Ortiz de Zevallos, Pilar and Lía del Río de Calmell

1978 Las Lagunas como Fuentes de Recursos Naturales en el Siglo XVI. *In* Ethnohistoria y Antropología Andina: Primera Jornada del Museo Nacional de Historia. Marcia Koth de Paredes and Amalia Castelli, eds. pp. 57–62. Lima.

Palacios Ríos, Felix

1977 Pastizales de Regadío para Alpacas. *In* Pastores de Puna. Jorge Flores Ochoa, ed. pp. 155–70. Lima: IEP.

Platt, Tristan

1982 El Estado Boliviano y el Ayllu Andino. Lima: IEP.

Pulgar Vidal, Javier

n.d. Las Ocho Regiones Naturales del Perú. Lima: Editorial Universo.

Rhoades, Robert and Stephen I. Thompson

1975 Adaptive Strategies in Alpine Environments: Beyond Ecological Particularism. American Ethnologist 2 (3):535–51.

Rostworowski, María

1985 Patronyms with the Consonant *F* in the *Guarangas* of Cajamarca. (In this volume.)

Saignes, Thiery
1978 De la filiatión a la residénce: les ethnies dans les vallées de Larecaja. Annales: Ecónomiés, Sociétés, Civilisations. 33e Année 5–6: 1160–81.

Shaner, W. W., P. F. Philipp, and W. R. Schmehl
1981 Farming Systems Research and Development: Guidelines for Developing Countries. Boulder, Co.: Westview Press.

Smith, Clifford, William M. Denevan, and Patrick Hamilton
1981 Antiguos Campos de Camellones en la Región del Lago Titicaca. *In* La Tecnología en el Mundo Andino: Runakunap Kawsanin-kupaq Rurasqankunaqa. Heather Lechtman and Ana María Soldi, eds. pp. 25–50. México: UNAM.

Soldi, Ana María
1982 La Agricultura Tradicional en Hoyas. Lima: PUC.

Thünen, Johann Heinrich von
1826 Der Isolierte Staat. C. M. Wartenberg.

Tosi, Joseph Jr.
1960 Zonas de Vida Natural en el Perú. Boletín Técnico No. 5 Instituto Inter-Americano de Ciencias Agrícolas de la OEA, Zona Andina. Lima.

Troll, Carl
1968 Geo-Ecology of the Mountainous Regions of the Tropical Americas. *In* Colloquium Geographicum 9. Bonn: Ferd Dümmlers Verlag.

Valée, Lionel
1971 La Ecología Subjectiva como Elemento Esencial de la Verticalidad. Revista del Museo Nacional 37:167–75. Lima.

Webster, Stephen
1980 Parentesco y Afinidad en una Comunidad Indígena Quechua. *In* Parentesco y Matrimonio en los Andes. E. Mayer and R. Bolton, eds. Lima: PUC.

Winterhalder, Bruce R. and R. Brooke Thomas
1978 Geoecology of the Southern Highlands of Peru: A Human Adaptation Perspective. Occasional Paper No. 27, Institute of Arctic and Alpine Research, University of Colorado.

Yamamoto, Norio
1981 Investigación Preliminar sobre las Actividades Agro-pastoriles en el Distrito de Marcapata, Departamento del Cuzco, Perú. *In* Estudios Etnográficos del Perú Meridional. Shozo Masuda, ed. pp. 85–137. Tokyo: University of Tokyo.

5

The Ecological Complementarity of Agro-Pastoralism: Some Comments

Norio Yamamoto

Introduction

Recent comparative studies of mountain populations in such diverse areas of the world as the Alps, Himalayas, and Andes have demonstrated parallels in ecological adaptations (Rhoades and Thompson 1975; Brush 1976a; Guillet 1983). However, these studies have not yet offered an adequate explanation of the continuing viability of distinctive Andean ecological complementarity (Murra in this volume). Although Murra's ethnohistorical work (1972, 1975, 1978) has shed much light on traditional Andean sociopolitical organization and its relationship to ecology, in general, cultural ecological studies by ethnographers have not explored in sufficient depth the subtleties and significance of the interdependent relationships among various components of the Andean highland ecosystem, such as farming and camelid pastoralism.

A major question that needs to be examined is how the Andean highlanders have successfully sustained a vast population and enjoyed high production over a long period of time (Murra in this volume), without permanently deteriorating their environment, which is regarded today as fragile and low yielding (Eckholm 1975; Guillet 1983; Thomas and Winterhalder 1976). Also, this is a region that has been continuously inhabited for at least 15,000 years, gave birth to such notable prehistoric high cultures as the Tiwanaku and Inca, and today supports a dense human population (Dolffus 1982).

Recent comparative ethnographies on mountainous regions in various parts of the world, however, offer some possible answers to the above question. Perhaps the most plausible explanation may be the widespread mixed agro-pastoral economy, as noted by Rhoades and

Thompson (1975) who consider it to be one of the several remarkable similarities that emerge from various comparative studies of mountain cultural ecology. Thus, this paper examines this economy as a possible explanation for the long-lasting viability of Andean ecological complementarity. I will draw primarily upon the data collected during my one year study (Yamamoto 1981, 1982) in Marcapata, a Quechua-speaking agro-pastoral community in the eastern part of the Department of Cuzco at an altitude of approximately 1,000 to 5,000 m above sea level, that began in 1978. My discussion will focus on the situation on the eastern slopes of the southern Central Andean highlands.

Variable Production in the Montane Environment

The Central Andes, particularly the southern area, is characterized by the steep gradients of the high Cordillera and extensive high plateaus which are much higher and wider than in the Northern and Southern Andes. The area features tropical alpine climates which permit utilization of the highlands throughout the year (Rhoades and Thompson 1975: 544). Thus, the great altitudinal differences in this area provide ecological diversity and consequently several different life zones (see Craig and Mayer in this volume). In general, the Andean people recognize four life zones: the *puna* of high altitudes, typically ranging between 4,000–5,000 m above sea level, the *suni* of mid/high altitudes (3,000–4,000 m), the *quechua* of mid-altitudes (2,000–3,000 m), and the *yunga* of low altitudes (less than 2,000 m; cf. Pulgar Vidal, n.d.).

The Central Andean highlands, however, are not an environment of inherently high productivity, because of soil aridity, cold temperatures, low levels of organic matter, and other factors (Thomas and Winterhalder 1976; Moran 1979: 161–69). Low temperatures with great diurnal fluctuation adversely affect the various biological and chemical processes crucial for maintenance of soil fertility. In addition, the lengthy wet season, which lasts several months, erodes and leaches vital soil, and triggers landslides. As a result, highland soil exposed to such severe climatic changes, artificial deforestation, and other human abuses discussed later in depth can easily deteriorate and lose its fertility. According to plant ecologist Ellenberg (1979), for example, the Upper Montane to Sub-Alpine belt found in the Central Andes is not original vegetation but a result of anthropogenic successions.

However, Andean populations have successfully maximized the potential of the environment by developing appropriate domesticates, as well as innovative technological and social practices.[1] Enrique Mayer (in this volume) describes some examples of such creative dynamism.

It should be emphasized that the Central Andes constitutes one of the five major domestication centers (Vavilov 1949/50), where complexes of animal and plant domesticates form a series of complementary and interdependent roles. Most of the crucial subsistence crops and animals, such as potato (*Solanum spp.*), *oca* (*Oxalis tuberosa*), *olluco* (*Ullucus tuberosus*), *quinua* (*Chenopodium quinua*), llama (*Lama glama*), alpaca (*Lama pacos*), and guinea pig (*Cavia porcelus*) appear to have been domesticated in the central and southern highlands (e.g., Sauer 1950; Franklin 1982).

Moreover, the domestication process in the Andes has produced a series of cultigens adapted to diverse *pisos ecológicos* along the vertical gradients, encompassing *yunga* to *puna* zones. For example, different species of Andean tubers with impressive variability can be culitvated at various elevations. In the *puna* and *suni*, the aforementioned potato, *oca,* and *olluco*, as well as *isaño* (*Tropaeolum tuberosum*) are widely grown, while in the *quechua*, *llacon* (*Polymnia edulis*) and *racacha* (*Arracacia xanthorhiza*) are commonly cultivated. On the other hand, *achira* (*Canna edulis*), manioc (*Manihot esculenta*), and sweet potato (*Ipomoea batatas*) form important *yunga* crops. Importantly, the variability found within each cultigen described above allows its cultivation in a range of ecological habits.

The potato, the best studied of the Andean tubers, in reality encompasses eight species (from diploid to pentaploid) and several thousand varieties that are grown in the *puna* through *quechua* zones (Zósimo Huamán: pers. com. 1984). In other words, variability in and among the cultigens under discussion permits maximization of the potential productivity of the numerous microenvironments found along the vertical dimension of the Central Andes.[2]

The complementary role of domesticated animals, particularly llamas and alpacas, to agriculture for full utilization of the Andean landscape must be noted here. Their maintenance involves forms and areas that are complementary to farming pursuits. More specifically, llamas and alpacas are kept in high altitude zones (ca. 4,000–5,000 m) characterized by severe aridity and coldness that effectively inhibit cultivation of even such high altitude crops as potatoes. As Webster (1971) notes, camelid herding effectively and significantly extends the production zone well beyond the upper limits of agriculture. These upper limits of human exploitation are among the highest in the world, comparable to the northern region of the Himalayan range (Dollfus 1982).

Despite the above similarity, there is an important difference between these two regions of the world: due to the tropical mountain climate, Andean animal husbandary is possible year round in the high altitude zones which lie directly above the agricultural zone.

Agro-pastoralism as a Production System

Contemporary Andean ethnographies demonstrate that the self-sufficient agro-pastoral subsistence system is widespread on the eastern slopes of the southern Central Andes (e.g., Webster 1971; Yamamoto 1982; Mankhe 1984). Operation of the system is facilitated by contiguous, condensed microenvironments along steep slopes that are accessible within reasonably short travel times to the local inhabitants (Brush 1976b). In addition to the topographic features, ecological factors must be taken into account in explaining the pervasive nature of the agro-pastoralism. Since the higher parts of the agricultural zone have a tendency to deteriorate through aridity, coldness, and erosion, fertilization by animal grazing and conscious addition of their dung is more important. Camelid dung that can be collected at known communal voiding areas is crucial to maintenance of the quality of the agricultural lands.

The farming system in Marcapata presents striking evidence for such a complementary relationship between animal herding and cultivation. Among the wide range of both indigenous and introduced crops and animals raised in Marcapata, potatoes, maize, and domesticated Andean camelids and sheep form the three foci of the local subsistence economy.

Three groups of potatoes, *papa maway, papa puna,* and *papa ruki* are grown on the higher eastern slopes around Marcapata, ranging in altitudinal sequence: *papa maway* in the lowest zone, *papa puna* in the intermediate zone, and finally *papa ruki* in the highest zone. The land for each type of potato is farmed according to a system of sectorial fallow, which dictates that a new plot be used each year. A four-year fallow is the minimum employed, requiring a longer fallow period in general to cultivate *papa ruki,* the frost-resistant species of potato grown at the upper limits of agriculture. The fields in fallow for *papa puna* and *papa ruki* are covered by alpine grass, and used frequently for grazing camelids and sheep. Furthermore, dung from the herd animals is always given to the land as fertilizer sometime after potato planting.

On the other hand, land for *maway* is not used for grazing llamas and sheep and not fertilized with dung. Since the land for *maway* in

Table 5.1 Marcapata: Ecological Zones and Land Control

Life Zone	Ecological Zone	Elevation	General Characteristics	Control
Puna	Alpine Rain Tundra	5,000–4,200 m.	Major grazing zone of llamas and alpacas	↑ Communal
Suni	Subalpine Wet Paramo	4,200–3,600 m.	Major tuber cultivation zone (*papa ruki, papa puna*) Major population zone of *campesinos*	
Quechua	*Ceja de Montaña*	3,600–3,100 m.	Cultivation of *maway patao*	
		– 3,100 –	Pueblo Marcapata and major population zone of *mestizos*	↓
		2,600 m.	Major maize(*llacta sara*) cultivation zone	↑ Individual
Yunga	Subtropical Temperate Rainforest	2,600 – 1,500 m.	Major chili pepper and *wari sara* cultivation zone Cultivation zone of cash crops and *yunka sara* maize	
	Subtropical Rainforest	1,500–1,000 m.	Major population zone of immigrants	↓

fallow is characterized by small trees and shrubs by virtue of its lower, warmer, and rainy location, the weeds are burned late in the dry season and subsequently potatoes planted. Thus the land is fertilized by weed ashes, as in the case of slash-and-burn cultivation.

Three groups of maize, *llacta sara, wari sara,* and *yunka sara* are cultivated on the lower eastern slopes around Marcapata, and, as in the case of potato cultivation, form an altitudinal sequence: *llacta sara* in the highest zone, *wari sara* in the intermediate zone, and finally *yunka sara* in the lowest zone. Interestingly, maize cultivation does not form a complementary relationship with camelid and sheep herding in the *puna* and *suni*. Since *yunka sara* and *wari sara* are grown by slash-and-burn cultivation, animal fertilizer is not used for their cultivation. Although *llacta sara* is cultivated in the same plot for successive years, only a limited quantity of camelid and sheep dung is used. However, European domesticates, such as cows and horses, are allowed to graze in the post-harvest fields, effectively fertilizing the fields.

There is yet another important fertilization process observable in Marcapata. In plots where maize has failed to germinate, due to a large extent to worm damage, cultivators plant a considerable number of beans. As a result, the fields for maize present an appearance, at a glance, of mixed planting. Since beans are well-known nitrogen-fixing crops, fields are fertilized in part by this practice. Although the available data for the relationships between herding and maize cultivation in regard to soil fertilization are limited, mixed maize and bean planting is often reported and the practice is considered to reduce the need to fallow (Sauer 1963; Donkin 1979; Dolffus 1982).

Fallow System and Community Management of Agricultural Land

A fallow system is an important means for effective recovery and maintenance of soil quality.[3] Effective implementation of such a system often necessitates supervision and control of land use under communal organization. When proper rotation of cultivation plots is not carried out, land under individual control often deteriorates to the point where rejuvenation is difficult. As a result, the fallow system under the community's control is the most pervasive form of land management in the Andean highlands.

On the other hand, eastern lowland agriculture, endowed with a warm and temperate climate and abundant water, is typically characterized by high productivity. These favorable conditions seem to be important underlying reasons for the recent "privatization" or the trend toward individual ownership and control of land use seen in the lowlands (Guillet 1981a, b).

The land use pattern observed at Marcapata offers important and useful insights into the basic issue at hand (see Table 5.1). The majority of the inhabitants in Marcapata are engaged in agro-pastoral activities under community supervision. However, the lowest portion of the slope below Marcapata is now occupied by recent immigrants from Puno, Cuzco, and other southern highland regions, who, under individual control, are devoted to the cultivation of a variety of cash crops, such as sugar cane, plantains, and citrus. In addition to the above example of individual control of land use, we see that the management of a portion of communal maize cultivation land has been given to individual control (Yamamoto 1981). Similar shifts in land use management have been observed in other highland communities. For example, Guillet (1981b: 20) notes:

> Communal control of land with extensive grazing and sectorial fallowing has been found in association with paleotechnic technology in the tuber zones. In contrast, intensive continuous irrigation and specialized horticulture is found in conjunction with private control of land and European technology in the maize zone.

Although the association defined above by Guillet may be explained as an effect of population pressure and/or the penetration of a market economy in the area under study, other factors, such as the aforementioned regional environmental conditions and ecological complementarity, must also be considered. Generally speaking, the juxtaposition of communal tenure and control of high altitude pasture for camelids and individual control of low altitude agricultural land is a phenomenon found not only in the Andes but also in other highland regions of the world, such as the Himalayas and the Alps (Rhoades and Thompson 1975; Brush 1976a; Guillet 1983).

The pervasiveness of the pattern of communal tenure and control of high altitude land suggests that the fragile environments can be best managed at the community level. Regularly scheduled fallowing of high altitude agricultural land, which permits animal grazing and attendant fertilization, is clearly best executed under communal control.[4] It has been noted by various workers (Ellenberg 1979: 411; Guillet 1981b: 24) that the sectorial fallowing of land for potato cultivation within mixed agro-pastoralism has been a remarkably stable system for centuries. In sum, potato cultivation and camelid herding are ecologically complementary and the resultant agro-pastoral subsistence system with communal land tenure and control has considerable antiquity and persists to this day.

On the other hand, plots for maize cultivation in the lowlands, in general, are primarily under individual control. Various communities not only on the eastern slopes but also in the intermontane valleys manifest a trend toward private control away from traditional communal management (Guillet 1981a, b).

There is yet another important consideration in respect to the management pattern of maize cultivation on the eastern slopes; it is likely that, fundamentally, maize cultivation has not been an integral part of the Andean agro-pastoralism. Whether we are dealing with modern or Inca eras, the sort of ecological complementarity observable between potato cultivation and camelid husbandry in the higher altitudes is lacking in the lowland maize cultivation. Maize cultivation seems to have evolved autonomously in its own low altitude temperate environment, independent from developments in the higher zones. That is to say, within the Andean mixed agro-pastoral system, maize cultivation has had only limited interdependence with other aspects of the system, thus preconditioning or allowing detachment away from communal management.

In other words, maize cultivation in successive years in the same plots seems to be a post-Conquest phenomenon. Dolffus (1982:40) argues that in the Inca period animal fertilizers were not utilized for maize cultivation in the *quechua* zone, as nitrogen was supplied in part by legumes and ashes providing additional nutrients. Also, ethnohistorical studies (Murra 1975, 1978) suggest that large scale exploitation and maize cultivation in the *quechua* zone began only after the formation of the Inca state. In addition, the European domesticates such as the cows, horses, sheep, and goats that the Spaniards introduced were better adapted to the lower *quechua* than the higher *puna*. Their local presence, in turn, made grazing in the post-harvest fields quite feasible and widespread. Except where *guano* was available (see Julien in this volume), I suspect the maize cultivation of that period employed a sectorial fallowing system with green manure.

Overall, available data argue that fundamentally maize cultivation in the *quechua* zone has no readily appreciable ecological complementarity with the llama-alpaca husbandry of the high *puna*. On the other hand, potato cultivation has an intimate interrelationship with herding and breeding of these Andean camelid domesticates. It is evident that without the use of camelid dung as fertilizer, the productivity of potato cultivation in the adjacent, lower zones would drastically decline (Orlove 1977). Without its continuing use, irreparable soil deterioration is likely to occur. Although the camelid's dung as fertilizer has not been extensively studied, the soil survey data for Nuñoa situated on the *altiplano* of 4,000 m are available (Winterhalder et al. 1974). The data show that the soils are deficient in nitrogen, phosphorous, and organic matter, in addition to having drainage and erosion problems. In contrast, the fields fertilized with sheep dung have increased organic matter sufficiently enough to grow potatoes. In addition, it must be noted that organic matter improves the physical qualities of the soil: aeration, soil moisture relationships, and the water-retention capacity of the soil (Moran 1979: 164).

The preceding seems to be a reasonable explanation for the pervasiveness of self-sufficient, agro-pastoralism in the southern highlands of the Central Andes, where potato cultivation has been most important and llamas and alpacas are particularly numerous. The complementarity that exists between potato cultivation and camelid husbandry, then, can be seen as the best adaptive strategy in minimizing adverse effects, such as soil erosion and deterioration, while maximizing potential productivity within the limitations set by the Andean highlands.

Agro-pastoralism and Food Consumption Patterns

In the southern Central Andean highlands, contemporary ethnographies and ethnohistorical studies have shown that, at least since the Inka period, three important exploitation patterns have existed for the three basic life zones: camelid pastoralism in the *puna,* potato cultivation in the *suni,* and maize cultivation in the *quechua* and *yunga* zones. From the standpoint of ecological complementarity, however, we can recognize two basic production systems composed of different permutations of the above three exploitation patterns; one formed by interdependent potato cultivation and camelid herding in the high altitudes, and the other, by autonomous maize cultivation in the low altitude zones.

Differences between the two production systems are also apparent in regard to food consumption patterns. No separate pastoral economy has developed anywhere in the Andes apart from the tuber cultivation (Troll 1931:263–64; Murra 1965:188), suggesting that neither one alone provides a sufficient dietary base. Dietary autonomy based on camelid pastoralism is greatly limited by the traditional cultural practice of utilizing neither milk nor blood (Webster 1973:117). At the same time, the *suni* and *puna* inhabitants whose diet is dominated in volume by Andean tubers, which are relatively low in fat and proteins, require meat provided by their domesticated camelids and guinea pigs.

It should be noted, however, that there are some indigenous communities in the *puna* and *suni* of the southern highlands that maintain self-sufficiency based solely on tuber cultivation and animal herding. The topography of the extensive *altiplano* poses considerable difficulty to households and other small social groups in gaining access to the maize cultivation zones. It is among these groups in the *altiplano* that we see a self-sufficient economy.

Although available data on food consumption patterns in the Andes are limited, the survey conducted by Picón-Reátegui (1976) and others in Nuñoa offers strong dietary evidence for this self-sufficient economy. Due to the isolated location and some socioeconomic characteristics of the communities in the district of Nuñoa (Fig. 5.1), food habits have been long linked to local *puna* food production. Studies by Mazess and Baker (1964) showed that foods not native to the Nuñoa or *altiplano* districts, such as maize and wheat, made up only 2.5 percent, while tuber crops and animal meat covered approximately 90 percent of the bulk of food eaten.

In Sincata, a small native Quechua community situated at 4,000 m

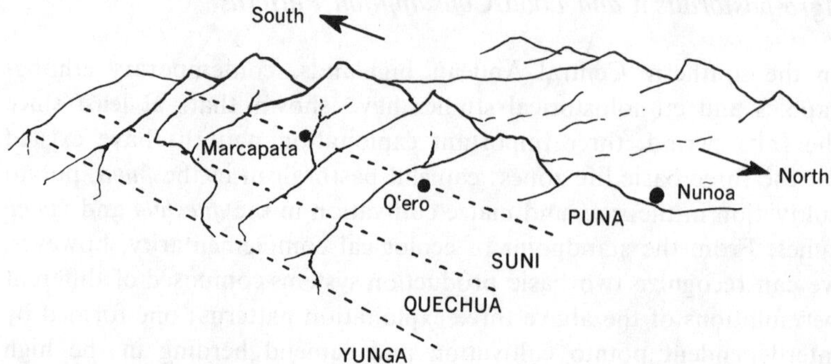

Fig. 5.1. Schematic drawing showing the relative locations of the key case studies mentioned in the text.

above sea level 20 km southeast of the town of Nuñoa with the same *puna* food production system, only about 3.5 percent of the bulk of food ingested was identified as foreign produce (Picón-Reátegui 1976:211). This evidence strongly suggests that local *puna* produce, such as potatoes and animal meat, enable the inhabitants to maintain self-sufficient subsistence.

In addition to the Nuñoa, various populations on the eastern flanks of the Cordilleras also show similar subsistence self-sufficiency based on animal herding and interdependent potato cultivation in the *puna* and *suni*. These populations, including Marcapata, augment high altitude production with maize cultivation in the *quechua* and *yunga*. However, in terms of their diet, they depend mainly on *puna* and *suni* products. For example, 80 percent of the bulk of food consumed in Marcapata consists of fresh and dehydrated potato (Yamamoto 1983: 98–100). Although maize cultivation occupies the majority of land belonging to the community and individual inhabitants of Marcapata, the dietary contribution of maize to their diet is considerably less than that of potato. Much of the maize is devoted to special dishes as well as the manufacture of *chicha* used for ceremonies and fiestas. In this light, maize cultivation is mainly for ritual purposes, rather than for daily food.

Similar food production and consumption patterns have been noted for Q'ero, on the eastern slope near Cuzco, by Webster (1971:178–79), who observes:

> Potatoes are the overwhelming diet staple throughout the year, constituting fully 80% of the gross consumption. . . . Corn is central

> in diet, but crucial in ritual. It is required for the manufacture of *chicha,* the ritual drink which is the *sine qua non* of fertility ceremonies, religious cargo execution and assumption of political office.

Overall, there are some basic differences between potatoes and maize in regard to production, consumption, and cultural values. It is likely that such differences were more prominent in Inca times. Murra (1975, 1978) points out a clear distinction between two kinds of agriculture simultaneously practiced in the Inca state to produce the more delicate but prestigious maize, as well as the lowly but crucial Andean tubers. In addition, he notes:

> Las diferencias botánicas y ecológicas entre las dos clases de agricultura también tenían correlaciones económicas: los sistemas de pesos y medidas y la tenencia de tierra eran diferentes para las dos especies de cultivos. (Murra 1975:49).

Conclusion

The preceding discussion as a whole suggests that maize and potatoes have completely different histories in the Central Andes. Maize introduced later into a production system of mixed agro-pastoral subsistence based on camelid herding and potato cultivation. I have argued elsewhere (1982:55) that the utilization of root crops coupled with herding in the highlands was subsequently amplified to such an extent that a self-sufficient production system based on the potato and camelids evolved.

The above data and lines of argument, in turn, strongly suggest that the production system composed of tuber cultivation and camelid herding represents an ancient adaptation to the biological and physical environments of the southern Central Andean highlands. It follows that Andean highlanders have been able to maintain this self-sufficient subsistence utilizing the products from the *puna* and *suni.* Onuki (in this volume) characterizes this subsistence pattern as the "llama-*papa* complex." In fact, the primary *quechua* and *yunga* products acquired by the Inca state through their archipelago system that spanned both the eastern and western slopes of the Central Andes were non-subsistence goods, such as coca, maize, wool, and guano (Murra 1972; Julien, Harris, and Morris in this volume). As a generalization, in regard to control of the vertical gradient by an ethnic group on the eastern slopes of the southern Central Andes, the cultural ideal is to gain access to and/or control over production zones in the *puna* through *yunga.*

It seems self-evident that the archipelago system of the Inca state and the exploitation pattern of contemporary groups are different, not only in scale, but also in the sociopolitical organization to manage the vertical control. However, it must be remembered that the basic feature of the Andean environmental exploitation system is the utilization of the great vertical gradient from *puna* to *yunga,* although self-sufficient agro-pastoral subsistence can only be established or maintained through exploitation of the *puna* and *suni.* In respect to Q'eros and Marcapata, such vertical control is indeed a cultural reality.

NOTES

I would like to thank Izumi Shimada, Shozo Masuda, Robert Rhoades, and Melody Shimada for their thoughtful comments on the contents and style of this paper.

1. One notable example of such technological practices are tuber preservation techniques. According to Troll (1968:33), without the invention of tuber preservation higher civilizations such as those of the Tiwanaku or Inca would not have developed at these great heights.

2. In addition, the potato is one of the most nutritious plant food sources for human consumption. The ratio of protein to carbohydrates is higher in potatoes than in many cereals and major tuber crops. The quality of potato protein is higher than that of most other food crops. Furthermore, the potato is superior to almost every other cropping food production per hectare per day (Centro Internacional de la Papa 1982).

3. Longtime fallowing is also effective in order to protect potato plants from the golden nematode (Brush 1980:163).

4. It must be noted also that community control over land for both agriculture and herding facilitates the scheduling of subsistence tasks (Guillet 1982, Yamamoto 1982).

REFERENCES CITED

Brush, Stephen B.

1976a Introduction to Symposium on Mountain Environments. Human Ecology 4(2):125–33.

1976b Man's Use of an Andean Ecosystem. Human Ecology 4(2): 147–66.

1980 The Environment and Native Andean Agriculture. America Indígena 40(1):161–72.

Centro Internacional de la Papa

1982 World Potato Facts. Lima: The International Potato Center.

Dollfus, Oliver.

1982 Development of Land-Use Patterns in the Central Andes. Mountain Research and Development 2 (1):39–48.

Donkin, R. A.

1979 Agricultural Terracing in the Aboriginal New World. Viking Fund Publications in Anthropology, No. 56. Tucson: The University of Arizona Press.

Eckholm, E. P.

1975 The Deterioration of Mountain Environments. Science 189:764–70.

Ellenberg, H.

1979 Man's Influence of Tropical Mountain Ecosystems in South America. Journal of Ecology 67:401–16.

Franklin, William L.

1982 Biology, Ecology, and the Relationship to Man of the South American Camelids. *In* Mammalian Biology of South American. M. A. Mares and H. H. Genowayas, eds. pp. 457–89. Pittsburgh: University of Pittsburgh.

Guillet, David

1981a Land Tenure, Agricultural Regime, and Ecological Zone in the Central Andes. American Ethnologist 8(1):139–56.

1981b Agrarian Ecology and Peasant Production in the Central Andes. Mountain Research and Development 1(1):19–28.

1983 Toward a Cultural Ecology of Mountains: The Central Andes and the Himalayas Compared. Current Anthropology 24(5):561–74.

Mankhe, Lothar

1984 Formas de Adaptación en la Agricultura Indígena de la Zona de los Callahuayas. *In* Espacio y Tiempo en el Mundo Callahuaya. pp. 59–71. La Paz: Instituto de Estudios Bolivianos.

Mazess, R. B. and P. T. Baker

1964 Diet of Quechua Indians Living at High Altitudes: Nuñoa, Peru. American Journal of Clinical Nutrition 15:341–51.

Moran, Emilio F.

1979 Human Adaptability: An Introduction to Ecological Anthropology. Belmont, Calif.: Wadsworth Publishing Co., Inc.

Murra, John V.

1965 Herds and Herders in the Inca State. *In* Man, Culture, and Animals: The Role of Animals in Human Ecological Adjustments, A. Leeds and A. Vayda, eds. pp. 185–215. Washington, D. C.: American Association for the Advancement of Science.

1972 El "Control Vertical" de un Máximo de Pisos Ecológicos en la Economía de las Sociedades Andinas. *In* Visita de la Provincia de

León de Huánuco 1562, Tomo II, John V. Murra, ed. pp. 427–68. Huánuco: Universidad Nacional Hermilio Valdizán.

1975 Formaciones Económicas y Políticas del Mundo Andino. Lima: Instituto de Estudios Peruanos.

1978 Las Organizaciones Económicas del Estado Inca. Mexico: Siglo Veintiuno.

Orlove, Benjamin

1977 Integration through Production: The Use of Zonation. American Ethnologist 4(1):84–101.

Picón-Reátegui, E.

1976 Nutrition. *In* Man in the Andes: A Multidisciplinary Study of High-Altitude Quechua. P. T. Baker and M. A. Little, eds. pp. 208–36. Philadelphia: Dowden, Hutchinson & Ross, Inc.

Pulgar Vidal, Javier

n.d. Las Ocho Regiones Naturales del Perú. Lima: Editorial Universo.

Rhoades, Robert E. and Stephen I. Thompson

1975 Adaptive Strategies in Alpine Environments: Beyond Ecological Particularism. American Ethnologist 2(3):535–51.

Sauer, Carl O.

1963 Cultivated Plants of South and Central America. *In* Handbook of South American Indians, Vol. 6. J. H. Steward, ed. pp. 487–543. Washington, D.C.: Bureau of American Ethnology.

Brooke, R. Thomas and Bruce P. Winterhalder

1976 Physical and Biotic Environment of Southern Highland Peru. *In* Man in the Andes. P. T. Baker and M. A. Little, eds. pp. 21–59. Philadelphia: Dowden, Hutchinson & Ross, Inc.

Troll, Carl

1931 Die Geographische Grundlagen der Andinen Kulturen und des Inca Reiches. Ibero-Amerikanisches Archiv 5:258–294.

1968 The Cordilleras of the Tropical Americas: Aspects of Climate, Phytogeographical and Agrarian Ecology. *In* Geoecology of the Mountainous Regions of the Tropical Americas. C. Troll, ed. pp. 15–56. Bonn: Ferd Dummlers Verlag.

Vavilov, N.I.

1949/50 The Origin, Variation, Immunity, and Breeding of Cultivated Plants, Vol. 13. Waltham, Mass: The Cronica Botanica Co.

Webster, Steven S.

1971 An Indigenous Quechua Community in Exploitation of Multiple Ecological Zones. Revista del Museo Nacional 37:174–83.

1973 Native Pastoralism in the South Andes. Ethnology 12(2):115–33.

Winterhalder, Bruce, Robert Larsen and R. Brooke Thomas

1974 Dung as an Essential Resource in a Highland Peruvian Community. Human Ecology 2(2):43–55.

Yamamoto, Norio

1981 Investigación Preliminar sobre las Actividades Agro-Pastoriles en el Distrito de Marcapata, Departamento del Cuzco, Peru. *In* Estudios Etnográficos del Perú Meridional, Shozo Masuda, ed. pp. 85–137. Tokyo: University of Tokyo.

1982 A Food Production System in the Southern Central Andes. *In* El Hombere y su Ambiente en los Andes Centrales. L. Millones and H. Tomoeda, eds. pp. 39–62. Senri Ethnological Studies 10. Senri: National Museum of Ethnology.

1983 Food Basis of Andean Highland Society (in Japanese). Kikan Zinruigaku (Quarterly Journal of Anthropology) 13(3):76–128.

III

Ecological Complementarity in the South-Central and Southern Andes

The nine papers brought together in this part test and elaborate Murra's vertical archipelago model. Beginning with Mujica's paper that takes us back to 1500 B.C., they are chronologically ordered. Spatially, all but Harris deal primarily with the *altiplano* and western slopes of the Andes. Julien and Masuda extend this coverage to the shore and offshore of the Pacific, reminding us that marine resources and the Pacific are integral parts of Andean ecological complementarity and cognition of the world. That the vertical ecology, on the one hand, and social organization and cosmology, on the other, are intimately linked is illustrated by Harris and Tomoeda. Flores, Harris, Hidalgo, Julien, Masuda, and Pease explore processes involving the destructuring of supra-communal patterns of ecological complementarity during the Colonial and modern eras. What emerges from their discussions is the persistence of traditional values and understandings linking various communities at different elevations in spite of inroads by the cash/market economy and modern legislation. Such interrelationships are predominantly voluntary in nature, although Mujica suggests the establishment of vertical archipelagos spanning both eastern and western slopes was partially based on the coercive power of the state-level Tiwanaku polity. The data base of Murra's model is scrutinized by Julien who emphasizes the critical importance of tight chronological control in any reconstruction of resource control patterns and thus questions the adequacy of Inca and pre-Inca distinctions.

6

Altiplano-Coast Relationships in the South-Central Andes: From Indirect to Direct Complementarity

Elías Mujica

When John Murra published his thesis in 1972 about the "vertical control of a maximum number of ecological levels," he significantly enriched our knowledge about Andean economic systems and obliged us to reformulate political, social, and economic models that had been postulated to define specific pre-European societies. Moreover, a few of the more common concepts established earlier such as transhumance (seasonal migration), *mitmaq* (the movement of people directed by the state), and conquest (the direct control and submission of territory), to cite only a few (F. Salomon in this volume), were complemented and enriched with a new, and for us innovative, possibility: the exploitation of resources controlling a maximum of ecological niches (verticality) by permanent populations (colonies) settled in the periphery (islands) separated physically from their nuclear territory or origin (archipelagos), but who did not lose their rights with their ethnic group. (Murra 1976:144–45; and in this volume.)

Although Murra's model began to be used with considerable regularity, the archaeologists left aside two fundamental aspects for better understanding and application:

1. What is the material manifestation of verticality? That is, how does one know that archaeological materials are proof of permanent colonies and not transhumance, exchange, migration, or other mechanisms of economic complementarity?

2. When and how did the system originate and what are its antecedents? By what process was it implemented and developed?

The above, and other questions, also posed by Murra, were put aside or answered only partially.

Archaeologists have advanced little with the first question even though solving it should be one of the basic points for the empirical understanding of the vertical control of multiple ecological levels. Nevertheless, practically from the first moment the archipelago was proposed by Murra, it was enthusiastically embraced by investigators who saw verticality everywhere, interpreting as such the most varied situations. As proof, it was sufficient to find any cultural element such as a ceramic fragment or decorative element outside of its point of origin or nuclear area.

Despite Murra's early warnings such as during the First International Congress of Andean Culture (Chile, 1973), verticality practically replaced other economic mechanisms—even Andean ones. The vertical archipelago model began to be used in such a generalized, uncritical manner that it ceased to have the special elements that made it an alternative to other mechanisms. In the same meeting in Chile in 1973, in the session at Iquique, Luis G. Lumbreras was critical of the way verticality was applied to data that could reflect other economic patterns which he generically called environmental macroadaptation, such as transhumance, migratory expansion, conquest, and so forth.

New investigations designed with a different perspective are necessary to define the physical manifestation of verticality. In a recent article, therefore, we (Mujica, Rivera, and Lynch 1983) tentatively outlined a methodology for the case of the south-central Andes (Fig. 6.1). Here I should like to concentrate on the second group of questions proposed above, with special emphasis on the conditions which stimulated and permitted the implementation of the archipelago system on the coast by societies which inhabited the high plateau of Lake Titicaca.

Background

In the South-Central Andean area (Lumbreras 1979:30–43; 1981: 75–94) the archipelago model proposed by Murra had a very special impact. On one hand, it presented new criteria for a better understanding of the relationships among the inhabitants of the various regions of the area. On the other hand, it permitted an understanding of the spatial distribution of certain archaeological materials. Moreover, because of both of these contributions, it has been possible to redefine with a more solid base the political and economic organization of the Tiwanaku culture (ca. A.D. 500–1200) which represented the highest level of development in the area.

Since the beginning of research in the area, there has been evidence that high plateau (*altiplano*) ethnicities had access to the valleys of the western Andean slopes. The interpretations of the forms and implications of this access in the prehistoric development of the area have varied through time.

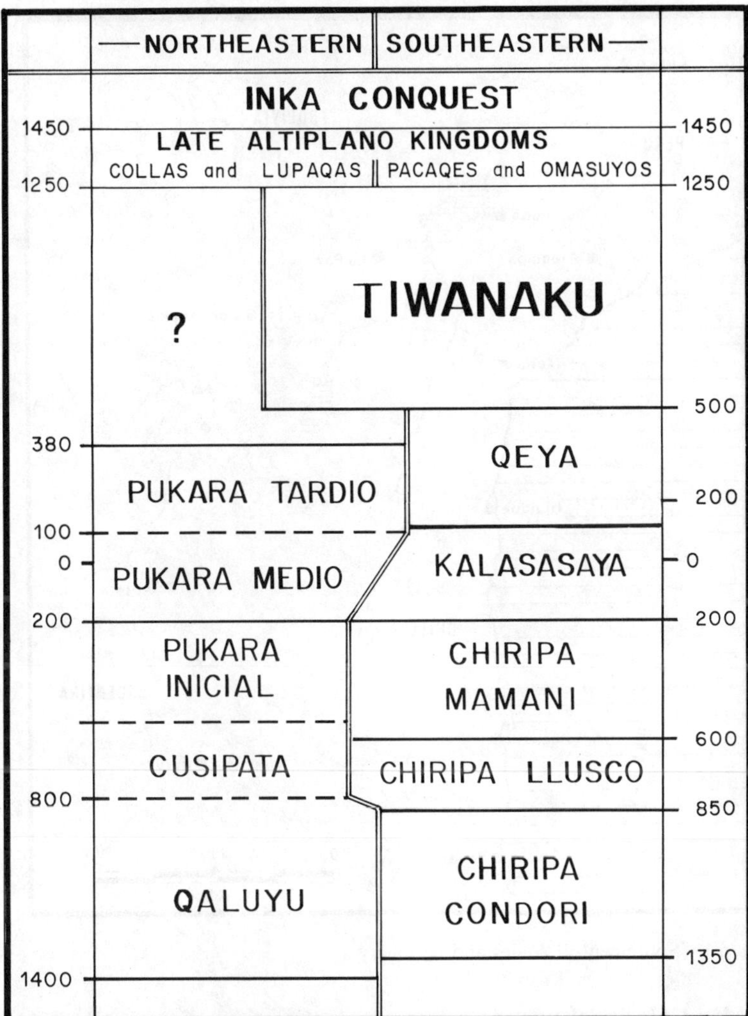
NORTHEASTERN
SOUTHEASTERN
INKA CONQUEST
1450
1450
LATE ALTIPLANO KINGDOMS
COLLAS and LUPAQAS
PACAQES and OMASUYOS
1250
1250
?
TIWANAKU
500
380
QEYA
PUKARA TARDIO
200
100
0
PUKARA MEDIO
KALASASAYA
0
200
200
PUKARA
INICIAL
CHIRIPA
MAMANI
600
CUSIPATA
CHIRIPA LLUSCO
800
850
QALUYU
CHIRIPA
CONDORI
1350
1400

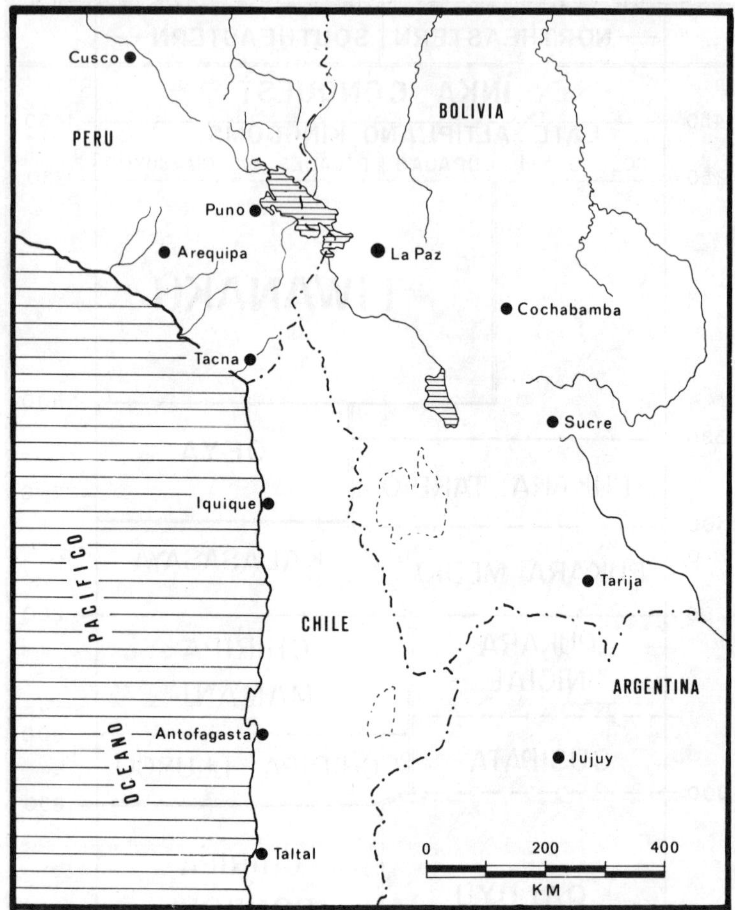

Fig. 6.1 South-central Andes and periphery

Max Uhle was the first to propose high plateau presence on the coast. The evidence was the discovery of Tiwanaku elements in his excavations in the valleys of the far south of Peru and north Chile, and in archaeological collections from the *puna* of Atacama, and Calama and Chiu-Chiu in the middle and upper parts of the Loa River (Uhle 1911, 1913a, 1913b, 1915, 1917, 1918, 1919, 1922). Another pioneer of Chilean archaeology, Ricardo Latcham, discovered and excavated cemeteries with Tiwanaku elements in Ancachi (Quillagua) and Chorrillos (Calama), and studied chronologically similar materials from Tchecar (San Pedro de Atacama) (Latcham 1927, 1928, 1936a, 1936b, 1938, 1941). Such discoveries permitted both pioneers to postulate a Tiwanaku period within the north Chilean sequence, and to postulate coastal-altiplano and altiplano-coastal influences. Latcham (1942: 11) even proposed that in the region of Tarapacá most valleys were colonized (*sic*) by Aymara-speaking Colla groups from the Bolivian high plateau at the time of the Tiwanaku expansion.

Later research has confirmed the original propositions of Uhle and Latcham, and has offered new evidence during different periods about the access of *altiplano* people to the valleys of the western Andean slopes and to the ravines and oases of the coastal desert. An exception was Junius Bird, who at first did not accept Tiwanaku presence in Arica (1943: 202), and who later concluded that the rare Tiwanaku pieces in Arica and Pisagua were exotic (1946:590). Otherwise, most archaeologists have accepted that the prehistoric developments of the high plateau of Lake Titicaca and of the Pacific coast were strongly linked.

In the far southern valleys of Peru, the physical presence of high plateau populations was confirmed by the research of the First Japanese Mission (Ishida 1960), Vescelius (1960), Disselhoff (1968a, 1968b, 1974), Flores Espinoza (1969, 1973, 1979), Trimborn (1973a, 1973b, 1975a, 1975b, 1975c, 1977, 1978, 1981), and Kleemann (1975, 1978, 1981). All found Tiwanaku and post-Tiwanaku evidence in their surveys and excavations. In north Chile the coastal-*puna* ties were emphasized by Richard Schaedel (1957), and Munizaga (1957:122) confirmed Tiwanaku presence in the material excavated by Junius Bird. Still later, research by Guillermo Focacci (1960, 1961a, 1961b, 1969, 1973), Percy Dauelsberg (1961a, 1961b, 1969) and Lautaro Núñez (1963a, 1963b, 1965, 1966, 1969), among others, helped to fill diverse chronological aspects, to define basic problems about the cultural development of the region, and to debate the probable influence of coastal Tiwanaku presence over later cultural developments. As regards Tiwanaku presence in the Atacama region, the work of Uhle and especially Latcham (1938) was continued by Gustavo Le Paige (1961, 1963, 1965), Mario Orellana (1963, 1964), Myriam Tarragó (1968, 1976, 1977), and George Serracino (1980), all of whom offered new evidences for Tiwanaku presence in that region so distant from the Tiwanaku nuclear area. They also described the contexts in which the high plateau elements appeared, and opened the road for a reinterpretation of the high plateau-coastal desert link.

Given the above-described history of research, it is not strange that when John Murra proposed the verticality thesis, the archaeologists of the south-central Andean area were the first to apply it to prehistoric societies, reinterpreting Tiwanaku presence on the coast as high plateau colonies in search of complementary resources (Espoueys

1971:94; Lumbreras 1972:29, 1974:55; Núñez 1972a:32, 1972b:28, 1976:185–86, 192–94). There was a dual and immediate effect: on the one hand, high plateau-coastal relationships through "verticality" made more sense and there was a more solid interpretation of the archaeological evidence; on the other hand, the old idea of the Tiwanaku empire was replaced by that of a colonizing state, following that proposed by Murra ([1972]1975, 1976), within an evidently more coherent and logical scheme in accord with the general characteristics of the South-Central Andean prehistoric development.

It is important to note that Murra's thesis was adopted by archaeologists to interpret Tiwanaku populations on the coast because it offered not only a better explanation for the composition and distribution of archaeological materials, but also, and fundamentally because from the administrative inspections and other sixteenth century legal documents (Diez de San Miguel [1567] 1964; Gutiérrez Flores [1574] 1964; Gutiérrez Flores y Ramírez Zegarra [1573] 1970, 1574; Ramírez Zegarra 1575; Osirio de Quiñozes y Ramírez Zegarra 1581–83), ethnohistoric investigations (Cúneo Vidal 1977; Murra [1955] 1978, 1964, [1968] 1975, 1970, 1979; Pease 1973, 1979, 1980, 1982; Soldi 1978) and ethnological research (Flores Ochoa 1972; Fujii 1980; Masuda 1981, 1982; Onuki 1980) also agree that this was a common pattern in our area of study since the European invasion. For example, the Lupaqa located in part of the old Tiwanaku nuclear territory had colonies from the valley of Lluta in Arica to Sama and Moquegua, oases also occupied earlier by Tiwanaku (Fig. 6.2).

The Character of Altiplano Presence on the Coast

Now not only is it accepted that Tiwanaku access in coastal valleys was by colonies (Berenguer 1975, 1978; Berenguer, Castro, and Silva 1980; Rivera 1975, 1976a, 1976b, 1977, 1980a, 1980b; Mujíca 1978, 1981a; Núñez and Dillehay 1979; Munoz 1983b), but researchers are also studying the *altiplano* coastal relationships of the pre-Tiwanaku epoch (ca. 1500 B.C. to A.D. 500) and are proposing very provoking hypotheses about the varied character of the Tiwanaku occupation in the coastal valleys and deserts (ca. A.D. 500–1200). The results of these investigations will be of great importance to know the historical depth of complementarity and its development through time. Due to this, I shall summarize the state of this matter so as to analyze later the existing conditions in the *altiplano* which permits us to understand the causes which stimulated and enabled permanent access to the coast.

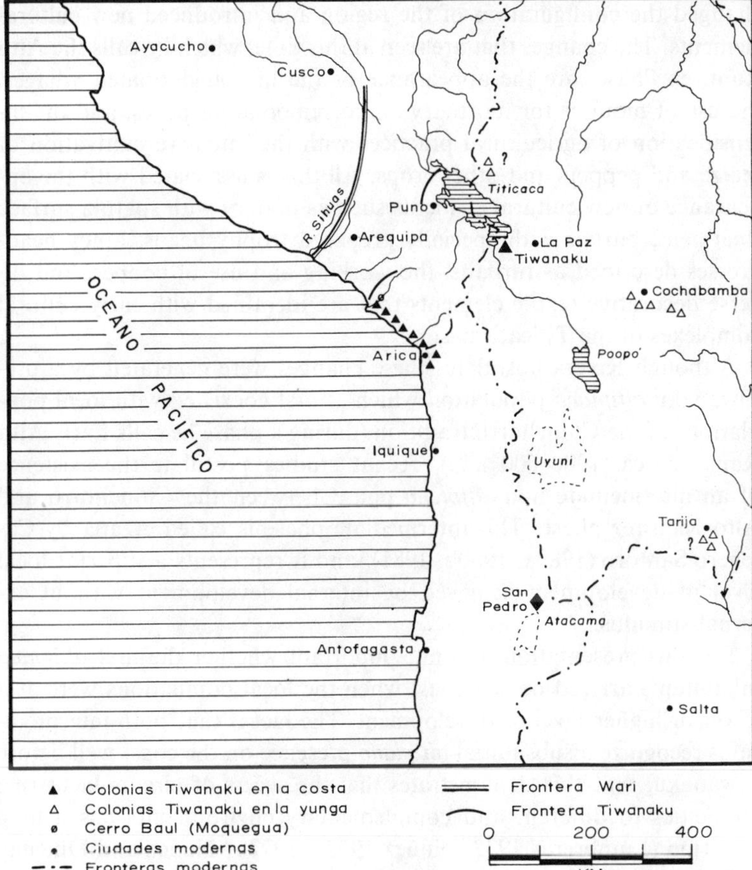

Fig. 6.2 Distribution of Tiwanaku colonies on the coast and in the *yungas*

1. *Pre-Tiwanaku Altiplano-Coast Relationships* (*ca. 1500* B.C.–A.D. *500*)

At the beginning of the 1970s, thanks to the progress of research by archaeologists in Arica (Lumbreras 1974:74) and to the interdisciplinary analysis of early remains from the region (Rivera et al. 1974), it was postulated that approximately between 1500 B.C. and A.D. 500, before Tiwanaku, *altiplano* populations arrived on the extreme north coast of Chile.

According to Mario Rivera (1975, 1976a, 1976b, 1977, 1978, 1980a, 1980b) diverse *altiplano* waves superimposed themselves on local, less-developed inhabitants represented by the complexes Chinchorro, Faldas El Morro, and El Laucho, and imposed a new form of life that changed the configuration of the region and introduced new cultural elements. The changes that are seen at this time, which he calls the Alto Ramírez Phase, are the appearance of the first agglutinated villages, the use of mounds for mortuary and ceremonial purposes, and the intensification of agricultural practices with the intensive cultivation of maize and peppers and other crops. All this is associated with the appearance of new cultural elements such as pottery with spatula surface treatment, burials with specially prepared trophy heads, fancy headdresses described as turbans, the working and use of copper, and diverse decorative textile elements that are identified with early cultural complexes in the Titicaca basin.

Although Rivera postulates these changes were generated by a pre-Tiwanaku *altiplano* population which at first coexisted with local populations of the Chinchorro tradition (during a phase he calls Early Alto Ramírez—ca. 1000–500 B.C.), recent studies postulate the existence of an intermediate non-*altiplano* phase between the Chinchorro and Alto Ramírez phase. This intermediate phase is called Azapa by Calogero Santoro (1980a, 1980b, 1981), and it represents a superior local level of development achieved by internal development without external stimulus.

For this presentation it is not important whether the first *altiplano* inhabitants arrived on the coast when the local populations were at a lower or higher level of development. The fact is that both interpretations recognize a substantial *altiplano* presence on the coast well before Tiwanaku, and this demonstrates that the access of circum-lacustrine ethnicities to different and complementary environments has a long tradition (Lumbreras 1972; Núñez 1972a, 1972b; Núñez and Dillehay 1979; Mujica 1978, 1981a). Now the important point is to determine the kind of access it was and its implications in *altiplano* development.

One hypothesis is that the access of *altiplano* populations to the coast was similar to later times (Lumbreras 1972:29; Rivera 1976a:80) with permanent colonies such as proposed by Murra. The problem is that the available coastal information is very scarce, we are talking about a period that lasted more than 1000 years when the situation was very complicated and unclear to us today, and finally we do not know much about the *altiplano* before 500 B.C. that could offer us comparative material.

Apart from probable transhumant movements suggested by Lautaro Núñez (1972b:31–32) for the Chinchorro tradition, it seems that between 1000 and 500 B.C. what happened (according to archaeological evidence) was that *altiplano* populations, probably related to the Wankarani and Chiripa cultures, moved through the temperate western valleys, beginning to control the economies of the valleys (Núñez 1972b: 32). The mechanism of access would be, then, a migration to zones of new economic resources of mesothermic agriculture, not to complement the high plateau resources, but rather to exploit independently new ones. Following this logic, the groups moving toward the coast did not maintain links with their nucleus as did colonists, but rather became independent, cutting themselves off from the *altiplano* development. A similar model has been proposed by Karen Mohr-Chávez (1977:1060) for the populations which arrived in the area of Cuzco around 1400 B.C.

For the period from ca. 500 to 100 B.C. we are fortunate to have more diagnostic cultural elements on the coast and a better understanding of the *altiplano* region. Here I shall limit this presentation to the coastal evidence.

In the mound of San Miguel de Azapa 15 km upriver from the city of Arica, an assemblage of textiles of clear *altiplano* origin was excavated (Focacci and Erices 1971:59, lámina III; Rivera 1977:44, 1980a: lámina I; Muñoz 1980a: fotos 31 and 33, 1983a:17; Mujica, Rivera, and Lynch 1983: 98, lámina 5). The most notable aspect of these pieces is the iconography which is completely different from that known earlier, and which represents that traditionally identified as Pukara in the *altiplano*.

As I expressed in the Symposium of Atacama Archaeology (San Pedro de Atacama, January 1983), the textiles from Azapa most probably come from the basin north of Lake Titicaca, and the existing dates for their contexts (496 ± 100 B.C. and 410 ± 901 B.C.) are in accord with what was happening in the *altiplano*. During the last years we have discovered in our excavations at Pucara sculptures (Plate 6.1) and ceramics with identical iconographic motifs in a chronologically similar place within a pre-classic Pukara context that I call Initial Pukara, which corresponds to a period of emerging complexity in the region (Mujica 1981a, 1981b; Mujica and Wheeler 1981).

However, the appearance of these Initial Pukara elements in the Azapa valley is not sufficient evidence to prove, at least for the moment, that permanent *altiplano* populations (colonies) were present on the coast. According to the contexts in which these pieces were found (Focacci and Erices 1971; Muñoz 1980a, 1980b), they should be interpreted as mortuary offerings associated with local elements. On the other hand, they are the only solid evidence on the coast of cultural elements from the basin north of Lake Titicaca. Up to now there has been no discovery of sculptures, typical *altiplano* pottery, or even villages, which one might expect to find if a permanent *altiplano* population lived there.

Plate 6.1 Polychrome stone sculpture, from an Initial Pukara context in the Pukara-type site, north Titicaca basin

For now, I suggest that high plateau-coastal relationships during the development of Pukara were not through permanent colonies, but through exchange links in which textiles could play an important role.

2. Tiwanaku Presence on the Western Periphery (ca. A.D. *500–1200)*

The archaeological evidence for the period of Tiwanaku influence differs substantially from the earlier period both in composition and density, and it reflects a different type of access to the coast. We have already mentioned that various authors postulate it means the presence of colonies; that is, permanent populations exploiting complementary resources and which are enclaves that do not lose their rights with their original ethnic group.

Although this last condition is difficult to prove with archaeology, the other requirements seem to be met. Tiwanaku settlements are found located principally in the agriculturally-rich middle areas of valleys.

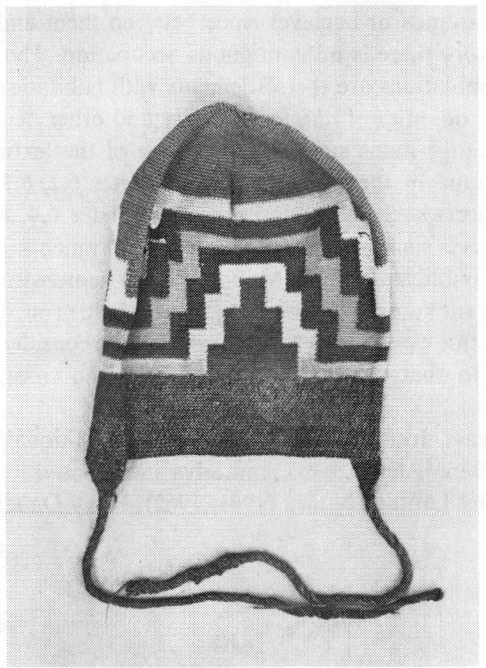

Plate 6.2 Wool cap from Azapa 70, north coast of Chile
(Museo de Azapa, Arica)

Plate 6.3 Wool bag from Azapa 70, north coast of Chile, with Pukara iconographic motifs
(Museo de Azapa, Arica)

They are like islands or enclaves since between them and the nuclear *altiplano* territory there is no contiguous occupation. The evidence for permanent populations are the settlements with habitations and cemeteries, and the quantity of *altiplano* pottery and other items. These are not only exchange items such as in the case of the textiles from San Miguel de Azapa of the previous period (Plates 6.2, 6.3), but rather utilitarian objects such as fabrics, ceramics (Plates 6.4, 6.5, 6.6, 6.7), and wood objects such as cups, spoons, and adornments.

In a recent publication, Ivan Muñoz (1983a) demonstrates the coexistence of Tiwanaku populations with local ethnic groups. He (1983b) has discussed this evidence at length, and adds a considerable amount of new data to that already described about the coastal Tiwanaku presence.

In recent years, José Berenguer has made an additional contribution (1975, 1978; Berenguer, Castro, and Silva 1980) based on preliminary observations by Lautaro Núñez (1961, 1962), Percy Dauelsberg (1963:

Plate 6.4 Tiwanaku ceramic from Ilo, extreme south coast of Peru (Museo Nacional de Antropología y Arqueología, Lima)

Plate 6.5 Tiwanaku ceramic, Loreto Viejo style, extreme north coast of Chile

Plate 6.6 Tiwanaku ceramic, Loreto Viejo style, extreme north coast of Chile

Plate 6.7 Tiwanaku ceramic, Loreto Viejo style, extreme north coast of Chile

203–204), and Oscar Espoueys (1972:67), and on a careful review and analysis of the Tiwanaku materials from Chile. He proposes that Tiwanaku influence in Arica (and, I would add, southern Peru) is different from that in San Pedro de Atacama, both in terms of the remains and their contexts. In San Pedro Tiwanaku materials that do not appear in coastal valleys predominate, such as finely made pottery (Plates 6.8, 6.9), *rapé* snuff tubes and palettes (Plates 6.10, 6.11), gold *keros* (Plate 6.12) and other wood objects finely worked and decorated with feline faces, human heads (Plate 6.13), and personages such as the sacrifices or the staff personage of the Tiwanaku sun gate. Moreover, even if these objects come from burials, no purely Tiwanaku cemetery is yet known, nor is there even a Tiwanaku settlement.

There is no question that the cultural manifestations of the two areas are different, and because of this they must reflect different types of Tiwanaku presence. Therefore a current hypothesis is that Tiwanaku maintained coastal colonies and, at the same time, participated in a big long-distance exchange network whose point of convergence was San Pedro de Atacama where ethnic groups from other places arrived (Berenguer 1975, 1978:33–35; Núñez 1976:194; Berenguer, Castro, and Silva 1980; Mujica 1981a:34–35; Mujica, Rivera, and Lynch 1983:86–88).

In summary, *altiplano* populations arrived in coastal valleys ca. 1500 B.C. by diverse ways. Although the studies needed to understand

Plate 6.8 Tiwanaku ceramic from San Pedro de Atacama

Plate 6.9 Tiwanaku ceramic from San Pedro de Atacama

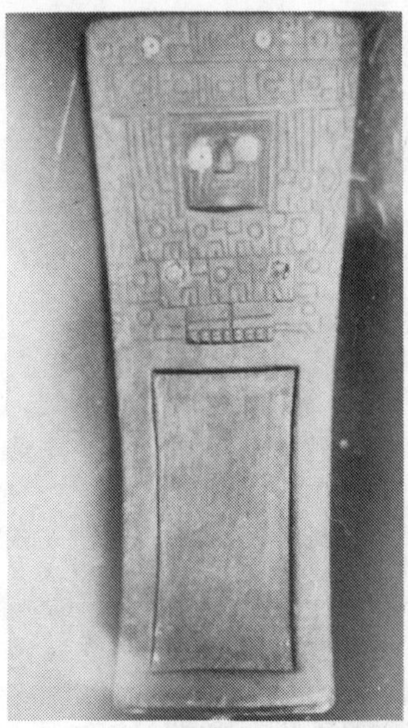

Plate 6.10 *Rapé* snuff palette from San Pedro de Atacama (Museo Arqueológico San Pedro de Atacama)

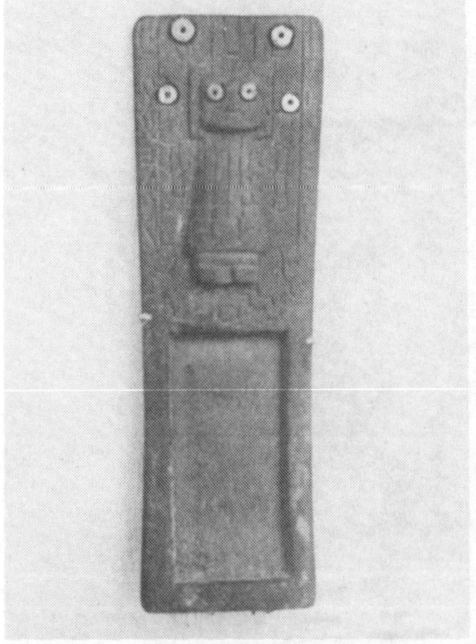

Plate 6.11 *Rapé* snuff palette from San Pedro de Atacama (Museo Arqueológico San Pedro de Atacama)

Plate 6.12 Gold *kero* from San Pedro de Atacama
(Museo Arqueológico San Pedro de Atacama)

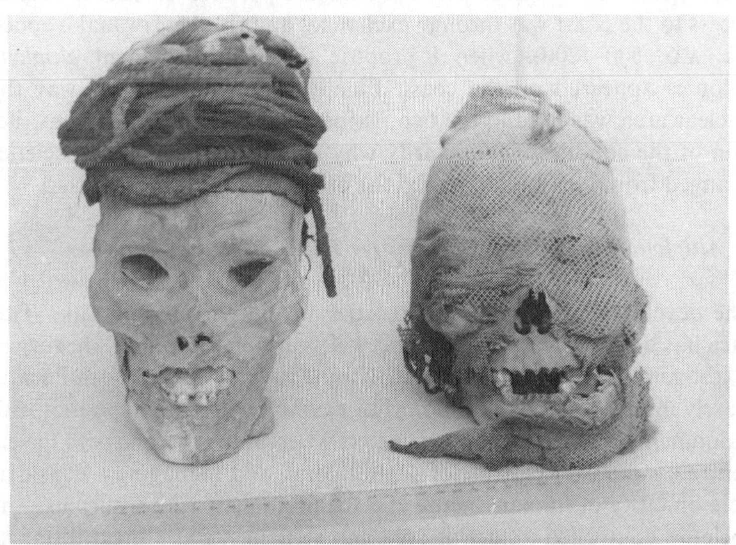

Plate 6.13 Heads with netting and turban from Azapa 70, north coast of Chile, with an associated date (Gak 5818) of 490 ± 100 B.C.
(Museo de Azapa, Arica)

how they did so are still insufficient, one can hypothesize a sequence of models. Between about 1500 to 500 B.C. *altiplano* groups migrated to the coastal valleys in search of new productive zones but were cut off from their nuclear area. Between about 500 B.C. to A.D. 300 or 500 the *altiplano*-coast relationship seems to have been exchange, without permanent *altiplano* populations on the coast. During the Tiwanaku period (ca. A.D. 500 to 1200) evidence indicates that there were permanent *altiplano* populations on the coast interacting with local groups, and this developed parallel with an active long-distance exchange network through San Pedro de Atacama.

The Nuclear Area of Altiplano Populations

First I shall propose some of the *altiplano* region characteristics that permit us to understand the conditions that encouraged the implementation of the previously described mechanisms and the limitations of the region that stimulated the highland populations to search for resources in other environments. Second, principally through a study of site distribution, I shall analyze how *altiplano* society used its environment during two different prehistorical periods: (a) the Pukara and Qeya epoch (ca. 500 B.C.–A.D. 500), when I propose the mechanism of access to the coast was through exchange; and (b) the Tiwanaku epoch (ca. A.D. 500–1200), when I propose the first permanent *altiplano* colonies appeared on the coast. Finally, by comparing the way the nuclear area was used in the two periods, I shall attempt a reconstruction of the conditions that clarify why and how the *altiplano* societies changed from one mechanism to the other.

1. Altiplano Environment: Productive Potential and Limitations

The development of complex societies in the *altiplano* of Lake Titicaca has been an accepted fact since very early in the region's history of investigations. First, the studies at Tiwanaku, and then those in Pucara, clearly indicate that assumption. For example, they were societies with monumental urban-ceremonial centers where it was necessary to have a centralizing power capable of agglutinating and managing a considerable quantity of human energy and maintaining it with a surplus. The societies controlled a nuclear area and settlements at a great distance, and all this was accompanied by a high technology demonstrated in metallurgy, pottery, textiles, and lithic sculpture.

The nuclear area where these cultures developed is at an average altitude of 4,000 m and between 15 to 18 degrees south latitude. It rests at the upper limits of animal and vegetable life, and thus as a productive center it has apparently certain limitations. Therefore defining the economic bases which permitted the complex development is a matter of special interest.

In spite of the harsh conditions of the ecology of the Titicaca basin, there was a development of agriculture and animal husbandry based on various plant and animal species. In both cases it is suspected that the process of domestication could have occurred in the *altiplano* but to date the archaeological investigations necessary to prove such a hypothesis have not been carried out (Mujica and Wheeler 1981:9).

The botanists Hawkes (1956, 1967), Ochoa (1962), and Ugent (1970) have pointed to the Titicaca basin as the most probable center of domestication for the potato (*Solanum tuberosum*). They base this hypothesis on the presence there of the wild form (*Solanum stenototum*) and on the existence of more than 400 varieties recognized by the present-day inhabitants. This amount exceeds the total of varieties known in any other part of the Andes (Yamamoto in this volume). As concerns the grain *quinoa* (*Chenopodium quinoa*) and *cañihua* (*Chenopodium pallidicoule*), there is even less evidence about their point of origin, although Simmonds (1965), Heizer and Nelson (1974), and Pickersgill and Heizer (1977) have suggested that their domestication took place within the basin or nearby. Whatever the case, it is clear that the domestication and cultivation of native Andean plants, well adapted to the *altiplano*'s difficult ecological conditions, played an important role in the development of *altiplano* societies. In addition to the above-noted species, it is necessary to add *oca* (*Oxalis tuberosa*), *mashwa* (*Tropeaolum tuberosum*), and *olluco* (*Ullucus tuberosus*), tubers which, with the grains, compose the cordilleran complex (Lumbreras 1970: 28; 1974:197).

It is also suspected that the Titicaca basin was the most probable epicenter for the domestication of the South American camelids. There the Spaniards found the highest concentrations of camelids (Murra [1964] 1975), including the wild forms such as the *guanaco* (*Lama guanicoe* Müller 1776) and the vicuña (*Lama vicugna* Molina 1782), and the domesticated forms such as the llama (*Lama glama* Linneaus 1758), and the alpaca (*Lama pacos* Linneaus 1758). Ricardo Latcham (1922:82; 1936b:611) suggested that the llama as well as the alpaca were domesticated in the Titicaca basin because it is in the center of the camelids' north-south geographical distribution over the Andes Mountains. Carl Troll (1931:277) expressed the same hypothesis noting among other factors that the Titicaca basin represents the densest and highest quality concentration of pastoral resources in the Andes (Troll 1931:265). Other authors such as Gilmore (1950), León (1932, 1939), and Lumbreras (1967, 1970) have noted that because the llama is found extensively outside the *altiplano,* its domestication could have taken place outside of the Titicaca basin, while the alpaca was purely of the *altiplano* and domesticated later—a point suggested earlier by Maccagno (1912:2).

The hypothesis of a late domestication of the alpaca as a deliberate attempt to improve the quality and productivity of wool was suggested by the archaeologists Bennett and Bird (1949:260; Bird 1954:3), and Lumbreras (1967, 1970) who also postulate that it took place in the Titicaca basin. Whatever the case, archaeology and ethnohistory indicate that the camelid pastoralism played a major role in the economy of the *altiplano* through its later prehistory whether or not they were domesticated in that region.

It is most probable that the combination of both productive strategies permitted overcoming the natural limitations of the *altiplano* habitat and made possible the development of complex societies. But to this one should add the very special geo-economic situation permitted by a large lake (Mujica 1978:289). However, it seems that even this was not sufficient since from very early in *altiplano* prehistory we find its inhabitants interacting with others settled in the Pacific coastal valleys, in the mesothermic highland valleys, and in the eastern Andean slopes, allegedly to have access to other resources (Mujica 1981a). The persistence of this interaction through time and by diverse mechanisms seems to indicate that economic complementarity through access to non-*altiplano* resources should be considered basic to the prehistoric process of the Titicaca basin. Thus complementarity creates a triple base, together with high-altitude agriculture and animal pastoralism.

A series of limitations in the *altiplano* could only be overcome by resorting to environments with different conditions, and this permits an explanation why economic complementarity was crucial in the prehistory of the region. On the one hand the Titicaca *altiplano* has unstable, irregular, and difficult or impossible-to-control conditions such as freezing sleet, droughts, and floods that are common but which follow no regular pattern. On the other hand, economically and socially important resources in the Andean world such as maize, peppers, and cotton among others can not be cultivated with certainty in the *altiplano,* at least not in the required quantities. The only way to acquire them was to travel many days where they could be exchanged for *altiplano* products or exploited directly by colonies.

In the following pages we shall see how the *altiplano* region was used by populations which descended to the coast during two different prehistoric periods.

2. *The Pre-Tiwanaku Altiplano (ca. 500* B.C.–A.D. *500)*

In figures 6.3 and 6.4 one can see the distribution of sites of the Pukara and Qeya cultures which developed in the *altiplano* before Tiwanaku. Although it has been thought traditionally that Pukara was chronologically before Qeya (the Early Tiwanaku of Bennett, or the Epoch III of Ponce), there is now new evidence to postulate that the two cultures are in part contemporary. First, the site distribution indicates a clear and systematic territorial division. The Pukara sites are concentrated to the north of the lake and the Qeya sites are to the south, a situation which implies that during this period the lake region was shared by two ethnic groups. There is only one Qeya site in Pukara territory, Tumatumani in Juli (No. 34 in the Pukara map and No. 12 in the Qeya map), but the Qeya ceramic in this site was very insignificant, and could have arrived by exchange or another mechanism that did not represent a stable southern Qeya population. Second, Pukara was considered earlier than Qeya principally because of radiocarbon dates collected by Kidder in 1955 and because of stratigraphic and stylistic studies from Bennett's time. Recent dates permit a lengthening of the Pukara culture up to about A.D. 400 (Beta 3430 = 1570 ± 100 B.P.; Beta 3428 = 1790 ± 90 B.P.). Third, in Kallamarca a few kilometers south of Tiwanaku a ceramic has been found that shares stylistic characteristics of both cultures (Lumbreras 1974: 61) (Plate 6.14), evidence for the contemporaneity of each style (*Gaceta Arqueológica Andina* 1982:8).

Since earlier (Mujica 1981a) I described basic characteristics of both cultures with special emphasis on their settlement patterns, here I should like to enlarge on the implication of the site distributions as concerns environmental usage.

(a) Pukara

The Pukara site dispersion reaches from Batan Urgo (site 1, Fig. 6.3) near Cuzco southward to the Ilave River on the western side, and north of the Suches River in the eastern side of Titicaca Lake. The sites can be grouped into three sectors or principal regions on the basis of their environment:

(1) the nuclear region (sites 5 to 2, Fig. 6.3)
(2) the northern region (sites 1 to 4, Fig. 6.3), and
(3) the lacustrine region (sites 22 to 34, Fig. 6.3).

The nuclear region sites appear to have emphasized the exploitation

Plate 6.14 Kallamarca ceramic, with shared Pukara and Qeya features

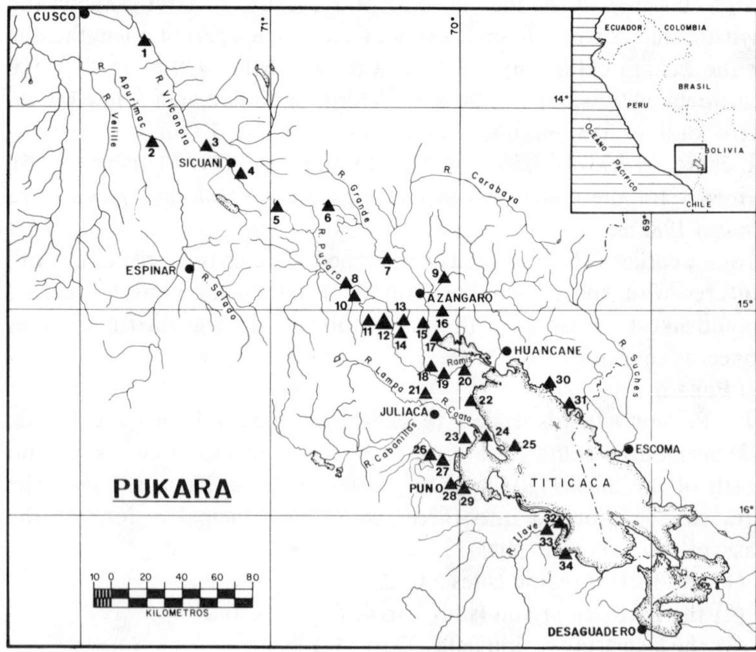

Fig. 6.3 Distribution of Pukara sites on the Lake Titicaca *altiplano*

of purely *altiplano* resources such as high-altitude agriculture and camelid pastoralism. The lacustrine sites demonstrate the interest in the exploitation of lake resources on both the shores and the islands. The northern sites are located in a fertile valley with mesothermic agricultural production.

If we compare the number and distribution of Pukara sites with those of the earlier period (Mujica 1981a), notable changes are evident. On one hand, there are more sites, reflecting a population increase, and on the other hand, they cover a greater territory, indicating access to ecological niches previously not used. In the same publication (1981a) I noted that only beginning with Pukara is there territorial control by one economic unit which intensively exploits three productive systems: the lake resources (birds, fish, amphibious animals, and so on), the *altiplano* valleys with high-altitude agriculture (potato, *quinoa, cañihua, oca, mashwa* and *olluco*), and the pastures for camelids. This domination of three principal and complementary *altiplano* environments coincides with the rise of complex society in the Titicaca basin (Mujica 1981b). Moreover, the incorporation of three productive systems within one centralizing economic unit could be reflected in the hierarchical organization of Pukara's settlement pattern. I have hypothesized (1981a:17) the existence of three different types of Pukara sites based on their size, location, and components: (1) the great urban and ceremonial center Pucara, the only one of this kind for this period; (2) various notable complex sites not as large as Pucara; and (3) various village-like settlements dispersed through the basin. Based on the characteristics and locations of these three settlement types it is not an exaggeration to postulate that the villages were responsible for the extraction of basic materials (clay, minerals, salt, etc.) and for the production of the basic agricultural and pastoral subsistence; that the secondary or intermediate centers functioned as collection and redistribution points for the goods; and finally that the great center Pucara's purpose was the centralization and transformation of goods into urban resources and their later redistribution. The fabrics found in the Azapa valley probably came from the site of Pucara, a hypothesis which requires verification.

The distribution of Pukara sites and traits allow us also to observe other types of changes compared with the earlier epoch, and they show the magnitude of the use of the *altiplano* and its periphery. In addition to the sites on the shores of the lake and those in the *altiplano* valleys of the north basin, unquestionably Pukara nuclear territory, there are others which indicate the access of lake populations to non-*altiplano* regions. On one hand, there are sites that are away from main *altiplano* that are not only toward pastoral resource zones, but that also have access to mesothermic valleys. Pukara begins to expand the traditional *altiplano* boundaries towards the Carabaya, Apurímac, and Vilcanota valleys by means not yet clearly understood. On the other hand, in the case of the Vilcanota Valley, the occupation seems to have been intense, and, although the evidence is scarce, this could be *altiplano* colonies permanently exploiting the mesothermic resources between Sicuani and Cuzco, or perhaps it could be a migration of *altiplano* inhabitants toward the north, which would allow a partial explanation of the gap in the Cuzco cultural sequence between Chanapata and Wari. At any rate, it is important that during the Pukara period there is a thoroughly *altiplano* society which dominates its environment, exploiting the available resources, and which opens its frontiers toward zones of complementary resources and, as noted earlier, achieves exchange with coastal groups settled in the Azapa valley. It is also probable that an exchange relationship was established with the eastern slopes. The evidence is limited to some intrusive pottery that we call Ramis (Mujica and Wheeler 1981: 51–52).

(b) Qeya

This period was originally called Early Tiwanaku by Bennett (1934: 448) due to its stratigraphic depth in his excavations in 1932 at the site Tiwanaku. Carlos Ponce (1961, 1972) renamed it Epoch III in his attempt to present an integrated cultural sequence for the *altiplano*. We prefer to use the term Qeya as does Wallace (1957) to avoid erroneous *a priori* conclusions about *altiplano* development (Lumbreras and Mujica 1983), and we establish that only the late phases of the development (IV and V of Ponce and the Classic and Decadent of Bennett) should be called Tiwanaku culture.

Construction began at the great center Tiwanaku but in fact little is known about the Qeya period due to the fact that there has been little systematic site survey, that most sites of the time were re-utilized during later Tiwanaku times, and that the extensive excavations at Tiwanaku itself during the last 25 years have not been published in detail.

The distribution of Qeya sites indicates a clear concentration on the shores of the lake, on the lake islands, and on the floodplains south of the lake. One Qeya site is located in a different environment, in the La Paz Valley (site 16, Fig. 6.4), but more will probably appear.

Since there are no Qeya cultural traits outside of the area described, for the purposes of this article it is important only to point out that Qeya represents a cultural group different from Pukara and that between A.D. 100 and 400 it shared the *altiplano* economically and politically.

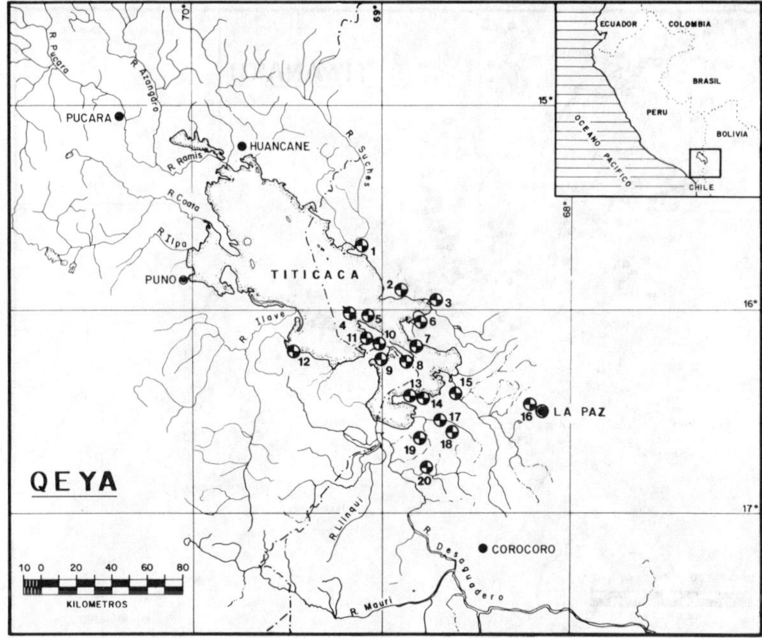

Fig. 6.4 Distribution of Qeya sites on the Lake Titicaca *altiplano*

3. *Altiplano Tiwanaku (ca.* A.D. *500–1200)*

The situation of the Titicaca *altiplano* during the Tiwanaku period, when it is postulated that the first coastal colonies were installed, changes considerably in relation to the previous period. In figure 6.5 one can see the distribution of sites and compare it with those of Pukara (Fig. 6.3) and Qeya (Fig. 6.4).

Since the Tiwanaku settlement pattern has been described several times previously, I shall only point out here some notable aspects of that pattern. The majority of sites are found concentrated around the lake and on the islands from Ayrampuri some kilometers from Azángaro in the valley of the same name (site 1, Fig. 6.5) to the valleys south of the lake. Various dispersed sites also exist in the southern part of the *altiplano* between the lake and Oruro. A third concentration is found in the La Paz Valley around the modern city. In addition, there are Tiwanaku sites on the eastern side of the lake (sites 2 and 5, Fig. 6.5), and various others in the Mizque-Cochabamba region that are not on the map but that are noted in figure 6.2.

This site distribution is important to understand how the *altiplano*

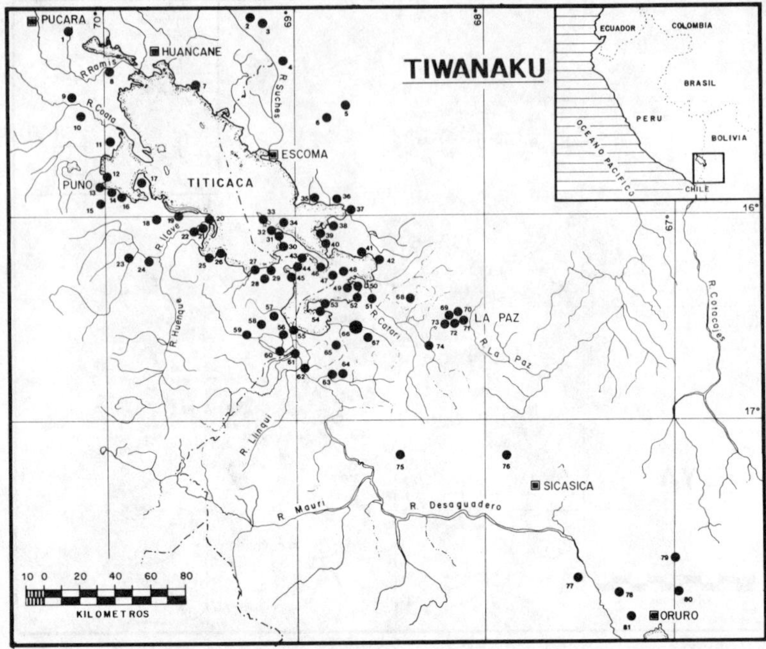

Fig. 6.5 Distribution of Tiwanaku sites on the Lake Titicaca *altiplano*

and its periphery was used by the Tiwanaku culture. The fact that the majority of sites are found on the periphery of the lake and in the islands and valleys of the south seems to indicate the use of lacustrine resources and *altiplano* agriculture. There was also the use of camelids on the shores of the lake during dry periods, and in higher places during humid periods (sites 15, 23, 58, 59, and 75 to 80; Fig. 6.5). The site concentration in the La Paz Valley indicates valley resources were important; however, the number of sites in this very reduced area could also mean a rapid saturation of its resources.

It is necessary to consider briefly the sites located outside of what I would call the nuclear *altiplano* area. The sites located to the east of the lake such as those of the Misque-Cochabamba region ten days walk away are exploiting rich agricultural resources that complement those of the *altiplano*. Although this is not this paper's central theme, these sites could be *altiplano* colonies placed on the eastern Andean slopes. I proposed this idea earlier (Mujica 1981a: 33–34), and it is a hypothesis that is also based on ethnohistoric information which documents Lupaqa and Pacaqe colonies in the same region during later times. At any rate, it is thus apparent that during Tiwanaku times the control of the *altiplano* was complete with an intensive exploitation of all types of resources and with a direct use of ecologically complementary zones such as in the La Paz Valley and in the eastern Andean slopes.

Pukara–Qeya vs. Tiwanaku: A Comparison

If one compares the maps of the site distributions of Pukara and Qeya with that of Tiwanaku, one will note significant differences between one period and the next that may help to understand the factors that encouraged and permitted the access to the coast through permanent colonies. It is important to distinguish between factors that "permit" versus those that "encourage" the establishment of an economic mechanism such as archipelagos, as will be discussed later.

The first main difference rests in how the circum-lacustrine territory is utilized during the Pukara-Qeya period when the *altiplano* is shared by two distinct ethnic groups or divided by two independent political entities. The second important difference is that during the Tiwanaku period the quantity and size of sites are considerably larger, a point which suggests a considerable population increase. The third difference is that the Tiwanaku culture, based on previously-noted factors, controls a greater range of resources and more varied environments.

The number of people, political unity, and control of all resources seem to be the three most important variables associated with the appearance of the vertical control of multiple ecological levels in the South-Central Andes. I shall now attempt a hypothetical reconstruction of how these factors acted.

Previously I noted it was necessary to distinguish between "encouraging" and "permitting" conditions of an economic situation. One deals with need; the other deals with the ability to achieve. The first encouraging factor is the number of people that the *altiplano* supported. Although it could theoretically produce more to support the state and population growth, to do so beyond the carrying capacity would endanger the whole system (Hyslop 1976).

The second encouraging factor is the state itself which was larger and complex in the Tiwanaku period than during the Pukara-Qeya period. On one hand, the state needs to establish mechanisms for the domination and control of a population, and the sending of people many days away from the nucleus without losing control of them (colonies) could have been one of these mechanisms. On the other hand, when the state grows, as happened with Tiwanaku as compared to the earlier ones, it is necessary to consolidate and reproduce the system with socially and economically important products such as maize, coca, and minerals that were only available at great distances. Although the Pukara and probably Qeya cultures had access to these products (archaeologically documented at least in the case of Pukara) it is one thing to acquire them through tenuous exchange links and quite another to obtain them through solid direct exploitation. In this sense exchange is defined as an indirect complementarity because it depends on interacting groups which could endanger the transaction if one of the groups breaks the link. On the other hand, the archipelago is a direct complementarity in the sense that exploitation by colonies is more direct and to a degree more certain. The state is assured of access to desireable and necessary resources for its continuation.

As concerns factors which permitted the implementation of archipelagos during the Tiwanaku period, I would like to consider of primary importance the density of its population, since without a sufficient or excess population the nucleus cannot establish colonies without running the risk that the basic self-sufficient *altiplano* economy be limited.

The complete understanding of its nuclear area, and the exploitation of all its resources should be considered a second factor which permitted the Tiwanaku culture to establish colonies on the coast. Contrary to the Pukara or Qeya cultures, the Tiwanaku culture controls all the resources around the lake and even extends the productive area to a region with considerably more variation—the lake islands, higher terrain, and even the complementary zones such as the La Paz Valley and the eastern and western Andean slopes. This understanding and exploitation of the *altiplano* environment, which is restricted by being in the upper limits of animal and vegetable life, can nevertheless generate surpluses to supply colonies with products which they do not produce. This surplus is indispensable since ethnohistoric and archaeological information indicate that coastal colonies consumed *altiplano* products.

I have left until last perhaps the most important condition that permitted colonization by the Tiwanaku culture: the political unity of the region and the absence of similarly-developed political groups in the periphery which could have caused some type of conflict or competition. Between approximately A.D. 500 and 1200, all of the *altiplano* is under the control of Tiwanaku which was at a superior level of development. Thus a solid nuclear zone seems to have been an important factor enabling the establishment of colonies, and this condition was met in the *altiplano* only with Tiwanaku.

(Translation by John Hyslop)

REFERENCES CITED

Bennett, Wendell C.
1934 Excavations at Tiahuanaco. Anthropological Papers of the American Museum of Natural History 34 (3):359–494. New York.
1936 Excavations in Bolivia. Anthropological Papers of the American Museum of Natural History 35 (4):329–507. New York.

Bennett, Wendell C. and Junius Bird
1949 Andean Cultural History. American Museum of Natural History, Handbook Series No. 15. New York.

Berenguer, José
1975 Aspectos diferenciales de la influencia de Tiwanaku en Chile. Tesis de Licenciatura, Departamento de Ciencias Antropológicas y Arqueología, Universidad de Chile. Santiago.
1978 La problemática Tiwanaku en Chile: visión retrospectiva. Revista Chilena de Antropología 1:17–40. Santiago.

Berenguer, José, Victoria Castro and Osvaldo Silva
1980 Reflexiones acerca de la presencia de Tiwanaku en el norte de Chile. Estudios Arqueológicos 5:81–93. Antofagasta.

Bird, Junius B.
1943. Excavations in Northern Chile. Anthropological Papers of the American Museum of Natural History 38 (4):171–318. New York.
1946 The Cultural Sequence of the Northern Chilean Coast. Handbook of South American Indians 2: 587–94. Washington.
1954 Paracas Fabrics and Nazca Needlework. The Textile Museum, Washington, D. C.

Cuneo Vidal, Rómulo
1977 Historia de los antiguos cacicazgos hereditarios del sur del Perú. Obras Completas, II Ignacio Prado Pastor, ed.: pp. 295–489. Lima: Grafica Morsom.

Dauelsberg, Percy
1961a Algunos problemas sobre la cerámica de Arica. Boletín del Museo Regional de Arica 5:7–17.
1961b La cerámica de Arica y su situación cronológica. Actas del Encuentro Arqueológico Internacional de Arica. mimeograph.
1963 Congreso internacional de arqueología de San Pedro de Atacama: resúmen de actas. Anales de la Universidad del Norte 2: 187–206. Antofagasta.
1969 Arqueología de la zona de Arica: secuencia cultural y cuadro cronológico. Actas del V Congreso Nacional de Arqueología: 15–19. La Serena.

Diez de San Miguel, Garci
[1567] 1964 Visita hecha a la Provincia de Chucuito por Garci Diez de San Miguel en el año 1567. Lima: Casa de la Cultura del Perú.

Disselhoff, Hans Dietrich
1968a Oasenstadte und Zaubersteine im Land der Inka. Archäologische

Forschungsreisen in Peru. Berlin.
1968b Huari und Tiahuanaco. Zeitschrift für Ethnologie 93 (1–2): 207–16.
1974 Das Imperium der Inka und die indianischen Frühkulturen der Andenländer. Berlin.

Espoueys, Oscar
1971 Tipificación de cucharas de madera de Arica. Boletin de Prehistoria de Chile, número especial del VI Congreso Nacional de Arqueología, pp. 63–109. Santiago.
1974 Tipificación de keros de madera de Arica. Chungara 4: 39–54. Arica.

Flores Espinoza, Isabel
1969 Informe preliminar sobre las investigaciones arqueológicas en Tacna. Mesa Redonda de Ciencias Prehistóricas y Antropológicas 2: 295–302. Lima: Pontificia Universidad Católica del Perú.
1973 Exploraciones Arqueológicas en Tacna. Tesis, Universidad Nacional Mayor de San Marcos. Lima.
1979 Los petroglifos de San Francisco de Miculla, Tacna. *In* Arqueología Peruana, Ramiro Matos, ed. pp. 173–81. Lima.

Flores Ochoa, Jorge
1972 El reino Lupaca y el actual control vertical de la ecología. Historia y Cultura 6: 195–201. Lima.

Focacci, Guillermo
1960 Excavaciones en Chaca 5. Boletin del Museo Regional de Arica. Arica.
1961a Excavaciones en San Miguel de Azapa. Boletin del Museo Regional de Arica. Arica.
1961b Descripción de un cementerio Inca en el valle de Azapa. Museo Regional de Arica. Trabajos presentados al Encuentro Internacional de Arica.
1969 Arqueología de Arica: secuencia cultural del período agroalfarero—Horizonte Tiahuanaco. Actas del V Congreso Nacional de Arqueología: 21–26. La Serena.
1973 Excavaciones en túmulos de San Miguel de Azapa. Boletín de Prehistoria de Chile, número especial del VI Congreso Nacional de Arqueología, pp. 47–62. Santiago.
1980 Síntesis de la arqueología del extremo norte de Chile. Chungara 6:3–23. Arica.
1981 Nuevos fechados para la época del Tiahuanaco en la arqueología del norte de Chile. Chungara 8:63–77. Arica.
1983 El Tiwanaku Clásico en el valle de Azapa. *In* Asentamientos Aldeanos en los Valles Costeros de Arica, pp. 94–124. Documentos de Trabajo 3, Instituto de Antropología y Arqueología de la Universidad de Tarapacá. Arica.

Focacci, Guillermo and Sergio Erices
1971 Excavaciones en túmulos de San Miguel de Azapa, Arica. Actas

del VI Congreso de Arqueología Chilena: 47–62. Santiago.

Fujii, Tatsuhiko
1980 Prehispanic Cultures of the Western Slope of the Southern Peruvian Andes. Bulletin of the National Museum of Ethnology 5 (1): 83–120. Senri.

Gaceta Arqueológica Andina
1982 Kallamarka: relaciones con Pukara y Paracas 1 (3): 8. Lima: Instituto Andino de Estudios Arqueológicos.

Gilmore, Raymond M.
1950 Fauna and Ethnozoology of South America. Bulletin 143 of the Bureau of American Ethnology 6: 345–464. Washington, D. C.

Gutiérrez Flores, Pedro
[1574] 1964 Padrón de los mil indios ricos de la provincia de Chucuito. *In* Diez de San Miguel, 1964, pp. 305–6. Lima: Casa de la Cultura del Perú.

Gutiérrez Flores, Pedro and Juan Ramírez Zegarra
[1573] 1970 Documentos sobre Chucuito. Historia y Cultura 4: 4–48. Lima.
1574 ms. Vista y tacha hecha de origen y por comisión del virrey del Perú don Francisco de Toledo a los Yndios de la Provincia de Chucuito . . . . Contaduría 1787, Archivo General de Indias.

Hawkes, J. G.
1956 Taxonomic Studies on the Tuber-bearing Solanums I: *Solanum tuberosum* and the Tetraploid Species Complex. Proceedings of the Linnean Society of London 166: 97–144.
1967 The History of the Potato. Journal of the Royal Horticultural Society 92:207–24, 249–52, 364–65.

Heizer, G. B. Jr. and D. C. Nelson
1974 On the Origin of the Cultivated *Chenopods* (*Chenopodium*). Genetics 78:503–5.

Hyslop, John
1976 An Archaeological Investigation of the Lupaqa Kingdom and its Origin. University Microfilms International, Ann Arbor, Michigan.

Ishida, Eiichiro, ed.
1960 Andes. The Report of the University of Tokyo Scientific Expedition to the Andes in 1958. Tokyo.

Kleemann, Otto
1975 Excavaciones en los valles del Caplina y Sama. *In* Investigaciones Arqueológicas en los valles de Caplina y Sama (Dept. de Tacna, Perú). Hermann Trimborn et al., ed. Studia Instituti Anthropos 25:87–118.
1978 Die Frühkoloniale Kirche von Sama Grande. *In* Amerikanistische Studien—Estudios Americanistas I, Libro Jubilar en Homenaje a Hermann Trimborn, R. Hartmann y Udo Oberen, ed., Collectanea Instituti Anthropos 20: 309–19.
1981 El reconocimiento arqueológico y la estructuración de los restos

visibles en Sama. *In* Collectanea Instituti Anthropos 25. Sama, Hermann Trimborn, eds. pp. 29–47.

Latcham, Ricardo

1922 Los Animales domésticos de la América Pre-Colombina. Publicaciones del Museo de Etnología y Antropología de Chile 3:1–199. Santiago.

1927 Las influencias de la cultura Tiahuanaco en la antigua alfarería. Revista Universitaria 12 (3):220–37. Santiago.

1928 La Prehistoria Chilena. Santiago: Imprenta y Litografía Universo.

1936a Prehistoria Chilena. Santiago: Oficina del Libro.

1936b Atacameño Archaeology. American Anthropologist 38:609–19.

1938 Arqueología de la Región Atacameña. Santiago: Prensa de la Universidad de Chile.

1941 Correlaciones arqueológicas entre Perú y Chile. Actas y Trabajos del 27 Congreso Internacional de Americanistas, pp. 267–75. Lima.

1942 Antropogeografía prehistórica del norte de Chile. Boletín del Museo Nacional de Historia Natural 20:5–17. Santiago.

Leon, A.

1932 Les Auchenides: notes phylogenique et zoologiques, étude zootechnique. Tesis Doctoral, Escuela de Medicina Veterinaria, Alfort, Francia.

1939 Algunas consideraciones sobre los camélidos en los Andes. Boletín del Museo de Historia Natural Javier Prado 3:95–105. Lima.

Le Paige, Gustavo

1961 Cultura Tiahuanaco en San Pedro de Atacama. Anales de La Universidad del Norte 1 (1):17–23. Antofagasta.

1963 Continuidad o discontinuidad de la Cultura Atacameña. Congreso Internacional de Arqueología de San Pedro de Atacama, Anales de la Universidad del Norte 2: 7–25. Antofagasta.

1965 San Pedro de Atacama y su zona. Anales de la Universidad del Norte 4. Antofagasta.

Lumbreras, Luis Guillermo

1967 La Alimentación Vegetal en los orígenes de la Civilización Andina. Perú Indigena 2 (26): 254–73. Lima.

1970 Proyecto de investigaciones arqueológicas en Puno, sobre el papel de la domesticación y el uso de los auquénidos en el desarrollo de las culturas altiplánicas andinas. Informe Anual de las Actividades del Museo de Arqueología y Etnología, Anexo 9. Lima: Universidad Nacional Mayor de San Marcos.

1972 Sobre la problemática arqueológica de Arica. Carta a Lautaro Nuñez y Percy Dauelsberg. Chungara 1:27–29. Arica.

1974 Los reinos post-Tiwanaku en el area altiplánica. Revista del Museo Nacional 40:55–85. Lima.

1979 Críticas y perspectivas de la arqueología andina. Documento de Trabajo No. 1, Proyecto Regional del Patrimonio Cultural Andino. Lima: UNESCO/PNUD.

1981 Arqueología de la América Andina. Lima: Editorial Milla Batres.

Lumbreras, Luis G. and Elias Mujica

1983 50 años de investigaciones en Tiwanaku. Gaceta Arqueológica Andina 1 (3):6–7. Lima.

Maccagno, Luis

1912 La raza de alpaca Suri. Anales de la Dirección de Fomento 11: 1–6. Lima.

1931 Los auquenidos peruanos. Lima: Ministerio de Agricultura.

Masuda, Shozo

1981 Cochayuyo, machas, camarón e higos charqueados. *In* Estudios etnográficos del Perú Meridional. Shozo Masuda, ed. pp. 173–192. Tokyo: University of Tokyo.

1982 Dinamismo inter-regional en los Andes. *In* El Hombre y su Ambiente en los Andes Centrales. Luis Millones and Hiroyasu Tomoeda, ed., Senri Ethnological Studies 10: 93–106. Senri.

Mohr-Chávez, Karen

1977 Marcavalle: The Ceramics from an Early Horizon Site in the Valley of Cuzco, Peru, and Implications for South Highland Socio-Economic Interaction. University Microfilms International, Ann Arbor, Michigan.

Mujica, Elias

1978 Nueva hipótesis sobre el desarrollo temprano del altiplano del Titicaca y de sus areas de interacción. Arte y Arqueología 5–6: 285–308.

1981a The Southern Connection: Historical Process in the South-Central Andes. Manuscript written for a volume tentatively titled The Precolumbian Time of Troubles in the Andes: Diagnostic Archaeological Features in the Middle Horizon. R. P. Schaedel, I. Shimada, and J. N. Vreeland, eds.

1981b Emerging Complexity in the Altiplano of Lake Titicaca, South-Central Andes. Fourth Andean Archaeology Colloquium, University of Texas at Austin.

Mujica, Elias and Jane Wheeler

1981 Producción y recursos ganaderos prehispánicos en la Cuenca del Titicaca, Perú. Final Report of the 1979–1980 Field Work Season, National Institute of Culture, Lima.

Mujica, Elias, Mario A. Rivera and Thomas F. Lynch

1983 Proyecto de estudio sobre la complementaridad económica Tiwanaku en los valles occidentales del Centro-Sur Andino. Chungara 11: 85–109. Arica.

Munizaga, Carlos

1957 Secuencias culturales de la zona de Arica. *In* Arqueología Chilena,

Contribuciones al Estudio de la Región Comprendida entre Arica y la Serena. Richard P. Schaedel, ed. pp. 77–122. Santiago: Centro de Estudios Antropológicos de la Universidad de Chile.

Muñoz Ovalle, Iván

1980a Tumulos Funerarios: Evidencias del Proceso de Agriculturación en los valles bajos de Arica, Chile. Memoria para optar al título de arqueológo, Departamento de Arqueología, Universidad del Norte. Antofagasta.

1980b Investigaciones arqueológicas en los túmulos funerarios del valle de Azapa (Arica). Chungara 6:57–95. Arica.

1981 Dinámica de las estructuras habitacionales del extremo norte de Chile (valle-costa). Chungara 8:3–32. Arica.

1982 Las sociedades costeras en el litoral de Arica durante el Período Arcaico Tardío y sus vinculaciones con la costa peruana. Chungara 9: 124–51. Arica.

1983a La Fase AltoRàmírez del extremo norte de Chile. *In* Asentamientos aldeanos en los valles costeros de Arica, Documentos de Trabajo 3:3–42. Instituto de Antropología y Arqueología de la Universidad de Tarapacá, Arica.

1983b El poblamiento aldeano en el Valle de Azapa y su vinculación con Tiwanaku (Arica, Chile). *In* Asentamientos aldeanos en los valles costeros de Arica. Documento de Trabajo 3:43–94. Arica, Instituto de Antropología y Arqueología de la Universidad de Tarapacá.

Murra, John V.,

[1964] 1975 Rebaños y pastores en la economía del Tawantinsuyu. *In* Formaciones Económicas y Políticas del Mundo Andino. pp. 117–44. Lima: Instituto de Estudios Peruanos.

1964 Una apreciación etnológica de la Visita. *In* Diez de San Miguel. 1964, pp. 421 44. Lima: Casa de la Cultura del Perú.

[1968] 1975 Un reino aymara en 1967. Formaciones económicas del mundo andino. pp. 193–223. Lima: Instituto de Estudios Peruanos.

1970 Información etnólogica e histórica adicional sobre el reino Lupaqa. Historia y Cultura 4: 49–62. Lima.

[1972] 1975 El control vertical de un máximo de pisos ecológicos en la economía de las sociedades andinas. Formaciones Económicas y Políticas del Mundo Andino. pp. 59–115. Lima: Instituto de Estudios Peruanos.

1976 Los límites y las limitaciones del archipiélago vertical en los Andes. *In* Homenaje al R. P. Gustavo Le Paige, S. J. pp. 141–46. Universidad del Norte, Chile.

1979 El valle de Sama, isla periférica del reino Lupaqa, y su uso dentro de la economía minera colonial. *In* Estudios Americanistas II. Libro Jubilar en Homenaje a Hermann Trimborn. R. Hartmann and Udo Oberem, eds. Collectanea Instituti Anthropos 21: 87–91.

Nuñez Atencio, Lautaro
1961 Aspectos comparativos entre labrados de madera del Depto. de Arica y Provincia de Antofagasta. Actas del Encuentro Arqueológico Internacional de Arica (mimeograph)
1962 Tallas Prehispánicas en Madera. Contribución a la Arqueología del Norte de Chile. Memoria de Prueba, Facultad de Filosofía y Educación, Universidad de Chile.
1963a Problemas en torno a la tableta de rapé. Actas del Congreso Internacional de Arqueología de San Pedro de Atacama. Anales de la Universidad del Norte 2:149–68. Antofagasta.
1963b Los keros del Norte de Chile. Antropología 1 (2):71–88. Santiago.
1965 Desarrollo cultural prehispánico en el norte de Chile. Estudios Arqueológicos 1:37–115. Antofagasta.
1966 Recientes fechados radiocarbónicos de la arqueología del norte de Chile. Boletín de la Universidad de Chile 64:32–38. Santiago.
1969 Panorama arqueológico del norte de Chile. Mesa redonda de ciencias prehistóricas y antropólogicas 2:197–217. Lima: Pontificia Universidad Católica del Perú.
1972a Carta respuesta a Luis G. Lumbreras sobre la problemática arqueológica de Arica. Chungara 1:30–37. Arica.
1972b Sobre el comienzo de la agricultura prehistórica en el norte de Chile. Pumapunku 4:25–48. La Paz.
1976 Geoglifos y tráfico de caravanas en el desierto chileno. Homenaje al R. P. Gustavo Le Paige, S. J. pp. 147–201. Chile: Universidad del Norte.

Nuñez Atencio, Lautaro and Tom D. Dillehay
1979 Movilidad giratoria, armonía social y desarrollo en los Andes meridionales: Patrones de Tráfico e Interacción Económica. Antofagasta, Dirección de Investigaciones Científicas y Tecnológicas de la Universidad del Norte.

Ochoa, Carlos M.
1962 Los solanum tuberiferos silvestres del Perú. Lima: Instituto de la Papa.

Onuki, Yoshio
1980 Environmental Exploitation of the Western Slope of the Andes of Southern Peru. Bulletin of the National Museum of Ethnology 5 (1):44–82. Suita.

Orellana, Mario
1963 Problemas de la arqueología de San Pedro de Atacama y sus alrededores. Actas del Congreso Internacional de San Pedro de Atacama, Anales de la Universidad del Norte 2:29–39. Antofagasta.
1964 Acerca de la cronología del complejo cultural San Pedro de Atacama. Antropología 2:96–104. Santiago.

Osorio de Quiñones, Luis and Juan Ramírez Zegarra
1581–83 Parecer de la visita a Chucuito. Ms., Archivo de Indias, Lima 129.

Pease, Franklin
1973 Cambios en el reino Lupaqa (1567–1661). Historia y Cultura 7:89–105. Lima.
1979 La formación del Tawantinsuyu: Mecanismos de colonización con las unidades étnicas. Histórica 3:97–120. Lima.
1980 Las relaciones entre las tierras altas y la costa del sur del Perú: fuentes documentales. Bulletin of the National Museum of Ethnology 5 (1):301–10. Senri.
1982 Relación entre grupos étnicos de la sierra sur y la costa: continuidad y cambios. *In* El hombre y su ambiente en los Andes Centrales. Luis Millones and Hiroyasu Tomoeda, eds. Senri Ethnological Studies 10:107–22. Senri.

Pickersgill, Barbara and Charles B. Heiser, Jr.
1977 Origins and Distribution of Plants Domesticated in the New World Tropics. *In* Origins of Agriculture. C. A. Reed, ed. pp. 803–35. The Hague: Mouton Publishers.

Ponce Sanginés, Carlos
1961 Informe de labores. La Paz: Centro de Investigaciones Arqueológicas en Tiwanaku.
1972 Tiwanaku: Espacio, tiempo y cultura. La Paz: Academia Nacional de Ciencias de Bolivia.

Ramírez Zegarra, Juan
1575 Informacion que hizo . . . porregidor de la provincia de Chucuito . . . de la taza que pagaban los yndios. . . . Mss. Archivo de Indias, Contaduria 1787.

Rivera, Mario A.
1975 Una hipótesis sobre movimientos poblacionales altiplánicos y transaltiplánicos en las costas del norte de Chile. Chungara 5:7–31. Arica.
1976a Nuevos aportes sobre el desarrollo altiplánico en los valles bajos del extremo norte de Chile durante el período Intermedio Temprano. *In* Homenaje al R. P. Gustavo Le Paige, S. J. pp. 71–82. Chile: Universidad del Norte.
1976b Desarrollo cultural en el norte árido y semi-árido de Chile: proposición de un modelo de periodificación. Actas y Memorias del IV Congreso Nacional de Arqueología Argentina, Revista del Museo de Historia Natural 3 (1–4):95–104. Mendoza.
1977 Prehistoric Chronology of Northern Chile. University Microfilms International. Ann Arbor, Michigan.
1978 Cronología absoluta y periodificación en la arqueología chilena. Boletín del Museo Arqueológico de la Serena 16: 13–41. La Serena.
1980a Algunos fenómenos de complementaridad económica a través de los datos arqueológicos en el Area Centro Sur Andina: la fase Alto Ramírez reformulada. *In* Temas antropológicos del norte de Chile, Estudios arqueológicos. Número Especial, pp. 71–103. Antofagasta: Universidad de Chile.

1980b Arqueología andina en el panorama de las investigaciones arqueológicas en Chile. *In* Temas antropológicos del norte de Chile, Estudios arqueológicos. Número Especial, pp. 46–69. Antofagasta: Universidad del Norte.

Rivera, Mario, Patricia Soto, Liliana Ulloa and Diana Kushner

1974 Aspectos sobre el desarrollo tecnológico en el proceso de agriculturización en el norte prehispánico, especialmente Arica (Chile). Chungara 3:79–107. Arica.

Santoro, Calogero

1980a Estratigrafía y secuencia cultural funeraria: fases Azapa, Alto Ramírez y Tiwanaku (Arica, Chile). Chungara 6:24–44. Arica.

1980b Fase Azapa: transición del Arcaico al Desarrollo Agrario inicial en los valles bajos de Arica. Chungara 6:46–56. Arica.

1981 Formativo Temprano en el extremo norte de Chile. Chungara 8:33–62. Arica.

Schaedel, Richard

1957 Informe general sobre la expedición a la zona entre Arica y La Serena. *In* Arqueología chilena: Contribución al estudio de la región comprendida entre Arica y la Serena. Richard P. Schaedel, ed. pp. 5–41. Santiago: Centro de Estudios Antropológicos de la Universidad de Chile.

Serracino, George

1980 Tiwanaku desde San Pedro de Atacama. Estudios Arqueológicos 5:95–106. Antofagasta.

Simmonds, G. G.

1965 The Grain Chenopods of the Tropical American Highlands. Economic Botany 19:223–35.

Soldi, Ana María

1978 Nuevos datos sobre la antigua provincia de Chucuito. *In* Etnohistoria y antropología andina. M. Koth de Paredes and A. Castelli, eds. pp. 123–33. Lima.

Tarrago, Myriam Noemí

1968 Secuencias culturales de la etapa agroalfarera de San Pedro de Atacama (Chile). Actas y memorias del 37 Congreso Internacional de Americanistas (Buenos Aires, 1966) 2:119–144. Buenos Aires.

1976 Alfarería típica de San Pedro de Atacama (Norte de Chile). Estudios Atacameños 4:37–64. Universidad del Norte, Museo de Arqueología.

1977 Relaciones prehispánicas entre San Pedro de Atacama y regiones aledañas: la quebrada de Humahuaca. Estudios Atacameños 5: 50–63. Universidad del Norte, Museo de Arqueología.

Trimborn, Hermann

1973a Nuevas fechas radiocarbónicas para algunos monumentos y sitios prehispánicos de la costa peruana. Atti del XL Congresso Internazionale degli Americanisti 1: 313–15. Genova.

1973b Investigaciones arqueológicas en el Departamento de Tacna

(Perú). Atti del XL Congresso Internazionale degli Americanisti 1:333–35. Genova.

1975a Los valles de Caplina y Sama. *In* Investigaciones arqueológicas en los valles de Caplina y Sama (Dpto. Tacna, Perú). H. Trimborn, et al., eds. Studia Instituti Anthropos 25: 13–60.

1975b Sama. Zeitschrift für Ethnologie 100 (1–2):290–99.

1975c Radiometrische Daten zur Kulturgeschichte des alten Peru. Die Naturwissenschaften 62 (10):476–81.

1977 Excavaciones en Sama (Dpto. Tacna, Perú). Indiana 4:171–78. Berlin.

1978 Investigaciones arqueológicas en la Vituña (valle de Sama, Dpto. de Tacna). *In* Historia y promesa. F. Miro Quesada, F. Pease, and D. Sobrevilla, eds., pp. 601–5. Lima: Pontificia Universidad Católica.

1981 Excavaciones en Sama, 1972 y 1975. *In* Sama. H. Trimborn, ed. Collectanea Instituti Anthropos 25:9–28.

Troll, Carl

1931 Die Geographische Grundlagen des Andinen Kulturen und des Inkareiches. Ibero-Amerikanisches Archiv 5:258–94. Berlin.

Ugent, Donald

1970 The potato. What is the botanical origin of this important crop plant, and how did it first become domesticated? Science 170:1161–66.

Uhle, Max

1911 La esfera de influencia del país de los Incas. Actas del IV Congreso Cientifico y Primero Panamericano 2:260–81. Santiago.

1913a Tabletas de madera de Chiuchiu. Revista Chilena de Historia y Geografía 8:454–58. Santiago.

1913b Los indios atacameños. Revista Chilena de Historia y Geografía 9:105–11. Santiago.

1915 Las tabletas y tubos de rapé en Chile. Revista Chilena de Historia y Geografía 16:114–36. Santiago.

1917 Los aborígenes de Arica. Museo de Etnografía y Antropología de Chile 1 (4–5):151–76. Santiago.

1918 Los aborígenes de Arica. Revista Histórica 6 (1):5–26. Lima.

1919 La arqueología de Arica y Tacna. Boletín de la Sociedad Ecuatoriana de Estudios Históricos Americanos 8:1–48. Quito.

1922 Fundamentos etnicos y arqueológicos de Arica y Tacna. Quito: Sociedad Ecuatoriana de estudios Históricos, Universidad Central.

Vescelius, Gary S.

1960 Rasgos naturales y culturales de la costa del extremo sur. *In* Antiguo Perú: Espacio y tiempo. pp. 381–83. Lima.

Wallace, Dwight

1957 The Tiahuanaco Horizon Styles in the Peruvian and Bolivian Highlands. Ph.D. dissertation, Department of Anthropology, University of California, Berkeley.

7

Cases and Variations of Verticality in the Southern Andes

Franklin Pease G. Y.

Introduction

There has been much discussion of the relevant variables and limitations of Murra's (1972) hypothesis on vertical control. Although the discussion generated by this hypothesis deserves careful consideration, this paper deals with limited aspects of the notion of verticality or diverse ecological control of resources in the Andes. Specifically, I address the concept of territory and how it relates to the notion of exchange, and present cases that show variations of verticality in the southern Andes during the Colonial period.

Territory and Exchange

Undoubtedly, the data available to Murra at the time that he formulated his hypothesis supported his ideas. Much of his discussion centered on the apparently exceptional Lupaqa case which has one of the more striking sets of documentation of any Andean ethnic group. On the other hand, the reports of Iñigo Ortiz de Zúñiga provide another exceptional source of information that has not been adequately utilized. Also, new variants and options of verticality continue to be identified. In all of these cases, the problem of territorial control by ethnic groups constitutes one of the essential issues. In fact, ethnic groups managed a system of ecological complementarity that certainly suggests a discontinuous territory. That distance was not an obstacle is evident in the well known case of the Lupaqa. Nevertheless, Gabriel Martínez (1981) recently pointed out the complexity of the problem when he tried to determine territorial control in the nuclear zone of these same Lupaqa, known in the documentation as the province of Chucuito. It is evident that the question of the existence of "islands" (in the sense Murra gave to the term to designate colonies from the valleys of Sama and Moquegua, for example) is still open in the Lupaqa nuclear territory. Studies done in other areas (Collaguas, for example) have made it clear that the nuclear zones of those ethnic groups were also crossed by discontinuous territories controlled by various kinship groups. It has also been proposed that they could have been forced to occupy a certain location in the *reducciones,* although in Collaguas it is evident that a single *ayllu* remained divided in different *reducciones,* indicating that these subdivisions controlled different ecological zones (Pease 1977: 145).

All this discussion, however, is bogged down by the way sixteenth century Spaniards conceptualized territory and its use. From the earliest information provided by the chroniclers it is clear that the Spanish imposed their own territorial designations, such as *provincias,* in the European sense of that time. Possibly, if they had considered older European patterns, for example, those of the early feudal estate, they might have realized that geographic denomination did not always correspond to the political jurisdiction. The notion of a province under a hierarchically organized authority, in turn connected to a central bureaucracy, almost represents a Utopian order for the chroniclers. A good deal of the known decimal hierarchy of Inca authorities falls, due to Spanish ethnocentric perceptions, within this confused realm. As a result, their almost chaotic definition of *provincias* cannot be completely matched with the ethnic units and the territorial dispersion recognized in recent studies. Undoubtedly, the issue discussed above is one of the most important areas for research. The use of different criteria may be one of the reasons why certain classificatory units, for example, *guarangas* and *pachacas,* appear more clearly defined in northern Peru than in the more thoroughly studied region of the southern Andes.

Possibly, the solution is not to attribute this fact solely to the later occupation of the northern Andean territories by *Tawantinsuyu.* As I have pointed out earlier (Pease 1979), the nature of articulation between *Tawantinsuyu* and different ethnic groups varied considerably and requires further analysis. If *Tawantinsuyu* varied in conduct in dealing with different ethnic units, it is difficult to imagine today applying a uniform standard of control (*criterio uniforme de control*) to the whole Andean area that seems more responsive to the Utopian view of the chroniclers than the reality they observed.

On the other hand, even though the Spaniards from the beginning applied a uniform criterion by means of a central legislative system, they did not escape confusion in territorial designations. Ramirez (1981:283) has pointed out that the primary sources "contain terminological confusion, even in something so essential as the basic administrative units of the kingdom of Peru. An example of this is that the chroniclers mention concepts such as 'provinces' and 'valleys' without characterizing or defining them."

Since the *encomienda* was demographically—not territorially—ordered, the Spaniards distributed the people of different ethnic groups as they found them, identifying them through the *curacas* and, as was well stated by Ramírez-Horton (1981:283–84), without considering the existing administrative units. However, there might have been exceptions. Nevertheless, they mentioned ethnic units to point out the dependency (*dependencia*) among *curacas,* which was not always coincidental with the notion of a continuous administrative territory. In this way, it is known that two orders of relationships (*órdenes de relaciones*) were superimposed; that derived from interdependency between the *curacas,* and that originating from the *encomiendas* themselves. But the situation thus created was not stable. There is evidence that by the end of the sixteenth century the *encomenderos* were trying to unify their rights into continuous territories. Subsequent to the creation of the *corregimientos* new administrative and territorial guidelines were established. The *reducciones* complicated the situation and matters were driven to extremes when, in the seventeenth century, the increase of foreigners substantially modified the demographic landscape. These circumstances led to a *microdefinición* of the units, now centered in kinship groups, related to the crisis of the ethnic lords of the *Hatun Curacas* rank, studied by María Rostworowski (1977).

In the midst of this complex situation, a generalized conflict developed among the *curacas* who were trying to delimit their geographic domains, which were now contained within a newly delineated administrative territory. This becomes evident in the many lawsuits over lands, which, on the one hand, affirm the urgency of these *curacas* to redefine their domains (now "territories") and, on the other hand, testify to their ancestral rights over domains located in different ecological zones located outside of the territory considered to be a nuclear area. This paradox is not irresolvable, nor was it then, since the *curacas* succeeded many times in recovering domains located far away from their nuclear areas (Pease 1978, 1982). Nevertheless, it can be observed that the Colonial administration favored ethnic fragmentation when it gave the privilege of independence to *mitmaqkuna* groups; evidence exists of litigation between these and indigenous groups.[1]

Since the first moments of the Spanish invasion, the Crown had expressly forbidden any move that allowed the return of the *mitmaqkuna* to their places of origin. However, this order was not followed, as is evident from the conduct of Pizarro himself and later individuals (Porras 1948:II, 263–64; Levillier 1921:22–3).

It is against this background that we have to set the analysis of the ecological control and complementarity. Recent studies have made possible the discussion of variants, such as the cases of micro-verticality described by Oberem ([1976]1981) and Salomon (1981). In these studies, the close relationship between ecological control and the *mitmaqkuna* is evident (Moreno 1981). In fact, what is already known about ecological control and complementarity should lead to a redefinition of the role and condition of the *mitmaqkuna* in the Andes.

Discussion of possible variants of ecological control in the Andes runs into the problem of exchange (*intercambio*) and the possible existence of markets. This issue requires further research. Clearly, the demand for goods existed; however, it is not clear whether this demand was in reality met by markets. The evidence used, whether derived from chronicles or administrative documents, is insufficient to demonstrate the existence of the market or an exchange conducted as a peripheral part of the kinship relationship in which equivalences were established by the products themselves in a set of "prices" or by a central authority. Even when barter (*trueque*) is mentioned, documents do not specify if it was regulated by kinship relationships, as seems most likely; only with some difficulty can we determine that they go "buying and selling as is the use and custom among the Indians" ("*conprando y vendiendo como es uso y costumbre entre yndios*"; cited in Rostworowski, 1977: 258—because of the preceding quote, Rostworowski speaks of merchants (*mercaderes*) "a modo de indios" [1977:261]).

Thus an apparent duality existed as suggested by abundant evidence for ecological control at different distances and scales manageable through traditional kinship mechanisms and coordinated by ethnic authorities, on the one hand, and exchange that could integrate with markets and professionals engaged in generalized barter, on the other.

Although the existence of a system of verticality in the southern Andes is generally agreed upon, strong evidence of its existence in other areas has not been established. This is especially the case for the coastal region of present-day Peru, perhaps because we lack the sort of documentation available for Chucuito and Huánuco. Nevertheless, there are data available on ethnic groups that controlled territories in the highlands (Murra 1975:88ff.; Rostworowski 1977:Chapter 1). There are additional examples which are less well-documented and evaluated, such as the case of the land controlled by the settlers of Ilo located in the Moquegua valley (April 8, 1597; Diego Dávila:I, 129f–30r).

In the above described work of Oberem and Salomon for the Caranqui zone, they distinguish micro-verticality from the macro-verticality described by Murra (Oberem [1976]1981:79). In their work, there are also indications of macro-verticality of the type found in southern Peru, i.e., stable colonies for salt production (Oberem [1976]1981).[2] Both Oberem and Salomon favor the opinion that this form was introduced into Ecuador by the Incas. In contrast to the above situation is the ethnohistorically documented existence of professional traders (*comerciantes profesionales*), the renowned *mindaláes*.

There are data, however, that question the accepted independence of the *mindaláes* from the *curacas,* inasmuch as "the Indian merchants [*mercaderes*] . . . did not serve their *caciques* as the others, they only paid tribute in gold and *mantas* and beads of white or red bones" (Oberem [1976]1981:81).[3] This question touches once again on an issue derived from Murra's model regarding their relationship with the central authority—what the Spaniards always considered 'tributary' in accordance with the organization they wanted to implant in the Andes —which was generally, if not always, characterized by the delivery of manpower rather than goods. In fact, the well known list of Huánuco (Mori and Malpartida [1549]1967) makes the problem clear for this region—all deliveries of goods were governed by the nature of available manpower (Murra 1975; and, for a recent comment on other testimonies, Murra 1982).

Certainly, a review of all the models and variants is beyond the scope of this paper. However, it is clear that it would be useful to carry out an in-depth analysis of the lines of evidence supporting the hypothesis of prehispanic markets and trade. One of the most often cited cases, that of the Tumbes raft captured by the Spaniards recorded in the Sámano-Xerez account, speaks of numerous objects apparently being transported for trade since *rescatar* is clearly stated in the text. Now, one can glimpse some of the doubts and problems:

1. When the Sámano-Xerez account was written between November 1527 and July 1528 (Porras 1937:21), the Spaniards may not have been able to translate well. Observers took note of the existence of goods (*mercancías*) being carried from one place to another; however, they identified this movement as commercial without considering reciprocal kinship or redistributive relations.

2. However, one cannot be certain that this was definitely an instance

of trade (*comercio*); it is perfectly possible that this movement was an exchange of gifts, perhaps a ritual exchange, captured by the Spaniards and confused with mercantile exchange.

3. The record of goods allows, moreover, an interesting comparison with later information for which more reliable translations exist (for example, the Huánuco list). The Tumbes list speaks of raw materials (e.g., emeralds) and processed goods (e.g., silver and gold jewelry, clothes, beads). We know that the latter items constituted part of gifts as well offerings to the divinities.

In the Huánuco list, raw materials are measured in terms of human energy. The finished goods were likewise produced by the manpower made available to the authority. In all cases, the contribution consisted of labor and not goods.

4. There is no definite prehistoric evidence of the general use of gold and silver objects except by the leadership, Cuzqueña or local, aside, of course, from their use in ritual. This suggests that the metal objects indicated in the Sámano-Xerez account, including perhaps the tongs, rattles, strings of beads, and others, could have been destined for offerings or ritual delivery of presents. It is likely that (given the evidence from the list of Huánuco) that these goods were products of manpower administered by the *curacas*. On the other hand, clothes are in general described in documents both as the products of conscribed labor service, as well as gifts from the authority.

The evidence of exchange cannot be denied. It can best be understood as limited to only kinship, or at least to ceremonial or *tributario*-redistributive context. If either of the latter two contexts is accepted, it would be well to recall the value that was assigned to gifts from the Inca, such as precious metal objects or *cumbi* clothes.

It may well have been that the exchange of ceremonial gifts among coastal populations fed such movements of goods as those reported by Sámano-Xerez. It should not be forgotten that the sanctuary of Pachacamac in Lurin must have attracted important gifts and offerings of this type.

Considering the above, it is possible to see that the information on goods (in the sense of merchandise) in transit or exchange reported by the chroniclers was highly conditioned by the ideas of the trade that the sixteenth century Spaniards already held. Through an interpretation that all the deliveries of goods to *Tawantinsuyu* could be organized under the same guidelines of labor service evident in the Huánuco list, an impression of a centralized trade organized by the authority could have arisen, adding to the extant confusion.

The Colonial Curacas and Ecological Control

A second theme I want to address has to do with the activities of the *curacas* and the changes in their situation under Colonial rule. Their conduct shows their control of necessary resources for the establishment of the complementarity of zones occupied by ancient distant colonies and the nuclear region.

It should be noted at the onset that the *curacas* sought either to keep or recover their control of the population; for example, succeeding in including the *mitmaqkuna* from Sama and Moquegua in the Toledan *tasa* of Chucuito (Pease 1978:136ff.; 1982:113–16). At the same time, in the notarial registries of Arequipa and Moquegua one notes how the *curacas* and other settlers similarly sought individual title to lands located in the same areas as the prehispanic colonies, entering in this way into a new European property system. This attitude relates to the defense of resources that complemented production in the nuclear areas.

The activities of *curacas* during Colonial times are still a matter for discussion, as they are viewed both as part of the disintegration which started with the Spanish invasion and as allies of the Spaniards and thus participants in the generalized exploitation of the Andean labor force. When the accruement of wealth by the *curacas* is described, we are dealing with the latter case. At the same time, it can be seen that the *curacas* were an active part of the resistance in its early stages, whereas most authors prefer to emphasize the struggle organized by the Inca military bureaucracy. The activities of the *curacas* in this early stage still requires much more research because their conduct was not that simple. At the same time, their alliance with the Spaniards may have been more a response to the confusion provoked because the Spaniards did not perform the mediator role that the Inca once exercised. The alliance has been especially emphasized in the ethnohistorical studies of Espinoza (1971, 1974). In fact, the *curacas* quickly took advantage of their *méritos*—real or not—as allies demanding payment and benefits, generally in the form of tribute exemption, grants, and privileges. The documents make it clear that, supported by the Lascasianism of the missionaries, they tried to break the power of the *encomenderos* and place themselves under the direct jurisdiction of the Crown. Echoes of this persisted until the seventeenth century, as can be seen in the well known writing of Felipe Guaman Poma de Ayala (Pease 1980).

Requests for privileges and tribute exemptions represented a considerable expense of time and money, and the *curacas* became advocates both for themselves and their people. This led to a special situation; the best known example, that of the ethnic leaders of Jauja (Espinoza 1971) makes it clear that an exceptional state of affairs existed since the decade of the 1640s. The Jauja *curacas* not only requested that they be treated as Spaniards and *encomenderos,* but also mobilized considerable economic resources toward that end, first traveling to Lima and then to Spain, paying lawyers and notaries to transcript their *quipus.* It is very possible they made illegal payments to facilitate the processing of their proceedings and the validating of their travel licenses (Espinoza 1971). At the same time, they had to learn to negotiate with local-level royal officials just as they had earlier with the *encomenderos.* More careful studies of the relationship between *curacas* and Spaniards in the sixteenth century are needed in order to explain certain cases that today seem to be extraordinary, such as that of Diego Caqui. By 1588, he commanded a truly great fortune consisting of ships for wine transport, mule trains for surface transport, production of the wine and wine skins, the cultivation of grapes, etc. This was only possible if he could have simultaneously made use of traditional Andean forms of access to resources—especially manpower—and of systems of exchange which began with the Spanish invasion (Pease 1981).

But greater precision is still needed on this issue. What is clear is that along with their acculturation we must consider the *curacas*' role in resistance. Their use of legal and bureaucratic avenues of resistance did not prevent them from taking part in repeated subversive endeavors that sometimes went beyond the level of local rebellions. Finally, there is abundant testimony that, thanks to these activities, the *curacas* maintained a system of multi-ecological control of resources utilizing even judicial power and mercantile contracts. Below I present some cases to illustrate these points.

Notarial Documentation of Moquegua: The Curacas in Action

Elsewhere (Pease 1981, 1982) I have emphasized the existing notarial materials, especially regarding the first books from Moquegua. Certainly, it is possible to carry out an ample study on the region, relying on the information recorded continuously since 1587. Here I limit myself to cases relating to the activities of *curacas* between 1587 and 1601, i.e., in the region covered by the first two notarial books of Moquegua. Significant information on the activities of ethnic lords as parties to lawsuits and other bureaucratic proceedings may be found in a view of these sources.

On October 27, 1590, the *curacas* of Juli, Pomata, and Yunguyu authorized Pedro Balaguer de Salcedo and Father Felipe Leandro S. J., Solicitor of the Company of Jesus, both residents of Lima, to present documents on behalf of the above *curacas* and their Andean subjects to Viceroy García Hurtado de Mendoza (Diego Dávila: I, 89 r-v). Subsequently, the same *curacas* and *principales* of Copacabana signed another power of attorney, jointly with the Prior of the convent of this town, so that the attorney could collect the debts of the confraternity. The first case deals with a frequent claim that needs some explanation: the *curacas* acted as attorneys for the people demanding provisions or the fulfillment of given dispositions, generally tribute. Similar examples appear frequently in the notary books. In the second cited case we are dealing with a matter that acquired great importance in light of the conclusions reached by Celestino and Mayers (1981).[4] Interesting data on the attitude of the *curacas* and ethnic groups can be obtained if the earlier confraternities can be studied, mainly after the augmentation of their property.

A different situation may be inferred in regard to the power of attorney bestowed by the *curacas* of Torata (*repartimiento* of the Crown), in their names and in those of the settlers of their respective *parcialidades* to a Spanish resident of Chucuito (Lorenzo de Robles) so that he could present the decree of Viceroy García Hurtado de Mendoza ("by which he commands that the gold *pesos* and other specie that should be returned to us by reason of the *revisita* and the *rebaja* [*tributaria*] that the said Lord Viceroy sent to be done for the said Indians *parcialidades,* and likewise the accounts that on the aforementioned we did and I, the said Pedro Conta, did and adjusted with Captain Miguel de Contreras, corregidor of this party of Moquegua and Torata and province of Colesuyu. . . ." [April 13, 1594; Diego Dávila 1587–95; I, 326f-32r]) to the governor of the province of Chucuito, where tribute from the region of Moquegua had been sent since the times of Toledo. This may be similar to the case mentioned above of the *curacas* of Juli, Pomata, and Yunguyu, since the *revisita* done after the general *visita* of Toledo should have affected the entire dependent population of Chucuito. Such is also the case for Moquegua, although some doubts may arise due to the observed dependency of the province of Colesuyu and from the intervention of the *corregidor* of Moquegua which could be due, in an extreme case, to those areas that were not dependent on the *curacas* of Chucuito but had existing tributary dependency in that city. Conversely, the dependents of the *curacas* may have been outside of the Colonial administrative jurisdiction of Chucuito. This could explain the reference to Colesuyo.[5]

Naturally, the bureaucratic activity of the *curacas* was complicated by the Spanish system of inheritance. The *curacas* had to face lawsuits over the rights to the *curacazgos* apart from meeting the administrative efficiency that the Crown demanded from them. Plentiful testimony to this is known, besides the cases that can be found in the notary books of Moquegua, since Pedro Conta, the *curaca* of Torata mentioned above, apparently was deprived of his position through legal channels by Martín Cutipa. In the case reviewed above, Conta and Cutipa appear as past and present *curacas*, respectively, both signing the request for reimbursement of the tribute paid in excess. In a later notarial registration (November 19, 1594; Diego Dávila 1595–97:I, 357f-r), Pedro Conta gave power of attorney to Pedro de Beceda, royal notary in Los Reyes, so that he would represent Conta in front of the Royal Audience in the suit filed against him by Martín Cutipa, native of Torata over his *curacazco*. Note that the conflict existed when the communal claim was made, in April, as noted. This situation was not an obstacle to the litigants in working on the common lawsuit. It would be interesting to verify if in other cases a distinction was made between the personal lawsuit of a *curaca* and his obligations to his ethnic group.[6] There are many situations in which the *curacas* of Chucuito and Moquegua allocated people to cover the chartering agreement; they themselves were sometimes the contractors, and actually operated with a power of attorney from the Spanish party to the contract. Such is the case of a document signed in Moquegua on August 6, 1595, between Pedro Pablo Corso and Baltasar Tumba, *segunda persona* of the town of Torata who agreed to carry 200 earthenware jugs of wine from the valley of Moquegua to the town of Juli, in Chucuito. Baltasar Tumba promised to furnish the necessary llamas and people to deliver the shipment within a period of 36 days; a freight charge of 300 *pesos* in wine (100 earthenware jugs) was fixed.[7] It is interesting to observe that don Martín Pari, brother of Baltasar Tumba, signed on behalf of Pedro Pablo Corso. In another paper it is stated that the same Martín Pari remained as attorney for Baltasar Tumba to continue the proceedings to collect initiated by don Pedro Conta and don Martín Cutipa heard by the authorities of Chucuito five years before (Diego Dávila 1587–91: I, 406f-407r). It becomes evident once more that the proceedings of the *curacas* were part of their inherited responsibility given the slowness of the judicial proceedings of the times.

It can be seen that to the claims and dealings mentioned above, the *curacas* had to add those initiated in order to collect their own salaries, established in Colonial *tasas*. On October 17, 1595, Pedro Cutipa, "*cacique principal* of the *parcialidad* of Hurinsaya of this town of Pomata" gave power of attorney to Juan Erda, resident of Chucuito, to collect the two years' back salary due him in addition to other debts (Diego Dávila 1587–91:I, 422f–4). Many examples can be added; testimony of the representative activities of the *curacas* of Moquegua is found repeatedly in the notary records, as are those of the *curacas* of Chucuito, tied as they were to the region.

Without doubt, the conflicts stemming from the tribute collection occupied the attention of the *curacas*. It can be seen, in addition to the above-mentioned cases, that the *curacas* of Moquegua had to begin their proceedings in the first instance before the lieutenant governor in Chucuito, first authority of Moquegua, as is evident from some of the powers of attorney recorded. It is also evident, as stated, that the proceedings could outlive the principals; in 1599, Baltasar Tumba, *curaca* of Torata, must have given power of attorney to his brother Martín Pari to represent him in front of Gonzalo Gutiérrez de Figueroa, General Inspector of the province of Chucuito, since he had to present the accounts of the *ejercicio tributario* of his predecessor and of himself (Diego Dávila 1596–1601: II, 259f-r). These cases should make it clear just how complicated the task of the Colonial *curaca* became when the channels through which he exercised his duties multiplied. Here it was not a matter of defending rights, for example, for reduction of tribute, but of presenting proofs of their good performance as collectors of royal tribute. The stability of the position of the *curaca* depended greatly on this. It can be recalled here that, apparently a few years later and into the seventeenth century, some *curacas* could regard the pressure of Spanish administration as excessive, possibly due to the demographic crisis in the *altiplano* which began somewhat later here than in other regions of the Viceroyalty of Peru. From this time, there is evidence of *curacas* who wanted to abandon duties that such a position carried with it during the Colonial administrations; the captaincy of *mita* in Potosí is an example.

The aforementioned cases relate essentially to the activities pertaining to proceedings that the Colonial *curacas* had to accomplish. Little is known in this regard aside from common reports of the many activities, proceedings, and lawsuits already in those times thought to be a vice to be eradicated (although one stimulated by the Colonial organization itself). The activities of the *curacas* were certainly many but we should also consider that the above observations allow new insight into the consequences of the Colonial situation on the ethnic units, well known already in the case of the Lupaqa. Since Moquegua had been an area where the people of Chucuito had colonies to produce maize,[8] it is not strange that we find testimony of the presence of the Lupaqa, known within the colony as settlers from the province of Chucuito. It is important to determine whether all of the cases that we subsequently examine relate to the classic model of mono- or multi-ethnic colonies, or whether we should seek evidence of important changes brought about by Colonial rule.

Relationships Originated by Ecological Control

The notarial books of Moquegua provide testimony to many cases in which the *curacas* of the Colonial province of Chucuito appear working in the region of Moquegua between the end of the sixteenth and beginning of the seventeenth centuries. Certainly, on some occasions it was apparently pure mercantile activity. For example, the *curacas* Francisco Collanqui and Baltasar Paca from Juli, as well as Francisco Callisaya of the *parcialidad* of Hurinsaya and Pedro Cutipa from the Ayancas, gave a letter of payment to Luis Osorio de Quiñones for the amount of 1147 *pesos* for "renting" 60 men to take wine from Arequipa to Chucuito, and from there to La Paz (May 15, 1588; Diego Dávila 1587–91:I, 40f-r). This case is of special interest, since Osorio de Quiñones had been Protector of Natives of Chucuito in the time of Viceroy Martín Enríquez (López de Zúñiga and Ramírez Zegarra 1581–83), and his persistent presence subsequently, visible in the notary books cited here, is an example of how easily commerce grew out of bureaucratic functioning, undoubtedly taking advantage of contacts and influence gained in the latter. Thus, Osorio appears to have exploited on his own behalf not only the existing ancestral linkages between the *altiplano* and Moquegua, which he knew well, but he also, as did others, utilized the movement of Andean muleteers between these two zones, stimulating the expansion of the route's wine commerce. In fact, the notary books of Moquegua offer much evidence of the delivery of Andean labor for trade in Moqueguan wine and its transport to the *altiplano* in quantity only explainable by consumption already introduced among the Andean population. It can clearly be seen that the *curacas* acquired the obligation to deliver not only the labor force, but the indispensable llamas for transportation of an increasing traffic (Diego Dávila 1587–91:I, 220f–221r, 222f–223r, 225f–226r, 227f–228r, 246f–247r, 248f–r, 406f–407r). In this way, the Colonial traffic was superimposed on an extant route originally not mercantile in character. It should be remembered here that in the Toledan *visita* the *curacas* were accused of charging the Spaniards similar "rent" for a labor force without providing a salary for the porters themselves. It can be seen that twenty years later, the activity continued without any evidence that the payment was made directly to the porters; rather that it continued to be administered by the *curacas*. The destructive intent seen in the time of Viceroy Toledo seems to have disappeared, given the Spaniards' utilization of the same system (Pease 1978:113ff).

The selling and acquisition of land by *curacas* constitutes an interesting chapter in regional history. In some cases the linkage is not evident between the ethnicities of different areas, although it is known that the notary Diego Dávila often acted as a go-between (*transhumantes*) in the jurisdiction of the Colonial province of Chucuito. A good example that provides interesting information is the following:

> In the town of Xuly of this province of Chucuito on the twenty-second day of the month of January of the year One thousand Five hundred ninety-four . . . there appeared present don Sancho Cutipa, *cacique* of said *parcialidad* and don Diego Ticunipa and Alonso Casquiqui and don Carlos Asayaya and don Lorenzo Pomahaba *hilacatas* of said *parcialidad* and don Rodrigo Nina Calisaya, governor of the *parcialidad* of Chanuilla, and don García Mollalla and Martín Auapora y Tomás Calisaya *hilacatas* of said *parcialidad,* and as an interpreter, don Diego Chuqui, notary of this town. . .

sold 30 *topos* of land to Father Juan Fonte S. J. in Suana,

> which is an old deserted town more or less a league from this said town . . . which thirty *topos* of land they said were formerly lands of the Ynga that were given to the *cumbe camayos* and after that [306r] . . . Company [of Jesus] resides in this town [of Juli] they gave it said lands for keeping their cattle, as common places and lands and in such times they have been cultivated for a few years by some Indians from said *parcialidades;* these lands not being part of the general distribution [*partición*] done by don Francisco de Toledo in the *redusión* of the Indians, and nevertheless, neither for this reason nor for any other in time and memory [the Jesuits] have not acquired rights or part of them. (January 22, 1594; Diego Dávila 1587–91:I, 306f–308r).

Aside from some specific annotations on the noted *curacas,* some of them known through other documents, there is new evidence of the activity of Andean *curacas* as notaries, a matter that requires future investigation. Also the preservation of the "lands of the Ynga" and their communal character calls for attention. Additional information of this type should shed much light on lands such as these. It is quite peculiar that this contract was registered with an itinerant notary, such as Diego Dávila; perhaps this occurred because, as former lands of the Inca, these zones had a special legal situation, and it was convenient to register the contract with an outside notary who did not make the local inspection. This incident is made more curious by the fact that the notary of the town of Juli, Martín Chiqui, appears only as an interpreter. From another viewpont, this case is of interest for it sheds light on the transformation of land tenure from ancestral to European norms.

Other cases refer more precisely to the maintenance of control over lands in Moquegua by ethnic groups of the *altiplano*. On April 8, 1597, Simón Rodríguez Barreda requested Diego Fernández Maldonado, lieutenant to the *Corregidor* in the valley of Moquegua, for authorization to employ 17 natives of the neighboring valley of Torata in his wheat and maize fields in the Moquegua valley. His basic argument was that they "are natives, born and raised in this valley of Moquegua."[9] Likewise, when referring to his fields, he pointed out that "they have sustained and continue to sustain many Indians from this valley and from the province of Chucuito, Pacaxes, Collao, and if in this valley the mentioned plantings had not been done, these Indians from the said *puna* would have died because in the *puna* for seven years running no food has been collected" (Diego Dávila 1596–1601:II, 109f–114r). Here one can see the presence of an *altiplano* population whose diverse ethnic origins clearly show the multiple utilization of Moquegua as a settlement of *altiplano* colonies.

Other examples raise the problem of the introduction of European concepts of property. In September 1599, Hernando Caballero Páez, resident of the plain of Moquegua, and María de Estrada, his wife, sold to Francisco Rodríguez two *topos* of land in the valley of Moquegua near the city of that name. María de Estrada was the daughter of Alonso de Estrada and Mencía Llanquicaña, native of Chucuito and former owner of the lands in dispute (see Diego Dávila 1596–1601:II, 303f–304r, 316f–4, 348f–350r). In a later document from 1600, Caballero, a widower, sold lands inherited from his wife, indicating the value of one of them as 200 *pesos* (Diego Dávila 1596–1601:II, 397f–398f, 411f–4, 412f–413r, 450r–451f). The same Caballero had bought in public auction part of the property left by Pedro Anagua, *curaca* of the Capangos in the valley of Cochuna, bordering on the land sold by Estrada and his wife (Diego Dávila 1596–1601 II,388f–390f). Undoubtedly, the main issue here is that individuals, natives of Chucuito, had registered as their own property lands located in Moquegua. Unfortunately, there are no indications of how those individual titles originated.

A similar situation is reflected in the power of attorney given to Diego Fernández Maldonado in June 1600, by the same Francisco Rodríguez in which he authorized Fernández to buy in his name "from don Prudencio, *yndio principal,* of the city of Chucuyto . . . a piece of land that he has and owns in said valley on the plain of Moquegua between some standing walls that border on the upper part the vineyard of the community of the Indians of Torata and on one side with my own lands and on the other with lands of an Indian of said province . . . ." (Diego Dávila 1596–1601:II, 428f–r). Moreover, a little more than a month later, the same notary book recorded a sale between Spaniards of an orchard bordering "the lands of don Fernando Cari, *cacique principal* of the city of Chucuito and its province. . . ." (Diego Dávila 1596–1601:II, 434f–435r).

Other ways in which the Europeans increased their lands at the expense of the Indians can be clearly seen. Although an issue amply discussed, it is appropriate here to describe a case I have just mentioned. On May 10, 1599, Pedro Anagua made his will; he was the *curaca principal* "of the Indians of Cochuna called Capangos, native of the town of Escapagua." He declared, among other things, that "I arranged with His Majesty the lands that are called Sualanay above Yacango and, despite the titles quoted as mine, my Indians in common with them, as they know, they did not give anything in the agreement and I paid two hundred and sixty *pesos* of eight *reales* of my belongings. I will that my Indians are charged (for the lands) and that such lands be returned to them (after payment) and in the interim while they are not paid for this be part of my goods. . . ." Although the provisions of his will affected his property in Sualanay, the *curaca* emphasizes not only the purchase of land from the Crown, but also that the same lands were registered as common property, although he preserved his own right to the money he had invested in them (Diego Dávila 1596–1601: II, 283f–286r). In March of the next year, 1600, Hernando Caballero Páez, who had acquired Sualanay at auction, passed it on to Juanes de Zaconeta (Diego Dávila 1596–1601: II, 283f–286r). In the next transaction, the latter sold it, in turn, to Hernán Bueno de Arana for 270 *pesos;* Bueno agreed to fulfill the arrangements of Pedro Anagua's will which stipulated that when the Capangos paid the money of the original agreement, the lands would be returned to them (Diego Dávila 1596–1601:II, 391f–r). A little later, on October 1, 1600, the Capangos, represented by their respective *curacas,* transferred the definitive rights to Sualanay to Hernán Bueno, indicating that Bueno had them 140 *pesos* to pay their taxes aside from the 260 that were necessary to fulfill the will of Pedro Anagua; likewise, they recorded that, as it was impossible for them to cancel such debts, they gave over the land (Diego Dávila 1596–1601:II, 449f–450r). This is how the matter was finally settled, and the lands stayed in the hands of Hernán Bueno. There must have been many similar cases, where the taxpayers had to borrow what they owned for taxes; in this manner the dispositions that limited the selling of Andean common goods could be avoided.

Finally, there is evidence of the purchase of land by Andean *curacas* in a manner different from the arrangement mentioned in the will of Pedro Anagua. On December 1, 1599, Captain Alonso de Estrada and his wife Jerónima de Miranda, sold to don Martín Estaca, *curaca principal* of the *repartimiento* of Carumas "a piece of land" in the settlement of Coanto, in the valley of Omo, of approximately 20 *fanegadas* of *sembradura.* Because such lands bordered others belonging to the Carumas (entrusted to Hernán Bueno and María de Avalos), it can be understood that the *curaca* was increasing the common lands with this acquisition (Diego Dávila 1596–1601: II, 355f–356r).[10]

Conclusion

Careful research of notary and town council books, both in Moquegua and in Arequipa, is necessary in order to determine the true extent of the *curacas'* activities. Such activities can be seen as closely related to the maintenance of control over coastal valley resources by the *curacas* of Chucuito. Without any doubt, the different politics of the various *curacas* can be seen, from the negotiations for the return of the *mitmaqkuna* keeping their residence in the coastal valleys (Pease 1982) to the multiple cases registered, for example in Moquegua, of land tenure, now property of the men of Chucuito. It is apparent that we need more comprehensive study of the way that land control varied under the norms of the European concept of property. It can be similarly seen that notary records offer evidence of land control by local ethnic groups, e.g., Carumas or Capangos, and call for more documentary research on this region.

(Translation by Mariana Mould de Pease)

NOTES

1. In a recent study, John H. Rowe (1982:106) analyzed the problems of the *mitmaqkuna,* pointing out the Colonial variation in its administrative con-

ceptualization in the case of Cajamarca. For examples of lawsuits between *mitmaqkuna* and natives, see Archivo Nacional de Bolivia, Sucre EC 1611, No. 2; Zorrilla 1977; Espinoza 1978; and Pease 1980.

2. Nevertheless, among the Chupaychu there were also resources accessible in one day and whose exploitation did not imply residence (Murra 1975: 66).

3. However, this assertion is somewhat late (1582). Salomon carefully analyzes the possibilities for the control of resources in multiple zones in Ecuador. Both observations deserve careful discussion beyond these pages. Nevertheless, one might suggest that if the Andean people told the Spaniards that the *mindaláes* were not subject to ordinary services (read delivery of manpower), and that they only paid tribute in goods, one may be dealing with an attempt to place them outside the Colonial status of tributaries, maintaining the important movement of essential goods for redistribution and sidestepping the personal service requirements establishing during Colonial times.

4. Celestino and Meyers 1981; the inference of Fuenzalida (1970) concerning relationships between *ayllu* and Colonial confraternity should also be recalled.

5. Similar cases took place in Collaguas; see, for example, the power of attorney given by don Diego Ala, "*cacique principal* de los Collaguas questán en la corona real residente que soy en esta, ciudad de Arequipa," on behalf of Luis de Murcia, to collect debts and even to sell goods and to collect settlers that had fled from the *reducciones*. Although this is a different case, since it designates a Spaniard as general attorney of the *curaca* to fulfill practically all the functions that the Spanish administration assigned to the *curacas* themselves, it deserves attention. The above allows us to assume that the services of an attorney were contracted frequently. Also, I should emphasize the residence of the *curaca* in Arequipa and the deliberate disposition of the collected tribute in his name in said city, or, failing this, the delivery of said tribute to his brother Juan, resident in the region of Collaguas "so he will bring it to be" (Archivo Departamental de Arequipa, Gaspar Hernández, 1561–62: 81f-82r).

6. The fact that in August 1595, don Pedro Conta appeared once again in the notary records of Moquegua as *cacique principal* of Torata leads us to assume that he was successful in his demands before the Audiencia of Lima (see Diego Dávila, I:406f-407r).

7. The price of each earthenware jug was fixed at 3 *pesos*; it is important to note that on August 13 the wine from Moquegua was sold in Zepita at 8 *pesos* and one *tomín* per earthenware jug, leaving a considerable margin of profit (Diego Dávila, I:408f-4).

8. The examples mentioned earlier allow us to see, once again, the presence of other groups from the *altiplano* in the valley of Moquegua.

9. Undoubtedly he wanted to avoid problems like the ones that orginated when (in July of the same year) another Spaniard, Diego Narváez, took to Moquegua settlers from Pacaxes and Chucuito who died of the plague that afflicted the region. The notary books contain the brief of exoneration

presented by Narváez (Diego Dávila, II:115f-210r; Pease 1982:112), in which he argues they died of the plague and not as a consequence of the change of habitat.

10. Certainly, there are similar cases elsewhere; for example on June 7, 1564, Juan Chacha, *curaca* of Collaguas, paid 1300 *pesos* for an agricultural field in Arequipa "from this part of the river of this city" bordering on another field that had been purchased earlier by Miguel Guasuri (possibly also a native of Collaguas). The road to Cuzco ran through the middle of both fields (Archivo Departamental de Arquipa, Gaspar Hernández, 1564:219f-r).

REFERENCES CITED

Celestino, Olinda and Albert Meyers

1981 Las Cofradías en el Perú: región central. Frankfurt/Main: Verlag Klaus Dieter Vervuert, (Editionen der Iberoamericana: Reihe 3, Mongraphien u. Aufsätze, 6).

Dávila, Diego

1587–95 Protocolos Notariales I. Notary Archives of D. Víctor Cutipé, Moquegua.

1596–1601 Protocolos Notariales II, Notary Archives of D. Víctor Cutipé, Moquegua.

Espinoza Soriano, Waldemar

1971 Los Huancas aliados de la conquista. Tres informaciones inéditas sobre la participación indígena en la conquista del Perú. Anales Científicos I. Huancayo: Universidad Nacional del Centro del Perú.

1974 La destrucción del imperio de los Incas. La rivalidad política y señorial de los curacazgos andinos. Lima: Retablo de Papel Ediciones.

1978 Los Chachapoyas y Cañares de Chiara (Huamanga): aliados de España. Historia, Problema y Promesa. Homenaje a Jorge Basadre, Vol. I. F. Miró Quesada, F. Pease G. Y., and D. Sobrevilla, eds. Lima: Fondo Editorial, Pontificia Universidad Católica del Perú.

Fuenzalida V., Fernando

1970 La matriz colonial de la comunidad de indígenas peruana: una hipótesis de trabajo. Revista del Museo Nacional XXXV. Lima (1967–68). Reprinted in La Hacienda, la Comunidad y el Campesinado en el Perú. Perú Problema No. 3. Lima: Instituto de Estudios Peruanos.

Levillier, Roberto

1921 Gobernantes del Perú. Cartas y Papeles. Vol. I. Madrid.

López de Zúñiga, Diego and Juan Ramírez Zegarra

1581–83 Parecer de visita a Chucuito. Mss. Archivo General de Indias, Sevilla, Lima, 129.

Martínez, Gabriel

1981 Espacio Lúpaqa: algunas hipótesis de trabajo. *In* Etnohistoria y Antropología Andina. Segunda Jornada del Museo Nacional de Historia. A. Castelli; M. Koth de Paredes, and M. Mould de Pease, eds. Lima.

Moreno, Segundo

1981 Colonias Mitimas en el Quito incaico; su significación económica y política. *In* Contribución a la Etnohistoria Ecuatoriana. S. Moreno and U. Oberem, eds. Colección Pendoneros No. 20, Serie Etnohistoria, Instituto Otavaleño de Antropología, Otavalo.

Mori, Juan de and Hernando Alonso Malpartida

[1549] 1967 La visitación de los pueblos de indios. *In* Visita de la Provincia de León de Huánuco en 1562, Vol. I. John V. Murra, ed. Huánuco: Universidad Hermilio Valdizán.

Murra, John V.

1972 El control "vertical" de un máximo de pisos ecológicos en la economía de las sociedades andinas. *In* Ortiz de Zúñiga 1972.

1975 Formaciones económicas y políticas del mundo andino. Lima: Instituto de Estudios Peruanos.

1982 The Mit'a Obligations of Ethnic Groups to the Inka State. *In* The Inca and Aztecs States. 1400–1800: Anthropology and History. G. Collier, R. I. Rosaldo and J. D. Wirth, eds. New York: Academic Press.

Oberem, Udo

[1976] 1981 El acceso a recursos naturales de diferentes ecologías en la sierra ecuatoriana. Siglo XVI. *In* Contribución a la Etnohistoria Ecuatoriana. S. Moreno and U. Oberem, eds. Colección Pendoneros No. 20, Serie Etnohistoria. Instituto Otavaleño de Antropología, Otavalo.

Ortiz de Zúñiga, Iñigo

1967–72 Visita de la provincia de León de Huánuco en 1562. 2 vols. Huánuco: Universidad Nacional Hermilio Valdizán.

Pease G. Y., Franklin

1977 Collaguas: una etnía del siglo XVI. Problemas iniciales. *In* Collaguas I. Fondo Editorial. F. Pease G. Y., ed. Lima: Pontificia Universidad Católica del Perú.

1978 Del Tawantinsuyu a la Historia del Perú. Lima: Instituto de Estudios Peruanos.

1979 Formación del Tawantinsuyu: mecanismos de colonización y relación con las unidades étnicas. Histórica. III (1). Lima.

1980 Estudio preliminar a Felipe Guaman Poma de Ayala. Nueva Corónica y Buen Gobierno. Caracas: Biblioteca Ayacucho.

1981 Las relaciones entre las Tierras Altas y la Costa del Sur del Perú: Fuentes Documentales. *In* Estudios Etnográficos del Perú Meridional. Shozo Masuda, ed. Tokyo: University of Tokyo.

1982 Relaciones entre los Grupos Etnicos de la Sierra Sur y la Costa:

Continuidades y Cambios. *In* El Hombre y su Ambiente en los Andes Centrales. Senri Ethnological Studies, 10. Luis Millones and Hiroyasu Tomoeda, eds. Senri.

Porras Barrenechea, Raúl

1937 Las relaciones primitivas de la conquista del Perú. Paris.

1948 Cedulario del Perú. Siglos XVI, XVII, and XVIII. Vol. II.: Ministerio de Relaciones Exteriores, Lima.

Ramírez-Horton, Susan E.

1981 La organización económica de la Costa Norte: un análisis preliminar del período prehispánico tardío. *In* Etnohistoria y Antropología Andina. Segunda Jornada del Museo Nacional de Historia. A. Castelli, M. Koth de Paredes, and M. Mould de Pease, eds. Lima.

Rostworowski de Diez Canseco, María

1977 Etnía y Sociedad. Costa Peruana Prehispánica. Lima: Instituto de Estudios Peruanos.

Rowe, John. H.

1982 Inca Policies and Institutions Relating to the Cultural Unification of the Empire. *In* The Inca and Aztecs State. 1400–1800. G. A. Collier. R. Rosaldo, and J. D. Wirth, eds. New York: Academic Press.

Salomon, Frank

1981 Los señores etnicos de Quito en la epoca de los Incas. Colección Pendoneros Serie Etnohistoria. Otavalo: Instituto Otavaleño de Antropología.

Samáno, Juan and Francisco de Xerez

Relación . . . (attrib.). *In* Porras 1937 (63ff).

Zorrilla A., Juan

1977 La posesión de Chiara los los indios Chachapoyas. Wari 1. Ayacucho.

8

Ecological Complementarity and Tribute in Atacama: 1683–1792

Jorge Hidalgo Lehuede

In an analysis of the prehispanic situation in the south-central Andes, the presence of individuals or families permanently established in places far away from their place of origin or political center could be interpreted as a variant of the simultaneous vertical control of a maximum of ecological niches (Murra 1972). It would be necessary to verify that they were settlers who had not lost their political rights within their original ethnic group, with which they exchanged their products. In that case we would then be dealing with a dispersed, but probably prosperous ethnic group.

If we move to the Spanish colonial situation, the same initial features may be interpreted as a phenomenon of disorganization, disarticulation, or destructuring of the ethnic group principally caused by pressures of taxes or private interests. The "Indian of the community" fled from his place of origin to avoid the abuses of the *encomenderos*, the tribute to the king, the *Potosí mita*, and the system of *repartos* imposed by the *corregidores*. When moving into another community he was accepted as a *forastero* or outlander where he paid lower taxes, was not subject to the *mita* of Potosí, and had no political rights. If he entered a *hacienda* he could be an *agregado* or a tenant and remain linked to the land through debt. In both cases he tried to cut the ties with his community of origin which, when the number of its tributaries was reduced, had to increase the burden on those who were left (Sánchez Albornoz 1978). It was a process of dispersion which created marginality, poverty, and the weaking of the original community.

In the prehispanic situation described, the dispersal occurred because of the need to diversify production in a self-sufficient manner, an ideal of self-sufficiency pursued that still left a margin for barter (Murra 1978: Chapter 7). This was noticeable even at the domestic unit level, where clothing, food, housing, and simple implements were produced. This relative self-sufficiency was broken by the Spaniards when they replaced the manpower that the ethnic groups delivered to the Inca state (Murra 1975:Chapter 1, 1983:77–94) with the payment of tribute in kind and then converted those amounts into money.

The pursuit of cash to fulfill these obligations and to obtain new products that became essential with increased specialization pushed the Andean peasants to look for temporary work on *haciendas*, in mines, and in textile workshops, at the same time that the proportion of their agricultural and handicraft production for sale was increased.

Dispersal in pursuit of monetary economic resources and through this the break-up of the community of origin was the essence of the process that melted ethnic variety into that unique species "the colonial Indian."

Nevertheless, we find in the *corregimiento* of Atacama at the end of the seventeenth century a process of dispersal and population mobility whose causes seem to correspond in their general outline with monetary economic pressure, but which, in its formal structure, preserve many elements of the prehispanic tradition. The process lasted until the end of the eighteenth century when a definitive crisis took place and the Atacameños living outside of Atacama were added to the tribute lists of the provinces where they were living as *forasteros*. This was an intermediate situation between the prehispanic centripetal type of movement and the colonial centrifugal movement. The latter become predominant by the end of the Colonial period. In other words, faced with the need to secure money, a large percentage of the Atacameños had to leave their province. They preferred to establish themselves on the borders of the *puna* from where they could keep in touch with their *ayllus*. They worked in mining mills, or on *haciendas*, and even raised their own livestock. However, they regularly paid tribute in Atacama through the *cacique* of their *ayllu* of origin, who traveled to collect it from them. Normally payment was made in coin. The *revisita* of Atacama carried out by the order of the Duke de la Palata in 1683 gives some clues concerning the social, political, economic, and cultural mechanisms that permitted the maintenance of the cohesion of the *ayllu* despite intense mobility and enormous dispersal. We shall try to reinforce this information with the data from the period in which the system was in crisis.

There are not many sources which study this process, and they leave large conceptual and temporal gaps, but still they offer enough hints to delineate the general characteristics that have been pointed out. Future research may confirm or modify these observations, through archaeological or historical research or through ethnographic work and may clarify problems of regional contacts.

The hypothesis that the pattern of settlement of the Atacama *ayllus* of the seventeenth and eighteenth centuries belongs in part to an Andean tradition of handling long-distance resources, is based both on historical data presented in this paper, and on ethnographic and archaeological information about systems of complementarity, above all that of double residence in a pattern that combines agriculture with livestock and transhumance (Bowman 1942:289–90). Another example is the case of the inhabitants of Peine who controlled agricultural land in Tilomonte and had to move there for short periods of time during the agricultural season (Mostny et al. 1954:10–11). The so-called *minifundismo* or dispersal of property that contemporary authors wrongly assign to inheritance patterns should also be considered (Valenzuela 1970; Beaulieu 1967; Hernández 1947; and the criticism of the model of the latter in Platt 1975). To this background should be added the archaeological data that suggest Atacameños settlements in both northwest Argentina and southern Bolivia, without forgetting evidence that might be explained by migratory movements or by the traffic of groups that looked for complementarity through barter (Núñez et al. 1975). The history of this dynamic configuration greatly surpasses our expectations.

The documentary starting point will be, not the sixteenth century, as we would wish, but the end of the seventeenth century, when in 1683 the *Corregidor* Alfonso Espejo, under the orders of the Duke de la Palata, made a *revisita* of the province. We are not going to analyze this document extensively. We are going to limit our data to the married or adult males of tribute-paying age (18 to 50 years old) and verify where they established residence according to this source. We have synthesized these data in Tables 8.1–8.4.

In the *corregimiento* of Atacama which is located in the desert zone of the same name, the settlements are found in oases, valleys, and high ravines, except for Cobija, the port to the Pacific, which at the time of our document (1683) was inhabited by fishermen who spoke a different language from the one native to Atacama which modern researchers have called *Cunza,* which translates as *our*.

In the properly Andean area, Atacama was divided into Baja (Lower) and Alta (Upper) Atacama. The separation into Alta and Baja apparently corresponds to Andean dual division since the altitude of San Pedro is less than that of Chiuchiu. Lower recognized as its *cabecera* the town of Chiuchiu, around which clustered the towns established in the basin of the Loa River, the only river of the Atacama desert that flows into the Pacific Ocean. Upper, headed by San Pedro de Atacama, was a group of dwellings set up in the high oases which are located to the east of the Salar de Atacama, and into which flow the squalid rivers that dry up in the area. The open woods of carob and *chañares* trees create a characteristic landscape of patches of green against the absolute desert. The heterogeneity of the soils, the irregularity of the water resources, and the importance of the carob trees, which played an important role in the Atacameñan cultural habits and diet, favored dispersion and made demographic concentration difficult (Bowman 1942: 287–389). Aside from these settlements, Upper Atacama included some of the towns located in the zone which today is the Argentinian *puna*, such as Susques and Incahuasi. In the area east of La Puna, Salta, and Jujuy, the highlands are cut by ocean-bound rivers which create relatively short corridors to the western forests of the Chaco with its coveted tropical products (Tarrago 1983). The production of maize and quinoa in prehispanic times and that of wheat in Colonial times in the terraces along the rivers, such as the San Juan, was higher than now (Krapovickas 1978:153).

Apparently Chiuchiu was culturally more heterogeneous than San Pedro. The sector of Toconce had suffered a settlement of people from the *altiplano* which is evident in the ruins of *Chulpas* (Aldunate and Castro 1981). According to Espejo, at the date of the *revisita*, everybody spoke the mother tongue or *Cunza*, the *lengua general*, and Spanish, except women who spoke only the indigenous languages. The reference in the document to "la Genl." [la lengua general] probably refers to *Quechua*, as well as to Aymara. Aymara was spoken in the northeast sector of Atacama and in the province of Chichas and probably Lipes. So by the end of the eighteenth century it would not be strange to find Atacameños who spoke all of the five languages mentioned: *Cunza*, *Quechua*, *Aymara*, the language of the coast, and Spanish. This linguistic ability should have facilitated communication with the neighboring provinces.

In Table 8.1 are shown the different types of tributaries counted in the *revisita* of 1683. In Lower Atacama, present tributaries included a category of men of tribute-paying age but who were exempt while holding office such as *caciques*, *alcaldes*, *cantores*, and *sacristanes*; they constituted 84.61% of the total. There were 12 permanent absentees, or 13% of the total, who still paid taxes to their *caciques*. Travellers in transit from or to Atacama were not registered. Absentees of unknown whereabouts or authentic runaways accounted for only 2.2%. On the other hand, in Upper Atacama the proportions are notably different. Those present number 83, representing a percentage of only 28.8%. There were 168 absentees who paid taxes; that is, 58.33%. Transient absentees who paid taxes in Atacama numbered 18 or 6.3%. Absentees of unknown whereabouts were 19, or 6.6% of a total of 288 tributaries counted in the census. The high percentage of individuals and families who lived permanently away from Atacama, when expressed in the terminology of the vertical model, presents us with the contradictory situation of the political *cabecera*, the nucleus, being demographically weaker than the periphery.

How can the marked difference observed between the two Atacamas be explained? This is very hard to answer adequately due to the lack of available information. In the *revisita* Espejo points out that Lower Atacama

> is in itself unproductive and does not have any more land to sow than the river banks, where the Indians cultivate by [making] steps [of land], having access to nothing more than the strength of their arms and stones. And they do this more as a form of entertainment than for fruit, because it is a rare year that yields fruits due to the continuous frosts. The Indians support themselves by their mules, since all of them are muleteers, and the said river provides them with some pasture, where they keep the mules. They were and still are of use to their province, carrying freight, which comes from the Kingdom of Chile, with which they would pay their taxes and bring clothing to get through the year. (Revisita de Atacama 1683, A.G.A., 9–7–7–1. f.1)

Thus the area of Chiuchiu solved its monetary problems by mule driving, to which one must add the copper of Calama and the gold of other places which was surely the reason for the presence of the few *forasteros* in the province. Mule driving and trade replaced for the Indians of Chiuchiu the simultaneous use of distant and complementary resources. Nevertheless, the existence of the category of "absentees who pay taxes" in Caspana and Chiuchiu (26% and 10% respectively of total tributaries in each of these units) implies some remnants of a complementary system, if not merely a result of colonial evolution.

Cobija, on the other hand, is a special case. The fishermen, as the *revisita* of Espejo states, had their own language and consequently their dealings with the *caciques* of Atacama in the sixteenth century as described by Lozano Machuca ([1581] 1965, II: 61) reflect political subordination and not colonization. The steep coast, without coastal valleys, did not offer the Atacameñan *señoríos* the possibilities available to the Lupaqa kingdom.

The situation of the sub-unit headed by San Pedro is described by Espejo in the following terms:

The other [town] of Atacama La Alta is bigger and they have land in excess to sow although [only] by the strength of their arms. And the Indians that sow are so few that they barely support themselves because [torn in the original] the *ayllus* are deserted as Your Excellency will be made aware of in the *padrón* and *revisita* which fulfill all the specifications. I maintain that those absences of the Indians are necessary because they cannot obtain in this province the whole of their taxes, so they go to the neighboring ones where there are mills, to hire themselves out. The mill owners in a short time set up a credit account with them of two hundred and three hundred pesos. They never get rid of the debt; as a result, they stay there without coming back to their towns or seeing their women, and when the *caciques* want to get them out, they close the door and they inflate the taxes. With this I maintain that it is impossible for those few who are still present (with the absentees staying where they are) to carry the burden of the taxes, which, prorating the taxes that correspond to them, comes to more than thirty pesos, in each third. (Revisita de Atacama, 1683, A.G.A., 9–7–7–1a, F. 1r–2f)

The presence of Atacameños from the *ayllus* of San Pedro working in the mills of Lipes is registered in 1643 when Ines Casma, widow of Martin Tuctipur and mother of Pedro Viltipoco, deceased, issued a letter of pardon to stay the execution of Martin Chico of the mill of Rosario de Lipes, for causing the death of her son. All of them were natives of the town of Sorco, of Upper Atacama and employees in the service of that mill. . . (A.N.B.E.P. Alvarez 1643, fs. 78–83, Vol. 137, catalogue of Mines).

Undoubtedly the "capturing by debts" on the part of the miners and landholders was a common procedure to alleviate the scarcity of labor and legally hold the Indians communities. We shall see in 1792 that the majority of the Atacameños who were in northwestern Argentina were engaged in agricultural tasks on someone else's land. Nevertheless, in the same *revisita* of 1683, another reason for their dispersal is given. In the *ayllu* Solo of Atacama La Alta, one absentee is registered in Tucuman and two in Lipes who had gone to the specified places "because of the convenience of pastures for their cattle" (Revisita de Atacama, 1683, A.G.N.A., 9–7–7–1, f. 21). We are dealing, then, with independent stockbreeders in search of more stable or richer resources, but who do not break the ties with their communities of origin. In several cases it is mentioned that the absentees are in places which are recognizable by the name of a river. This could be an indication of the complementary agricultural and pastoral interests which were looked to for the solution of monetary demands.

That the pastoral products played a role in paying tribute and thus, in ecological complementarity, seems evident in the report of don José Agustín de Arze, the census-taker of Atacama 100 years later in 1786/7. This officer, who knew Atacama well, points out the great sacrifices that the *caciques* had to make in order to collect tribute from the Atacameños who lived in the *intendencia* of Salta. It took eight days for the *caciques* to cross the mountain range and then they had to travel long distances to reach the houses of the Atacameños which were scattered between Jujuy, Salta, Tucuman, and Cajamarca. He adds:

> Although all or most of the tributaries pay their respective assignment with the fruits of their labor, or in other types of industry, they previously have settled equivalent prices or estimates with the collectors. This way the taxpayers never suffer losses, but rather the *caciques* suffer from setbacks due to delay, which they often suffer when they have to make expenditures in order to cover themselves for the money which in many cases they regularly advance, especially those *caciques* who do not have many possibilities; with this understanding there is no discord among them which could motivate other disagreements. (Hidalgo 1978:79)

Were the products of manual labor and handcrafts with definite monetary value taken directly to Atacama or sold or bartered by the *caciques* en route? Did the fact that the chieftains advanced money mean that they bought these products and that the fiscal authority received only coin, or did it also receive products that could be sold? What products did the *caciques* bring to Atacama and where did they get the money to pay for them? As yet we know nothing about this, except that the *corregidor* in 1750 accepted the payment of tribute in wheat. We should ask if the political heads of the *ayllus* limited themselves to taking surpluses from their tributaries or took some of those presents from the community in order to ease the tax load and secure the ties of solidarity indispensable to the perpetuation of this institution through time. Regrettably, the sources found to date do not allow us to answer these questions.

It would be convenient to return to the pattern of dispersion before analyzing its dissolution at the end of the eighteenth century. As we have seen in Table 8.1, the major part of the *ayllus* of Atacama, were, from a social point of view, remarkably disperse structures, although they had a geographic location, especially the ones from the sector of San Pedro. Where were the long-term absentee tributaries who regularly paid their taxes? In Table 8.2 we have edited the data provided by the *revisita* of 1683. The *corregimiento* of Lipez was the province that attracted the greater number of people from both Atacamas. Next in importance for La Alta came the jurisdiction of Tucuman (particularly in the Río de San Juan). The next largest number of Atacameños is 29 settled in Chichas, 17.26% of all tribute-paying absentees. The rest, numbering two or three, were distributed between Guatacondo, Pica, and Loa, in the jurisdiction of Tarapacá, and also in Chile and Sinti. Only in three cases is the place of residence not indicated.

If any particular *ayllu* is observed, such as the *ayllu* of Condeduque, Cantal, and Acapana, its extraordinary dispersion and the scanty number of tributaries present are surprising. Of the seven taxpayers present in this *ayllu*, four were indigenous authorities, who because of their functions had to be absent often, and the other three included a blind man, an unmarried youth of 22, and a "Chilean". Considering

Table 8.1 *Revisita of Atacama*, 1683: Categories of Tributaries

Ayllu	Present tributaries	Absentees who pay taxes	Transient absentees	Absentees of unknown residence	Total	Foreigners
Chiuchiu	19	2			21	
Calama	13			13		
Cobija	18	3		1	22	
Caspana	27			1 (delinquent)	35	
Atacama La Baja	77	12		2	91	
Solo	11	14	6	6	37	
Sequitur	6	9	7	5	27	
Soncor	9	5	3		17	
Solcor	3	14			17	
Coio & Veter	10	19			29	
Condeduque, Cantal, & Acapana	7	31⁺	2	5	45	
Toconao	26	34		2	62	
Socaire	3	30		1	34	
Peine & Cama	8	12			20	
Atacama La Alta	83	168	18	19	288	
Total Atacama	159	180	18	21	379	[10]

⁺ Includes a youngster of 19, disabled, who is present in his *ayllu*.

Table 8.2 *Revisita of Atacama* 1683: Tributary Atacameños with prolonged absences and those born outside of Atacama

Native of:	Resident in: Guata-condo	Pica	Loa	Lipez	Tucu-mán (Río de Sn. Juan)	Casa-bindo	Chichas	Chile	Sinti (Pilaya & Paspaya)	Un-known	Total	Born in another jurisdiction
Chiuchiu	2										2	
Calama												
Cobija			3								3	
Caspana				7							73	
Atacama La Baja	2		3								12	
Solo				8	6						14	2
Sequitur				2	7						9	1
Salcar				7			5	1		1	14	5
Soncor					1		3		1		5	5
Coio & Vecter				14	3		1			1	19	
Condeduque, Cantal, & Acapana		1		17	3		9			1[+1]	31	9
Toconao				12	13	1	6	1 (Copiapo)	1		34	7
Socaire				9	17		3			1	30	9
Peine & Cama		1		6	3		2				12	8
Atacama La Alta		2		75	54		29	2	2	4	168	
Total Atacama	2	2	3	82	54		29	2	2	4	180	

[+1]Includes a youngster 19 years old, disabled, present in his *ayllu*

that the *revisita* registered 45 men as heads of families or bachelors who had to pay tribute, only 15.5% had their residence in Atacama. The extent of geographical dispersion can be seen in figure 8.1.

In Table 8.3 we have noted the dispersion of transient absentees that come and go over a region encompassing Lipez, Tucuman, Chichas, and Chile. This listing is incomplete since it does not register the movement of the muleteers from Chiuchiu, but it does not support the idea that perhaps they helped to maintain communication between the *ayllus* and their distant tributaries, particularly in the case of the *ayllu* mentioned: Condeduque. On the other hand, in the case of Sequitur these travelers could have collaborated in the task of keeping up direct ties between authorities and tributaries or between the latter and their families.

In Table 8.4 I have noted the periods of absence both for the tributaries who were traveling and for those who permanently resided outside of the province in 1683. The highest number among these categories is for those born in other jurisdictions—as high as 29.34% of the total of the absentees who paid taxes in Upper Atacama. In other words, 17% of the tributaries of Upper Atacama in 1683 had been born outside of the province. More than 56% of the absentees who paid taxes had left the province more than 11 years previously or had been born outside of it. Considering how long such periods of time are in individual life histories together with the pattern of use of multiple resources, which are at a distance of days or weeks of traveling time, we ask ourselves how was the cohesion and solidarity of those groups maintained? How could individuals who had been born in other provinces and who had lived outside all their lives continue to belong to the *ayllu*?

Undoubtedly the chieftains, travelers, and muleteers played a role in the survival of the *ayllus*, even though, as we have pointed out, it is difficult to attribute to them the entire responsibility. Every link has

Table 8.3 *Revisita of Atacama* 1683: Transitory absentees

	Chichas R. San León	Lipez	Chile	Tucumán (Río de Sn. Juan)	
Solo	3	2	1		
Sequitur		4	2	1	
Soncor		1		2	
Condeduque, Cantal, & Acapana			2		
Total	3	7	5	3	18

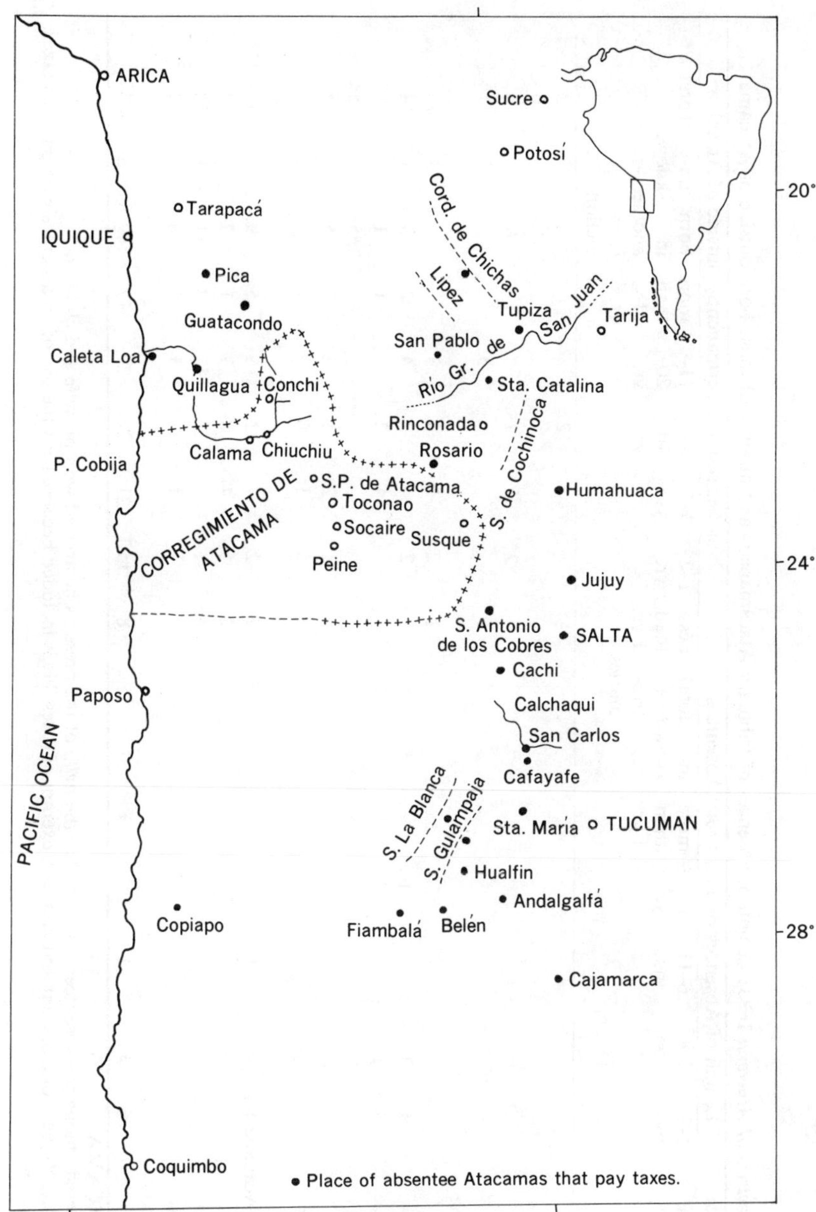

Fig. 8.1 Distribution of tributary absentee Atacameños

Table 8.4 *Revisita of Atacama* 1683: Length of absences of tributary Atacamanans and number of those born outside of Atacama

Ayllu of Origin or Affiliation	Length of Absences of Transitory Absentees							Number residing permanently outside of Atacama								
	1–2 mo.	3–4 mo.	6–11 mo.	1 yr.	more than 1 yr.	un-known	total of trib-utaries	Less than 1 yr.	1–2 yr.	3–5 yr.	6–10 yr.	11–20 yr.	more than 21 yr.	born in another juris-diction	un-known	Total
Chiuchiu											2					2
Calama																0
Cobija									2*1	1	1					4
Caspana								1				3			3	7
Total Atacama La Baja								1	2	1	3	3			3	13
Solo	1	3		1		1	6		2		2	4	· 2	3	1	14
Sequitur	4	1		2			7	1		4	2		1	1		9
Soncor					3		3							5		5
Solcor								1	1	2	1	2	2	5		14
Coio & Veter								3	3	3	6	1	1		2	19
Condeduque, Cantal, and Acapana	1		1				2	1	2	7	1	3	5	9	2	30+1*2
Toconao								2	5	4	8	7	1	7		34
Socaire									1		2	11	4	11	1	30
Peine & Cama									1	1		1	1	8		12
Total Atacama La Alta	6	4	1	3	3	1	18	8	15	21	22	29	17	49	6	167
TOTAL ATACAMA																

*1 One registered among the absentees, who "closed the *ayllu* of the presents he arrived with his wife and children."

*2 A youngster, 19 years old, present and disabled, exempt of taxes. He is included because he is the son of an absentee who pays his taxes.

two ends and the man or family group that left Atacama could keep or cut these links. The absentee would be interested in keeping them to preserve his rights to water and land in Atacama, a right that was kept until the seventeenth century. But if these rights were not exercised, what would be the interest in fulfilling obligations without receiving anything in exchange? This does not seem to have been the situation at the end of the eighteenth century. In a great number of cases (33.33% of the absentees who paid taxes) the male head of the household had left the province but his wife or some of his children remained, enjoying the resources provided by the *ayllu* or inherited from relatives.

Economic interest was not the only one that motivated tributaries to keep up their ties to the native *ayllu.* It also seems that a tendency toward endogamy played a significant role. Only 24 of the 168 absentees who paid taxes were married to outsiders or women who did not originally belong to the same *ayllu*; that is, only 14% of the migrants had married foreigners. The number of single men and widowers was 48, or 28.57% of the total 168 absent tributaries who paid taxes in Atacama La Alta.

To be sure, a set of cultural features, among them language, dress, festivities, kinship systems, systems of authority and exchange, besides the economic interests already mentioned—land, water, pastures, etc.—all were possible insurance against extreme poverty and contributed to maintaining cohesion of the *ayllus* despite dispersion and the colonial pressures we have described.

Nevertheless a factor that should not be underrated in the preservation of this pattern of disperse settlement was the acceptance and the knowledge of it on the part of the fiscal authorities which was the way in which the system received legal support. At least since the *revisita* of Espejo, the authorities assumed that the Atacameñan Indians would continue to pay their tribute wherever they were living. Espejo in his report states his fear that Atacama would become depopulated if the driving of mules in Chiuchiu was suspended and if the absentees were registered as foreigners in their places of residence. In this last case, the residents of Atacama would have had to pay excessive taxes, above the annual 60 pesos per tributary. The *corregidores* and *caciques* of Atacama therefore were legally authorized to continue collecting tribute from outside their provinces and to be tolerated by the authorities of the other jurisdictions. The person who did not pay tribute could be forced to do so by being made to return to Atacama and by being imprisoned. The *revisita* of 1752, carried out by the *corregidor* Manuel Fernândez Valdivieso, confirms this situation in several cases. An example is "Joseph Gregorio, 20 years old, single, having been brought from Salta, had run away again" (Ayllo Condeduque, revisita de Atacama 1752, A.G.N.A. 9–7–7–1). Another is Francisco, 54 years old, from the *ayllu* Condeduque, resident in Copiapo "who was put in jail in this town several times because he did not want to pay his taxes when he was of an age to do so." (idem).

In the *revisita* of 1752, the category "absentees who pay taxes" does not appear because these normally were included among the native tributaries. Also this seems to be the case of some of the categories of absentees, but preferably this last category was saved for those who had fled. That is why some locations that were not very popular in 1683 increased in population in 1752, such as Copiapó and Coquimbo in the Kingdom of Chile for tributaries from Upper Atacama, and Guatacondo in Tarapacá for the tributaries from Lower Atacama. We are not going to make a careful analysis of those changes at this time, but the point we want to stress is that there was no questioning of or any other indication that anyone found it strange that natives from Atacama resided in other provinces. A case that is surprising to us, but not to the *revisitador*, is that of the *cacique* of the *ayllu* Soncor who resides in "the Laguna Blanca, jurisdiction of Salta" and not in the town of Atacama that bears the name of the *ayllu.*

Nevertheless, in 1750 there are clear signs that the system was in crisis and that a question of identities was appearing. The *revisitadores* of Jujuy, Juan Antonio de Herrera and Juachín Romualdo Velásquez, met in the town of Cochinoca on March 20, 1750 with the second lieutenant don Juan de Araya, resident of Atacama, who, on behalf of the *corregidor* don Manuel Fernández Valdivieso, had come to collect "tribute from the Indians, which is recorded in memory" with a request that in 1730 the "corregidor" of Atacama had made to the Governor of Tucuman to exclude from the lists the Indians from Atacama who were in his jurisdiction since in the last ten years there had been" continuous litigations among the collectors and the governors of both jurisdictions" over who should pay. The more than fifty Indians benefited from this by "not paying to one or to the other the Royal Tributes to Her Majesty" (Revisita de Atacama, 1752). Consequently the census takers ordered: "and in order to clarify which ones belong to each jurisdiction and paying attention to the serious damage done to Her Majesty . . . we send the said don Juan de Araya lieutenant of the *corregidor* and the Governor and the *cacique* of the sector of Río de San Juan, don Martín Caucota, to appear in person at the town of Rinconada at the time when the listing of the said *ayllu* is to be started so that henceforth it will be clearly stated who belongs to each jurisdiction. . . ." (Revisita de Atacama, 1752).

On May 2, 1750 began the inspection, the "*Padrón* of native Indians originating from the province of Atacama, from whom the governor don Martín Caucota should collect taxes adjusted to the royal *provisiones* from the archive of the Royal Audiencia of La Plata obeyed by the lords, Governor of the Province of Tucumán and his subordinates; year of a thousand seven hundred and forty eight." Then followed a list of 20 tributaries and one *reservado.* The following nine were excluded from the list "because they had presented legitimate proof" of not belonging to it. But "in this state don Martín Caucota appeared and proved that Lorenzo Sânchez and his children Domingo and Pascual were of the said Province of Atacama," these were added to the first 20 (Revisita de Atacama, 1752).

It is evident that distinctions as to which province native people were from were no longer clear and that belonging on a list of tributaries or the inclusion in it was not voluntary but forced by the *cacique* authority and supported by Spanish law.

Undoubtedly, the *corregidores* tried to use this knowledge for their own benefit. In what way could the obligatory delivery of merchandise take place with this distribution of the population? The *caciques* probably suffered more direct pressure from the *corregidor* than the tributaries, who always were able to hide themselves, fleeing, or other forms of resistance. In the two Atacamas we find examples of how intolerable were the demands that these *caciques* had to suffer. In Chiuchiu, Antonio Bernardo Echevarría, a widower, 33 years old with four children, fled to Copiapó "because on being elected *cacique* he threw down the list and left." In the accounts of Manuel Fernández Valdivieso, there figures the *cacique* of the town of Toconao, Francisco Roque, who was removed from office because he owed 187 pesos and five *reales* "without any hope of collecting them since he had no goods whatsoever." In fact, all the goods of this chieftain had been expropiated by the *corregidor* (Hidalgo 1982). These are not the only examples. The same *corregidor* had under him two more chieftains who owed him between 100 and 160 pesos without any hope of collecting them, and he complains of the lack of individuals that guarantee with their own goods the money to be collected (Revisita de Atacama, 1752).

If it was difficult to collect tribute, even greater difficulties should have been encountered in demanding extra payments. To do so it was necessary to have recourse to violence, in different forms, which consequently yielded a greater number of cases of Indians who fled from Atacama, abandoning their land and families, or tributaries who paid their taxes against their will. In this way the visit of the *cacique extrac-*

tor was no longer an occasion for the interchange of news and goods among relatives; the *cacique* turned the official of the realm who squeezed the payments in an unbalanced relation.

Nevertheless the solidarity between the "absent" Atacameños and their ethnic authorities had not completely disappeared in 1775 when the rebellion in Incahuasi took place and the *corregidor* of Atacama fled to Tucumán. From there he intended to recruit troops to return to punish the rebels, but the rebels received information from the Atacameñan peasants, who inhabited the area where the counterattack was being organized and who threatened to abandon the province en masse, causing the *corregidor* to abandon his project (Hidalgo 1982).

By April 1791, Dr. don Vicente Anastasio de Isasmendi, parish priest and vicary of the *beneficio* of Calchaquí, had asked the *Intendente* Governor in Salta that the Atacama Indians residing in his province be registered and made to pay their tributes there, so that he could be paid or receive the synod that was due to him because it was he who attended them in spiritual matters and not the parish priest of Atacama. He pointed out:

> for many years there have been residing in my parish (Cachalquí) Indians who pay tribute in the Province of Atacama, the majority of them being natives of that district and descendants of people who moved. They are completely subject in spiritual matters to the said parish; and since their establishment here this parish priest has never received the due synod, undoubtedly because the Indians have not registered themselves in the past *revisita* as they should have and demanded their continued residence.

Isamendi argues in his favor: "so if the laborer is worthy of reporting his stipend, he who serves the altar must live from that same altar to which he dedicates all his watchfulness. . . ." He adds that the Indians from Atacama continuously suffer the collections of tributes of the *Intendencia* of Potosí, and since they had to travel great distances to collect them, the costs were charged to the poor Indians, and as a result they paid double tribute in ratio to the rest of the natives. This is why they feared the collectors. When these officers came through the province they fled to the mountains to avoid payment. On the other hand, because they were not tributaries in Calchaquí, these Atacameños from Salta had to pay for parochial rights as "pure soldiers." This seems to indicate that they were subject to paying more than the natives of the province (A.G.N.A. 9–30–4–9, "Testimonio del expediente formado sobre el empadronamiento en Salta de los indios del partido de Atacama, revisitado en aquellas jurisdicciones"; also notes on the proceedings published by John Murra, 1974).

The *Real Hacienda* of Salta considered that the petition was "fair and in accordance with the law" and in consequence recommended those who resided in that province to register of the Atacameños in Salta.

Another report that answered the request of Isasmendi, written by the ministers Guemes and Rabaza, recalls Article 120 of the *Real Ordenanza de Intendentes* which established that "all the inhabitants subject to this tax residing in the province should be registered in every sector of the province." Its conclusion was that since the Atacameños were in Calchaquí, a separate list of them should be made there, so they could make their payments, without bothering the dwellers of Atacama. If the taxes were withdrawn from Atacama and collected in Salta, the Royal Treasury would not suffer. They deliberated that although "in Atacama such Indians go by the name of natives because they have their own land there, in Calchaquí they would be seen as *forasteros* and in this class the same would be collected from them that they would pay in their old province." In their opinion, to exile the Atacameños from Salta would be harmful to them because of "the incomparably better land they occupy now than that left behind by their ancestors" (A.G.N.A., 9–30–4–9, "Testimonio . . .").

The proceedings in question were sent to Potosí, and there the opinion of the sub-delegate from Atacama was to support the segregation of the residents in Salta from the list of those of his province, although his reasons differed from those of the officers of the *Intendencia*. Considering the benefit to the Royal Treasury, he supported the execution of the measure as soon as possible. His point of view reflected the opinion of the *caciques* of Atacama. He argued that between Salta and Atacama there was more than 200 leagues

> the major part depopulated and high *cordillera,* and transportation from one territory to another was necessary for the miserable *caciques* . . . twice a year they had to travel during inclement weather, the work and cruel hungers that such deserts offer, and the small travel allowance that was assigned to them for that purpose. . . . And then they were made to believe that immediately upon their arrival in these parts of Salta, they could achieve the ends of their rough trip with the prompt satisfaction of payment of the taxes. It so happened that the native tributaries, spoiled with the protection of being

in an alien jurisdiction and throwing off the yoke of subordination, postponed payment or even hid, or even tried to inflict bodily injuries upon the *caciques* even to the point of pursuing them with a lasso and knife which intimidates them. (A.G.N.A., 9–30–4–9, "Testimonio . . ." f.8.f.)

The sub-delegate of Atacama finishes complaining that in this way it was very hard for the chieftains to collect the total of what was owed and they were forced, along with the sub-delegate, to pay the difference out of their own pocket. That is why you could not find in Atacama young men who of their free will would accept the position of collector *cacique*. With this in mind, he recommended extending the proposal of the *Intendente* of Salta to the "towns named Fiambala, San Carlos, Santa María, and Belem" (Idem f9).

Then, according to the opinions of the Spanish authorities of Salta and Atacama, the preservation of the system of registration according to place of origin, not by that of residence, was no longer satisfactory to anybody. On the contrary it had become a very hard burden for everybody to support. Even the principal *cacique* of Atacama and his "second" greeted enthusiastically the possibility of a separation. They say in one of their letters: "since the piety of the lord *Intendente* of this province has consented to the separation of our worst enemies who are settled in the jurisdiction of Salta," they requested a new *revisita*. (A.G.N.A., 9–30–4–9, "Testimonio . . ." f. 36r).

I think that for the subject of this paper it is unnecessary to reiterate the legal and social arguments that the officer of the treasury put up in favor of or against changing the lists of Atacama and Salta. The fact is that the measure was put into practice before it was completely approved. In the *revisita* of Atacama of 1792, the sub-delegate Benito Antonio de Goyena, under orders of the *Intendente* of Potosí arranged a meeting with the *caciques* to form a "punctual reason of the Indians of this sector who were found absent in the province of Salta with the purpose of confronting them with the testimony of the *revisita* which once again should be put into effect in that jurisdiction for the families living there . . . . they will appear before me the governor, seconds, *caciques* knowledgeable of the doctrine of this capital, and under the solemnity of oath declare and state all and singly the Indians who are registered in their respective lists as residents of the jurisdiction of Salta who are absent from that part, expressing their names, ages, places of residence, and in the order kept in the last *revisit* which took place in the year 1786" (A.G.N.A., 13, 19, 1, 1, f. 78). Following this are declarations of *caciques* of the six *ayllus* of San Pedro and of Toconao,

Soncor, Peine, and Susques, with the items requested. The information appears slightly corrected farther on in the same *revisita*. The number of tributaries, according to one summary or another, are given in Table 8.5.

In the *revisita*, there is also a summary of the places where tributaries reside and their number (Table 8.6).

The total sum matches that of the second list and the *revisita* points out that there are 43 places "where at present reside the two hundred thirty three tributaries who have separated from their place of origin, Atacama, June 18, 1792" (A.G.N.A., 13–9–1–1, f. 109r). It should be pointed out that the majority of the places mentioned coincide with archaeological sites of the Intermediate and Late periods of the Argentinan northwest. This coincidence of prehispanic tradition of settlement and Colonial establishments should be evaluated by the archaeologists of the area to determine if there is evidence for late Atacameñan colonization in prehispanic period or if it is a phenomenon that appeared in the Colonial period. Figure 8.1 shows the distribution of these places.

All the documentation from the end of the eighteenth century concentrates on the Atacameños in Salta and Tucumán, and nothing is said of those who inhabited Lipez and Chichas, the other two provinces in which were concentrated an important number of tributaries absent from Atacama in 1683.

Finally, we are left with the question: how did the Atacameños of the end of the eighteenth century productively insert themselves in those areas of what is now northwest Argentina? Fortunately we can answer

Table 8.5 Salta Tributaries and Residents

Ayllu	Chieftain	Absent Tributary Indians	
		f.88r	f.108v
Condeduque	Dn Pedro Gerardo Liquitay	15	19
Sequitur	Dn Andrés Chávez	4	4
Coyo	Dn Martín Andrés	14	15
Solo	Dn Juan Manuel	14	14
Betere	Dn Agustín Lucas	13	13
Solcor	Dn Santos Manuel	13	13
Toconao	Dn Joseph Mathias	6	7
Sorcor	Dn Martín Matheo Fabián	24	26
Socayre	Dn Martín Matheo Fabián	41	42
Peine	Dn Bernardo Lázaro Reyes	41	64
Susques	Dn Thomas Manuel Puca Puca	38	34
Total of Absentee Tributaries		223	233

Table 8.6 Number and Place of Tributaries

Place	No. of Tributaries	Place	No. of Tributaries
Santa María	28	Fiambala	22
Laguna Blanca	18	San Carlos	7
Calchaqui	30	Andargala	2
Cachi	4	Angastaco	5
San Antonio del Cobre	10	Culampaja	5
Rinconada	1	Guandacal	1
Bolson	14	Tolombon	2
Cafayate	3	Gualfin (Hualfin)	1
Tacuil	7	Jacton	1
Belem	11	Pucara	3
Concho	6	Pacta	1
Cajoncillo	1	Cajón	7
Cajones	13	Salta	2
Payogasta	1	Vicuña Pampa	3
Palo Blanco	1	Suracatao	1
Loconte	3	Tolar	1
Tactil (Tastil)	7	Frume Arco	1
Rosario	1	Capillas	1
Altos de Tonco	1	Cortaderas	1
Jujuy	1	Pampa Grande	1
Guasamayo	1	Uturunco Guasi	1
		Frontera	2
Total Tributaries: 162		Total Tributaries: 71	

this question in some detail since we have found in the General Archive of Argentina "the list of Indians originally from Atacama who reside in the area of Calchaquí, and who, when asked by my 'revisitor' if they had land in the community of their origin, answered that they did but that it was sterile and without water and for that reason they had moved to the abovementioned valley and parish to be able to support themselves." (A.G.N.A. S. XIII. 17, 2, 1, Revisita de Salta, 1791). The summary is presented in Table 8.7.

The *revisitadores* of Salta found 441 persons and 126 tributaries (which afterwards was reduced to 111), a number much smaller than the 223 or 233 tributaries registered in Atacama. It is evident that in Salta there was interest in hiding natives and protecting them from fiscal control. The *Contaduría General de Retasas* points out that the difference is due to the fact that neither in Salta (Calchaquí) nor in Catamarca (Santa María, Belem, and Fiambala) was it required that the owners of estates, farms, and mines declare the number and origin of the *forasteros* who worked for them (A.G.N.A. 9–30–4–9; Tax list

Table 8.7 Her Majesty's Tributaries of Atacama Origin

Reserv.	Girls	Widows	Single Women	Married Women	Parishes	Tribut.	Absent.	Prox.	Boys
17	45	—	14	57	Calchaqui	69	1	3	65
2	15	1	6	20	Santa María	28	—	3	6
3	15	—	4	18	Belem	25	—	2	13
2	2	—	2	4	Fiambala	4	—	2	3
24	77	1	26	99	Total	126	1	10	77

in Salta of Atacama Indians, information from tax accounts and tribunal of superior council, 1806).

Regarding Salta and the specific situation of the Atacameños there, the report mentioned above analyzes it as follows:

> The Treasury has recognized with special attention both the general registration lists that were made in the district of Salta, last year, 1791, and the one that independently was ordered to be done of the Indians from Atacama; at the same time it advises that from the 582 tributaries which is the total of the main register and 67 retired due to age, a total of 649. Two thirds are Indians from the inner divisions of the Kingdom, most of whom are tenants, others collected and contracted by the farms and estates adjoining to that city.
>
> In the report that was made of the Indians of Atacama settled in the estates of the district of the parish or *repartimiento* of San Pedro Nolasco de Calchaquí in the district of Salta, there were registered 86 individuals, 69 tributaries and 17 adults, but from this number only two have land, one through marriage, that is Juan Ignacio Valencia, married to Justa Cañisares who lives on her lands named Seclantes, and in the annex of San Antonio, Pablo Fabian who has his own lands, and the rest survive as tenants and laborers to those landowners.
>
> The 57 tributaries and the 7 retired of the district of Atacama who were registered in the district of the city of Catamarca have this same occupation and it can be said that the province of Salta is the asylum of these who have fled, since they found among the inhabitants all kinds of protection and shelter and were able to live in freedom not bothered by the Crown's justices or priests and exempt of the services of their obligation in their town of origin." (A.G. N.A., 9–30–4–9, Expediente. . .).

The situation described in the last quotation does not qualify for a system of complementarity of control of multiple resources. It deals with the breakdown of the remnants of that system during the Colonial period; that is, the breaking of the links with the communities of origin and the reassignment to a private owner of agricultural land or mine holdings. The two exceptional cases who were able to own lands in Salta emphasizes even more the absence of any community control over them.

NOTE

This work was written thanks to funding provided by the Dirección de Investigaciones de la Universidad de Tarapacá for the project Las sociedades indígenas de los corregimientos de Arica, Tarapacá y Atacama . . . which allowed me to research in the Archivo Nacional de la Nación Argentina, Buenos Aires, and the Archivo Nacional de Bolivia, Sucre, where are found the majority of the documents consulted. A preliminary version of this paper was presented to the Simposio de Arqueología Atacameña organized by the Universidad del Norte, in San Pedro de Atacama, January 10–15, 1983 under the title "Movilidad Atacameña, 1683–1792."

MANUSCRIPTS

Archivo General de la Nacion Argentina, Buenos aires (A.G.N.A.)

9–7–7–1. Colonia-Gobierno. Atacama, varios padrones de. . . 1683–1777.

— Revisita de Atacama de 1683 efectuada por el Corregidor Espejo obedeciendo orden del Duque de La Palata.

— Revisita de Atacama de 1752 efectuada por el corregidor José Manuel Valdivieso.

13–19–1–1. Sección Colonia, Contaduría, Patrones Potosí, 1791–92.

— Revisita de Atacama de 1792, efectuada por el subdelegado B. A. de Goyena.

9–30–4–9. (Leg. 33, Exp. 33). "Testimonio del expediente formado sobre el empadronamiento en Salta de los indios del partido de Atacama, residentes en aquella jurisdicción".

13–17–2–1. Sección Colonia, Contaduría, Patrones Provincia de Salta, Revisitas de indios, 1785–92.

— Revisita de Salta 1791, (Leg. 2. Lib. 5).

Archivo Nacional de Bolivia, Sucre (A.N.B.)

Catálogo de Minas. Lipez, 1643. II, 14. Ingenio del Rosario de Lipez. Carta de perdón de muerte: Inés Casma, viuda de Martín

Tuctipur, y madre de Pedro Viltipoco, difunto, en favor de Martín Chico. Todos ellos indios Atacama, naturales del pueblo de Sorco, de Atacama La Grande, y empleados en el servicio de este ingenio por la muerte que éste último dió al dicho Pedro Viltipoco. (A.N. B.E.P. Alvarez 1643, Fs. 78–83) Vol. 137.

REFERENCES CITED

Aldunate del Solar, Carlos and Victoria Castro

1981 Las Chullpa de Toconce y su relación con el poblamiento altiplánico en el Loa Superior, período tardío. Tesis para optar al grado de Licenciado en Filosofía con mención en prehistoria y arqueología. Universidad de Chile, Santiago.

Beaulieu, Andrés

1967 El habitat humano y la economía agrícola en el Oasis de Chiuchiu. *In* Revista de la Universidad del Norte 4:81–101. Santiago.

Bowman, Isaiah

1924 Desert Trails of Atacama. Special Publication No. 5. American Geographical Society, New York.

1942 Los senderos del desierto de Atacama. Emilia Romero, Transl. Santiago: Sociedad Chilena de Historia y Geografía.

Hernández Aracena, Roberto

1974 Chiuchiu: La desintegración de la comunidad tradicional. *In* Antropología, segunda época 1:17–33. Universidad de Chile, Santiago.

Hidalgo, Jorge

1978 Incidencia de los patrones de poblamiento en el cálculo de la población del Partido de Atacama desde 1752 a 1804. Las revisitas inéditas de 1787, 1792, y 1804. *In* Estudios Atacameños 6:53–111. Museo de Arqueología, San Pedro de Atacama, Universidad del Norte, Chile.

1982 Fases de la Rebelión indígena de 1781 en el Corregimiento de Atacama y esquema de la inestabilidad política que la precede 1749–81. Anexo: 2 documentos inéditos contemporáneos. *In* Chungará 9:192–246. Dpto. de Antropología, Universidad de Tarapacá, Arica.

Krapovickas, Pedro

1978 La agricultura prehispánica en el Puna. *In* Actas V Congreso Nacional de Arqueología, Argentina, San Juan.

Lozano Machuca, Juan

[1581] 1965 Carta del factor de Potosí Juan Lozano Machuca al Virrey del Perú, en donde se describe la provincia de los Lipes. Relaciones Geográficas de Indias, Perú, Tomo II, Biblioteca de Autores Españoles 184, Madrid.

Mostny, Grete, Fidel Geldes, Raul González, and F. Oberhauser

1954 Peine, un pueblo Atacameño. Publicación No. 4, Instituto de Geografía, Universidad de Chile, Santiago.

Murra, John

1972 El "control vertical" de un máximo de pisos ecológicos en la economía de las sociedades andinas. *In* Visita de la Provincia de León de Huánuco en 1562 por Iñigo Ortíz de Zúñiga. I:427–76. Huánuco.

1974 Notas del Archivo de Buenos Aires sobre—Atacameños en Salta. (Our Title). Estudios Atacameños No. 2:108–10. Museo de Arqueología de San Pedro de Atacama. Universidad del Norte, Chile.

1975 Formaciones económicas y political del Mundo Andino. Lima: Instituto de Estudios Peruanos.

[1955] 1978 La organización económica del Estado Inca. México: Siglo Veintiuno.

1983 La mit'a al Tawantinsuyu: Prestaciones de los groupos étnicos. *In* Chungará 10:77–94. Universidad de Tarapacá, Arica.

Núñez A., Lautaro, Vjera Zlatar M. and Patricio Núñez H.

1975 Relaciones prehistóricas trasandinas entre el N. W. Argentino y Norte Chileno (período cerámico). *In* Serie Documentos de Trabajo 6:11–24. Grupo de Arqueología y Museos. Departamento de Ciencias Sociales, Universidad de Chile, Antofagasta.

Platt, Tristán

1975 Reseña Bibliográfica del artículo de Roberto Hernández: Chiu-Chiu: La desintegración de la comunidad tradicional. *In* Chungará 5:153–157, Arica.

Sánchez Albornoz, Nicolás

1978 Indios y Tributos en el Alto Perú. Lima: Instituto de Estudios Peruanos.

Tarrago, Myriam Noemí

1983 La Historia de los Pueblos Circumpuneños en relación con el Altiplano y los Andes Meridoinales. Paper presented at Simposio de Arqueología Atacameña, Jan. 1983. Universidad del Norte, San Pedro de Atacama.

Valenzuela Rojas, Bernardo

1970 Epítome etnográfico de la cuenca del Río Salado. Provincia de Antofagasta Chile. *In* Boletín de Prehistoria de Chile. Año 2, No. 2–3, 1969–70: 75–99. Universidad de Chile, Santiago.

9

Guano and Resource Control in Sixteenth-Century Arequipa

Catherine J. Julien

To the people who lived in the region surrounding Lake Titicaca, resources from the adjacent lowlands were particularly important. Large, dense populations lived near the limits of cultivation where agricultural disasters were common. These people traditionally sought foodstuffs from the lowlands. Their principal source of wealth was the domestic camelid, and their animal wealth was a means of obtaining the foodstuffs needed from the lowlands, principally maize. One option open to them was to take up residence in the lowlands and cultivate the desired foodstuffs themselves. Polo de Ondegardo observed this Andean adaptation in the sixteenth century (1940:177–78) and John Murra returned it to our attention over a decade ago (1968, [1972] 1975).

A primary focus of interest for cultivators from the Lake Titicaca region at the time of the Spanish arrival in the Andes was the district of Arequipa.[1] There, groups of cultivators participated in a local agricultural economy adapted to the arid coastal environment. Cultivators in Arequipa produced large quantities of maize with the aid of *guano*, bird droppings from the coast and offshore islands, incorporated into the soil to supply needed nitrogen and phosphorus. *Guano* was thought to be essential by sixteenth century cultivators in Arequipa:

> . . . The Indians of Moquegua grow a little wheat and maize, although not very much because maize cannot be grown unless bird dung from the coast, that they call *guano*, is put on the fields when the plants are somewhat grown. Without *guano*, the maize does not form kernels. They bring it 20 leagues [100 km] from here, from some islands in the sea, and because of this problem and because the Indians have very few animals, they are poor. (Diez de San Miguel 1964:245; author's translation)

Diez de San Miguel's observations call attention to the distances *guano* was transported. An examination of the scattered documentation for the sixteenth century reveals that settlement in Arequipa was concentrated in the upper coastal valleys where maize was the principal crop. *Guano* was an important means of securing high maize yields in the area.

A particularly close relationship existed in the Spanish colonial era and afterward between the Lake Titicaca and Arequipa regions. In addition to cultivated foodstuffs, large quantities of fish and shellfish were dried and imported inland as were seaweeds (Masuda 1981 and in this volume; Coker 1908:346–51; Vázquez de Espinosa, lib. IV, cap. LXVII, 1969:349). Assembling the scattered information related to *guano* is only one means of documenting the complex pattern of resource control and use involving people from the coast to the highest elevations.

The ties between coast and highlands clearly extend further into the past. Archaeological research on the northern Chilean coast has documented the appearance of high altitude foodstuffs on the coast before cultivation was practiced locally (Núñez 1974:123, 128–29). Two millenia or more before the present, camelid wool textiles appear to have almost entirely replaced an earlier cotton textile tradition (Bird 1943:271–72). Even in these earlier times, the outline of a strong bond between coast and highlands is visible.

In the discussion which follows, two cases have been examined in some detail. People from the Lupaca province on the southwest shore of Lake Titicaca resided permanently in the coastal valleys of Arequipa. Information about them illustrates the position of outside cultivators in the agricultural economy of the Arequipa region. The residents of Puquina territory, who lived in the upper Tambo valley, demonstrate the situation of local cultivators (Fig. 9.1).[2]

The Ecology of the Arequipa Region

The involvement of people with resources in the district of Arequipa was circumscribed to a great degree by natural factors. These factors affected the supply and distribution of both cultivable land and *guano*, and so influenced the pattern of resource use in the area at the time of the Spanish arrival. Much of the Pacific coast of South America is an extremely arid desert, and the availability of water and aids to soil fertility are critical factors which determine where cultivation may occur.[3]

The availability of water is the most serious limit to cultivation. In

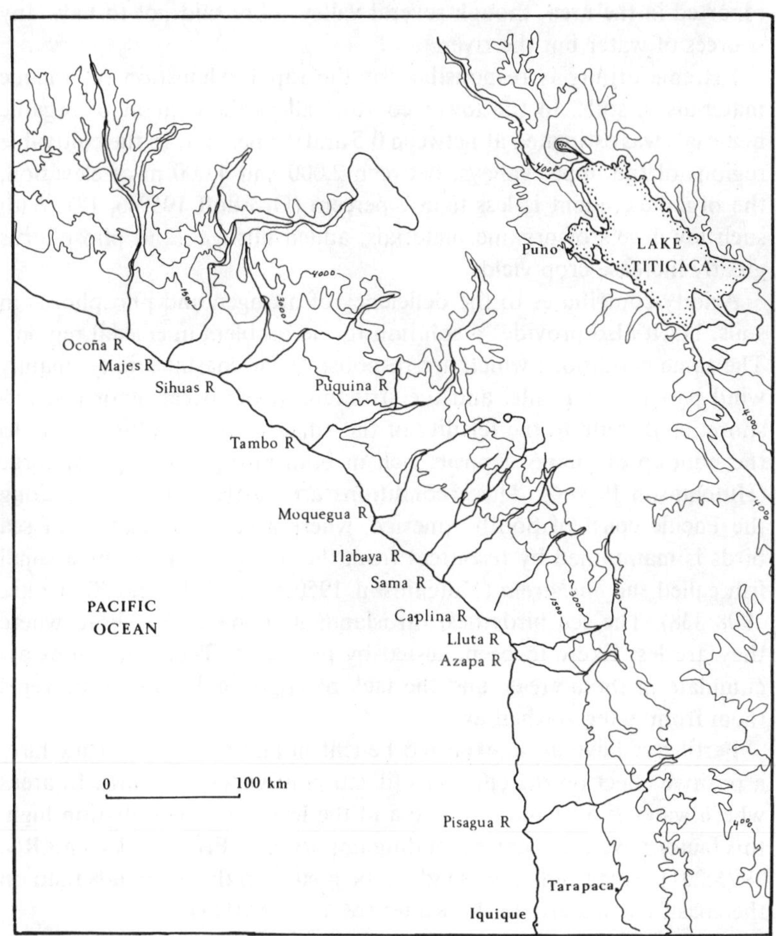

Fig. 9.1 The Arequipa region

Arequipa very little rain falls below 1,600 m of elevation (Murphy 1936:I, 264; Meigs 1966:table 8, 133). Even in areas above 1,600 m rainfall is scarce and not dependable enough for dry farming, except in some areas above 3,000 m (Diez de San Miguel 1964:127). Cultivation depends mainly on irrigation, using water redirected from the rivers which crosscut the coastal strip. South of the Sama River, the only river to flow all the way to the coast throughout the year in recent times is the Lluta (Alan Craig, pers. comm.). In several valleys, even during the summer rainy season, the rivers do not provide enough water to till all of the cultivable valley land.[4] Other sources of water have been reported in the area, though several valleys were said not to have any sources of water but the river.[5]

Extreme aridity is responsible for the rapid exhaustion of organic materials in soils. In the lower coastal valleys the content of organic materials was estimated at between 0.5 and 0.3 percent. In the cultivable regions of the upper valleys, between 2,000 and 4,000 m of elevation, the organic content is less than 2 percent (Drosdoff 1959:6, 12). With such low levels of organic materials, added nitrogen and phosphorus greatly increase crop yields.

Aridity contributes to the deficiency of nitrogen and phosphorus in soils, but it also provides a solution to the problem in coastal regions. The same conditions which are responsible for coastal aridity, mainly wind patterns, currents, and the structure of the ocean floor just offshore, contribute to the fertility of the adjacent seas, and indirectly to the buildup of guano deposits rich in both nitrogen and phosphorus (Hutchinson 1950:4). These conditions are particularly evident along the Pacific coast of South America, where a large population of sea birds is maintained by resources from the sea, particularly by a small fish called the *anchoveta* (Hutchinson 1950:5–8, 13–15, 18–20; Coker 1908:338). The sea birds nest on islands and the rocky shore where they are less likely to be molested by predators. Their excretions accumulate in these areas, and the lack of appreciable rainfall prevents them from being washed away.

Fertilizers have an unexpected benefit in an arid region. They have a positive effect on the efficient utilization of water by plants. In areas where water is a scarce resource and the level of solar radiation high, this factor develops a corresponding importance (Frère, Rijks, and Rea 1975:221). Solar radiation tends to be greater in the highlands than on the coast, particularly in the winter (Meigs 1966:111).

Another phenomenon contributes to agricultural productivity in the area. If there is some degree of topographic relief near the coast, a seasonal rise in humidity creates abundant fog vegetation.[6] Called *lomas* vegetation, it provides seasonal forage for animals. Seasonal humidity can also have an effect on water loss through evaporation in the lower valleys (Barriga 1941–48:II, 292, 321; III, 25). Cultivation may have been aided in this way, though its chief support in the Arequipa region was still irrigation.

Native settlement was affected by all of these factors, as well as by native preferences for specific crops. In the sixteenth century settlement was densest in the upper valleys (p. 206). Varieties of maize preferred by native consumers today are cultivated in this area (Flores 1970:196–99). Food preferences may have been a principal reason for settlement at these altitudes, but there are environmental advantages as well. The upper valleys received comparatively more rainfall than the lower valley area. Settlement higher up the river presumably would have been advantageous when water was in short supply. Still, the upper valleys had poorer quality soils than the lower valleys. Cultivation there was unaided by seasonal humidity. The upper valley was also subject to higher levels of solar radiation. A fertilizer supplying both nitrogen and phosphorus would have been comparatively more important under such conditions.

Guano Use

References to where and how *guano* was used are scattered throughout the literature, and there is no single comprehensive treatment of the subject at any point in time.

The word *guano* is a hispanicization of the Inca word *wanu* meaning "dung for fertilizer."[7] Cieza de León is the first person to describe *guano* use. He travelled through southern Peru in 1548–49, and though he did not travel along the coast in Arequipa, he reported that *guano* from islands near Quilca, Chuli, and Tambopalla (at the mouth of the Tambo River), Ilo, and Tarapacá was used to fertilize maize:

> . . . The Indians go out to them [the *guano* islands] on floats, and from the rocks in the upper part of the islands they gather great quantities of bird dung to use in planting their fields of corn and other crops which support them. Its use is advantageous to them because the earth where they plant is made rich and fertile instead of sterile, because if they had not used this dung, they would harvest very little maize. They would not be able to support themselves if the birds, reposing on the rocks of the islands already mentioned, did not leave their droppings which when harvested are of considerable value to the Indians. Because of the value of this dung, the Indians trade it among themselves like a precious substance (*Crónica*, cap. LXXV, 1932:232–33; author's translation).

Vázquez de Espinosa, who travelled along this section of coast in 1617–19, documents the use of *guano* in the valleys from Majes south to Arica, noting that *guano* was mined even further south on an island near Tarapacá, probably the island in front of Iquique (lib. IV, cap. LVIII, 1969:336; lib. IV, cap. LXV, 1969:346; lib. IV, cap. LXVII, 1969:348; Cobo, lib. II, cap. XIV, vol. 91, 1956:85; see p. 221). He also noted that *guano* increased yields enormously. By using *guano* on a *fanega* of land (1.6 a.), 300–500 *fanegas* (1.5 bu. or 52.9 l) would be reaped at harvest (Vázquez de Espinosa, lib. IV, cap. LXV 1969: 346; lib. IV, cap. LXVII, 1969:348).

Guano application was described sketchily by several early writers. Diez de San Miguel said that *guano* was incorporated into the soil after the plants had sprouted and were "somewhat grown" (p. 185). Another method was mentioned by Vázquez de Espinosa who noted that *guano* was applied at planting, and then again some time afterward (lib. IV, cap. LXVII, 1969:348). López de Caravantes notes that a fist full of *guano* was incorporated into the soil with the seeds, and these were planted a handful at a time (Jiménez de la Espada, vol. I, app. II, 1880–97: CXXXVIII). This technique of planting was likened to the method used in Spain at the time in the cultivation of broad beans (*habas*) and was referred to as seeding in handfuls (*en macollas*) (Vázquez de Espinosa, lib. IV, cap. LXVII, 1969:349).

In 1846, Johann Jakob von Tschudi described *guano* application in some detail:

> . . . The Peruvians use it chiefly in the cultivation of maize and potatoes. A few weeks after the seeds begin to shoot, a little hollow is dug round each root, and is filled up with *guano*, which is afterwards covered with a layer of earth. After a lapse of twelve or fifteen hours, the whole field is laid under water, and is left in that state for some hours. Of the Guano Blanco a less quantity suffices, and the field must be more speedily and abundantly watered; otherwise the roots would be destroyed. The effect of this manure is incredibly rapid. In a few days the growth of the plant is doubled. If the manure is repeated a second time, but in smaller quantity, a rich harvest is certain. At least the produce will be threefold that which would have been obtained from unmanured soil. (1854:169)

Tschudi's account agrees more closely with Diez de San Miguel's than with the other two early accounts. It may have been that *guano* was used either at the time of planting or some time shortly afterward. Both Tschudi and Vázquez de Espinosa note that two *guano* applications were made, although Tschudi indicates that the second application could be omitted. The dictionary of González Holguín also makes reference to two applications. *Huanunchapuni* means "to apply fertilizer a second time" (1952:178). Tschudi is the only observer to link *guano* use with irrigation, but it is clear from his account that prompt irrigation was necessary. Tschudi is also the only observer to provide an idea of the dose: *guano* was applied in small amounts directly to the individual plant in its naturally occurring concentration. Little *guano* was wasted.

Access to Guano

Information about *guano* procurement is nearly nonexistent, despite the probable continuance of native methods of obtaining the substance. Some of the factors which circumscribed its acquisition can be identified. Both coastal technology and highland animal resources were put to use in procuring *guano* for cultivators.

The skills and technologies of the coastal fishing peoples were clearly important in the quest for guano. Obtaining *guano* from offshore islands necessitated ocean travel, and the vessel commonly used along the coast for fishing was a float made of two sea lion skins. If inland cultivators were to do the actual mining of *guano* themselves, they probably either obtained floats from the fishermen or made them.[8] Cobo describes the floats made in the province of Arica:

> . . . They make [the floats] from sea lion skins full of air which they tie together in the same two bundle style as those of reeds. On each float only one Indian rides, and in the water [the float] draws as much water as the other kind of float [reed]. It can even draw more because these floats sometimes deflate in water. So that they do not sink, each Indian takes a piece of cane, and from time to time in mid-sea, unfastens the closure and reinflates the float by blowing into it, as if it were a ball of air. These floats are very light and swift in the water, like the air they are composed of; [the Indians] never put sails on them as they never do on the reed ones, and they are navigated by oar, as in the reed version. (Cobo, lib. VII, cap. XVIII, vol. 91, 1956:295; author's translation)

These craft were also used to unload freight from the frigates entering Spanish ports and were described and illustrated by a number of other writers, as they were in use through the beginning of the twentieth century (Vázquez de Espinosa, lib. IV, cap. LXVII, 1969:349; Tschudi 1854:176).[9] Their buoyancy was notable. They were preferred for use as landing craft because they were stable in high surf conditions that would have capsized an ordinary boat (Edwards 1965:19). Despite their small size and delicate appearance, these craft would have been excellent for short ocean voyages.

A voyage to the *guano* islands often involved a trip of a kilometer or more from the shore (Cobo, lib. II, cap. XIV, vol. 91, 1956:85). A certain amount of navigational skill must have been required. Although fishing was the only use attributed to these floats in descriptions of them, one writer noted that fishermen could spend two to three days at sea on them (Latcham, cited in Edwards 1965:19).

Some of the *guano* islands were located near the mouths of rivers, but others were some distance from a source of fresh water (Fig. 9.2). Permanent settlement near these islands is not likely, although some of the fishing people living on the north Chilean coast in the nineteenth century were located 8 to 10 km from drinking water (Bird 1947:596). Travel, either overland or by sea, to islands any distance from the river mouths is indicated. Watertight bags, with a seam lashing analogous to the technique used in joining sea lion skin floats, were in use in the area.[10] A water supply could be carried in this way to the site of *guano* mining.

Another factor which affected *guano* acquisition was scheduling. Birds deposited *guano* on offshore islands because there they were safe from predators and other disturbances during nesting. Nesting occurs mainly between November and March, although there is really no time of year when nesting would not be disturbed (Coker 1908:364). Permanent settlement on the islands is therefore not indicated. Control was desirable and some informants note that *guano* was harvested in alternate years (Raimondi 1948:252). *Guano* may have been harvested on a similar schedule in antiquity.

The quantity of *guano* extracted made the use of pack animals a great convenience. The administrator of a 1792 survey said that half a *fanega* (26.5 l) of *guano* was not sufficient for the needs of a Puquina cultivator. That quantity is about 15.5 kg, one-third to one-half of a llama load.[11] People from the highlands were excellently equipped to transport the *guano* back to the cultivation site. Llamas, and the ropes and sacks made from llama fiber, were available to them.

Cultivators in Arequipa

Who actually travelled to the *guano* islands and mined *guano* cannot be determined from sixteenth century sources, but the relationships between people and resources in the Arequipa region can be studied. Identifying the location of groups of cultivators and gathering information about local organization are necessary preliminaries to a discussion of resource control in Arequipa. The story must be pieced together from a variety of sources. Both outsiders and local cultivators had reason to seek *guano*, and each group will be considered in turn.

Outside Cultivators

The people of the Lake Titicaca region and adjacent high altitude pasturelands, who live near or above the limits of cultivation, have traditionally sought foodstuffs from the lowlands (Flores 1968, 1970; Custred 1974; Casaverde 1977). Their food quest can be documented in the sixteenth century. Juan Polo de Ondegardo, an administrator who was both an authority on the native economy and an *encomendero* in the Lake Titicaca region, wrote:

> In addition to not reaping anything but potatoes, and on some land not even potatoes can be grown, out of five years three are bad, although they always need to leave the land, taking their animals to look for maize to eat. They acquire it through exchange in the lowlands, the closest area being more than 60 leagues [300 km] away. I mean that they have to leave their land in order to acquire any quantity, because they have to work on the coast or in the valleys of Cochabamba . . . so that in any of these [last] years, which have really been very ordinary, most of the people leave the land, some with livestock belonging to the community and to widows and minors and to fulfill some obligation kept track of by their community. With the livestock they take wool, sacks, and other livestock, principally young animals about two years old which are used for carrying maize, and they return to their land where they remain all year long. In accounting for and distributing the things they bring, it is curious and difficult to believe, but no one is wronged. And in this customary trade, even when the year is good, many times the people will be gone a year and eight months, because all their dealings are that slow. Some people even rent lands there and plant and wait for the harvest. They are so settled that they seem like native residents there to those who do not know them, and they load the livestock with the things they have traded for or harvested and send it back with others. This happens when the year is good, because it is customary. If there is a drought, most of the people leave the land and spend four or five months in the valleys working just to get enough to eat. They are happy if they can return well fed and with a couple of loads of maize on the livestock they all take with them. [In such years] the [highland] towns are depopulated. (Polo de Ondegardo 1872: 136–38; author's translation)

Polo describes people, organized at the household or community level, who appear to have acted on their own initiative, being guided by their food preferences and the periodic unavailability of food resources at home. Exchange was a feature of the pattern documented above, but so was actual residence in the lower growing zones for the purposes of cultivating food crops.

Polo wrote several decades after the European arrival and may have documented a pattern that was at least partially a response to Spanish colonial demands from the native population. Permanent settlements of people from the highlands in the coastal valleys were a feature of earlier organization, however. In Arequipa, groups of outside cultivators having the same place of ethnic origin can be documented (Table 9.1). People from the Cuzco area and from the Canas and Canchis province (Julien 1983: map 2) were located in the valley of Arequipa. Two groups from Chucuito, capital of the Lupaca province, were located in the Azapa Valley near Arica, and two groups from Hatunqolla, capital of the Qolla province of 'Urqosuyu, were situated in Cochuna near Moquegua (Barriga 1939–55: III, 17–20, 28–30).[12] People from the Pacajes province were reported to have lands assigned to them in Arequipa by Thupa 'Inka for their use in maize cultivation (Jiménez de la Espada 1880–97:II, 58).

Permanent settlements of people outside of their provinces was an important part of the Inca resettlement program. Colonies were established for different administrative purposes (Cieza de León, *Señorío*, cap. XXII, 1936:127–34; Julien 1983:78–81). Groups of colonies having diverse origins characterized Inca administrative centers and other sites of Inca activity (Cobo, lib. 12, cap. XXV, vol. 92, 1956:114; Ramírez Velarde 1970:287–88; Ramos Gavilán 1976:43).

Other colonies of people from the Lake Titicaca region were located in the Pacific coastal valleys only to secure resources unavailable at home (Cieza de León, *Señorío,* cap. XVII, 1936:106–7). Such colonies were still subject to the local authorities (*kurakas*) of their home province. The colonies of people from Chucuito settled in Azapa were subject to Qari 'Apaza, *kuraka* of Chucuito. The Hatunqolla colonies may have been in the same category. Though the Incas are given credit for founding such colonies (Jiménez de la Espada 1880–97:II, 58; Diez de San Miguel 1964:125; Gutiérrez Flores 1970:45), there is a strong possibility that people from the Lake Titicaca region had maintained colonies in the Arequipa region before the Inca conquest (Murra 1964:429; Rowe 1982:106–7).

Table 9.1 Early Encomienda Grants in Southern Arequipa

Location	Origin (if not local)	Encomendero	Kuraka	No. of Tributaries
Arequipa		Diego Hernández	Caya	359
Arequipa		Lucas Martínez		
Ahuela Yumina	Canas		Cacha	30
Otra Parcialidad	Canchis (?)		Canchis	35
Otra Parcialidad	not given		Curimaqui	10
Yumina	Pisquicancha		Mora	25
Arequipa		Pedro Pizarro		
Coquiguaya	Urcos		Chuquimaqui	25
Otra Parcialidad	Cuzco		Chuquimaqui	4
Curane [Colani]	Canchis		Ninacanchis	35
Otra Parcialidad	Pomacanche		Yanquichoque	30
Otra Parcialidad	Cangallo		Sica	15
Otra Parcialidad	not given		not given	6
Tambopalla Chuli		Diego Hernández	not given	36
Omate		Martín López	Caila	287
Puquina		Diego Hernández	Ate	234
Ubinas		Francisco de Noguerol	Sisquicha	1075
Cochuna		Hernando de Silva		125
Suhuba	Hatunqolla		Alique	
Capavaya	Hatunqolla		Alique	
de Catari [Carumas]		Hernando de Silva	Catari	249
Tacna		Pedro Pizarro		
Tacna			Istaca	800
Sama-Arica Coast			not given	206
Tacna		Hernando de Torres	Cata	600
Ilo and Ite		Lucas Martínez	Pola	194
Lluta and Azapa		Lucas Martínez		
Lluta and Azapa			Cayoa	200
Yllavaya	not given		not given	70
Auca	Chucuito		Aura	50
Hinchichura	Chucuito		Canche	94
Arica	Tarapacá		Yano	30
Tarapacá		Lucas Martínez	Tuscasanga	900
Sama		Juan de San Juan	not given	not given

Note: Information for all of the grants in the above table was taken from Barriga (1939–55:I, 40–48; III, 14–22, 28–30; 1954:91–93), except for the grant to Sama (see Diez de San Miguel 1964:126, 207–8). The portion of Tacna held by Torres was mentioned in the Tacna grant to Pizarro; there is no separate award document. The awards were organized by *encomendero*. In the above table I have separated the various awards to show each portion separately.

Case 1: The Lupacas (Fig. 9.2)

Information about the Lupaca colonies in Azapa is contained in a 1567 administrative survey (*visita*) and other documents (Diez de San Miguel 1964; Gutiérrez Flores 1964, 1970; AGNA 9. 17. 2. 5). These documents contain a wealth of information about Lupaca involvement in the Pacific coastal valleys because the province was a personal *encomienda* of the Spanish Crown and special care was taken to insure that the agricultural economy of the Lupacas be preserved.[13]

In spite of the notable wealth of some individuals in the Lupaca province (Gutiérrez Flores 1964), a large number of people lived at the poverty level. Stratification was marked, resulting in the concentration of wealth in the hands of the *kurakas* and their relatives (Gutiérrez Flores 1970: 44–45; Diez de San Miguel 1964:140, 146, 147). A Dominican interviewed in the 1567 *visita* said that the Lupacas traded for high altitude products, such as potatoes and *chuño*, in neighboring provinces because they could not grow enough themselves (Diez de San Miguel 1964:139–40, 143, 156). Frosts, droughts, and flooding were specifically mentioned as problems, flooding because it made potatoes more susceptible to worm damage, and presumably, to mold (Diez de San Miguel 1964:151, 163).

The food quest as described by Polo is also apparent from the Lupaca documentation. The testimony taken in the *visita* documents the activities of people from the Lupaca province in several lowland areas. On the eastern Andean slopes, people from the Lupaca province were active in the Larecaja area, near the modern Bolivian town of Sorata, and in the Capinota-Chicanoma area southeast of La Paz in the Bolivian Yungas. On the western slopes of the Andes, in Arequipa, there were people from the Lupaca province in Sama and Moquegua, as well as in Azapa.

Table 9.2 Lupaca Population in 1572

	No. of Tributaries	No. of Kurakas
Lupaca Province		
Aymara	12,596	218
Uru	3,469	16
Larecaja	68	2
Chicanoma	22	—
Sama	328	6
Moquegua	297	6
Hinchichura	11	—
Total	16,791	248

Population (Table 9.2)

A general census of the Lupaca population was taken for the purposes of setting a *tasa* by Viceroy Toledo (1975:78–81). In this census, a separate accounting was made of Lupaca tributaries residing permanently in the lowlands (Table 9.2). Very early population figures to compare with this census are available only for the Azapa colonies mentioned in the text of the 1540 *encomienda* award (Table 9.1). A total of 144 tributaries was recorded. In 1572, the number of tributaries totalled 11. If Auca and Hinchichura were the only two Lupaca colonies in Azapa, the population had suffered a marked decline. Population decline since the time of the Spanish arrival is likely due to the combined effects of conquest and introduced disease, but the degree of decline in this case (92 percent) is extreme. The Auca and Hinchichura colonies were situated near Arica, a port city where the death tolls from disease were particularly high in the later sixteenth century (see note 12); Vázquez de Espinosa, lib. IV, cap. LXVI, 1969: 347; Barriga 1941–48:III, 65, 69–70). The decline in areas away from the coast and away from Spanish settlement was probably not as extreme.

Both the Toledo *tasa* and the 1540 grant to Azapa referred to the people counted in the Lupaca colonies as *mitimas*, a term denoting someone who was not residing in his place of ethnic origin (Rowe 1982: 96). The use of this term appears to be correct in the case of the Azapa colonies. Auca and Hinchichura are listed with a third *mitima* town following an accounting of the local population in the 1540 grant (Barriga 1939–55:III, 18).

The Lupaca tributaries in Sama and Moquegua were also specifically referred to as *mitimas* in the 1574 *tasa* of the Lupaca province (Diez de San Miguel 1964:78–83). In the case of Sama, however, native lowlanders (*yungas*) may have been included in the counts:

> And he found that there were 540 Indians, more or less, who would be able to pay tribute, and that among these were 40 older people who could still pay tribute and that there were another 40 older people who were not able to [pay] and that in these [figures] were included all of the native Indians called *yungas* and *mitimas* put there by the Incas as well as Indians from outside who had been there for years. (Juan de Matute in Diez de San Miguel 1964:125; author's translation)

Both the *mitimas* and *yungas* of Sama were accounted as part of the Lupaca province in 1567 following the return of this group to Lupaca jurisdiction (see note 13). The *encomienda* of Sama was held by Juan de San Juan before its return to Chucuito, and no other *encomienda* awards appear to have been made to people in Sama.

The *yungas* of Sama appear to have been subject to Lupaca jurisdiction during the later Inca empire as well. A group of *yungas* were counted in the last Inca census of the province, a *khipu* read into the record of the 1567 *visita* (Diez de San Miguel 1964:64–66; Julien 1982: Table 5.2). Following the accounting of each political division of Lupaca province proper, a separate entry recorded 200 *yungas* for Sama.

Moquegua was not accounted in the same way as Sama in the Inca census.[14] The people subject to the Lupaca province in Moquegua appear to have been people with origins in the Lupaca province only. People from the Lupaca province were not the only inhabitants of the Moquegua valley, either. A group of *mitimas* from Hatunqolla were located in the Moquegua area at Cochuna (see p. 194), and people from Carumas, who may have been the local population, resided in the valley as well.[15]

Location

Little precise information about the location of the western Lupaca colonies was provided in the 1567 *visita.* Crops raised by colonists were sometimes mentioned, and modern cultivation of these crops can be used to suggest possible locations for Lupaca settlement. An upper valley location for colonies in Moquegua and Sama can be documented, though lower valley land was occupied in Azapa and perhaps Sama as well.

Maize and *ají* were the two crops specifically identified with the western Lupaca colonies in the 1567 *visita* (Diez de San Miguel 1964: 17, 33, 80, 124, 126). These two crops were the principal cultigens in the area (Cobo, lib. IV, cap. III, vol. 91, 1956:159–60; Vázquez de Espinosa, lib. IV, cap. XXV, 1969:172). Maize and *ají* can be grown over a range of altitudes in these valleys, but *ají* cultivation is commonest in the middle valley zone (1,000–2,200 m). Maize can be grown at any altitude up to 3,814 m, but different varieties have different altitude preferences (Cárdenas 1960:86). Today, people from the Lupaca area seek varieties of maize cultivated at elevations near 3,000 m (Flores 1970:196–99).

The Lupaca colonies of Sama and Moquegua appear to have been located in the upper valley where maize was the principal cultigen. In Moquegua, the prime area for cultivation in historic times is the cultivable strip, about 25 km long and 2 km wide, in the area of the modern city of Moquegua. This area was an early center for Spanish settlement, and by 1790, most of the non-Spanish population lived higher up the valley. A witness in the 1567 survey mentioned Lupaca settlement at the town of Torata (about 2,200 m) (Cusi in Diez de San Miquel 1964:27; Barriga 1939–55:vol. 2, 129, 133). Another witness talks about maize cultivation 100 km up the Moquegua river from the coast, putting Lupaca settlement at about the altitude of Torata (Garci Diez in Diez de San Miguel 1964:245). Maize was the only cultigen mentioned in the visita in connection with the Lupaca colonies in Moquegua, and Lupaca settlement appears to have concentrated at Torata or at a similar altitude in the Moquegua drainage.

Sama, unlike any other valley in the area, has a narrow cultivable strip along its entire length. The strip is about a kilometer wide and extends about 110 km inland. A town at about 3,000 m, Tarata, was named as a site of Lupaca settlement (Diez de San Miguel 1964:27). In addition to maize, *ají* was grown by Lupaca cultivators in Sama (Diez de San Miguel 1964:247). Several valleys, including the Tambo, Ilabaya, Sama, Azapa, and Lluta valleys, were important centers of *ají* cultivation during the Spanish colonial era (Peru 1926:146; Vázquez de Espinosa, lib. IV, cap. LXV, 1969:346). All had some lower to middle valley land under cultivation where *ají* was probably the most important crop.

Less water was available for cultivation in Azapa than elsewhere. The river was usually dry from about 1,500 m down to the coast, and cultivation depended on spring water. In the early seventeenth century spring water was used for cultivation 15 km up the valley and in a second oasis 5 km up the valley. Near the mouth of the Azapa River, a fresh water spring provided water for a large *totora* stand and for the Spanish port of Arica. When these springs dried up, the people moved to the nearby Lluta valley (Peru 1926:376). As noted earlier, Auca and Hinchichura were situated near Arica (note 12). No crops were mentioned in the 1567 *visita* associated with the Lupaca settlements, but *ají* was an important crop in this area, and *coca* and cochineal were harvested locally (Barriga 1941–48:I, 61; IV, 147; 1939–55: III, 18)].

Organization

Considerable detail about the personal wealth of the *kurakas* was collected in the 1567 *visita,* and some of this wealth included rights to land and labor in the coastal valleys. Community holdings were not closely examined, but with additional information from a 1574 *visita,* a case can be made for the existence of colonies producing food in the coastal valleys for the Lupaca province as a whole.

Pedro Gutiérrez Flores, administrator of the 1574 *visita,* recommended a number of administrative policies, including the planting of community fields in Moquegua and Sama:

> If this [recommendation], that the Indians from this province plant such lands seems inconvenient, it is not, because [the Indians] have the custom of going and coming from those valleys because there are a great number of Indians from this province populated there who plant fields for the *kurakas* and other important individuals in this province. The rest go there ordinarily to look for food. The natives of those valleys who pay tribute with the people of this province should be obligated only to plant the fields mentioned earlier in place of their tribute and those [people] from this province obligated to bring the harvest with [community] livestock for the purpose described. The execution of this task could be turned over to the person your excellency names since the Indians that are on the coast were put there from this province by the Inka as *mitimas* for this purpose, and this is what we have learned from the inquiries we have made, that the large amounts of food that the *mitimas* produced for this province during Inca times were brought and placed in the storage houses. (Gutiérrez Flores 1970:45; author's translation)

Although Gutiérrez's statement is a little obscure, he was clearly describing two different time periods. His first remarks concerned the present (1574) and he described the private holdings of the *kurakas* and other individuals who were occupied in obtaining foodstuffs from the lowlands. His recommendation, that the *yungas* and *mitimas* subject to the Lupaca province be allowed to produce foodstuffs for the province in lieu of other tribute obligations, was based on Inca practice. He implies that all of the people who produced for the *kurakas* and other important individuals in the 1570s were originally put there by the Incas to produce for the province as a whole.

Gutiérrez's statement may explain the status of the *yungas* of Sama, separately accounted in the *khipu* census. If so, the only service this group owed to the Inca administration was the production of foodstuffs for the Lupaca province. In 1567 the *yungas* of Sama still produced food for consumption in the Lupaca province, but in exchange for highland products:

> The Indians of the province of Sama are *yungas* and *mitimas* put there by the Inka. They grow maize, wheat, and *ají*, and they have a little livestock that the highlanders bring them in exchange for the foods just mentioned. (Garci Diez in Diez de San Miguel 1964:247)

If Gutiérrez was correct in giving credit to the Incas for organizing *yungas* to produce on behalf of the Lupaca province, then clearly a change had occurred in this relationship by 1567. The relationship established under the aegis of Inca rule had been replaced by individual efforts to obtain foodstuffs through exchange of some kind.

Gutiérrez's statement suggests that *mitimas* from the Lupaca province had been obligated to provide transport of the foodstuffs back to the Lupaca province with animals from the Lupaca community herds. If each household was only assigned the type of labor service by the Inca administration, then transport service was the obligation owed by the Lupaca *mitimas* (Bandera 1968:509).

In the 1560s the situation was different, and *kuraka* and other individual holdings were very much in evidence. The two head *kurakas* of the Lupaca province, Martín Cari of the Hanansaya division and Martín Cusi of Hurinsaya, were extensively interviewed in the 1567 *visita*. When questioned about Lupaca activities in the lowlands, Cari gave a very general reply:

> The *kurakas* and other important individuals have maize fields in Moquegua, Sama, Capinota, and Larecaja. Other people also have maize fields in Moquegua, Sama, Capinota, and Larecaja. . . . The Indians from this province go to Arequipa, to the coast and to Moquegua most years to trade for maize, and to obtain it they take camelids and wool and *charqui*. (Diez de San Miguel 1964: 17; author's translation)

Cari's statement left no one out and echoes both Gutiérrez Flores and Polo who wrote during roughly the same time period.

Both Cari and Cusi gave lists of services owed to them, and some of these services involved labor in the coastal valleys. Cari was provided with transport services by 40–50 people who could be sent on long trips to the lowlands. Once sent, they were excused from additional duty for the remainder of the year. Retainers given to his family by the district of Juli before the time of Inca rule were being sent to the lowlands to pick up maize in 1567 (Diez de San Miguel 1964: 21). He was also entitled to the services of 25 retainers in Moquegua who were there to plant maize for him.

Cusi provided less information about retainer service, but included important details about the reciprocal nature of the obligation:

> In Moquegua, which is in the *yungas*, they give him 12 Indians who plant and tend 9 *topos* of maize fields. He gives these Indians

> llamas and sacks to use in bringing *guano* to the fields because maize does not grow without it. He also gives them *coca*, livestock, wool for clothing, and *charqui* to eat. In Sama they give him three Indians who plant corn for him there, and he gives them what he gives the others. The Chinchaysuyu people, *mitimas* of Juli who are in Moquegua, give him another two Indians to tend the fields he has there, and he gives them the same things as he gives the others (Diez de San Miguel 1964:33; author's translation).

The people who produced for the *kuraka* were provided with a number of staples from their province of origin and with the necessary equipment to carry out their task. Such provisions indicate the reciprocal nature of the retainer relationship. (Murra 1968:135–36).

Cusi's statement also records the cultivator's involvement in obtaining *guano* themselves. The cultivators travelled to the coast to bring it back. Two Spaniards resident in Sama noted that local cultivators travelled to the coast to obtain *guano*, taking animals with them, thus generalizing Cusi's statement to other local residents (Juan de Matute and Pedro de Bilbao in Diez de San Miguel 1964:126–27). They made no distinction between *yungas* and *mitimas* from the Lupaca province.

Local Cultivators

A sizeable local population resided in the Pacific coastal valleys. Information about it is found mainly in early *encomienda* grants made between 1540 and 1548 (Table 9.1). These grants do not provide a complete coverage of Arequipa, although the southern part of Arequipa, from Majes to Tarapacá, is fairly well covered (Table 9.3). Since *encomienda* grants continued to serve as the basis for territorial division throughout the Spanish colonial era, later information about the territories of the people granted sometimes can be used to identify the gaps. The nearly complete listing of grants in the *tasa* of Toledo (1571–73) provides just such a control (Table 9.4).

The 1540s *encomienda* grants provide unique information about local organization. Most grants were described by reference to a *kuraka* and the places where people subject to his authority lived. Often, the places listed are near each other and a local territory can be roughly defined. If people lived outside a local territory, the grants often make reference to this fact. *Saya* divisions can sometimes be identified.[16]

In the southern part of the Arequipa district, the area from Majes to Tarapacá, several large groups subject to a single *kuraka* or pair of

Table 9.3 Coverage of Early Encomienda Grants

	Tributaries in 1540	Tributaries 1571–173
Corregimiento of Arica		
Lluta/Arica	444	186
Tarapacá	900	761
Pica and Loa	—	160
Tacna (Pizarro)	1006	
Tacna (Torres)	600	660
Ilabaya	—	299
Ilo/Ite	194	50
Corregimiento of Carumas and Ubinas		
Ubinas (Noguerol de Ulloa)	1055	532
Cochuna (Silva)	125	73
Carumas (Silva)	249	415
Pocsi	—	440
Puquina	234	125
Tambopalla Chuli	36	25

Note: *Mitimas* are included in 1540 figures.

kurakas can be documented. Such groups were present in Tarapacá, Tacna, Omate, Puquina, Ubinas, Ilo and Ite, Lluta, and Azapa and in the valley of Arequipa (*encomienda* of Hernández) (Table 9.1).

Mitimas living in the same area were listed separately in these awards. Each group of *mitimas* having a single origin was listed by reference to a particular town and a particular *kuraka*, suggesting that these groups were living apart from the local population and had their own ethnic leadership. Their number was not included in the total number of tributaries subject to a local principal *kuraka*, except in the case of Lluta and Azapa. The *mitima* towns of Lluta and Azapa were listed separately by reference to particular towns and *kurakas*, but their total was included with the total number of tributaries subject to the principal *kuraka* of Lluta. This treatment may be significant as a grant Pizarro made on the same day gave the usual separate accounting of *mitima* towns (Barriga 1939–55:III, 17–22).

Only one award was made to a coastal territory subject to a single *kuraka*, the grant to the area from Ilo to Ite subject to Pola, who was identified as a fisherman (Table 9.1). Three of the towns subject to Pola (Chiri, Tamanco, and Tacari) were listed as "towns of fishermen" (Barriga 1939–55: III, 18). Three others, Ilo, Ite, and Meca, were not labelled in this manner. Their location at the mouths of the Moquegua and Ilabaya rivers was specifically noted, placing them close enough to a source of fresh water to make cultivation possible. To the south,

Table 9.4 Local Population in 1571–73

	Trib.	Total		Trib.	Total
City of Arequipa			*Corregimiento of Condesuyo*		
La Chimba & Tiabaya	1059	4223	Chuquibamba	585	3175
La Chimba & Tiabaya	441	1807	Chuquibamba	426	2098
Mitimas from Nasca	21	—	Arones	434	1987
*Collaguas in La Chimba	141	565	Arones	500	2348
*Collaguas in La Chimba	159	639	Pampacolca	819	4016
*Collaguas in La Chimba	181	805	Viraco	558	2621
TOTALS	2002	8039	Andagua & Chachas	547	2082
			Chilpacas	269	1116
Corregimiento of Camaná			Machaguay	309	1151
Majes	139	334	Achanquillo & Ayanque	317	1412
Majes	164	566	Achamarca	385	1606
Acari	625	2404	Chachas & Ucuchachas	507	2461
Atiquipa	203	649	TOTALS	5656	26073
Caravelí & Atico	417	2247			
Molleguaca	78	332	*Corregimiento of Collaguas*		
Ocoña	110	376	Yanquecollaguas	4026	17548
Ocoña	109	304	Larecollaguas	2218	4848
Quilca	183	658	Larecollaguas	1333	5658
Cabanas in Camaná	25	191	Cabana	567	2364
Pampamico & Camaná	35	—	Cabana	728	3482
TOTALS	2088	8061	TOTALS	8872	33900

	Trib.	Total
Corregimiento of Arica		
Tarapacá	761	3933
Pica & Loa	160	636
Lluta	186	785
Ite	50	199
Tacna	660	2849
Ilabaya	299	1468
TOTALS	2116	9870
Corregimiento of Carumas and Ubinas		
Ubinas	532	2745
Carumas	199	975
Carumas	216	1121
Pocsi	440	2257
Cochuna	73	344
Puquina	125	642
*Omate	128	543
*Quinistaca	206	964
*Cheque	16	69
TOTALS	1935	9660

	Trib.	Total
Corregimiento of Characato and Vitor		
Paucarpata	127	551
Chiguata	113	532
Characato	245	978
Chule & Tambo	25	120
*Vitor	30	138
*Socavaya & Porongoche	65	343
*Quispillata, Socavaya, & Porongoche	82	380
*Yaravaya	116	523
*Copoata	113	522
*Guasacache	36	156
*Orejones Yuminas	72	227
*Guaypar Yuminas	12	60
*Yuminas & Canchis	52	265
*Canas & Canchis of Colani	46	232
*Cuquivaya & Colani	90	409
*Colca, Guayba, & Colani	101	487
*Yanaconas	514	—
TOTALS	1839	5923

Note: The *encomienda* grants of the Toledo *tasa* (Toledo 1975) have been grouped following the *corregimiento* division of Cristóbal de Miranda (1925). The Toledo *tasa* did not include Achanquillo and Ayanque, so totals have been supplied from the Miranda document. A number of *encomiendas* were not listed in Miranda, but can be assigned to particular *corregimientos* where the Miranda totals are different by the number of tributaries given in the *tasa*. The *encomiendas* which have been fit into the *corregimiento* division in this way are starred.

along the coast from Sama to Arica, a similar situation may have prevailed, but the language of the award document is not clear. Tacna was split between two *encomenderos*, apparently following *saya* division (Barriga 1939–55:I, 40–41). One of the *encomenderos*, Pedro Pizarro, also received a group of coastal people who were clearly separate from his Tacna *encomienda.* The award may have been defined by a reference to the *kuraka* Capanique, but again, the language is unclear. Fishermen at the mouth of the Sama river were specifically included; other groups, for example the people in Arica, may have been fishermen though no information was provided.

North and south of the section of coast just described, a different situation prevailed. A small group of fishermen at Tambopalla Chuli, near the mouth of the Tambo River (Cieza de León, *Crónica,* cap. LXXV, 1932:232–33), was awarded to Diego Hernández. Hernández received rights to Puquina territory located some distance up the river from the coast in the same award, but the fishermen were clearly separated from the Puquina group. No information for Pica and Loa exists, but the Tarapacá grant was awarded "with the fishermen," though no location for them was given (Barriga 1939–55:V, 18). Subject to Tarapacá, but accounted with the *kuraka* of Lluta, was a group of 30 fishermen located at Arica.[17]

One of the most significant observations to be made about the distribution of population in Arequipa is that a large share of the total population lived in the upper valleys. This situation is very clear in the Toledo *tasa* (Table 9.4). The *corregimientos* of Condesuyos, Collaguas, Characato and Vitor, Carumas and Ubinas, and the city territory of Arequipa were all landlocked. The *corregimientos* of Arica and Camaná covered the Arequipa coast. In Arica, both Tacna and Tarapacá included a sizeable population in the upper valleys; due to a water shortage very little lower valley land, if any, could be cultivated. These two *encomiendas* made up about 70 percent of the total population of the *corregimiento* of Arica in 1571–73.

In the 1540s a similar situation may have prevailed, at least in the area south of Majes. Comparing the population count for the coastal strip from Tambopalla Chuli to Arica (436 tributaries) with the upper valley population of the other grants in Arica in 1540 (5,082), the coastal population formed only 8.6 percent of the total. Without relying on the accuracy of this figure, it is still probable that a large share of the population lived in the upper valleys.

The upper valley areas were the center of maize production in Arequipa. Because of the importance of this cultigen to both local cultivators and outsiders from extreme high altitudes, the concentration of population at this altitude is not suprising.

Case 2: The Puquinas (Figs. 9.2, 9.3)

Puquina territory was awarded by Francisco Pizarro to Diego Hernández in 1540. The people of Puquina were subject to a *kuraka* named Ate who resided in the town of Puquina, called a *tambo* in the 1540 document. No *saya* division is evident from the document. Instead, the names of towns subject to Ate and the number of tributaries in each were given. This information is reproduced in the order given (Table 9.5).

All of the locatable towns named in the 1540 grant are situated near the Puquina River. The most distant is Yalaque. The lowest in elevation is Seche at 2,750 m and the highest is Seque at 3,400 m. The territory defined is fairly consistent with a 1792 description of Puquina territory, except that some of the places named in 1792 were lower down the

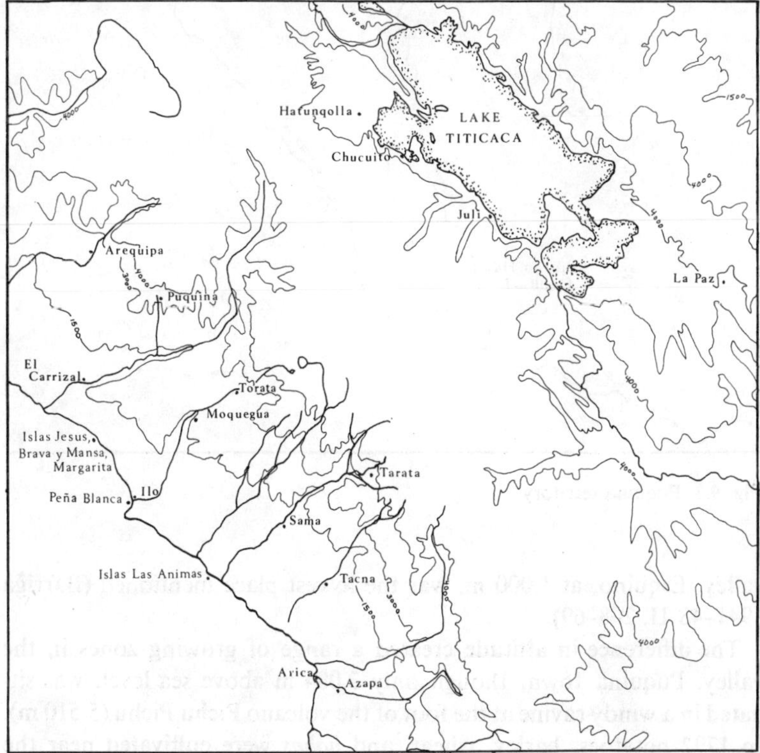

Fig. 9.2 Lupaca and Puquina sites

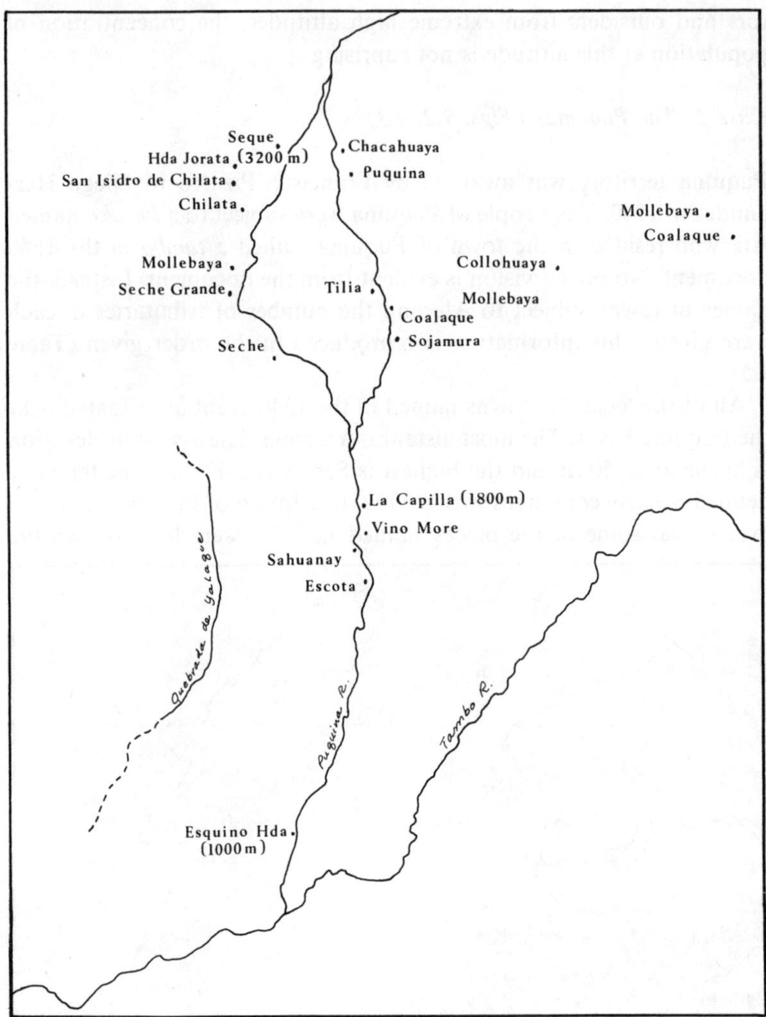

Fig. 9.3 Puquina territory

valley. Esquino, at 1,000 m, was the lowest place mentioned (Barriga 1941–48:II, 268–69).

The difference in altitude created a range of growing zones in the valley. Puquina town, though only 3,084 m above sea level, was situated in a windy ravine at the foot of the volcano Pichu Pichu (5,510 m). In 1792 potatoes, barley, wheat, and *habas* were cultivated near the town. Water was scarce and frosts were a problem. Lower down the

Table 9.5 Towns Named in the 1540 Encomienda Grant to Puquina

Pusquea	20	Siche [Seche?]	8
Chilata	20	Molleguaha [Mollebaya]	6
Curata [Jorata?]	10	Puquina	55
Seque	12	Llata	30
Chacobaya [Chacahuayo?]	0 or 17	Congona	7
Tila [Tilia?]	24	Mollillaca	—
Capoco	12	Culluguaya [Colloguaya?]	20
		Yalaca [Yalaque?]	6
			230 or 247

Note: 234 was the total given in the award document.

valley maize was grown and fruit orchards were noted at Esquino (Barriga 1941–48:II, 268–69).

Access to land in different growing zones was probably important to Puquina cultivators. A description of traditional land holdings in Puquina from the 1792 survey illustrates native use of different local growing zones. One of the goals of the survey was to set up a community chest in Puquina using revenues from the produce of land held by the community, and each *saya* division was to contribute land for the purpose. A list of the holdings of each division was provided (Table 9.6) (Barriga 1941–48:II, 274–75).

Table 9.6 Traditional Land Holdings in Puquina, 1792

	Place	No. of *Tupus*	Holder
Hanansaya:	Chacahuayo	6	Hanansaya
	"	3	Segundas
	Caspaya	4	Hanansaya
	Caspata	1	Hanansaya
	Coalaqui	1	Camayos
	Vino More	6	Guaca
	"	3	Segundas
	Yalaque	3	Guaca
	"	6	Segundas
	"	6	Hanansaya
	La Capilla	3	Hanansaya
Hurinsaya:	Jerusalén (Puquina)	5	Hurinsaya
	Coalaque	6	Hurinsaya
	"	1.5	Hurinsaya
	"	1	Camayos
	Toxe More	4.5	Segundas
	Vino More	6	Guaca

Note: In addition, the list of lands included an unspecified number of *tupus* belonging to each *saya* division at El Carrizal, perhaps the El Carrizal near the mouth of the Tambo River (Fig. 9.2).

When the location of these holdings is taken into account, a pattern of land holding in different growing zones becomes apparent. Several groups named had access to land in more than one growing zone. Lands at the elevations of Coalaque and Vino More were listed most frequently (Fig. 9.3). In the 1540s the largest share of the population resided near Puquina Table (9.5). If the pattern of land holding documented in 1792 has any antiquity, cultivators may have had access to lands near Puquina and to lands in a lower growing zone as well.

Details of this land holding pattern cannot be confirmed using the 1540 *encomienda* documents. The only reference to land holding in the 1540 award was a note that the grant included "all of the Indians in the towns visited and in other towns not visited plus the *aji* fields and places where livestock was pastured and people [subject to Puquina] wherever the *caciques* mentioned have them" (Barriga 1939–55:I, 47; author's translation). *Ají* fields and high altitude pasture lands fall mainly outside of the range of altitudes covered by Puquina territory. Other 1540s grants contained similar clauses which may have been included as legal language so that the grants would be considered all inclusive. The existence of a general clause such as this one is still interesting, for although it may not be applicable in all cases, it describes a general pattern of *kuraka* holdings at elevations both above and below the upper valley zone.

No mention of *guano* can be found in the 1540 document, but the 1792 survey contains information about traditional rights to *guano* from the coast. *Guano* was recognized as essential to cultivation in Puquina at that time "because without this aid and practice [the Indians] would not even be able to bear the costs of planting their fields" (Barriga 1941–48:II, 276; author's translation). In 1792, people in Puquina territory exercised some rights to *guano* from offshore islands (Barriga 1941–48:II, 276–77).

Alvarez y Jiménez had considerable authority to reorganize local affairs, and he describes *guano* rights in the act of reorganizing them. The heads of Hanansaya and Hurinsaya divisions each had rights to *guano* from offshore islands (Table 9.7, Fig. 9.2). In 1792, the *saya* division positions were held by men with Spanish surnames who may not have been native *kurakas*. These posts were then being given to people with no ancestral ties to the local population. The holders had the same role in the Spanish colonial bureaucracy as the *kurakas*; that is, they were important chiefly as tax collectors. Alvarez y Jiménez assigned 12 *tupus* of land to each *kuraka* from the lands requisitioned for the community chest. He then reduced the *guano* claims of these

Table 9.7 Rights to Guano in Puquina Territory in 1792 (Fig. 9.2)

	Limited Rights	Entire Island
Don Francisco Rosas Head of Hanansaya		Frailes Empinadas Perica Blance
Don Manuel Lajo y Olim Head of Hurinsaya		La Margarita
Community	*Las Animas *Islas Jesús	"from Taranto to the Island of Alfaro" *Pocoguata *Brava *Manza

*Possession disputed in 1792.

two men and left each with rights only to enough guano for the lands assigned to him. *Saya* division heads in Puquina may have had traditional rights to the produce of lands worked on their behalf by the community, as did the *kurakas* of the Lupaca province. *Guano* rights may have been linked to these rights. In the eighteenth century, however, claims to *guano* could be purchased, and the two *kurakas* may have acquired their rights to *guano* through purchase.

The community itself had corporate rights to *guano* along the coast "from Taranto to the Island of Alfaro." No breakdown by *saya* division was given. Each cultivator received only half a *fanega* of *guano* every other year, which Alvarez y Jiménez considered to be insufficient for their needs. A larger supply appears to have been available to Puquina cultivators in the past, as a claim to three offshore islands, said to be ancient, was then in dispute with a Spaniard (Table 9.7).

Alvarez y Jiménez noted that in 1792, the inner islands along the Arequipa coast were held as the exclusive property of individuals or communities while the outer islands could be mined by anyone (Barriga 1941–48:I, 86). The only other valley for which he gives specific information about *guano* claims was Ilabaya, where the community claimed four *guano* islands "from time immemorial" (Barriga 1941–48: II, 324).

Community rights to *guano* may have existed in the sixteenth century as well. Pedro de Avendaño, writing in 1564–65, described differences over rights to *guano*:

> . . . The natives, for whom this fertilizer was of great benefit, had great differences over it, because some groups said that [the *guano*]

> that was deposited on the islands bordering their territory was theirs, and other groups said it was available to anybody (Jiménez de la Espada, vol. I, app. II, 1880–97: CXXXVIII–CXXXIX; author's translation).

Avendaño leaves the situation in doubt, but the disputes he described were clearly between native groups. Community claims to *guano*, like the Puquina claim described by Alvarez y Jiménez in 1792, existed in the mid-sixteenth century.

Resource Control in Sixteenth-Century Arequipa

Through an examination of the activities of Lupaca and Puquina cultivators in Arequipa during the Spanish colonial era, a number of general features of the local agricultural economy can be documented. Particular food preferences, local technologies, the availability of an effective fertilizer, and the food demands of outsiders living at or near the limits of cultivation appear to have been constant features of the Arequipa agricultural economy over a fairly long span of time. Because of the relative longevity of such features, they can be detected even in the scattered and incomplete source materials available to us. What results is a general picture of the relationships between population and resources in this desert coastal region.

To address a subject like resource control, a more precise chronological analysis is required. A fairly detailed knowledge of the structure of political authority and how it changed over time is also necessary, as control exercised over productive resources was dependent on the lines of political authority operative at a given moment. Here our sources provide a very fragmentary record, for any part of the sixteenth century. Most administrative documentation was generated for contemporary use, and except for moments when administrators were concerned with pre-Spanish administration, only offers direct testimony about contemporary affairs. Attributing antiquity to bits of organization identified in these documents requires the exercise of extreme caution and begs for corroboration by archaeological evidence.

Let us consider what kind of information we have about resource control in Arequipa before the Spanish arrival. At present, administrative documentation for the period from 1540 to 1585, and particularly from 1567 to 1574, contains the best and earliest information about population and resources in Arequipa. This period was an extremely eventful one for Arequipa, and native settlement was probably affected by the events. Major campaigns of the Spanish civil wars (1543–48 and 1553–55) were fought in the southern highlands along the principal roads in the *altiplano* and from the *altiplano* to Arequipa (Crespo 1972). Many Inca towns were located along these roads, and the movement of people in these areas is a likely result. From the early years of the *encomienda*, excessive tribute and *mita* burdens may have made Arequipa a haven for residents of the Lake Titicaca region (Sânchez-Albornoz 1978:45–56). Migration within Arequipa was encouraged by the founding of Spanish cities and villas in the coastal valleys and by the rapid establishment of routes to the Potosí-Porco mining areas from the 1540s on. The existence of important routes to the mining areas involved the local population in the production of food for these centers and in raising pack animals and alfalfa. Andean people very early became involved in colonial commerce related to the mining centers (Murra 1978a). The movement of people described by Polo in 1571 (p. 193) may have been intensified by any of the circumstances just cited, and not be due only to the agricultural disasters common near the limits of cultivation. Population movement in this period probably had serious effects on the relationship between population and resources.

The disruption which brought about altered relationships between population and resources also brought about considerable changes in the structure of political authority. At the time of the Spanish arrival (1532) Arequipa formed part of the Inca empire and had for perhaps a century. The story of how Inca control ended anywhere in the provinces is as yet poorly known. In Arequipa, Inca control may have been broken first by independent Inca governors, *kurakas* from the *altiplano* or local *kurakas* prior to the establishment of any meaningful Spanish colonial authority (Julien 1982:142–44). By 1567, the date of our first detailed information about cultivators in Arequipa, control was in the hands of the *kurakas* who headed groups awarded in *encomienda*. A number of colonial administrators noted that the *kurakas* they dealt with were the direct inheritors of Inca rule (Sarmiento de Gamboa 1906:7–8; Santillán 1927:47–51). The *kurakas* may have benefited personally from labor service formerly owed directly to the Inca government. *Kuraka* holdings in the 1560s and 1570s may not reflect an earlier situation in detail.

Besides a bias in our sources in favor of *kuraka* control, a preponderance of our information concerns the people of the Lupaca province, so our point of view is dominated by the concerns of outside cultivators. The Lupacas were privileged to be a Crown *encomienda*. Their *kurakas* successfully reclaimed rights to lowland resources held by the province at the time of the Spanish arrival (note 13). We do not have similar information for adjacent provinces in the Lake Titicaca region or for any local population in Arequipa. The return of colonists to any other Lake Titicaca province has not been reported, either.

Even so, the Lupaca sources are particularly valuable as a source of information about Inca administration because, for the Lake Titicaca and Arequipa regions, only in the case of the Lupaca province did an Inca political unit survive well into the era of Spanish dominance. Although other Inca provinces were awarded in *encomienda* to particular Spaniards when awards were first made, the only grant in the area to survive partitioning in the 1540s was the Crown *encomienda* to the Lupaca province (Julien 1983:10–29). The preservation of an Inca political unit is a major reason why we can detect elements of the Inca provincial administration in the Lupaca source materials (Julien 1982).

One such element may be the group of cultivators organized in Sama to provision the Lupaca province with maize. A *khipu* of the last Inca census recorded a group of 200 *yungas* (2 *pachakas*) with approximately 20,000 Lupaca tributary households (2 *hunu*). In the same *khipu*, the people who resided outside the Lupaca province proper appear to have been accounted with their groups of origin within the province. A group of Lupaca *mitimas* settled in Sama were therefore not accounted separately. Gutiérrez Flores, administrator of a 1574 *visita* and *tasa*, noted that the obligation of the Sama cultivators was to cultivate maize for the Lupaca province and the obligation of the Lupaca *mitimas* was to transport it to the province (p. 200). In the absence of the Incas, the tributary relationship had apparently ceased to exist (Diez de San Miguel 1964:247). Gutiérrez Flores attempted to reestablish it, though he did not make different assignments to the *yungas* and *mitima* groups, but rather, globally assigned a fixed amount of metal tribute and an amount of maize for consumption in the Lupaca province (AGNA 9.17.2.5:f. 254r).

What is interesting about this arrangement is that this group of *mitimas* from the Lupaca province and *yungas* were the only units of population recognized in Sama. The group was awarded in *encomienda* to Juan de San Juan and later taken from him in exchange for another award (note 13). No other *encomienda* for the Sama area can be traced, even in the Toledo *tasa* which provides a full accounting of the *encomiendas* of Arequipa. This situation suggests that, at some point, the productive activity of the Sama valley was reoriented to serve the needs of outside cultivators. The accounting of two *pachakas* of indigenous residents in the Inca census of the Lupaca province suggests an Inca hand in reorganizing the local population.

The Incas were involved in relocation projects of this kind, and several examples of projects in the southern highlands can be documented. In Cochabamba, south and east of the Lake Titicaca region, the Incas relocated the indigenous population of the valley and reoriented agricultural production to benefit outsiders. The Arequipa valley may have been depopulated by natural causes and then repopulated by outsiders, except for a small group of native residents (Morúa, lib. IV, cap. XI, 1946:397–98). Ayaviri, in the northern Lake Titicaca region, is another example of Inca removal of a local population and its replacement with outsiders (Cieza de León, *Señorío,* cap. LII, 1936, 246–47). In the first two cases, the purpose of the undertaking, at least in part, appears to have been to supply maize to people living at higher elevations.

The Sama organization appears to be different from the contemporary organization of either Moquegua or Azapa. In Moquegua, not only groups from the Lupaca province but groups from a Qolla province in the northern Lake Titicaca region were settled. People identified as Carumas, who may have been a local population, were also located in the Moquegua drainage. The Lupaca settlements in Azapa were located in relative proximity to groups from Tarapacá, and the outsiders formed enclaves in what appears to have been a much larger local population.

Individual holdings were also described in the Lupaca sources. Whether the *kurakas* inherited control of groups organized by the Incas to provision the Lupaca province as a whole or whether the *kuraka*'s antecedents or other individuals had retainers cultivating for them in the lowlands during the time of the Inca empire or before it cannot be determined from our sources. The tradition of retainer service appears to have antedated the Inca empire, on the basis of direct testimony in the Lupaca sources, but the question of where these retainers served their lords was not addressed. So far, the only archaeological evidence which suggests the presence of people from the Lake Titicaca region in Arequipa is from a site in Sama, where stratified ceramic materials indicate use of the site by people with close ties to the southern Lake Titicaca region during the time of Inca control and later.[18]

To provide a model for earlier organization in the area, some investigators have taken the organization of the Lupaca province and the Arequipa valleys found in the 1567 *visita* and extended it backwards into the past, arguing that the Incas altered Lupaca organization very little (Pease 1978:64–65, 92). The colonies of *mitimas,* returned to the Lupaca jurisdiction in the 1550s, are interpreted as distant outposts from the lakeshore territory of the Lupacas in pre-Inca times, and this spatial arrangement has been described as an "archipelago." Because people from other parts of the Lake Titicaca region and elsewhere were also present in the area in the later sixteenth century, an earlier multiethnic character of settlement in the lowlands is also hypothesized (Murra [1972] 1975:74, 76). The question of control then becomes how did outsiders manage to coexist with each other and with local people at a time when no centralized authority mediated their affairs (Pease 1979:100)?

While the body of Lupaca materials can be appreciated as sources of much new information about local people, the assumption that the political organization of 1567 is a reflection of the pre-Inca past is probably unwarranted. The Incas were indeed active in the southern part of the empire, and there is a growing body of administrative materials to document both the imposition of the Inca decimal administration (Julien 1982) and the relocation of people on a large scale (Morales 1977; Wachtel 1982; Murra 1978b). Inca provincial limits can be reconstructed for the Lake Titicaca region because they were revived in the late sixteenth century for the purposes of mine labor recruitment (Julien 1983:9–29).

One means of assessing whether or not the Lupaca polity of 1567 reflects a pre-Inca polity in any way is to consider information provided in accounts of the Inca conquests of the Lake Titicaca and adjacent areas. The evidence from these sources indicates that the territory of the Lupaca province had a very short-lived history as an autonomous polity and that this polity achieved its independence from a much larger polity less than a generation before annexation of the Lake Titicaca region by the Incas. Moreover, the 1567 Lupaca territory has essentially the same territorial limits as the Inca province reflected in the mine labor recruitment organization.

Particularly detailed accounts of the Inca conquest of the southern part of the empire were recorded by Pedro Sarmiento de Gamboa and Pedro de Cieza de León. These two versions were written independently of each other (Rowe 1945:269), and as will be seen, reflect different local biases in the telling of the round of Inca conquests. Both writers document a polity larger than the Lupaca province with its seat in the Lake Titicaca region, which controlled adjacent territories including a good portion of Arequipa, and which existed two or more generations before the time the area was incorporated into the Inca empire. Information about this polity is also contained in their story of Inca conquests in the south through the time of Thupa 'Inka, the tenth Inca ruler.

Sarmiento de Gamboa collected information in Cuzco in 1572 from members of the Inca royal lineages.[19] Their story was that when Chuchi

Capac, the Qolla king whose seat was at Hatunqolla near Puno, was conquered, a large territory came under Inca control:

> Chuchi Capac had oppressed and subjected more than 160 leagues [800 km] from north to south, because he was a *cinche*, or as he called himself, *capac* or Qolla Capac, from 20 leagues [100 km] away from Cuzco to Chichas and the entire territory of Arequipa and the coast to Atacama and the slopes above Mojos. (Sarmiento de Gamboa, cap. 37, 1906:76)[20]

Sarmiento is very definite about including the entire district of Arequipa. After making a trip to Hatunqolla to threaten Chuchi Capac with a military campaign if he did not submit to Inca rule (cap. 37, 1906:75), Pachacuti returned with an army. During a pitched battle, Pachacuti tried to capture Chuchi Capac. He succeeded, and with his hostage, went to Hatunqolla where he waited for all of the people subject to Chuchi Capac to come to acknowledge their submission to him (cap. 37, 1906:76).

The story Sarmiento tells about successive campaigns also helps to define Qolla territory. After a Qolla rebellion, two sons of Pachacuti who had directed the reconquest, headed south where they met with armed resistance from the people of Paria, Tapacari, Cotabambas, Poconas, and Charcas, who were assembled in the teritory of Chichas and Chuies to defend themselves as a group against the Incas (cap. 41, 1906:83). After subduing a second Qolla revolt occurring on the death of Pachacuti, Thupa 'Inka headed south to conquer Chile. He conquered the Chileños and placed his boundary markers at the Maule River, heading north to conquer Coquimbo. At this point Condesuyos and Chumbivilcas decided to submit peacefully to Inca rule (cap. 49, 1906: 96; cap. 50, 1906: 96–97). The Condesuyos he referred to was probably the territory which later became the *corregimiento* of Condesuyos, located within the limits of the sixteenth century district of Arequipa, and bordering on Chumbivilcas in the district of Cuzco.[21]

A second, and very different, version of the conquest of the Lake Titicaca region was given by Cieza de León. Cieza travelled through the area and, at one point, credits a source in Chucuito for some of his information. Because of the amount of local history contained in his account and the clear contrast between his account of the Inca conquests and Sarmiento's, Cieza's version appears to be local and not an Inca view of their conquests. The lords of Chucuito are clearly important in his story, while they are not mentioned at all by Sarmiento, and Cieza may have gotten a fair amount of information in Chucuito.

Cieza describes a rivalry between two local lords, Zapana of Hatunqolla and Cari of Chucuito. The rivalry began at least a generation before the time of Viracocha, because Cieza speaks of the descendants of Zapana when he describes Viracocha's reign (*Señorío*, cap. XXXVII, 1936:191). The Zapana Cieza first mentions had subjected a large part of the Lake Titicaca region to his dominion (*Señorío*, cap. VI, 1936: 39) when he was challenged by Cari from the valley of Coquimbo, apparently the valley in Chile. Cari arrived in Chucuito, settled there, and then waged a campaign on the island of Titicaca which he won (*Señorío*, cap. IV, 1936:41). For this last piece of information, Cieza credits Chirihuana, a "governor of Chucuito," who may have been an Inca governor since Cieza mentions having met a number of them in his travels (*Señorío*, cap. XX, 1936:121). Having taken an important island shrine, Cari then turned to campaigns for control of other islands. He then began to occupy more of the Lake Titicaca shore, founding the towns of Ilave, Juli, Zepita, and Pomata. Cari's next campaign was against the Canas, to the north of Qolla territory, where he also met with success, travelling as far north as Lurocachi (just south of modern Maranganí). At this point Viracocha became involved, as both Zapana and Cari solicited an alliance with him to defeat the other. Viracocha elected to aid Cari and was on his way to the area with an army when Cari succeeded in defeating Zapana and killing him. Viracocha continued on to Chucuito where he made a pact with Cari (*Señorío*, caps. XLI–XLIII, 1936:205–14).

The conquest of the Lake Titicaca region was not effected until the reign of Pachacuti, when two Chanca captains set off to conquer the Lake Titicaca region at the behest of Pachacuti (*Señorío*, cap. XLVIII, 1936: 320). The Chanca captains fought battles all the way to Chucuito, at which point their objectives were apparently acheived, and the territory subject to Chucuito fell into their hands. The terms of the pact between Viracocha and Cari and the alliance between Pachacuti and the Chancas are not at all clear (*Señorío*, cap. XLVI, 1936:224–25; cap. XLVIII, 1936:230–32, cap. LII–LIV, 1936:245–57), but Pachacuti apparently had to personally secure the Lake Titicaca region himself after the alliance with the Chancas came to an end because of Chanca treachery in another campaign under the alliance.

The territorial worth of Zapana or Cari at any given point is hard to assess in Cieza's account, but further information about Inca conquests again helps to delineate Qolla territory. Once the conquest of Chucuito was effected, Cieza does not describe other military campaigns until late in Thupa 'Inka's reign. Then, Thupa 'Inka travelled to Chucuito and from there he solicited submission from the Charcas,

Carangas, and "others in those lands" (*Señorio*, cap. LX, 1936: 279). Some people submitted while others fought. After these victories in Charcas he conquered as far as the Maule River in Chile. The Arequipa area, except for Condesuyos which was taken by the Chanca captains at the time of the alliance (*Señorio*, caps. XLVI, 1936:224–25; cap. XLVII, 1936:228–29; cap. XLVIII, 1936:231) and reconquered along with Chumbivilcas by Pachacuti after his personal visit to the Lake Titicaca region (*Señorio*, cap. LIII, 1936:249), was apparently annexed when Chucuito was taken.

Cieza gave a description of Qolla territory which included Arequipa:

> This part that they call Qollas is the largest region, in my view, of all Peru and the most populous. Qollas begins in Ayaviri and extends to Caracollo. In the east they have the slopes of the Andes; in the west, the peaks of the mountain ranges and their slopes, reaching to the ocean. Without the land that they occupy with their towns and tillage, there are large depopulated areas, full of wild game. (*Crónica*, cap. XCIX, 1932:288).[22]

Cieza's description of Qolla territory differs from Sarmiento's (p.217), and the differences may be due to a difference in what each author was describing. The southernmost place in Qolla territory in Cieza was Caracollo, the last *tambo* in Pacajes province before Paria. Sarmiento included more territory to the south. Cieza may have described a region unified by an ethnic identity, and ethnographic information from a variety of sixteenth century sources can be used to document the coincidence of Cieza's limits with a particular headdress and the head deformation associated with it (Julien, 1983:42–45; Cieza de León, *Crónica*, cap. C, 1932: 291). Cieza never mentions Lupacas or Pacajes, and clearly for him, these people were Qollas. This ethnically identified group may, of course, reflect a former polity of some sort during which a fair degree of cultural unification was achieved. Sarmiento, who clearly described a territory subject to a particular lord at the time he was defeated by Pachacuti, may have described an expansive period in the history of Qolla polity.

If Cieza was talking about a region which shared an ethnic identity, then this identity extended to the headwaters of the rivers which drained the Pacific slopes of the Andes. The only information which confirms the use of Qolla headdress and head deformation in the Arequipa valleys is for Collaguas, where the Collaguas used these symbols of Qolla identity; their neighbors further down the Colca River, the Cabanaconde, did not (Jiménez de la Espada 1885:II, 40–41).

Several major differences are evident in the accounts of Cieza and Sarmiento in the retelling of the Inca conquests. Cieza adds a powerful lord in Chucuito who defeats and executes the lord of Hatunqolla on the eve of incorporation into the Inca empire. In Sarmiento's account, Pachacuti defeated the lord of Hatunqolla and took him to Cuzco for execution. Sarmiento also adds detail about Qolla rebellions to the story. Moreover, Sarmiento describes two separate campaigns following the conquest of the Lake Titicaca region, one undertaken by two sons of Pachacuti for control of Charcas, and the other a campaign by Thupa 'Inka to win coastal Chile. Cieza combines these two campaigns into one, under the leadership of Thupa 'Inka. In Cieza's version, the annexation of Condesuyos and Chumbivilcas is timed with the conquest of the Lake Titicaca region, while in Sarmiento, this area submitted peacefully after Thupa 'Inka's conquest of Chile.

Both versions of the Inca conquest reflect a pre-Inca polity with its seat in the Lake Titicaca region larger than any of the Inca provinces in the area, whether subject to a lord at Hatunqolla or more recently conquered by a lord at Chucuito.[23] Cieza's story about the emergence of a lord at Chucuito, named Cari, is not repeated anywhere else, though a Cari lineage was clearly in control of the Lupaca province at the time of the Spanish arrival. A Cari had distinguished himself in the campaigns of Huayna Capac, and his descendants were in control of the Lupaca province in 1567 (Cabello Valboa, tercera parte, cap. 21, 1951:368).[24] Though Cieza's story is unique, it helps to explain the basis for the political division effected by the Incas in the Lake Titicaca region. Both Cieza and Sarmiento describe the political organization of the Lake Titicaca and Arequipa regions as something quite different from the political organization evident in the 1560s. Control exerted by a centralized authority over the upper valleys and perhaps over the lower valleys and coast is a clear possibility in the period before the Inca empire.

While there is also a story to be told about resource control, our sources do not tell it. Qolla interest in the upper valleys of Arequipa has been documented through the course of this study, and political control of lowland territory would have given them an advantage in securing resources there.

Even for the time of Inca control, there is only a slight amount of information about resource control. The Incas were involved in redistribution of land and other productive resources, and such activities would have involved a redistribution of irrigation waters especially where water was in short supply as in the valleys of Arequipa. Garci Diez, in the 1567 *visita* of the Lupaca province, noted in his opinion that the distribution of water in Moquegua should continue to be effected in the same manner as in Inca times (Diez de San Miguel 1964: 247).

Since the productivity of land was linked to the use of guano fertilizers, a redistribution of land might well affect the distribution of rights to *guano*, if such rights existed at the time the region was annexed to the Inca empire. One bit of evidence that the Incas were involved in authorizing claims to *guano* is Avendaño's statement, cited earlier (pp. 211–12). The disputes which arose in the 1560s over whether claims to *guano* from nearby islands existed under the Incas or a free-for-all situation prevailed are precisely what might be expected if a centralized authority involved in recognizing claims suddenly ceased to do so. Garcilaso de la Vega, "El Inca," gives a detailed but possibly imaginative description of Inca control over *guano*, describing bounded claims mined by the cultivators themselves on a scheduled basis. Sanctions against killing the birds, against travelling to the islands during nesting season, and against mining *guano* from the claims of others were also described. Although Garcilaso details a reasonable program for controlling the exploitation of *guano*, his unreliability is notorious, and his information cannot be checked against information from other sources (lib. 5, cap. III, vol. 2, 1959:70).

Even following the Spanish arrival, when the written record began, we have very little information on resource control. By the late sixteenth century, the trade in *guano* had become a lucrative colonial enterprise. As in the case of *coca*, *guano* was a high demand substance for the native population, and it was easily transported and not available locally in much of the Andean area. It was easily commercialized. Europeans sold it to native cultivators or took it inland to sell (Cobo, lib. II, cap. XIV, vol. 91, 1964:85). In 1617–19, Vázquez de Espinosa described this trade:

> In this land there is a rich mine of benefit to everyone, and many people have enriched themselves in it and its trade. . . . Forty leagues [200 km] from this city [Arica], near Tarapacá and visible from the land, is a small island where a great number of frigates travel to load the earth found on that island. . . . The frigates bring it to the city, and to all the ports and valleys, and sell it by the *fanega* at the usual price of 12 to 14 reales. All of the cultivators buy it for their planting, and the Indians take it away on their llamas. It is so important that first they would quit eating before they would quit buying *guano*, because by putting *guano* on a *fanega* of planted land it will yield 300, 400, and 500 *fanegas* . . . it has enriched many who have entered

into the trade with frigates. (Vázquez de Espinosa, lib. IV, cap. LXVII, 1969:348; author's translation)

Vázquez' description probably referred to the island facing Iquique, an important source of *guano* through the Spanish colonial era. *Guano* from this distant island may have increased the supply available to cultivators in the valleys near Arica, at least in the late sixteenth century. To the extent that commercialization of *guano* focused on this source, European activities may not have interfered much with native claims to *guano* during that same period. The effects of Spanish entry into commerce in *guano* are difficult to interpret, but certainly, the Spanish commerce in *guano* had consequences for local cultivators.

Our picture of the activities of native people in the Andes is usually obscured by the disruption which occurred following the arrival of the Spanish. Still, some aspects of the relationship between population and resources can be documented. In the agricultural economy of sixteenth century Arequipa, productivity was linked to a very effective source of organic compounds available at a distance from the cultivation site. Local productivity supported not only the local population, but contributed to the support of a large population in the *altiplano* where foodstuffs were often in short supply and preferences for maize turned attention to the adjacent lowlands. This relationship should be kept in mind when thinking about the earlier history of the Arequipa region.

NOTES AND ACKNOWLEDGMENTS

1. Both John H. Rowe and Patricia J. Lyon read and commented on an earlier draft of this paper. Their comments provoked considerable rethinking about the use of scattered, non-contemporaneous source material and served to focus my presentation of the issues. I am also indebted to Franklin Pease, Bill Denevan, and Alan Craig for their comments on different sections of the paper; to Alex Georgiadis for help with the bibliography; to Dick Weaver of Chemurgic Company for information used in calculating the weight of *guano*; and to Tom Abercrombie for letting me use a copy of the 1574 Toledo *tasa* of the Lupaca province.

The limits of the Spanish city district of Arequipa can be identified in Toledo 1975:217–53.

2. Puquina is the name of both a language, spoken mainly on the northeast side of Lake Titicaca (Bouysse-Cassagne 1975:315–16; Julien 1983:47–49), and a group of people, settled along a confluent of the Tambo River near Arequipa (Figs. 9.1, 9.3). At present there is no reason to think that the people from Puquina territory spoke the Puquina language.

3. The dryest section of the Peruvian desert is the Desert of Atacama where summer (October-April) rain only occurs above 2,200 m. Maximum aridity is reached at Iquique (Meigs 1966:111, Table 8; Murphy 1936:I, 263–64).

4. Barriga 1941–48: II, 307; III, 11, 66–67, 96. This eighteenth century survey will be cited many times. It was conducted in 1790–92 by the *intendente* of Arequipa, Antonio Alvarez y Jiménez. This administrator visited all of the parishes in the *intendencia* of Arequipa. Though he does not give parallel information for each parish, for some he provides detailed information about resources and economic activities.

5. Meigs 1966:113; Barriga 1941–48:II, 189, 262, 281; III, 126, 162. The Omate River flowed underground in places (Barriga 1941–48:II, 253).

6. Barriga 1941–48:II, 309–10, 321; III, 157; Vázquez de Espinosa, lib. IV, cap. LVIII, 1969:336–37; cap. LX, 1969:339–40; cap. LXIV, 1969: 346.

7. González Holguín 1952:520. "Estiercol para estercolar. Huanu."

8. In a 1549 *tasa* of Ilabaya, sea lion skins were required as tribute (Barriga 1939–55:205).

9. Raimondi describes their use at Ilo in 1864 (1948:252). Two examples were collected for museums (Means 1942:plate 19; Lothrop 1932:144, figs. 4, 5, plate XXa-c).

10. These water bags, made of gut, were associated with the oldest agricultural remains at the site of Punta Pichalo, near the mouth of the Pisagua River (Bird 1943:271–72, fig. 29s).

11. This calculation was based on the weight of poultry droppings (55 cu. ft. is equivalent to 1 tn.).

12. The colonies of Auca and Hinchichura have been located in Azapa because of the wording of the 1540 *encomienda* award where they are clearly included with towns in that valley (Barriga 1939–55:III, 18; Trelles 1982: 157; for a differing view, see Pease 1979:102–103, note 5). Other evidence for this location comes from a 1574 *tasa* of the Lupaca province: "*y onze yndios del pueblo de Hinchura que estan en la costa junto a Arica, han de pagar veinte y seis pesos y quatro tomines y onze fanegas de maiz . . .*" (AGNA, 9.17.2.5:f. 271r; Toledo, 1975:80).

Cochuna was located in Moquegua. The 1574 *tasa* of the Lupaca province, cited above, specified that Juan de Castro had to pay some of the expenses of the parish priest in Moquegua because he had an *encomienda* there (AGNA, 9.17.2.5: f. 307r). Juan de Castro was the *encomendero* of Cochuna. Garcilaso de la Vega located it at 5 leagues (25 km) from the town of Moquegua (lib. III, cap. IV, vol. 1, 1959:223–25).

13. *Mitimas* originally awarded in *encomienda* to Lucas Martínez Vegaso (Azapa) and Juan de San Juan (Sama) were recognized to belong to the Lupaca province and were returned to the jurisdiction of Chucuito in 1557 (Diez de San Miguel 1964:126, 174; Pease 1980:113–14).

14. The early *encomienda* of Sama, held by Juan de San Juan, may have included the Moquegua *mitimas*. There is a Cédula Real of 1568 which refers to a Repartimiento of Çuma [Sama] and Moquegua (Pease 1980:114). This

cédula refers to the return of this *repartimiento* to the jurisdiction of the Lupaca province under Cañete (1557), an apparent reference to the *encomienda* of Juan de San Juan. In the 1567 *visita* of the Lupaca province, close in date to the *cédula* cited above, Sama and Moquegua are handled separately. Sama alone is repeatedly described as having been the former *encomienda* of Juan de San Juan. Still, if the reorganization carried out by Cañete affected only the *encomiendas* of Juan de San Juan and Lucas Martínez Vegaso (Diez de San Miguel 1964:174), then there is a fair likelihood that the Lupaca tributaries in Moquegua had been a part of the *encomienda* of Juan de San Juan.

15. An 1804 description of the parishes of Arequipa describes a former occupation in Moquegua by people from Carumas, mentioning habitation sites at the Pago de Omo, Samehua, Estuquiña, Huaracani, and Yaracachi (Barriga 1939–55:IV, 129). Confirmation for the placement of Carumas in the valley comes from the 1574 *tasa* of the Lupaca province. In addition to Juan de Castro, the *encomendero* of Cochuna, Doña Elvira Davalos had to contribute to the support of a parish priest in Moquegua (AGNA, 9.17.2.5: f. 307r). Doña Elvira Davalos was the mother of Doña Maria Davalos who inherited the *encomienda* of Lucas Martínez Vegaso through marriage to him on his deathbed (Trelles 1982:136–37). At the time of the Toledo *visita* in Arequipa (1573), Doña Maria Davalos held Martínez's *encomienda*, which included a group of Carumas. If her mother held a claim to an *encomienda* in the Moquegua area, it was probably the Carumas portion of the former *encomienda* of Lucas Martínez Vegaso, transferred to her by her daughter.

16. Most of the 1540s grants were not the initial awards made in Arequipa, but resulted from Pizarro's and others' attempts to create additional *encomiendas*. In some ways these grants are more valuable than the first awards because the population had to be redescribed to be split, and more was known about the composition of the local population than before. Valuable references to outsiders living in the area or rights held by the *kurakas* elsewhere are often included. For example, people from Tarapacá were settled in Azapa; people from Ubinas were living in Omate (Barriga 1939–55:III, 18, 21).

17. Tarapacá is the only case where fishermen were accounted as part of a group with a large upper valley population.

18. Trimborn 1975:293–96, Abb. 2. An excavated building yielded two floors with associated refuse. The earliest was associated with ceramics influenced by the Cuzco-Inca style and above it ceramics with colonial affiliation were found (p. 294). Some of the bowl fragments illustrated exhibit base thinning and profiles characteristic of materials of Phase 3 in the Hatunqolla sequence. Nothing shown appears to be stylistically earlier than Phase 3 at Hatunqolla, a site which appears to have been founded after the area came under Inca control (Julien 1983:90, 224–34).

19. Sarmiento's history was read to a group of these nobles so that they could correct it before it was sent to the King of Spain (1906:130–34). Although he collected it for Viceroy Toledo, Toledo also collected information on the Inca conquests and his account differs from Sarmiento's (John Rowe, pers. com.).

20. "*Tenía Chuchi Capac opresas y subjetas más de ciento y sesenta leguas* [800 km] *de norte sur, porque era cinche, ó, como él se nombraba: capac, ó Colla Capac, desde veinte leguas* [100 km] *del Cuzco hasta los Chichas y todos los términos de Arequipa y la costa de la mar hacia Atacama y las montañas sobre los Mojos. . . .*"

21. Sarmiento's use of the term Condesuyos, and Cieza's (pp. 217–19), is problematic because the name also applied to the western quarter of the Inca empire. A territory larger than the *corregimiento* of Condesuyos may be implied. The only early writer to provide any details on the itinerary for this trip was Juan de Santa Cruz Pachacuti, a native of Canchis province, near Cuzco. He notes that Pachacuti, the ninth Inka, travelled: ". . . *yendo por el Collao, en donde tope con los yndios Ccoles y Camanchacas, grandes hechizeros, y de alli baja por Arequipay, passa á Chacha y Atunconde y á los Chumbivilcas, y de allí a Camana, y le da la vuelta á su ciudad por los Aymaraes y Chilques y Papres, y entra al Cuzco*" (Pachacuti Yamqui Salcamaygua 1879: 279). Colesuyo was a territory which included the upper Tambo River and may have extended further south and southeast along the coast. Pachacuti appears to have travelled to Arequipa along the road described by Vaca de Castro (1908:439–40). All of the places he visited after Arequipa were to the north. Sarmiento's description of the territory subject to Chuchi Capac is therefore contradicted in some degree, because the *corregimiento* of Condesuyos falls within the limits of Arequipa. To extract him from this contradiction, a Condesuyo subject to Chuchi Capac would have had to have refused to come to Hatunqolla on the defeat of Chuchi Capac, remaining independent until later.

22. "*Esta parte que llaman Collas es la mayor comarca, a mi ver, de todo el Perú y la más poblada. Desde Ayavire comienzan los Collas, y llegan hasta Caracollo. Al oriente tienen las montañas de los Andes, al poniente las cabezadas de las sierras nevadas y las vertientes dellas que van a parar a la mar del sur. Sin la tierra que ocupan con sus pueblos y labores, hay grandes despoblados, y que están bien llenos de ganado silvestre.*"

23. The idea of a larger polity in the Lake Titicaca region is also reflected in the account of Martín de Morúa, who as parish priest in Capachica at the north end of Lake Titicaca had access to local information. Morúa described the territorial worth of a Lake Titicaca lord, but without reference to time or to place of residence: "*Dicen que antiguamente había Rey en el Collao, y que se llamaba Javilla, y que fué señor deste Vilcanota hasta Chile y aún más adelante comenzó el término de su jurisdicción desde una raya que viene bajando desde un cerro que hasta hoy se parece y se ve desde el Camino Real, empezando con el dicho cerro que está a mano derecha yendo desde el Cuzco a Potosí, en el propio asiento y paraje de Vilcanota. . .*" (Morúa, cap. XXI, 1946:214–15).

24. Cieza's story also suggests an explanation for the distribution of archaeological materials at a site near Chucuito, Arku Punku, located on the Puno-Moquegua road. The site is on a direct line between Chucuito and Qutimpu, the hypothesized burial grounds of the Cari dynasty during the

time of Inca control. The materials on the surface of the site are domestic refuse from an earlier habitation of the site and indicate affiliation with the Hatunqolla area. The materials associated with the burial towers are not affiliated with the Hatunqolla area but are characteristic of materials from Chucuito during the time of Inca control. Cieza's story indicates that Cari exerted control first over the lakeshore. The Arku Punku area was clearly subject to the lords of Chucuito in 1567, and presumably in Inca times. The changing affiliation suggested by the materials at Arku Punku may reflect a change in territorial control (Julien 1981:140–41).

REFERENCES CITED

AGNA

1785 Taza de la Provincia de Chucuito [1574]. *In* Retasa de Francisco de Toledo, ff 243–315v. Archivo General de la Nación, Buenos Aires, Argentina.

Bandera, Damian de la

1968 Relacion del origen e gobierno que los Ingas tuvieron [1557]. *In* Biblioteca Peruana, ser. 1, vol. 3:493–510. Lima: Editores Técnicos Asociados.

Barriga, Victor M.

1939–55 Documentos para la Historia de Arequipa. 3 vols. Arequipa: Editorial La Colmena, S. A.

1941–48 Memorias para la Historia de Arequipa. 4 vols. Arequipa: Editorial La Colmena, S. A.

1954 Historia de la fundación del nuevo pueblo de San Fernando de Socabaya. Arequipa: Imprenta Portugal.

Bird, Junius Bouton

1943 Excavations in Northern Chile. Anthropological Papers of the American Museum of Natural History 38 (4), New York.

1947 The Cultural Sequence of the North Chilean Coast. *In* Handbook of South American Indians, Vol. 2. Julian H. Steward, ed. pp. 587–97. Bureau of American Ethnology, Bulletin 143. Washington: Smithsonian Institution.

Bouysse-Cassagne, Thérese

1975 Pertenencia étnica, status económico y lenguas en Charcas a fines de siglo XVI. *In* Tasa de la Visita General de Francisco de Toledo. Noble David Cook, ed. pp. 312–28. Lima: Universidad Nacional Mayor de San Marcos.

Cabello Valboa, Miguel

1951 Miscelánea antárctica, una historia del Perú antiguo [1586]. Lima: Universidad Nacional Mayor de San Marcos, Facultad de Letras, Instituto de Etnología.

Cárdenas, Martín

1960 Manual de plantas económicas de Bolivia. Cochabamba: Imprenta Icthus.

Casaverde R., Juvenal

1977 El trueque en la economía pastoril. *In* Pastores de puna; uywamichiq punarunakuna. Jorge A. Flores Ochoa, comp. pp. 171–91. Estudios de la Sociedad Rural, 5. Lima: Instituto de Estudios Peruanos.

Cieza de León, Pedro de

1932 La Crónica del Perú. Madrid: Espasa-Calpe, S. A.

1936 Del Señorio de los Incas. Prólogo y notas de Alberto Mario Salas. Buenos Aires: Ediciones Argentinas "Solar."

Cobo, Bernabé

1956 Historia del nuevo mundo [1653]. Francisco Mateos, ed. Biblioteca de Autores Españoles, desde la formación del lenguaje hasta nuestros días (continuación): Vols. 91–92. Madrid: Ediciones Atlas.

Coker, Robert E.

1908 The Fisheries and the Guano Industry of Peru. Bulletin of the Bureau of Fisheries 28:333–65. Washington: Government Printing Office.

Crespo R., Alberto

1972 El corregimiento de La Paz. 1548–1600. La Paz: Empresa Editora "Urquizo Ltda."

Custred, Glynn

1974 Llameros y comercio interregional. *In* Reciprocidad e Intercambio en los Andes Peruanos. Giorgio Alberti and Enrique Mayer, comp. pp. 252–89. Perú Problema, 12. Lima: Instituto de Estudios Peruanos.

Diez de San Miguel, Garci

1964 Visita hecha a la provincia de Chucuito por Garci Diez de San Miguel en el año 1567. Waldemar Espinoza Soriano, ed. pp. 3–287. Documentos Regionales para la Etnología y Etnohistoria Andinas, Vol. 1. Lima: Ediciones de la Casa de la Cultura del Perú.

Drosdoff, Matthew

1959 Suelos del Sur del Perú. Los Suelos, PS/A/2, Plan Regional de Desarrollo del Sur del Perú: Vol. 1. Lima: Ministerio de Fomento.

Edwards, Clinton R.

1965 Aboriginal Watercraft on the Pacific Coast of South America. Iberoamericana 47. Berkeley: University of California Press.

Flores Ochoa, Jorge A.

1968 Los pastores de Paratía; una introducción a su estudio. Instituto Indigenista Interamericano, Serie: Antropología Social: Vol. 10. Mexico.

1970 El reino Lupaca y el actual control vertical de la ecología. Historia y Cultura 6:195–201. Lima.

Frère, M., J. Q. Rijks, and J. Rea

1975 Estudio agroclimatológico de la Zona Andina (informe técnico). Proyecto Interinstitucional FAO/UNESCO/OMM en Agroclimatología. Rome: Organización de las Naciones Unidas para la Alimentación y la Agricultura.

Garcilaso de la Vega, "El Inca"

1959 Comentarios reales de los Incas [1604]. 3 vols. José Durand, ed. Lima: Universidad Nacional Mayor de San Marcos.

González Holguín, Diego

1952 Vocabulario de la lengua general de todo el Peru llamada Qquichua, o del Inca [1608]. Raúl Porras Barrenechea. Lima: Imprenta Santa María.

Gutiérrez Flores, Pedro

1964 Padrón de los mil indios ricos de la provincia de Chucuito. *In* Visita hecha a la provincia de Chucuito por Garci Diez de San Miguel en el año 1567. pp. 306–63. Documentos Regionales para la Etnología y Etnohistoria Andinas, Vol. 1. Lima: Ediciones de la Casa de la Cultura del Perú.

1970 Resultas de la visita secreta [1574]. Historia y Cultura 4:5–48. Lima.

Hutchinson, George Evelyn

1950 The Biogeochemistry of Vertebrate Excretion. Survey of Existing Knowledge of Biogeochemistry 3. American Museum of Natural History, Bulletin: Vol. 96. New York.

Jiménez de la Espada, Marcos

1880–97 Relaciones Geográficas de Indias. Perú. 4 vols. Madrid: Ministerio de Fomento, Tipografía de Manuel G. Hernández.

Julien, Catherine Jean

1981 A Late Burial from Cerro Azoguini, Puno. Ñawpa Pacha 19: 129–54. Berkeley.

1982 Inca Decimal Administration in the Lake Titicaca Region. *In* The Inca and Aztec States 1400–1800: Anthropology and History. George A. Collier, Renato I. Rosaldo, and John D. Wirth, eds. pp. 119-51. New York: Academic Press.

1983 Hatunqolla: A View of Inca Rule from the Lake Titicaca Region. Series Publications in Anthropology: Vol. 15. Berkeley: University of California Press.

Lothrop, Samuel K.

1932 Aboriginal Navigation Off the West Coast of South America. Journal of the Royal Anthropological Institute, Vol. LXII (July-Dec.): 229–256. London.

Masuda, Shozo

1981 Cochayuyo, macha, camarón, e higos charqueados. *In* Estudios Etnográficos del Perú Meridional. Shozo Masuda, ed. pp. 173–92. Tokyo: University of Tokyo.

Means, Phillip Ainsworth

1942 Pre-Spanish Navigation Off the Andean Coast. The American Neptune 2 (2):1–20.

Meigs, Peveril

1966 Geography of Coastal Deserts. United Nations Educational, Scientific and Cultural Organization (UNESCO), Arid Zone Research: Vol. XXVIII. Paris.

Miranda, Cristóbal de

1925 Relación hecha por el Virrey D. Martín Enríquez de los oficios que se proveen en la gobernación de los reinos y provincias del Perú [1583]. *In* Gobernantes del Perú; Cartas y papeles del siglo XVI. Roberto Levillier, ed. Vol. 9, pp. 114–230. Colección de Publicaciones Históricas de la Biblioteca del Congreso Argentino. Madrid: Imprenta de Juan Pueyo.

Morales, Adolfo de

1977 Repartimiento de tierras por el Inca Huayna Capac (Testimonio de un documento de 1556). Cochabamba: Universidad Boliviana Mayor de San Simón, Departamento de Arqueologia, Museo Arqueológico.

Morúa, Martín de

1946 Historia del orígen y geneología real de los Incas del Perú [c. 1605]. Introducción, notas y arreglo por Constantino Bayle. Biblioteca "Missionalia Hispánica," vol. II. Madrid: Consejo Superior de Investigaciones Científicas, Instituto Santo Toribio de Mogrovejo.

Murphy, Robert Cushman

1936 Oceanic Birds of South America. 2 vols. New York: American Museum of Natural History.

Murra, John Victor

1964 Una apreciación etnológica de la visita. *In* Visita hecha a la provincia de Chucuito por Garci Diez de San Miguel en el año 1567. pp. 421–44. Documentos Regionales para la Etnología y Etnohistoria Andinas, Vol. 1. Lima: Ediciones de la Casa de la Cultura del Perú.

1968 An Aymara Kingdom in 1567. Ethnohistory 15 (2):115–51. Seattle.

[1972] 1975 El control "vertical" de un máximo de pisos eológicos en la economía de las sociedades andinas. *In* Formaciones Económicas y Politícas del Mundo Andino. Historia Andina 3:59–115. Lima: Instituto de Estudios Peruanos.

1978a Aymara Lords and Their European Agents at Potosí. Nova Americana I:231–43. Torino: Einaudi.

1978b Los olleros del Inka: hacia una historia y arqueología del Qollasuyu. Historia, Problema y Promesa: Homenaie a Jorge Basadre: 415–23. Lima: Pontificia Universidad Católica del Perú.

Núñez, Lautaro A.

1974 La agricultura prehistórica en los Andes meridionales. Colección Testimonios. Antofagasta: Universidad del Norte.

Pachacuti Yamqui Salcamaygua, Juan de Santa Cruz

1879 Relación de Antigüedades deste Reyno del Piru. *In* Tres Relaciones de Antigüedades Peruanas, pp. 231–328. Publícalas el Ministerio de Fomento. Madrid: Imprenta de M. Tello.

Pease García Yrigoyen, Franklin

1978 Del Tawantinsuyu a la Historia del Perú. Historia Andina 5. Lima: Instituto de Estudios Peruanos.

1979 La formación del Tawantinsuyu: mecanismas de colonización y relación con las unidades étnicas. Histórica, Vol. III, No. 1 (julio): 97–120. Lima: Pontificia Universidad Católica del Perú.

1980 Relaciones entre los grupos étnicos de la Sierra Sur y la Costa: continuidades y cambios. *In* Senri Ethnological Studies, No. 10, pp. 107–22. Senri: National Museum of Ethnology.

Perú

1926 Arbitraje de Tacna y Arica. Documentos de la Comisión Especial de Límites: Vol. 5. Lima: Ministerio de Relaciones Exteriores, Casa Editora "La Opinion Nacional."

Polo de Ondegardo, Juan

1872 Relación acerca del linaje de los Incas y como conquistaron y acerca del notable daño que resulta de no guardar á estos indios sus fueros [1571]. *In* Coleccion de Documentos Ineditos, relativos al Descubrimiento, Conquista y Organización de las Antiguas Posesiones Españolas de América y Oceanía. D. Luis Torres de Mendoza, ed. Vol. XVII, pp. 1–177. Madrid.

1940 Informe del Licenciado Juan Polo de Ondegardo al Licenciado Briviesca de Muñatones sobre la perpetuidad de las encomiendas en el Perú [1561]. Revista Histórica, Vol. XIII: 125–96. Lima.

Raimondi, Antonio

1948 Notas de viajes para su obra "El Perú". Vol. 4. Lima: Imprenta Torres Aguirre.

Ramírez Velarde, María

1970 Visita a Pocona (1557). Historia y Cultura 4:269–308. Lima.

Ramos Gavilán, Alonso

1976 Historia de Nuestra Senora de Copacabana; Segunda edición completa, según la impressión príncipe de 1621. La Paz: Academía Boliviana de Historia.

Rowe, John Howland

1945 Absolute Chronology in the Andean Area. American Antiquity 10 (3) (January): 265–84. Menasha.

1982 Inca Policies and Institutions Relating to the Cultural Unification of the Empire. *In* The Inca and Aztec States 1400–1800: Anthropology and History. George A. Collier, Renato I. Rosaldo, and John D. Wirth, eds. pp. 93–118. New York: Academic Press.

Sánchez-Albornoz, Nicolás

1978 Indios y tributos el el Alto Perú. Historia Andina:6. Lima: Instituto de Estudios Peruanos.

Santillán, Fernando de

1927 Origen, descendencia, política y gobierno de los Incas [1563].

Colección de Libros y Documentos referentes a la Historia del Perú, tomo IX (2a. serie): 1–124. Lima: Imprenta y Librería Sanmartí.

Sarmiento de Gamboa, Pedro

1906 Geschichte des Inkareiches von Pedro Sarmiento de Gamboa [1572]. Herausgegeben von Richard Pietschmann. Abhandlungen der Königlichen Gesellschaft der Wissenschaften zu Göttingen, Philogisch-Historische Klasse, Neue Folge, Band VI, No. 4. Berlin: Weidmannsche Buchhandlung.

Toledo, Francisco de

1975 Tasa de la visita general de Francisco de Toledo [1571–73]. Noble David Cook, ed. Lima: Universidad Nacional Mayor de San Marcos.

Trelles Arestegui, Efraín

1982 Lucas Martínez Vegazo: Funcionamiento de una Encomienda Peruana Inicial. Lima: Pontificia Universidad Católica del Perú.

Trimborn, Hermann

1975 Sama. Zeitschrift für Ethnologie, Band 100, Heft 1 und 2:290–99. Braunschweig: Verlag Albert Limbach.

Tschundi, Johann Jakob von

1854 Travels in Peru, On the Coast, In the Sierra, Across the Cordilleras and the Andes, Into the Primeval Forests. Thomasina Ross, transl. New York: A. S. Barnes & Co.

Vace de Castro, Cristóbal

1908 Ordenanzas de tambos, distancias de a otros, modo de cargar los indios y obligaciones de las justicias respectivas hechas en la ciudad del Cuzco en 31 de Mayo de 1543. Revista Histórica, tomo III: 427–92. Lima: Instituto Histórico del Perú.

Vázquez de Espinosa, Antonio

1969 Compendio y descripción de las indias occidentales [c. 1629]. B. Velasco Bayón, ed. Biblioteca de Autores Españoles, desde la formación del lenguaje hasta nuestros días (continuación): Vol. 231. Madrid: Ediciones Atlas.

Wachtel, Nathan

1982 The Mitimas of the Cochabamba Valley: The Colonization Policy of Huayna Capac. *In* The Inca and Aztec States 1400–1800: Anthropology and History. George A. Collier, Renato I. Rosaldo, and John D. Wirth, eds. pp. 199–235. New York: Academic Press.

10

Algae Collectors and *Lomas*

Shozo Masuda

The Importance of the Marine Resources

In discussions of the formation of civilization, the spotlight always falls on agriculture. The entry of agriculture marks the appearance of pottery-making, weaving, metallurgy, and temple-cults. However, in the case of Central Andean civilization, one cannot ignore the existence of another very important *dramatis personae*—the exploitation of marine resources. The Peruvian Current furnished inestimable resources to pre-agricultural Andean peoples. Consideration is occasionally given to the maritime foundation of Andean civilization, but, with the rise of so-called intensive agriculture, all the attention seems to be diverted from the ocean to the land, as if agriculture fully substituted for the utilization of maritime products, at least as far as alimentation is concerned. In spite of the innumerable iconographic representations of marine life in the plastic art of the Moche and Nazca cultures, scarcely a question has been raised as to what extent maritime products might have complemented those of agrarian or of stockbreeding origin, or as to what kind of social and political role was played by the people who devoted themselves to the exploitation of sea foods in prehispanic times. An important contribution has been made by María Rostworowski, who has shown us the existence of fishermen in Chincha and in other areas of the central and north coasts of Peru. Many of them did not have access to land for cultivation and subsisted on marine products, often paying their tribute in Colonial times by selling fish (Rostworowski 1977, 1981). Indeed there exists a large number of references to fishing and to the utilization of marine products for food in Colonial sources (Rostworowski 1981:84–88; Masuda 1982). A large quantity of fish and maritime products was consumed not only in the coastal area but in the highlands as well. For example, the city of Potosí consumed annually "six thousand *arrobas* (150,000 pounds) of marine fish" in the second half of the sixteenth century, according to the information provided by *Relaciones Geógraficas de Indias* (Jiménez de la Espada 1965:I, 381). Bernabé Cobo, speaking about the Spanish and Indian fishermen of Callao, affirms that many people of Lima preferred fish to meat for dinner (Cobo [1653] 1956:I, 286). Such demand for marine resources may very well date back to the prehispanic period. An Andean predilection of marine flavor is still detected nowadays in the daily preparation of food.

Among coastal products of importance which are transported to the highlands at the present time are some marine products, such as fish, salt, shellfish, and algae. What is interesting is that it is not coastal people but *altiplano* inhabitants who are engaged in the collection of certain shellfish and seaweeds, at least on the southern coast of Peru. The collectors of *macha* (*Mesodesma donacium*), for example, who work on the beach of Camaná in the Department of Arequipa, and in Palos, Santa Rosa, and Boca del Río in the Department of Tacna, are mostly from the highlands. The same holds true for the collectors of seaweeds.

Andean Seaweed Collectors

Among Latin American countries, Peru and Chile are remarkable for their interest in and utilization of algae. In both countries, algae have the generic name of *cochayuyo*, which in Quechua signifies aquatic plant. Freshwater algae are distinguished from marine algae, and both are utilized as a food source. The former mostly belongs to a genus called *Nostoc* and has various local appellations. The latter includes *Gigartina* spp., *Porphyra* spp., *Durvillea antartica,* and *Ulva lactuca* (Masuda 1981:183; Acleto 1971:13–16; Etcheverry 1958).

In Chile, the word *cochayuyo* always means *Durvillea antartica.* It is a kind of coffee-colored algae and falls under the class called Phaeophycae together with *Macrocystis integrifolia* and *Macrocystis pyrifera,* both of which are commonly called *huiro* (Marti Silva 1975:3). According to Rojas Labarca, "its adhesive apparatus and the lower part of its stalk are eaten in salads, under the name of *ulte*, *huite*, or *coyofe* (*collofe*)" (Rojas Labarca 1975:3). The Mapuche-Spanish Dictionary by Esteban Erize (1960) informs us that *collov* is the generic name of edible aquatic plants, and that it signifies specifically one called *cochayuyo*, a seaweed very much liked by the coastal native inhabitants of Chile. "Above all they take to *huilte*, part of the plant that extends from a disk-shaped adhesive part (by which the plant attaches itself to rocks) to its ramified stalk" (p. 79). Indigenous taste for *cochayuyo* seems to date back to the prehispanic period, since chronicler Alonso de Ovalle refers to it: ". . . . some roots grow, and from them is born a stem resembling a wrist (*muñeca*), which is called *ulteu*. When cut and toasted over a fire for a little while, it is peeled into something like the stem of lettuce or that of artichoke, although the taste is quite different. From those stems grow several very large *vainas* (pods) of more than three or four *varas* (yards) and four, six, or eight *dedos* (fingers) wide. It is called *cochayuyo*" (Ovalle 1969:60). *Durvillea antartica* inhabits southern regions of Chile and its northern limit is located somewhere around 33° south latitude and it is normally found together with *Lessonia nigrescens* (Alveal 1970:71). The latter is not edible, though collected in quantity for industrial use nowadays. According to Ovalle, "there are two kinds of *cochayuyo*, although their color and shape are almost alike. The Indians make a strict distinction between them, because they cut the good one, dry it, and prepare a dish for Lent, but leave the bad one in the sea. They uproot and throw it on the beach, and they have the custom of making very large heaps of it, but it is useless and cannot be utilized for anything" (Ovalle 1969:60).

What is called *cochayuyo* in Peru is of a completely different sort, and even within Peru local varieties differ from south to north. South of Nazca, the word *cochayuyo* indicates almost always *Porphyra columbina* which belongs to a class called Rhodophyceae. It is a small, leaf-like seaweed growing on rocks, and is collected systematically by local people. In Chile, the same plant has the vulgar name of *luche* or *luchi* and is sold in markets in a ball-shaped mass called *pan de luche* (loaf of *luche*). Marti Silva says that *Porphyra columbina* is called *luche rojo* (red *luche*), while there is another kind called *luche verde* (green *luche*), which is identified as *Ulva lactuca*. Both are edible and used in preparing *guiso* (stew) (Marti Silva 1975:43). Here again we are dealing with a very ancient custom, since Ovalle writes as follows:

> *Luche* is pulled off the rocks where it grows like an ordinary terrestrial plant. It is collected in spring when it grows up most. Placing it in the sun to dry, the Indians make large loaves of it (*pan*). These are prized much in interior regions, especially in Peru, in Cuyo (present Mendoza) and Tucumán, because they serve for many kinds of stew in which they are eaten (1969:59–60).

In central and northern Peru, a seaweed of a totally different kind is in vogue. It is a long weed shaped like a cord with many stems and is classified as *Gigartina chamissoi.* It belongs to the class Rhodophyceae (Acleto 1971:58–59). This species is also collected in quantity and its use is diffused far into the highlands.

The biological distribution and diffusion of the use of these different species of *cochayuyo* is significant. The most suitable habitat for *Durvillea antartica*, the *cochayuyo* of the Chileans, is restricted to southern Chile; therefore it is not surprising that only the Chileans are interested in it. However, *Gigartina* exists all along the coast of Peru and extends south far into Chilean territory and yet only the inhabitants of central and northern Peru show any interest in it. Neither Peruvians from the south coast nor Chileans use it. Finally, *Porphyra columbina* is most abundant in the central and south coasts of Peru and in Chile, its presence diminishing as we move along the Peruvian coast. Thus it is surprising to find that the people of the central and north coasts of Peru exploit only *Gigartina chamissoi* and make nothing of *Porphyra* as foodstuff, since this variety is so appreciated in southern Peru and Chile. Of this interesting phenomenon, we shall consider more in a later section.

Who collects these seaweeds? Carlos Aldunate del Solar, in his *Cultura Mapuche,* informs us that *lafkenche* (men of the sea) collect *erizos, choros, machas, jaibas*, and *pancoras*, while women collect *cochayuyo, luche*, and *lúa.* (Aldunate del Solar 1971:29). In central and northern Peru, it is also women and children who collect *cochayuyo.* In many cases, they are of fishing families. The fishermen seldom engage in such collection since such a simple job as seaweed collecting does not need expertise. In southern Peru, the situation is different. There it is not coastal inhabitants but highland people who collect *cochayuyo, Porphyra columbina.* The fishermen on the south coast do not engage in seaweed collection. Instead, peasants and pastoral people from the southern highlands, that is to say, those from the Departments of Ayacucho, Apurímac, Arequipa, Cuzco, and Puno, seasonally go down to the coast to devote themselves to the collection of *cochayuyo*. As Ovalle says, *cochayuyo* "grows up most" in springtime, which corresponds to the months of September and October. The highland people, be they peasants or pastoralists, have the busiest time in May and June for the harvest of maize. Peasants do the harvesting and herders help them in transporting the crop. It is a difficult task because the land cultivated is often located on steep, and sometimes jagged slopes. The herders of llamas use their animals to carry the crop and obtain a portion of it as reward. Finishing the harvest, the highland people have a brief spate of leisure time, and some of them travel to the coast for the collection of marine products, the most desirable being *cochayuyo* and *machas*.

The coastal zone of the Department of Arequipa provides the most suitable areas for the collection of *cochayuyo*. The collectors converge on two different areas and display varied life styles. One group occupies a littoral to the northwest of Matarani, between Punta Coloca and La Huata. The other locates itself more to the northwest, dispersing between Tanaka and Ocoña. Both areas are characterized by steep rocky cliffs washed incessantly by raging, billowing waves, an ideal habitat for *Porphyra columbina*. Therefore the collection of *cochayuyo* involves seeking perilous places, which requires pluck to brave the danger. It is not rare to hear that a collector was carried off by high waves during his work.

Algae Collectors of Sibayo

The first group of algae collectors is constituted almost exclusively of the people of Sibayo, which is situated in the highlands at 3,900 m above sea-level in the Province of Cailloma, Department of Arequipa. Edmundo Corrales conducted an intensive study of these people which throws light on their activities on the coast. According to his research, they are agro-pastoral, and have a strong sense that they have a right to the littoral where they have collected *cochayuyo* "since the time of our ancestors" (*desde el tiempo de nuestros abolengos*) (Corrales 1979: 21). They used to form three *utañas*, "places to live." The three *utañas* are called Coloca, Carrizal, and La Punta (La Huata) respectively. An *utaña* is a small colony characterized by the concentration of several dwellings and a spring of fresh water. Each *utaña* has access to *lomas*, a seasonal meadow nurtured by a thick fog called *garúa*. The dwellings are shacks made of piled stones (*piedras pircadas*) with thatched roofs and conform to the style of highlands housing. A few permanent residents live in the three *utañas*, three in Carrizal, one in La Huata, and two in Arantas. They are called *orilleros* (Corrales 1983:49). The Sibayo families who come down to the coast to reside in an *utaña* are related to the *orilleros* by the tie of *compadrazgo*, which guarantees their temporal residence for the collection of *cochayuyo*. In other words, the *utaña* contitutes a rather closed world to people other than those of Sibayo.

The access of the Sibayo people to the coast seems to have a long history. Franklin Pease cites an interesting oral tradition concerning Inkarrí and his relationship to Sibayo.

> They say that Incarrí at one time descended to a high region called Callalli and started there. In Callalli the *ayllus* esteemed him much: He gave Callalli and Sibayo no more than firewood and livestock, because, situated so high, they could not have land for sowing. He left them especially firewood and pasture. He gave the Sibayo people the sea or the lomas. . . . Every year to this day they go fishing and for bringing those greens called *cochayuyo.* (Pease 1977:148–49)

The Sibayo people arrive at the coast in wintertime, between July and September, and stay there until November or in some cases until December, exploiting marine resources, principally algae. The algae collected include *cochayuyo*, *piscunchaqui* (*Almfeltia durvillaei*), and *huancapaqui* (*Gigartina tuberculosa*). The former is edible and the latter is used for medicinal purposes, but far greater emphasis is given to *cochayuyo.*

The seaweed collectors, once settled down in their *utaña,* begin working in the section which they call *chacra* (farmland). The *chacra* is a portion of coastline assigned to the head of each family by a *cabecilla* or president who acts on behalf of the community. This property grant was hereditary, and when a family head died without an heir, his *chacra* was returned to the community to be redistributed to someone else by the same procedure.

Collected seaweed is dried in the sun in wooden frames to be made into *planchas* (plates or sheets) (Masuda 1981:Foto 2). Every *utaña* possesses *planchaderos*, enclosures where *planchas* are made, and *hornos* (ovens), hermetically-made stone storehouses to store *planchas* under dry conditions. An oral tradition gathered at La Huata tells about a powerful god who once came down to the coast to partition *chacras* and about the first *hornos* contructed by the god (Corrales 1983:47).

Algae Collectors of Chala and Atico

The seaweed collectors who work on the northwest coast of Arequipa form a considerable number of colonies between Tanaka and Ocoña. All along the coastal strip between Tanaka and Chala, which corresponds approximately to the District of Atiquipa, one finds small villages of collectors in almost every arid gorge—Quebrada de la Vaca, Quebrada de Moca, Jihuay, and Tarillo among them. Between Chala and Atico, are Piedra Blanca, Punta de Lobos, Chorillos, and Playa Hermosa among others, and beyond Atico toward Ocoña are La Bodega, Oscuyo, and others.

The majority of the seaweed collectors are migratory. Like the people of Sibayo, they come down to the coast in July or August, where they stay until November or December. But unlike the Sibayo collectors, they do not object to the intrusion of outsiders, although there is a tendency for those of the same origin to group together. They do not assign *chacras* or use any other system of demarcation. Each one is quite free to choose a spot where he can collect seaweed and shellfish. Predominant in number are people from southern Ayacucho and northern Arequipa, such as Parinacochas and La Union. In Agua Salada, for instance, of the 25 families residing there in 1978, 22 were from the Parinacochas region and the rest from Cotahuasi in highland Arequipa. In Chorillos, the majority were from the Chuquibamba-Pampacolca region. However, there is a mixed type also. Punta de Lobo is a case in point. The residents in the winter of 1981 represented Pampacolca and Andagua (Arequipa), Parinacochas (Ayacucho), Sicuani (Cuzco), and Yunguyo (Puno).

It is possible to classify the villages of *cochayuyo* collectors in this region into three types. The first type preserves the simplest life style of algae collectors. They live in small caves or under ledges on a rocky shore and work individually. The craggy cliffs which lie between Tanaka and Chala are studded with rock-shelters which retain the traces of human habitation, and in the *cochayuyo* season they are occupied by people newly arrived from the highlands. They live there for two or three months in isolation. Sometimes, an area which abounds in caves and shelters is selected by a group of the same provenance. One good example is Tarillo near Atiquipa. Several families live there seasonally who are all from a highland village called Pisquicocha in the Department of Apurímac. Most people there are pastoralists of llamas and alpacas. As they are from the same community, to a certain extent they show social coherence and collectivity. But they lack any kind of integrated organization and governing mechanism, excepting the leadership sometimes wielded by some "big men." Yet this leadership is not strong enough to regiment other people's opinions about internal and external matters, and the residents are completely dependent on the will of the merchants and intermediaries of nearby towns for the sale of their products and food supply. Once the season is over, the place becomes vacant. All the people go back to their highland homes or travel to other places to look for temporary jobs.

The second type may be the most popular one among the collectors' colonies which lie around the towns of Chala and Atico. It is a congregation of straw huts, which has the outward appearance of a village. But it shares social characteristics with the first type in that it is devoid of systematic organization. It is amorphous, without any focus and direction. Though a resident's stay is temporary, naturally there can be certain forms of Andean reciprocity among the members of one group of dwellings. But it is surprising to see that in a place of this type, people are generally indifferent to what their neighbors do and they are often ignorant of the name and provenance of a nextdoor family. There is an incessant coming and going, depending on harvesting conditions.

The third type represents a sedentary colony which displays a nascent village-like organization. It is far from the type officially recognized as an administrative unit, with its heads and governing body. But its members are permanent residents, many of whom live in adobe huts with corrugated tin roofs. There is always a "big man" in this type of community, active and full of enterprising spirit. He knows how to direct and integrate people. He knows what to do to maximize profits by combining the labor of his fellow villagers and by finding the most remunerative way of selling products. An example of this can be seen in the history of Agua Salada, situated on a tableland between Tanaka and Atiquipa. Some influential families of the village participated actively in the affairs of collecting and selling products and transporting them in small vans to Chalhuanca, Abancay, and even as far as Cuzco. One man from one of the above families undertook to supply food and drink for the people of Tarillo and bought the seaweed collected by them. He was from the highland region of Arequipa and therefore bilingual. His fluent Quechua won him the confidence of the Tarillo neighbors. Therefore he took an active hand in the matters of Tarillo, capitalizing on the fear and distrust the highland people have of the *mestizo* population of the coast. He also played a positive role in the construction of the school and the church in the village. Chorillos, which is near Atico, has grown considerably in recent years, and the inhabitants are planning to establish a school for their children, thus following the example set by Agua Salada some twenty years ago.

Transformation of the Traditional Way of Life

The seaweed workers in the Chala-Atico region seem to be adapting themselves fairly well to the socio-economic changes which have been going on in the coastal zone of southern Peru over the last decades. Similarly, the people of Sibayo are now undergoing radical changes in their traditional way of life, as they receive more and more influence from the market economy of bigger cities. Formerly, they used to migrate to the littoral seasonally, organizing llama caravans. They drove herds of llamas following difficult mountain trails far from the roads frequented by cars, and arrived at their coastal *chacras* after an arduous trip of two weeks. Since a series of elaborate rituals were involved in the preparation and execution of the trip, they had to prepare not only provisions for their own consumption, but also some ritual objects such as yellow corn and llama fat. At the time of departure, they performed *tinka* to insure a peaceful journey and success in *cochayuyo* collection. Arriving at his *chacras*, each individual had to perform the *tinka* ceremony again, offering wine and barley chicha and "pay" (*pegamento*) to the traditional sea-goddess Mamacocha, mumbling an incantation. This is a practice which the Andean people have observed since prehispanic times, and Pablo José de Arriaga condemned it as one of the most unpardonable sins committed by Andean idolaters (Arriaga [1621] 1968: 201). This centuries-old tradition is now falling into obsolescence among the young generation of Sibayo (Corrales 1983:57–62). Today everybody takes the bus at Chivay and arrives at Matarani in a day. Contact with urban centers has strongly affected their lives, and some of the former algae collectors have ended up by becoming fishermen, merchants, and employees in Arequipa, Mollendo, and Matarani. Others have become middlemen and now go between urban markets and producers of *planchas* of *cochayuyo*. They have given up their *chacras*, which have fallen into the hands of relatives. The assignment procedure of *chacras* mostly remains a memory, and strict observance of demarcation is no longer expected. Undoubtedly, this phenomenon has much to do with the penetration of a market economy, and the development of road systems and bus transportation. However, there is something more. Edmundo Corrales thinks that the Sibayo people have been losing their traditional way of life for many reasons, but one natural phenomenon is largely responsible for it: the disappearance of the *lomas* (Corrales 1979: 68). I completely agree with him.

According to the information which Corrales obtained from an informant, the last herd of llamas arrived at the Matarani coast in 1953 (Corrales 1979:78). Since that time, there has been no llama caravan of Sibayo seen, simply because there has been no pasturage. In fact, a drought began in the middle fifties, not only in the *mitañas* of the Sibayos, but also on all of the southern coast of Peru. Climatological data bear this out: precipitation has diminished markedly since 1955 and is still low today. The absence of precipitation in the form of thick *garúa* has prevented the formation of *lomas*, thus depriving the Sibayos of valuable forage which is essential to the maintenance of their llamas in the *mitañas*. The herders and peasants of Sibayo can no longer observe the traditional system of vertically controlling *chacras* on the coast depending on llama herds.

The Lomas of Chala and Atico

Today, traveling along the Pan American Highway between Yauca and Ocoña in any season of the year, we hardly see anything green except in those few places where there is an irrigation system utilizing springs. The area is as arid as any other on the Peruvian coast, and villages such as Atiquipa and Chala Viejo are inactive places where people eke out a scanty livelihood. "There is no water for cultivation," the local people complain. Poor cattle and dying olive trees are all they have around them. The young people have gone. Even in broad daylight, the villages have the aspect of ghost towns, there being only a few aged men and women shut inside their houses.

But before the drought started in the 1950s, this coastal strip was very famous for the formation of *lomas*, perhaps one of the most fecund in all Peru. According to the aged of Atiquipa, they used to have dense *garúa* annually starting from August or September. Consequently, stock-breeding flourished, and the cultivation of olive trees and other plants prospered. Ramón Ferreyra, who conducted important investigations in the 1940s and 1950s on *lomas*, concludes that the place where there is a major concentration of vegetable species is the *lomas* of Chala, Atico, and Atiquipa (Ferreyra 1960:52–53). The fame of the *lomas* of the region dates back to the Colonial period. Father Bernabé Cobo, who devotes two entire chapters to the description of *garúa* and *lomas,* writes as follows:

> The most abundant *lomas* and pasture in all the coast is found in the diocese of Arequipa, i.e., the hills of Ilo, Atico, and Atiquipa, and in this diocese of Lima, i.e., the mountains of La Arena and the lomas of Pachacama and La Chay. It rains most there, grass grows most and lasts the longest. Pasture grows in those *lomas* one or two months after the appearance of *garúas,* and lasts as long as that stays or even more, i.e., until November and December. However, if there is not this strong moisture, it dries up in less than two months, and the hills regain natural sterile aridity. Thus those who saw so much green and colors at the time of *garúa* wonder how it turns into dryness in two months. They do not feel certain that such dry, sterile, and for the most part sandy places could nurture so much grass and

pasture, and that in such a short time all the flowers and green could dry up and disappear (Cobo [1653] 1956: I, 88).

Another chronicler, Vázquez de Espinosa, touches on the *lomas* and exuberant vegetation and cattle raising in the same region.

> Twelve leagues from the Valley of Hacari toward the south is situated the Valley of Chala, where they produce the best olive oil and fruits in all this Kingdom and some wine. Before reaching there and in the same mouth of the valley to the sea, there is the *lomas* of Atiquipa, which is the best of the coast. All the year round, livestock farming prospers there—cattle, mules, horses, goats, and sheep, and the number is great. There are fountains and streams all the year round. This is quite rare in other *lomas*, and because of this, animals can graze comfortably. In these *lomas*, there are some farmhouses and ranches, with gardens and orchards of Spanish and native fruits. Very good fig and olive trees grow. A quantity of wheat, corn, and other crops are harvested. Many become rich raising stock, because of the advantage they have over other regions. These *lomas* are near the seashore and extend into the interior more than two leagues (Vázquez de Espinosa [1629] 1969:334–35).

This situation prevailed as late as the 1950s. The aged informants of Chala and Atiquipa testify to the great crowd of domestic animals which filled the *lomas* fields. There were many which belonged to the farmers of Atiquipa, Chala, Cháparra, and Yauca. At the same time quite a few came from the mountain areas led by herders —cattle, sheep, and even llamas. The season of *garúa* and *lomas* exactly coincides with the time of drought in the highlands when there is a shortage of pasture. Naturally the herders of Parinacochas and Aymaraes did not fail to utilize the plentiful resources which *lomas* offer for their animals.

A very important fact in connection with our topic is that those pastoral people who used to come to the *lomas* of Chala and Atiquipa frequently availed themselves of maritime resources including *cochayuyo*. We have testimony of an algae collector of Pisquicocha, aged 37 in 1981, who used to go to Agua Salada accompanying his father. In the early 1950s, he says, they traveled all the way from Apurimac down to the coast walking with a herd of llamas. They used to bring 15 or 20 llamas on each trip. Starting from Pisquicocha, Apurímac, they passed through Incuyo, and, entering into the Valley of Cháparra, arrived in Chala on the eighth day. The first thing they did upon their arrival was to construct a shanty, leaving their llamas to pasture. Then they engaged in *cochayuyo* collection for two or three weeks. Already in those days buyers of seaweed went to and fro along the coast, and collectors sold the better part of their harvest to them. They did not prepare *planchas* as they do now but loosely piled up the dried weed. The dried weed was packed in bags, each of which contained two or three *arrobas* (one arroba is 11.5 kg). On their return journey 80 percent of their bags were filled with articles they bought with the money obtained by the sale of *cochayuyo*—dried figs, dried olives, rice, sugar. The rest, that is to say, three or four bags, were of *cochayuyo.* On each trip, some ten *arrobas* of *cochayuyo* were transported to their native place. It was important for barter with other highland peasants rather than for their own consumption. One ounce of *cochayuyo* could be bartered for ten or twenty ears of maize. Some of the peasants bought as much as four or five ounces, because they liked *picante* with *cochayuyo,* as the informant says.

The Importance of Lomas to Herders in Their System of Vertical Control

We have already seen how the maritime activity of pastoral people is related to the formation of *lomas.* At the time when *lomas* used to appear periodically, the traditional form of pastoral life followed the well-established pattern of transhumance, combined with the exploitation of marine products. It is significant that the algae collectors of Sibayo employed the term *chacra* to denote the place of maritime production. To them, *cochayuyo* and shellfish hunting were an efficacious way of utilizing lowland resources, just as in the case of agrarian production in Sama and Moquegua by the Lupaqa people. We do not know why the Lupaqas produced corn and wheat in Colonial times. They might have been important as complementary foodstuff, or they might have been used for barter. But in the case of algae, we are inclined to think that it constituted one of the important media of economic exchange employed by pastoral people. Important resources are out of reach for the pastoral people who live in the *puna* more than 4,000 m high. To come by complementary foodstuffs such as maize, potatoes, and wheat, they have to barter with their products—jerked meat and wool. Certainly *cochayuyo* could be a welcome addition, because it is a product much coveted in the highland region. The witness from Pisquicocha shows us the importance of purchasing merchandise with the money obtained from the sale of *cochayuyo*, and testifies as to the relatively limited amount of *cochayuyo* transported to the mountain areas. In his youth the monetary economy was already beginning to penetrate into remote, provincial areas. But in the days of Vásquez de Espinosa, the circulation of money was extremely limited and the rural area hardly felt the impact of the market economy. To the Andean people of the early Colonial period, cash was something to be used for tax payment. It had very little to do with subsistence, which largely depended on self-production and barter. In such circumstances, *cochayuyo* must have had much more importance as a means of gaining basic materials necessary for subsistence. Indeed, it would not be excessive to say that it might have played a role as a "special purpose money" in older days, something like cacao in the prehispanic commerce of Mesoamerica.

María Rostworowski, in her significant contribution to the study of *lomas,* points up its importance in prehispanic and Colonial economy. She claims that "*lomas* and their natural resources were in the power of coastal people, at least until the sixteenth century," and that desire for pasturage by highlanders was satisfied after the Spanish invasion, when the coast suffered the demographic catastrophe and economic disorganization of the *reducciones* (Rostworowski 1981:53–54). This may hold true for the smaller *lomas* dotted along the central coast. However, in the rich *lomas* such as those of Atiquipa and Chala, there is a possibility that the highland herders could have had access to pasturage without disturbing the peasants and herders of the coast. One informant of Atiquipa testifies to the peaceful coexistence between coastal herds and highland animals in the *lomas* of his region in the 1940s and 1950s. There is no reason to assume the same did not hold for preceding centuries. If so, it might be said that the vertical control of *lomas* by the pastoralists of the *puna* had its roots in prehispanic times.

Botanically, several kinds of *lomas* can be distinguished. Mikio Ono classifies five sorts (cf. Craig in this volume)—Herbaceous *lomas*, Shrubby *lomas*, Bromelian *lomas,* Tillandsia *lomas,* and Cacti *lomas*. Herbaceous *lomas* is most suited for pasturing. Though *lomas* have an extensive distribution, perhaps from Trujillo (see Craig in the volume) to Antofagasta, Herbaceous *lomas* are confined to central and southern Peru (Ono 1982). According to a study of the distribution of *lomas* vegetation by Shuichi Oka and Hajime Ogawa, Herbaceous *lomas* abound more on the south than on the central coasts (Fig. 10.1) Moreover, on the central coast, Tillandsia *lomas* predominate in lower altitudes, while in the south, especially between 15°50′S and 17°S (that is to say, between Tanaka and Mollendo approximately), Herbaceous *lomas* show a major extension in altitude, and cover a zone from 1,200 m high down to the seashore (Fig. 10.2).

Here we go back to a point which we dealt with at the beginning of

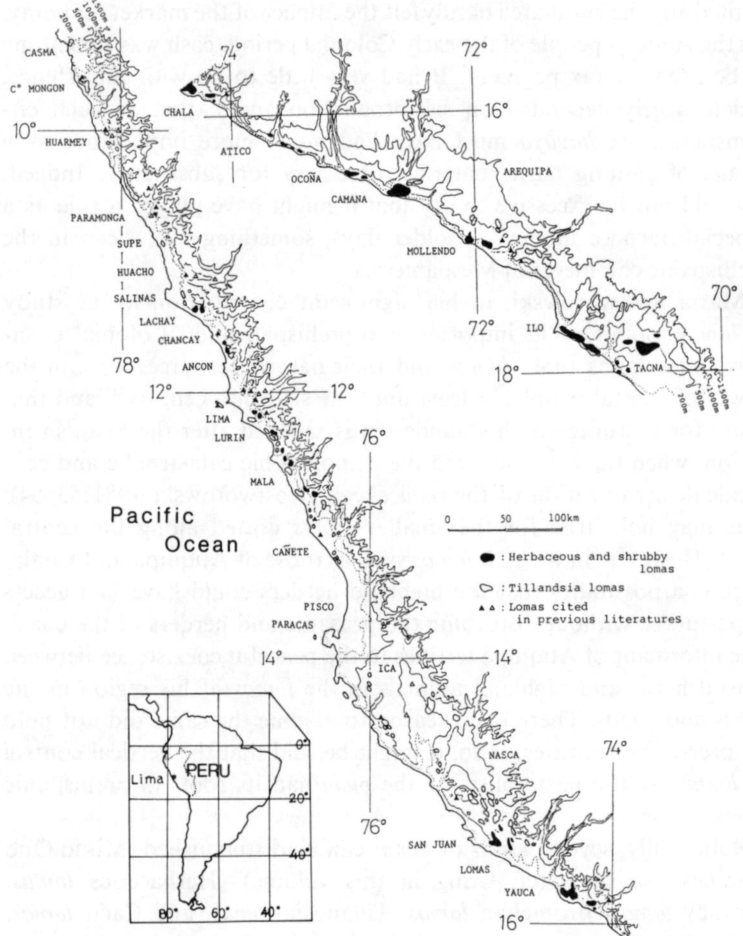

Fig. 10.1 Distribution of *lomas* vegetation along the Peruvian Pacific Coast (Oka and Ogawa 1984)

this article: the distribution of different kinds of seaweeds on the Peruvian coast. As was already explained, south of Nazca *Porphyra columbina* is the predominant seaweed collected and utilized for food. The northern limit is defined somewhere between Ica and Nazca. North of that extends a vacuum zone where there is no ethnographic utilization of seaweed. For instance, the inhabitants of the valleys of Chincha and Cañete show little interst in *cochayuyo*, and it is not sold in their markets. North of Lima, perhaps from Chancay to the north

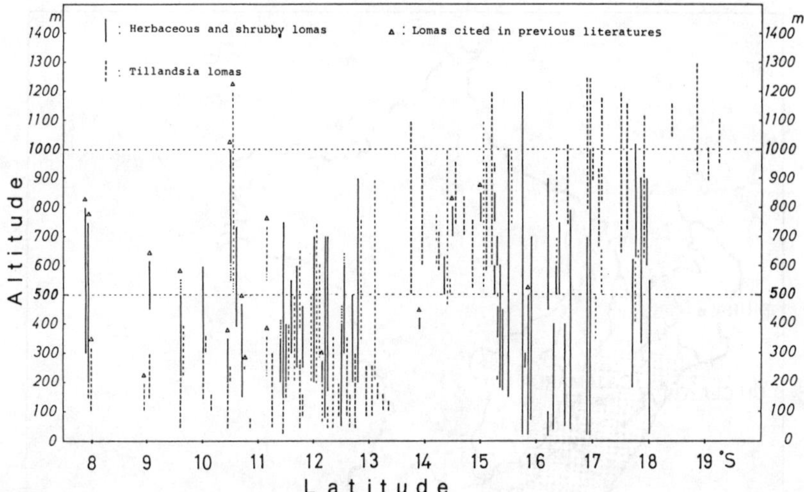

Fig. 10.2 Vertical distribution of *lomas* vegetation (Oka and Ogawa 1984)

begins another zone of seaweed-eating. There, a different kind called *Gigartina chamissoi* is collected and eaten. This zone extends as far north as Chiclayo. But strangely enough, at the Sechura desert this interest in *cochayuyo* ends and in the extreme north of Peru people are quite indifferent to seaweed as a food resource. Both *Porphyra* and *Gigartina* exist on all parts of the Peruvian coast, but the people of the south are not interested in *Gigartina* and those of the north neglect *Porphyra.* (Fig. 10.3). Evidently, it is a cultural selection, and as in any other case of cultural difference, the reason will be complex and hard to answer. However, we are at least able to say that the collection of *cochayuyo* in the south by highlanders has been supported by ecological conditions favoring the formation of *lomas,* which extend down to the seashore and make it possible for herders to bring their llamas to the coast.

Before concluding, it will be worth while asking how people reacted to the socio-economic changes which resulted from climatological alteration. Certainly, the drought caused much hardship to local peasants and herders. But the algae collectors, facing the disappearance of pasture, resorted to another means of transportation and continued their work. They arrive at the coast by bus, and, instead of carrying back dried seaweed to their mountain homes on the backs of llamas, they sell the product directly in the market, thus penetrating further into the urban economy and getting hold of more cash. It is to be noted

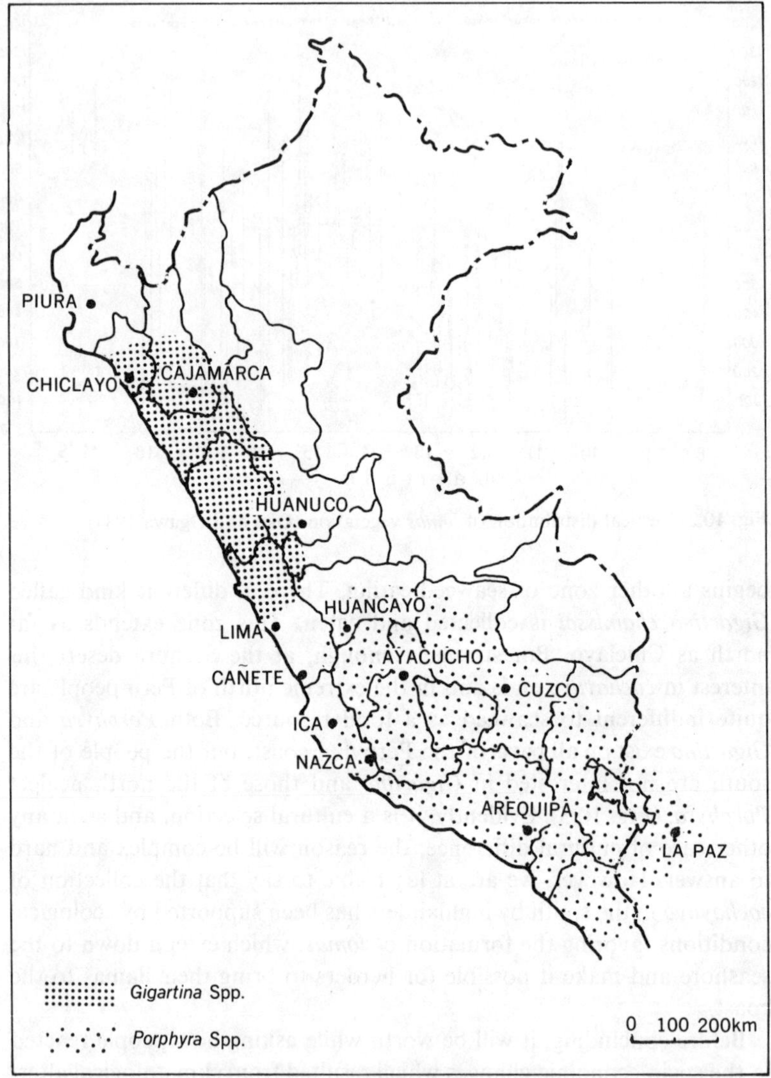

Fig. 10.3 Distribution of two species of *cochayuyo* in Peru.

that a group of algae collectors began to settle down in Agua Salada precisely at the moment when the drought began, in spite of the protests of the Atiquipa people. They began to coordinate the production of *cochayuyo*, looking for lucrative markets for sale, and even selling *planchas* themselves by van or motorcycle. They also seek other sources of income, and are hired for rice-planting in Camaná or for the harvest of olives in Yauca (Masuda 1981:186–87). The descent of El Niño in 1983 was another catastrophe which caused a serious problem for them. The rise of water temperature affected seaweeds and shellfish disastrously. Yet the *cochayuyo* collectors of Chala and Atico hold on in one way or another. However, the kind of climatological changes which we are witnessing at present, the drought and the change of ocean current, could have occurred in past years. We want to ask, therefore, how such natural changes affected the system of vertical control in older days, when there were few mechanisms to defend oneself against the forces of nature. Could the herders of the past find any other means of subsistence, or did a great climatological change mean a radical deformation or even destruction of their system and their culture?

REFERENCES CITED

Acleto, César

1971 Algas marinas del Perú de importancia económica. Universidad Nacional Mayor de San Marcos, Museo de Historia Natural "Javier Prado," Departamento de Botánica, Serie de Divulgación 5.

Aldunate del Solar, Carlos

1971 Cultura Mapuche, Santiago, Chile.

Alveal, K. L.

1970 Estudios ficoecológicos de la región costera de Valparaiso. Revista de Biología Marina 14 (1):7–88.

Arriaga, Pablo José de

[1621] 1968 Extirpación de la idolatría del Perú. *In* Crónicas peruanas de interés indígena. Francisco Estebe Barba, ed. pp. 191–277. Madrid: Editorial Atlas.

Cobo, Fray Bernabé

[1653] 1956 Historia del Nuevo Mundo, Madrid: Editorial Atlas.

Corrales Valdivia, Edmundo Luis

1979 Litoral de Isla y Piso Ecológico Collagua. Tesis presentada a Universidad Nacional de San Agustín de Arequipa, Perú.

1983 El mito tenía razón. *In* Historia 2:43–66 Arequipa.

Erize, Esteban

1960 Diccionario Mapuche-Español. Santiago, Chile.

Etcheverry D., Hector

1958 Biblíografía de las algas chilenas. Revista de Biología Marina 7 (1–3):63–182. Valparaíso.

Ferreyra, Ramón

1960 Algunos aspectos fitogeográficos del Perú. *In* Monografías y

Ensayos. Publicaciones del Instituto de Geografía, Serie 1, No. 3: 41–88. Lima.

Jiménez de la Espada, Marcos, ed.
1965 Relaciones geográficas de Indias, Perú. Madrid: Editorial Atlas.

Marti Silva, Eduardo Alberto R.
1975 Composición y aprovechamiento de algas marinas. Tesis presentada a Universidad Austral, Valdivia.

Masuda, Shozo
1981 Cochayuyo, macha, camarón e higos charqueados. *In* Estudios etnográficos del Perú meridional. Masuda, S., ed. pp. 173–92. Tokyo: University of Tokyo.
1982 Dinamismo inter-regional en los Andes Centrales. Senri Ethnological Studies 10: 93–106.

Oka, Shuichi and Hajime Ogawa
1984 The Distribution of Lomas Vegetation and Its Climatic Environments Along the Pacific Coast of Peru. Geographical Reports of Tokyo Metropolitan University 19. Tokyo.

Ono, Mikio, ed.
1982 A Preliminary Report of Taxonomic and Ecological Studies on the Lomas Vegetation in the Pacific Coast of Peru. Tokyo.

Ovalle, Alonso de
[1649] 1969 Historia del reino de Chile. Santiago, Chile: Instituto de Literatura Chilena.

Pease G.Y., Franklin
1977 Collaguas: Una etnía del siglo XVI. Problemas inciales. *In Collaguas I,* Pease G. Y., Franklin, ed. pp. 148–49. Lima: Pontificia Universidad Católica del Perú.

Rojas Labarca, Julio A.
1975 Evaluación nutritiva de *Ulva lactuca.* Tesis presentada a Universidad Austral, Valdivia.

Rostworowski, María
1977 Etnía y sociedad: Costa peruana prehispánica. Lima: Instituto de Estudios Peruanos.
1981 Recursos naturales renovables y pesca. Siglos XVI y XVII. Lima: Instituto de Estudios Peruanos.

Vázquez de Espinosa, Antonio
[1629] 1969 Compendio y descripción de las Indias Occidentales. Madrid: Editorial Atlas.

11

Interaction and Complementarity in Three Zones of Cuzco

Jorge Flores Ochoa

Introduction

Three zones of Cuzco (Fig. 11.1) are described which do not correspond to three cases but rather to three levels of social complexity in order to appreciate the differences and similarities in the way in which present day communities at different altitudes interact and complement each other. The communities have certain predominant forms of agricultural production as well as agricultural products which they use to obtain products from other ecological zones or the surplus of which they can make use of.

We will go from least to greatest complexity, beginning with the zone which shows the most isolation in terms of the kind of urban life in the main centers of population, the presence of roads for motorized vehicles, and the presence of the market system and marketplaces.

Vilcabamba

Vilcabamba is a district of the province of Convención, which, according to the 1981 census, has 14,705 residents of which 183 live in the district's main town, the capital, at an altitude of 3,500 meters above sea level.

The area studied lies three days' walk from Vilcabamba above the Apurimac River basin, which in that region forms a warm valley below an altitude of 2,000 meters. Here the departments of Apurímac, Ayacucho, and Cuzco come together, conscribed by the Apurímac and Pampas rivers and near where the latter joins the former. The department of Apurímac makes a rapid descent from 4,000 to 2,000 meters

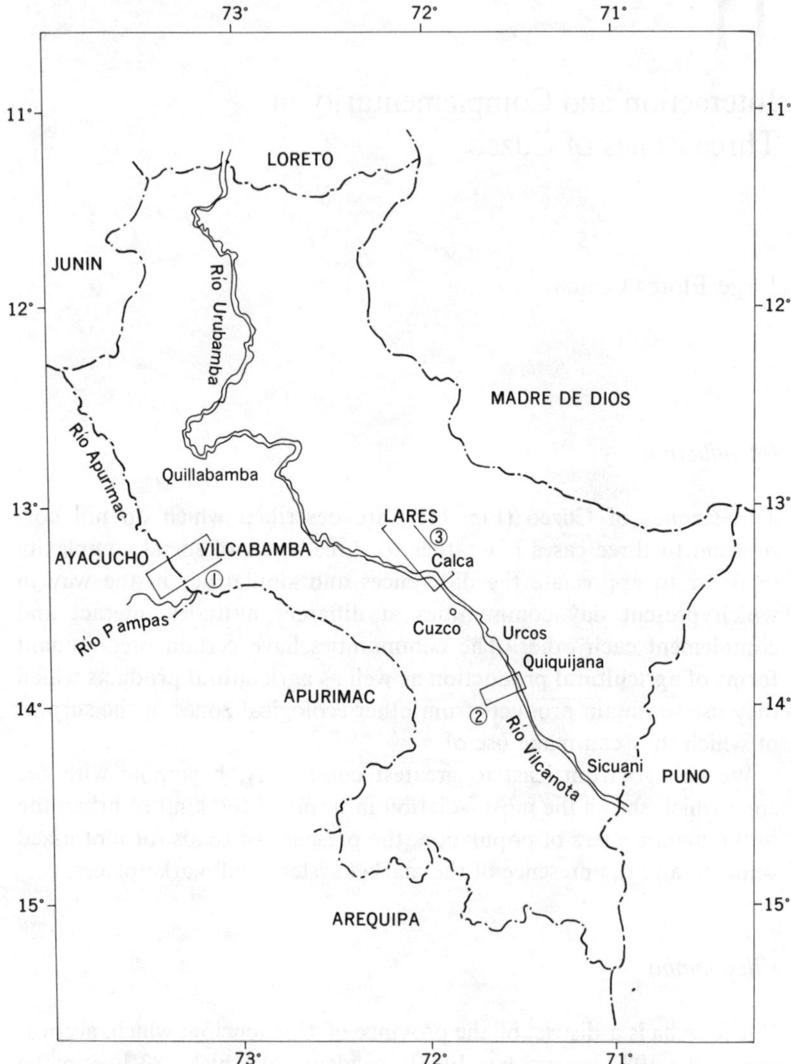

Fig. 11.1 The Department of Cuzco

at the bottom of the valley through which flows the Apurímac River. Heat and humidity in the form of fog which ascends the valley modify the temperature of the high parts, including the *puna* located above 3,900 meters. A road which is sometimes passable by vehicles is under construction to Vilcabamba, and the intention is to extend it to the department of Ayacucho.

There are several indigenous peasant communities distributed over different altitudes in the zone (Fig. 11.2). I shall refer to Incawasi and Choquetira[1] which are located at intermediate elevations between altitudinal zones typical of the southern Peruvian highlands. Choquetira has lands from the *qeshwa* and the *puna*[2]; Inkawasi has lands in the *qeshwa* and in the *yunga*.

The hamlet of Choquetira has the greatest population and exercises a certain type of jurisdiction over the people of Trancapata and Ligiana in the *puna*, over Aqobamba, Paltaytamba, and Lucuypata in the *qeshwa* zone, and over Cedrobamba and Tronca in the *yunga*. The settlements of the community of Inkawasi are spread out along the Mapillo River which descends into the Apurímac River. In the *qeshwa* one finds San Martín (formally Qasapata), Inkawasi itself, and Uchupuqru; in the *yunga* there is Erapata, Sarpampa, Apaylla, Aquililla, and Pacaypampa.

There are important archaeological sites in the region. The monuments are of the Inca period, and one should mention the Inca road which joined Cuzco with Ayacucho by crossing the Apurímac River at the Pumachaca bridge of which only the stone bases remain.

On the slopes above the Apurímac River there are populations such as Carco, San Fernando, and Pipiqata. On the shores of the river on the beach located in the *yunga* is Yauyaco which is rather important because it functions as a "port"[3] facilitating the exchange of products with the residents of the opposite shore of the river belonging to the departments of Ayacucho and Apurímac.

The main *yunga* products are coca, yuca, coffee, sweet potato, hot peppers (*ají*), *unkucha*, "valley maize", peanuts, broadbeans, and sugar cane. In the *qeshwa* one has maize, broadbeans, squashes, and pumpkins. In the *puna* potatoes, *oca*, *mashua*, *olluco*, *tarwi*, and *quinua* predominate. The following varieties of potatoes are cultivated: *puca*, *palta*, *cusi*, *vacahuasi* (in three colors—black, white, and red), *bole*, *huspa talega* (a potato representative of Vilcabamba; *kañigua*, and *huywan* (two types—yellow and red). The potatoes which have been introduced into the region are: *cuzco*, *mariva*, *ilave*, *yungay*, and *wayro*. Cows, horses, and goats are properly found in the *yunga*; in the *qeshwa* and *puna* sheep predominate with some cattle and horses. Choquetira has direct access to sheep and potatoes as its main products.

Incawasi has the following main varieties of maize: *Valle grande*, *Valle cubano*, *Valle chico*, *Janca sara* with *Yuroc* (white), *almidón*, *morocho colorado*, *morocho* with *punya*, and *pirisinco*. Incawasi has very few potatoes and no direct access to cattle. Communities such as Yunkay, which is very small with little land, have only patches planted

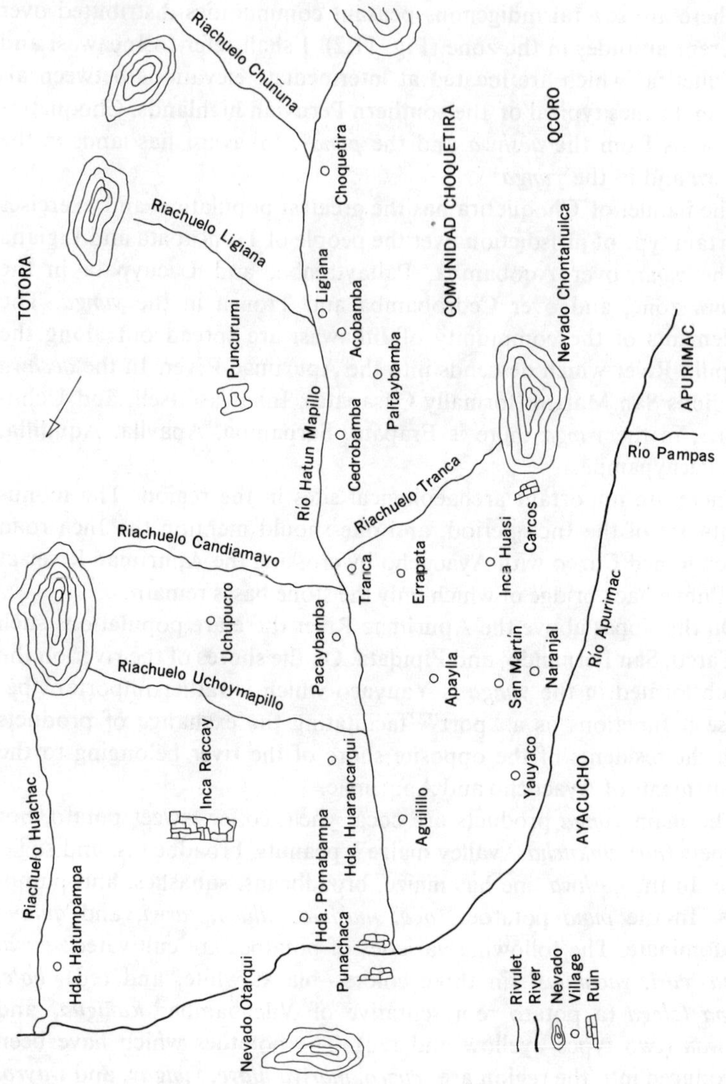

Fig. 11.2 Vilcabamba

with coca. In the lower sectors of its territory, Choquetira has successfully planted *puca sara*, the *puna* maize. The heat and humidity which ascend the Apurímac River create a special microclimate modifying the influence of altitude, and in the Andes this is very important for differentiating the environments and their typical products.

The cultivation of coca on the shores and the lands along the Apurímac River is of great commercial importance because it is an exchange product for which buyers come great distances—including even the pastoral people from the *punas* of Ayacucho and Andahuaylas.

The best coca (*moqllu*) seeds are brought in on horseback from Quillabamba. They are also acquired in Vacachacra where coca is planted on a greater scale. While other crops are growing, coca is cultivated on the same land. A process called *pisado* is applied to the coca harvest, and this gives it greater commercial value, because it is considered sweeter than the non-*pisada* or *hacha coca.* The coca which grows at higher altitudes is the best because it is sweeter, softer, and has thin leaves. The coca from lower lands is thick and bitter. *Awki* coca comes in two varieties, long-leaved and round-leaved, and the latter is considered better because it does not become diseased. The coca from the region of Incawasi is well known and is preferred to that from other valleys of the Convención. Those of the *banda*, as those of Ayacucho and Apurímac are called, and also the peasants from nearby Choquetira hold the coca from Incawasi in high regard. Those of the *banda* bring in exchange smoked and salted meat, potatoes, wheat, wool, cheeses, flour, dried and salted meat, ropes, llama and vicuña fat, sheep, horses, cows, and pigs, in addition to other industrial, craft, or other agricultural products. They first want to obtain coca, but they are also attracted by the coffee, *achiote*, cane, cattle hides, oranges, avocados, and *chirimoyas.*

Those of the *banda* transport their products on llamas and horses. Those from Pampachiri in Andahuaylas are most common in the number and frequency of their trips. The llamas cross the Apurímac River on rafts. Commerce is more intense from May to August. Other visitors who bring potatoes come from the communities of Chicmo, Champacocha, Argoma, Hascatoy, Huancarama, Talavera, and Andahuaylas, all from Apurímac. Those from Ayacucho come from Chapi, Mollebamba, Umaca, Chanta, Troja, Qasi, and Huamanga.

The measurements used for exchange remain relatively stable. Some of those utilized in 1981 were:

A cow is worth two *quintales* of coca[4]
A pig for an *arroba* of coca

An *arroba* of potatoes for a pound of coca
A *quintal* of wheat for one *arroba* of coca
A load of potatoes for a load of yuca
A young ram for a load of yuca
A sheepskin for three loads of yuca
A pound of coca for a load of yuca
A load of maize for a load of potatoes
An *arroba* of potatoes for three pounds of coffee
An *arroba* of potatoes for four pounds of salt
An *arroba* of potatoes for four pounds of sugar
Seven loads of potatoes for one sheep
One load of potatoes for one load of corn
One sheep for six to eight loads of corn
One yearling bull for 20 to 25 loads of corn
One arroba of hot peppers (*ají*) for two loads of corn
One *arroba* of hot peppers (*ají*) for two loads of potatoes
Three *arrobas* of hot peppers (*ají*) for one sheep
One *arroba* of hot peppers (*ají*) for a costal of wheat

In 1981 a load of coca cost 1,500 to 1,800 *soles*; a load of yuca costs 1,000 *soles*.[5]

Maize and coca go together as do potatoes and cattle in the relations among the communities of the Mapillo basin which have direct access to these products and establish a transverse relation to obtain products that neighboring communities have available for exchange. Thus there is a direct relation which permits the supply of what they do not produce. These relations are established among the communities of the eastern edge of the Apurímac River, but they are not carried out with communities from the other side of the river since they produce the same things.

People of the *puna* like yuca because it is a special food, and in June and July the inhabitants of Choquetira and Yanahuanca come down to obtain it in exchange for potatoes and young rams. Goods and people are transported by horse or mule, the most-used means because muleteering is still very much alive. The families up high have horses and do not raise llamas or alpacas. The *mio-mio* pasture poisons them.

People from Inkawasi acquire horses and mules in Quillabamba which come from Cuzco, Chumbivilcas, Yauri, Espinar, Paucartambo, and Chinchaypuqyu. Those of the *banda* bring them from Andahuaylas, Grau, Huancarama, Pampachiri, and occasionally from Ayacucho. On the average, a young mule costs 100,000 *soles*; a horse 80,000.

A horse for two *quintales* of coca
A horse for eight *quintales* of coffee
A horse for 15 loads of potatoes

Pigs are valued for their meat and for the lard they produce. A pound of lard is worth three pounds of coffee and a pound of coca. Pigs are also used to get additional labor for agricultural work. One pound of pork or one pound of lard is given for a day's work. Very rarely is lard or pork sold. A pig is worth five or six thousand *soles*. Chickens are abundant and cost 1,800 *soles*. They are exchanged in the following way:

One chicken for a *vellón* (sheepskin)
One chicken for a guinea pig
One chicken for two pounds of coca

The value of chickens is relatively high because they are used for community and family *fiestas*. They are used to prepare fancy dishes that are essential to certain rites such as the first haircutting, All Saints' Day (Nov. 1), the Day of the Dead, "rooster grabbing" contests (horse races to grab roosters suspended from a crosspiece), and religious *cargos* and communal work. Similarly expensive are guinea pigs which are valued at 500 *soles*, and are very desirable. They are used to prepare special dishes for festive and ritual occasions such as marriages (especially in the *warmi horgoy* part of a marriage when the bride leaves her father's household), birthdays, communal work, and similar activities. Also, guinea pigs are exchanged for coca, rice, sugar, or chickens.

There are no market sites[6] where buyers and sellers come together periodically. The Mapillo River basin interacts by way of roads between the communities of the high part (*puna-qeshwa*) and those of the low part (*yunga*). The variety of products available to them is complemented and supplemented through the llama trains that come from the *banda*.

The lack of market sites does not mean that there are no commercial monetary transactions. Outside products are bought with money. Also, one goes out to sell, even to Vilcabamba and Quillabamba. Money is acquired by selling products or by going to work for a salary. In the houses of some peasants there are little shops which sell outside goods such as sugar, alcohol, canned fish, beer, matches, candles, cigarettes, kerosene, crackers, candies, or noodles. Sometimes the shops only offer alcohol. To get other goods, people go to Yupanca at the end of the highway under construction with potatoes, *moraya* (fine white *ch'uño*), and sheep to sell or exchange for coca, coffee, yuca, fruits, and hot peppers (*ají*). With money from sales they buy sugar, salt, noodles, and similar goods.

Professional travelling merchants visit the zone. They come from outside the area, going from community to community carrying merchandise on their backs or sometimes on animals borrowed from friends. One can distinguish at least three types of itinerant merchants. There are the *bayeteros* who offer homespun cloth of sheep's wool. They may be intermediaries or the weavers themselves. They come from the provinces of Canchis, Yauri, or Espinar which are the "high provinces" of the Department of Cuzco, and they belong to agricultural-herding communities with sheep, alpacas, and llamas. They are also known as *sicuaneños* or *qollas*, a name which today is given to natives of the *altiplano* and, in a broader sense, to those who come from south of Quiquijana. They also sell clothing or exchange it for coca, coffee, or hot peppers (*ají*).

Other merchants are the *wasaq'epi* (bearers, in *runa simi*) who come from different provinces of Cuzco. Their name was originally limited to travelling traders from the province of Acomayo in the Department of Cuzco. They distribute merchandise from cities or other distant zones of production such as rice, noodles, sugar, flour, alcohol, canned goods, tools, utensils, radios, sandals, harmonicas, flashlight batteries, spoons, knives, pots, plates, and scales for weighing called *romanas*. They sell them, or exchange them, for coca, coffee, hot peppers (*ají*), and skins. Equivalents such as the following are used in exchange:

A sack of sugar for two and a half *quintales* of coffee
A sack of noodles for two and a half *arrobas* of coffee
A box of lard for two and a half *arrobas* of coffee
An *arroba* of salt for an *arroba* of coffee
A box of canned tuna fish for a *quintal* of coffee

The third group are the cattlemen who specialize in the buying and selling of beef cattle. They are from various places including the *banda*. The general consensus of opinion identifies cattle merchants with outsiders from urban centers. They carry money and pay in cash, although it is not uncommon to pay with manufactured items such as radios, record players, and tape recorders. They drive the cattle to urban centers to sell it as meat in the supply markets.

These intermediaries also occasionally deal in products which more properly belong to other ecological levels. As good businessmen, they do not neglect any opportunity presented them to gain profits, given that each transaction enlarges their take. A big part of their activities is accomplished by walking or using animals to carry burdens. They go from community to community, leaving what they acquire or offer in houses of friends or acquaintances whom they treat as *compadres* and with whom they have a fluid relationship of a permanent type. Roads and trucks have increased their mobility and extended their range of activity. The intermediaries known as *huamanguinos* who come from the *banda* bring their products on llamas traveling several days or even weeks. In the region, as I said, they do not raise llamas or alpacas and use other types of animals for transportation and for cargo.

In an aside I shall now make some reference to the commerce of *qochayuyu* (seaweed) and other important maritime products (Corrales 1983, Masuda 1981). The best quality of *qochayuyu* is said to come from Hoyelos and Hojas, and it is bought in Quillabamba and Andahuaylas. The *huamanguinos* are the suppliers who provide the best *qochayuyu* which comes from Chiclayo. Heed should be paid to this statement, since a great distance separates Vilcabamba from Chiclayo. It is improbable that the merchants make such long trips. There is evidence that the herders of Huancavelica go to the highlands of Arequipa for llamas which they then take to Cerro de Pasco (Timoteo Trucios Ayuque, pers. com., F. Valderrama 1983).

Qochayuyu is sold or exchanged for coca. The *planchas* (blocks)[7] are sold by the pound or by *arroba*. A pound costs 1,000 *soles*. It is used to make fancy dishes on special days like marriages, the first haircutting, and communal agricultural work.

The high cost of *qochayuyu* makes some people replace it with *monte qochayuyu,* a plant that grows on the trees and rocky terrain.

The equivalences for the exchange of *qochayuyu* are:

A pound of *qochayuyu* for a pound of coca
Two cakes of *qochayuyu* for a pound of peanuts
Two cakes of *qochayuyu* for a pound of hot peppers (*ají*)

Quiquijana

The capital of the district of the same name, Quiquijana is located in the province of Quispicanchis. It lies at an altitude of 3,210 meters on the edges of the Vilcanota River, above the highway (currently being paved) which connects Cuzco with Puno, and above the railroad, which similarly connects the two cities. The district has 8,940 inhabitants, of which 1,213 live in the capital; the remainder is the rural population.

The Quiquijana as a district capital has schools, a civil guard post, and a parish church. It is also a railroad station. Sellers of articles of primary necessity are to be found daily in its big plaza. Sunday is market day. A great number of sellers and buyers, mainly from nearby communities, come together, as do intermediary sellers who bring merchandise from outside for local consumption that complements the peasants' needs.

In the communities and ex-*haciendas* of the valley maize is the chief crop. It is of good quality and thus sold in the city of Cuzco. The other crops come from the *qeshwa* zone (Gade 1975).

The valley is narrow, created by the very steep slope toward the communities. Passing rapidly from the *qeshwa* zone to the *puna,* one finds pastures for herding.

The communities of Pataquehar and Waqwaqocha (Fig. 11.3), also called Waqwalaguna, are found on the left bank of the Vilcanota River looking downriver. Pataquehuar is located at an altitude of 3,900 meters and is also called Pataquehuar Alto as opposed to Pampaquehuar, or Quehuar Bajo. It is divided into five sectors that are *kancha* (*kancha*, in *runa simi*, means "place with corrals") Waman, Pumawasi, Antallaqta, and Mancoran. The population varies by sectors. The most numerous has no more than 300; the least does not exceed 100.

Agricultural production predominates over cattle raising. The main crops are potatoes, *oca*, *lisa*, *año*, and *broadbeans*. The number of varieties of potatoes shows their importance and the role they play in the communal economy. The varieties are: *pukapaltuna*, *yanapaltuna*, *muru paltuna*, *inkalo*, *yurak paltuna*, *chimu*, *puka chimu*, *pitikiña*, *chalka*, *yuraq pitikiña*, *yana pitikiña*, *qompis*, and *waña*. The *yanapaltuna* with the *pukapaltuna*, and the *inkalo* are the best for making *ch'uño*. For *moraya*, the finest white *ch'uño*, *wañu* is preferred. Because of its high location, the community has fine conditions for making *ch'uño* and *moraya*, both forms of dehydrating the potato by nightly cold and daily heat.

Animal herding centers around sheep. Each family has 30 or 40 head. The useful llama does not exceed 10 or 20 animals per family, and each family's four or five alpacas is too limited for them to have any economic importance other than to provide fiber for family use. Families never have more than two or three burros or horses, and not all have them. Sheep are the source of wool for domestic use or for exchange for products of low zones, and of meat for eating, sale, and exchange. Llamas follow in importance for their ability to carry burdens because the people can use them to transport products that they wish to use in commercial exchanges, and to take care of their own needs

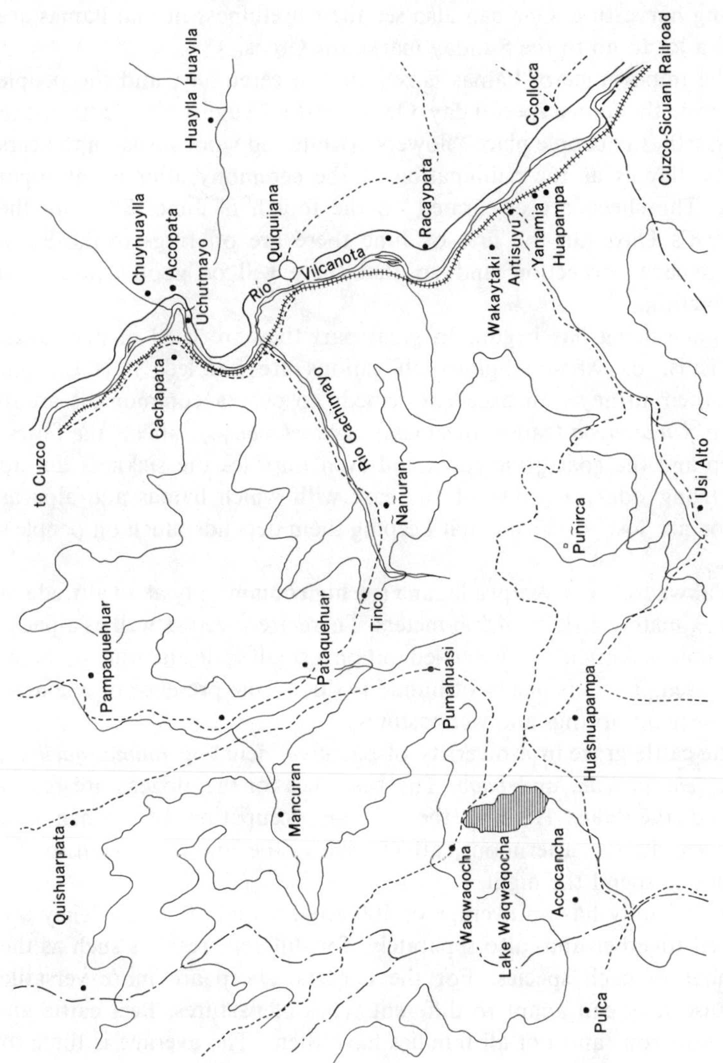

Fig. 11.3 Quiquijana

during harvesting. One can also see their usefulness in that llamas are used a lot to go to the Sunday market in Urcos.

The importance of llamas is reflected in ceremony, and the people celebrate them on a special day. On the first of August also dedicated to the Earth, the people place "flowers" (white-red wool yarns) in the ears of the llamas as the culmination of the ceremony after an all-night vigil. The sheep are celebrated on the fourth of June, St. John the Baptist's Day. On the first of June there are offerings to the Earth to concede protection and so that there will be good agricultural production.

Goat raising has begun. In great part they are used in marriages, baptisms, or when religious obligations are fulfilled. It is thought that their urine is an excellent remedy to cure a common disease in sheep. *Umamuyoq* (causes dizziness) or *mucho onqoy*, affects the fattest sheep and the goat urine cures and even impedes the sickness due to its strong odor. Because of the ease with which llamas and alpacas die or are lost, it is said that keeping them depends much on people's luck.

Wakwaqocha or Waqwa laguna is a high community at an altitude of approximately 4,200 to 4,500 meters. There are sheep as well as alpacas and llamas. Agriculture is carried out on a small scale and only potatoes are raised. There is plenty of humidity due to the presence of a lake as well as many springs and wet pastures.

The cattle graze in a diversity of pastures including *tullma*, *quellma*, *chele*, *chora*, *ichu*, and *paqo*. The best ones for the alpacas are found around the lake. Herding them is an occupation of women and children. In the afternoons, after grazing, the animals return to the corrals to spend the night.

Each family has an average of 100 alpacas and 50 sheep. They are herded together and, also separately, for different reasons such as the number of each species. For the herders, sheep are more versatile because they can adapt to different types of pastures. Beef cattle are not numerous and not all families have them. The average is three to four cows per family. They are sent to the hills to graze.

They also care for animals of people from other communities in exchange for agricultural products like potatoes, *moraya*, or *ch'uño*. Some have lands in nearby low areas such as in the zone of Quiquijana, Pataquehua, and Nañuran, where they can get potatoes. They do not have direct access to maize which grows in the valley. They live permanently in Waqwaqocha, only farming in the lowlands without living in them. Thus some have their own supply of potatoes and some maize.

The ceremonies for alpacas, *ch'uyasqa*,[8] takes place between the Day of the *Comadres* and the Carnival (Mardi Gras). Llamas are celebrated in August with the *T'ikachay*.

Llamas are used in commercial exchanges, and they are used to go to the Sunday markets in Urcos, Quiquijana, and Acomayo.

The interrelationships among Pataquehuar, Waqwaqocha, and Quiquijana are aimed at supplying each with the products which are not produced in its territory. The concern is domestic, to have a full range of food. The relations are set up through trade, cash payments, or a combined means including working additional days, caring for animals from elsewhere, helping out at harvest time, and transporting products from the fields to the home storehouses.

In Waqwaqocha, alpacas, llamas, and sheep are sold alive as well as for meat. The live animal is sold; the rule is that it is not exchanged for agricultural produce. This is also true for cows, which cost 80,000 *soles*. It is one of the most direct ways to get money. The sales are called "barter for money." The meat of the alpaca is sold in the market in Quiquijana. Some carry it to more distant places like Quillibamba more than 180 km away. This market is very important because it is in a region where the demand for meat is very high by the urban as well as the peasant populations. Due to the production of export items (coffee, cacao, tea, coca), the peasants share money, and also because they give coca which is a product of high value and importance which has increased in recent years because of restrictions on its sale and political control over its movement.

Also, merchants and residents from towns like Quiquijana and Urcos go up to the high communities to buy live sheep for their use or as a business investment for sale as meat in Sicuani and Cuzco.

An alpaca costs 20,000 to 30,000 *soles*; sheep 7,000. They are exchanged for coca in the following way:

An alpaca for an *arroba* of coca
A sheep for a half *arroba* of coca
An alpaca for four *arrobas* of maize
A sheep for two *arrobas* of maize

The exchange of meat for potatoes is limited or almost non-existent since the community havests only part of the potatoes it eats. They rarely sell or exchange an entire animal, and prefer to do it in parts. The fiber of llamas or alpacas, as well as sheep's wool, can be sold or exchanged. There are commercial middlemen who travel around the zone accumulating wool and fiber for businesses in Sicuani. They are the *compadres* who come once a year with gifts (coca, alcohol, cigarettes) to feast the herders. A pound of white alpaca fiber costs 250 *soles*. A pound of colored costs 450 *soles*. Less sheep's wool is sold, because it is used to weave the cloth used for their own clothes. They have looms on which they weave homespun wool. Sheeps' wool is sold at 150 *soles* a pound. March and April are the best months to sell meat because it is of higher quality, has fat, and the animals weigh more.

Since maize cultivation is reduced or nonexistent in Wakwaquocha, it is acquired from Quiquijana or in nearby communities. Also those from Quiquijana can go up to Waqwaqocha carrying maize which they exchange for potatoes. An *arroba* of maize can be exchanged for one of potatoes. In this manner, those of Quiquijana who do not cultivate potatoes, fill their larders with potatoes.

Other products such as coca, hot peppers (*ají*), candles, and kerosene are acquired in Quiquijana, by purchase or by exchange. The agricultural products which they do not produce are obtained by exchange with the producers of the communities of the *qeshwa* zone.

Those of Pataquehuar who have potatoes and some maize use the same methods to obtain the products they do not produce or which they produce in small quantities—wool, alpaca fiber, meat, maize, and broadbeans. They sell their animals in order to obtain cash. Llamas will bring up to 15,000 *soles* and goats 5,000. They do not sell live animals, because, they say, they keep the hides in order to sell them separately and thus make more money. Sales increase when there are festivals to the patron saints in the neighboring communities, in Quiquijana, and in the other villages of the valley. Also merchants come from Cuzco, Sicuani, and Quiquijana who travel throughout the high altitude areas buying live animals to satisfy the urban demand. The sales take place in a cordial atmosphere in which exchanges of gifts are made, gifts of portions of coca leaf, alcohol, cigarettes, and other treats.

The people of Pataquehuar sell little sheep's wool, keeping what they produce to knit garnments for themselves. Since their production of alpaca fiber is insignificant, they sell what they do get to the merchants who accumulate it, travelling throughout the zone exchanging industrially produced goods for cash or for agricultural products for those who do not have access to them or whose harvest is insufficient. The rates of exchange are:

One sheep is exchanged for 1/2 *arroba* of coca leaf
One sheep is exchanged for 4 *arrobas* of maize
One llama is exchanged for 6 *arrobas* of maize

The price of yellow corn is 1,800 *soles* per *arroba*; white corn costs 2,500 *soles* per *arroba*; and an *arroba* of coca leaf costs 27,000 *soles*.

Part of the harvest of potatoes, barley, broadbeans, and the rest of what they obtain is destined for exchange in the nearby communities or for sale in the Sunday market in Quiquijana. They need cash in order to buy in Quiquijana what they do not produce, such as candles, kerosene, salt, sugar, oil, matches, alcohol, coca, noodles, and canned foods. When they go down to the town they try to avoid the *alcanzadores* who are the merchant women from Quiquijana, Urcos, Sicuani, and even Cuzco who post themselves at the entrances to the town and try to buy products from the country by force or by offering small gifts, or through social relationships which they have established with the country folk.

The Sunday market of Quiquijana is rather busy, usually receiving 2,000 people. When it is nearing the time of a festival, such as Christmas, All Saints' Day, Carnival (Mardi Gras), or when it is time for the ceremonies to the Earth or the livestock, attendance rises in number, reaching 3,500 and even passing 4,000. This figure is very high when one takes into account that the *comunidades* do not have very large populations, usually an average of 100 to 200 members, and the population of the town itself is barely 1,200 permanent inhabitants.

Those of Waqwaqocha and Pataquehuar call going to the market *rantikuy*. The market takes place in the main plaza. The Sicuani-Cuzco road crossed the plaza and the route of the present asphalted road has been modified in that it goes through the periphery of the town. The authorities have decided to construct a new market near the new road, planning to make it a daily market and not just a Sunday market.

Apart from the traffic of people from neighboring communities, the Sunday market receives merchants who come from nearby centers. The objective is to carry out transactions for a profit. Products from the higher altitudes are offered, such as potatoes, barley, *oca*, wheat, and *lisas,* and also from the valleys—maize, broadbeans, green peas, chickpeas, and *tarwi*. There is *Ch'ini challwa*, small sun-dried fish, which comes from the provinces of Canas and Espinar. Hot peppers (*rocoto*) and cotton are brought from Qosñipata and Quincemil which are to the east in the hot lowlands. Carrots, lettuce, and cauliflower come from valley communities such as Wakaytaki, Antisuyu, Noqorayse, Pampaquehuar, and Ñañurau. Potatoes, *ch'uño*, and meat are brought from communities on the *puna*, such as Kallatiya, Pataquehuar, Sanchaq, Waqwaqocha, Lampa, and Jayuni. Maize also comes from the lower areas such as Jolqa, T'io, Arkopata, and Quiquijana itself. Onions are from Sicuani, and pottery from Pukara, in Puno Department.

Itinerant merchants offer manufactured goods such as clothes, plastic objects, kitchen utensils, toys, detergent, salt, sugar, matches, cooking oil, canned goods, crackers, noodles, flour, cigarettes, and some pharmaceuticals. These same goods are offered in the stores of the town. They are acquired with cash, although there is no lack of opportunities in which barter is accepted, especially in the case of some storekeepers who thus supply themselves with agricultural produce.

A lot of what is offered is being resold; for example, the hot peppers (*rocotos*) which are required in Urcos by middlemen. They buy them by the sack, which costs 10,000 *soles* each. They are sold in Quiquijana *al menudeo*; that is, by the unit. Coca is sold in the same way. The sellers come from Cuzco; they may be Pilpinteños or *pilpis* (from Pilpinto, a district in the province of Paruro) who are specialists in coca. They get to Cuzco at about 9:30 A.M. and at midday leave the market in trucks or in their own vehicles. An *arroba* of coca costs them 27,000 *soles* in Cuzco, which, selling it bit by bit, by the pound or by the *maki* of coca for three piles of potatoes (each pile is 6 potatoes); two *maki* of coca for two piles (of 5 units each) of *ch'uño*. A pound of coca was sold at 1,200 *soles* and two and a half *maki* of coca for 100 *soles*.

In 1981 some of the established equivalents for exchange were:

6 onions for 6 ears of corn
1 onion for a pile of *ch'uño*
3½ handfuls of potatoes (more or less 6 potatoes) for 2½ handfuls of carrots
6 bags of potatoes, each of 4 medium-sized potatoes, for 5 cebolla, plus a handful of *asnapa*

Pottery is sold or exchanged. Equivalencies are established taking into account the contents of a vessel. They are exchanged for maize, *ch'uño,* potatoes, barley, wheat, green peas, and broadbeans. A *tomín,* a kind of pitcher, which costs 600 *soles,* can be exchanged for an *arroba* of potatoes.

Pottery is brought by merchants, who prefer to sell for cash, or by the potters themselves. They come in trucks which arrive on Saturday, leaving for the return trip on Monday. Sometimes they go to the communities of the *qeshwa* or the *puna* to offer their wares.

In the various transactions *yapa* is customary, which is a gift made between sellers and buyers, which might be an increase of produce, such as an extra potato, a bit of maize, or something extra such as a cracker, or a piece of candy.

Some residents of the town are of the opinion that barter is on the decrease, because the major part of transactions are carried out with money. There are even those who do not accept exchanges of products. This leads to the fact that the peasants need more money in order to acquire other goods. The market has also grown; there are more vendors and a larger variety of merchandise than there were 10 years ago, when the town had fewer inhabitants.

The market begins to quiet down at midday, and by two in the afternoon it has all but concluded; by four o'clock the larger number of people has left. They return to their communities in groups, arriving drunk at their houses, since a bottle of alcohol is an "obligatory" purchase. Market day is special, even to wearing new *fiesta* clothes. They eat a light late-morning meal in the plaza, exchanging food with those of other communities. Those from the *puna* offer boiled potatoes and *ch'uño* for hominy[9] and salads from the *qeshwa*.

As in the case of Vilcabamba, we will make special reference to the commercialization of *qochayuyu*. Those of Waqwaqocha and Pataquehuar acquire it in Quiquijana, in the Sunday market or in the shops. It is bought wholesale once a year for the Feast of All Saints' Day by merchants from Atico, Camaná, Chala, and Mollendo in the Department of Arequipa. On Sundays it is offered for sale by middlemen. When there is not any *qochayuyu* to be had in Quiquijana, they go as far as to Cuzco to get it. The price in the shops in town is always higher. A "block" (*plancha*) costs 1,500 *soles* and small blocks (*planchitas*) from 100 to 150 *soles*. In 1981 there was only one vendor of *qochayuyu*. It is not sold by weight nor is it bartered.

Qochayuyu is used as an ingredient for special dishes for holidays or communal work groups. *Picante* is one of the dishes in which it is most used. It is a mixture of green peas, chick peas, *qochayuyu*, chopped onion, cheese, *challwa* (dried fish), and ground hot peppers (*ají*). It is eaten during rest periods when doing agricultural work. Other dishes are *soltero* (lit. "bachelor") in which the seaweed is accompanied by carrots, potatoes, broadbeans, and hot peppers (*rocoto*); *kahuchi*, consisting of potatoes, broad beans, and *qochayuyu*; and *chiriucho*, made with the meat of hens and guinea pigs and which is different from the *chiriucho* of the city of Cuzco, where it is eaten only on the holiday of Corpus Christi and which also is made using *qochayuyo*.

Calca

We use the name Calca to refer to the region of the province of the same name, which includes populated centers of different sizes and communities dedicated to various agricultural activities. Calca is the capital of the province of the same name. It is at 2,980 meters of altitude on the right bank, looking downriver, of the Vilcanota River. According to the census of 1981, it has 6,112 inhabitants; the whole province having 59,210 inhabitants. It is the fifth largest of the thirteen populated centers of the department, after Cuzco, Sicuani, Quillabamba, and Espinar.

As the provincial capital, Calca is the seat of the subprefectural court. There are primary and secondary schools and private schools, a public health post, running water, sewers, and electricity.

There is an asphalt road to Cuzco, integrating the so-called tourist circuit of the Sacred Valley of the Incas. It has a market of foodstuffs which functions every day of the week, with vendors who have permanently installed stands. In the entire area the only comparable market is that of Urubamba, although it is smaller and has less diversified merchandise, both agricultural and manufactured, than other regions of the country or outside the country. On Sundays the number of vendors increases, with the attendance of peasants from communities of the area as well as sellers and buyers from Cuzco.

Part of the jurisdiction of Calca is a region which extends to the northwest (Fig. 11.4) through which runs the road from Calca to the Valley of Lares. It ascends the Vilcanota Valley up to an altitude of 4,880 meters, then descends to Lares at 1,200 meters, in less than 150 km in a straight line.

The presence and importance of Calca as an administrative and political center began in Inca times. In the town one finds archaeological remains which evidence an urban center of finely finished Inca architecture. An Inca road crosses it going in the direction of Antisuyu, from which were extracted coca, lumber, feathers, wax, and other resources of hot lands. Historically documented information exists from the sixteenth century, which throws light on the importance which this area continued to have under Spanish domination.

The Vilcanota Valley stands out in the Cuzco area for its maize production, which is of such high quality that it is produced for export. It also produces fruit such as peaches, apricots, apples, and pears; flowers; and vegetables such as onions, cabbage, carrots, forage barley, alfalfa, chick peas, and green peas. Production is for market, supplying the city of Cuzco and cities outside the department.

To the east of Calca following the course of the Qochoq River, begins a narrow ravine, which ascends rapidly and through which winds an old Inca road which was used as a road for travelling by

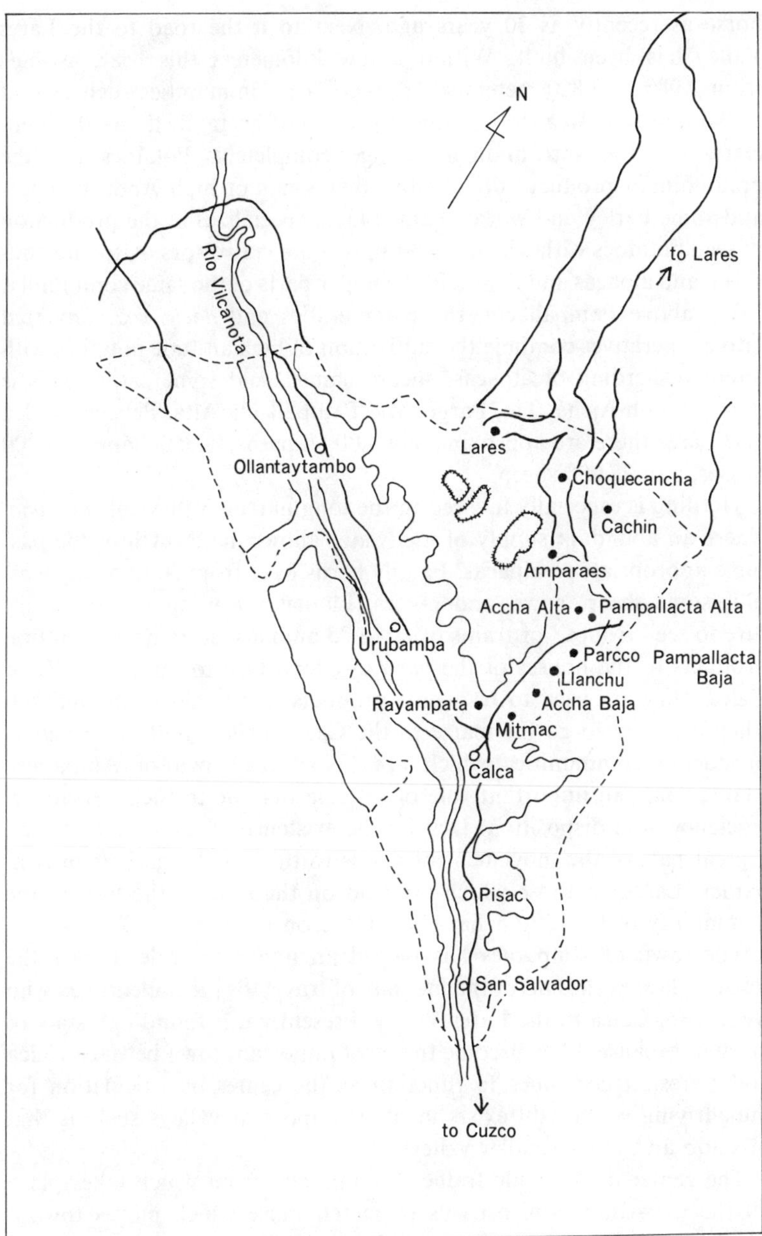

Fig. 11.4 Calca

horse as recently as 30 years ago. Next to it the road to the Lares Valley has been built. Within a few kilometers this road ascends from 2,980 to 3,800 meters where there are communities such as that of Pampallacta. In a straight line it would not be more than 10 kilometers, but the surroundings change completely. Potatoes are the predominant product, along with other kinds of high Andean tubers and some barley and wheat. Pampallacta specializes in the production of seed potatoes with which they supply other cultivators. Also one finds sheep and alpacas and llamas in the upper parts of the same community.

Up above Pampallacta, the communities and *haciendas* converted into cooperatives combine the cultivation of high altitude potatoes with intensive herding of alpacas, sheep, llamas, and some cattle. This is the case with Ajcha, Tío, Pargo, and Pampallacta Alta. Between Calca and Lares there are approximately 4,000 alpacas, 8,360 llamas, 3,000 horses, and 27,000 sheep.

Herding is especially favored in the long narrow valleys of the *puna,* where an abundant supply of meltwater allows the growth of the pastures appropriate to alpacas. Family herds have from 30 to 50 alpacas, plus some sheep, cows, and horses. Llamas are numerous. It is not rare to see "troops" or trains of 20 to 25 animals, carrying agricultural products to the houses of the *puna* dwellers. Due to the proximity to Calca, they are used to transport products to be sold in the market. They are used to go for maize to the Calca Valley itself or to maize-producing communities which are below the town of Amparaes. Llamas play an important role of articulators due to their versatility, efficiency, and disposition. Despite the existence of the road to Lares, a great part of the movement of goods to the weekly markets in Amparaes, Lares, or those which are held on the road at the foot of the community of Choqekancha, takes place on the backs of llamas.

The town of Amparaes has played an important role. It was the resting place at the end of the first day of travel for the muledrivers who went from Calca to the Lares Valley. Presently it is found in a state of growth, because it has become the most important town between Calca and Lares. It continues to function as the center of articulation for muledriving which still exists in other important valleys such as that of Laqo and other smaller valleys.

The center of the mule traffic is Amparaes, from which takes place all the departures and arrivals of merchandise which moves toward the valleys not reached by the road. It has a daily market with a handful of buyers and sellers. It possesses several stores well-stocked with merchandise of all kinds, aimed at urban and rural consumption.

A lot of potatoes, barley, and broadbeans are cultivated. Maize appears a few kilomaters away, which is feasible because the descent to the hot valleys is very rapid. In two or three kilometers one can descend several dozen meters. Amparaes is next to archaeological ruins, which shows continuity of occupation from pre-Inca times to the present.

The valley of Lares itself, which gives its name to the entire region, is a tropical zone. The district capital, which is also called Lares, is at an altitude of 3,050 meters. Between these two zones there is not much movement back and forth, except for political-administrative functions. In the Lares Valley various towns have formed which are growing due to the migration to this zone for its valuable agricultural products. Worth noting is the cultivation of coffee, cacao, *achiote,* coca, citrus fruits, bananas, papayas, pineapples, and other fruits; yuca, pumpkins, and all the products which are used for sale in urban markets. Cattle predominate; there are no sheep because humidity and heat rule the environment.

In this article we have not considered Lares as the district capital. In the project presently under way will be seen its relationship in the interaction of Calca with the valley, because since the opening of the road, it has remained marginal, being accessible only by a secondary branch road to the principal road.

This third case corresponds to an area more extensive and complex, with components at several levels, from peasant communities to a city such as Calca, which as provincial capital represents an important center of articulation. The historical antecedents show that this function was also very important in the past as shown by thc several kinds of Inca roads which cross-cut the area going in different directions, the existence of an Inca urban center in the Vilcanota Valley, and archaeological remains which are found right up to the Laqo Valley and the Lares Valley itself (Gutierrez n.d.). The dominant role of Calca persisted until 1960, when the road to Amparaes was inaugurated, which would later be continued to the Lares Valley finally uniting Calca with Quillabamba which is the capital of the province of La Convención.

The opening of the road produced important changes in the articulation of the region. Calca lost part of its function as the end point for the valley products which were carried by muletrains. Trucks began to transport directly from Amparaes at first and then from the valley itself, passing through Calca, which then lost its function as a "port" as the Calqueños called it, falling into a decadence from which it is now recovering very slowly.

With the panorama so briefly discussed for this region, one sees clearly the communities and towns established at diverse altitudes which have in common several aspects of interaction and complementarity. The communities keep on functioning in terms of relationships based on exchanges of agricultural products. Those from Pampallacta exchange potatoes for maize, barley, and broadbeans with communities from lower zones as well as from the Vilcanota Valley and the area surrounding Amparaes. They also obtain coca by exchange with the peasants of Lares and Laqo. Some have direct access to wool and meat which they also use in their relations with the agricultural people of the *qeshwa* region. As has been indicated several times, the steepness of the slope allows many different zones of production within a short distance, similar to the type of compact ecological relations which Brush establishes (1974:292), although with the difference that direct access and control do not go beyond two ecological zones, which makes necessary exchange and complementarity by means of barter, sale, or working in exchange for goods.

The market of Calca supplies the urban population, as do the smaller markets such as that of Amparaes, Lares, and recently sprung-up markets such as at the crossroads at the foot of Choquekancha.

The market of Calca is for buying and selling. Peasants take part of their production in order to obtain money with which to buy what they do not produce, such as factory-made articles or those of urban origin although barter has not completely disappeared. Something similar, though on a smaller scale, is happening in Amparaes, given that in these places there is more barter going on. What is important is the peasants' participation in the marketplace and the market system; it is not the end for which they are producing, but rather one of the means they have for acquiring other products of cash which they can use to acquire what they need for their subsistence and thus meet the demands of the urban population (Appleby 1978). The special annual fair held in Calca on the fifteenth of August deserves to be mentioned. On that date they celebrate the feast of the patron saint, the Virgin de la Asunción. Hundreds of peasants come from the communities under the political and religious jurisdiction of Calca. The producers from diverse regions are represented, such as potters or middlemen who bring pottery from Pukará, producers of wool, weavings, sacks, fiber, *charki*, suet, potatoes, and products from the hot valleys of the east. The peasants who offer potatoes and maize exchange them for pottery. Those who come for maize or potatoes, barley, or wheat, do not sell for cash. This is not to say that large volume transactions are not in cash, because middlemen come from the Vilcanota Valley as well as from neighboring departments in order to make wholesale purchases of maize, potatoes, barley, wheat, coffee, *achiote*, and cacao.

The potters who have not exchanged their entire production at the end of the fair travel to neighboring communities to barter, and return to their homes with agricultural products. Sellers of other goods vacate the fair as soon as it is over.

The Sunday market is increasing in attendance, of buyers as well as sellers, but these people are from the urban populations of Urubamba, Pisaq, and Cuzco who buy in large volume for their own consumption.

In Calca *qochayuyu* is sold at the fairs, the various markets, and in the shops. The peasants who use it require money to acquire it. Merchants bring *qochayuyu* from Cuzco or from sellers from Arequipa who offer it for sale. It is eaten in family feasts, agricultural work-groups, and ceremonial occasions, such as religious *cargos*.

Discussion and Conclusions

The foregoing descriptions give us an appreciation of three situations which are markedly different. Vilcabamba is a zone without roads for motorized traffic, of peasant communities which are not directly related with any other populated center of any importance. Through interaction and complementarity the communities manage to obtain goods for daily consumption which they do not produce, because the communities have access only to products of two ecological zones. More strongly commercial relationships are produced with producers from far away zones, which supply the goods which are not found on the complementary upper or lower ecological floors of the region. The volume of sales is small-scale, not constituting the main line of the economy—neither to acquire other products nor to dispose of their own, although it is the form in which to obtain cash. There is a lack of marketplaces and the presence of shops is unnecessary because travelling vendors can supply goods from the outside.

Quiquijana is of an intermediate complexity, which, as district capital, exercises a major influence over its jurisdiction. The weekly market is important in terms of meeting the demands of the population of the place, as well as for peasants who can acquire the goods which are not produced in the countryside and other rural regions. It provides the opportunity to get hold of money for their purchases.

Communities have direct access to at least two production zones which they must complement through direct exchanges with neighbors. Thus the region is integrated by weak, infrequent contact with producers from other regions. This relationship is achieved by means of a Sunday market and by itinerant merchants who also frequent the communities. Quiquijana then is the center of articulation, although its influence has not largely affected the interaction and complementarity which exist between the various ecological floors.

The situation in Calca is more complex. It takes in a more extensive region with a small city which is the provincial capital, and a wider range of centers of population and indigenous peasant communities. The road as the central axis permits communication and displacement of goods and people. The daily market of Calca is more important for meeting the demands of the urban population than those of the rural one. For the peasants complementarity and interaction are effected through direct relationships with neighboring communities. As was true in Vilcabamba and Quiquijana, the majority of peasants control at least two altitudinally different production floors. Direct exchange is facilitated by the close proximity of ecological floors. The market as a place and as a system is peripheral; it is not the customary medium for the acquisition of agricultural products for consumption. Markets are used to sell part of their production in order to buy products complementary to their economy.

The close proximity of hot lands allows the peasants to count upon the supply of coca which is very important for ritual ceremony and the proper etiquette of social relations. They obtain it through barter or through purchase in the towns, or in travelling to the valley with their products which have a sure market among the farmers of export products from the valley, who always need what comes from the highlands.

We have not here considered the historical aspects which are important given that the archaeological and historical evidence show a continuity of occupation. Calca was a commercial center in Colonial times and Vilcabamba was important to the Inca economy, in as much as it was the refuge of the last Incas from Cuzco. Despite the lack of historical argument, the description of the three zones shows that changes since the Spanish invasion have modified more the form than the base of the diverse relations of interaction and vertical control among peasant communities. The lines established by Murra (1975) evidence the continuity which through some invisible conduit links the past to the present, given that these links originate in ecological factors which are the tangible reality of the Andean *montaña* in which verticality is important, especially in the tropics where the altitude and not the latitude is what exercises the major influence for establishing productive differences between the zones which are controlled and utilized by peasants. The market system and marketplaces are secondary and even peripheral to the peasant economy. Even now the circulation of complementary goods is not yet predominant. Indigenous peasant communities still follow the very Andean lines of verticality. The continuous opening of ways of communication for motorized vehicles is an important factor in transformation and change. The next years will be of greater gravitation against systems which have shown strong persistence for centuries.

(Translation by Freda Wolf de Romero)

NOTES

This work was made possible by the contribution of Dr. Shozo Masuda of the University of Tokyo which permitted anthropology students from Cuzco National University, Washington Rozas, Alberto Moscoso Flores, and Manuel Silva, to do field work in the three zones described. With Dr. Masuda's help, Washington Rozas is working in Calca, the axis of the Lares Valley, as part of a project in which the anthropologists Jorge Sánchez Farfán and David de Rojas Silva are also participating. Sánchez is investigating potato farmers in the community of Pampallacta, and de Rojas is searching for the documentary historical information. The author is studying the upper ranges where the herding of alpacas takes place.

This work has been written with the collaboration of Washington Rozas and Alberto Moscoso Flores.

1. Quechua names of sites, places, and towns are written as they figure on commonly used maps and other documents.

2. *Yunga, qeshwa,* and *puna* are the three principal ecological zones of the *sierra*. Altitude is one of the most important aspects of differentiation.

3. In Cuzco they call any town which serves as a center of articulation a "port."

4. A *quintal* weighs about 100 pounds, an *arroba* 11.5 kilograms, and a pound 453 grams.

5. All prices are indicated in Peruvian *soles* of 1981.

6. The concepts of site and system of the market are taken from Bohannan and Dalton (1965).

7. The *planchas* are blocks of *qochayuyu* (seaweed), like small adobe bricks.

8. This denomination is usual in several places in Cuzco (Flores 1977).

9. Boiled maize. A much appreciated food.

REFERENCES CITED

Appleby, Gordon

1978 Exportation and Its Aftermath: The Spatioeconomic Evolution of the Regional Marketing System in Highland Puno, Peru. Ph.D. dissertation. Division of the Humanities and Social Sciences, California Institute of Technology.

Bohannan, Paul and George Dalton

1965 Markets in Africa. The Natural History Library: Anchor Books.

Brush, Stephen B.

1974 El lugar del hombre en el ecosistema andino. Revista del Museo Nacional 40:279–302. Museo Nacional de la Cultura Peruana. Lima.

Corrales V., Edmundo

1983 El mito tenía razón. Historia 2:43–66. Departamento de Historia, Geografía y Antropología, Universidad Nacional de San Agustín. Arequipa.

Figueroa, Adolfo

1981 La economía campesina de la sierra del Perú. Lima: Pontificia Universidad Católica del Perú.

Flores Ochoa, Jorge A., ed.

1977 Pastores de Puna. Uywamichiq punarunakuna. Lima: Instituto de Estudios Peruanos.

Gade, Daniel W.

1975 Plants, Man, and the Land in the Vilcanota Valley of Peru. Biogeographica N. 6. The Hague: W. Junk B. V. Publishers.

Gutiérrez Pareja, Salustio

n. d. Ciudades ocultas del Cusco milenario. Cuzco.

Masuda, Shozo

1981 Cochayuyo, macha, camarón e higos charquoados. Estudios etnográficos del Perú meridional:173–92. Shozo Masuda, ed. Tokyo: University of Tokyo.

Moscoso Flores, Julio Alberto

n.d. Trabajo de campo realizado en las comunidades de Huathua Laguna. Ms. Cuzco.

Murra, John V.

1975 Formaciones económicas y políticas del mundo andino. Lima: Instituto de Estudios Peruanos.

Rozas, Washington

n.d. Datos sobre las comunidades de Incahuasi y Choquetira. Ms. Cuzco.

Valderrama, Ricardo and Carmen Escalante

1983 Arrieros, troperos y llameros en Huancavelica. Allpanchis 18: 65–87. Cuzco: Instituto de Pastoral Andina.

12

The Llama is My *Chacra*: Metaphor of Andean Pastoralists

Hiroyasu Tomoeda

Introduction

To understand how simultaneous control of ecological niches (Murra [1972] 1975) is maintained today is important and leads us, logically, to examine the relationships and interaction between agriculture and pastoralism in the Andes. In this paper, I present the total configuration of these relationships in its three dimensions: economic, social and ideological, focusing my observations on the Apurimac region of southern Peru.

It is necessary to take into account the different ecological regions according to altitude differences. Therefore, following Pulgar Vidal's (n.d.) classification I will divide the region of Apurímac into four zones: *puna*, 4,500–4,000 meters above sea level; *suni*, 4,000–3,500 meters; *quichua*, 3,500–2,300 meters; and *yunga*, 2,300–1,000 meters. In agreement with the local inhabitants, the *quichua* is subdivided into two zones, higher *quichua*, 3,500–3,000 meters, and lower *quichua*, 3,000–2,300 meters.

As regards livestock, the agriculturalists (especially those of the high *quichua*) raise cows and sheep on a small scale, while the pastoralists are dedicated to camelids. These latter are called *punaruna* or *uywamichic* by the former, who are, in turn, called *llaqtaruna* or *chacareru*. These terms imply two distinct habitats, different forms of production, technologies, and lifestyles. The habitat of the herders is the cold *puna* where agriculture is almost impossible, but this does not mean that they do not have access to cultivable fields. On the contrary, the herding communities in Apurímac have land in the *suni* zone where they cultivate tubers.

For the agriculturalists in the high *quichua*, the *suni* zone is the potato zone *par excellence* and their source of subsistence. In the upper valleys maize is cultivated through the construction of terraces. Those of the lower *quichua* dedicate themselves exclusively to maize and to cereals. The amount of cultivation carried out by herders in the *suni* is insufficient to cover their needs and they are therefore dependent on the agriculturalists; conversely, those in the *quichua* have no direct access to the *puna* and depend on the herders. This interdependence is the basis of the economic relationship between agriculturalists and herders (compare this study with the agro-pastoralism described by Yamamoto in this volume. Also see Harris in this volume).

The Economic Dimension

For Apurímac we have an excellent description of the economic relationships between agriculturalists and herders (Juan de Dios Concha Contreras 1975). In 1971, Concha Contreras studied the province of Antabamba which borders the region of Aymaraes where we carried out research in 1981. The data we collected corroborates his descriptions. I will only mention that overall, the same system operates in these two regions in Apurímac, Antabamba-Abancay, and Aymaraes-Andahuaylas. The Antabamba herders establish their most intimate and important relationships with the agriculturalists of the high *quichua* of Antabamba (Antabamba, Huaquilca, Antilla, Mollebamba, etc.) and with the people of Abancay in the lower *quichua* (Cachora, Taquebamba, Huanipaca), while the Aymaraes herders establish their relationships with the agriculturalists of Caraybamba, Cotaruse, Pampamarca, and with the people of Andahuaylas of the lower *quichua* (Huancaray, Huancarama).

In order to subsist, Apurímac herders need to obtain tubers and cereals through barter with agriculturalists, a matter of prime importance. In order to achieve this, different but superimposed means exist. One of them is direct exchange of *puna* products (wool, fresh meat, *charqui*, textiles, and ropes of their own manufacture) for agricultural products from the *quichua* (maize, potatoes, barley, wheat, etc.). The second method is to receive these products as payment for providing transportation services using their llamas. The third method is a combination of two exchanges with agriculturalists of different agricultural or ecological regions. With this combination the pastoralists seek to double the benefits of the exchange. The fourth method consists in raising camelids for the agriculturalists from the high *quichua* through a contractual arrangment by which the herders will receive agricultural products. Barter exchanges are quite common in this region, though the intervention of the monetary system is undeniable.

Herders travel to the communities on the western flanks of the Andes during March and April where they exchange their products for fruit such as figs, olives, apples, and *ají* (*Capsicum*), or they journey to the salt mine (Huarhua, in La Unión, Arequipa) to obtain this product (*Huarhuacachi*). In May they travel to the lower *quichua* villages where they exchange the products obtained in the previous trips and/or *puna* products for maize. Llamas are used to transport the herders' products and, when requested, to carry the harvests at the agriculturalists' fields.

The maize harvest in the *quebradas* (side valleys) of the high *quichua* is later than that of the lower *quichua,* and some pastoralists take advantage of this difference to supply themselves with the maize they lack. Nevertheless, the main interest in undertaking short trips to the higher valleys is to obtain potatoes which are harvested in the *laymes* (communal land in the *suni* cultivated by annual rotation) in May. Apart from the travels mentioned, herders undertake other treks on different occasions to obtain necessary foods. They frequently visit the valleys before planting time.

In Concha Contreras' (1975) detailed description there are some surprising exchange rates between pastoralists and agriculturalists. These are the data for the year 1971:

1. The wool from one sheared sheep (*vellón*) which has a market price of 20 *soles* is exchanged for one *topo* of apples whose value is 200 *soles;* that is, in the national market the apples have ten times the value of the wool. According to the observer, there is a higher demand for wool by the agriculturalists, while the demand for apples is more secondary; it is an *antojo* (a whimsy and thus something they can do without).
2. One *vellón* is exchanged for three *cuartas* of maize in the lower *quichua,* which have a value of 120 *soles*; that is, the maize has six times the value of wool.
3. One *arroba* of rock salt which can be bought for 10 *soles* in the mine of Huarhua is exchanged for 3 *cuartas* of maize.
4. For transporting 10 loads of harvest the herder receives one load in payment.

The discrepancy in value of the products which are exchanged is "fantastic" according to Concha Contreras (1975). Some decades ago, the herders had an even greater advantage because:

1. In the 1950s one *vellón* was exchanged for 4 *cuartas* of maize; in the 1960s for 3 *cuartas*; and in the 1970s for two.

2. In the decade of the 1940s one fourth of an *arroba* of salt was exchanged for four *cuartas* of maize; in the 1950s half an *arroba* of salt for four *cuartas* of maize; in the 1960s one *arroba* of salt for three *cuartas;* and in the 1970s one *arroba* of salt for two *cuartas* of maize. At present (1981) I can vouch that one *arroba* of salt is exchanged for one *arroba* of maize.

To use market standards of value in the exchanges between herders and agriculturalists is not justified, since these are established on the basis of traditional exchange values. Nevertheless, we have the impression that the herders have maintained certain advantages in the last decades. We must thus ask ourselves why the agriculturalists of the *quichua* have permitted and continue to permit this. Or, vice versa, why have the herders responded to the increase of value of the agriculturalists' products in relation to the goods that they bring? There are many interrelated factors which must be considered in order to answer these questions: (1) the relative reduction in demand by agriculturalists for the products that herders have to offer; (2) the difference in the character of the products exchanged by both; that is, today, that which the herder has to offer is considered a "treat"by the agriculturalist that he can do without, while the agriculturalists' goods are indispensable to the herder; (3) the integration, ever more accelerated, of the products of both parties in the national and/or international market; and (4) the strengthening of the position of the herder, due to an increase in wool prices, which has permitted him to respond to adjustments in the price of agricultural goods.

All these factors, and perhaps others that are also interrelated, are difficult to disentangle. Here I am interested in only one aspect: How do the agriculturalists and herders perceive the situation of the discrepancy of the exchange rates, which, let us say, they themselves have become aware of?

According to Concha Contreras, the municipal authorities of each community in the *quichua* zone used to advise the peasants so that they would not let themselves be cheated by "those Indians in the *puna*" and would say, "How is it possible that you give away so many potatoes or maize, for the little things that the herders give?" To be "cheated" by the Indians of the *puna* sounds a bit strange considering the reality of the situation and should not be taken literally. This expression is one way of conceptualizing the situation of disproportional exchange rates, which are the result of the factors already mentioned and which exist today. Here is a commentary given by an Antabamba peasant woman with respect to the readjustment, which is quite understandable.

> We have to give like we used to, because they (the herders), poor people, have to travel far to search for a livelihood. We would not like the same to be done to us. Sure, the authorities tell us that we are allowing the Indians to take advantage of us, but these gentlemen do not know the many sacrifices of searching for food.

I interpret these comments in this way: The herders have taken advantage of the disproportionate exchange rate because of their lower economic status with respect to the agriculturalists, who can cede surplus production to those who lack these goods and who need them for survival. The generosity that a *llaqtaruna* shows towards a poor *punaruna* is a determining factor that intervenes in the establishment of the unequal exchange rates or economic complementarity between both parties. The economic disadvantage of the agriculturalist is compensated by the superior status accorded him by the herders, which permits him to show generosity.

Nevertheless, this situation is changing. Many *llaqtaruna* no longer believe that the *punaruna* are as poor as before. I do know some herders who abandoned their trips with llama caravans to the lower valleys, going there by taking advantage of modern transportation facilities and coming back loaded with quantities of maize in a hired truck. The maize was bought with money that they obtained from the sale of alpaca wool. They readily admitted that barter offers them an advantage in comparison with cash purchases, but they also said that it was a waste of time to go from house to house to barter for products. Nowadays the agriculturalists like to tell jokes about the "millionaire herder," where the stereotyped image of the poor, humble, and ignorant herder is superimposed on the image of a rich man.

Without doubt, the basis of the exchange rates between agriculturalists and herders is the supply and demand of the goods both of them have; yet, the herders, for whom the provision of agricultural products is indispensable, need some kind of institution that will channel and regulate the supply and demand in such a way that the basic goods that they need are permanently guaranteed.

To date we do not know of the existence of any kind of market or other system that could provide the above-mentioned regulation. I can only describe a social relationship established on a personal basis through the ties of friendship or *riqsisqa* (a person that is known). This relationship between a herder and an agriculturalist becomes more binding when *compadrazgo* and *padrinazgo* relationships are established between them.

For a herder the primary motive is to insure a sufficient quantity of agricultural products for his consumption, and for that he will seek out and maintain relationships with agriculturalists of known economic solvency. It is thus important to note that the roots of this friendship lie in the differences in their respective statuses.

The Social Dimension

We saw that exchange is vital for the herders, and to achieve success they put in a lot of effort. At this stage I have the following question: Wouldn't a marriage tie between these two groups provide greater and more fruitful advantages (Tomoeda and Fujii in this volume)? With a marriage alliance the steady supply of goods between different ecological zones favorable to herding and to agriculture could be achieved. The simultaneous control of ecological zones would then be taken care of through a group of families united by ties of matrimony and kinship. This kind of union could be made feasible and would be of mutual benefit to herders and agriculturalists in the higher *quichua*, if we take into account the shorter distances involved.

But reality is different, and the tie of friendship does not go any further. A marriage alliance between the two groups is inconceivable for reasons that were explained to me. A poor agriculturalist told me that he was ashamed to introduce his wife to relatives and acquaintances because she was from the *puna*. A young *llaqtaruna* told me that he "would not get used to the loneliness." Another added: "Who can stand to live in the *puna*?" The predominant criteria in the answers were the differences in life styles and the implicit notion of the lowly status of the *punaruna*. In order to corroborate this statement, we have examined the ecclesiastic records for one region from the beginnings of this century and we present the statistical data in another paper (Tomoeda and Fujii in this volume). We can confirm that the percentage of marriages between agriculturalists and pastoralists is minimal. In conclusion, the two groups exchange products but not women and the result is thus two sub-societies forced into interdependence.

The Ideological Dimension: The Ritual of Vispera

Having dealt with the economic and social aspects I will now examine the ideological angle, in this case, from the herders' point of view. In order to do so, I will describe the details of a ritual I observed on 13 August 1981 on the *estancia* of Chicurumi, District of Cotaruse, Province of Aymaraes, Department of Apurímac. It was called *víspera* and forms part of the *Ayllusqa* or *Agustukuy* and it makes reference to camelid fertility. *Víspera* is the preparation of the *despacho* or offering which will be carried out the next day. It took place at three in the afternoon and lasted approximately three hours. In contrast to the more elaborate ritual and because of its simplicity it is called the *uchuy tinka* (little *tinka*) in opposition to the big or *hatun tinka*.

3:00 P.M. In a corner of the house of a herder, the man puts on an improvised table the *mesaqepi*, a bundle, which when opened reveals its contents: *illa*, a lithic zoomorphic figurine; *kirwa* or *kiqmi*, braided ropes of llama wool; *pichuwira*, male llama fat; sea shells; three *waiqa*, small coca bags; *llampu*, maize flour, and incense (a rosin powder); several *chuwa*, wooden receptacles; a drinking cup in zoomorphic form; *taku*, a piece of fine clay; mineral objects such as those called "white stone," "pepper gold," and *winchurumi*; three *qeros*; and *kipuna*, small woolen cloths used to wrap things. On the wall are hung bronze bells and woolen llama ropes.

In addition, the owner places on a shawl (*qepi*) ears of maize of different colors, a small drum (*tinya*), and a bottle of rum (*aguardiente*).

3:05 P.M. The man brings burning embers in a broken ceramic pot which he places under the *mesaqepi*, and adds incense and coca leaves which produce smoke that is offered to the *mesaqepi*. The man and his wife kneeling before the *mesaqepi* embrace each other three times. Then the man takes five ears of maize and places them one by one in the *chuwas*. The couple seat themselves to the side of the *mesaqepi* and in front of the woman there is a mortar (*muray*), and pestle (*kutana*). The man shucks one ear of yellow *muruchu* maize and places the kernels in one *chuwa*, which he then gives to his wife; she turns the *chuwa* over into the *muray* and proceeds to grind the kernels with the *kutana*. The man, seated to the right of the woman, chooses three coca leaves (*kintu*) and adds them to the ground corn while the woman pauses in her task. She then places *chapchu* (roughly ground maize) into the *chuwa*, to which he adds a piece of *pichuwira*, three leaves of *coca kintu*, and a bit of incense.

3:10 P.M. The man throws the *chapchu* into the fire as an initial offering; then he offers a shot of rum to the *illa*, spilling some drops on the *mesaqepi* and drinking the rest (act of *tinka*). The woman and the other observers carry out the *tinka* in the same manner. The man then brings one *chuwa* from the *mesaqepi*, takes an ear of yellow *muruchu* maize which he then shells into the *chuwa* and gives to his wife, who proceeds to prepare *llampu.* The process of grinding is interrupted briefly so that the husband can add three *kintus* and a little bit of pulverized *taku*, and the white flour turns into a reddish brown powder.

The first *llampu* (finely ground maize) prepared by the woman is placed back into the *chuwa* together with its cob. The husband returns it to the *mesaqepi* and taking another *chuwa* which contains *granada* maize, proceeds to remove the kernels and hands them to his wife.

3:28 P.M. The woman begins once more to prepare a second *llampu* for *canta*, a figure of a female alpaca. The previously prepared *llampu* was for the *canta* of a female llama. The new *llampu* is finished and is returned to the *chuwa*, which the man takes back to the *mesaqepi.* He then gives his wife a new *chuwa* which contains red maize *chumpi* which he has already shelled. The wife begins to grind the corn in order to prepare the third *llampu.* One kernel is spilled from the mortar. She picks it up and, taking a cup of rum, spills some drops on the *muray* and *kutana* while she mumbles "*ay Chicurumi, Pachamama*" and drinks the rest, pausing so that the husband can add three *kintus* and *taku.* This *llampu* will be used for the *canta* of the male llama.

3:48 P.M. The third *llampu* is ready, the man hands a *chuwa* of white maize to his wife, who begins once again to grind the kernels while the man takes the last *chuwa* from the *mesaqepi* and the three ears of *muruchu* corn that had been left there, loosening the kernels. While doing this, the bottle of *aguardiente* (a type of rum), which was at his side tips when he moves his arm. Taking a cup he spills some drops of liquor on the floor and says, "*Pachamama* is asking for *aguardiente.*"

3:58 P.M. The preparation of the fourth *llampu* for the *canta* of the male alpaca is finished and the man takes it in its *chuwa* to the *mesaqepi.* The woman takes the kernels of the white corn and begins to grind them, while the husband adds the ground clay. This time he does not add the *kintus,* although he has selected them. The *llampu* for the baby llamas is ready and the man places it on the *mesaqepi.* Having concluded the grinding, the woman receives from her husband three *kintus,* and chews them, and then drinks the liquor from the cup.

4:11 P.M. The man, holding a copper *tumi*, proceeds to scrape the following materials in this order: *illa,* shell, pepper gold, *winchurumi*, and white stone. These scrapings are added to the five *chuwas* that contain *llampu.*

The wife grinds three ears of *muruchu* corn one by one to prepare three *chapchus.* The husband adds some *pichuwira*, three coca leaves, and incense. The three *chuwas* with *chapchu* in them are also placed on the *mesaqepi*. The owner does a *tinka* in front of the *mesaqepi* and bids the others do the same.

4:25 P.M. When the *tinka* is concluded, the man places the five *chuwas* which contain the *llampu* on the floor, and the couple proceed to do a *tinka* to them with the rum. Then the woman plays the drum (*tinya*) for some minutes and begins to sing:

Sumaqllata mamallay	Beautifully, mother
Muyurinki mamallay	You will go around, mother
Hermanay Paisanaqa	My sister, townswoman
Mamallay allpaqaqa	My mother *alpaca*

4:29 P.M. The man takes a piece of llama fat (*pichuwira*), divides it in two, gives one half to the woman and keeps the other; both vigorously knead the fat until they form balls, which they mix with *llampu*. They continue to knead and mix it with *llampu* to shape the mixtures into the form of a male llama and a female llama (the figures are made by the man and his wife, respectively). In the process they use all the *llampu* without leaving any residue. While this is going on, a chicken enters the room, and the owner does not permit the fowl to eat the maize left on the floor, because, if it did, "in the same manner the condor will eat one of our little alpaca babies." Neither chicken nor dogs are allowed to come near the place of the ritual.

The daughter, who has remained behind in the kitchen brings a pot of hot *chicha,* and the mother interrupts her activity to fill the two *qeros* with the beer, which she hands to her husband. He then spills some of it on the floor and drinks the rest; the woman does the same, and then the spectators are invited to drink the *chicha*.

4:46 P.M. In the dough kneaded by the husband the head, neck, and body of the male llama are already distinguishable. With one finger he makes a small hole in the part that corresponds to the back of the llama, and placing in it pieces of incense he closes the opening. When the figurine is finished, it is placed in the *chuwa*. The man places next to the head a leaf of *kintu* and two *kintus* on each side of the back of the figurine.

The man begins to another knead piece of *pichuwira* for the *canta* of the male alpaca. The woman, finishing the *canta* of the female llama, opens its back, places incense inside and closes the opening. She places the *canta* in a *chuwa* and sprinkles a handful of coca leaves over the figurine.

4:56 P.M. The woman asks her husband to give her some *pichuwira* to make the figure of the young animals; both are vigorously kneading the fat and from time to time add some *llampu.* The man notices that the woman has made a mistake; she has made only one figurine instead of three. The man begins to give shape to the figurine of the male alpaca; the front part of the neck is retouched so that the shape of *piscayoq* becomes more visible. He perforates the back, places the incense inside, and deposits the figurine in the *chuwa.*

The man takes the *canta* of the female llama that his wife has made and kneads it again. He divides the ball into three equal parts and with one of them begins to shape a small figurine.

5:08 P.M. The man finishes the three small figurines. He places them on a *chuwa* and spreads incense over their backs. He again kneads *pichuwira* to make the figure of the female alpaca. The woman gives kneaded dough to her husband so that he may shape the *canta* or *musoqkancha* (new corral) or offspring. The woman now kneads the dough left by her husband, while he opens the back of the *canta* of *musoqkancha* to introduce the incense and places the figurine in a *chuwa.* The woman gives the dough to her husband, who breaks it into three pieces and shapes the three figurines of the little alpacas and *allpachas* (female alpacas) and places them in a *chuwa* and spreads incense on their backs.

5:23 P.M. In front of the owners are five *chuwas* in which one can see nine figurines (or *cantas*) of camelids made of *pichuwira,* maize flour (*llampu*), *coca kintu* leaves, incense, and mineral scrapings. In the first *chuwa* there are three *maqesanas* (female llamas); in the second, three *allpachas* (female *alpacas*); in the third, a *piara* or *carguero* (male transportation llama); in the fourth, a *wanso* (male alpaca); and in the last one, *musoqkancha* or offspring. Together with the cobs of the corn that have been used, the figures are placed in their *chuwas* in such a way that their posteriors face the couple.

5:26 P.M. The man proceeds to carry out the first *tinka* of the *piara* with liquor, invoking these phrases (this act is called *samay*):

> *Wanso . . . piara samaykamusaq qampuchkanqa, pionninpas qampuchkanqa, maqesanakuna qamuchkanqa, clasin clasin riatillunpas qamuchkanqa, todo completo qamuchkanqa, waskanpas kimsa docena sartalla qamuchkanqa, gastunpas waranqa mediollalla qamuchkanqa, pichuwiranpas Chalhuanca urayllamanta qamuchkanqa, chuyallanpas Chalhuanca urayllamanta qamuchkanqa*" (*Huanso, piara* I desire to come, its peons should come, *masqesana* should come, her ear ribbons of all colors as well, it should all come complete, three dozen rope bundles should come too, its expenses of one thousand

and a half should come too, its *chuya* (*aguardiente*) from far below Chalhuanca).

He allows some drops of liquor to fall on the *piara* figure and drinks the rest. Then the wife does a *tinka* with the *aguardiente* provided by the husband and also makes invocations. The man asks the observers likewise to make *tinkas*.

The *wanso* is also invoked in a *tinka* in the same order: by the man, his wife, and the spectators. Then the *tinka* of the *maqesana* and of the *allpachas* are invoked, and while one person recites invocations, the rest shout "*wajoo, wajoo.*" The wife begins to play the *tinya* and to sing.

5:56 P.M. The man proceeds to wrap all the *cantas* in a shawl with their *chuwas*, taking care not to damage them, and places the bundle on the *mesaqepi*. One of the three *chapchus* is burned as the ritual of *víspera* is concluded, while the others are kept for the next day.

The Ideological Dimension: The Ritual of the Día

I will now narrate the ritual of the day which, together with the "preceeding evening" (*víspera*), forms a whole unit known as *Ayllusqa*. Because of snow, *día* had to be postponed for one week, and during that week the owner suffered continuous nightmares due to the delay in offering the *cantas* to the mountain spirits. The ritual took place on 21 August in one *cancha* of Chicurumi.

8:20 A.M. Men and women invited by the owners begin to gather and converse inside the house. They are offered some rum while they are solicited by the owners to help in the ritual. Those who accept are called *peones*. Then the owner addresses an old man and asks him to take the role of *masa* (son-in-law) since he knows the rituals well, and because the owner is ignorant of them, as he is not from these parts.

8:42 A.M. All go to the *tinka corral*. The owner carries the *mesaqepi* on his back and in one hand the *tinya* drum, while his wife carries a full huge earthenware *chicha* jar. One *peón* carries *taya* (a bush) firewood and embers, others carry diverse packages, while from a nearby corral, the old *masa* drives the animals towards the *tinka corral*.

8:53 A.M. Together with the herd which is about 80 head, mostly alpacas, the owners arrive at the *tinka corral* where they are welcomed by two men and a woman.

The *tinka corral* which is shaped like a figure eight is located some 400 meters from the owners' house. One of the circles measures eight meters, and the other five meters. At the junction there is an opening of 1.50 meters, wide, the wall is stone *pirka* and is 1.30 meters high. On the eastern part of the larger circle there is an entrance which was later closed off with a blanket.

9:08 A.M. The *mesaqepi* is left in a corner of the corral. The owner unties the bundle, removing coca leaves and selecting *kintus*. The *masa* prepares a fireplace by digging to a certain depth and, after making the sign of the cross, places firewood in it.

The *masa* receives from the owner 25 leaves of *coca kintu*, lights the fire with the embers and adds *kintus* and *llampu* while the others converse and chew coca. The owner, taking off his hat and facing east, kneels in front of the *mesaqepi* and unties the bundle.

9:27 A.M. Following the instructions of the *masa*, the owner approaches the fire pit, takes a *chuwa*, and drinks *aguardiente* from it, sprinkling some drops over the fire. The wife does the same and the old *masa* closes this act.

The old man places incense in three *chuwas*. The woman feeds it to the fire slowly in order to create smoke and not fire.

9:38 A.M. The wife offers two *qeros* of *chicha* to her husband. He proceeds to make a *tinka* in front of the fire, first with the vessel in his right hand in honor of *Pachamama*, and then with the left hand vessel in honor of the *Apus* or mountains.

The owner carries out *tinkas* to the *chapchu* which is placed in a *chuwa* on the *mesaqepi* with two *qeros* of *chicha*, while invoking *samay*. He drinks the *chicha* that he has in his right hand, and once finished, he switches the vessel to his left hand, and the one in that hand to his right hand, and drinking that, returns the empty *qeros* to his wife. When this *tinka* is completed, the man picks up the *chuwa* in both hands, lets his breath fall on the *chapchu*, and sprinkling it over the fire lets some drops of *chicha* fall on it.

The owner's wife asks an old woman to play the *tinya* during the ritual; she is offered a small bottle of rum in payment. The old woman plays the *tinya* and presently begins to sing. When she is finished, only the men shout, "*wajoo, wajoo*." The owner distributes coca while the old lady continues with the singing, and a discussion arises about the order in which the *cantas* should be burned.

10:00 A.M. The first *samay* begins. The owner standing in front of the *maqesanas* (female llama *cantas*) says the following:

Samaykamusaq, qamuchkanqa maqesana qamuchkanqa, qamuchkanqa Huayunca pasaqmanta, Parionakunapa, don Fabian Huarcapa qamuchkanpa, Huamanikunapa qamuchkanqa, Sallcatamanta quimsa corralla qamuchkanqa, wasi gastonpas Chalhuanca uraymanta qamuchkanqa, tragullanpas pichuwira, todo completo qamuchkanqa (I am going to ask that the *maqesana* come, that she come from the sector of Huayunca, from the Parionas, from that of don Fabian Huarcapa, that she come from the *Huamanis*, from the area of Sallcata three corrals, that the food for the house come from far below Chalhuanca, the drink, the chest grease, everything complete, that everything complete may come.).

Then the wife does a *tinka* with two *qeros* of *chicha*, while the owner does it with a *chuwa* full of rum. The other people also do their *tinkas* one by one, while the *masa* kneeling in front of the *mesaqepi* shakes the *waiqa* (the small bag that containd coca leaves) over the *cantas* of the *maqesanas*. When each invited person has finished his invocation, the *masa*, shaking his bag reiterates, "*Jampuchun, jampuchun*" (let them come, let them come!).

10:06 A.M. The *maqesanas* have received their *tinka,* and the old woman passes the drum to the *patrón* who plays it, and when he concludes, all the men shout "*wajoo, wajoo.*" The wife takes the *tinya* and sings, and once the song is finished, returns the instrument to the old woman, who continues with the recital.

The congregation has finished the third *tinka* to the *maqesanas* (the first two with *chicha* and the third one with rum) imploring the *samay* (desire). The *masa* takes the figurines to the fire pit, spreads coca, grease, and incense, and puts them in the fire with the heads facing east. The fire is moderate so that the offering burns slowly and smokes sufficiently. The old woman continues singing. One of the guests places a pot of *chicha* on the fire in which the figurines have been placed moments before.

10:15 A.M. The second *samay* directed to the female alpacas (*allpachas*) is begun. The ritual repeats itself, and once it is over, the wife of the owner sings while playing the *tinya.* The *masa*, making invocations, carries out the *tinka*, and at the end, sings accompanying himself on the *tinya.* The old woman continues with the songs. During the second *samay*, a couple arrives at the corral, and the visit of these people is taken as a good omen. The ceremony ends, and the old *masa* burns the figures while the old woman sings, and we hear some invocations.

10:38 A.M. The third *samay* to the *piara* (male llama) is carried out in the same way as those preceding. At the completion of three consecutive *tinkas*, each participant receives coca leaves from the owner or from the *masa.* The old woman continues singing while the old *masa* completes a *tinka* and implores:

Ay inka piaralla qamuchkanqa, macho Cucuchimanta vecinokunapas qamuchkanqa pachaq peonninpas allin yuyayniyoq qamunqa (Oh! that the inca *piara* from the great Cucuchi [a mountain] might come; that his neighbors might come; that one hundred peóns with good memory might come.)

11:06 A.M. The old man and a helper bring some braided ropes (*kiqmi*) and woolen ribbons (pink and carnation red). The ribbons are called *waita* or *tika* (flower), and the *samay* of the *piara* continues.

One *peón* selects 25 coca leaves, braids them together with a skein of pink wool, and leaves them in one *chuwa.* He then begins to make another bundle.

11:20 A.M. The *samay* to the *piara* is finished. On the *mesaqepi* there is now one *chuwa* with the figures of the *piara* and another with those of the *wanso* (male alpaca) whose *tinka* now begins. The ceremony takes place as before.

11:30 A.M. The *masa* picks up the braided ropes and hands them to the wife of the owner, who hangs them around her neck. Three male helpers go to the center of the corral and bring three male llamas that have been previously selected by the herder. They are young animals. They face east. The wife hands over one of the ropes, and the herder ties the hind legs of the llamas forcing them to sit. The seated llamas are tended by the three men who place their hands on the necks and backs of the animals. The owner sprays water called *ñawin yacu* (water from the fountain's eye) over the heads and backs of the llamas, and then he repeats it with *ñawin aqa* (chicha).

The herder then gets a piece of *taku* (fine clay) and with it draws three branching lines over the backs of the llamas. His wife then hands him three *kintu* leaves and *llampu* which he buries between the shoulder blades of the animals.

11:40 A.M. The *masa* brings the 25 bundles of *coca* leaves that have been selected previously. He digs a small hole of about 5 cm with a knife in which he places the leaves and the *llampu* and covers them. Meanwhile, the owner perforates the ears of the llamas and adorns them with the pink ribbons. The owner sprinkles coca leaves over the backs of the animals and places a coin on the middle llama's back. All those attending surround the llamas and take the coca leaves which, they chew.

11:48 A.M. The wife takes off her shawl (*lliqlla*) and covers the llama's heads with it. The *masa* burns incense in front of the animals' noses, and the owner, carrying the *illa*, shakes it over the covered heads of the animals. The owner breaks a handful of the *huayllaichu* grass into three portions and places each bundle along the backs of the llamas, tying the grass with the animal's own wool.

11:53 A.M. The *masa* burns the figures of the male alpaca and llama, and they begin the *tinka* to the bound llamas. The owner places himself behind the llamas. A man places some bells around the neck of the central llama and causes the bell to sound while the *tinka* is continuing. As the bells sound, the *masa* distributes coca leaves from a shawl spread out in front of the llamas to those people who have finished the *tinka*. The owner's wife also performs the *tinka* with two *qeros* of *chicha* and one *chuwa* of liquor and recites an invocation. When she is finished, she too receives coca leaves.

12:20 P.M. The *tinka* of the young llamas is ended, and the owner frees the animals, while "*wajoo*, *wajoo*" is shouted in unison. The old man advises that now is a good moment to give names to the llamas and the central one is named *Rompecalle* (streetbuster).

12:35 P.M. The three helpers bring three young male alpacas to the center of the corral, and place them close together facing east. The owner forces them to sit using the *kiqmi* rope which is handed to him by his wife. The owner sprays the alpacas with *ñawin yaku* and *ñawin aqa*, and with the *taku* draws the branching lines on the wet parts. The *masa* hands him three *kintu* leaves and with the *llampu* given him by the wife, the herder buries the leaves in the thick wool between the shoulder blades of the alpacas. Then they tie the three bundles of *huaylla* grass on their backs and sprinkle coca leaves on them. As before, a coin is placed on the back of the middle animal.

The congregation once more surrounds the alpacas and takes coca leaves from their backs which they chew or place in their coca bags. The owner adorns the ears of each alpaca with a pair of ribbons and they are also named: *Nueve décimos* (a valued silver coin), *Huamanpusaq* (eight condors), and *Cerro Blanco*. The owner's wife covers the head of the alpacas with her shawl and the *masa* gives them incense. The congregation carries out one by one the *tinka* and *samay* with two *qeros* of *chicha* and one *chuwa* of rum while the owner shakes his *kipuna* bag which contains coca leaves. Before beginning the *tinka* some of the attending parties place coins on the animals, which are termed *voluntad* or good will.

The *masa* brings the figurines of the *musoqcancha* from the *mesaqepi* and repeatedly passes them under the noses of the alpacas. Then he burns them in the pit. The *tinka* and *samay* are ended, and the owner frees the animals.

1:31 P.M. The herder and his wife, carrying in their right hands *qeros* full of *chicha*, go around the inside of the corral, driving the animals towards the exit, and as the animals get out of the corral, the herder and his wife spill the contents of their *qeros*. During this phase one hears repeated "*wajoo, wajoo*." In the middle of the empty corral the owner's wife and a female guest dance to the *tinya* and the songs they sing.

1:35 P.M. The owner takes the last *chapchu* to the fire pit and burns it as the final offering.

The *masa* counts the coins given by the guests during the *tinkas* of the animals and, handing them over to the owner, informs him of the amount of donated money. The man deposits the money in separate *waiqa*, or coca bag. The old man puts all the things on the *mesaqepi* in order while informing the owner.

2:12 P.M. Helped by the *masa*, the owner ties the *mesaqepi* on his back. Everybody returns to the house. The camelids driven out of the corral are seen dispersed in the distance.

Songs of the Ayllusqa Ritual

The *Ayllusqa* is carried out with songs from which springs the whole world of the herders and which help us understand the deep meanings of the ritual. The rite is repetitive, cyclical, and becomes monotonous. The prime objective for the person performing the ritual is, without doubt, the increase of the camelid herd. The initial phases of the ritual are expressed in song as if man and domestic animal have met again after a year has passed (this ritual is an annual event), and as if both have lost their force and vitality. This is expressed in the following song:

Chaychallaraqmi yuyarinki	Only now do I begin to remember you
Pisikallpalla wawallaykiqa	Your son with little strength
Perdonawanki licenciawanki	You will forgive me, give me licence
Chicurumillay perdonawanki	Chicurumi, forgive me
Chayllaraqmi yuyarimuiki	Only now do I remember you
Pisikallpalla patronayki	Your *patrona* with little strength
Pisikallpalla patronchallayki	Your little *patrón* with little strength
Ñam hermana hermanachayqa	Yes, sister, my little sister

The I-you address in the song refers not only to the pair man-beast, but also to the man-spirit world (*Pachamama*, the *Apus*' and other tutelary gods). The meeting (*tinkoq*) of these three beings (man, beast, and divinity) is a necessary pre-condition for animal fertility which the herder so ardently desires, and his desire is satisfied only by the offering of the gifts in the ritual to the gods. Should he neglect them, the gods would be come angry and any kind of ill luck could befall him, such as the diminution of his herd through sickness or theft, or even his own death (human death is sometimes interpreted as a result of the mountain having devoured a man's heart). Thus the day of the meeting is crucially important and is expressed in the following song:

Kunan punchaoqa qollqe kurralpi	Today in the silver corral
Lunes punchaoqa qori kurralpi	Monday in the golden corral
Imayllamantam dueñollay ruwawanki	Out of what are you making me, owner mine?
Qaykallamanta dueñollay ruwawanki	Out of how much are you making me, owner mine?
Vierneschalla punchaochalla mamallay	Friday, mother
Diallaykiqa, santuykiqa, mamallay	It is your day, it is your saint's day, mother

As I mentioned before, the three beings, who meet in a special place (*wiwa tinkana corral*) and at a determined time, are all in a state of near exhaustion and tiredness, and it is necessary to replenish the lost forces in order to achieve an increase in fertility:

Patronchallay dueñochallay	My *patrón*, my owner
Kamaqchallayman igualaykuway	Please even out my forces
Kamaqchallayman kabalaykuway	Please replenish my forces
Inciensollaykiwan chuyachaykiwan	With your incense and your liquor
Wirallaykiwan llampullaykiwan	With your fat and your *llampu*
Kukachaykiwan kintuchaykiwan	With your coca and your *kintus*
Qollqe platupi, qori platupi	On the plate of silver, on the plate of gold

Kamaq can, perhaps, be translated as soul or spiritual force. From the context of the song we can derive that incense, *chuya* liquor, *wira* llama grease, *llampu* from ground corn, and *coca kintu* are material representations of the concept of *kamaq*. *Kamaq*, once materialized, becomes tangible to the senses in that incense is to smell, the *llampu* to touch, and the coca to taste, and therefore perceived by man.

It seems that it is the llamas who sing the song asking these things to be given (*alcanzarles*); yet, these are no more nor less than offerings given to the gods. Of all these offerings, the most important is, as we shall see, coca. The herder who made the *cantas* explained the force that coca has, and why he added it to the ground corn. Only when *kamaq* has been *alcanzado* (succored) and has revitalized itself in the exhausted beings, is it possible to increase the herd, which is what men desire:

Kamaqchallayman alcanzaykuptikiqa	If you would succor me, my force
Kikichallaysi chauchorikasaq	I would be sprouting roots by myself
Kikichallaysi mallkirichkasaq	I would be shooting branches
Mallkicha jina wayllacha jina	Like the tree, like the *huaylla* grass
Chiri wayrapi chauchorichkasaq	In the cold wind I would be taking root

Many of the songs collected need to be studied in depth. Here I will only deal with one aspect of them. The songs that sing of the desire to increase the herd, with their bucolic character, inherently contain the force of green nature. Herders use a series of metaphors when they refer to the increase or fertility of the herd; we can appreciate "I would be shooting branches/ Like the tree, like the *huaylla* grass."

Not only in ritual, but also in daily life, herders compare their camelids to plants. A colleague of mine, who carried out fieldwork in Arequipa (in the province of La Unión), told me that a herder said to him, "My llama is my *chacra*" while he was showing him his herd. This is abundantly clear if we take into account the important role that the llama has in the pastoral life of the Andean peoples.

With alpacas a similar expression was noted. The herders of the Apurimac region, when they shear the alpacas, frequently refer to the wool "harvest." In a figurative sense, they compare the llama to the fields, and the wool to the plants growing in them. According to a herder, the favorable time for the wool "harvest" is in February and March, because "*paray tiempu rutuninku para mayllanampaq, caqmanta wapo wiñamunanpaq*" (We shear in the rainy season so that the rains wash the bodies and they can rapidly sprout again like plants). Another herder, as he was exchanging alpaca meat for ears of corn said," Let us exchange my tender *choclo* for yours." That camelids are likened to maize is evident in the ritual just described.

The *cantas* were made out of ground maize with llama fat, *coca kintu*, incense, *taku*, mineral scrapings, and others things. Five types of maize corresponded to five kinds of *cantas* (*piara* male llama: red *chumpi*; *maqesana* female llama: yellow *muruchu*; *wanso* male alpaca: white *almidón*; and offspring: white and small *almidón*). I also remind the reader that five cobs remain in each *chuwa* until they are burned as offerings.

According to the man who was shaping the animals from the *llampu*, the ground corn represents the body of the animal while the coca represents its force (*kamaq*). Coca plays a symbolic role of great importance. For example, it is the "shawl" that envelopes the animal (it is said that the wool grows rapidly if the animal is wrapped in the shawl). It is the "grass" that the animal eats, while the rum is water (the *chuwa* full of liquor is called *qocha* [lake]). The participants chew the coca leaves spread on the backs of the animals. The ears of the *canta piara* and the loads of the llamas are represented with coca leaves. Coca leaves in the bag are shaken over the heads of the llamas as they receive the *tinka* (the coca can be replaced by the *illa* when it represents *kamaq*). Twenty-five leaves of coca *kintu* are buried in a hole dug in front of the llamas. (In another ritual I observed that the seeds of coca [*muqllu*] were buried under the *churana* stone at the center of the corral). And, finally, when the animals receive the *tinka*, three *kintu* leaves are mingled with the animal's wool so that it may grow rapidly and abundantly (in the case of the alpaca) or so that the animal may have great strength (in the case of the llama).

The metaphor used to express the increase of the herd through the *huaylla* grass has already been mentioned. This plant, a variety of *ichu*, grows in the *puna* and is eaten by the camelids. The three branching lines drawn on the foreheads and backs of the animals are associated with *huayllariy* (branching like the *huaylla*). We also observed that a handful of *huaylla* grass was tied along the spine of the animal with its own wool. Coca and *huyalla* are used as symbols of increase and abundance of wool. *Huaylla* is the clothing and finery of the camelids according to the following song:

Qollqe kanchapi sayallachkani	I am standing in the silver corral
Qori wayllallay pakanayoqlla	With my veil of golden *huaylla*
Qollqe kaywilla kayllayoqlla	With my silver collar
Qori wayllalla kurunayoqlla	With my crown of golden *huaylla*
Qori wayllalla día pachayoqlla	With my clothing of golden

	huaylla
Ima kuyayllam bajaykamuni	Oh! how much admired have I come down
Qayka kuyayllam hermana purisaq	How greatly admired, my sister, I will walk
Dueñullay qollqe wayllawan tipawanki	With silver *huaylla* you will sit me down
Waylla siantas akuykuspa mamallay	While chewing[1] the *huaylla* flower, mother
Ichu muqunta kutuykuspa mamallay	Eating *ichu* seeds, mother
Chicurumillay wayllallapi mamallay	With the Chicurumi *huayllas*, mother
Qayka kuyaysi dueñulla cani	How admired I am, my owner
Qori wayllalla kapachayoqlla	With my golden *huaylla* cape
Qori wayllalla tapanayoqlla	With the golden *huaylla* shawl
Qollqe wayllalla tapanayoqlla	With the silver *huaylla* shawl

Clothing is made out of spun and woven wool. It is very interesting that in a figurative way, wool derives from anot her vegetable material. The woolen ribbons which adorn the animals' ears are also figuratively plants, since they are called *tika* or *waita* in the following song:

Amapola tikawan churawanki	You will adorn me with the poppy flower
Arequipachallay multicolores	Many colors from Arequipa
Tupawasqachu? luciasqachu?	Do I look good? Do I look fine?
Ima kuyayta qayka kuyayta	How loved and how much admired
Amapola tikari lucillawasqapaschu?	Doesn't the poppy flower look good on me?
Terciopelo tikari liciawasqapaschu?	Doesn't the velvet flower look nice on me?
Anqoripa loqochayoqlla mamay	With my *anqoripa* hat, my mother
Clavelina loqochayoqlla mamay	With my carnation hat, my mother
Sumaqllata mamallay waytarinki	Beautifully you will adorn me
Wawa sapallay warmichallaqa	Woman with many children
Tikaykukuskan, hermanallay	That which has flowered, sister
Tupaqllaychu, manachu?	Does it make me look nice or

	not?
Humanga tikari Arequipa tikari	Huamanga flower, Arequipa flower
Ima kuyay tupani amapola tikayoq	How beautiful I look with the poppy flower

Once the vitality (*kamaq*) of the camelids has been regenerated through the the ritual process, the animals, figuratively dressed in *huaylla* clothes and decorated with flowers, express their happiness and contentment, and demonstrate their latent power in the next song:

Chicurumillay patachapiqa	On the slopes of Chicurumi
Chicurumillay pampachapiqa	On the *pampas* of Chicurumi
Ima kuyayllam patronay kani	How admired I am, my *patrona*
Qayka kuyayllam dueñollay kani	How admired I am, my owner
Acerollas kallpayqa	My force is like steel
Acerollas tulluyqa	My bones are like steel
Ima munayraq purimuchkasaq	How loved will I walk about
Qayka kuyayraq pasiamuchkasaq	How much admired will I strut around

The vital force thus replenished becomes usable by the herders. They prefer to express this by relating it to their customary treks to the valleys. During the phase when they carry out the *tinka* and *samay* for the male llamas, they sing as follows:

Kaylluchallayta churakapuway	Put on my chest adornment
Sillwichallayta churakapuway	Put on my saddlecloth
Viajero kachkani, pasajero kachkani	I am a traveller, I am a passer-by
Wasichallanchi pasallasaqña	I am already leaving our house
Ama pañallay waqapuwankichu	Don't you cry for me, my little sister
Hermanullayiki kallachkaniraq	I am still your brother
Qari qariraq kapullawan	Very brave
Chicurumillay jovenchallaqa	Is the young man from Chicurumi
Riqsisqalla kachkani	I am renowned
Llaqtan llaqtan purimunaypaq	For going from town to town
Calle calletan pasiamunaypaq	For strutting from street to street
Ima kuyayraq sayarichkani	How admired I am standing

Qayka kuyayraq sayarichkani	How much admired I stand
Chacarerupa punkuchallanpi	At the door of the *chacarero*
Chacarerupa corralchallanpi	In the corral of the *chacarero*
Arequipallay llipipiyoq	With Arequipan finery
Huamangalla vestidoyoq	With Huamangan clothing
Cerruy Pascucha kaskachayoq	With my bells from Cerro de Pasco
Comun comunchu ñoqa puriyman	I do not go like just anyone
Mancha manchachu ñoqa puriyman	I do not walk fearfully
Llaqtayoqkuna tapuwaptinpas	When the townspeople ask me
Wasiyoqkuna tapuwaptinpas	When the owners of the house ask me
Sara mamaqa sasa kayllanallas	It is difficult to bring mother maize
Sara mamaqa sasa sillwinallas	It is difficult to carry mother maize
Apamuchkani karguchalla ruwananchipaq	I am bringing it to pass the *cargo*
Obligacionllata rurachkanchik	So that we discharge our obligation
Santo Santata servichkanchik	To serve the saints
Maykamaraqcha purillasaqpas	How far need I go
Maykamaraqcha samarisaqpas	And where will I rest?
Pero maqtaqa qari qarilla	But I am a strong young man

In these songs I find phrases that subtly reflect the mentality of the *punaruna* with respect to the *llaqtaruna*, confirming the low status of the herder that I mentioned before. But this latent discrimination is not always present. There are times when it disappears, and then the llama, exalted in song and with the ritual force of coca and a body of maize, ears of coca, wool of *huaylla* or coca, is garlanded with flowers. Then he multiplies and grows like the plants. I dare not, at this time, compare other kinds of pastoralist societies, but surely, this characteristic sentiment towards green nature, towards the plants, be they wild or domesticated, is typical of Andean pastoralism.

If the *llaqtaruna* show their respect for the world of vegetation, since they are very dependent on it, then both pastoralists and agriculturalists share a common ideological cosmos. And it is certain that the latter respect the magico-religious knowledge of the former.

(Translation by Enrique Mayer)

NOTE

1. *Akulli* is the Quechua word for the act of chewing coca and should not be confused with animals chewing grass, though the poetic expression does equate the two on purpose.

REFERENCES CITED

Concha Contreras, Juan de Dios
1975 Relación entre pastores y agricultores. Allpanchis 8:67–102 Cuzco.

Murra, John V.
[1972] 1975 El control vertical de un máximo de pisos ecológicos en la economía de las sociedades andinas. *In* Formaciones Económicas y Políticas del Mundo Andino. pp. 59–115, Lima: Instituto de Estudios Peruanos.

Pulgar Vidal, Javier
n.d. Geografía del Perú. Lima: Editorial Universo.

13

Marriage Relations Between *Punaruna* and *Llaqtaruna*: The Case of Pampamarca Parish, Apurímac, Peru

Hiroyasu Tomoeda and Tatsuhiko Fujii

In this brief essay we will analyze the marriages contracted between herders (*punaruna*) and agriculturalists (*llaqtaruna*) in the parish of Pampamarca, which encompasses the districts of Caraybamba and Cotaruse, in the Province of Aymaraes, Department of Apurímac, in the southern highlands of Peru. The parish is on the upper Chalhuanca River, where we can identify three ecological zones; *puna* (4500–4000 m above sea level), *suni* (4000–3500 m), and upper *quichua* (3500–3000 m; see Fig. 13.1).

The high and extensive *puna* zone is the domain of the herders who are dispersed in four communities (Totora, Pisquicocha, Mestizas, and Iscahuaca), while the very steep and narrow valleys are home to four agricultural communities (Pampamarca, Cotaruse, Colca, and Caraybamba). These agriculturalists cultivate mostly Andean tubers in the *suni* zone and grow maize and other cereals on the terraces in the valleys. The pastoral communities are exclusively dedicated to raising Andean domesticated camelids, alpacas and llamas, although we should also note that they do cultivate tubers on a small scale. The agriculturalists also raise some Old World domesticated animals, cattle and sheep, in the *suni* and lower parts of the *puna*.

From an economic point of view, the herders and agriculturalists are linked, complementing each other's production with produce from their respective zones. If this economic link is so vital, why don't they intermarry and become relatives? This is precisely the question we address. That is, what are the patterns of intermarriage, if any, between agriculturalists and herders within this relatively confined area? We examined the marriage records in the parish of Pampamarca, going back some 70 years (i.e., starting in 1903).

Tables 13.1a through 13.1h show the number of marriages by place of origin of the spouses. The total number of marriages in the 70–year period is given in Table 13.1h, showing the high rates of village en-

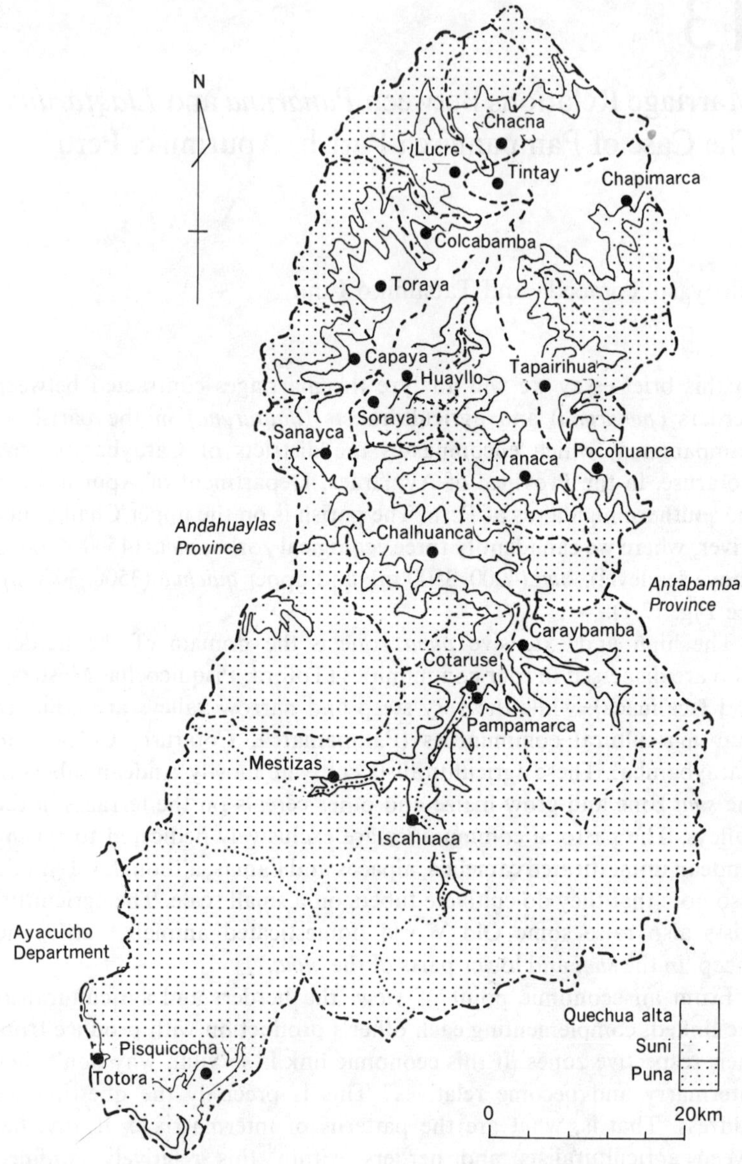

Fig. 13.1 Aymaraes Province

Table 13.1a Primary data on endogamous and exogamous marriages by parish, 1903–10

Husband \ Wife	Toto	Pisq	Mes	Isca	Pam	Cot	Col	Car	O-p.	No m.	Ill.	Subtotal
Totora	1								1			2
Pisquicocha									1			1
Mestizas			5						2			7
Iscahuaca												0
Pampamarca				1	20	2			2			25
Cotaruse						16				1		17
Colca						1	3	1				5
Caraybamba								11				11
Out-parish					2	1		4	1			8
No mention			1							1		2
Illegible												0
Subtotal	1	0	6	1	22	20	3	16	7	2	0	Total 78

Table 13.1b Primary data on endogamous and exogamous marriages by parish, 1903–20

H \ W	Toto	Pisq	Mes	Isca	Pam	Cot	Col	Car	O-p.	No m.	Ill.	Subtotal
Totora	6								2	3		11
Pisquicocha		2							1			3
Mestizas			20						2	2		24
Iscahuaca			1	6	3				2			12
Pampamarca			1	3	39	2		2	2	3		52
Cotaruse					2	38	1	1	2	2		46
Colca					2	1	10	1				14
Caraybamba					1		1	48		4		54
Out-parish			2		3	2	1	6	3			17
No mention			1		1					12		14
Illegible											1	1
Subtotal	6	2	25	9	51	43	13	58	14	26	1	Total 248

dogamy in which partners come from the same community. Village endogamy shows up equally among the communities of the *puna* as well as those of the upper *quichua*.

There is a high percentage of village endogamy during the period of 70 years. (cf. Tables 13.1a to 13.1g). Eighty-nine percent (201/226) of Caraybambinos chose a wife from the same community, and the same is

Table 13.1c Primary data on endogamous and exogamous marriages by parish, 1903–30

H \ W	Toto	Pisq	Mes	Isca	Pam	Cot	Col	Car	O-p.	No m.	Ill.	Subtotal
Totora	6								2	3		11
Pisquicocha		5							1			6
Mestizas			24						2	2		28
Iscahuaca			1	10	3				3			17
Pampamarca			1	3	53	2		2	2	4		67
Cotaruse					4	48	1	1	2	2		58
Colca					2	1	19	1				23
Caraybamba					1		2	70	1	6	1	81
Out-parish			2		4	3	1	6	5			21
No mention			1		1					69	1	72
Illegible											1	1
Subtotal	6	5	29	13	68	54	23	80	18	86	3	Total 385

Table 13.1d Primary data on endogamous and exogamous marriages by parish, 1903–40

H \ W	Toto	Pisq	Mes	Isca	Pam	Cot	Col	Car	O-p.	No m.	Ill.	Subtotal
Totora	6								2	3		11
Pisquicocha		5							1			6
Mestizas			29	2	1				2	2		36
Iscahuaca			1	17	3				3			24
Pampamarca			1	3	79	4	1	2	3	5		98
Cotaruse				1	4	65	1	2	3	4		80
Colca					3	2	28	1				34
Caraybamba					1	1	3	137	5	7	1	155
Out-parish			2		5	4	1	9	11			32
No mention			1		1					85	1	88
Illegible											1	1
Subtotal	6	5	34	23	97	76	34	151	30	106	3	Total 565

evident in Mestizas with a figure of 82 percent (56/68). In the four communities of the valley, we first note the high percentage of endogamy, then marriages between two members of valley communities within the same parish. We observe that 7 percent (12/162) of men from Cotaruse married someone from the valley. Lastly are marriages between a local person with someone outside the parish. For example,

Table 13.1e Primary data on endogamous and exogamous marriages by parish, 1903–50

H \ W	Toto	Pisq	Mes	Isca	Pam	Cot	Col	Car	O-p.	No m.	Ill.	Subtotal
Totora	14								2	3		19
Pisquicocha		6							1			7
Mestizas			37	4	1				2	2		46
Iscahuaca			1	18	5			1	3			28
Pampamarca			1	3	116	5	4	4	4	6		143
Cotaruse				2	5	115	1	3	3	6		135
Colca				1	7	2	53	3		1		67
Caraybamba					2	1	4	155	7	7	1	177
Out-parish			2		8	7	1	12	16	1	1	48
No mention			1		2		1			85	1	90
Illegible											1	1
Subtotal	14	6	42	28	146	130	64	178	38	111	4	Total 761

Table 13.1f Primary data on endogamous and exogamous marriages by parish, 1903–60

H \ W	Toto	Pisq	Mes	Isca	Pam	Cot	Col	Car	O-p.	No m.	Ill.	Subtotal
Totora	22								3	5		30
Pisquicocha		10							1	1		12
Mestizas		1	54	4	1				3	4		67
Iscahuaca			2	23	6	1		1	4	1		38
Pampamarca			4	3	134	6	4	4	5	13		173
Cotaruse				2	9	124	1	3	4	9		151
Colca				1	9	3	62	3		3		81
Caraybamba				1	3	2	4	175	9	10	1	205
Out-parish			3		9	9	1	14	31	4	1	72
No mention			1		2		1	1		91	1	97
Illegible									1	1	2	4
Subtotal	22	11	64	34	172	145	73	201	61	142	5	Total 930

4 percent (7/162) of men from Cotaruse and 3 percent (6/187) of men from Pampamarca married outsiders from agricultural villages of the upper *quichua*, people from Chalhuanca, Antilla, Yanaca, Sañayca, and other communities. The rest of the marriages are with people from distant places, such as Cuzco, Andahuaylas, and Huancavelica.

It is clear that marriages between *puna* and valley residents are the

Table 13.1g Primary data on endogamous and exogamous marriages by parish, 1903–70

H \ W	Toto	Pisq	Mes	Isca	Pam	Cot	Col	Car	O-p.	No m.	Ill.	Subtotal
Totora	24								3	5		32
Pisquicocha		15							1	1		17
Mestizas		1	56	5	2				4	4		72
Iscahuaca		1	2	23	6	1		1	4	1		39
Pampamarca			5	3	138	6	4	4	6	13	1	180
Cotaruse				2	8	131	1	3	7	9		161
Colca				1	9	3	69	4		3		89
Caraybamba				1	4	3	4	194	13	10	1	230
Out-parish			3		10	10	2	14	34	4	1	78
No mention			1		2	1	1	1		91	1	98
Illegible									1	1	2	4
Subtotal	24	17	67	35	179	155	81	221	73	142	6	Total 1000

Table 13.1h Primary data on endogamous and exogamous marriages by parish, 1903–72

H \ W	Toto	Pisq	Mes	Isca	Pam	Cot	Col	Car	O-p.	No m.	Ill.	Subtotal
Totora	24								3	5		32
Pisquicocha		15							1	1		17
Mestizas		1	56	5	2				4	4		72
Iscahuaca		1	2	23	6	1		1	4	1		39
Pampamarca			5	3	145	6	4	4	6	13	1	187
Cotaruse				2	8	132	1	3	7	9		162
Colca				1	9	3	69	4		3		89
Caraybamba				1	4	3	4	201	13	10	1	237
Out-parish			3		10	11	2	15	34	4	1	80
No mention			1		2	1	1	1		91	1	98
Illegible									1	1	2	4
Subtotal	24	17	67	35	186	157	81	229	73	142	6	Total 1017

least frequent, since only 1 percent (2/162) of men from Cotaruse and less than 1 percent (1/237) of men from Caraybamba married someone from the *puna*. We should note, however, that among the marriages between *puna* and valley residents, we include those that took place among herders, because some herders do live in communities in the higher parts of the valley.

Table 13.2 Endogamous and exogamous marriages by zone

a. 1903–10

	Puna	Valley	Out-parish
Puna	6	0	4
Valley	1	54	2
Out-parish	0	7	Total 74

b. 1911–20

	Puna	Valley	Out-parish
Puna	29	3	3
Valley	3	95	2
Out-parish	2	5	Total 142

c. 1921–30

Puna	11	0	1
Valley	0	58	1
Out-parish	0	2	Total 73

d. 1931–40

Puna	14	1	0
Valley	1	127	6
Out-parish	0	5	Total 154

e. 1941–50

Puna	20	3	0
Valley	2	146	3
Out-parish	0	9	Total 183

f. 1951–60

Puna	36	2	3
Valley	4	65	4
Out-parish	1	5	Total 120

g. 1961–70

Puna	11	1	1
Valley	1	45	8
Out-parish	0	3	Total 70

h. 1971–72

Puna	0	0	0
Valley	0	10	0
Out-parish	0	2	Total 12

i. 1903–72

Puna	127	10	12
Valley	12	600	26
Out-parish	3	38	Total 828

In some pages of the marriage records (1903–72), we find mention of the husband's occupation. Of the 316 cases where the occupation is known, 83 are herders, 194 agriculturalists, 25 merchants, and 14 of other occupations. The total of registered marriages for these years is 1,017. Table 13.3a, which shows the origins of the 83 herders, makes clear the fact that there are also some herders in the upper *quichua* communities (see central section; from Pampamarca to Caraybamba).

Table 13.3b indicates marriages registered among the 194 agriculturalists by village of origin. When we compare this table with Table 13.1h, we note that in the former there are no marriages between *puna*

Table 13.3a Endogamous and exogamous marriages among herders

H \ W	Toto	Pisq	Mes	Isca	Pam	Cot	Col	Car	O-p.	No m.	Ill.	Subtotal
Totora	7								1			8
Pisquicocha		1							1			2
Mestizas		1	19		1					1		22
Iscahuaca			1	10	3	1			1			16
Pampamarca				1	12		1	1			1	15
Cotaruse				1		1						2
Colca							3					3
Caraybamba							1	4	2		1	8
Out-parish			1		1			1			1	4
No mention											2	2
Illegible												0
Subtotal	7	2	21	12	17	2	5	6	5	1	5	Total 83

Table 13.3b Endogamous and exogamous marriages among agriculturalists

H \ W	Toto	Pisq	Mes	Isca	Pam	Cot	Col	Car	O-p.	No m.	Ill.	Subtotal
Totora										2		2
Pisquicocha												0
Mestizas												0
Iscahuaca												0
Pampamarca					37				1	6		44
Cotaruse					3	31			2	3		39
Colca					2	1	26			1		30
Caraybamba					1	2		64	2	2		71
Out-parish						2		1	2			5
No mention									1	2		3
Illegible												0
Subtotal	0	0	0	0	43	36	26	66	7	16	0	Total 194

and valley residents (see left-central quadrant), which demonstrates that not all marriages that show up in the same quadrant in Table 13.1h can be considered marriages between agriculturalists and pastoralists.

In Tables 13.2a to 13.2i, we show the number of marriages according to place of origin of the marriage partners grouped in three zones; valley, *puna*, and outside the parish. In Table 13.2i we can see that during a period of 70 years only 12 men of the valley married pastoralist women, and only 10 pastoralists married women who came from the

Table 13.3c Endogamous and exogamous marriages among merchants

H \ W	Toto	Pisq	Mes	Isca	Pam	Cot	Col	Car	O-p.	No m.	Ill.	Subtotal
Totora												0
Pisquicocha												0
Mestizas												0
Iscahuaca												0
Pampamarca			1			1						2
Cotaruse									1			1
Colca										1		1
Caraybamba								15	3			18
Out-parish						1		1				2
No mention										1		1
Illegible												0
Subtotal	0	0	1	0	0	2	0	16	4	2	0	Total 25

Table 13.3d. Endogamous and exogamous marriages among employees, *arrieros*, musicians

H \ W	Toto	Pisq	Mes	Isca	Pam	Cot	Col	Car	O-p.	No m.	Ill.	Subtotal
Totora												0
Pisquicocha												0
Mestizas												0
Iscahuaca					1							1
Pampamarca				1		1		1	1			4
Cotaruse						2						2
Colca												0
Caraybamba										1		1
Out-parish					1	2		1	1			5
No mention							1					1
Illegible												0
Subtotal	0	0	0	1	2	5	1	2	2	1	0	Total 14

valley, giving a total of 22 interzonal marriages, a small number indeed. Further, according to the reasoning above, the actual marriages between zones should be even fewer than 22.

In sum, even though we cannot give a precise figure, it is evident that marriages between *puna* and valley residents have rarely taken place.

(Translation by Enrique Mayer)

14

Ecological Duality and the Role of the Center: Northern Potosí

Olivia Harris

Discussion of ecological complementarity in the Andes by historians and archaeologists has understandably given particular attention to the archipelago model in which an ethnic population concentrated in one area has colonists working on its behalf in sometimes far-flung "islands" and exploiting different resources. It was this dramatic discontinuity of territory that led John Murra to point to the hitherto unappreciated particularities of Andean social and economic organization;[1] and since his original formulation new research has helped to confirm and refine his model.

The evolving ethnohistorical map of Qullasuyu and Kuntisuyu is revealing a pattern of population concentrated at high altitudes, with territory stretching down into maize lands on eastern and/or western slopes, and various islands settled far away from their lands of origin.[2] This exploitation of distant islands continued through colonial times, although evidence for continuous occupation of a particular island by the same ethnic group is rare. Thus, for example, the Qaranqa, based in the *altiplano* in the western part of what is today the Dept. of Oruro in Bolivia, controlled maize lands on the western slopes until the seventeenth century (Rivière 1982:20–25) and also worked maize lands in Pocpo (Dept. of Chuquisaca) and in Tomina (Dept. of Tarija). In addition, until the eighteenth century they retained control of some of the land assigned to them in 1556 in the valley of Cochabamba; under Inka rule they had worked this land mainly for the state, and in colonial times its produce was used to support those serving the *mita* in Potosí (Rivière 1982; Morales 1977; Wachtel 1981; Espinoza 1981). For the late nineteenth century there is a reference to a Qaranqa *hacienda* in the Canton Moromoro of the province of Chayanta.[3]

Comparable evidence can be pieced together for the Killaka/Asanaqi nation, to the east and south of Qaranqa. From the sixteenth to the twentieth centuries there are references to members of this ethnic group in the valleys of the eastern flank far from their main territory. Espinoza Soriano points out that in the sixteenth century they were said to have land "in many places" (Espinoza 1981:182), including the coca-producing *yungas* of Pocona,[4] and that in the Cochabamba valley "at harvest time for two or three months of the year there are more than six hundred Indians of the said province of Carangas, Quillacas, and Asanaques who have come to obtain food."[5] In the early seventeenth century they worked lands below San Pedro de Buenavista surrounded by the *ayllus* of Chayanta;[6] at the end of the eighteenth century Cajias reports that they had "enclaves" in the valleys of Yamparaez (Dept. of Chuquisaca) and Arque (Dept. of Cochabamba) as well as maintaining access to extensive pastures in the neighboring

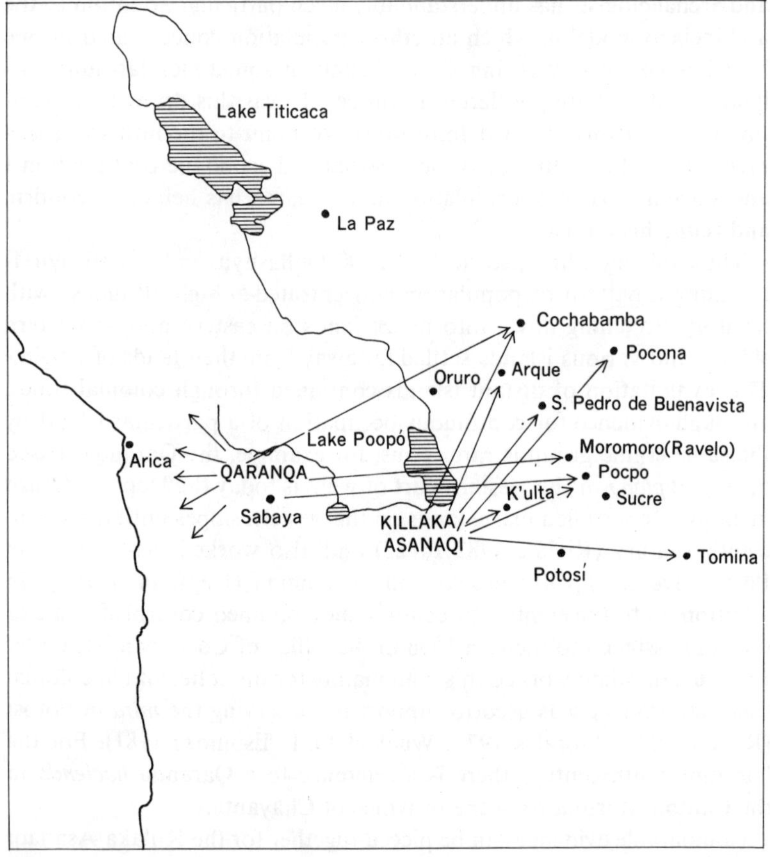

Fig. 14.1 Valley lands of the Qaranqa and Killaka/Asanaqi (sixteenth-twentieth centuries)

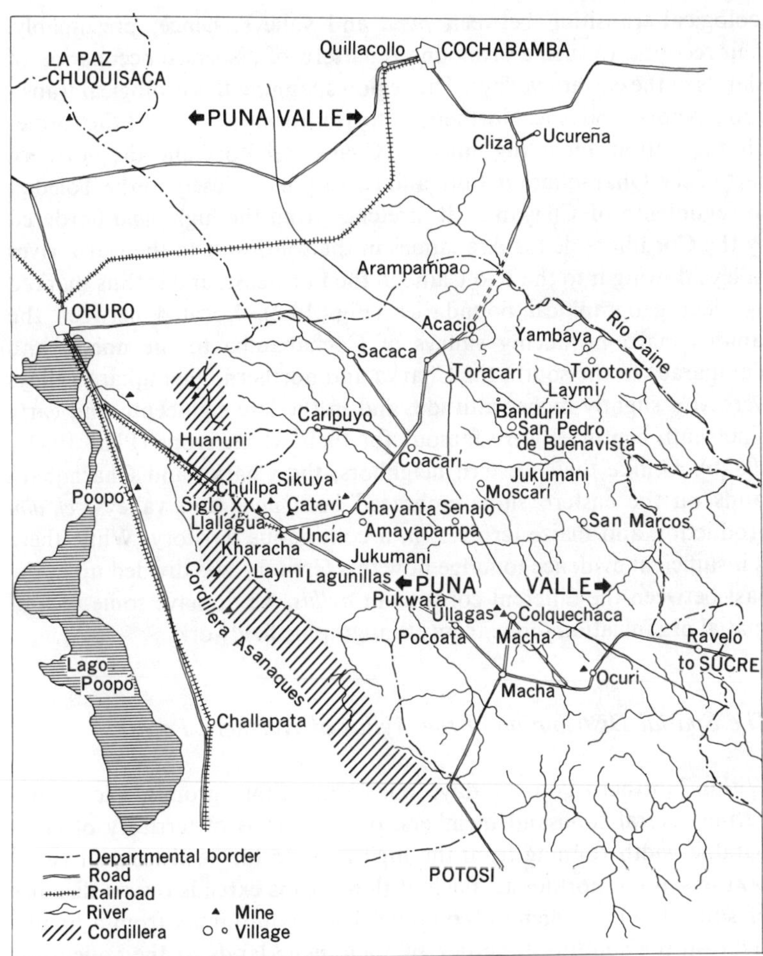

Fig. 14.2 Northern Potosí

partido of K'ulta. Today according to Rivière, some households from Quillacas and Pampa Aullagas still cultivate in Pocpo (Dept. of Chuquisaca) (Cajias 1978; Espinoza 1981; Rivière 1982) (Fig. 14.1).

The main territory of the Qaranqa and the Killaka/Asanaqi falls within the ecological zones characterized by Troll as Dry *Puna*, Thorn *Puna*, and Desert *Puna* (1968:37–8). While on the western flank of the cordillera the Qaranqa used to have direct access to maize-producing valleys, with which to complement the specialized production of the *punas*, to the east, they, and the Killaka/Asanaqi, were cut off by the intervening territory of other ethnic populations, occupying the crucial ecological transition between *puna* and valleys; hence, presumably, their recourse to such a pronounced pattern of dispersed occupation of islands in the eastern valleys. The region spanning this ecological transition is known today as Northern Potosí; it forms the core of the former Charka nation, including much of Charka territory and the northern part of the Qharaqhara nation, and corresponds closely to the Toledan corregimiento of Chayanta. It stretches from the high *puna* bordered by the Cordillera de los Asanaques in the southwest to the warm river valleys flowing into the Río Caine in the northeast, and is thus marked by clear geographical boundaries (Fig. 14.2). Located between the famous maize-producing valleys of Cochabamba to the north, and Yamparaez to the south, the Charka and northern Qharaqhara valleys were at a slightly higher altitude, and in the late eighteenth and early nineteenth centuries were famous for their wheat crops (Platt 1982a, 1982b). Unlike their western neighbors, the Charka and Qharaqhara lands on the eastern slope embraced both *puna* and valleys, *ch'uñu* production and maize terraces, in a continuous territory. While there is insufficient evidence to judge how this territory was divided up in the past between the different constituent *ayllus*, we do have some idea of spatial organization today from ethnographic fieldwork.

The Spatial Distribution of the Ayllus of Northern Potosí

Within Northern Potosí today, four large ethnic groups, each numbering several thousand members, occupy strips of territory of comparable width running from the high *puna* to the semi-tropical valley bottoms in the northeast.[7] Each of these strips extends over a distance of some 120 km; when I accompanied a Laymi family from a hamlet right on the southwest border of their *puna* lands to the valley, the journey took seven days with unladen llamas, and some sixteen days returning upwards with llamas and people fully laden. Unaccompanied and with a light load, a man walking can cover the same distance in some three days and nights (Fig. 14.3, and Fig. 14.4—a schematic version of the same area as Fig. 14.3, but including also the approximate boundaries of the northern strip of Sakaka).

In Northern Potosí today the lands of the maximal ethnic units are organized such that each in its own "strip" spans the entire ecological range of the region. Spatial organization appears, then, to be similar on a larger scale to the "strip" pattern which has been identified by N. Wachtel, whereby agricultural land is divided into long strips of more or less equal width but variable or indeterminate length so that those working each strip have access to a similar or identical range of ecological variation along the length of the strip. Wachtel has himself described the *tsvi* strips of Chipaya agriculture, and he argues that Wayna Qapaj's distribution of *suyos* or *urcos* in Cochabamba to different groups of *mitmaqkuna* to work for the Inca state operated on the same principle (1981:303). Gilles Rivière has shown that the way that the communities bordering on the Salar de Coipasa in Carangas today distribute strips along the dried edges of the salt lake follows this principle also (1982:309).

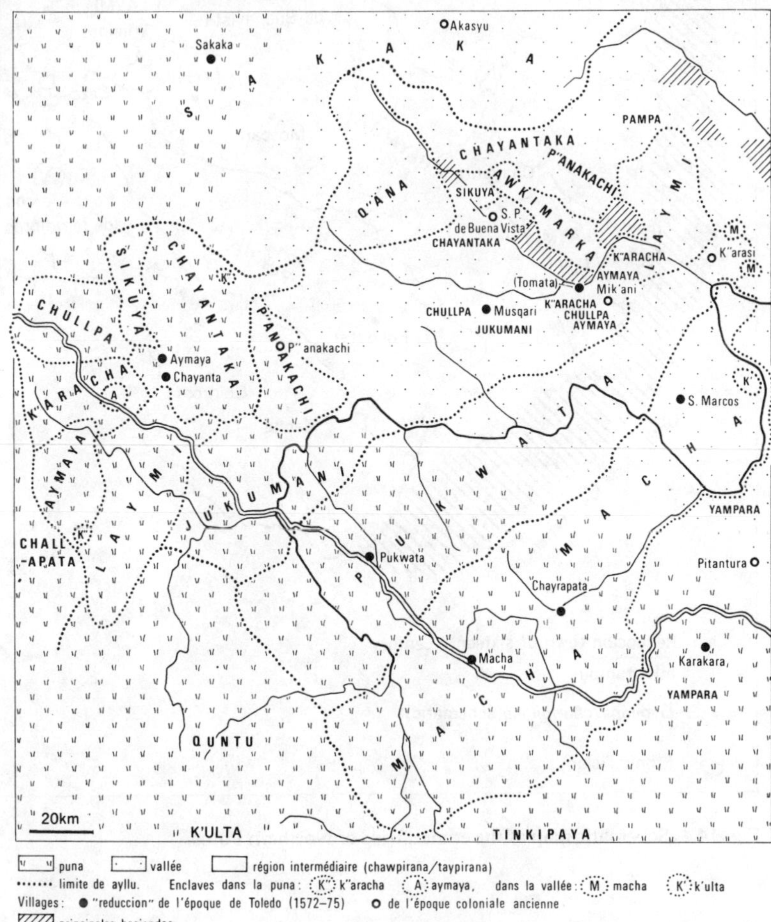

puna   vallée   région intermédiaire (chawpirana/taypirana)

······ limite de ayllu.   Enclaves dans la puna: K'' k''aracha   A aymaya,   dans la vallée: M macha   K' k'ulta

Villages: ● "reduccion" de l'époque de Toledo (1572–75)   ○ de l'époque coloniale ancienne

principales haciendas

Fig. 14.3 The *ayllus* of Northern Potosí

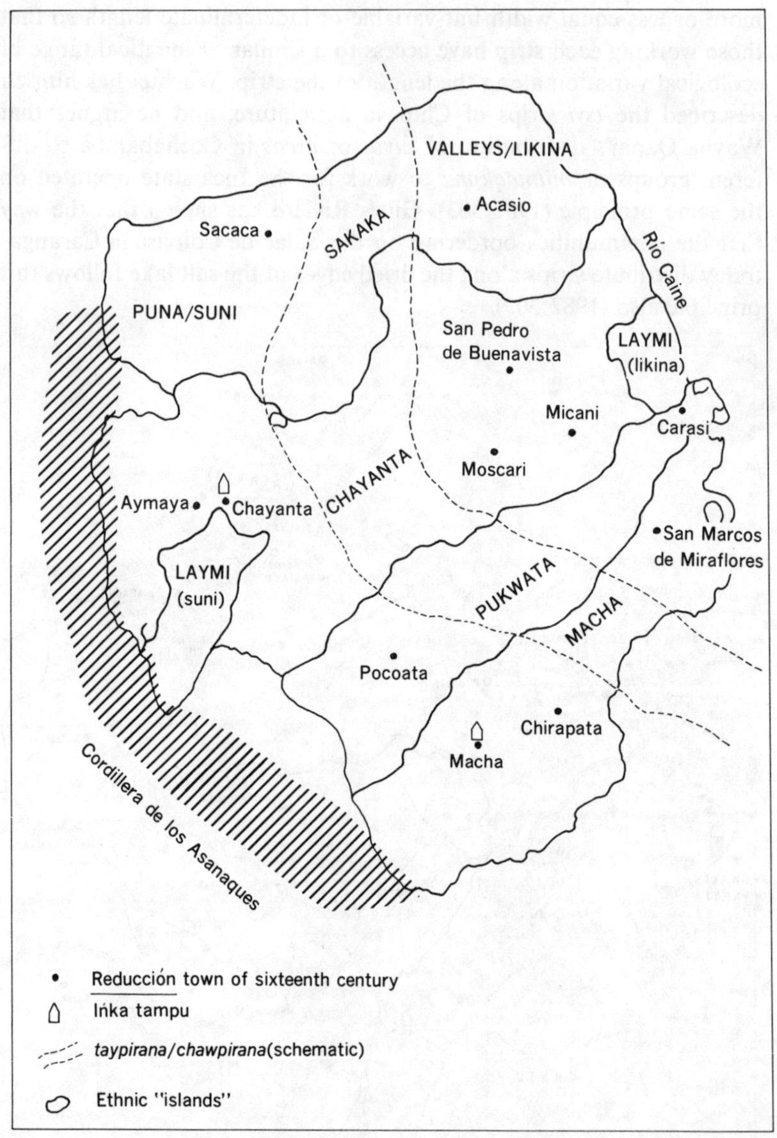

Fig. 14.4 Schematic map of the ethnic strips of Northern Potosí

In the case of the strips of Northern Potosí the scale is of a quite different order from the Chipaya *tsvi* strips or those on the salt lake; given their size it is important to ask how the different ecological resources within each ethnic strip are distributed. My evidence comes entirely from recent ethnographic fieldwork, and it is impossible at this stage to say whether present dispositions within each strip reflect an ancient pattern, or are the product of adaptation to recent political and economic conditions. In the vertical economy operating today in the *ayllus* of Northern Potosí, most households have access to *puna* and valley products through a combination of direct production and kin ties. The circulation of ecologically-specialized produce is today uncentralized, not organized by *ayllu* authorities.

The Laymi *ayllu* was part of the Colonial *repartimiento* of Chayanta; the highland area known by the Laymi as *suni* became part of the Colonial *doctrina* of Chayanta, while the valley lands (known as *likina*) and their inhabitants were assigned to the *doctrinas* of Micani and Carasi. Aymara-speakers, they number some 7,000–8,000 souls today. As can be seen from figures 14.3 and 14.4, the two halves of Laymi territory are widely separated within the Chayanta strip: the *suni* lands lie at an altitude of 3,800–5,000 m, and the subsistence base is a mixed economy of livestock raising and cultivation; llamas are kept above the level of cultivation on the mountain tops, and nearly all households have a flock of sheep. They produce tubers (potatoes, *ch'uñu*, *ullucu*, *oca*, *mashwa*) together with some beans, wheat, and barley. In the *likina* (2,000–3,500 m) the main crops are maize and squashes, with some wheat, beans, and certain species of tuber and *quinoa* that prosper in the warmer climate; goats and some sheep are reared. About two thirds of the Laymi population live today in the *suni*, and one third in the *likina*.

In spite of the distance separating the two parts of their land, and their allocation to different provincial administrations in the Dept. of Potosí today, the Laymi form a distinct and recognizable ethnic group. Their weaving style and their mode of dress are their own, distinguished from neighboring *ayllus* by a series of markers readily identifiable to all those who share the local code of appearance. Above all, the reproduction of *ayllu* identity over time derives from the practice of endogamy, such that the vast majority of *ayllu* members marry within the group. Some households cultivate directly in both ecological zones, a practice known to Spanish-speaking administrators as *doble domicilio*; but even those who do not practice double cultivation directly are familiar with the other half of Laymi territory, and at some point in their lives are likely to stay there for an extended period. The close kin ties between *suni* and *likina* and the frequency of traffic between them gives rise to a distinctive economic system that I have termed the "ethnic economy": within the *ayllu* and between *ayllu* members, ecologically specialized products circulate according to a number of different principles, including unreciprocated donations, immediate purchase and sale for money, exchange of use values between direct producers, and delayed reciprocal transfers. However in almost all cases, the terms, the circumstances, or the objects of such exchanges and forms of circulation are different between *ayllu* members than they are with outsiders. Even though a part of product circulation between the two ecological zones is mediated by the money form, relations between them cannot be understood simply in terms of trade or market[8] (Harris 1978b, 1982; Platt 1982a, 1982b; Godoy 1983).

As we made the long journey from *suni* to *likina* in early July after the harvest, I had much time to reflect on what seemed to me an unfair distribution of land. All the other *ayllus* through whose territory we passed on our descent through the Chayanta strip seemed to have much shorter journeys to make from *puna* to valley, valley to *puna*; Laymi lands appeared to lie at opposite extremes of the Chayanta strip. Footsore, I wondered why the distribution of land in the different ecological niches had developed in this way, rather than being organized such that all the different *ayllus* had journeys of comparable length between highlands and valleys. When I spent some months in the *likina* region, this sense of unfairness was compounded by the discovery that within the lands of the *ayllu* the same discrepancy was repeated. Different areas of the *likina* land are identified by a close association with particular *suni cabildos*. They are the places where most members of a *cabildo* go to cultivate or to obtain maize and other *likina* products, and marriage alliances between these connected areas of *suni* and *likina* tend to reproduce the link over time. While my information is far from complete, it indicates that the *suni cabildos* furthest to the north (that is, closest to the *likina*) have most of their *likina* lands to the south (that is, closer to the *suni*) while those *suni cabildos* furthest from the *likina* frequently have access to valley lands at the opposite extreme of *likina* territory

The Laymi *suni* as a whole is divided into an upper half (*patxasaya*) and a lower half (*manqhasaya*) which correspond to relative altitude. The lower *cabildos* in the *suni* have valley lands at a higher altitude than the higher half of the *suni*, whose valley lands tend to be further down, and therefore further away. Thus, Lagunillas in the northeast of the Laymi *suni* has valley lands around Micani (Mik'ani) at the southwest extreme of Laymi *likina* lands. Households of Qalaqala, the largest

Laymi village which also forms part of *manqhasaya*, mostly go to cultivate or obtain valley produce to the area immediately beyond Micani. The *suni cabildo* of Muruq'umarka on the other hand, which is situated in the southwestern *patxasaya*, has to travel several leagues beyond Micani to reach the valley lands of most of its members (in the hamlets of Nikrutampu, Saychani, Kunturpampa, Qutani, and Puqusuqu) while the *cabildo* of Kututu at the furthest extreme of the *suni*, has most of its *likina* lands near the Río Caine to the northeast (Fig. 14.5).[9]

This correlation is not perfect; indeed it could not be since *ayllu* members state explicitly that valley lands are "mixed up" (*ch'axruta* Aymara; *ch'ajrusqa* Quechua). While most highland *cabildos* are associated with a particular hamlet or hamlets in the valleys, a survey of any valley hamlet would reveal households whose *puna* lands were elsewhere, sometimes widely separated.[10] Platt has argued that the reason for this derives from the developmental cycle of households, and the ways that female inheritance and strategic marriages can be used to ensure to each household access to adequate land, and products from both ecozones (1982b:42–43). In his model, *cabildos* (or "minimal *ayllus*") that have sufficient land practice a higher rate of intra-*cabildo* endogamy, thus reproducing a close link over the generations between the *puna* and valley sections of the *cabildo*. Where land is scarce, there is a greater tendency to marry out of the *cabildo*, and therefore to introduce new alignments of the kin ties uniting the two ecological zones (Platt 1978a:1106 n.6).

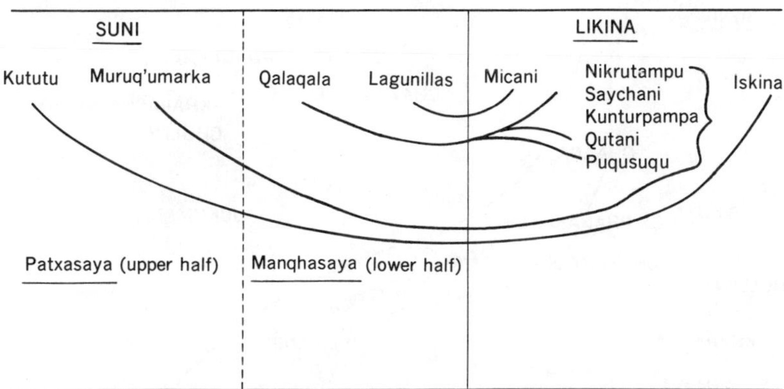

Fig. 14.5 Schematic representation of the relationship between *suni cabildos* and *likina* lands, *ayllu* Laymi, Northern Potosí

Taypirana/Chawpirana: The Center or Intermediate Ecology

Within one *ayllu* of the Chayanta strip, then, the location of land and resources in the two contrasted ecological zones seems to follow the principle—stated simply—that the further away your lands in one direction, the further you have to travel in the other: the nearer your lands in one direction, the less distance you travel in the other. If we turn back to the distribution of the different major *ayllus* of the Chayanta strip as a whole, the same pattern emerges in many cases (Fig. 14.6).[11]

And what of those ethnic groups whose lands straddle the ecological transition itself, a region known as the *taypirana* (Aymara) or *chawpirana* (Quechua)? Laymi lands present an unambiguous opposition between highlands and valley since they are removed from this intermediate zone. However there is one *ayllu* in the Chayanta strip which appears precisely to straddle the region of ecological transition. Known as Qhaana, it does not have a divided territory, unlike all the other *ayllus*. Significantly, I was told that Qhaana is *puro centro* (*taypipini*).

The case of Qhaana *ayllu*, stiuated in the region of ecological transition—in the middle—is unambiguous because its territory forms a single bloc. What of other ethnic groups occupying this intermediate zone? The best case to consider is that of the Jukumani *ayllu*, also in the Chayanta strip, which has recently been studied by Ricardo Godoy (1983) (Figs. 14.4, 14.6). Many Jukumani identify the main part of their

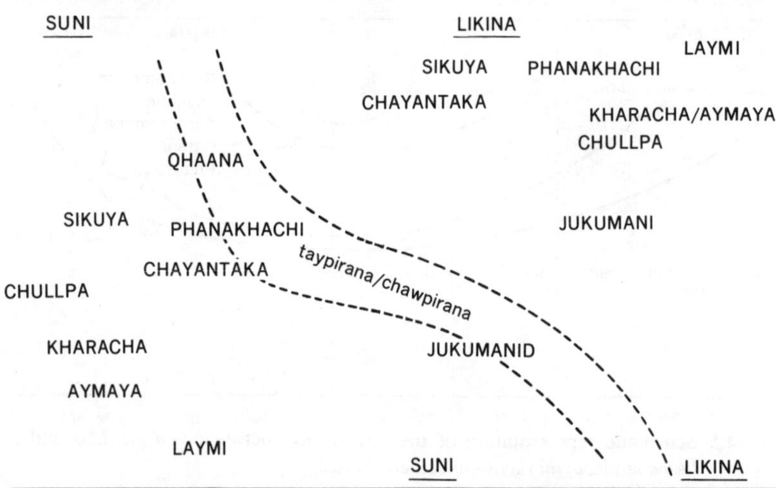

Fig. 14.6 Schematic representation of Fig. 14.3, showing distribution of *ayllus* of the Chayanta strip with reference to the *taypirana/chawpirana*.

territory as *chawpirana*. It lies to the northeast of the Laymi, and in Godoy's detailed account it is clear that it embraces both a small area of *puna* ecotype, and also many protected *quebradas* where even at quite a high altitude maize is grown. Jukumani households living at the highest altitudes apparently do not simultaneously cultivate in the river-bottoms, although the distances involved are small. Specialized produce from each ecozone circulates mostly by barter: wool, *ch'arki*, potatoes, and *ch'uñu* from the *puna*, against peaches, *tunas*, peas, beans, some maize, and wood from the *chawpirana*.

Jukumani is an *ayllu* whose intermediate ecological position allows it access to the basic subsistence crops through exchange within a small geographical area. However, unlike the Qhaana, the Jukumani *ayllu* also has separate lands in the valley region, and perhaps for this reason I never heard Jukumani referred to as *puro centro*. From Godoy's account it seems that the valley lands, in spite of the great distance from roads and markets, and the smaller range of crops that grow there, are still important to Jukumanis in the higher altitudes, and a small proportion of households live permanently in the valley, cultivating maize in part for their *puna* and *chawpirana* kin (100 households, as opposed to approximately 1,800 households in the higher region).

The information provided by Godoy on Jukumani spatial dispositions provides some confirmation for the hypothesis that those who live furthest from the valley lands also have to travel furthest. Even for maize-producing hamlets in the *chawpirana* valley, maize is a necessary security since the harvests in the two ecozones may differ dramatically. However, it is the high-altitude *cabildos*; i.e. those producing little or no maize, who are most likely to cultivate maize in the valley, or maintain close economic links with valley residents. And it appears to be the case that the valley lands at the lowest altitudes are significantly associated with those highland villages or *cabildos* that cannot themselves grow maize. Conversely the *chawpirana* (i.e. lower) *cabildos* are more likely to have land or kin in the higher altitude valley lands.[12]

Perhaps even more interesting than this spatial correlation of high with low, less high with less low, is that Godoy describes *chawpirana* households (that is, those in the main territory whose lands are low enough to produce maize) as more "sedentary" than others. Other households come to them, passing through their land on their journey farther up or farther down. One might suggest for the Jukumani that the *chawpirana* is the meeting place of those who come with *puna* products from higher up and those who come from lower down with valley products. The whole of the large upper half of Jukumani territory is sometimes referred to as *chawpirana*; for example, in contrast with neighboring *ayllus* such as Laymi, whose highland territory is overall at a higher altitude. Conversely, according to Godoy "Jukumani valley dwellers regard their highland relatives as *suni* residents because the latter do not produce maize in abundance" (1983:35). Again, "*suni* and *likina* dwellers might have different perceptions of which and how much of [the diagnostic staple crops of *suni* and *likina*] they have to grow in an area for that area to be classified as *chawpirana*" (Godoy 1983:35). It is clear that to some extent the term selected to classify a particular ecological zone will depend on the position of the speaker. However within the main part of Jukumani territory a distinction is made between *suni*, *likina*, and the intermediate *chawpirana* zone, even if the allocation of particular *cabildos* to a particular zone may vary between one speaker and another. Unlike Qhaana, Jukumani is not *puro centro* because it includes a small *puna* area, and a small separate valley area.[13]

Taypi/Chawpi in the Organization of Space

How is this configuration to be explained? Part of the reason must surely lie in the nature of subsistence organization itself. *Chawpirana* households in Northern Potosí may be more self-subsistent than those cultivating further away from this intermediate zone. However, they are not autarkic in any absolute sense: they require typical *puna* products, such as *ch'uñu*, wool, and salt, and also supplement their own maize production with valley maize.[14] A more significant factor is undoubtedly that of the availability of pack animals. *Cabildos* located in the high *punas* have access to abundant llama flocks, while those at lower altitudes have little pasture suitable for rearing pack animals. Those living at the highest altitudes are in a better position to make long journeys and transport produce in bulk than those at lower altitudes. Today the commonest pattern of inter-zonal mobility is for highlanders to travel down to the valleys after the harvest to acquire maize. Valley-dwellers, dependent on Old World pack animals (donkey and mules) until the opening up of the region to motor transport, have made the upward journey less frequently. Archaeological evidence indicates that this pattern is very ancient (Lorandi 1978, Browman 1981; Mujica et al. 1983); it clearly helps to explain how the llama-rich communities of Qaranqa and Killaka/Asanaqi were able to maintain rights to "islands" of maize lands so far from their main nucleus of population (often further from the *taypirana/chawpirana* region than the maize lands of Charka and Qharaqhara, just as their *puna* lands were also further from the ecological transition).

However, important as the availability of pack animals undoubtedly is and was, it seems insufficient to explain the striking configuration of spatial organization in Northern Potosí. I wish to suggest that an explanation must be sought also on another level, in terms of the *conceptualization of space*, to complement more material explanations. In particular, the ways that Andean cultures organize space in terms of the "center" must be taken into account.

The Aymara concept of *taypi* refers most commonly to an intermediate position. In Bertonio's *Vocabulario de la Lengua Aymara* of 1612, the word is translated as *Cosa que esta medio* (sic); examples cited in illustration include the middle finger (*taypi lukana*), the middle child of three (*taypi huahua*), midday (*taypi,* vel *Chica uru*), and a person of middling size (*taypi haque*). The position of *taypi*, then, is defined by what is on either side, rather than corresponding to the more concentrically-organized idea of the center common in Western thought. The definition given by Bertonio for the word *taypirana* needs to be understood in this light: "*Taypirana*: *Lugar del medio, o lo que esta en medio de alguna llanada, o cerro, o pueblo. Taypirana yapu. Chacara que esta en medio de otras. Taypirana uta. Casa en medio del pueblo. Pirca taypirana*: *El medio de la pared.*" (II:340). The Quechua *chawpi* seems to share a very similar semantic field.

Therèse Bouysse-Cassagne has done much to alert us to the significance of the *taypi* in Aymara spatial and political organization, emphasizing how Qullasuyu was divided in two halves—Urcosuyo and Umasuyo—whose meeting point was formed by an axis running between Río Azangaro to Lake Poopo, centered on Lake Titicaca (Bouysse-Cassagne 1978; Wachtel 1978; Julien 1983). At the same time the pioneering work of Veronica Cereceda on the semiology of Andean textiles has shown that spatial organization is fundamental for understanding the aesthetics of weaving. In her analysis of the meanings embodied in the *talega* sacks of Isluga (formerly a western valley of the Qaranqa, today a community in Northern Chile), the central stripe along the rectangular space is known as the "*heart*":

> The *chhima* (heart) is a place both of meeting and of division between the two sides; it plays a double, ambivalent role: it separates, it creates two sides, and at the same time it reconnects them and establishes the "territory" which is common to them both. The center is thus defined as the articulating point of the woven space,

> the unambiguous axis which divides the bag longitudinally following the threads of the warp. (1978:1020)

The stripe at the heart of the woven space of the *talega* is not, then, a rupture between the two opposed halves, but a possibility of mediation. However, the space of the *talega* is not simply divided in two halves, but also subdivided by a series of stripes on either side of the "heart." What is important for our purposes is that the stripes within each half are balanced by an identical stripe at the same distance from the "heart" or center on the other side. The woven space of the *talega* is dual, and within the duality each side is a mirror image of the other: a stripe on one side is balanced by a corresponding stripe on the other.[15]

The aesthetic principles underlying the organization of space in these textiles offer a striking similarity to the pattern of access to land and different ecological resources among Northern Potosí *ayllus*, one which finds echoes in some pre-Spanish political structures of the Aymara region. How far is it applicable to other regions of the Andes? We have noted the congruence of meaning between the Aymara *taypi* and Quechua *chawpi*. The communities of the Chaupiwaranga River far to the north in the Peruvian Dept. of Pasco offer suggestive points of comparison. The name of Chaupiwaranga itself serves to underline its position as an intermediary (*chawpi*) zone between the ecologically opposed *puna* and valleys. Enrique Mayer in his account of one of the communities of Chaupiwaranga—Tangor—stresses that the Tangorinos have direct access to both potato and maize lands, so that "the internal market in Tangor is tiny in comparison with the amount of exchanges of labor and services" (1974:64–5).

The significance of the *chawpi* is made explicit by Cesar Fonseca Martel. The twenty communities of the Chaupiwaranga Valley differ in altitude, but all have both *kechwa* and *jalka* lands; that is, tuber lands and maize lands. In comparison with the high *puna* community of Cauri which is *jatun jalka*, or the Huallaga valley which is *jatun kechwa*, they are all "medium or lesser *kechwa*": though there are differences in altitude between them, all maintain access to both maize and tuber fields (1973:29–31). However, within the *quebrada* of Chaupiwaranga the concept of the *chawpi* also has a more limited and precise meaning. In the description of the community of Yacan, it is the *marka* or village itself that constitutes the *chawpi*, the point of meeting and division.

> The *marca* is situated almost midway between the river and the *altiplanos*. It is the nucleus, the *chaupi* or navel of the community.

> The landscape is organized around this fixed point, especially the dirt roads which provide easy access to the maize and tuber fields and the natural pastures. In the *marca* the lands of the *kechwa* and the *jalka* "meet"—the lower part with the upper part. That is why the *marca* has a climate which is neither "hot" nor "cold" but "mild" (*cordial*). (1973:35)

The *marka* represents the meeting point, the mediation between the ecology of the *jalka* and that of the *kechwa,* between tubers and maize. Indeed to judge from Fonseca's own diagram of the community of Yacan, the *chawpi* extends outside the *marka* in the form of a road that runs horizontally between the lower *jalka* and the upper *kechwa,* through the center of the *marka,* and expresses the "meeting" of the two contrasted ecozones as a line etched directly onto the landscape (Fonseca 1973:36). This example illustrates the *range* of meaning incorporated in the concept of *chawpi*: at one extreme an intermediate region which spans the ecological transition, and within which householders have direct access to the contrasted ecological resources deemed fundamental for subsistence; at the other, a line and a *marka* which divide ecological space above and below in balance with each other.

Chaupiwaranga, and in particular the community of Yacan, reveal a similar organization of space around a center as we have indicated for Northern Potosí. In economic terms there are certainly differences, especially in the greater emphasis on direct cultivation of both tubers and maize by each community in Chaupiwaranga, in contrast to the *chawpirana* region of the Jukumani *ayllu* where ecologically-specialized products circulate in the form of barter between the *cabildos* located at different altitudes. How far is the conceptual orientation described so vividly by Fonseca common to both regions? Is ecological space also classified as duality in Northern Potosí? And does the *marka* stand at the center, dividing and uniting what lies above and below?

Dualist Classification of Vertical Space

Platt has drawn attention to the way that ecological space in Macha is classified as dual in a form that seems to minimize the significance of the intermediate zone—the *chawpirana* or *taypirana*:

> One might suggest . . . that the Macha model is dualist in spite of the natural organization which, both empirically and ideally, ensures the mediation between the opposed poles. . . . Troll and the Macha

> agree on which are the distinctive or major ecological features of the landscape; but while a scientific representation can eliminate the *chawpirana* by reducing it to a line on a map, the Macha have to eliminate in the realm of ideas a zone which exists in reality, by reinforcing the supplementary contrasts which operate without mediation. (1978:1087)

Empirically the transitional zone exists. It can be characterized by a low level of exchange (Tangor), or a low level of mobility (Jukumani), or an absence of land in either ecological extreme (Macha, Qhaana). But in symbolic thought it can be "reduced" to a line which opposes and joins two halves. In Northern Potosí, the duality of space is reiterated in many symbolic forms. Both Laymi and Macha identify the two contrasted ecozones as male and female, although they differ in how they make the gender attributions. *Puna* and valleys are also characterized as kitchen and storehouse respectively, an allusion to the two separate rooms of which each household is constituted (Platt 1978a; Harris 1978a).

In conversations with Laymi householders, evaluations of the relative merits of the two ecozones frequently polarized around the contrast of staple foods (Fig. 14.7). The diagnostic food of the *suni* is potatoes and *ch'uñu*; the diagnositc food of the *likina* is maize. In Laymi symbolic classification maize is thought of as male like the *likina*, while potatoes, like the *suni* itself, are female. The dual opposition of crops extends also into the conceptualization of forms and rates of exchange. One of the major exchange cycles is that by which *suni* people obtain maize for money. Money enters the Laymi economy principally through the sale of potatoes, and therefore is closely identified with potatoes; thus while *likina* producers do not obtain potatoes directly in exchange for their

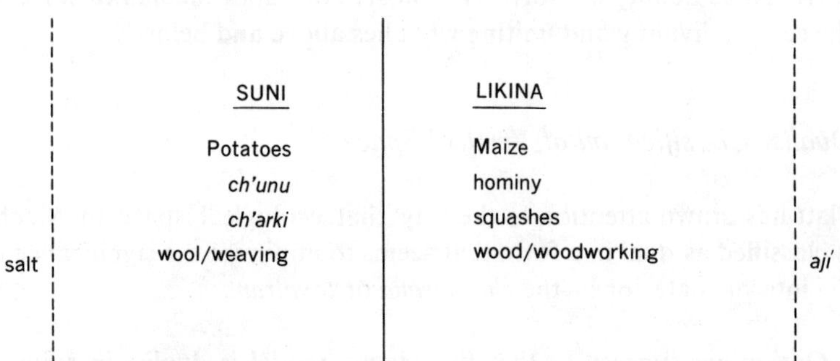

Fig. 14.7 Ecological duality in Laymi thought, as expressed in the contrast of diagnostic products.

maize, it is potatoes which provide the means for maize to be exchanged so that the dualism of potatoes and maize is retained indirectly. A transmuted version of the same dualism can be detected in the exchange rates for *ch'uñu*. *Ch'uñu* can be exchanged directly for maize, but not in equal quantities; the "balanced opposition" of *ch'uñu* in terms of exchange rates is not maize itself but hominy (*maiz pelado*; one unit of *ch'uñu* is equivalent to two units of maize and to one unit of hominy). The logic of this equivalence is that both *ch'uñu* and hominy involve the investment of much labor to transform the original crop: potatoes in the first case, maize in the second. *Ch'uñu* is produced through the process of freeze-drying, and hominy by cooking white maize in ash for many hours and then washing it repeatedly.

A complementary example can be drawn from ecologically specialized products which are not directly exchanged or purchased, but which circulate in the form of gifts to kin from the other ecozone. In the *likina* squashes play this role: *likina* producers do not sell or barter them, but give them "for nothing" to *suni* kin. The equivalent product of the *suni* is *ch'arki,* which *likina* people obtain as gifts from their *suni* kin.

The polar contrasts in which ecological variation is thought can also be illustrated by the craft specializations which typify each zone. *Suni* householders have access to abundant quantities of wool from their flocks of sheep and llamas, and are said to be great weavers (*suma sawuri*). In the *likina,* by contrast, wool is scarce, but wood which is non-existent in much of the *suni* is plentiful. *Likina* dwellers are said to be experts in carpentry, woodcarving, and the manufacture of different flutes.

Finally, there are two products not obtainable within Laymi territory at all, which play a central role both in food preparation and in rituals: salt and *aji*. Both are purchased for cash in the mining towns, but both can also be obtained by direct exchange with neighboring ethnic communities. Salt in this part of the Andes is a highland product *par excellence*; it is brought by llama trains from the huge salt lakes of Coipasa, Garci Mendoza, and Uyuni (Depts. of Oruro and Potosí). *Aji* is evidently a product of low-lying valley lands, and Laymi sometimes obtain the hot pepper from communities on the Río Caine, beyond their own *likina* territory. Salt and *aji* lie today beyond the extremes of *ayllu* land.[16] They are the primary seasoning for food, and are also employed as a pair in many rituals. The conjoining of these two products, the first typical of the barren *puna*, the other of the semitropical valleys, surely reiterates on a vaster scale the dual oppositions expressed within the two contrasted parts of Laymi territory.

The Location of the Marka

In Chaupiwaranga the *marka* of Yacan is situated on the point of ecological transition itself. In Northern Potosí today, each of the ethnic strips has an eponymous town (Sacaca, Chayanta, Pocoata (Copoata), and Macha). Sacaca and Macha were the pre-Spanish *cabeceras* of the Charka and the Qharaqhara nations respectively. In the words of Don Fernando Ayavire y Velasco:

> [*el*] *pueblo de San Luis de Sacaca que en el tiempo de los ingas y antes de ellos fue uno de los más principales pueblos que hauia en esta provincia de los Charcas y Su Partido y cabecera a donde se juntauan todos los caciques y principales de la nación y hábito y traje de los Charcas y lo mismo de otras naciones, pues fueron senores mis pasados y aguelos de este dicho pueblo de San Luis de Sacaca naturales.*[17]

The towns of Macha, Chayanta, and Pocoata are all named in the *encomienda* granted by Francisco Pizarro to his brother Gonzalo in 1540; in 1575 Copoata is listed as one of the four *pueblos anexos* of Macha, but in the same document is recorded the successful petition of the *caciques* of Copoata to pay their *tasa* independently of Macha.[18] In addition, both Chayanta and Macha were *tambos* on the Umasuyo branch of the Inka road (Bouysse-Cassagne 1978:1074).

The four eponymous towns of the four ethnic strips were all important centers before they were redefined as *reducción* towns by the Toledan reforms. While the status of all of them is not as clear as that of Sacaca, it is noteworthy that all these towns lie in the highlands (Fig. 14.4) and that the position they occupy seems to be intermediate between the southwestern limits of the *ayllus* defined by the Cordillera de los Asanaques, and the *taypirana/chawpirana* zone. All enjoy a climate that evades the worst cold of the *puna*, and around Pocoata there is even some cultivation of highland maize (*sara ch'isiwayu*); however, all are situated away from the *quebradas*.

There is an obvious geo-political logic to these locations, given the comparative ease of communications on the plateau. Indeed, the road system itself going southeast from Paria to Yampara follows much the same route today between Oruro and Sucre. As we have mentioned, both Chayanta (site of Inka tin mines) and Macha were *tambos* on the Inka road. However, the strikingly similar position of the four eponymous towns within their strip cannot be explained just in terms of the route of the road, since Sacaca, at a similar altitude to the other three, lies some distance to the northeast of the probable route of the road.

The locations of the early Spanish towns in the valley region is also suggestive. While there is as yet no evidence that they existed as important sites before the Toledan reforms, in several cases (notably Moscari, Acasio, and San Marcos de Miraflores) they occupy a similarly "intermediate" position between the *taypirana/chawpirana* and the lower reaches of the valley territory (Fig. 14.4). It appears that the ritual and administrative centers were in this region located away from the intermediate ecological region itself, in contrast to much of the ethnographic evidence from the eastern slopes of the Peruvian Andes, including Yacan. It is to be hoped that future archaeological and archive research will enable us to move beyond such speculative hypotheses.

Conclusion

The classification of space outlined here is based on a duality which is in some contexts defined by the center that divides and unites the two halves. At its most clear-cut, it opposes *puna* and valleys, *suni* and *likina*, and their characteristic products. However, within each half there are also subdivisions, distinctions in terms of relative distance from the center. In the design of the *talega*, a stripe of a particular color on one side of the center is balanced by an identical stripe at the same distance on the other side of the center; the dual classification of vertical space also reveals internal subdivisions within each half, the land of the *ayllus* within each ethnic strip, the *cabildos* within each *ayllu*, located with reference to its distance from the center. Andean thought finds constant homologies between textile design, particularly stripes, and social groups (Harris 1984; Bradby 1982). The relationship proposed here between the *talega* and the distribution of groups in the vertical space of Northern Potosí is not that the latter is directly determined by the aesthetic principles of textiles, but rather that space is perceived and classified in terms of certain categories and relations which find their purest, most ideal expression in the self-contained space of a single piece of cloth. Nor would it be right to extrapolate from the *talega* and assume a single set of principles for all Andean textiles; clearly there are many. Cereceda has pointed out the importance of recognizing that the *talega* is a bag, used for storing and transporting food. It is perhaps significant that the two Laymi textiles which appear to share the aesthetic principles of the *talega*—the *costal* and the *walqipu*—are also food containers. Might there not be some as yet unrecognized connection between the social and economic organization of subsistence on a grand scale, and the design of the woolen containers manufactured by each household to store that subsistence and transport it across the vertical space, from *puna* to valleys, from valleys to *puna*?

Many issues remain outstanding, amongst them the problem that in political and economic reality the two ecological zones were not and are not in equilibrium. What balance there is exists in the formal relationship: the way it is thought symbolically and spatially, rather than the way power is distributed. It is revealed in the conceptual bases for establishing proper rates of exchange rather than in the sum of actual exchanges that occur. Traditionally the administrative and ritual centers of this region, as in other parts of Qullasuyu, have lain in the *puna* zone; there is no evidence to date that the valley towns of Northern Potosí were seen as balancing the highland *markas*. While the modes of circulation of ecologically-specialized produce between *puna* and valleys is entirely decentralized, and dependent on the needs and decisions of individual households, it is likely that this is a recent development. We do not know to what extent peasant households in the past had independent access to such produce, or whether production and circulation was centralized by *ayllu* authorities. And how and when did the pattern of *ayllu* organization with reference to the *taypirana/chawpirana* evolve?

The historical and ethnographic record indicates that at an inclusive level the *ayllus* of Northern Potosí occupy the same areas that they were working in the sixteenth century; that is, taking into account all the alienation of *ayllu* land and *ayllu* members over the last four centuries, a certain continuity of territorial occupation is apparent. On the other hand, it is clear that with the imposition of European administrative units based on bounded territories, the "scattering" of ethnic populations across the landscape, the primacy of rights over people rather than land, which are evident in the early *quipu* transcriptions, were progressively "tidied up." Within the main Charka and Qharaqhara area, ethnic "islands" were doubtless in many cases absorbed into the surrounding group. The same must be true of more distant islands. One outstanding question that requires archaeological and archival research is where these nations cultivated coca leaf, and whether they had islands intercalated with the ethnic populations of the western flank of the *cordillera*.

Nonetheless, the occupation of widely-dispersed discontinuous lands still endures in Northern Potosí. While at the level of the ethnic strips into which the region is divided, the fragmented descendants of the Charka and Qharaqhara do not appear to occupy territory archipelago-style, at a less-inclusive level, of course, they do. Fig. 14.3 indicates islands of *ayllu* land far from the main territory, and there are doubtless many more cases than Tristan Platt and I have documented. Most of these islands offer access to a climate or ecological resource not available in the main territory. However in at least one case there seems to be no such rationale. While the discontinuous pattern of land occupation at its broadest must be explained in terms of the multiplicity of specialized resources provided by the unique Andean ecology, it is important not to forget how embedded is this mobile and flexible pattern in Andean social organization. It would be a mistake to explain every case of an island inserted into the territory of a different group as "diversification of resources." In some cases the explanation is due to the scattered distribution of population to available land *within* a single microzone.

Leaving aside these "islands" where a small group is inserted in the territory of a different ethnic population, the whole organization of vertical space that I have described typifies the pattern of discontinuity in ethnic landholding. This is evident in the Chayanta strip where all the constituent *ayllus* have a divided territory except for Qhaana which is pure center. In the other strips too, although *ayllu* organization at its broadest level embraces the whole strip, its segmentary character, as described by Platt for Macha (1978a), means that the operative affiliation of particular households and kin groups is to a lower-level group. At this lower organizational level, territory is not continuous. From the perspective of the internal subdivisions of the ethnic groups, only those *ayllus* or *cabildos* occupying the *taypirana/chawpirana* itself can be said to have continuous territory, and their intermediate position deprives them of direct access to the specialized resources of the more extreme ecologies: the livestock, wool, textiles, *ch'uñu* of the *puna,* and the abundant maize, squashes, wood, and musical instruments of the valleys.

NOTES

This essay was presented to the seminar on Andean Thought at the 1984 Conference of the Society for Latin American Studies in Cambridge. I would like to thank those who discussed it with me there and at the Wenner-Gren Conference at Cedar Key, and especially Tristan Platt for his detailed comments.

1. Murra 1972, 1978. Murra evokes this discontinuity with the image of the archipelago and scattered islands of the ethnic unit.

2. See *inter alia* Pease 1977; Cajias 1978; Saignes 1978; Bouysse-Cassagne

1978; Wachtel 1978; Espinoza 1981; Rivière 1982; Rasnake 1982; Mujica, et al. 1983; Platt forthcoming; Murra 1975.

3. Archivo Histórico de Potosí PD 56 1881. My thanks to Tristan Platt for this information.

4. *Visita a Pocona* 1557 in *Historia y Cultura* 4, Lima 1970.

5. "y queal tiempo de la cosecha los dos o tres meses del año ay más de seisciento yndios de la dha provincia carangas, quillacas y asanaques buscando comyda." Repartimiento de tierras por el Inca Huayna Capac 1556, Morales (1977).

6. 'Los yndios de santiago de aymaya con Gaspar de la rua Hinohoza sobre las tierras' Archivo Nacional de Bolivia T&I 533 (1618).

7. Three of these ethnic strips, Sakaka, Pukwata, and Macha, have a similar organizational structure, being composed of ten constituent *ayllus* (or twelve in the case of Sakaka), half of which compose the upper moiety, the other half the lower moiety. Each moiety is, or was until the Agrarian Reform, headed by an indigenous authority. Chayanta is different, being composed of a number of separate *ayllus* which today are the largest units which remain under the jurisdiction of indigenous authorities. At least one of these *ayllus* (Aymaya) was until 1572 an "island" of the Qharaqhara nation (AHP Cajas Reales 18).

8. The Laymi "ethnic economy" is discussed in detail in Harris 1982.

9. The lowest-altitude lands formerly worked by Laymi are no longer in their control. As early as the late sixteenth century Laymi lands around Torotoro on the Río Caine had passed into Spanish hands (ANB TI 149 1592).

10. Qalaqala is the most obvious example. The people of Qalaqala are particularly associated with the valley lands north of Micani; but there are also Qalaqala households working land much further to the north; for example in Puqusuqu and Qutani, side by side with people from high-altitude *suni cabildos*. While this is an important exception to my argument, it is explained partly by the large concentration of population in Qalaqala, drawn presumably from many parts of Laymi territory.

11. The most obvious exception seems to be the *ayllu* of Phanakhachi. It should be pointed out that an analysis in terms of cartographic distances "as the crow flies" is highly artificial, since the journey between *suni* and *likina* in the Chayanta strip is circumscribed by the small number of places in which the Chayanta River—the *jach'a jawira* or *jatun mayu*—can be forded. Some *ayllus* have been abandoning their valley lands in recent years (Isko 1983).

12. I am grateful to Ricardo Godoy for sending me an early draft of his thesis, and also various unpublished papers on Jukumani. The two lowest-altitude valley areas worked by Jukumani are Ullchu and Umaje: of the nine *puna* and *chawpirana cabildos* working lands in them only two (Belen and Tojoria) are situated low enough to produce their own maize. Similarly the higher-altitude valley lands (Ch'apirusa, Kanuani, Aramani, Mosokunka, and Samichua) are more associated with *chawpirana cabildos* than high altitude *puna cabildos* (six as opposed to four). These figures are obviously im-

pressionistic, since they do not indicate what proportion of the different *cabildos* are involved in each case.

13. The idea of *chawpirana/taypirana* as mediation is further strengthened by Platt's statement that in the Macha strip, households in the *chawpirana* tend not to have lands in either extreme of the *ayllu* territory (1982b:34)

14. Godoy 1983. Platt, however, comments that for Northern Potosí as a whole, households growing high altitude maize rarely also cultivate maize in the valleys (1982b:49).

15. Lest there be some confusion, let me make explicit that the unit that reveals an organization of space similar to the *talega* is the individual ethnic strip, with its "center" running from northwest to southeast (Fig. 14.4), and *not* the whole of Northern Potosí with its four strips or stripes.

16. The lands where *aji* is grown were probably formerly under Laymi control (see note 9 above). Platt notes the presence of ten Macha *uchucamayocs* near Carasi mentioned in a document of 1579 (1978a:1082); Macha also has some salt mines within its territory.

17. "The town of San Luis of Sacaca which in the time of the Incas and before them was one of the most important towns in this province of Charcas and its jurisdiction; and was the capital where all the *caciques* and principals of the nation and customs and garb of the Charka would gather, and likewise those of other nations. For my forefathers were lords, natives of the said town of San Luis of Sacaca" (Memorial de Charcas, 1582 [Espinoza 1969]).

18. Archivo General de Indias, Sevilla, Charcas 56. I am grateful to John Murra for showing me a copy of this document. AHP Cajas Reales 18; see also Platt 1978b: 102–3.

REFERENCES CITED

Bouysse-Cassagne, T.
1978 L'espace aymara: urco et uma. Annales 33 (5–6):1057–80.

Bradby, B.
1982 Plan, Market, and Money: A Study of Circulation in Peru. Ph.D. thesis, University of Sussex.

Browman, D.
1981 New Light on Andean Tiwanaku. American Scientist 69 (4):408–19.

Cajias, F.
1978 La población indígena de Paria en 1785. Estudios en homenaje a Gunnar Mendoza. pp.41–100. La Paz.

Cereceda, V.
1978 La sémiologie des tissué andins: les *talegas* d'Isluga. Annales 33 (5–6):1017–35.

Espinoza Soriano, W.
1969 El Memorial de Charcas; cronica inédita de 1582. Cantuta. Revista de la Univ Nac de Educ, Chosica.

1981 El reino aymara de Quillaca-Asanaque. siglos XV and XVI Rev. del Mus. Nac. 45:175–274.

Fonseca Martel, C.
1973 Sistemas económicas andinos. Biblioteca andina. Lima.

Godoy, R.
1983 From Indian to Miner and Back Again: Small-scale Mining in the Jukumani Ayllu, Northern Potosí, Bolivia. Ph.D. thesis. Columbia University.

Harris, O.
1978a De l'asymétrie au triangle: transformations symboliques au nord de Potosí. Annales 33 (5–6):1108–25.
1978b El parentesco y la economia vertical del ayllu laymi, norte de Potosí. Avances 1:51–64. La Paz.
1982 Labour and produce in an ethnic economy, Northern Potosí, Bolivia. *In* Ecology and Exchange in the Andes. D. Lehmann, ed. pp. 70–98. Cambridge: Cambridge University Press.
1984 Comment on Urton. Revista andina 3. Cuzco.

Isko, X.
1983 Condores y mastakus: vida y muerte en los valles norpotosinos. Dimensiones socio-culturales de la fecundidad y mortalidad en Bolivia. Min. de Planeamiento y Coordinacion, La Paz.

Julien, C.
1983 Hatunqolla: A View of Inca Rule from the Lake Titicaca Region. Anthropology Vol. 15: Univ. of California Publications.

Lorandi, A.M.
1978 Les "horizons" andins: critique d' un modèle. Annales 33 (5–6): 921–25.

Mayer, E.
1974 Las reglas del juego en la reciprocidad andina. *In* Reciprocidad e intercambio en los andes peruanos. G. Alberti & E. Mayer, eds. pp. 37–65. Lima: IEP.

Morales, A.
1977 Repartimiento de tierras por el Inca Huayna Capac (1556). Museo Arqueológico, Univ. de San Simon, Cochabamba.

Mujica, E., M. Rivera, and T. Lynch
1983 Proyecto de estudio sobre la complementaridad ecológica Tiwanaku en los valles occidentales del centro-sur andino. Chungará 11. Arica.

Murra, J.
1972 El 'control vertical' de un máximo de pisos ecológicos en la economía de las sociedades andinas. *In* I. Ortiz de Zúñiga, Visita de la Provincia de León de Huánuco en 1562. Vol. II. Huánuco.
1975 Formaciones económicas y políticas del mundo andino. Lima: IEP.
1978 Los limites y las limitaciones del 'archipiélago vertical' en los Andes. Avances 1:75–80.

Pease, F.
1977 Collaguas: una etnía del siglo XVI. *In* Collaguas I. Franklin Pease, ed. pp. 136–67. Lima: Univ. Católica.

Platt, T.
1978a Simétries en miroir. Le concept de *yanantin* chez les Macha de Bolivie. Annales 33 (5–6):1081–107.
1978b Mapas coloniales de Chayanta: dos visiones conflictivas de un solo paisaje. Estudios bolivianos en homenaje a Gunnar Mendoza. La Paz.
1982a Estado boliviano y ayllu andino. Lima: IEP.
1982b The role of the Andean ayllu in the reproduction of the petty commodity regime in Northern Potosí (Bolivia). *In* Ecology and Exchange in the Andes. D. Lehmann, ed. pp. 27–69. Cambridge: Cambridge University Press.
forthcoming Los aymaras frente al estado. J. Albó, ed. Cultura y sociedad aymara.

Rasnake, R.
1982 The kurajkuna of Yura: A case study of indigenous authorities and national society in rural highland Bolivia. Ph.D. thesis. Cornell University.

Rivière, G.
1982 Sabaya: structures socio-économiques et representations symboliques dans le Carangas. Bolivie. Doctorat de 3ème cycle d'ethnologie, Paris.

Saignes, T.
1978 De la filiation a la résidence: les ethnies dans les vallées de Larecaja. Annales 33 (5–6):1160–181.

Troll, C.
1968 The Cordilleras of the Tropical Americas: Aspects of Climatic Phytographical and Agrarian Ecology. *In* Geo-ecology of the Mountainous Regions of the Tropical Americas. Geog. Inst., Univ. of Bonn.

Wachtel, N.
1978 Hommes d'eau: le problème uru (XVI-XVIIe siecle). Annales 33 (5–6):1127–59.
1981 Les *mitimas* de la vallée de Cochabamba. La politique de colonisation de Huayna Capac. J. de la Soc. des Amer. 67:297–324.

IV

Variations in the North: Comparative Perspectives

The five chronologically ordered papers in this part present overall coherence and varied patterns of ecological complementarity that are in many ways significantly different from those seen in the preceding section. Each paper focuses on different aspects of ecological complementarity, thus effectively dovetailing with the others in temporal and topical coverage. Onuki, from the vantage of the North Highlands, emphasizes the crucial role of the *yunga* zone and its non-staple crops for coastal and highland populations throughout prehistory, while Shimada adopts a processual view of copper alloy metallurgy and explores its implications for attendant organizations and etic and emic perceptions of non-subsistence resources, particularly ores and metals. Shimada examines the coast-highland relationship from a coastal perspective which encompasses the Ecuadorian and Peruvian coasts. Rostworowski focuses on the social and historical significance of linguistic peculiarities found in the recently transcribed *Visita* to Cajamarca and speculates on the geographical and ethnic origins of various populations permanently settled in the North Highlands. The concept of "discontiguous territoriality" raised by Rostworowski should be carefully compared with that of "*dominio salpicado,*" which Ramírez defines in her ethnohistorical study of the social and economic roles of *kurakas.* The latter concept features "share cropping" and the distinction of absolute control over land or resources versus actual use or the right to sublet land. Schaedel reconstructs ethnic boundaries and their interrelationships over time in north Peru, effectively utilizing archaeological, documentary, linguistic, and ethnographic data.

15

The *Yunga* Zone in the Prehistory of the Central Andes: Vertical and Horizontal Dimensions in Andean Ecological and Cultural Processes

Yoshio Onuki

Introduction

Murra's (1972) thesis of vertical control has contributed greatly in providing a new direction for anthropological research and, at a more specific level, interpretation of the long cultural tradition of the Central Andes. Since then, many ethnographic studies of environmental utilization have appeared, throwing light on a rich variety of actual cases. However, no representative recent ethnographic case has been reported that supports Murra's ethnohistorical model of large-scale archipelago-type vertical control. Many ethnographic studies have examined utilization of the environment between the *puna* and *quechua* zones or the relatively small scale of environmental utilization from the *yunga* to *puna* zones, principally on the eastern slope of the Andes. However, in general, the role of the *yunga* zone for cultural developments has not been adequately considered in these recent studies.

In contrast, archaeological and ethnohistorical studies document intensive utilization of the *yunga* zone. Human activity in the *yunga* zone from the late preceramic to the Formative period has been one of my concerns in Andean prehistory. Elsewhere I have argued that, at least during the third and second millenium B.C., there was a distinctive sociocultural pattern which exploited the natural resources of the *yunga* zone in the intermontane valleys which could be conceptualized as the *Yunga* Tradition (Onuki 1982).

There are several classificatory schemes for the Andean natural environment, some of which use the term *yunga* to refer to the coastal region in general as well as the lower part of the eastern slope of the Andes. I follow Pulgar Vidal's (1963) scheme which limits the *yunga* zone to the interior part of the coastal valleys (*yunga marítima*) and the lower part of the intermontane valleys (*yunga fluvial*), the former encompassing elevations ca. 500–2,400 m above sea level and the latter from 1,000–2,400 m. Admittedly, altitudinal demarcation is somewhat variable according to local conditions.

Looking at the list of prehistoric Andean cultigens, the importance of the *yunga* zone in the history of agriculture is obvious. With the exception of the potato, *quinoa*, maize, and a few others, most plants can only be cultivated in the *yunga* and lower zones. All the known cultivated plants of the preceramic and Early Formative periods are rarely grown in the area above the *yunga* zone. As the native society was driven away from the *yunga* zone during the Colonial period, we cannot observe the traditional system of *yunga* exploitation. It is possible, however, to shed light on the role of the *yunga* zone in prehistoric times through archaeological investigations. This paper offers a tentative framework for the interpretation of Andean cultural processes with emphasis on *yunga* utilization over time, following the outline of my earlier work (Onuki 1982).

The Preceramic Period

During the late Lithic period (8000–4000 B.C.), the hunter-gatherers of the Andean highlands hunted camelids and cervids, exploiting resources found in the valleys far below the hunting areas. Lithic period rock paintings are known from Lauricocha and Toquepala and there are other examples of rock art extensively distributed in the coastal, as well as intermontane valleys, many assignable to the Lithic period based on clear stylistic affinities with paintings at Toquepala and Diablo Machay. The above distribution of rock art suggests that the *yunga* zone both on the cis-Andean side and in the intermontane valleys was frequently visited by the hunter-gatherers.

A very important discovery was made at Guitarrero Cave in the Callejón de Huaylas (Lynch ed. 1980). Although located about 2,600 m above sea level in the lowest end of the *quechua* zone, the adjacent valley floor, only about 150 m below, can be classified as belonging to the *yunga* zone based on the variety of plants cultivated there today (e.g., *pacae*, *lúcuma*, sugar cane; the last of Old World origin). The above implies that Guitarrero Cave is situated on the borderline between the *quechua* and *yunga* zones and served as a base for exploitation of *yunga* resources on the valley floor just below, especially plant resources such as *pacae*, *lúcuma*, *achira*, squash, and chili, all of which were recovered through excavations (Smith 1980:96–104). The most important data to emerge provide evidence of the cultivation of two kinds of beans, *Phaseolus lunatus* and *Phaseolus vulgaris*, around 7000 B.C. (Kaplan 1980). Lynch (1971, 1980) has argued for a system of transhumance between Guitarrero Cave and the *puna* zone; a similar pattern of environmental utilization may well have been widespread throughout the Andean highlands during the Late Lithic period.

On the other hand, Rick (1980:270) suggests the possibility of self-sufficient subsistence within the *puna* and *suni* zones on the Junín plateau. Certainly, self-sufficiency based on *puna-suni* exploitation may well have been possible in a region where the *puna* was extensive, the camelids abundant, and lakes and the upper ends of valleys supplied useful resources such as small animals, birds, fish, and some plants.

It is interesting to note that deer was preferred over camelids in the Cajamarca basin, the Callejón de Huaylas, and the upper Huallaga basin. In these three regions the *puna* was not so extensive and it may have been necessary to cover the valley and its slopes to exploit resources distributed from the *puna* to the *yunga* zones, depending more on deer than camelids.

It is likely that dependence on *yunga* resources was accelerated in the system of transhumance during the Archaic period, perhaps favored by the good climatic conditions which also brought about expansion of the *yunga* zone into a slightly higher elevation. In the Ayacucho region a notable increase of habitation sites was observed in the Chihua phase (4300–2800 B.C.) especially in the hot and dry xerophytic zone of the *yunga* where MacNeish (1977:780–82) reported maize, *lúcuma*, beans, coca, and cotton were cultivated. In the Late Archaic period, we have the well-known Mito period temple complex found at Kotosh, Shillacoto, and Wairajirca sites in the upper Huallaga basin. Constructions almost identical to the Huallaga complex were discovered at La Galgada around 1,200 m in a tributary of the Santa River (Bueno and Grieder 1979; Grieder and Bueno 1981).

These data suggest that in the Archaic period a distinctive system of intensive exploitation of the *yunga* zone was elaborated and remarkably effective. Although a great many of the details of this system remain to be clarified, I propose to call it the *Yunga* Tradition, a counterpart of the contemporary Pacific Littoral Tradition defined by Willey (1971) for the coastal region. The *Yunga* Tradition most likely evolved from the Andean Hunting-Collecting Tradition. The *Yunga* Tradition may encompass the Mito period of the upper Huallaga basin, La Galgada, Huaricoto in the Callejón de Huaylas (Burger and Burger 1980), and the Chihua and Cachi phases of the Ayacucho basin (MacNeish et al. 1975).

The Formative Period

The *Yunga* Tradition continued in those complexes as Pandanche A in northern Cajamarca, the Early Huacaloma period at Huacaloma in the Cajamarca basin, the Kotosh-Wairajirca and Kotosh-Kotosh periods in the upper Huallaga basin, and possibly the Andamarka phase in Ayacucho. These complexes or cultures, like the Initial period on the coast, differ little from the preceding Late Archaic period as far as subsistence and site location are concerned. The principal differences lie in the use of pottery and textiles which certainly enhanced the effectiveness of the *Yunga* Tradition but did not necessarily cause a substantial change in it. Agriculture in the *yunga* zone was productive and played the most important role in subsistence, supplemented by hunting and collecting activities. During the Early Formative period in the highlands this subsistence system can be viewed as a continuation of the *Yunga* Tradition.

Cultural aspects of the Early Formative in the highlands have been clarified somewhat in the upper Huallaga basin and the area around Pacopampa in Cajamarca. Archaeological research carried out in 1979 and 1982 in the Cajamarca basin provides interesting data for the Formative period (Terada and Onuki 1982). Some of the data related to the present discussion are summarized below.

Excavations in 1979 elucidated three periods for the Formative at Huacaloma; that is, Early Huacaloma, Late Huacaloma, and Layzón. The Early Huacaloma period (1500–1000 B.C.) is characterized by Huacaloma Coarse Brown pottery which has thin walls, is not polished, and ranges from brown to dark brown. The principal forms are neckless jars with thin, plain rims, and composite silhouette bowls with carinated shoulders. The neckless jars are decorated with punctation and narrow, short appliqué, and the bowls with punctation and sharp, deep incised lines. At Huacaloma two rectangular rooms were found whose walls and floors were thickly coated with yellowish white plaster. One of the two rooms had a circular hearth in the center of the floor.

The Late Huacaloma period (1000–500 B.C.) is found above a layer of hard yellow soil, three to five meters thick, which completely covered the construction and platforms of the Early Huacaloma period. During the 1979 excavations, we thought this thick, sterile soil was artificially accumulated at the onset of the Layzón period, but 1982 excavations produced definite evidence that the thick layer was deposited by Late Huacaloma period people in order to build a huge ceremonial platform complex. While the coarse pottery of the Early Huacaloma period continued in reduced quantity, smoothed types of red and dark brown increased conspicuously. Newly emerged traits include neckless jars and open bowls with red-painted rims, bowls and short-necked jars with line-burnished designs, and highly polished bowls, short-necked jars, and bottles. Red-on-Orange painted jars, and bowls with incision and post-fired painting in red, white, and yellow are also new characteristics. Among the stone implements, polished points of slate, hammerstones, handstones, mortars, and a T-shaped axe are worth noting.

The Layzón period (500–200 B.C.) inhabitants thoroughly destroyed the Late Huacaloma constructions and built their own structures for ordinary habitations on top of the debris. Although some earlier traits can still be observed, the most abundant types are Layzón White and Layzón Red-on-White. Short-necked jars with wide mouths are newly introduced, while the neckless jars so common during the preceding two periods almost completely disappear. No change was noticed in relation to stone implements. The most significant change is observed in the faunal remains; while in the two Huacaloma periods deer bones predominante, the abrupt increase of camelids and decrease of deer is remarkable in the Layzón period (M. Shimada 1982).

The site of Huacaloma is situated 2,700 m above sea level, very close to the valley floor which extends from 2,750 to 2,500 m for a distance of some 20 km between the modern city of Cajamarca and the town of Jesús. Thus, the Cajamarca basin in general belongs to the lowest limit of the *quechua* zone. However, as exemplified by the *chirimoya* trees in the patio of San Francisco Church in the heart of Cajamarca city, some plants of the *yunga* zone are viable, if they are adequately protected, and therefore the Cajamarca basin can be said to be situated on the borderline between the *quechua* and *yunga* zones. If it was slightly warmer during the second to third millennium B.C. than today, it is possible that the whole valley floor constituted a *yunga* zone. Indeed, even today, oranges, avocados, and *pacae* trees are grown on the valley floor below Jesús. As a consequence, it is highly likely that the people of Huacaloma in the Formative period could fully utilize the plant resources of the *yunga* zone and that their subsistence system shared many common characteristics with that of the *yunga* zone in other regions. The pottery of the Early Huacaloma is quite similar to that of Pandanche A (Kaulicke 1981; Morales 1981) and that of the Yesopampa period at La Pampa, Ancash (Terada 1979). The pottery of the Late Huacaloma is very close to Pacopampa Pacopampa or Pandanche B, and also to the Bagua complex (Shady and Rosas 1979), and shares some basic traits with that of the Kotosh-Wairajirca and Kotosh-Kotosh periods, and to a lesser degree, with Chavín de Huántar (Terada and Onuki 1982:259–61). Except for Chavín de Huántar, all related sites are located in the *yunga* zone.

A truly exciting find was reported from the Jequetepeque Valley.

Pottery identical to that of the Early Huacaloma period was found at Monte Grande and its surroundings near Tembladera (Ravines 1982: 149–54, 164, 181–206; Tellenbach 1982, personal communication). The area is very extensive, and Monte Grande has separate habitation and ceremonial areas.

The preceding suggests that people of the same cultural tradition lived in both the highland and coastal valley at the same time during the Early Formative period. The area around Tembladera definitely lies in the *yunga* zone (*yunga marítima*), and in the Early Formative period, it shared the same culture with the adjacent highland region extending at least from Pandanche to Cajamarca.

In the Late Huacaloma period, the Jequetepeque Valley was separated from the Cajamarca basin and it became closely connected with a coastal tradition emanating from the region, extending from the Lambayeque to Moche valleys. The Cajamarca basin developed its own style, maintaining a close relationship with northern partners like Pandanche B or Pacopampa Pacopampa. The situation of the Layzón period is not clear, since little data exist on the distribution of related contemporaneous sites.

An interesting report was presented from Cerro Arena in the Moche Valley which had pottery very similar to Layzón Red-on-White (Brennan 1980, 1982; Mujica 1975), but we are not certain whether the similarity is the result of exchange between highland and coast or whether both regions shared the same culture. Brennan assigns Cerro Arena to the Salinar culture, and, if so, the Layzón culture would belong to a different tradition, since pottery of the Layzón period lacks the distinctive traits of Salinar such as modeled stirrup spout jars.

During the Middle Formative period, the *quechua* zone began to be exploited, as well as the *chala* zone on the coast. We know very little about the early phase of maize cultivation, and preceramic maize is rarely found; however, it seems that maize was present almost every place where the later "Chavin" style flourished, and the two traditions, the *Yunga* Tradition and the Pacific Littoral Tradition, merged into the Peruvian Tradition defined by Willey (1971).

The Classic and Postclassic Periods

Based upon the distribution of Classic period archaeological sites, we can infer utilization patterns of the *chala* and *yunga* (*marítima*) zones by coastal societies and the more complicated highland systems of environmental exploitation that encompassed the *puna* to *yunga* zones.

In both regions, the principal crops were maize and tubers. *Yuca* (manioc) is frequently represented in Moche and Chimú ceramics, while Nasca pottery depicts *yuca* and *achira.* For example, Carrión Cachot (1959:62–66) illustrates Chimú jars showing a person holding maize and *yuca.* On the coast, during the Classic and Postclassic periods, an effective agricultural system was carried out in which maize and probably tubers as principal crops were supplemented with beans, *ají*, fruits, and other products.

A similar pattern is observed for the highlands. In the upper Huallaga basin, many Classic and Postclassic period sites are found around or over 3,000 m above sea level; however, there are contemporaneous sites of smaller scale found in the valley bottom, access to which was facilitated through sites at intermediate elevations. For example, the Chupachus' territory ranged from the valley bottom to the *puna* zone.

The situation seems to have been the same in the Cajamarca Valley in which sites with Cajamarca style pottery are distributed from the *yunga* to *suni* zones. The *yunga* zone of the Cajamarca basin today is located around the town of San Marcos and confluence of the Cajamarca and Condebamba rivers. There, *yuca* is grown and carried to Cajamarca city markets in the *quechua* zone almost every week.

Lathrap (1973), in his iconographic analysis of the famous Tello Obelisk, argues that *yuca*, *achira*, gourds, and *ají* are depicted and that the Obelisk as a whole represents or symbolizes a pre-Chavín agricultural system with tropical jungle origins. However, while we do not have direct evidence of *yuca* cultivation, the other three plants were cultivated by the preceramic period in both the coastal regions and highland intermontane valleys. Therefore, it may be possible to say that those plants depicted in the Tello Obelisk were components of the *Yunga* Tradition agricultural system. Further, the origins of this system may lie not in a remote jungle but rather in the *yunga* zone on the eastern slope of the Andes. This may lead us to argue that a maize and root crop based agricultural system originated within the process of *yunga* exploitation in the preceramic period, developed further during the Early Formative period, and eventually, in the Middle Formative period, determined the direction for later development of a variety of agricultural systems in the whole Andean area. This may explain why root crops and other products of the *yunga* zone were not abandoned in the Classic period when the *quechua* zone became the most favored ecological niche for maize cultivation.

Although the major population centers were shifted to the *quechua* zone in the Classic period, the *yunga* zone continued to be utilized as intensively as before for products like *yuca*, sweet potato, *ají*, beans, gourds, squash, fruits, cotton, and coca, all indispensable for the highland people and not securable anywhere but in the *yunga* zone.

On the other hand, another maize-tuber complex emerged from the *puna-quechua* exploitation system. This complex combined maize and quinoa with potatos, *olluco*, *oca*, and other tubers (Yamamoto in this volume). We do not have sufficient data to conclude when and how cultivation of the potatos was established. As already stated, during the Late Archaic and Early Formative periods, the *Yunga* Tradition was rapidly developing, and the highland hunter-gatherers must not have been indifferent to that development. The *Yunga* Tradition may have given the idea of root crop cultivation to highland people already experimenting with camelid domestication in the *puna* zone and eager for some way of food production. By the Middle Formative period, these people established an effective mode of food production which may be called the llama-*papa* complex, contrasting with the maize-*yuca* complex in the valleys. When the *quechua* zone became extensively populated, the llama-*papa* complex was combined with the maize-*yuca* complex, eventually culminating in large scale vertical control of the Andean highlands. At the same time, regional variations of the vertical control system appeared reflecting the environmental and historical peculiarities of each region.

The Cajamarca culture was a long tradition which began in the Initial Cajamarca period, as represented at Huacaloma, and lasted until incorporation into the Inca empire. Most sites of the Cajamarca culture are located on the hills and foothills surrounding the valley from 2,800–3,300 m above sea level. Steep slopes and precipitous cliffs make access to the sites difficult, suggesting strategically defensive locations.

These sites look down on the Cajamarca basin and valley bottom of San Marcos which can be reached in a couple of hours on foot. We may suppose that the agricultural fields may once have extended to the gentle slopes below the sites and on the valley bottom. The peasants' houses may have been scattered in the fields or, if they lived in the hilltop sites, it would not have been a heavy burden to make a daily roundtrip to the fields.

There are habitation sites of the Cajamarca culture on the terraces around the confluences of the Cajamarca and Condebamba rivers, and they provided the base for exploitation of the *yunga* zone around 2,000 m above sea level. It would not have been possible to make a daily roundtrip between the hilltop sites and these low floodplain settlements and the latter probably represent the habitation sites for a group especially allotted for the *yunga* exploitation.

The Cajamarca culture also occupied the western slope of the Andes, looking down upon the Jequetepeque and Chicama valleys (Schaedel and Shimada in this volume). Large sites have been reported near San Miguel and Contumazá, to the north and south, respectively, of the Jequetepeque Valley. In the fifteenth century, the *waranqa* Guzmango extended down to Cascas, and it is possible that the Cajamarca culture directly exploited the uppervalley *yunga* of the Chicama valley (Espinoza 1967). If the silver mine of Chiquelete was somewhere near modern Chilete, this implies that the Cajamarca culture held sway over the narrow bottom of the upper Jequetepeque Valley. On the other hand, the *yunga* zone around Tembladera, once dominated by highland people in the Early Formative period, seems to have been incorporated into the Chimú domain. I. Shimada (1982:184; and in this volume) argues that the Cajamarca culture had control over the irrigation water of the Jequetepeque Valley based on strategic positions in the upper valley, but we do not have definite evidence for that argument.

While powerful societies like Moche and Chimú took control over the coastal *yunga*, the Cajamarca culture incorporated the intermontane *yunga* in the Cajamarca and Condebamba river area. It is likely that the Cajamarca people averted conflict with the Moche or Chimú peoples over the *yunga* zones of the coastal valleys, choosing the alternative of more peaceful interdependence (I. Shimada 1982 and in this volume; Ramirez, in this volume.)

There are many large stone masonry sites in the mountains at 3,000 to 3,500 m around the upper parts of the Chillón and Chancay valleys (Casana 1976). These sites share the same construction technique and form with high elevation sites in the upper Marañón area and the Cordillera Negra of Ancash, and it seems likely that they belong to the same cultural tradition. The sites of this Chillón-Chancay group, like those of the Cajamarca culture in the upper part of the Jequetepeque Valley, are situated in the mountains overlooking the *yunga* zones of the valleys. However, it is interesting that there are a few sites such as Ayacoto or Huaynacoto, located in the valley bottom of Pacaybamba *quebrada*, an affluent of the Chancay River, at an elevation of about 1,300 m. There, we see rectangular or quadrangular *chullpas*, three-by-four m rectangular rooms with walls over two m high, and split-level floors with *batans* set into them.

Many sherds found at the sites are of red painted jars with strong highland affinity. Yet, it is interesting to find among them many sherds of Chancay Black-on-White pottery, suggesting these sites were built and used by a highland people who carried out exchange with coastal Chancay valley people. The highlanders who came down to the valley did not accept the coastal way of house building but retained mud-mortared stone architecture. These sites may have been bases for highland people directly exploiting the coastal *yunga* zone (Dillehay 1979). The adjacent highland area of the upper Chillón and Chancay valleys would have had difficulty in gaining access to the intermontane *yunga* zone on the eastern side of the Andes which was separated by an extensive *puna* and also occupied by other groups.[1]

The Nature of Environmental Utilization

The Central Andes are divided into two major natural regions, the highlands and coastal lowlands. In the former, high mountains and deep valleys intermingle, and different kinds of resources are vertically distributed. In the latter, human occupation is primarily confined to the valley plain where resources are horizontally distributed. What is the cultural significance of vertical versus horizontal resource distribution for Andean prehistory?

First, let us examine the highlands. Since the ecological zones are arranged according to altitude, the exploitation of multiple resources can only be accomplished by vertical movement. This way of combining vertically distributed resources is inherent not only in the Central Andes, but in different mountainous regions of the world, not only in the Himalayas but also in Ethiopia and New Guinea (Rappaport 1968). Thus, the issue is not verticality itself but local strategies for exploiting vertically distributed resources.

The physiography of the Andean highlands often impedes traffic and transportation. Many mountain slopes are so steep that they cannot effectively be cultivated. Due to these topographical and climatic conditions, the highlands, except for some wide basins with favorable conditions, have had limited productivity. Local groups tend to be isolated from each other and social integration across wide geographical areas is only realized with hardship. In some regions, it is very hard to maintain subsistence systems which utilize all zones from the *puna* to *yunga*. This is notable particularly in the south highlands where the *puna* zone is extensively spread out, and the *yunga* is found only in the narrow bottoms of deep, intermontane valleys or on the very remote eastern slopes of the Andes. As exemplified in Q'ero, a system of exploitation of multiple resources is viable on the eastern slopes, taking advantage of the continuous distribution of different ecological zones within a fairly short distance (Yamamoto in this volume). However, in the region of

Lake Titicaca, access to the *yunga* or even *quechua* zones is difficult, the nearest zones lying on the western slopes.

A similar case is found in the Junín plateau and the upper Mantaro region which are obliged to seek the *yunga* zone in the upper parts of the coastal valleys. A major difference from the Titicaca region can be seen in the fact that, here on the Central Coast, highly organized societies with large populations existed. In consequence, the effectiveness and form of *yunga* exploitation were dependent on the nature of the relationship with those coastal societies.

These peculiarities of the highlands make it necessary that the people choose among alternatives. One was to establish a system of direct exploitation of all zones from the *puna* to the *yunga.* The second alternative was to separate the *quechua-yunga* and *puna-suni* systems of exploitation and to combine them into an interdependent or complementary relationship. The third option was whether to directly control the coastal region or maintain a complementary and, in general, peaceful relationship.

In striking contrast to the highlands, the resources of the coastal region are horizontally distributed. Moseley (1975:13–16) differentiates nine resource zones or complexes within the *chala* zone. A similar delineation of microenvironments must be attempted for the coastal *yunga* zone. I. Shimada (1982:163) describes two such microenvironmental zones for the Lambayeque region.

It should be noted that the *chala* zone on the coast has the potential to be an extension of the *yunga* zone, while the *quechua* zone higher up does not possess this potential. In other words, the highland *yunga* has productivity limited to that zone, while on the coast it is possible to expand *yunga* productivity to the *chala* zone. Consequently, the coastal region could maintain higher productivity of the *chala* zone and enhance the productivity of the *yunga* zone by expanding fields for *yunga* plants down into the *chala* zone. Undoubtedly, this potential for expanding *yunga* productivity contributed to the formation of societies with larger and denser populations on the coast than in the highlands. Economic self-sufficiency was more easily accomplished within the coastal region with less dependency upon interchange with the highlands. If llamas were reared on the coast as is argued by the Shimadas (I. Shimada 1982; Shimada and Shimada, in press), there were only a few things, exotic materials and mineral ores (Shimada in this volume), to be sought in the highlands.

Exploitation of the *quechua* zone in the highlands and the *chala* zone on the coast as the principal production areas opened the possibility of maintaining large populations. Both zones had circumscribed environments as defined by Carneiro (1961) in which increasing population pressure preconditions the emergence of highly organized, stratified societies. Therefore, any idea which strengthened or effectively maintained a stratified society would have been "adaptive" in both regions regardless of origin. The evolutionary process of Andean civilization was inevitable both on the coast and in the highlands, whether the resources were distributed horizontally or vertically.

Vertical control, however, cannot be explained solely in terms of the biological need to survive. It would have been possible for men to live either on the resources of the *quechua-yunga* zones or those of the *puna-suni* zones (Yamamoto, in this volume). There must have been cultural reasons other than economic necessity to have systematically exploited a wide area ranging from the *puna* to *yunga* or even to the *ruparupa* zone. In this respect, *yunga* products deserve special attention.

Ethnographies of the *puna* or *quechua* inhabitants always mention the use of such *yunga* products as *ají*, coca, gourds, and fruit. Bastien (1978: 137–38) describes how eager the highland people are to obtain *yunga* products for rituals. The use of *yunga* products originated in the preceramic period, and the persistence of this tradition may be one of the reasons why large scale vertical control was sought during the Classic and Postclassic periods. Further, while two specialized forms of environmental utilization evolved in some regions, the *puna-suni* and *quechua-yunga* complexes, maize and *yunga* products led to a mutually interdependent economic linkage. This, in turn, formed a base for eventual sharing of the same cultural tradition. Their interdependence was reinforced by a long, persistent religious tradition which gave important symbolic meaning to the *yunga* products. Thus, the significance of vertical control is as much symbolic as economic, and it would be invaluable to elucidate the underlying symbolism that integrated these complexes into a coherent whole (Bastien 1978:192).

Yunga exploitation was not so crucial for the coastal region as for the highlands, since the extensive *chala* zone could provide *yunga* products. However, the coastal people could not completely abandon the *yunga marítima*, because of its importance for deer hunting, cultivation of coca, cotton, fruits, and *ají*, as well as control of irrigation water. If those plants were cultivated in the *yunga* zone, the vast plain of the *chala* zone could have been used principally for the cultivation of staple foods, such as maize and *yuca*. The coastal people, too, must have been greatly concerned with the *yunga* zones in the upper valleys. We may conclude that the *yunga marítima* played the most important role in linking the coast and highlands, so that they might exchange ideas and goods, and ultimately, share what Willey (1971) identifies as the Peruvian Tradition.

During the Colonial period, the indigenous populations on the coast rapidly declined, while the highland people were driven out of the *yunga* and lower *quechua* zones. They barely maintained their traditional way of life in the poorest and/or remotest areas, appropriately called the refuge region by Aguirre Beltrán, and developed the closed corporate society as documented in Mesoamerica (Wolf 1957). By the end of the sixteenth century, for example in the upper Huallaga basin, the Spanish had already converted the *yunga* zone into sugar plantations and stock farms (Varallanos 1959:271–73). In the eighteenth century, the planting of fruits, coca, cacao, and tobacco flourished (Varallanos 1959:274). I suspect future ethnohistorical studies will reveal similar processes in the Callejón de Huaylas, the Cajamarca basin, and other fertile valleys. In any case, modern ethnography can provide little information concerning traditional patterns of *yunga* utilization by highland people. Rather, we may have to rely on archaeological materials, hoping at the same time that ethnographers will locate some area in which the traditional way of *yunga* utilization still survives.

Conclusion

Utilization of the *yunga,* both the *marítima* and *fluvial* of Pulgar Vidal's (1963) classification, has played an extremely important role in the process of prehistory of the Central Andes. It was already present in the Late Lithic period. I am inclined to think that plant cultivation originated in the process of *yunga* exploitation carried out by the highland people, and that even the cultivation of manioc (*yuca*) and the peanut may have begun not in the tropical forest but rather in the slightly higher, adjacent Andean valleys.

Whether the coastal *yunga* belonged to sea-oriented or highland people in the Archaic and Early Formative periods seems to have depended on the local situation, but in the Jequetepeque Valley the highland people of the Cajamarca basin held sway well down to the valley bottom around Tembladera. The importance of the *yunga* zone during the Middle and Late Formative periods is attested to by the great frequency of sites, although an increase of sites in the *quechua* and *chala* zones is also noted.

Demand for *yunga* products encouraged the eventual emergence of vertical control spanning the *puna* to *yunga* zones in the highlands, and also made the coastal people maintain special concerns with the *yunga marítima* during the Classic and Postclassic periods. There were cases in which highland people had to seek *yunga* resources on the western side of the Andes in the upper parts of the coastal valleys. This situation favored the interchange of ideas and goods between the coast and highlands, certainly encouraging them toward sharing of the same cultural tradition.

We suffer from a paucity of data concerning traditional forms of *yunga* utilization. Multidisciplinary research is sorely needed. Since economic self-sufficiency for biological survival could have been attained by dependence on the resources of one or two ecological zones, the Andean type of vertical control must be explained not only from the economic or ecological point of view but also in terms of ideology and culturally prescribed values. I suspect the *yunga* and its products were more important symbolically than economically, that verticality or horizontality by itself had no significance and that what was more important was control of the *yunga* zone or acquisition of its products. It may be that thus motivated contact or interchange through the *yunga* zone was responsible for the formation and persistence of the Peruvian Tradition common to both coastal and highland regions.

So far, I have stressed the significance of the *yunga* zone in the cultural processes of the Central Andes. Before concluding, I would like to add one more point.

Both in the highlands and coastal regions, the environment had several zones with micro-niches within each zone, and various systems were elaborated to exploit a variety of resources distributed in them. Those systems were elaborated based on the idea of ecological complementarity which, early in prehistory, was always sought after either within the limits of the highlands or the coastal lowlands. Each society or ethnic group was autonomous with social and economic self-sufficiency maintained by exploiting a variety of environmental potentialities. In other words, all societies or groups in the highlands depended on the same basic system of vertical control of the highland environment, at least since the Classic period. Coastal societies, on the other hand, depended on the same basic system of horizontal control.[2] Consequently, ecological complementarity was not seen among different ethnic groups either in the highlands or on the coast. The importance of ecological complementarity lay within the same ethnic group or a smaller unit. The relationship among the different ethnic groups, either in the highlands or in the coastal lowlands, can be interpreted in terms of competition rather than complementarity.[3]

Central Andean cultural processes, seen from the ecological point of view, may be summarized as the formation processes of ecological complementarity within each ethnic or smaller social unit to achieve and/or maintain economic self-sufficiency and sociopolitical autonomy. At the same time, they may be seen as the processes of competition among units (either within the highlands or the coastal region), with the competition ceasing when the units were subsumed within a single, extensive system of either vertical or horizontal control under a strong, integrative political force.

NOTES

1. Based on his extensive surface survey in the Nepeña Valley, Proulx (1982: 90) has recently argued that the Recuay culture influenced or perhaps even controlled the upper valley, namely the *yunga* zone, while the Moche occupied primarily the middle valley area around Pañamarca. He (Proulx 1982:91) describes interaction between them as being marked by mutual respect. The parallelism between the Chancay and Nepeña valleys is remarkable. The frontier area, noted by Patterson and his colleagues (Patterson, McCarthy, and Dunn 1982), is also located in the *yunga* zone of the Lurín Valley where they have found contact between upper valley and lower valley peoples (Dillehay 1979).

Although I did not think that the coastal *yunga* zone sustained any independent ethnic group, Schaedel (in this volume) interprets various lines of evidence, though still sparse, as "substantiating the existence of what appear to be early autonomous *etnías*." His view is highly stimulating and may put me deep in the valley bottoms and keep me there for the rest of my life.

2. Consider the divergent views presented in this volume by Ramirez and Rostworowski. Also see Schaedel and Shimada in this volume.

3. Schaedel (in this volume) uses the terms *etnia* and *macro-etnia*. My "ethnic group" and "smaller unit" roughly correspond to his *macro-etnía* and *etnía* (or subdivision of *etnía*), respectively.

REFERENCES CITED

Bastien, Joseph W.
1978 Mountain of the Condor. Metaphor and Ritual in an Andean Ayllu. St. Paul, Minnesota: West Publishing Co.

Brennan, Curtiss T.
1980 Cerro Arena: Rise of the Andean Elite. Archaeology 33 (3): 6–13.
1982 Cerro Arena: Origins of the Urban Tradition on the Peruvian North Coast. Current Anthropology 23: 247–54.

Bueno Mendoza, Alberto, and Terence Grieder
1979 Arquitectura precerámica de la sierra norte. Espacio, No. 5. Lima.

Burger, Richard L., and Lucy Salazar Burger
1980 Ritual and Religion at Huaricoto. Archaeology 33 (6):26–32.

Carneiro, Robert L.
1961 Slash-and-Burn Cultivation Among the Kuikuru and Its Implications for Cultural Development in the Amazon Basin. *In* The Evolution of Horticultural Systems in Native America: Causes and Consequences. A Symposium. Johannes Wilbert, ed. pp. 47–67. Caracas.

Carrión Cachot de Girard, Rebeca
1959 La religión en el antiguo Perú. Lima.

Casana Robles, Teodoro
1976 Restos arqueológicos de la Provincia de Canta. Huaral.

Dillehay, Tom
1979 Pre-hispanic Resource Sharing in the Central Andes. Science 204: 24–31.

Espinoza Soriano, Waldemar
1967 El primer informe etnográfico sobre Cajamarca. Año de 1540. Revista Peruana de Cultura. 11–12:5–41.

Grieder, Terence, and Alberto Bueno Mendoza
1981 La Galgada: Peru Before Pottery. Archaeology 34 (2):44–51.

Kaplan, Lawrence
1980 Variation in the Cultivated Beans. *In* Guitarrero Cave: Early Man in the Andes. Thomas F. Lynch, ed. pp. 145–48. New York: Academic Press.

Kaulicke, Peter
1981 Keramik der frühen Initialperiode aus Pandanche, Depto. Cajamarca, Peru. Beiträge zur Allgemeine und Vergleichende Archäologie 3:363–89.

Lathrap, Donald W.
1973 Gifts of the Cayman: Some Thoughts on the Subsistence Basis of Chavín. *In* Variation in Anthropology. D. W. Lathrap and Jody Douglas, eds. pp. 91–105. Urbana: University of Illinois Press.

Lynch, Thomas F.
1971 Preceramic Transhumance in the Callejon de Huaylas, Peru. American Antiquity 36:139–48.
1980 Guitarrero Cave in its Andean Context. *In* Guitarrero Cave: Early Man in the Andes. Thomas F. Lynch, ed., pp. 293–320. New York: Academic Press.

Lynch, Thomas F., ed.
1980 Guitarrero Cave: Early Man in the Andes. New York: Academic Press.

MacNeish, Richard S.
1977 The Beginning of Agriculture in Central Peru. *In* Origins of Agriculture, Charles A. Reed, ed. pp. 753–801. The Hague and Paris: Mouton.

MacNeish, R. S., T. C. Patterson, and D. Browman

1975 The Central Peruvian Interaction Sphere. Papers of the Robert S. Peabody Foundation for Archaeology 7.

Morales Chocano, Daniel

1981 La Cerámica Pre-Chavín de Pacopampa y la Fase Inicial de Pandanche. Boletín de Lima 15: 23–25.

Moseley, Michael E.

1975 The Maritime Foundations of Andean Civilization. Menlo Park: Cummings Publishing Co.

Mujica, Elias

1975 Excavaciones Arqueológicas en Cerro de Arena—un Sitio del Formativo Superior en el Valle de Moche, Perú. B.A. thesis, Pontificia Universidad Católica del Perú.

Murra, John V.

1972 El control vertical de un máximo de pisos ecológicos en la economía de las sociedades andinas. *In* Visita de la Provincia de León de Huánuco (1562). John V. Murra, ed. Vol. II, pp. 429–76. Huánuco: Universidad Nacional Hermilio Valdizán.

Onuki, Yoshio

1982 Una Perspectiva Prehistórica de la Utilización Ambiental en la Sierra Nor-Central de los Andes Centrales. *In* El Hombre y su Ambiente en los Andes Centrales. Luis Millones and Hiroyasu Tomoeda, eds. Senri Ethnological Studies 10: 211–28. Senri.

Patterson, Thomas C., John P. McCarthy, and Robert A. Dunn

1982 Polities in the Lurín Valley, Peru, During the Early Intermediate Period. Ñawpa Pacha 20:61–82.

Proulx, Donald A.

1982 Territoriality in the Early Intermediate Period: The Case of Moche and Recuay. Ñawpa Pacha 20:83–96.

Pulgar Vidal, Javier

1963 Geografía del Perú. Las ocho regiones naturales del Perú. Lima: Editorial Universo.

Rappaport, Roy A.

1968 Pigs for the Ancestors. Ritual in the Ecology of a New Guinea People. New Haven: Yale University Press.

Ravines, Rogger

1982 Arqueología del valle medio del Jequetepeque. Lima: Instituto Nacional de Cultura.

Rick, John W.

1980 Prehistoric Hunters of the High Andes. New York: Academic Press.

Shady Solis, Ruth, and Hermilio Rosas La Noire

1979 El complejo Bagua y el sistema de establecimientos durnate el Formativo en la sierra norte del Perú. Ñawpa Pacha 17: 109–42.

Shimada, Izumi

1982 Horizontal Archipelago and Coast-Highland Interaction in North Peru: Archaeological Models. *In* El Hombre y su Ambiente en los

Andes Centrales. Millones and Tomoeda, eds. Senri Ethnological Studies 10: 137–210. Senri.

Shimada, Melody
1982 Zooarchaeology of Huacaloma: Behavioral and Cultural Implications. *In* Excavations at Huacaloma in the Cajamarca valley, Peru, 1979. K. Terada and Y. Onuki, pp. 303–36.

Shimada, Melody and Izumi Shimada
In press Prehistoric Llama Breeding and Herding on the North Coast of Peru. American Antiquity.

Smith, C. Earle
1980 Plant Remains from Guitarrero Cave. *In* Guitarrero Cave: Early Man in the Andes. Thomas F. Lynch, ed. pp. 87–119. New York: Academic Press.

Terada, Kazuo, ed.
1979 Excavations at La Pampa in the North Highlands of Peru: 1975. Tokyo: University of Tokyo Press.

Terada, Kazuo and Yoshio Onuki, eds.
1982 Excavations at Huacaloma in the Cajamarca Valley, Peru: 1979. Tokyo: University of Tokyo Press.

Varallanos, José
1959 Historia de Huánuco. Buenos Aires: Imprenta López.

Willey, Gordon R.
1971 An Introduction to American Archaeology, Volume II: South America. Englewood Cliffs: Prentice-Hall.

Wolf, Eric R.
1957 Closed Corporate Peasant Communities in Mesoamerica and Central Java. Southwestern Journal of Anthropology 13:1–18.

16

Perception, Procurement, and Management of Resources: Archaeological Perspective

Izumi Shimada

Introduction

In a geographical setting as complex as that of the Central Andes, in theory, there are a vast number of potentially complementary ecological permutations. Identification of "realized" (as opposed to "potential") permutations is made difficult because of our limited understanding of such key factors as (a) the changing needs and choices of the human inhabitants, (b) the changing natural and anthropogenic environment (e.g., deforestation, tectonic movement, what Mayer in this volume calls "production zones"), (c) natural resources that were prehistorically exploited, and (d) the processing and management of resources once they were procured. I have already commented elsewhere (Shimada 1982) on the inadequacy of our knowledge of culturally significant resources in the prehispanic Andes. Craig (in this volume) offers a glimpse of the dynamic qualities of the Andean landscape. There are surprisingly few resources in the prehistoric Andes that have been examined in their totality (Julien on guano in this volume and Shimada and Shimada, in press on llama); i.e., the human perception or attitude toward them, availability in time and space, extractive and modifying technologies, transport mechanisms, functions (both latent and manifest), disposition/distribution of both raw materials and products, and attendant institutions (particularly administrative). Too often we speak of "interregional interaction," "state administration," and other broad cultural issues with only a very partial understanding of the natural and cultural dimensions of resources. The sort of holistic perspective on resources that I am advocating here is only possible with tightly focused, sustained interdisciplinary (as opposed to multidisciplinary) research.

Over the past six years, a large circle of specialists from various disciplines (such as ethnohistory, geology, zooarchaeology, and metallurgy) have been collaborating in research design formulation, fieldwork, and laboratory analyses of the Sicán metallurgy of prehispanic north coastal Peru, characterized by the large scale production of arsenical copper. Drawing upon an ever expanding body of data on the Sicán metallurgy, I will illustrate the value of this holistic perspective on resources. The paper begins with a characterization of the Sicán culture, followed by a discussion of changing perceptions of arsenical copper over time, which serves as an effective caution against our tendency to treat resources as static, invariable entities. The nature and source(s) of arsenic-bearing ores have not been satisfactorily determined and the conventional view of ore importation from the North Highlands must be considered as just one of various possibilities. Our understanding of the material and labor needs and logistical complexity of arsenical copper smelting and working allows us to establish the organizational capacity and territorial control that would have been required of the associated administrative/political entities. The preceding serves as the basis for discussion of the nature of interaction between the Cajamarca and Sicán polities. Finally, consideration of disposal and distribution of metal products leads us to hypothesize a key role for the Middle Sicán polity in prehispanic Ecuadorian-Peruvian exchange, possibly involving "primitive money" made of arsenical copper and archaeologically recovered in Batán Grande.

The Sicán Culture: A Characterization

An early Colonial document on the purchase of the extensive land dotted with many archaeological monuments in what is today Batán Grande in the central Leche Valley (Figs. 16.1, 16.2) describes the area as "Sicán" or "Signan," signifying the house or temple of the moon in the extinct, indigenous Muchik language (Kosok 1965:126, 162; Rondón 1966). The document also speaks of the area's reputation for "idols and treasures." Indeed, in the area of ca. 60 km shown in Figure 16.2, we find some 50 archaeological sites that together span 3000 years of regional prehistory in the extensive semi-tropical thorny forest and an estimated 100,000 looters' pits, some even dating to the Colonial period. Intensive archaeological research since 1978 has amply shown the appropriateness of the term "Sicán" as we have documented through excavations various monumental religious structures of different periods (Cavallaro and Shimada n.d.; Shimada 1981, 1982, 1983, in press; Shimada et al. 1981; Shimada, Elera, and Shimada 1982).

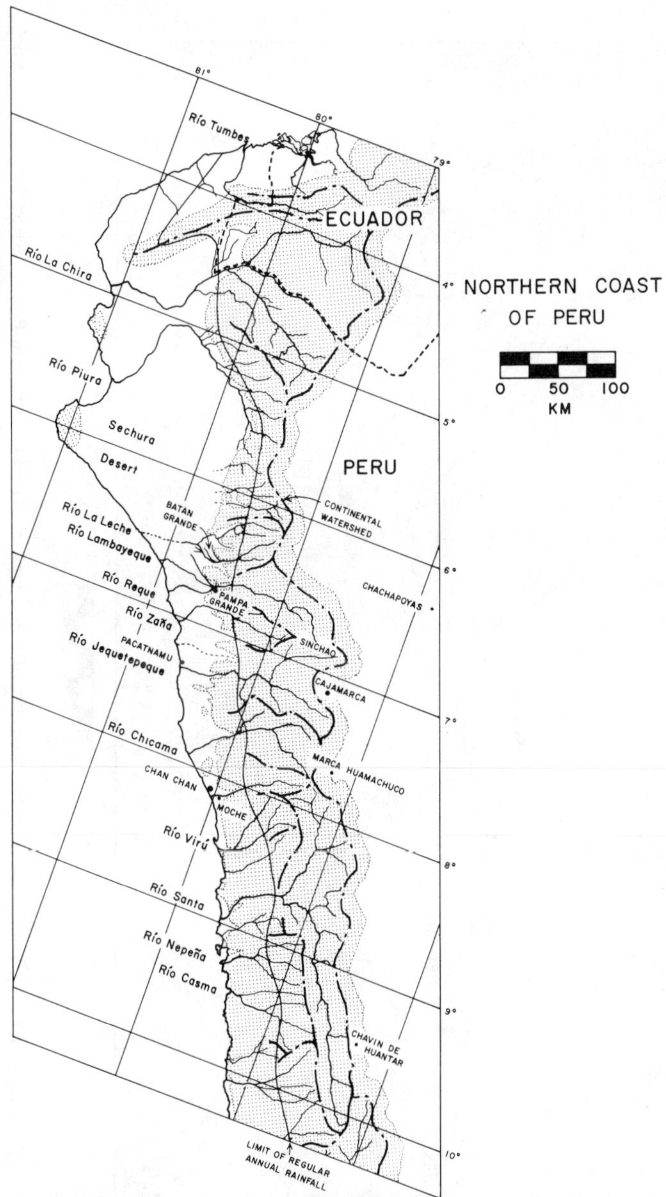

Fig. 16.1 Map of northern Peru and Southern Ecuador, showing the location of Batán Grande and other key sites and areas mentioned in the text.

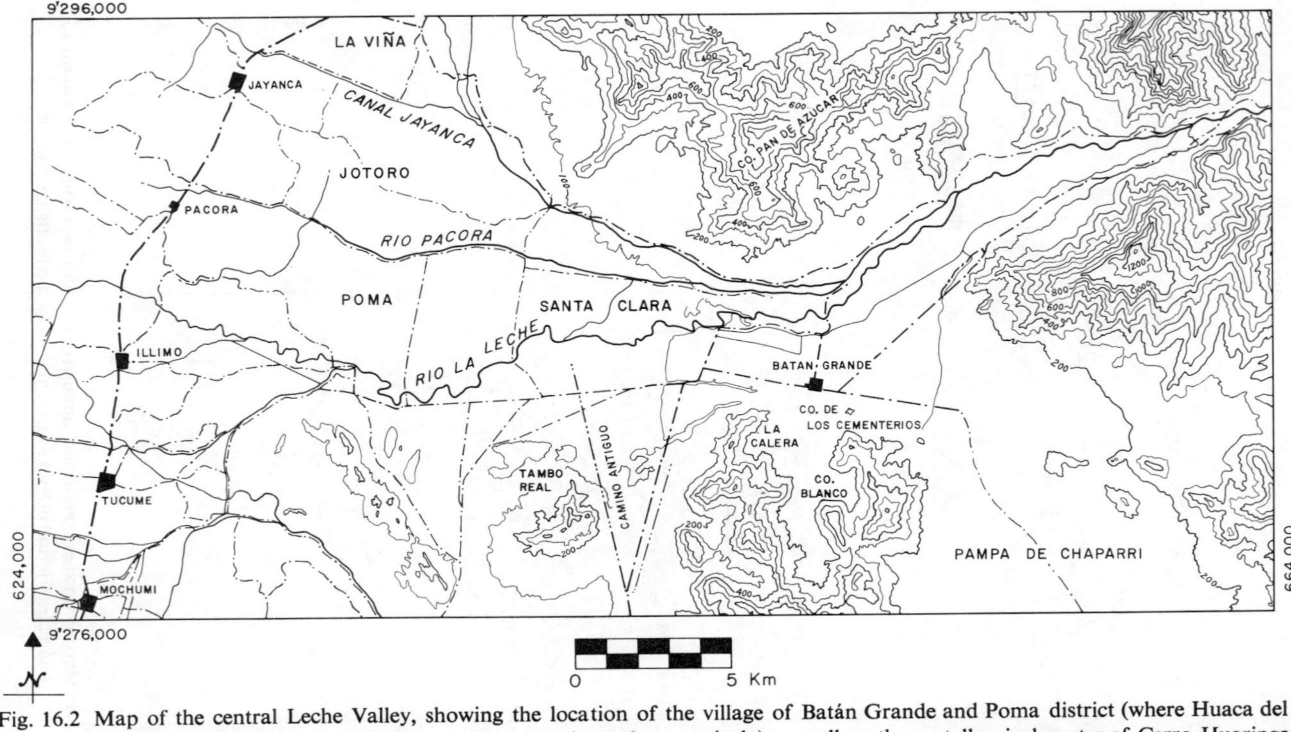

Fig. 16.2 Map of the central Leche Valley, showing the location of the village of Batán Grande and Poma district (where Huaca del Pueblo Batán Grande and the Sicán Precinct are situated, respectively) as well as the metallurgical center of Cerro Huaringa (also known as Cerro de los Cementerios).

Thus, we have adopted the term "Sicán" to describe the local cultural tradition subsequent to the demise of the intrusive Mochica intervalley polity around A.D. 700. This cultural tradition has been chronologically tripartitioned and below follows a brief characterization of the first two periods that are relevant to the basic thrusts of this paper (Table 16.1, 16.2).

The Early Sicán (A.D. 700–850) is poorly known. Its ceramics are heavily influenced by foreign styles such as Middle Cajamarca (based in the adjacent North Highlands), and Wari and/or Pachacamac of Middle Horizon Epoch 2. Specification of the exact sources of influence is difficult because of the limited sample and its provincial character. Concurrent with new ceramic forms and associated styles and iconography, we see a major change in funerary practices, perhaps reflecting adoption of a new religious ideology and cosmology. Whereas the earlier Mochicas often buried their deceased in an extended position within a rectangular adobe chamber, we now see cross-legged, seated burials in cylindrical pits. At the same time, we have not identified any population center, architecture or other physical expression of corporate undertaking, political centralization, or well-developed social hierarchy. Although we may envision Early Sicán as a period of transition, there were some important continuities with the preceding Moche Phase 5. Subsistence items and patterns remain largely unchanged. Llama herding and breeding on the coast that we established *by* the end of the Moche Phase 5 (if not earlier; Shimada 1982; Shimada and Shimada 1981; in press) appears to have remained a viable and important resource management during Early Sicán, in spite of the apparent absence of any regional political authority. However, as we see below, perception, exploitation, and management of natural resources underwent a significant change during the following period.

Excavations at the site of Huaca del Pueblo Batán Grande (HPBG) with five meters of excellent cultural stratigraphy have shown a *rapid formalization* of a distinct art style and iconography that represents integration of selective aspects of the Mochica and Early Sicán antecedents into a new configuration. Significantly, the above was associated with other varied material, ideological, and organizational change with far reaching impacts: initiation of construction of monumental adobe structures, large-scale copper alloy smelting and metalworking, and elaborate funerary tradition. These developments that were intricately interwoven emerged around A.D. 850–900, a matter of a few generations, and came to characterize the Middle Sicán, which corresponds to the "classic" period of the Sicán Culture. I have argued elsewhere (Shimada 1983) that the key and immediate mechanism of

Table 16.1 Regional Cultural Chronologies

Lambayeque Valley (Nolan 1980)		Relative Chronology (Rowe and Menzel 1967)	Batán Grande	Moche Valley (Donnan and Mackey 1978)	
Colonial	1600	Colonial		Colonial	
Chimu-Inca (A.D. 1450–1550)	1500	Late Horizon (1476–1534)	Chimu-Inca	Chimu-Inca (A.D. 1470–1534)	
Lambayeque C	1400		Chimu (A.D. 1350?–1460 to 1470)		
(A.D. 1250–1450)	1300				
	1200	Late Intermediate	Late Sicán (A.D. 1050–1350?)	Late	–AD.1470)
		(900–1476)			
Lambayeque B	1100			Middle Chimu	
(A.D. 1000–1250)					
	1000			Early	(A.D. 800–
	900		Middle Sicán (A.D. 850–1050)		
Lambayeque A		4 (800–900)			
(A.D. 700–1000)	800				
		3 (750–800) Middle	Early Sicán (A.D. 700–850)		
	700	2B (700–750) Horizon			
		2A (650–700)		V	–A.D. 800)
	600	1B (600–650)			
Late Moche (Mochica)		1A (550–600)	Late Moche	IV	
(A.D. 450–700)	500		(A.D. 450–700)		
				III	Moche (Mochica)
	400			II	
	300	Early Intermediate			
		(400 B.C.-A.D. 550)		I	
	200				
	100				
	A.D.			Gallinazo	
	B.C.				

Table 16.2 List of Carbon-14 Dates for the Batán Grande Region

Site Name	C - 14 Date	Laboratory No.	Cultural Phase	Sample Context and Material
HPBG	1520 ± 65 BP; AD 430	SMU-873	Mochica IV	T-1/2–'79, Stratum XII-N, charcoal from firepit
	1430 ± 60 BP; AD 520 f	SMU-901	Mochica IV	T–1/2–'79, Stratum XII-D-E, charcoal from firepit
	1385 ± 65 BP; AD 565	SMU-876	Mochica V	T–1/2–'79, Stratum XII, charcoal from buried urn
	1130 ± 70 BP; AD 820	SMU-1066	Early Sicán-Middle Sicán transition	T–1/2–'79, Stratum XI-D, charcoal from firepit
	1098 ± 67 BP; AD 852 p	SMU-1326	Middle Sicán	T–4–'83 charcoal from Smelting Furnace 6
	1084 ± 39 BP; AD 866 p	SMU-1324	Middle Sicán?	T–4–'83, burnt wooden post bottom intruding into Floor 5, Room 40
	1032 ± 79 BP, AD 918 p	SMU-1328	Middle Sicán	T–4–'83, charcoal from buried (inverted) urn, Floor 9, Room 33
	1010 ± 40 BP; AD 940 f	SMU-899	Middle Sicán	T–1/2–'79, Stratum XI-A, charcoal from firepit
	978 ± 56 BP; AD 972 p	SMU-1322	Middle Sicán ?	T–4–'83, burnt wooden post bottom intruding into Floor 3, Room 40
	940 ± 60 BP; AD 1010	SMU-1068	Middle Sicán ?	T–1/2–'79. Stratum VIII, charcoal from firepit
	930 ± 40 BP; AD 1020	SMU-875	Middle Sicán	T–1/2–'79, Stratum IX, charcoal from firepit
	908 ± 37 BP; AD 1042	SMU-1321	Late Sicán	T–4–'83, burnt wooden post, Floor 7, Room 29
	906 ± 49 BP; AD 1044	SMU-1320	Middle Sicán	T–4–'83, charcoal from firepit, Floor 5, Room 38
	876 ± 62 BP; AD 1074	SMU-1183	Late Sicán	T–3–'82, charcoal from firepit, floor, Room 10
	867 ± 52 BP; AD 1083	SMU-1175	Middle Sicán/Late Sicán transition	T–3–'82, charcoal from Smelting Furnace 1, Floor 28 between Levels 22 and 23
	814 ± 56 BP; AD 1136	SMU-1329	Late Sicán	T–3–'82, charcoal from firepit, Feature 27
	760 ± 40 BP; AD 1190 f	SMU-900	Late Sicán	T–1/2–'79, Stratum VI-A charcoal from firepit
	724 ± 55 BP; AD 1226	SMU-1176	Late Sicán	T–3–'82, charcoal from floor, Room 14
	700 ± 40 BP; AD 1250	SMU-902	Late Sicán	T–1/2–'79, Stratum IV, charcoal from firepit
Huaca Oro	1028 ± 52 BP; AD 922	SMU-1330	Middle Sicán	Part of well-preserved log used as flooring material of the pyramid of Huaca Oro

HLV	1090 ± 60 BP; AD 860	Beta-3403	Middle Sicán	Charcoal from firepit immediately below Wall 1, at the eastern base of the principal pyramid
	1050 ± 70 BP; AD 900	SMU-1070	Middle Sicán	Wooden beam of looted shafttomb roof, Southern Sector
	980 ± 50 BP; AD 970	Beta-3402	Middle Sicán	Burnt roof beam, adobe enclosure overlying shafttomb (SMU-1070), Southern Sector
H. Menor	915 ± 50 BP; AD 1035	GrN-5474	Middle Sicán	Wooden bow from gravelot of looted shafttomb
H. El Corte	985 ± 65 BP; AD 965	Beta-1802	Middle Sicán	Burnt roof beam atop Platform Mound 1
H. Julupe	980 ± 70 BP; AD 970	Beta-1803	Middle Sicán	Charcoal from burnt post, Trench 2
H. Soledad	1570 ± 40 BP; AD 380 f	SMU-897	?	Charcoal from a firepit, Test Pit 3, Cut A, Southern Cemetery
	1390 ± 65 BP; AD 560	SMU-833	Mochica V?	Charcoal from the "protective organic layer" covering Phase I construction, Mound II
	890 ± 50 BP; AD 1060 f	SMU-903	Middle Sicán?	Wood from plastered/painted column, Phase III construction, Mound II
Co. H	790 ± 50 BP; AD 1160	Beta-5671	Late Sicán	Charcoal from firepit below Floor 11, Excavation Area 1, Sector III
	760 ± 50 BP; AD 1190	Beta-5672	Late Sicán	Charcoal from firepit dug into sterile zone, top of T-shaped platform, Sector III
	660 ± 60 BP; AD 1290	SMU-1161	Late Sicán/Chimu transition?	Charcoal from smelting furnace, Excavation Area 1, Sector III
	450 ± 60 BP; AD 1500	Beta-2591	Inca	Charcoal from smetlting furnace, Excavation Area 1, Sector III

HPBG = Huaca del Pueblo Batán Grande; **HLV** = Huaca Las Ventanas; **H. Menor** = Huaca Menor; **H. El Corte** = Huaca El Corte; **H. Julupe** = Huaca Julupe; **H. Soledad** = Huaca Soledad; **Co. H.** = Cerro Huaringa (Cerro de los Cementerios)
f = fractionation corrected; p = preliminary date.
All dates are based on the halflife of 5568 years.

the rapid and varied cultural changes at the onset of the Middle Sicán was a religious revitalization, which provided the organizational framework for subsequent political and economic growth during this period.

The Middle Sicán Culture may be characterized by the following interrelated material, ideological, and organizational features:

1. A distinct art style with highly homogeneous and ubiquitous representation of the "Sicán Lord," a principal deity that has been variously described as a "tin-woodsman" (Scheele and Patterson 1966), "bird-man" (Carrion 1940), or "rotund figure" (Kroeber 1944), with a two-dimensional semicircular face, elaborate headdress, comma or almond-shaped eyes, conventionalized ears with pointed tips and large circular ornaments on the lobes, and a wide collar expressed in various media (metals, textiles, ceramics, murals, and wood; e.g., Kauffmann 1973; Shimada 1982, 1983; Zevallos 1971). The almost endless repetition of the same deity crosscutting time (the above features becoming more accentuated and eventually simplified over time) and space suggests strong, long-lasting ideological unification (Fig. 16.3).

2. The construction, occupation, and abandonment of the 1,000 by 1,600 meter T-shaped Sicán Religious-Funerary Precinct with at least 17 major truncated pyramids and platforms in the Poma area of Batán Grande (Fig. 16.4). The Precinct was the inferred symbolic and physical center of the Middle Sicán polity. Surveys and excavations in 1980–1982 showed that much of the Precinct was paved with adobes and a limestone flagstone floor, and principal constructions were accompanied by a series of platforms, elaborately constructed multi-room compounds, and deep shafttombs. Many, if not most, of the monumental constructions such as Huacas El Corte and Las Ventanas were built with marked adobes, whose size, soil, and distribution patterns suggest production under multiple sponsors (Cavallaro and Shimada, n.d.; Shimada 1983). Around A.D. 1050–1100, many of these constructions in the Precinct were burnt and abandoned, marking the end of the Middle Sicán.

3. Elaborate funerary practices, including elite shafttombs, some with numerous sacrificial burials and quantities of gold and other metal funerary objects (e.g., Pedersen 1976; Shimada 1981, 1982, 1983; Shimada et al. 1981; Tello 1937a, 1937b; Valcárcel 1937; Vreeland and Shimada 1981). Tello's only visit to Batán Grande was prompted by the impressive quantities of funerary gold objects discovered around the bases of the principal pyramids of Huacas La Merced and Las Ventanas. A rare photograph of a gravelot from a looted shafttomb in the Precinct shows some 200 Middle Sicán gold objects. Pedersen (1976) recorded a large shafttomb at Huaca Menor that measured 14 by 14 meters at the top with a depth of at least 20 meters. The tomb

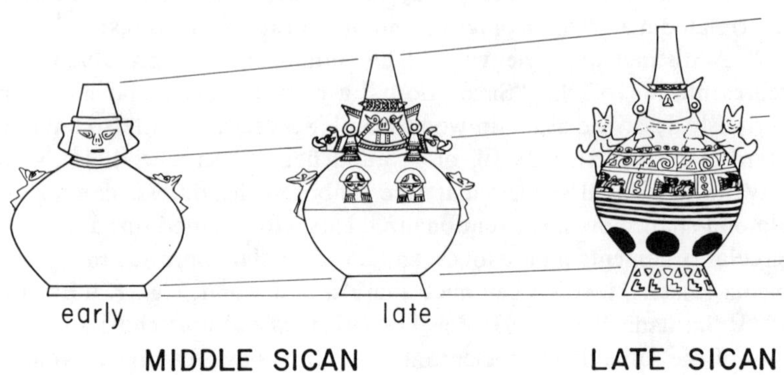

Fig. 16.3 Tentative seriation of the Sicán effigy jars with the Sicán Lord representation. The left vessel represents early Middle Sicán, while the right specimen dates to Late Sicán.

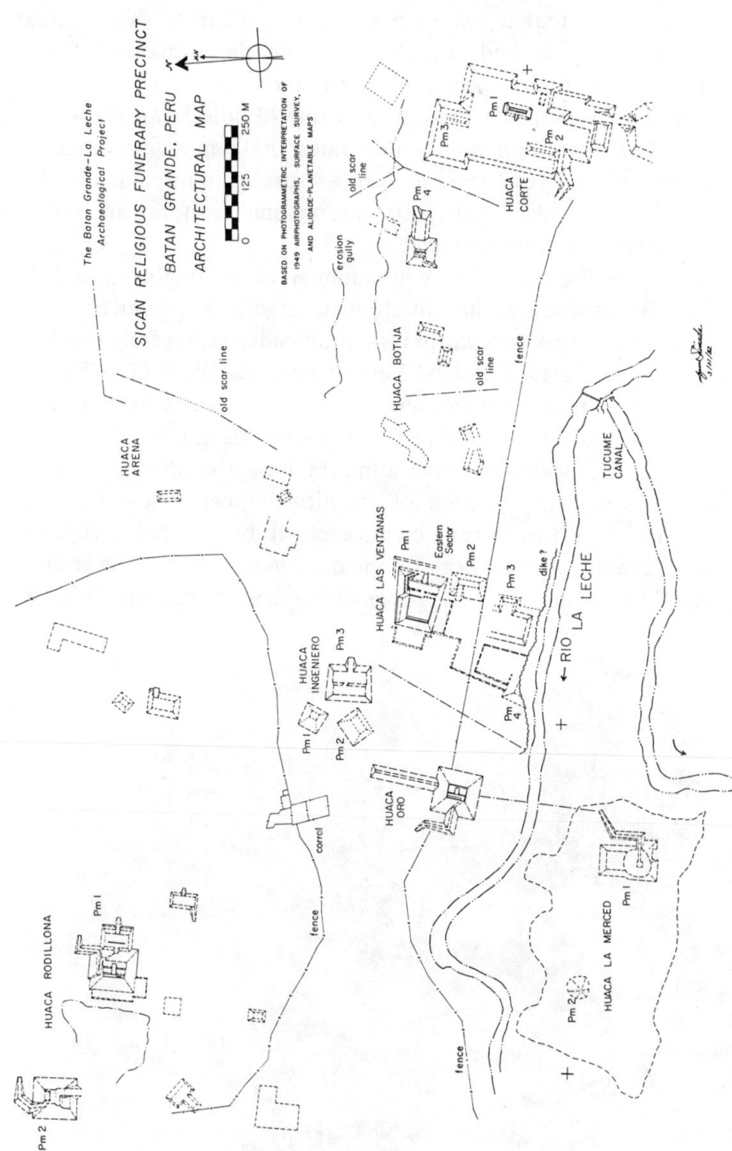

Fig. 16.4 Architectural map of the Sicán Religious-Funerary Precinct in Poma district of Batán Grande.

yielded 17 bodies, mostly sacrificial, mantles of *Spondylus princeps*, lapis lazuli and cinnabar, wooden scepters and arrow shafts, great quantities of gold foil and "copper" artifacts (an estimated 500 kg), discs of shell, one quartz necklace, many stacks of *naipes*, (double-T shaped "primitive money"), and at least one Middle Sicán blackware effigy jar. The preceding amply illustrates the impressive range of natural and cultural resources, as well as vast manpower at the disposal of the Middle Sicán polity. Its interregional economy and stratified social systems are also evident.

4. Paralleling the unprecedented quantity of sheet gold and gold alloy funerary artifacts is the initiation of large-scale production and use of arsenical copper (primarily utilitarian ends) successfully employing sulfide ores. The 1982 and 1983 excavations at HPBG (T-3-'82 and T-4-'83) revealed four complete sets and part of a fifth set of smelting furnaces in five successive Middle Sicán strata dating to ca. A.D. 850–1050 (Plate 16.1), clearly demonstrating the local technological know-how for large scale production of arsenical copper. These furnaces were associated with numerous ceramic blowtube tips called tuyeres, slag lumps, ground slag, and ore fragments, among others. The earliest evidence of *in situ* arsenical copper smelting dates to ca. A.D. 800–850

Plate 16.1 A panoramic view of the 1983 excavation at Huaca del Pueblo Batán Grande, showing three of the four stratified, complete sets of smelting furnaces dating to the Middle Sicán period.

(T-1/2-'79). Evidence of metallurgical activity is found in all three contiguous trenches, an area of 13 by 17 meters. Indications are that we exposed a portion of an extensive metallurgical workshop area. Large quantities of arsenical copper artifacts such as cast hoes, digging stick blades, spear points, and *naipes* commonly found in Middle Sicán tombs in Batán Grande were most likely to have been locally produced at HPBG and other nearby contemporary sites with metallurgical remains such as those around Cerro Jotoro (some 17 km west of the former site). The continuing importance of the arsenical copper smelting and metalworking over time (until the Spanish Conquest) has been well-documented through excavations at HPBG and nearby Cerros Huaringa (also known as Cerro de los Cementerios) and Sajino (Epstein and Shimada in press; Shimada et al. 1982, 1983). For example, initiation of intensive metallurgical activity at Cerro Huaringa dates to about A.D. 1100–1150, first supplementing production at HPBG but supplanting it during late prehistory. The indigeneous character of the metallurgy is seen in strong continuities and gradual improvements in smelting technology, furnace and tuyere constructions, as well as spatial organization of metallurgical activities.

Additional characterizations are possible. The distinctive Middle Sicán ceramics with the hallmark Sicán Lord head representation have been reported as far south as Ancón and Pachacamac (Menzel 1977 Reiss and Stübel 1880–87; Schmidt 1929; Uhle 1903) and as far north as Isla La Plata near Guayaquil, a center of *Spondylus* trade (Marcos 1982). Menzel (1977:59) observes that "during this time north coast ideas of art, religion, and technology appear strongly as far south as Pachacamac, and, through the agency of Pachacamac, to some extent at Ica and even Nazca on the south coast."

Where some detailed survey data exist (such as for the Lambayeque, Zaña, and Jequetepeque valleys; Kosok, 1959, 1965; Disselhoff 1959; Nolan 1980; Ravines 1982; Eling, personal communication, 1982), we see widespread distribution of Middle Sicán ceramics in funerary and habitational contexts. They are found up into the necks of these valleys and the relationship between the Middle Sicán and North Highland-based Cajamarca Culture has been described as one of "push and pull" and "checks and balances," i.e., political and territorial control of the crucial valley necks oscillated between them over time (Shimada 1982:184–5). It is significant that the intrusive Middle Sicán occupation is superimposed over that of the earlier Mochica (Phase 5) at such major sites as Pampa Grande, Cipán-Collique (Lambayeque), Chumbenique (Zaña), Cañoncillo, Moro Viejo, and Ventanilla (Jequetepeque). Available evidence, then, suggests political control of the area between the Leche and Jequetepeque valleys, inclusive.

The preceding discussion and data on the Middle Sicán projects a picture of a culture with a highly elaborate art and technology, differential accumulation, material wealth, and the ability to command a large labor force and impressive quantities of varied material resources, some of which had to be imported over considerable distances (e.g., *Spondylus*, gold nuggets, emeralds, lapis lazuli, and possibly arsenic-bearing sulfide ores). At least three levels of social classes are suggested by funerary treatments. Although these features argue for attribution of "state" status to the Middle Sicán polity, our settlement data are still inadequate to judge the presence of the three levels of decision-making or administration commonly expected from a state society. At the same time, ideological unity is suggested by the distinct and homogeneous art style and iconography.

Changing Perception and Knowledge of Resources: The Case of Arsenic-bearing Ores and Arsenical Copper

As seen in the preceding discussion, the metallurgy may well be the best understood aspect of the Middle Sicán Culture, which seems to have been responsible for establishing arsenical copper as the primary metal of later prehistoric north Peru. I believe the initiation and control of expanding metallurgical production stands as a major force underlying the economic and political power attained by the Middle Sicán polity. It is when we examine the implications of the preceding characterization of the Sicán metallurgy that we see various issues relevant to this symposium. These include changing perceptions of (a) the function and value of arsenical copper, (b) sources of arsenic-bearing ores (highlands vs. coast), and (c) the disposition and spatial distribution of the metal products. The last may lead to another major characteristic of Middle Sicán Culture, possible participation in an Ecuadorian-Peruvian exchange network. Basic issues here are the nature of correspondence between the emic and etic views of resources and Sicán geopolitics and the political economy.

Changing Perception and Function of Arsenical Copper

Copper, smelted by the first millennium B.C. and widespread throughout much of the Central Andes by the first few centuries of our era was the medium of experimentation and innovation for both North Peruvian and *altiplano* metallurgical traditions (Lechtman 1980; Ponce

1970). Although used primarily for utilitarian purposes, copper was clearly the mainstay of Mochica metallurgy, which in the opinion of Lechtman (1980) was in many ways never equaled in the Central Andes. Logically, it was on this sound technological foundation of copper metallurgy that arsenical copper metallurgy was built. As noted above, concurrent with the onset and florescence of the Middle Sicán Culture we see a definite, large-scale, permanent shift from copper to arsenical copper on much of the North Coast. The timing of this shift is rather curious as arsenical copper objects, though rare, were already being produced several centuries earlier by Mochica metallurgists. Why, then, did it take so long (up to 500–600 years) to attain preeminence in North Coast metallurgy?

Was the inhibiting factor organizational and cognitive in nature? Certainly the presence of a technological innovation does not necessarily lead to its rapid diffusion or acceptance without appropriate cultural receptivity. Innovations must be properly perceived and appropriate organizational and conceptual adjustments made. I concur with Lechtman (1979:12) who argues that the smelting of arsenical copper was a "self-generated technological change" among North Coast metallurgists and "though the alloy may have been an accidental one, the Mochica were aware of its properties and may well have tried to reproduce it." This assertion is based on compositional analyses of Moche Phase 3 and 4 artifacts excavated by M. Uhle at the site of Moche (Kroeber 1944, 1954; Patterson 1971). Although we are dealing with only 25 artifacts, arsenic appears in the highest concentration (up to 2%) and most consistently in ornaments (as opposed to ingots or utilitarian implements; Lechtman 1979:4). This differential use (to be further verified) is intriguing in terms of the intrinsic qualities of arsenical copper which are very similar to those of more widely known tin-copper bronze. Both alloys offer improved hardness, casting, and strength. These qualities are ideal for the production of utilitarian implements and during the Middle Sicán arsenical copper was indeed primarily used for this end. The Mochica perception of this alloy was apparently different. Lechtman (1979:4, 1980:314–5) suggests perhaps it was the color or luster that was valued as special and ornamental by the Mochica elite. At about 2% arsenic, color changes in the alloy would begin to be apparent.

The preceding discussion of the changing perception, value, and function of the same material resource serves as an effective caution against our tendency to treat resources as static, invariable entities. The cultural contexts of their procurement/production, including costs and availability, must be properly assessed.

If the Mochica metallurgists were aware of arsenical copper and differentiated its use, why did they not produce more of it? Since the awareness of the metal is already indicated, we must now concentrate on questions of the smelting technology and ore supply.

Sources of Arsenic-Bearing Ores: Changing Perspectives and Their Implications

Ongoing multi-faceted metallurgical research has shown thus far that copper-based implements archaeologically recovered from the Batán Grande region and dating to Middle Sicán or later periods, consistently contain ca. 2% to 6% arsenic (Epstein and Shimada in press; Shimada et al. 1982, 1983). Similarly, metallic copper prills or droplets in the smelting slag (metallurgical waste product from smelting) have been observed to contain arsenic in variable quantities from 1% to 30% (Epstein and Shimada, in press; Shimada et al. 1982, 1983; Merkel 1984).

Examination of slag has provided more information on the smelting process. Summarizing a large body of data resulting from technical analyses of the Middle Sicán slag, Merkel (1984:29–30) observes that in the prills recovered from HPBG the products are rich in arsenic and sulfur. Smelting at Batán Grande was based on reduction of copper ores using charcoal as fuel. Merkel (1984) concludes that the concentration of sulfur relative to arsenic "... indicates that in part copper sulfide ores were probably charged into the smelting furnace." Although the question of prehispanic sulfide ore smelting has been long debated (e.g., Mathewson 1915; Caley and Easby 1959; Patterson 1971), evidence from HPBG indicates Middle Sicán metallurgists were in the transitional stage toward the full exploitation of copper sulfide ores (Merkel 1984). It is our impression that Batán Grande metallurgists gradually improved their control over the smelting process and consistency in the products.

Numerous ore fragments were recovered from our excavations at HPBG. Analyses of these specimens are currently being carried out by MASCA, The University Museum, and University of Pennsylvania (under S. Fleming's direction) and only a few tentative observations can be presented here. Most of the samples are oxide ores with highly varying copper concentrations. Some are rich in iron and appear to have been used as flux. During smelting, flux is added to produce a slag from accessory copper-poor minerals contained in the gangue. This technique improves the recovery of the reduced copper. Importantly, there are several ore fragments high in arsenic and iron content and low in copper (arsenopyrite). The nature of the ores used in smelting, however, cannot be readily deduced from these specimens as they may represent those deemed inappropriate or discarded by the ancient metallurgists (Fleming, personal communication 1984). Likewise, data from analyses of smelting products do not allow a ready identification of specific ores charged in the smelting furnace, partly due to interaction between the charged ores and flux during smelting.

Nonetheless, at this intermediate phase of our research, we can offer a gross characterization of ores used in Batán Grande. Copper oxides seem to have been the major ore component in the smelting charge by volume and weight. The oxides were locally available. Prehistoric mines of various scale (e.g., Cerro Blanco, Cabeza de León, and Barranco Colorado) that yielded copper oxides and were linked by an ancient road network to the metallurgical center of Cerro Huaringa (and probably to the nearby HPBG) occur within 14 km of HPBG (Epstein and Shimada, in press; Shimada 1982; Shimada et al. 1982, 1983; Lechtman 1976). Similarly, iron ore (hematite) is quite common within the same area (e.g., Cerro Azul, Cabeza de León).

What we are concerned with here, however, are sources of arsenic-bearing ores. Based on her extensive survey of prehistoric mines and metallurgical sites, Lechtman (1976, 1979, 1980) concluded that there are no significant deposits of arsenic-bearing ores on the North Coast. They do, however, occur in abundance in the North Highlands. Lechtman (1976:15–16; 1979:9) observed:

> It seems much more likely that the source of the arsenic was not any of the arsenic minerals per se but rather the copper sulfarsenide ores that are so abundant in the northern sierra, particularly in the region of Quiruvilca (ca. 4,000 m) to Sinchao (3,850 m) which is NW of Hualgayoc, the important Spanish silver-mining center. These ores . . . are as scarce on the coast as they are abundant in the sierra. I found no evidence of them at all on the north coast . . . unless substantial quantities of arsenic mineral suddenly surface on the north coast, I think we must look to the northern sierra for the key to arsenic bronze and to sulfide smelting in the northern Andes.

At the same time, when we consider the emerging body of data on Sicán metallurgy as a whole, our picture of the arsenic-rich ore source(s) is not clear as the above passage may imply.

As noted earlier, the high concentration of sulfur in the prills and slag must have been due to the use in part of copper sulfide ores in the smelting charge. Arsenopyrite is a strong candidate. Merkel (pers. com. 1984) has observed that the level of sulfur in the HPBG prills is greater than would be expected from possible smelting charge additions for arsenic of such ores as arsenopyrite (FeAsS), realgar (AsS) or enargite (Cu_3AsS_4) (based on mass balance calculations for experimental smelting results). We must entertain the strong possibility of mixing of two or more copper ores. Conversely, some coastal polymetallic oxide ores along with flux (with other minor elements) and/or one of the aforementioned ores could well have produced the observed prill compositions.

With the present status of our research on the smelting charge and coastal and highland ores, we can neither support nor refute the possibility of ore importation from the adjacent North Highlands. At the same time, a brief survey (together with ore specimens collected) in 1983 by I. Shimada and J. L. Suarez (Peruvian mining engineer) of ancient mines in the vicinity of Batán Grande (Cerro Blanco) and Nueva Arica (Cerro Leque Leque) in the neighboring Zaña Valley suggests that arsenopyrite may have existed in abundance in prehispanic times in these coastal regions. A series of fine-grain surveys of coastal mineral sources, as well as continuing analysis of metallurgical remains are needed. Certainly, the preceding amply illustrates the premature nature of any argument on "coast-highland interactions" based on the possibility of ore importation. Questions surrounding the limited arsenical copper production by the Mochica metallurgists can be only partially dealt with at this point. Considering the evidence for gradual improvement of the smelting technology and consistency in the products seen in the Sicán metallurgy, we may venture to suggest that the Mochica metallurgists did not have sufficient technological control to consistently smelt arsenical copper. The coast-centric orientation of the Mochica economy and territoriality (Shimada 1982, n.d. 1) argues for a coastal source of arsenic-bearing ores.

Organizational Requirements and Features of the Sicán Metallurgy

Metallurgical production is a system of sequentially ordered activities that are temporally and/or spatially differentiated. The interdependent steps in production are sustained by a wide range of logistical supports. The interdisciplinary and holistic perspective being followed in this paper allows us to discuss various organizational requirements and features of this system and component activities.

Although the excavations at HPBG have failed to show the total range of material remains of the Sicán copper-based metallurgy, the knowledge we have acquired for the later periods (but technologically continuous metallurgical centers such as Cerro Huaringa) allows us to make a reasonably complete reconstruction of the activity organization at the former. For example, in spite of the absence of any *batán-chunga* set (the stable anvil and matching rocking stone used to crush slag and/or ores), we can confidently speak of their use due to the presence of ground slag. Thus, although our excavation is limited to a 13 by 17 m area, it is certain that the metallurgical activities covered a much larger area. Similarly, the presence of tuyeres with ground slag temper implies tuyere production nearby, perhaps by the metallurgists themselves. Three or four furnaces that form a group could have been operated independently, with different phases of the metallurgical operation, such as preheating, smelting, cooling, and melting represented at any one time. The excavational evidence from HPBG allows us to speak confidently of multiple steps in only one workshop.

Other lines of evidence, however, point to a much larger scale metallurgical production for the Batán Grande region as a whole during the Middle Sicán. For example, consider the estimated 500 kg of "copper" objects removed from the Huaca Menor tomb (Pedersen 1976:63). Most, if not the overwhelming majority, of these and other funerary non-ornamental "copper" objects, show no evidence of use along with poor craftsmanship (Lechtman 1981). This suggests that the objects were made rapidly for the exclusive purpose of internment as offerings. Merkel (1984:43–44) offers an estimate of the product size of the Sicán smelting based on furnace dimensions and the results of experimental copper smelting. A minimal volume of 1.25 liters of the molten mass in the furnace with an estimated slag density of 3.5 g per cubic centimeter represents approximately 4.375 kg slag. Experimental results (using an ore with ca. 30% copper) show that, at best, the slag to copper ratio is about ten to one (Merkel 1983; Tylecote, Ghaznavi, and Boydell 1977). With a copper recovery efficiency of 50–71% or better (Tylecote and Boydel 1978), 5 kg slag (allowing for some error in estimates) would yield 0.3 to 0.4 kg of impure copper product per smelting run (Merkel 1984:44). Since the furnace chamber volume varies depending on the number of "re-linings," the estimate of the molten mass in the furnace also varies from about 1.25 to 2.5 liters. Accordingly, we may speak of 0.3 to 0.6 kg of impure copper as the product of each smelting run. To produce a finished copper ingot of, let us say, 0.4 kg probably required a whole day by a team of several workers. Thus, the production of 500 kg funerary copper-based objects (even if we allowed for one week for digging a 14 m by 14 m by 20 m deep shafttomb and other funerary preparations) would have been a tall order for even a dozen smelting workshops devoted exclusively to this task. Clearly the above burial situation is atypical, but when we consider the fact that even a small Middle Sicán tomb invariably contains some "copper" objects and that there was a continuous demand for the production of secular implements, it becomes highly likely that we are dealing with a procurement level beyond the production capacities of a cottage industry. The inferred local production of the *naipes* believed to have served as "primitive money" leads us to suggest further that the control of the entire regional copper alloy production (smelting and metalworking) was in the hands of the central authority of the Middle Sicán Culture. This suggestion will be examined later in more detail.

As with earlier and later production setups, loci of the Middle Sicán smelting (and probably casting and a limited degree of metalworking) was likely to have been spatially segregated from loci involved in the manufacture of final products. At Pampa Grande, Chan Chan, and Huaca Chotuna only workshops involved in hammering, annealing, cutting, and/or shaping have been identified (Donnan 1981; Shimada 1978; Topic 1977). The ceremonial complex of Chotuna appears to have been exclusively involved in manufacture of finished products such as personal ornaments. In Batán Grande, those engaged in arsenical copper smelting had to contend with heat and fumes from the furnaces on a daily basis. Preparing charges to be placed in furnaces, cleaning furnaces, providing draft with blowtubes, and grinding slag to extract prills added up to busy, dirty, and physically taxing work.

Another important consideration for organization and management of the smelting activity was the constant and heavy demand for fuel. Experiments have shown that fuel consumption in primitive copper smelting is several times greater than ore consumption (Tylecote and Boydel 1978). According to Merkel's (1984:49) estimates from experimental results, to produce 5 kg of slag (a minimal figure) would have required about 2 kg of copper ore and 4 to 6 kg of flux, depending on the qualities of the ore, fuel, and refractories. If a dozen smelting workshops operated daily, the quantity of charcoal fuel consumed would be in the order of 150 kg. Preheating furnaces and consolidation of prills would have required much more fuel. In essence, a logical placement of the smelting operation would be close to ore and fuel sources. The metallurgical sites such as HPBG, Cerros Huaringa, and Sajino are all ideally situated economically in both regards. The extensive region from Batán Grande to Olmos and beyond toward Chulucanas has been famous at least since the Colonial era for the dense and extensive subtropical thorny forest and as the source of high quality charcoal (Hutchinson 1873; Rostworowski 1981). The inferred level of charcoal consumption for the metallurgical operations in Batán Grande would have decimated the local forest quite rapidly and I suspect the charcoal fuel had to be procured from a much more extensive area.

Based largely on ethnohistorical data, Netherly (1978:248) argued for "... strong state involvement in the production of metal objects" during the Chimu and Inca dominations of the North Coast. At the same time, she (1978:248) suggests that the "... organization of the metalworkers appears not to have been monolithic" and seems to have followed the general organizational pattern of the prehispanic North Coast: "... organization into *parcialidades* under a headman (who may have been some kind of master craftsman) or under a *principal* lord (whose functions may well have been more supervisory or administrative) and who presumably dealt with the paramount lord or state authorities."

Relevant archaeological data are insufficient to properly assess the above ethnohistorically based views. However, some important observations can be made. For the copper alloy smelting in Batán Grande under the Chimu and Inca administrations we have (Epstein and Shimada, in press; Shimada et al. 1982, 1983) noted that a certain degree of autonomy was allowed for individual groups of metallurgists in the manner of furnace construction, tuyere decoration, form, and size. The Middle Sicán tuyeres from HPBG display just as much, if not greater, variation, perhaps reflecting a considerable degree of autonomy at the level of the metallurgists manning individual workshops (Fig. 16.5).

In regard to the procurement and distribution of the fuel and arsenic-bearing ores, it is my contention that the central authority of the Middle Sicán state was involved. The location of major prehistoric smelting sites was dependent on ready local access to essential ingredients such as fuel and ores. It is a simple fact of Andean geography that such locations are neither uniformly distributed nor numerous. In the case of the Sicán metallurgy using copper-arsenic alloys, the overwhelming portion of smelting charges in furnaces consisted of locally available copper oxide and hematite ores. Arsenic-rich mineral addition may have represented a minor portion in weight of the charge. Many different arsenic-bearing minerals may have been used to "salt" the smelting charge to produce the observed alloy products. Proximity to arsenic-rich ore sources was by no means the overriding determinant of smelting site location. Thus, in order to effectively distribute arsenic-bearing ores to smelting sites whose locations were largely determined by local resource distribution, it is logical to expect the involvement of a state authority. Metalworking, on the other hand, has fewer environmental constraints and can be placed in a wider range of geographical settings perhaps based on cultural factors.

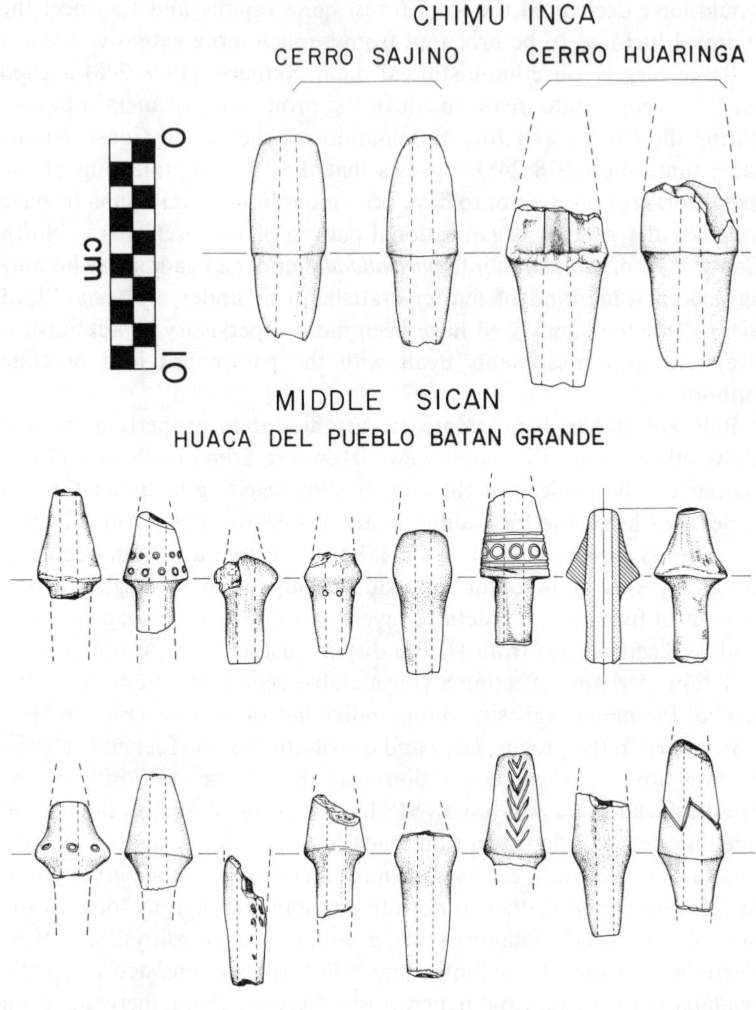

Fig. 16.5 Examples of the Sicán tuyeres excavated in 1983 at Huaca del Pueblo Batán Grande. Note the modified distal ends. The overall size and shape are quite different from that of later tuyeres at Cerros Huaringa and Sajino.

In addition, it is likely that the inferred level of fuel consumption could not be sustained for long by forest within the territorial boundaries of a single *parcialidad* (Netherly 1984) and once again management at a supra-*parcialidad* level could be necessary.

Copper oxide and hematite ores, on the other hand, could well have been supplied by a series of nearby mines all found on the south bank of the Leche River (e.g., Cerros Azul, Blanco, Chaparrí, Barranco Colorado, and Cabeza de León), and thus their procurement could have been directly handled by the local *parcialidad.*

One difficulty in attempting to test the applicability of Netherly's ethnohistorical model of organization is that no distinction is made between smelting and the metalworking. Sites engaged in these two phases of metallurgy may well have been in different *parcialidades.* Metallurgical production (encompassing both smelting and metalworking) must be seen as a multi-settlement system; examination of individual sites or component activities in isolation would yield a misleading picture of the overall organization. In other words, although individual component activities may have been managed at the level of local *parcialidades*, the metallurgical production as a whole seems to have been supervised by a state authority.

The Nature of Sicán-Cajamarca Interaction

In an earlier discussion, the provenience and exact identification of the arsenic bearing ores was described as indeterminate at this point. However, the North Highlands of Peru and its western slope remain a strong possibility as the source area, when one examines the broad spectrum of archaeological data, particularly ceramics. Diagnostic painted kaolin Cajamarca ceramics (particularly the Reichlens' Cajamarca IV and V [1949]), although not common, are widespread on much of the North Coast. Disselhoff (1959) surface-collected and excavated a considerable quantity of Cajamarca ceramics at the site of San José de Moro (Moro Viejo), strategically situated at the intersection of the traditional north-south coastal road and east-west road that follows the Jequetepeque River to the Cajamarca Basin. Surface finds include sherds of Cajamarca Phases I–V, especially III/IV and V. One tomb he excavated is of particular interest to us. Underneath some children's tombs with utilitarian paddled ware vessels, he found a body in supine position oriented south in packed clay together with two painted tripod bowls (red and dark-brown on cream), one pigeon-shaped tricolor painted vessel, three plain tripod bowls, two plates of light brownish clay, and one *Lambayeque* duplex handled jar with post-firing painting on light brown slip, among others. The *Lambayeque* vessel he described (no illustrations provided) seems to be in the Late Sicán style. Disselhoff notes that the custom of burying in packed clay still continues in Niepos in the headwater region of the Zaña Valley.

Certainly the supine burial position pointing south is not the Sicán pattern, which is seated, cross-legged, and facing north. This burial may represent someone with Cajamarca cultural affiliation. Significantly, Disselhoff reports another burial very close to the above that contained various blackware jars with the Sicán Lord head representation (but no Cajamarca ceramics). I believe there is a distinct possibility that during Cajamarca Phases III/IV to V there was a Cajamarca colony established at San José de Moro, coexisting at least for some time with a Middle and perhaps Late Sicán colony.

A burial with Cajamarca vessels was also excavated near Tembladera further inland along the Jequetepeque River (V. Pimentel, pers. com. 1983).

In extensively looted cemeteries in the Poma district of Batán Grande, we have recovered an appreciable number of fragments of kaolin, painted Cajamarca vessels, such as plates and tripod bowls, as well as a few whole whistles and spoons.

Elsewhere (Shimada 1982; Shimada and Elera 1982) I have described the possible significance of the widespread "Coastal Cajamarca" ceramics (Sicán Painted Plates or Ravines' (1982) "Lambayeque rojo blanco") in regard to Sicán-Cajamarca interaction. They are found from the valley necks to the lower portions of coastal valleys from the La Leche to the Jequetepeque. Key observations include: (1) in terms of form (plates with annular bases), decorative style, and designs, they strongly resemble Cajamarca plates; (2) their paste, however, is not kaolin but oxidized red, suggesting local manufacture; (3) they coexist with Early and Middle Sicán blackware and paddled ware in time and space but show no stylistic or iconographic blending; (4) none of the five excavated or salvaged Early to Late Sicán burials in Batán Grande included "Coastal Cajamarca" vessels as funerary offerings; (5) their utilitarian value is limited because of the fugitive nature of the painted designs; and (6) they occur in a wide range of cultural contexts, ranging from atop the T-shaped platform mound at Huaca El Corte to habitational areas at HPBG.

Overall, we must consider the distinct possibility of dispersed Cajamarca colonies on the northern North Coast during the second half of the Middle Horizon and Late Intermediate peacefully coexisting with indigenous coastal populations. "Coastal Cajamarca" plates excavated at HPBG span at least 300 years. Motives for their presence on the coast, however, are not apparent.

What about the possibility of Middle Sicán colonies in the North Highlands (cf. Murra 1972)? Although Rostworowski (in this volume) suggests *yunga* colonies in the North Highlands, archaeological evidence is hard to come by. My survey of the Incahuasi region at the headwaters of the Leche River revealed two sites with coastal paddled ware sherds. Associated ceramics show curvilinear designs against a cream background reminiscent of the Cajamarca ceramics known from further south. Some sherds with regular grid designs may date to Inca domination of the area. Unfortunately, these surface materials are ambiguous as to chronological and behavioral significance.

Even observations by Reichlen and Reichlen (1949) on the "Tiahuanaco-Chimu" materials they recovered at Cerro Chóndorko, upon closer examination, prove ambiguous. Their usage of the term "Chimu" approximates that of Menzel (1977:62), who defines it as the "tradition that originates in the time of the Huari Empire, long before the time of the Kingdom of Chimor." I feel a fusion of the Mochica and Wari traditions lies at the heart of the Sicán style. It is significant that the Reichlens (1949:166) recognize a definite relationship with "Lambayeque." Their illustrated materials (1949:Fig. 9, E-G) can be classified as Sicán. The burial they describe is clearly intrusive and of relatively high status with associated funerary goods such as *Spondylus*, turquoise ornaments, obsidian, a "Chimu type" copper *tumi* knife, a bronze *tupu*, and a small vase. It would be useful if we could identify the bronze as arsenical copper.

The preceding is tantalizing but not enough to argue for widespread *yunga* colonies. My hypothesis, nonetheless, is that such a reverse verticality originated as *mitimaes* established by the Wari Empire.

What the preceding discussion shows, in spite of tenuous and limited data, is that the suggestion that arsenic-bearing ores were imported from the North Highlands is quite reasonable. We have already suggested state-level control of arsenic-rich ore and fuel procurement and distribution. But what specific form did the control take? State-administered trade and central place redistribution? Emissary enclave or colonial enclave (Fig. 16.6)?

Based on her archival research, Netherly (1978:84) suggests: "Given the relative late date of the introduction of copper-arsenic bronze within the total North Coast developmental sequence, obtaining these (sulfarsenide) ores would seem to have been mediated, and probably initiated, by the state. I would hypothesize that the actual establishment of permanent enclaves of coastal miners or metalsmiths in the highlands is probably the least likely of the possible mechanisms used. . . ." In fact, she favors administered trade as the mechanism of procurement (1978:268–72, 333). In her conception, actual transport was provided by the subjects of the lord or king as part of their labor service, as opposed to involvement of full-time specialists under sponsorship of a

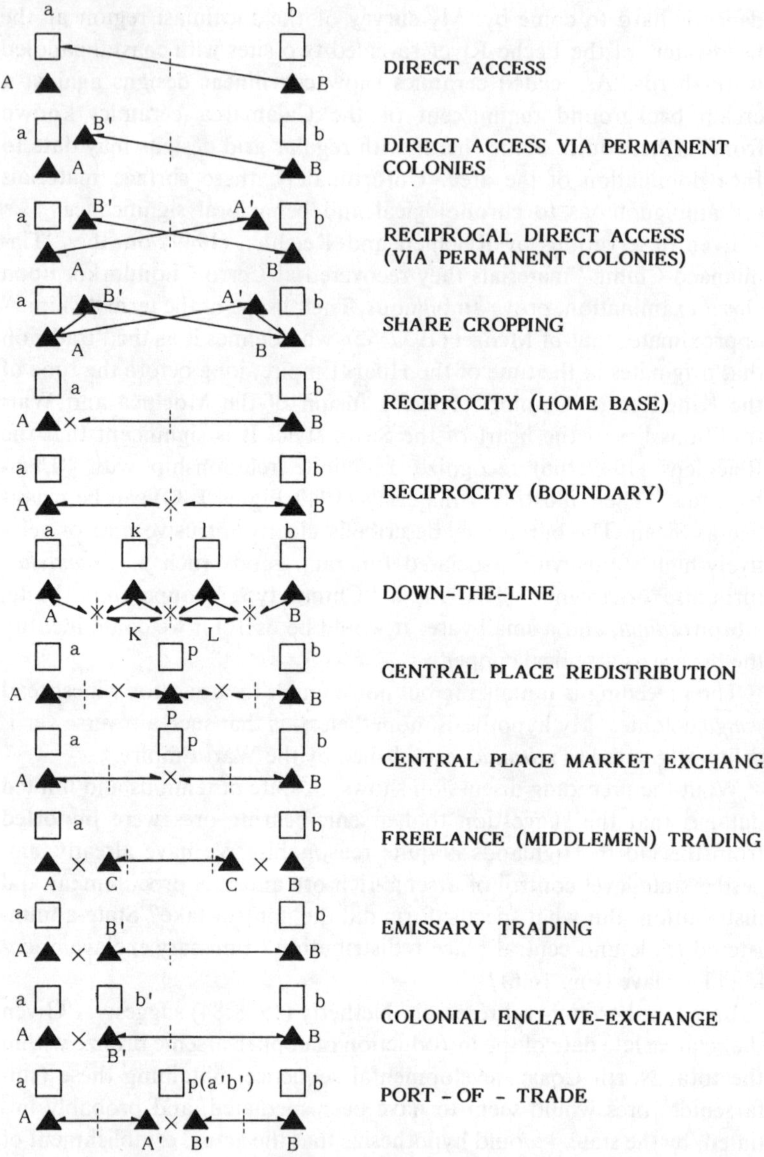

Fig. 16.6 Graphic representation of diversified modes of exchange and their spatial implications. Based on Figure 10, page 42, of Renfrew, 1975. Squares a and b indicate respectively the point of origin and the place of receipt of goods, triangles A and B the population at the source and the recipient. Square p is a central place and triangle P a central population. Exchange transactions are indicated by a cross and territorial boundaries by a broken line.

lord. She does not specify the time periods to which the above view would apply.

Kosok, (1965:98–100), based on Father Calancha's observation that the Chimor Capac employed 6,000 vassals to bring him highland gold, silver, copper, and other products, argued for a trade treaty between the Chimu and his Cajamarca allies. He felt that the North Highlands supplied "metals" (likely to have been ores) in return for "fine cotton textiles and other coastal products much in demand in the Sierra." The Chimor Capac is believed to have established a state monopoly over this trade.

Both Kosok and Netherly do not give sufficient consideration to the question of the nature and the degree of sociopolitical integration of the North Highlands populations involved in such trade (Shimada 1982:183–85). Even figure 16.7 taken from Renfrew (1975) does not specify the organizational complexity of groups engaged in varied forms of exchange or trade.

Archaeologists commonly treat the Cajamarca culture as a monolithic entity. Yet, Espinoza's ethnohistorical analysis (1967:13–14) suggests that during the fifteenth and sixteenth centuries the "Reino de Cajamarca" consisted of seven *huarancas*. The key mining area of Sinchao (for sulfarsenide ores) may have been controlled by the chiefdom level polity of *Huaranca* Pampamarca or Chota. Arsenic minerals, such as arsenopyrite have been reported from the area between Contumaza and Cascas in the headwaters region of the Chicama River (Lechtman 1976:15) within the domain of the *Huaranca* Cuismancu. Descriptions of these *huarancas* give the impression that most of them reflect older sociopolitical organization. If so, we must ask the level of organization of the North Highland polity with which the Middle Sicán state may have dealt in the inferred procurement of arsenic-rich ores. In an earlier publication (1982:185), I suggested that asymmetrical status of the participants in lowland-highland interaction would tend to lead to the establishment of colonial enclaves by the higher ordered group in the territory of the lower ordered polity.

Overall, if we assume a North Highland origin for the arsenic-bearing ores used in Middle Sicán smelting in Batán Grande, we seem to have a consensus of a sort in supporting state involvement in their procurement and distribution. However, it is clearly premature to specify the mechanism of the procurement and distribution until many of the issues raised above are resolved.

The Sicán Political Economy and the Question of Ecuadorian–Peruvian Economic System

Now, we come to the final major issue derived from a holistic perspective on Middle Sicán copper alloy metallurgy: disposition and distribution of resultant products. We will focus on the distinct possibility that the Middle Sicán polity controlled the production of what has come to be known as "copper axe money" and that it was a key element in an extensive prehispanic exchange network linking various parts of coastal Ecuador and Peru, an antecedent to ethnohistorically documented late prehispanic coastal Ecuador-Lambayeque-Chincha trade (Rostworowski 1970, 1975, 1977).

Among the variety of metal objects looted or excavated from Middle Sicán tombs are packages or stacks of double-T shaped metal objects known as *naipes* among looters (Plates 16.2, 16.3). *Naipes* are typically discarded by looters as worthless and corroded specimens soon disappear from the surface. The preceding accounts for the rarity of *naipes* mentioned by Pedersen. As described below, they are, on the contrary, quite common among Middle Sicán tombs in Batán Grande. Although form and size vary, they are all essentially double-T in shape. Our metallographic analysis of sample specimens from Batán Grande shows that they are all fashioned out of hammered and cut sheet metal. An

Plate 16.2 The range of size/form categories of the *naipes* recovered from Huaca La Merced.

Plate 16.3 The most common size/form category of the *naipes* found at Huaca Las Ventanas. The same category of *naipes* is found in large numbers at Huaca Menor.

important variable, however, is the quantity and the range of size/form categories found in tombs. In general, smaller tombs contain only one set of *naipes* of one size/form category. For example, a seated, cross-legged adult male burial excavated atop the Huaca Las Ventanas principal pyramid in 1981 (Shimada, n.d. 2) had a package of some 20 small (ca. 4.2 by 2.1 cm) specimens, while a partially looted burial salvaged at the west base of the Huaca La Merced principal pyramid in 1983 (Elera 1984) still contained at least four packages of small specimens (ca. 4.7 by 1.5 cm) wrapped in coarse cotton cloth and cords of plant fiber, together with fewer numbers of at least four larger size/form specimens (the largest being 10 by 8.5 cm and 44 g in weight). The largest cache reported thus far for Batán Grande comes from the enormous (14 by 14 m and at least 20 m deep) Huaca Menor shafttomb looted sometime around 1966. At the looting site Pedersen (1976:64) found various packages of *naipes,* each containing up to 500 of orderly stacked specimens of the same size/form category. The single specimen he illustrates (1976:Fig. 2) is nearly identical in size and form to those we have recovered from various looted tombs at Huaca Las Ventanas and the partially looted tomb at Huaca La Merced. A radiocarbon date for the Huaca Menor tomb and ceramics associated with burials containing *naipes* allows us to confidently specify that the *naipes* date to the middle to late Middle Sicán (ca. A.D. 900–1050). (See Table 16.3)

The above discussion shows that *naipes* had important cultural value and were differentially distributed and accumulated among different sectors of Middle Sicán society.

The inference that they served as "primitive money" is based on their similarity in form, material, and manufacturing to the abundant "copper axe money" specimens that have been recovered on coastal Ecuador (Easby, Caley, and Moazed 1967; Estrada 1961; Holm 1966/67, 1975). On coastal Ecuador, the largest number of "axe money" specimens comes from the middle and lower reaches of the Guayas River where the Huancavilca-Manteño and Milagro-Quevedo cultures flourished during the final prehistoric period, ca. A.D. 800–1532 (Holm 1982; Meggers 1966; Stothert 1984). During this period, Stothert (1984) sees the evolution of powerful local chiefdoms in the Manabí region and in the Guayas Basin. Archaeological and ethnohistorical evidence points to unprecedented centralization of specialized production of goods such as shell beads and textiles, a heightened degree of differential access to goods, use of "copper axes," settlement hierarchy, and the operation of specialized traders under the protection of paramount chiefs (Salomon 1978; Stothert 1984).

In regard to the coastal Ecuadorian specimens Holm (1975:2–3) points to such characteristics as portability, durability, standardization in shape, size, and probable weight, and intrinsic value of the raw material, in addition to extrapolation from historical descriptions of similar copper "axes" widely used in economic transactions in late prehispanic Mexico as the basis for their interpretation as a medium of exchange and status symbol. He (1975:3) regards them as one of various categories of "primitive monies" with rather limited circulation and value. The tentative nature of the above functional characterization is well underscored by Holm (1966–67:138, 140; 1975:2) who points out that:

We do not know yet of any descriptions . . . which relate the use of

Table 16.3 Elemental Composition of Copper Artifacts

Elemental composition (% by weight) defined by proton-induced x-ray emission of selected *naipes* from Huaca La Merced and Las Ventanas

MASCA No.	Provenience	Cu	As	Sn	Pb	Fe	S	Si	Ag	Sb	Ni	Cr	Bi
BG83–52A	Huaca La Merced; Middle Sicán; burial Lot 2	95.2	4.47	≤0.013	0.025	0.014	0.0033	0.026	0.058	0.026	≤0.013	0.0087	≤0.022
BG83–52B	Huaca La Merced; Middle Sicán; burial Lot 2	95.3	4.32	≤0.014	0.040	0.033	0.0064	0.034	0.123	0.020	≤0.013	0.010	≤0.022
BG83–52C	Huaca Las Ventanas, burial Lot 2	96.7	2.45	≤0.014	0.183	≤0.011	0.026	0.065	0.373	≤0.020	≤0.013	0.010	0.100
BG83–52D	Huaca Las Ventanas, burial Lot 3	95.9	3.66	≤0.012	0.024	0.023	0.0045	0.093	0.067	0.016	0.064	0.013	0.100

Elemental composition (% by weight) of a *naipe* specimen from the Huaca Menor tomb (after Pedersen 1976:65)

Cu	Mn	Si	Zn	Pb	Ag	Al	S	Fe
99.602	0.01	0.01	0.01	0.20	0.14	0.01	0.01	0.008

Elemental composition (% by weight) of an "axe money" specimen excavated from a burial at Garbanzal, Tumbes, Peru (after Minato 1960:517).

Cu	Ag	Zn	Sn	Pb	As	Sb	Fe	Mg	SiO_2	Ca
99.56	0.016	0.042	0.003	0.034	0.330	0.008	0.146	0.071	0.033	trace

> such money-axes in Ecuador at the time of conquest, when presumably they were in use. That the chronicles known to us are mute in this respect might be owing to the lack of observations, but it might just as well be due to a very restricted use of these money-axes; consequently, we have no proof of specific transactions in which these were employed. We are left to guess if the fractionary values suggested by our seriation of weights, of the smaller axes, are of commercial and measuring significance or not. . . . Most of the axes known come from graves and would consequently suggest an offering or wealth carried by the deceased to his new realm. From a monetary point of view this would restrict the currency available, and probably thus stimulates the value and the new production.

Certainly the specimens Holm (1966–67:139, Fig. 4) illustrates that measure 42 by 40 cm and weigh over 20 kg are unlikely to have been used for daily or general circulation as money. At the same time, Salomon's (1978) ethnohistorical study showed the presence of a group of specialized traders under the protection of paramount lords in late prehispanic Ecuador. In this new light, the presence and use of some media of exchange is highly plausible.

In coastal Ecuador, the most commonly found "copper axe money" specimens are inverted-T in shape and typically measure about 10 to 4.5 cm in length, 9 to 3.5 cm in width, 2 to 0.5 mm in thickness, and weigh 45 to 4 g (Holm 1966/67:136–37). However, double-T shaped specimens similar to those found in Batán Grande (compare Plates 16.2, 16.3; Fig. 16.7) also occur, though less frequently. The Ecuadorian specimens are reportedly fashioned out of hammered sheets of nearly pure copper, having a concentration of over 99% (Holm 1966/67:141, 1975:11). It should be noted that published results of compositional analyses are disturbingly rare (Minato 1960; Pedersen 1976; Wassen 1973).

Most Ecuadorian specimens lack contextual data and precise dating. Holm (1966/67:136, 1975:5) argues that the use of "copper axe money" began after A.D. 800–900 and lasted to the time of the Spanish Conquest.

In spite of its abundance on coastal Ecuador, Holm (1966/67:140–41, 1975:9–10) feels that the "money" was imported from elsewhere, such as northern Peru and the highland Ecuadorian region of Cañar, since the recent fluvial and alluvial formations of coastal Ecuador have no copper ore deposits.

Although definite similarities exist between the *naipes* from Batán Grande and the "copper axes" from coastal Ecuador, we do not have

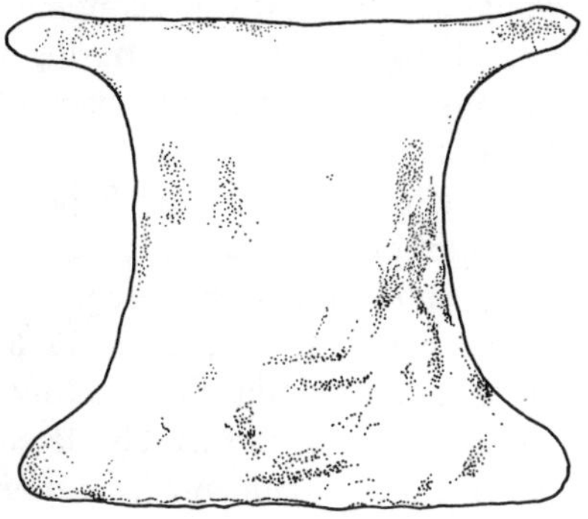

Fig. 16.7 Examples of "copper axes" found on coastal Ecuador. Note the similarities in size and form between some of the Ecuadorian specimens and the Batán Grande *naipes*.

an independent line of evidence to speak of the monetary function of the former. In fact, Wassen (1973) described an enigmatic object looted from the site of Cipán (or Sipán) in the Lambayeque Valley that is made of 49 double-T *naipes* stapled together (identical in shape and similar to one of the most common size /from categories of *naipes* from Batán Grande). He tentatively interprets it to be body armor. Cipán has a definite Middle Sicán occupation. This object casts doubt on the monetary function of the *naipes*, although we must consider the possibility of money used ornamentally.

However, just as Salomon's study has provided a new perspective on Ecuadorian "copper axes," a document discussed in a series of articles by Rostworowski (1970, 1975, 1977) provides support for the presence of prehispanic "copper" tokens of exchange in Peru. This newly discovered *Aviso* speaks of the prosperity and deference enjoyed by the Chincha population which included 6,000 specialized *mercaderes* who managed a long distance maritime economic network linking Chincha (extending into the adjacent *altiplano*), Lambayeque, and south coastal Ecuador (Puerto Viejo of Manabí) during the fifteenth and sixteenth centuries. These *mercaderes* are said to have employed "copper money" ("*compraban y vendían con cobre*"; Rostworowski 1970: 171, 1977:176).

I would suggest that this economic network had a considerable antiquity and may have begun during the Middle Sicán. Although some questions as to the true identity of the *mercaderes* still exist (Ramírez 1982; Pease in this volume; Netherly 1978:254–58), on the basis of the preceding, we can tentatively hypothesize that the *naipes* functioned as a medium of exchange/standard of value and status symbol.

The importance of the recent documentation of the *naipes* in Batán Grande (Elera 1984; Pedersen 1976; Shimada 1979, 1983; Shimada et al. 1981) can be summarized as follows (Shimada 1984): (1) they occur in funerary contexts securely dated to the Middle Sicán period; (2) there was well-documented, contemporary copper alloy metallurgical production of considerable intensity in Batán Grande; and (3) compositional analysis of sample specimens from Batán Grande (Table 16.2) shows them to be made of arsenical copper, the primary smelting product of the Middle Sicán metallurgy. Pedersen (1976:65) reports that a specimen from Huaca Menor is 99.6% copper. But this is misleading since he did not examine the specimen for the presence of arsenic (also see Wassen 1976:31).

Based on the preceding observations I hypothesize that the archaeologically recovered *naipes* in Batán Grande were locally produced and distributed under the Middle Sicán state centered in Batán Grande. A corollary hypothesis is that the *naipes*, like their Ecuadorian counterparts, served as true tokens of exchange and status symbols. The presence of "copper axe" specimens on coastal Ecuador similar in shape and size to the *naipes*, as well as ethnohistorical references to *mercaderes* in Lambayeque lead us to suggest that the Middle Sicán polity participated in Ecuadorian-Peruvian trade around the tenth and eleventh centuries. Further, we must explore the possibility that, in addition to producing the *naipes*, the Sicán polity exported the raw materials (blank sheets, ingots of copper and arsenical copper) to be processed further elsewhere; for example, on coastal Ecuador. Thus, I would expect some of the copper "axe" specimens found in coastal Ecuador to be made of arsenical copper. Concurrently, the possible inclusion of South Coast and Cajamarca cultures in the inferred interregional exchange or trade should be examined. An antecedence for such long distance contact exists; during the late Early Intermediate period (estimated at A.D. 400–550), North Coast Mochica ceramics and guano miners reached the South Coast (Kubler 1948; Shimada n.d. 1) as part of their horizontal expansion.

Elsewhere (Shimada 1979, 1981, 1982, 1983; Shimada et al. 1981) I have presented my thoughts on the nature of articulation between the Middle Sicán intra- and inter-regional economies. In regard to the

Middle Sicán-Cajamarca relationship, I have considered an economic symbiosis similar to the model Flannery (1968) offered for Olmecs in Veracruz and Oaxaca in the adjacent highlands. North Highland *huarancas* could offer arsenic-rich ores, charcoal fuel, and rights to irrigation water to the Middle Sicán population, who in turn, could reciprocate with coastal products such as dried and salted fish, salt, cotton, *aji*, and other agricultural produce (Netherly 1978:268–69). Significantly, however, the Middle Sicán polity could offer a wide range and large quantities of utilitarian and sumptuary metal goods to the North Highlands and other regions. In spite of the uncertainty surrounding the mechanism(s) involved, we must keep in mind the impressive distribution of Middle Sicán ceramics and textiles bearing their distinct iconography. As noted earlier, economic interaction with coastal Ecuadorian populations is suggested by the presence of Sicán ceramics on the Isla La Plata, similarities between "copper axes" and *naipes,* and the presence of *Spondylus* shells, coral, emeralds, and various semi-precious stones found in Middle Sicán elite tombs.

The Middle Sicán polity could have controlled not only the goods being distributed but the transport mechanisms themselves. There are now sufficient lines of evidence to speak of the breeding and herding of llamas on the North Coast at least since Moche Phase V (Shimada 1984; Shimada and Shimada, in press). Thus, llama caravans involved in horizontal or vertical long-distance exchange and trade should not necessarily be viewed as exclusively initiated and controlled by the highland polities. We must consider both coastal llama caravans and balsa rafts as transport media available to coastal polities. I suggest that the control over natural and cultural resources, as well as intra- and inter-regional economies provided the foundation of the Middle Sicán material wealth and political power (considering that the quantity and quality of sumptuary goods interred in many Middle Sicán tombs are unmatched in the Andes for their time).

Although highly speculative, we are speaking of an extensive prehispanic economic exchange network that may have linked coastal Ecuador and the northern North Coast, South Coast, and North Highlands of Peru. Batán Grande occupies the hub of the inferred network, not only in terms of geographical location but also production and distribution of a (if not the) key item of exchange. This ambitious conception is not unreasonable when we consider the unprecedented material accumulation we see in the Middle Sicán elite tombs. The mechanisms involved in this accumulation have long been a source of fascination among us and the above offers a promising avenue of future research.

Overall, the preceding has illuminated yet another reason for state involvement in the metallurgical production. It also serves to broaden our spatial perspective along the horizontal dimension and introduces an important alternative organization for resource procurement and management to the vertical archipelago.

Conclusion

Multi-year, interdisciplinary research into the Middle Sicán copper alloy metallurgy provides a sound foundation for a holistic or processual perspective on mineral and metal resources and serves as a jumping board for consideration of various issues of interest to this volume. Resources, however they may be defined, must not be seen as static entities. The given cultural value of a resource changes and must be empirically documented under different cultural conditions. The observed change in the functional significance of arsenical copper from Mochica to Middle Sicán times was shown to be closely linked to changes in broader cultural conditions. Emergent data on the Middle Sicán smelting technology show the complexity and magnitude of resource needs and management, and the necessity for state-level administration of essential ingredients such as arsenic-rich ores and fuel. Cultural reconstructions based on the understanding of component activities treated in isolation are likely to be misleading. At the same time, the uncertainty surrounding the provenience of arsenic-rich ores effectively illustrates the inadequacy of our (etic) current perception and knowledge of Andean resources and how future advances may significantly alter current views of coast-highland interaction. Too often we speak of "labor organization," "state administration," etc., when we barely have sufficient knowledge of the source areas and final products. Extensive deforestation, desertification, field burning, depopulation, and other environmental changes force us to scrutinize our current identification of source areas for organic resources such as lumber, bird feathers, and llamas. Improved understanding of manufacturing processes may lead us to emphasize the role of regional polities such as *parcialidades* and *huarancas*.

Despite the uncertainty regarding ore souce(s), other lines of archaeological data allow us to speak of the probable coastal presence of North Highland population(s). On the other hand, archaeological evidence for *yunga* colonies in the North Highlands is still tenuous.

Lastly, there is a strong possibility that the Middle Sicán polity controlled production of a key medium of exchange/standard of value (copper-copper alloys) that is believed to have been used in an Ecuadorian-Peruvian exchange network. If so, the ethnohistorically documented maritime exchange employing full-time middlemen and a medium of exchange along the western South American coast may have much more antiquity than heretofore discussed. It forms a contrasting situation for the well-known, traditional vertical resource control and management patterns that have dominated the literature on Andean ecological complementarity. Together with the horizontal archipelago and state-administered trade that I describe here and elsewhere (1982), the prehispanic North Coast cultures seem to have developed at least three major resource and management practices. Finally, the operation of the above three systems should not be considered as mutually exclusive of each other or traditional vertical control. One major future research area should be the articulation of the former with the latter, in what may be called organizational complementarity.

ACKNOWLEDGMENTS

Data for this paper were collected during the 1978–83 seasons with support of the National Geographic Society, National Science Foundation, and Latin American Studies Program of Princeton University. Many people assisted me in data collection and provided valuable comments. In particular, I thank P. Carcedo, K. M. Cleland, M. Cornejo, A. K. Craig, C. Elera, S. M. Epstein, S. Fleming, U. Franklin, A. Higueras, H. Lechtman, J. L. Merkel, M. I. Paredes, V. Pimentel, S. Ramírez, M. Shimada, and J. L. Suarez.

REFERENCES CITED

Caley, Earle R. and Dudley T. Easby, Jr.
1959 The Smelting of Sulfide Ores of Copper in Preconquest Peru. American Antiquity 25:59–65.

Carrion, Rebeca
1940 La Luna y su Personificación Ornitomórfa en el Arte Chimú. Lima: Actas y Trabajos Científicos del 27 Congreso Internacional de Americanistas, 1: 571–87.

Cavallaro, Raffael and Izumi Shimada
n.d. Sicán Marked Adobes and Labor Organization: Evaluating Hypotheses. Manuscript.

Disselhoff, Hans D.
1959 Tumbas de San José de Moro (Provincia de Pacasmayo, Perú).

Copenhagen: Proceedings of the 32nd International Congress of Americanists, pp. 364–67.

Donnan, Christopher B.

1981 Proyecto Chotuna-Chornancap: 1980 Season. Princeton: Willay, 8:3.

Easby, Dudley T., Jr., Earle R. Caley, and K. Moazed

1967 Axe-Money: Facts and Speculation. Mexico City: Revista Mexicana de Estudios Antropológicos 21:107–48.

Elera, Carlos G.

1984 Características e Implicaciones Culturales en Dos Tumbas Disturbadas de Huaca La Merced, Complejo Arqueológico de Batán Grande, Lambayeque, Costa Norte del Perú. Informe presentado al Instituto Nacional de Cultura, Lima.

Epstein, Stephen M. and Izumi Shimada

In press Metalurgia de Sicán: una Reconstrucción de la Producción de la Aleación de Cobre en El Cerro de los Cementerios, Perú. Bonn: Beitrage zur Allgemeine und Vergleichende Archäologie.

Espinoza, Waldemar

1967 El Primer Informe Etnológico sobre Cajamarca: Año de 1540. Revista Peruana de Cultura 11–12:1–37.

Estrada, Emilio

1961 Correlaciones entre la Arqueología de la Costa del Ecuador y Perú. Quito: Humanitas, 2 (2):31–61.

Flannery, Kent V.

1968 The Olmec and the Valley of Oaxaca: A Model for Inter-regional Interaction in Formative Times. *In* Dumbarton Oaks Conference on the Olmec. E. P. Benson, ed. pp. 79–110. Washington, D.C.: Dumbarton Oaks.

Holm, Olaf

1966–67 Money Axe from Ecuador. Copenhagen: Folk 8–9:135–43.

1975 La Pieza, No. 3. Guayas: Casa de la Cultura Ecuatoriana.

1982 Cultura Milagro-Quevedo. Guayaquil: Museo Antropológico y Pinacoteca del Banco Central del Ecuador.

Hutchinson, Thomas J.

1873 Two Years in Peru, with Exploration of Its Antiquities. 2 vols. London: Sampson, Low, Marston, and Searle.

Kauffmann, Federico

1973 Manual de Arqueología Peruana, 1973 edition. Lima: Ediciones Peisa.

Kosok, Paul

1959 El Valle de Lambayeque. Lima: Actas y Trabajos del II Congreso Nacional de Historia del Perú: Época Pre-Hispánica 1:69–76.

1965 Life, Land, and Water in Ancient Peru. New York: Long Island University.

Kroeber, Alfred L.

1944 Peruvian Archaeology in 1942. New York: Viking Fund Publications in Anthropology 4.

1954 Quantitative Analyses of Ancient Peruvian Metal. American Antiquity 20:160–62.

Kubler, George

1948 Towards Absolute Time: Guano Archaeology. *In* A Reappraisal of Peruvian Archaeology. W. C. Bennett, ed., Society for American Archaeology Memoir 4:29–50.

Lechtman, Heather N.

1976 A Metallurgical Site Survey in the Peruvian Andes. Journal of Field Archaeology 3:1–42.

1979 Issues in Andean Metallurgy. *In* Pre-Columbian Metallurgy of South America. E. P. Benson, ed. pp. 1–40. Washington, D.C.: Dumbarton Oaks.

1980 The Central Andes: Metallurgy without Iron. *In* The Coming of the Age of Iron. T. A. Wertime and J. D. Muhly, eds. pp. 267–334. New Haven: Yale University.

1981 Copper-Arsenic Bronzes from the North Coast of Peru. New York: Annals of the New York Academy of Sciences 376:77–122.

Lechtman, Heather N., Antonieta Erlij and Edward J. Barry, Jr.

1982 New Perspectives on Moche Metallurgy: Techniques of Gilding Copper at Loma Negra, Northern Peru. American Antiquity 47: 3–30.

Marcos, Jorge

1982 Isla La Plata y los contactos entre Mesoamérica y los Andes. Lima: Gaceta Arqueológica 1 (1):4–5.

Mathewson, C. H.

1915 A Metallographic Description of Some Ancient Peruvian Bronzes from Machu Picchu. American Journal of Science, 4th Series 40 (240):525–98.

Meggers, Betty J.

1966 Ecuador. New York: Praeger.

Menzel, Dorothy

1977 The Archaeology of Ancient Peru and the Work of Max Uhle. Berkeley: University of California.

Merkel, John F.

1983 Reconstruction of Bronze Age Copper Smelting, Experiments Based on Archaeological Evidence from Timna, Israel. Unpublished Ph.D. dissertation, Institute of Archaeology, University of London.

1984 Analysis of Copper Smelting Specimens from the Site of Huaca del Pueblo Batán Grande, Peru. Report submitted to MASCA, The University Museum, University of Pennsylvania.

Minato, H.

1960 Chemical Analysis of Copper and Bronze Wares. *In* Andes 1: Report of the Tokyo University Scientific Expedition to the Andes in 1958. E. Ishida, ed. pp. 516–17. Tokyo: Bijutsu-shuppansha.

Murra, John V.

1972 El Control Vertical de un Máximo de Pisos Ecológicos en la Economía de las Sociedades Andinas. *In* Visita de la Provincia de León de Huánuco, Vol. 2. J. V. Murra, ed. pp. 429–76. Huánuco: Universidad Nacional Hermilio Valdizán.

Netherly, Patricia

1978 Local Level Lords on the North Coast of Peru. PhD. dissertation, Cornell University. Ann Arbor: University Microfilms.

1984 The Management of Late Andean Irrigation Systems on the North Coast of Peru. American Antiquity 49:227–54.

Nolan, James L.

1980 Prehispanic Irrigation and Polity in the Lambayeque Sphere, Peru. Ph.D. dissertation, Columbia University. Ann Arbor: University Microfilms.

Patterson, Claire C.

1971 Native Copper, Silver, and Gold Accessible to Early Metallurgists. American Antiquity 36:286–321.

Pedersen, Asbjorn

1976 El Ajuar Funerario de la Tumba de la Huaca Menor de Batán Grande, Lambayeque, Perú. Mexico City: Actas del 41 Congreso Internacional de Americanistas 2: 60–73.

Ponce, Carlos

1970 Las Culturas Wankarani y Chiripa y su Relación con Tiwanaku. La Paz: Academia Nacional de Ciencias de Bolivia, Publicación 25.

Ramírez, Susan

1982 Retainers of the Lords or Merchants: A Case of Mistaken Identity? *In* El Hombre y su Ambiente en los Andes Centrales. L. Millones and H. Tomoeda, eds. pp. 123–36. Senri Ethnological Studies 10, Senri.

Ravines, Rogger

1982 Arqueología del Valle Medio del Jequetepeque. Lima: Instituto Nacional de Cultura.

Reichlen, Henri and Paule Reichlen

1949 Recherches archéologiques dans les Andes de Cajamarca: Premier Rapport de la Mission Etnologique Francaise au Peróur Septentrional. Paris: Journal de la Société des Américanistes 38: 137–74.

Reiss, Wilhelm and Alphons Stübel

1880–87 The Necropolis of Ancón, Peru, 3 vols. Berlin: Asher & Co.

Renfrew, Colin

1975 Trade as Action at a Distance: Questions of Integration and Communication. *In* Ancient Civilization and Trade. J. A. Sabloff and C. C. Lamberg-Karlovsky, eds. pp. 3–95. Albuquerque: University of New Mexico.

Rondón, Jorge

1966 Ferreñafe Prehispánico. Chiclayo: Ferruñap, Año III, No. 25: 7–15.

Rostworowski, María

1970 Mercaderes del Valle de Chincha en la Época Prehispánica: un Documento y unos Comentarios. Madrid: Revista Española de Antropología Americana 5:135–78.

1975 Pescadores, Artesanos y Mercaderes Costeños en el Perú Prehispánico. Lima: Revista del Museo Nacional 41:311–49.

1977 Coastal Fishermen, Merchants, and Artisans in Pre-Hispanic Peru. *In* The Sea in the Pre-Columbian World. E. P. Benson, ed. pp. 167–86. Washington, D. C.: Dumbarton Oaks.

1981 Recursos Naturales Renovables y Pesca, Siglos XVI y XVII. Lima: Instituto de Estudios Peruanos.

Salomon, Frank L.

1978 Ethnic Lords of Quito in the Age of the Incas: The Political Economy of North-Andean Chiefdoms. Ph.D. dissertation, Cornell University. Ann Arbor: University Microfilms.

Scheele, H. and T. C. Patterson

1966 A Preliminary Seriation of the Chimu Pottery Style. Berkeley: Ñawpa Pacha 4:15–30.

Schmidt, Max

1929 Kunst und Kultur von Peru. Berlin: Propyläen-Verlag.

Shimada, Izumi

1978 Economy of a Prehistoric Urban Context: Commodity and Labor Flow at Moche V Pampa Grande. American Antiquity 43:569–92.

1979 Behind the Golden Mask: The Research Problems and Preliminary Results of the Batán Grande-La Leche Archaeological Project. Paper presented at the 44th Annual Meeting of the Society for American Archaeology, Vancouver.

1981 Temple of Time: The Ancient Burial and Religious Center of Batán Grande, Peru. Archaeology 34 (5): 37–4.

1982 Horizontal Archipelago and Coast-Highland Interaction in North Peru. *In* El Hombre y su Ambiente en los Andes Centrales. L. Millones and H. Tomoeda, eds. pp. 137–210. Senri Ethnological Studies 10. Senri.

1983 The Formation of the Middle Sicán Polity: The Highland Connection and Revitalization Movement. Paper presented at the 48th Annual Meeting of the Society for American Archaeology, Pittsburgh.

1984 Llama and Cash Flow on the Prehispanic Peruvian Coast. Paper presented at the 49th Annual Meeting of the Society for American Archaeology, Portland.

In press Batán Grande and Cosmological Unity in the Andes. *In* Andean Archaeology, 1981. R. Matos and S. Turpin, eds. Los Angeles: UCLA Institute of Archaeology.

n.d. 1 Horizontal and Vertical Dimensions of the Prehispanic States in North Peru. *In* The Andean State: Origins and Development, J. Haas, S. Pozorski, and T. Pozorksi, eds.

n.d. 2 The Sicán Burials of Batán Grande, Peru. Unpublished manuscript.

Shimada, Izumi and colleagues.

1981 The Batán Grande-La Leche Archaeological Project: The First Two Seasons. Journal of Field Archaeology 8:405–46.

Shimada, Izumi and Carlos G. Elera

1982 Emerging Cultural Complexity on the North Coast during the Middle Horizon. Paper presented at the 47th Annual Meeting of the Society for American Archaeology, Minneapolis.

Shimada, Izumi, Carlos G. Elera, and Melody Shimada

1982 Excavaciones Efectuadas en el Centro Ceremonial de Huaca Lucía-Chólope, del Horizonte Temprano, Batán Grande, Costa Norte del Perú. Lima: Arqueológicas 19:109–210.

Shimada, Izumi, Stephen M. Epstein, and Alan K. Craig

1982 Batán Grande: A Prehistoric Metallurgical Center in Peru. Science 216:952–59.

1983 The Metallurgical Process in Ancient North Peru. Archaeology 36(5):38–45.

Shimada, Melody and Izumi Shimada

1981 Explotación y Manejo de los Recursos Naturales en Pampa Grande, Sitio Moche V: Significado del Análisis Orgánico. Lima: Revista del Museo Nacional 45:19–73.

In press Prehistoric Llama Breeding and Herding on the North Coast of Peru. American Antiquity 50.

Stothert, Karen

1984 A New Look at Guangala Society and Economy: A Discussion of the Origin and Development of Chiefdoms on the Santa Elena Peninsula, Ecuador. Paper presented at the 49th Annual Meeting of the Society for American Archaeology, Portland.

Tello, Julio C.

1937a Los Trabajos Arqueológicos en el Departamento de Lambayeque. Lima: El Comercio, January 29–31.

1937b El Oro de Batán Grande. Lima: El Comercio, April 18.

Topic, John R.

1977 The Lower Class at Chan Chan: A Qualitative Approach. Unpublished Ph.D. dissertation, Dept. of Anthropology, Harvard University.

Tosi, Joseph A., Jr.

1960 Zonas de Vida Natural en el Perú. Lima: Instituto Interamericano de Ciencias Agrícolas de la OEA, Zona Andina.

Tylecote, Ronald F. and P. J. Boydell

1978 Experiments on Copper Smelting Based on Early Furnaces Found at Timna. *In* Archaeo-Metallurgy. Institute for Archaeo-Metallurgical Studies, Monograph 1, pp. 27–49.

Tylecote, Ronald F., H. A. Ghaznavi, and P. J. Boydell
1977 Partitioning of Trace Elements Between the Ores, Fluxes, Slags, and Metal During the Smelting of Copper. Journal of Archaeological Science 4:305–33.

Uhle, Max
1903 Pachacamac: Report of the William Pepper, M.D., LL.D. Peruvian Expedition of 1896. Philadelphia: University of Pennsylvania.

Valcárcel, Luis E.
1937 Un Valioso Hallazgo Arqueológico en el Perú: Informe sobre los Hallazgos en los Yacimientos Arqueológicos de La Merced, La Ventana y Otros del Distrito de Illimo, Lambayeque. Lima: Revista del Museo Nacional 6(1):164–68.

Vreeland, James M. and Izumi Shimada
1981 Burial and Looting Traditions at Batán Grande, Peru. Paper presented at the 1981 Annual Meeting of the Institute for Andean Studies, Berkeley.

Wassen, S. Henry
1973 A Problematic Metal Object from Northern Peru. Göteborgs: Göteborgs Etnografiska Museum Arstryck 1972: 29–33.

Zevallos, Jorge
1971 Cerámica de Cultura "Lambayeque." Trujillo: Universidad Nacional de Trujillo.

17

Patronyms with the Consonant *F* in the *Guarangas* of Cajamarca

María Rostworowski de Diez Canseco

The document presented for discussion is a lawsuit in the Consejo de Indias between two wealthy *encomenderas*, doña Jordana Mexia, the widow of Melchor Verdugo, against doña Beatriz Ysaga, the widow of Captain García Holguin, over the ownership of the *repartimientos* of Pomamarca, Bambamarca, and Chondal in Cajamarca. In order to know the quantity of inhabitants and taxpayers a *visita* to the province of Cajamarca was carried out between 1571 and 1572 under the charge of Diego Velasquez de Acuña. The *visita* was finished after an interruption of 6 years, in 1578, by the *corregidor* Diego de Salazar.

In 1535 Francisco Pizarro granted the aforementioned *encomienda* to Melchor Verdugo, but on reviewing its great area and population, Vaca de Castro proceeded in 1542 to take away a thousand taxpayers which he adjudicated first to Hernando Alvarado, and later, after Alvarado's death, to García Holguín.

The importance of the first part of the *visita*, that is to say from 1571 to 1572, lies in the fact that the *reducciones* ordered by Viceroy Toledo had not yet been effected. The *guarangas*, *pachacas*, and villages were still found in their original locations. Thus, the second part, carried out in 1578, does not have the same informative value as the former part.

One cannot overemphasize the importance of this document for the investigation of the region and the information which it contains for the study of Andean history. Pilar Remy transcribed and studied the testimony and has studied and analyzed the part which deals with the demography of the *visita* (Remy 1982). She has, moreover, transferred the data to analytical tables and charts which facilitates working with them. Likewise she has located the villages, the *guarangas*, and the *pachacas* so that we shall refer back to her study and focus our attention on just two points which give us a new slant on things and which we will analyze in detail since they were not considered by Remy.

The extension of the *señorío* of Cajamarca included only the present day provinces of Cajamarca, Celendín, Contumazá, Chota. Hualgayoc, and San Miguel. The political division of *curacazgo* of Cajamarca was formed by six original *guarangas*, which were Cajamarca, Guzmango or Cuzmango, Bambamarca, Pomamarca, Chondal, and Chuquimango, plus a seventh one of *mitimaes*. The *curaca principal* of the seven *guarangas* was the lord of Guzmango, which it seems was the most important *guaranga*. Two of the *parcialidades* mentioned in the *visita* are never called *guarangas*; they are Colquemarca and Malcadan.

The *señorío* of Cajamarca was subdivided into 52 *pachacas* and 42 villages, and at the time of the *visita* they were composed of 23,691 inhabitants of both sexes and all ages.

Pilar Remy was kind enough to give me a copy of her report and of a transcription of the *visita*. In my judgment, it is a very important document, comparable only to the *visitas* made by Iñigo Ortiz de Zuñiga to Huánuco (1967; 1972) and by Garci Diez de San Miguel to Chucuito (1964). I hope that in this meeting we can find a way to publish the *visita* with the analysis and charts made by Remy.

Patronyms with the Letter F

In this paper we want to call attention to several points not mentioned by Remy: first, the persistence of feminine and masculine patronyms which contain the letter *F*; second, to the presence in Cajamarca of a group called Llacuaz whose existence in the region raises a series of questions; and lastly, it is interesting to point out that a topic for further investigation would be the fact that *pachacas* were divided up among different villages, a situation which for lack of a better term we will call *dis-contiguous territoriality*, a subject which Remy mentions without pursuing it.

We know that the different Quechua dialects, including that of Cajamarca (Quesada 1976), and the languages of the Aru group do not contain the letter *F* in their alphabets. The same can be said for the scarce bits of vocabulary known of the Culli language spoken in Huamachuco and listed in the comparative chart of Northern Peruvian languages collected by the bishop of Trujillo, Martinez Compañon in the eighteenth century.

The consonant *F* was found only in North Coast languages in the region of Chimor, Lambayeque, and Jayanca and also in the language spoken in Sechura farther to the north. In order to be convinced of this we can check the *visita* of Sebastian de la Gama to Jayanca in 1540 (W. Espinoza 1975), that of Ferreñafe of 1568 (Zevallos Quiñones 1975), and the Yunga grammar of Fernando de la Carrera of 1644.

In the legend of the arrival of the mythical Naymlap on the North Coast, various personages of his retinue carried names with an *F*, a letter frequently found in the patronyms of the lords of Lambayeque (Cabello de Valboa 1951). In a suit between indigenous pretenders to the *cacicazgo* of Reque (Rostworowski 1961) in 1595, there also appear here and there names with *F*.

Finally the Muchic dictionary prepared by Richard Schaedel, based on the grammar of Carrera and on the works and documents of Brüning, Middendorf, and others, contains words with the letter *F*. That is, we can say without much fear of being mistaken, that we can ascribe a North Coast origin to these patronyms with the letter *F*. Well then, in the *visita* to *Cajamarca* we find among its inhabitants 89 men and 171 women in whose names is found the letter *F* (the patronyms are listed in the appendix).

Let us look at the form and frequency of distribution of patronyms with *F* among the *pachacas*, first of women's, then of men's.

Feminine Patronyms—distribution

Pachaca	Pueblo	Guaranga	
Pingomarca	S. Rafael de Nipos	Chondal	1
"	S. Rafael de Nipos	"	1
"	S. Juan de Pingomarca	"	13
"	S. Joseph de Chanchan	"	12
"	S. Gregorio Mezique	"	12
"	S. Miguel Catamuche	"	3
Polloques	S. Rafael de Nipos	"	1
"	S. Pedro de Libie	"	18
"	S. Miguel de Catamuche	"	5
"	S. Miguel de Catamuche	"	11
Nipos	S. Rafael de Nipos	"	12
"	S. Bartolomé Tacabamba	"	1
"	S. Joseph de Chanchan	"	1
"	S. Miguel de Catamuche	"	3
Paiay Yungas	Sta. Cruz de Sochabamba	"	8
Paiay Yungas	S. Andrés de Llapa	Chondal	1
Paiaca	S. Matías de Payaca	"	1
Xaxaden	S. Pedro de Chalaques	Guzmango	8
"	S. Gabriel de Cascas	"	2
"	Sta. Magdalena de Lachan	"	2
Nachedon	S. Pedro de Chalaques	"	7
Collana	S. Salvador Mollebamba	"	2
"	S. Gabriel de Cascas	"	1
Pauxan	S. Benito de Cadachon	"	3

Feminine Patronyms—distribution

Pachaca	Pueblo	Guaranga	
Ayambla	Santiago Catazabolan	Gusmango	3
Faxan	S. Pedro de Chalaques	″	1
Chusan	Sta. Magdalena de Lachan	″	1
Baca	S. Antonio Caxamarca	Caxamarca	5
Lachan Yungas	S. Antonio Caxamarca	Caxamarca	2
Cayao	S. Antonio Caxamarca	″	1
Colquemarca	S. Joaquin de Puquio	Colquemarca	1
Viton	S. Pedro de Libie	Chuquimango	6
Xucat	S. Luis de Tambodon	″	4
Chiton	S. Luis de Tambodon	″	1
″	S. Gregorio de Mezique	″	1
Malcadan	S. Salvador de Mollebamba	parcialidad	11
Agomarca	S. Gabriel de Cascas	Colquemarca	3
Tacabamba	S. Bartolomé Tacabamba	″	2
Lleden	S. Martin de Agomarca	″	1

Masculine Patronyms—distribution

Pachaca	Pueblo	Guaranga	
Pingomarca	S. Rafael de Nipos	Chondal	1
″	S. Juan de Pingomarca	″	3
″	S. Joseph de Chanchan	″	8
″	S. Gregorio de Mezique	″	4
″	S. Miguel Catamuche	″	1
Polloques	S. Juan de Pingomarca	″	1
″	S. Gregorio de Mezique	″	2
″	S. Pedro de Libie	″	4
″	S. Miguel de Catamuche	″	4
″	″ ″	″	4
Nipos	S. Rafael de Nipos	″	3
″	S. Miguel Catamuche	″	2
Paiay	Sta. Cruz de Sochabamba	″	5
Xaxaden	S. Pedro de Chalaques	Guzmango	3
″	S. Salvador Mollebamba	″	2
″	Sta. Magdalena de Lachan	″	2
Nachedon	S. Pablo de Chalaques	″	5
Ayambla	Santiago de Catazabolan	″	2
Pauxan	S. Benito de Cadachon	″	1
″	S. Sebastian de Acaden	″	1
Cayao	S. Antonio Caxamarca	Caxamarca	2
Baca	S. Antonio Caxamarca	″	1

Lachan Yungas	S. Antonio Caxamarca	"	3
Yscan	S. Bartolomé Tacabamba	Bambamarca	1
Aspac	S. Pablo de Chalaques	Pomamarca	2
Chiton	S. Gregorio de Mezique	Chuquimango	1
"	S. Luis de Tamboden	"	1
Viton	S. Pedro de Libie	"	2
Malcadan	S. Salvador Mollebamba	Malcadan	6
"	S. Lorenzo de Malcadan	"	2
People brought from the Guambos			2

The *pachacas* which contain the largest number of words with *F* are those of Pingomarca, Polloques, and Nipos, all of which belong to the *guaranga* of Chondal. This frequency does not mean that the rest of the patronyms do not belong to the Muchic or Yunga language, but that, for lack of a dictionary, we cannot identify them as such.

The fourth *pachaca* which formed the *guaranga* of Chondal is that of Payaca and it is possibly the same that is mentioned as Paia in the same *guaranga.*

If we compare the names of the villages and *pachacas* of Chondal with the present day toponyms, we verify that the *guaranga* of Chondal was situated in the neighboring sierra of Chiclayo and Jequetepeque. Moreover, among the villages of the province of Cajamarca existed a hamlet called San Joseph de Chanchan and another called San Gregorio de Mochique.

These facts lead us to affirm that the members of the four *pachacas* which made up the *guaranga* of Chondal were people of North Coast origin. In the *visita* they are not mentioned as *mitimaes,* with the exception of the members of Paiay, inhabitants of the hamlet of Santa Cruz de Sochabamba, and those of Lanchan, both of which are indicated as Yunga. The rest of the people of the *guaranga* of Chondal do not appear in the document as a foreign element and were treated as though they were natives. In that sense the testimony of the *visita* clearly indicates who were *mitimaes*, such as the case of a fairly important group which is mentioned as a *guaranga* and composed of four *pachacas*, each one of which consists of people of separate origin; that is to say, Quechuas, Cañaris, Guayacondores, and Collas.

There is a marked difference between the members of the *guaranga* of Chondal, totally assimilated to the region of Cajamarca, and members of the *guaranga* marked as *mitimaes.* This circumstance leads us to sustain the hypothesis that the establishment of coastal people in Cajamarca dated from a much earlier time, prior to the Inca conquest, while that of the *mitimaes* took place under Cusco rule.[1]

The long lapse of time which passed from the beginnings of coastal settlement in Cajamarca is perceived by means of the existence of patronyms with *F* in many other *pachacas*, especially among women. This fact supports the possibility of a Mochica or Chimu conquest of the zone of Cajamarca at some time in the past. We know about the great expansion carried out by the coastal lords, about their wealth and power, so that it does not seem strange to us that a portion of the province of Cajamarca was dependent on Chimor rule at some time during the process of its development.[2]

Supportive of what we are sustaining is the affirmation of Fernando de la Carrera in 1644 that the language mentioned by some as Yunga and by others as Mochica was then spoken in Santa Cruz, Nepos, San Pablo, and also in the parishes of Balsas de Marañon and in Cachen of the Guambos. This diffusion of the northern language shows a great coastal influence in the highlands and, possibly, during the time of the apogee of the coastal kingdoms, the *yungas* controlled the land situated at the heads of the valleys and rivers.

A basic need of the inhabitants of the lowlands was the possession and control of the intakes of its rivers; that is, the jurisdiction of the waters which came down from the highlands and were indispensable to the irrigation of its fields and crops. Later on, with the fluctuations of the centers of power, the Yungas lost the territories which they possessed in the *sierra*. The limited influence which they managed to maintain in the highlands ended with the Inca conquest, and with it, their hydraulic controls which were situated up in the *sierra*.

Besides the Yungas, there was another group of outsiders which inhabited Cajamarca in an epoch previous to Cusco rule. They were the Llacuaz who in 1571 were congregated in the *parcialidad* of Colquemarca. It would be interesting to see the evidence of some other migration in the region and compare the motives of their settlement in the region with that of the Yunga people, in order to have a better view of the ethnic composition of Cajamarca.

According to the *visita* studied, the *pachaca* of the Llacuaz was divided, as was the custom in the region, into six villages which were the following:

San Joaquin de Puquio	41	members
San Felipe de Canchaden	85	〃
San Martin de Agomarca	135	〃
San Cristobal de Chumara	35	〃
San Alfonso de Chanta	23	〃
N. Sra. de la Asunción	72	〃
Total	391	

The number of members of the *pachaca* Llacuaz distributed among the six villages does not correspond to colonies or archipelagos but to a special feature of the social and territorial organization of the Cajamarca region. The same holds true for the other *pachacas*.

The Llacuaz are never mentioned as foreigners in the *visita*; nonetheless the Llacuaz phenomenon exists throughout the North and Central Highlands.

Very briefly we will state what we know about the Llacuaz. We find mention of these *ayllus* in Huarochiri in the central *sierra* situated in the Maritime Cordillera of the Andes, in the *guaranga* of Quinti, of Langasica, and of Colcaruna.

In the course of an administrative *visita* in 1571, the inspectors found an *ayllu* named Llacuaz in the *punas* and *cordilleras* of Quipucancha which had never before paid taxes (Rostworowski 1978).

In Laraos, in the same area of the central sierra, there existed an entire *guaranga* named Llacuaz.[3] We also find an *ayllu* Llacuaz in the *revisita* of the province of Tarma, in the *repartimiento* of Chaupiwaranga (AGN-Derecho Indígena cuaderno 220).

Another report of 1587 indicates the villages of Mito and of Orcotuna were inhabited by Llacuaz in addition to other hamlets that by that time were deserted (AGI-Patronato 109, Ramo 5). In Mito in 1629 there existed an *ayllu* Llacuaz in the *repartimiento* of Lurín Guanca in the north, in Ancash, Cajatambo, and Recuay. The documents on the extirpation of idolatry contain more interesting information on this indigenous group. Lastly, in the town of Huarmaca in the province of Piura, we find once more an *ayllu* called Llacuaz. The incidence of these people so far to the north as Piura obliges us to rethink everything that has heretofore been said on the subject.[4]

According to Arriaga (1968:248) the indigenous population in the zone of Cajatambo to Recuay had a double origin, and some were descended from the *Guari* or *Llactayoc* people native to that area, which had long been settled in the region, and distinguished themselves by possessing a large number of *huacas* near their villages.

The word *guari* has several meanings: it has to do with a god worshipped over a widely distributed area and also indicates an ancient population (Duviols 1973; Rostworowski 1983). A series of documents dealing with the extirpation of idolatry, the majority of which remain unpublished, contain information about these ethnic groups. According to their testimonies some Guari had the ocean as their *pacarina*, or place of origin, and were said to have arrived in the highland long before the other inhabitants. The god Guari taught the people agriculture and the techniques of building terraces and irrigation canals, besides bringing with him *coca* of the coastal variety (*Erytroxilum Novogranatense*, var. *Trujillensis*, Plowman 1979: Rostworowski 1973b; AAL Idolatrías, Leg. IV, Expediente 19, fol. 65r, año 1565).

In the town of San Juan de Machaca a man accused of sorcery said that his god Guari:

> bino de los llanos y se conbirtio en piedra y tuvo hijos que se llamaron Carua Rupai y es malqui que adoran por ser de los llanos y ablan la lengua materna como los de los llanos (AAL, Idolatrías, Leg. II, Exp. 2, fol. 13r y 13v, año 1657).

Nevertheless among the Guari themselves there was not one single place of origin. Some claimed the ocean as their *pacarina*, others said they came from caves situated in the snow peaks of Yarupajá (AAL, Idolatrías, Leg. II, exp. 18, años 1656–68).

The second group of inhabitants of the region, according to Arriaga, were the Llacuaz who were considered to be intruders. Their *pacarina*, or place of origin, was found in Lake Titicaca and in Lake Yarcaca, while the principal god worshipped by them was Libiac, the god of lightning (Hernandez Principe 1923; Duviols 1973). The Llacuaz were considered inhabitants of the *punas*, as opposed to the Guari, inhabitants of the villages (AAL, Idolatrías, Leg. VI, Exp. 10, año 1565).

In the documents dealing with idolatry among the natives of Ancash and Cajatambo, there are several myths about the arrival of the Llacuaz and the welcome they received in different villages. For example, in Mangas they were not allowed to settle and were obligated to pass on to the hamlet of Guancas, where, unlike the first place, they were received with festivities. According to the legends, the Llacuaz had received from their Apu Libiac Cancharcog a handful of earth, which would permit them to identify the place where they ought to settle permanently, after having found a similar kind of earth.

After passing a year in Guancas, they realized the earth they had been keeping was different from that of the village and they set off once again upon their wanderings. This episode shows the Llacuaz to be an agricultural people and not herders. Thus they arrived in Otuco where they posted themselves up above the hamlet while they sent a messenger with a llama as an offering, asking for food and to be welcomed by the natives of the valley.

The answer of the Guari was to kill the youth sent as a messenger and skin the llama alive, returning the remains to the watching Llacuaz. Then the Llacuaz cautiously went down to the valley where they found its inhabitants dancing the *guarilibiac* and laughing at their new emissary who had taken the form of a small bird. Infuriated, the Llacuaz created a storm with black mists and enormous hailstones and attacked the unwary dancers with their slings. The Guari were exterminated and the Llacuaz established themselves in the houses and fields of the vanquished (AAL, Idolatrías, Leg. VI, Exp. 18, fol. 11–11v. a; ps 1656–68).

The myths indicated above show a marked similarity with the conquests and methods used by Pariacaca and Macahuisa in the Central Highlands (Avila 1980), and it is also very similar to the search for fertile land undertaken by Manco Capac's group.

By the time of the seventeenth century documents which narrate these episodes, one finds mention of mixed *ayllus* of Guari and Llacuaz. By then both celebrated some *fiestas* in common and in them the Llacuaz went off to the *punas* to hunt deer and *guanacos* and, on returning to the villages, were received by the Guari with copious amounts of *chicha* and food. Together they danced for days their memorable dances and *taquis*.

In this very summarized mythical information on the ethnic composition of the population of Ancash and Cajatambo, we want to call attention to a similar narrative from other places between the coast and the highlands. In effect, in the valleys of Lurín-Lima and the Chillon on the Central Coast we discern through local traditions a general indication to which it is fitting to add the information from Ancash and Cajatambo, of a legendary time when the Yungas established themselves and inhabited the western slopes of the Maritime Cordillera. For some reason the circumstances changed and the coastal advance toward the highlands suffered retrogression and the Yungas had to abandon their possessions in the highlands (Rostworowski 1977 and 1978).

Something similar is found in Cajamarca with the presence of the Yungas in the highlands. Ethnohistory can only point out this phenomenon. To archaeology falls the task of continuing the investigation to prove or reject this hypothesis which comes from the documents in the archives.

The information about the Llacuaz in Cajamarca and in Piura and throughout the area from the central sierra northwards, obliges us to rethink the question of the presence of these groups and the reasons for their diffusion. We will present three hypotheses to explain the appearance of the Llacuaz in such far-flung and distant areas.

The first corresponds to what Duviols supposed was a division of the population between agriculturalists and herders; that is to say, between Guari and Llacuaz, in a system of dual division based on habitat and the type of work to which each group was dedicated. However, all Llacuaz are not herders and the myth to which we have referred shows them with agricultural and not pastoral preoccupations. On the other hand, there is an insistence on showing the Llacuaz as outsiders in opposition to local groups, settled in the region since times past. For these reasons we are inclined to suppose that we find ourselves confronted by massive migrations of ancient Andean populations. This dispersion could have started up already during the apogee of Wari culture or, failing that, as a consequence of its fall and termination. Let us analyze both possibilities.

In the case of the expansion of the Llacuaz people going back to the epoch of the greatest progress of the Middle Horizon, one could propose that the word *llacuaz* was a synonym or equivalent of the Quechua *mitmaq*; that is to say, that they were groups of populations sent by the central Wari government to different points of the sierra, according to the criteria and exigencies of the moment. We propose that the Andean custom of sending colonies as *mitmaq* to populate certain regions in order to serve the various ends of the central government was not a custom invented by the Incas, but on the contrary, was in use throughout the area.

If then, during Inca times great emphasis was placed on these massive transportations of ethnic groups in order to execute state objectives, then the custom itself must have been pan-Andean, belonging to cultures previous to the Inca enlargement.

The third alternative could have come about not as a consequence of Wari rule but rather upon its decadence, when subject peoples saw themselves free of rule imposed from above and took advantage of the situation to abandon the villages where they had previously lived and wander the *punas* in population movements which no one controlled.

In this case we would be dealing with an ethnic group which, for unknown reasons, advances from south to north, installing themselves in various locations in the high altitudes, in a zone in accordance with a transhumant pattern of life. Andean mythology indicates a time propitious to the wandering of ethnic groups, the Incas themselves being an example of a similar case. The reason for the migrations was due to the lack of political control after the disappearance of the power of Wari.

After the establishment of Tahuantinsuyu, the Cusco government prohibited native peoples from leaving their villages except by the express authorization of those in charge in compliance with the wishes of the sovereign. The Inca policy was to exercise very strict control of the population. The chronicler Miguel de Estete describes what he saw during his trip from Cajamarca to Pachacamac in the company of

Hernando Pizarro and he mentions that all the roads and bridges were watched (Fernández de Oviedo 1945). In other words, the Incas had stopped the previously free circulation of ethnic groups in the Andean environment. This control was indispensable in order to govern the country and to realize the great state enterprises such as roads, *tambos*, and administrative centers. Moreover, the fear of rebellions made it necessary to verify migratory movements (Fernández de Oviedo, tomo XII. 1945/1549).

As a result of the Spanish Conquest, the *mitimaes* and the *yana* tried to return to their former *señoríos*, but the vice royalty government restrained any attempts at change among the native population.

In summarizing the information about the ethnic composition of Cajamarca and thanks to the new information of the *visita* of 1571–72, we perceive three different types of foreign people installed in the area at the time of the Spanish Conquest. These groups arrived at different periods and had different causes for their settlement. Firstly, the Yungas appeared with the purpose of gaining free access to the intakes of their irrigation canals and perhaps a desire to exchange their goods with the inhabitants of the highlands (see our paper presented at the Tercer Seminario Nacional de Hidrología-ONERN, September 1983).

The coastal people installed in Cajamarca formed a *guaranga* within the sociopolitical system of the region. The presence of patronyms of the Yunga language, especially among women in the numerous *pachacas*, suggests an old occupation of the zone by coastal people.

The second group, the Llacuaz highlanders who had come up from the south, occupied isolated spaces along the Maritime Cordillera and it is possible that their arrival was due to the fall of the great Wari center which allowed people to wander along the *sierra*.

The latest newcomers to settle in Cajamarca were the *mitimaes* imposed by the Inca government, composed of people of various origins; that is to say, Quechuas, Cañaris, Guayacondores, and Collas.

Discontinued Territoriality in Cajamarca

One of the most remarkable features of the *curacazgo* of Cajarmarca is the socio-political structure linked with a discontinued or scattered territoriality. We are not dealing with archipelagos or colonies but with an overall system with a special organization which, even though we have observed it in other regions, is no where else as clear, as in Cajamarca.

My wish is to call attention to the facts to motivate a debate which will help to understand the intermeshing, the method of dispersion, and the objectives of this discontinued territoriality.

Pilar Remy has made several charts which help demonstrate the distribution of population by towns. Few villages were occupied exclusivey by a single *guaranga*. That of Guzmango or Cuzmango, because it is the most important is the one which possesses five villages inhabited only by members of its own *guaranga* without having others interspersed among them. These towns were the following:

San Francisco de Guzmango	678	inhabitants
Santiago de Catazabolan	932	〃
S. Benito de Cadachon	375	〃
Sta. Ana de Cimba	435	〃
S. Mateo de Contumazá	320	〃

The *guaranga* of Chondal counted one town inhabited only by its own people called San Joseph de Chanchan. The members of the *guaranga* of Chuquimango were the only inhabitants of the village of Espiritu Santo de Chuquimango.

As for San Antonio de Cajamarca, it was inhabited by all the *guarangas* and *parcialidades*. Of a total of 42 villages only 10 were populated exclusively by the members of a single *guaranga* without the intrusion of others. The rest of the villages, such as Pomamarca, Cajamarca, Mitimaes, and the *parcialidad* of Malcadan, were all shared with other *pachacas*.

What could have been the motive of this socio-political dispersion of the population and the lands of each *pachaca?* It is very difficult to settle upon even one hypothesis. In this case one is not dealing with vertical archipelagos, and even if the motives revolved around a similar concept, we find so-called verticality does not explain the configuration present in Cajamarca.

The only thing that occurs to us, but it seems unsatisfactory because it is too simple, is the possibility that this system of dispersed landholdings could have reduced crop losses. If each *pachaca* had access to land in different places, they had the opportunity to avoid local climatic catastrophes; for example, too much or too little rain, hailstorms, frosts, or plagues. It was a way of ensuring subsistence. In case the crops failed in one zone, there would still be hope that they would be successful in another.

(Translation by Freda Wolf de Romero)

NOTES

1. A very different situation was that of the potters, natives of Collique, who received the order during Inca times to move to Cajamarca in order to make tableware for the royal warehouses. They were sent to the site which they named Xultin. During the Colonial period, these *yana* formed part of the *pachaca* of Ayambla, of the *guaranga* of Guzmango.

W. Espinoza (1967 and 1970) changed the name of Chondal to Chonta and that of Ayambla to Ayamla and, finally, mentions the *pachaca* of Pucho as the *ayllu* which included the Yunga ceramic-makers. These changes only introduce errors and difficulties into research. In the *visita* of 1571–72, there is no mention of a *pachaca* named Pucho and we do not know where Espinoza took the reference.

2. The possible Chimu or Mochica territorial occupation to which we refer is different from the mention of the presence of coastal people in the *visita* to Cajamarca made by Barientos in 1540 (Espinoza 1967). In 1540 the lords of Pacasmayo, Saña, Collique, Chuspo, Cinto, and Túcume were said to serve the Inca with their people to transport the products of the lands of the Inca to the *tambos* of Cajamarca. The temporary presence of these coastal people acting as porters is substantially different from the long-term presence of coastal, Yunga, people in the *guaranga* of Chondal.

The *encomendero* of Cajamarca, Melchor Verdugo, took advantage of the Andean system to order and oblige the natives of his *encomienda* to transport the tribute which they owed him all the way to the city of Trujillo "*por sus pachacas y mitas.*" In this case we have the temporary presence of highland porters travelling on the coast.

3. Archivo General de la Nación. Protocolos Notariales, Francisco Roldán N° 925, ano 1735. "Carta de poder otorgada por Juan Bernardo de Mendoza, cacique segunda persona del pueblo de San Pedro de Larau de la guaranga de Llacuaz, en la provincia de Huarochirí, a Silverio Sebastián Yacharachin."

4. Biblioteca Nacional de Bogotá, Colombia. Miscelánea. Papeles del Obispo Martínes Compañón. Tomo 113, año 1782, ff. 872r–83v.

DOCUMENTS CITED

Archivo General de Indias (AGI)
Sección: Justicia 1063
Sección: Patronato 109, Ramo 5
Archivo Arzobispal de Lima (AAL)
Sección Idolatrías: Legajo IV, Expediente 19-año 1656
〃 II, 〃 2 〃 1657
〃 II, 〃 18 〃 1656–68
Archivo General de la Nación (AGN) (Lima)
Derecho Indigena Cuaderno 220.

REFERENCES CITED

Arriaga, Fray Pablo José de
[1621] 1968 Extirpación de la idolatría del Perú. Biblioteca de Autores Españoles. Ediciones Atlas, Madrid.

Avila, Francisco de
[1598?] 1980 See Taylor.

Cabello de Valboa, Miguel
[1586] 1951 Miscelánea antártica. Instituto de Etnología, Universidad Nacional Mayor de San Marcos. Lima.

Carrera, Fernando de la
1644 Arte de la lengua Yunga de los Valles del Obispado de Truxillo del Perú, con un confessonario y todas las Oraciones Christianas traducidas en la lengua y otras cosas. Impreso en Lima por J. Contreras.

Diez de San Miguel, Garci
1964 Visita hecha a la provincia de Chucuito. . .1567. Lima: Casa de la Cultura.

Duviols, Pierre
1973 Huari y Llacuaz. Agricultores y pastores. Un dualismo prehispánico de oposición y complementariedad. Revista del Museo Nacional 39:153–91. Lima.

Espinoza, Soliano, Waldemar
1967 El primer informe Etnológico sobre Cajamarca. (1540). Revista Peruana de Cultura del Perú 11–12:5–41. Lima.
1970 Los mitmas yungas de Collique en Cajamarca. Revista del Museo Nacional 36:9–57. Lima.
1975 El valle de Jayanca y el reino de los Mochicas. Siglos XV y XVI. Boletín del Instituto Francés de Estudios Andinos 4(3–4):243–74. Lima.

Estete, Miguel
See Fernández de Oviedo.

Fernández de Oviedo, Gonzalo
[1549] 1945 Historia general y natural de las Indias. Ed. Guaraní. Asunción, Paraguay, Vol. 12.

Hernández Príncipe, Lic. Rodrigo
1923 Mitología andina. Revista Inca, Vol. 1. Lima: Universidad Nacional Mayor de San Marcos.

Mogrovejo, Toribio Alfonso de
1920 Diario de la segunda visita pastoral del Arzobispo de Los Reyes, Don Toribio de Mogrovejo. Publicado por fray Domingo Angulo. Libro de visitas 1593. Revista del Archivo Nacional del Perú No. 1. Entrega 1 y 2.

Ortiz de Zúñiga, Iñigo
1967 Visita de la provincia de León de Huánuco en 1562. Universidad

Nacional Hermilio Valdizán, Huánuco. Vol. 1.

1972 Vol. II.

Plowman, Timothy

1979 Botanical Perspectives on Coca. Journal of Psychedelic Drugs 2 (1–2) Jan.–July.

Quesada, Félix

1976 Diccionario Quechua. Cajamarca—Cañaris. Ministerio de Educación-Instituto de Estudios Peruanos. Lima.

Remy Simatovic, Pilar

1982 Mss. Informe analítico del proyecto de investigación. Organización y cambios del Reino de Cuismanco, 1540–80.

Rostworowski de Diez Canseco, María

1961 Curacas y sucesiones. Costa norte. Lima.

1973a Urpay Huachac y el "Simbolo del Mar" Boletín del Seminario de Arqueología. PUC. N° 14 Enero-Diciembre.

1973b Plantaciones de coca prehistóricas en la vertiente del Océano Pacifico. Revista del Museo Nacional 39:193–224.

1977 Etnía y sociedad, costa peruana prehispánica. Lima: Instituto de Estudios Peruanos.

1978 Los señoríos indígenas de Lima y Canta. Instituto de Estudios Peruanos. Lima.

1983 Estructuras andinas del poder. Ideología religiosa y política. Lima: Instituto de Estudios Peruanos.

In press El derecho hidráulico entre los señoríos costeños prehispánicos. Paper presented at Tercer Seminario Nacional de Hidrología. Oficina Nacional de Evalución de Recursos Naturales (ONERN).

Taylor, Gerald

1980 Rites et Traditions de Huarochiri: manuscrit quechua du début du 17 siècle. Paris: Editions L'Harmattan.

Zevallos Quiñones, Jorge

1975 La visita del Pueblo de Ferreñafe (Lambayeque) en 1568. Historia y Cultura 9:155–78. Museo Nacional de Historia. Lima.

APPENDIX

Patronyms originally from the Muchic or Yunga language

Masculine Pachaca	Patronym	Feminine Pachaca	Patronym
Pingomarca	Eltef	*Pingomarca*	Funchon
en S. Juan de	Facchon	S. Juan de	Fecto
Pingomarca	Eltef	Pingomarca	Fistum
			Faccha
			Chufibi
			Fencun
			Susfil
			Chasfumi
			Fallen
			Fistun
			Filican
			Faychon
			Funchun
Pingomarca		*Pingomarca*	
S. Juan de	Estefo	S. Juan de	Fellen
Chanchan	Eltefel	Chanchan	Zonfen
	Estefe		Chozfui
	Esquen		Funchon
	Farquete		Esfuyo
	Fasique		Felchon
	Estefel		Xufil
	Chequinaf		Funchun
			Zonfel
			Fequen
			Feychen
Pingomarca		*Pingomarca*	
S. Gregorio	Retefe	S. Gregorio	Chilfon
de Mezique	Eltef	de Mezique	Chusfun
	Faymas		Fofoc
	Fano		Faychon
			Fequen
			Chufin
			Fan
			Sonfel
			Fayec
			Susfel
			Lusfyn
			Chufi

Masculine Pachaca	Patronym	Feminine Pachaca	Patronym
Pingomarca		*Pingomarca*	
S. Miguel de	Nafcol	S. Miguel de	Subfil
Catamuche		Catamuche	Chefel
			Fumep
Pingomarca		*Pingomarca*	
S. Rafael de	Tefel	S. Rafael	Chufel
Nipos		de Nipos	
		〃	Fili
Pollogues		*Polloques*	
S. Juan de	Falcuy	S. Rafael	Fellen
Pingomarca		de Nipos	
Polloques		*Polloques*	
S. Gregorio	Falseque	S. Pedro de	Uilfic
de Mezique	Alfel	Libie	Fallen
			Fexon
Polloques			Falla
S. Pedro de	Soliflus		Fanchun
Libie	Falxeque		Fulchon
	Fanec		Felton
	Felque		Fallen
Poyoques			Fedenon
S. Miguel	Palchec		Efelchop
Catamuche	Exfen		Filchon
	Falsec		Funa
	Fioy		Felgen
			Felenon
Polloques			Pecheful
S. Miguel de	Ustef		Efcho
Catamuche	Fequenan		Fizan
	Llenfon		Fioc
	Eltefe		
		Poyogues	
		S. Miguel de	Efechoc
		Catamuche	Tinfel
			Fillan
			Forcoi
			Chufel
		Polloques	
		S. Miguel de	Cusfil
		Catamuche	Chonfel
			Finchon

Masculine Pachaca	Patronym	Feminine Pachaca	Patronym
			Chifel
			Afon
			Zipan
			Actfel
			Chuyfem
			Chipfel
			Felchop
			Fusfel
Nipos		*Nipos*	
S. Rafael	Fapchon	S. Rafael	Felni
de Nipos	Estofe	de Nipos	Fonchon
	Fanoc		Chefel
			Fel
Nipos			Fenchen
S, Miguel de	Tifel		Cuzfin
Catamuche	Felele		Yofi
			Funchon
Paiay-Yungas			Yufe
St. Cruz de	Faman		Fisichon
Sochabamba	Segun		Efoc
	Efio		Funchon
	Chufino		
	Fazerque	*Nipos*	
		S. Bartolomé	
		Tacabamba	Adfel
Xaxaden		*Nipos*	
S. Salvador	Llufel	S. Joseph	Cuzfai
Mollebamba	Nafca	Chanchan	
Xanaden		*Nipos*	
Sta. Magdalena		S. Miguel de	Heyfan
de Lachan	Xefes	Catamuche	Funchen
	Chifoc		Xecfel
Nachedon		*Paiay-yungas*	
S. Pablo de	Faquien	Sta. Cruz de	Filio
Chalaques	Estefe	Sochabamba	Fallen
	Chifen		Felint
	Nofel		Chof
	Fellen		Felioc
			Filquen

Masculine Pachaca	Patronym	Feminine Pachca	Patronym
Ayambla			Fumo
Santiago de	Faminy		Fumi
Catazabolan	Chifomo		
Pauxan		*Paiay*	
S. Benito de	Fancoy	S. Matías de	
Cadachon		Payaca	Yfas
Payxan		*Xaxaden*	
S. Sebastián	Feyllan	S. Pedero de	Xafal
de Acaden		Chalaques	Ynfel
			Yfechen
Gayao			Filli
S. Antonio	Falme		Nonfel
Caxamarca	Estefel		Yunfel
			Fylman
Baca			Fylma
S. Antonio	Edfequen		
Caxamarca			
Lanchan-yungas		*Xaxaden*	
S. Antonio	Myfei	Sta. Magdalena	
Caxamarca	Fisaco	de Lachan	Farchon
	Naufen		Sulfain
Yscan		*Nachedon*	
S. Bartolomé		S. Pedro de	Fylpon
Tacabamba	Fuilon	Chalaques	Fycho
			Fanchon
Aspac			Fycon
S. Pablo de	Llefen		Fyllo
Chalaques	Felchon		Zelfel
Chiton			Etentan
S. Gregorio	Yecfan		
de Mezique	Llufel	*Collana*	
		S. Salvador	Llulfec
		Mollebamba	Nofeche
Chiton		*Collana*	
S. Luis de	Efequen	S. Gabriel	Lacfid
Tambodon		de Cascas	

Masculine Pachaca	Patronym	Feminine Pachaca	Patronym
Viton		*Pauxan*	
S. Pedro	Fayoc	S. Benito	Efechan
de Libie	Funchon	Cachadon	Pofay
			Chilfui
Malcadan		*Ayambla*	
S. Salvador	Etquem	Santiago de	Felnin
Mollebamba	Faclloc	Catazabolan	Fraychen
	Tefa		Fuenchen
	Chufen		
	Nofon	*Chusan*	
	Eltef	S. Benito	Pisni
	Eltef	Cadachon	
Malcadan		*Chusan*	
S. Lorenzo	Dofan	Magdalena	Efuchin
Malcadan	Funne	de Lachan	
Gente de	Fillque	*Baca*	
los *Guambo*	Fyquin	Antonio	Chamifle
			Chafles
			Facchun
			Fumen
			Fellen
		Lanchan-yungas	
		S. Antonio	Fellen
		Caxamarca	Fulchon
		Cayao	
		S. Antonio	Fupe
		Caxamarca	
		Colquemarca	
		S. Joaquin	Fempem
		de Puquio	
		Viton	
		S. Pedro	Chefel
		de Libie	Sisfel
			Chasfai
			Olfin
			Fellenta

Masculine Pachaca	Patronym	Feminine Pachaca	Patronym
			Quefel
		Xucat	
		S. Luis de	Fylchan
		Tamboden	Fechen
			Fellan
			Funep
		Chiton	
		S. Luis de	Fyllan
		Tamboden	
		Chiton	
		S. Gregorio	Holfon
		Mezique	
		Malcadan	
		S. Salvador	Efchot
		de Malcadan	Fallen
			Faye
			Casfen
			Funep
			Fellen
			Efan
			Yecfel
			Cecfel
			Xocfun
			Ficchan
		Agomarca	
		S. Gabriel	Filnon
		de Cascas	Colfyn
			Eful
		Tacabamba	
		S. Bartolomé	Fili
		Tacabamba	Chifel
		Llenden	
		S. Martín de	Feltiquilla
		Agomarca	

18

Social Frontiers and the Territorial Base of *Curacazgos*

Susan Ramírez

Introduction

Several recent ethnohistorical efforts to define and better understand late prehispanic Andean social and economic organization have focused on the spatial distribution or settlement pattern of one ethnic group or of the subjects of one paramount lord or *curaca.*[1] Guillermo Cock discussed the scattered settlement pattern, which he dubbed "*salpicado de territorios,*" in some detail for the Collaguas during colonial times (Cock 1976:113–16).[2] Gabriel Martínez, analyzing the scattered distribution of the Lupaqa found "*pueblos compartidos*" or "*duales,*" sharing territory (Martínez 1981: 265). María Rostworowski, elsewhere in this volume,[3] uses the phrase "*territorialidad salpicada*" or "*discontinua*" to describe shared towns and the widely scattered settlement pattern of the different ethnic groups censused in Cajamarca in the 1570s. And, in his analysis of the *visita* of Conchucos of 1543, David Noble Cook described the same phenomena, albeit without using such phrases (Cook 1976).[4] All of these scholars and the many not here cited[5] who recognize and note the pattern seem to build on the pioneering work of John V. Murra, when he published his seminal article describing the "archipelago" model and "*islas.*" (Murra [1972] 1975).

Most authors go no further than describing the pattern. One exception is Rostworowski, who in her important article on the coca lands of Quivi, postulates the use of force to gain access to land outside the immediate central area of an ethnic group (Rostworowski 1977: 179, 190). But, she adds that more information is needed to understand the tenancy of different ethnic groups (p. 195).

My purpose here is to describe the scattered settlement pattern in northern Peru, based on documentation that, for the most part, was written before the Toledan reorganization of 1572–73 of the area. The analysis will focus on the coastal polities that existed between Pacasmayo on the south and Jayanca on the north, and, of necessity, will include remarks concerning the highland hinterland of the region. I will try, to the degree the primary sources permit, to distinguish between core[6] and peripheral areas, despite the fact that the boundaries or frontiers of these areas are not precisely known or completely understood. In the process, I will discuss a mechanism, other than force, kinship, or another possibility, that explains the dispersed residences of members of one ethnic group or polity both on their own lands and on lands of others. Understanding how it was possible for one lord's subjects to live and work in close proximity to those of another will help refine the concept and definition of indigenous polities, especially with regard to the working of their political economy.

Scattered Site Settlements

Early primary sources on the North Coast show that within the core area of a *curacazgo* the population lived dispersed or scattered, sometimes near their fields or the resources they worked. Even though the *visita* of Jayanca of 1540, for example, is probably not complete, the visitor having confined his rounds to the settlements within two leagues of the *tambo,* it gives ample evidence of the spatial distribution of the population of the valley. In 1540 the subjects of the *curaca* of Jayanca lived in about 250 settlements within this two-league radius (Espinoza 1975:271). With very few exceptions, the population lived in *ranchos* and *pueblos* that often had more *casas* or *moradas* than *indios de visitación.* A "*pueblo grande*" was "*ve[i]nte moradas*" and had a population of seven families (assuming each *indio de visitación* was head of a household) (p. 265). Other "*pueblos grandes*" had ten, eleven, or thirteen families. But, in all the almost two weeks he spent in the *valle,* the visitor personally toured only about a dozen settlements, of hundreds, that were that large or larger. Evidence from a myriad of sources for the total coastal area under consideration also yielded the names of 55 towns in fifteen *encomiendas* that were created from six *curacazgos*, proving that the pattern was not valley or polity specific (Ramírez 1981:286–87).

These early sources, however, provide only a shadow, outline, or hint of what the demographic and political landscape was like in 1532. Already by that date, the populations of both coast and highlands had been decimated by disease. Soon thereafter, war and forced marches and service had also taken a toll. Furthermore, the Spanish did not respect indigenous administrative units when they adjudicated the Indians as *encomiendas*. They, starting with Francisco Pizarro himself, frequently divided a *curacazgo* into two or more *encomiendas*. In 1536, for example, he divided the Indians of Túcume between Juan Roldán and Juan de Osorno (BAH/Mata Linares, t. 82, 138v and AGI/J418, 1573, 132v). Pacasmayo was divided into four *encomiendas*: Chérrepe, Moro, Chepén, and Jequetepeque (ART/CoO, 28-IV-1559,18v). A contemporary summarized Pizarro's actions, saying:

> El marques don Fran[cis]co piçarro gov[ernado]r q[ue] fue deste reyno todos los repartimientos que hizo no los hizo en un dia syno en dias diuersos . . . parese que el d[ic]ho marques no hizo encomienda a todos de las cabeças e caçiques prinçipales que auia syno que a unos hizo encomienda del caçique pr[incip]al y primera perssona y a otros de la segunda y otros pr[incip]ales quedauan a otros aunque estos heran subjetos a la pr[incip]al y primera p[er]sona de los d[ic]hos caçiques (AGI/J457, 1144v-45).

Fray Domingo de Santo Tomás also remarked on this phenomenon in 1550 when he noted that the Spanish often divided a "province" into as many as three or four *encomiendas* (CVU, 1–1, 1-VII-1550).

Finally a series of *reducciones* greatly altered the demographic landscape. In the north the first systematic *reducciones* of which we have note were ordered by Dr. Gregorio González de Cuenca in 1566 (AGI/J456, 419). He resettled, for example, the scores of villages and hamlets of Jayanca in three towns (AGI/Patronato 189, R. 11, 1566). But, by reference we know that similar concentrations of Indians and resettlements had occurred years before this date. A *principal* of Túcume testified that there were five *principales* of Pácora in the 1530s. Only one survived in 1570 "*por lo qual los pueblos que tenian se an benido a resumir en el pueblo solo q*[*ue*] *dicen de pacora y hiçieron caçique de todos ellos don Joan pacora que agora es cacique*" (AGI/J418, 1573, 219–19v). The extent of the *reducciones* in the region in the sixteenth century is summarized in Table 18.1.

Thus, no one should be surprised that the transcriptions of the Toledo *visitas* show the extant population living in a few villages. The six known towns of Chérrepe, which itself was part of the original jurisdiction of the *curaca* of Pacasmayo, were first reduced to three and, then, further reduced to two (Ramírez 1981:287; Ramírez 1978). These sixteenth century *reducciones*, then, by forcing Indians of various lords to live together in one settlement or shared towns, accentuated

Table 18.1 Reducciones of Lambayeque

Settlement	*Reduced to*	*Source*
Tecapa	San Pedro de Lloco	AGI/J458, 1419
Chérrepe	Chérrepe (new asiento de)	AGI/J459, 3062v
Choloc		
Indos viejos del tambo real		
Noquique		BNP/A310, 1584
Quin cala	Culop(o)	AGI/J459, 3062v
Mitimaes of Saña	9 pueblos	AGI/J459, 3064–65v
14–15 pueblos in Chicama	4 pueblos	AGI/J460, 365v
3–4 pueblos in Licapa	2 pueblos	AGI/J457, 790
		AGI/J460, 365
c. 250 pueblos of San Salvador (de Jayanca)	3 pueblos	AGI/Patronato, l. 189, R. 11, 1566
Mocllo	Pololo	AGI/J455, 1689v
300 tributarios of Pololo	Chiclayo	AGI/J457, 832–34
Sinto	Picsi	ANP/DI, l. 19, C. 483, 1793, 31v
San Miguel de Picsi	Chiclayo	OCI/Monsefú, No. 110, 5345, 73
Sinto	Chiclayo	AGI/J457, 818v
Collique	Chiclayo	ART/CoC, 15–I–1781, 13–14 and 44v
3 pueblos of Collique	1 pueblo	AGI/J457, 732v
Chacchacalla	Llomonte	AGI/J457, 727v
Mayna	Reque	AGI/J457, 792v
Corñan	Lambayeque	ART/CoC, 15–I–1781
Callanca	Monsefú	ART/IC, 11–XII–1787
pueblo of fishermen, Callanca	Callanca	ART/Mata, 1587, 2v
100 Indians from the royal road to Saña	Moro	AGI/J460, 461

the earlier pattern, first clearly evident in the Conchucos document of 1543 (Cook 1976:30–31).

In addition to the villages or hamlets within one or two leagues from an administrative seat, a lord often had subjects living outside his core area of jurisdiction. Perhaps the earliest account for the North Coast is from Sebastián de la (da) Gama's 1540 *visita* that mentions some 200 Indians from Jayanca on lands of Túcume in the highland area of Guambos, now modern Cajamarca.

> Declaró Antón Cauallero que conosce a vn prencipal de Facollapa que se dice Labamy que tiene más de doscientos indios, e que cada tres lunas dan nueue platos de plata. E quel dicho prencipal está en los Guanbos e se sirve de él [el encomendero Lorenzo de] Vlloa, vecino de Trujillo. . . . E luego el dicho juez le preguntó al dicho

> Facollapa [*cacique*] si tiene noticia de Labany questá an Los Guanbos, y le preguntó si es suyo. Dijo que no. Preguntado de donde es, dijo que es natural de Jayanca e que era de su padre. Preguntado si ha seruido; dijo que al cacique de Jayanca pasado le seruia e que agora no le sirue. Preguntado a quien sirue agora; dijo que a Ulloa, vecino de Trujillo. Preguntado por qué no le sirue; dijo que porque no ha enviado por él . . . Preguntado qué tanto está su tierra del prencipal de Jayanca; dijo que en dos días llega allá a su pueblo, e que está en tierra de Tucume e que se fue en tiempo de sus padres. (Espinoza 1975:268–70)

These two responses can be interpreted as follows: about one lifetime ago, a lesser lord and his Indians left Jayanca to reside in and work resources found on lands of Túcume, another coastal *señorío,* in the nearby highlands of Cajamarca. The Indians once served the paramount lord of Jayanca, but no longer did because the lord had not sent for them (implying, perhaps, that he could still claim their services, if he cared to).[7] These passages further imply that Labamy and his subjects lived within two days' travel of Jayanca and had direct or indirect access to silver.

Finding coastal peoples in the highlands is not surprising. Santo Tomás noted in 1550 that, in general, one province consisted of hot and cold lands on which were settled various villages that exchanged products with one another and were subject to one paramount lord. The Spanish, he said, disrupted this trade and communication by dividing a province into as many as three or four *encomiendas* (CVU, 1–1, 1-VII-1550). More specifically, in 1549 the lord Copez (Copis) "que es en los llanos" had "unos [principales] que confinan con los Guambos"; and the *curaca* of Controilico "que es en los llanos . . . [had] otro principal en la sierra que se llama Penachi" (Loredo 1958:269–71).[8] Also, Don Hernando, the *curaca* of Saña, in 1566 had "sus y[ndi]os en distrito de mas de treinta leguas de la mar hasta caxamarca" (AGI/J458, 1829).[9] And finally, subjects of the lord of Túcume lived near Simbal, in the hinterland of Trujillo (ANP/Aguas 3–3–18–68 as cited by Rostworowski 1977:191).

Confirmation that the *curacas* had subjects in the highlands who were not there as *mitimaes* comes from the *Ordenanzas* that Dr. Cuenca wrote for Jayanca in 1566. He ordered that highlanders who were subjects to coastal lords should not travel to the coast in the summer, because they became sick and died: "los indios serranos a ellos [lords of Jayanca] sujetos por ninguna vía, en tiempo de verano, abajen a los llanos a trabajar ni a otra cosa" (AGI/Patronato, 1. 189, R. 11, 1566).

Thus, *curacas* had subjects living "*derramados en poblezuelos*," in the words of the 1560s, over relatively vast areas (CVU, 1–4, 1564). Such areas proved extensive enough to justify the petitions of numerous lords for a license to ride horseback. A typical petition stated that the lord's subjects "estan divididos en partes lejos y para visytallos es menester de andar a cauallo" (AGI/J458, 1830v).

While most subjects originally lived under their lord in their own villages or hamlets, by the 1540s, some subjects lived in close proximity, even in the same towns, with subjects of other lords. Others lived on lands of another, like those of Jayanca in Guambos.

Early colonial documents show this dispersement and intermingling to have been common and recognized by authorities. In the 1540 instructions that Pizarro gave Diego Verdejo for his visit to the North Coast, Pizarro asked him to find out, among many other things, "que indios advenediros subjetos a otro cacique e mitimaes tienen en la tierra de cada curaca" (BAH/A109, 112). In addition, a court case, dated 1558, records how the *curacas* of Sinto, Túcume, Ferreñafe, Lambayeque, Collique, Chuspo, and Saña gathered to claim subjects who were living within the jurisdiction of another. At the meeting, the *curacas* agreed to return the subjects to their rightful lord. Thus, the lord of Sinto recovered subjects from the lords of Lambayeque, Collique, Ferreñafe, and Chuspo. The *curaca* of Reque recovered Indians from the lords of Collique, Chuspo, and Lambayeque. The lord of Chuspo received Indians from Lambayeque, Túcume, Sinto, and Reque. The lord of Ferreñafe got Indians from Raco, Reque, and Chuspo (ART/CoJ, 29-III-1558). Eight years later lords still petitioned Dr. Cuenca to allow them to visit distant settlements to bring back (*recoger*) their subjects (AGI/J457, 829; and J461, 1490).[10]

A Curaca's Control over Natural Resources

Understanding what appears to be overlapping and complex jurisdictions requires a review of the role of the *curaca* in the management of natural resources. Theoretically, the *curaca* controlled the land and irrigation water of his "province" or "valley," to use the words of the chroniclers. The origin of this right and tradition goes back to pre-Inca times. Briefly, before the establishment of the kingdom of Chimor, local lords battled over land. Fernando Abad de Santillán, one of the few Spanish chroniclers to record pre-historic accounts regarding the North Coast, states that

> antes [de los Incas] en cada valle ó provincia habia su curaca, señor principal, y tenian sus principales mandones subjetos a el curaca, y cada valle destos tenia guerra con su comarcano, y desta causa no habia comercio ni comunicacion alguna entrellos; . . . y era uso que al que quedaba con la victoria y sujetaba al otro, le hacian los subjetos sementeras de maíz y coca y ají, y dábanle ovejas y de lo demas que tenian, en reconocimiento. Y desta suerte hubo algunos curacas que subjetaron algunos valles y provincias en particular, como fué el señor del valle que agora se dice de Trujillo, el qual se llamó Chimo Cápac, y señoreó la mayor parte de las Y[u]ngas (sic). (Santillán 1950:45)[11]

As the quote states, the price of peace, in this competition over resources, were fields of corn, coca, and pepper and other products or, in more Andean terms, the labor and the use of the physical resources to produce these goods. This is the earliest reference to this precedent-setting custom of working lands for another in acknowledgment of superior rank, status, and hegemony.

This practice probably was the culmination of a long process that antedated this reference to pre-history. Even before the time of the reference, one lord battled another for control over resources. The victor became paramount lord with some claim to the territory of the other, then his subordinate, by right of conquest.

An analogous situation followed the Inca conquest of the coast between 1462 and 1470 (Rowe 1948:40). The Inca, again, by right of conquest, took control and assumed the rights of disposition over the resources of the Chimu. In accordance, his agents reordered and balkanized the kingdom. Then Inca surveyors proceeded to divide and mark these units, a lord's physical domain, in several ways. Felipe Guamán Poma de Ayala says the Inca divided the highlands from the coast

> Términos y mojones de los yndios de la cierra y de los llanos, *yungas*, questauan puestas por Topa Ynga Yupanqui y de Uayna Capac Ynga y de sus mojonadores Yngas, . . . por su consejo rreal y principales y justicias deste rreyno, para que tubiesen jurisdición los yndios de la cierra con los llanos. (1980:852 [866])

He specifically states that Topa Ynga Yupanqui "mandó mojonar todos los mojones destos rreynos de los pastos y chacaras y montes . . ." (111[111]). And elsewhere,

> Y estaua amojonado hasta los rríos de coger pescados, camarones y

> llachoc, onquena, chinche hasta dalle tierra a un yndio, a una yndia, tanta pulicía. 1074[1084]

Martín de Murúa, another chronicler, elaborates on the types of resources that were regulated and delegated, entrusted and assigned, by the Inca to a *curaca's* discretion.

> tenian amojonados los terminos y jurisdiccion de cada suyo o provincia, y dicen que Topa Inga Yupanqui fue el que de nuevo amojono toda la tierra, con grande orden, conforme a los corrientes de los ríos, hasta los Andes, y puso limites en las chacras y montes, y todo género de minas de oro y plata y demas metales y minas de colores con que pintan, hasta las islas en la mar junto a la costa de cada pueblo; puso grandes penas para que no se quebrantasen ni entrasen los unos en los terminos de los otros a cazar ni pescar ni cortar leña ni sacar ningun genero de color, ni en las minas ni en las salinas, ni otra cosa alguna, si no fuese con especial licencia del Inga. (Murúa 1946:III–28, 233)

That this demarcation had been carried out on the North Coast by the Inca is evident from a petition brought before Dr. Cuenca by Don Garçia, the *cacique* of Moro, asking that the lands held by him and his counterparts of Jequetepeque, Chérrepe, and Chepén be confirmed "conforme a la traça que hizieron los d[ic]hos caçiques e Indios antiguos de los d[ic] hos repartimientos." He reiterated the need to restore the boundary markers "hecho(s) en tienpo del Ynca que las [the lands] partian" (AGI/J458, 2041-42).

Further evidence that the territorial domain of a *curaca* was indeed known and bounded comes from a viceregal decree, dated 6 December 1567, of Licenciado Lope de Castro, regarding the founding of the town of Santiago de Miraflores in the valley of Saña. It locates the boundary between the valleys, and by extension, the lords, of Pacasmayo and Saña, "en los arenales q[ue] ay entre el valle de caña y el de pacasmayo . . . conforme a como los indios antiguos . . . los tenyan partidos . . . (ART/CoR, 30-VI-1576).

These demarcations clearly were an administrative convention, designed to keep the peace and to order or structure relations between neighboring lords. Poma de Ayala says of the distribution of lands that "con esto se quitauan pleytos" (Poma de Ayala 1980: 1074 [1084]). They did not necessarily mean that the territorial dimension of a chiefdom was one compact unit, just that the Inca confirmed and delegated each lord's control of specific resources, including lands, perhaps scattered along the length of a river valley (as suggested by Netherly 1984:247) and in different ecological zones.[12]

The Inca confirmed one *curaca* per province or valley, who according to Poma de Ayala, expected obedience and respect from all who entered his jurisdiction (1980: 455 [457]). These lords, who were to become the *curacas* or *caciques principales* of early colonial times, were ordered to assign part of their delegated domain to be worked for the Inca—a situation not unlike that outlined above. A manuscript, entitled "Apuntamientos de Su Mag[es]t[ad] para el peru," reads:

> Resulta de la declaracion de los caciques e yndios biejos tomados en las visitas hechas de los naturales que los yngas señores unibersales fueron tan señores que hordenaron como cada rrepartimiento senalase para el d[ic]ho ynga una parte de tierras que son las que agora llaman las de ynga y las senbrase de comidas y benefiçiase la comunidad de cada rrepartimiento. (BAH/Muñoz, A92)

The *curaca* apportioned the rest of the land and other resources to the lesser lords under him, who in turn entrusted them to subordinates further down the hierarchical power structure until individual heads of households actually received them for use.[13] In a now moth-eaten and incomplete notarial register of the *cabildo* of Lambayeque, an Indian scribe recorded the oral testimony of old men to the effect that the lands that those born in Lambayeque still held in 1607 had been given and assigned to them ("q[ue] les fueron repartidas y señaladas") by the "*caciques antiguos*" of the town. Again, they declared that the lands "belonged" to the lords. They had been passed down, in some cases, according to the Indian witnesses, through as many as ten generations (ANCR/1586–1611, 12). The truth of this testimony is supported by a petition presented before Dr. Cuenca in which Don Xpoval Colloçi states that he and his Indians had been in possession of the lands since pre-conquest times: "emos tenido y gozado de muchos años aeste p[ar]te desde en tienpo de los yngas" (AGI/J461, 1515–15v).

In return for the use of the resources, the users customarily gave the lord a portion of the produce (*Relaciones Geograficas de Indias* 1881: II, 240). In the land register of Lambayeque, quoted above, one entry, regarding the lands called Colluci, reads that they "belonged" to the heirs of the *principal* Chum, because

> en los tiempos pasados los arrendava y pagava el alquiler al prençipal col[lo]cçi los d[ic]hos prencipales de chum. (ANCR/1586–1611, 23v-24v).

Thus, the lesser lords called *Chum* paid rent to the *principal Collocçi* and, by so doing, acquired the use and possession of the lands. So, too, the lord of Ferreñafe permitted a subject to plant only in exchange for "tribute" "por ellas [the lands] como hazian los yndios hasta aqui" (AGI/J461, 1563). Likewise, the *curaca* of Túcume had lands he inherited from his father and grandfather which he "rented" to other Indians (AGI/J461, 1525). And the lords of Jayanca divided (*repartia*) and subdivided the lands among their subjects in return for an annual "*terrasgo*" (land tax or rent) (AGI/G458, 2020; and J462, 1875).[14]

Irrigation water was also "owned" and subject to "rental" payment. In the 1530s, Jayanque, the *curaca* of Jayanca, for example, "hazia conprar el agua a sus yndios y no se los queria dar [el agua] syno se le pagava con buen oro" (AGI/J418, 1573, 459v-60). The cooks (*cocineros*) and deer slayers and leather workers (*venaderos* ?) of Túcume worked irrigated land that they rented from the owner of the irrigation canal, Don Andrés Cunun (or monon) Çeque.[15] In 1566 part of the rent (tribute) was paid in goods and part in labor: "le ayudamos a hazer sus sementeras . . . y trabajar en lo que dezimos, y es costumbre que se tiene entre nosotros . . ." (AGI/J461, 1521).

The interpretation of the words "*terrazgo*," "rent," "tribute," and "payment" in the above quotes cannot be taken literally. Most of the Indians on the coast, even in 1566, spoke only their native language. Spanish and mestizo scribes were putting words in their mouths when they wrote out their petitions. The number of different words used to embody the relationship between "owner" and "renter" suggests that no exact Spanish word that would clearly convey the essence and conditions of the exchange existed. Therefore, the terms must be understood, in their Andean context, in terms of labor service. Rostworowski, to whom we are so much indebted for information on the early native society of the coast, tells us that before the conquest to be a subject of a lord meant that he "tenía la obligación de acudir con su gente a la labranza de las heredades del curaca" (Rostworowski 1961:15–16). In Jayanca a lesser lord designated part of the lands he controlled to be tilled for the *curaca* in recognition of his hegemony.

> en todos los prencipalazgos dauan en aquel t[ien]po una suerte de tierra al caçique prençipal e que el d[ic]ho neptur [principal] tenia señalado un pedaço de tierra al caçique de jayanca como a su señor e que este testigo de presente a uisto que en la parçialidad del d[ic]ho neptur el d[ic]ho don fran[cis]co caçique de jayanca posehe un pedaço de tierra que haze senbrar (AGI/J418, 1573, 312).

The produce from planting and cultivating these lands constituted the "payment," "rent," and "tribute" for the others Neptur and his subjects used. Labor input was how the tribute was originally assigned and measured. The payment in "*buen oro*" expected by the *curaca* of Jayanca in 1539 was probably a Spanish idea and imposition. (AGI/J418, 1573, 459–60).[16]

"*Que haze sembrar*" in the above quote provides a clue to understanding the tenure system. The principal, Neptur, designated a piece of land in recognition of hegemony, but it was the *curaca's* responsibility to have it worked (Santillán 1950:48–49). The *curaca* had to go through the formality of asking his subjects to prepare the ground, sow, weed, irrigate, guard, harvest, and deliver the produce or, alternatively, to build a temple or repair an irrigation canal before they would help (recall also Facollapa's testimony, above, regarding Labamy) (see also AGI/J461, 866v and J458, 1778v-79). In response to the *curaca's* request, lesser lords brought their Indians to do his bidding, even if it meant leaving their homes and traveling some distance. One principal had to travel three leagues to obey his *cacique mayor* "para le obedescer y hazerlo que me quiere" (AGI/J458, 1801). Another had to travel two leagues to see his *cacique mayor* "para le obedescer y hacer lo que por el me fuere mandado . . ." (AGI/J458, 1801v).[17] In this case, the *curaca* probably asked Neptur to work the lands.

A lord could and did, however, also allow the subjects of another lord to work such parcels and other privately held lands[18] and resources in exchange for labor, manifested, at times, as part of the product.[19] Specific examples on the coast include the Indians of Sinto who used both the lands and waters of Lambayeque (AGI/J462, 1875v), and one *principal* of Lambayeque renting land to another *principal* of Lambayeque (ANCR/1586–1611, 24). In 1566, Doña María, widow of the late *curaca* of Collique, petitioned Dr. Cuenca to annul a rental agreement made without her knowledge and consent to a Spaniard

> para que yo las pueda alquilar a caçiques o a yndios myos o ajenos como hera my voluntad y no a españoles (AGI/J461, 1442v-43).

Likewise, Don Diego Çicha, *principal* and *segunda persona* of Sinto, asked Dr. Cuenca to recognize his rights to certain lands and irrigation water "para que las pueda senbrar y arrendar a yndios de otros rrepartimientos" (AGI/J461, 1531). Finally, the Indians of Chiclayo rented lands of those of Reque and Callanca after a severe flood in the 1570s. Although this example is late, it probably builds on the earlier tradition (BNP/A538, 1580).

In four of the five examples of one lord renting lands to subjects of another in the previous paragraph, the renters are specifically identified by community. In these cases, the rentals were between two parties that at the time of the conquest were part of the same *curacazgo*. Other early colonial documents contain information showing that the lord of one *curacazgo* also rented lands to individuals who had never been under his jurisdiction. In other words, *curacas* of the original pre-conquest *curacazgos* of Jayanca, Túcume, Sinto, Collique, Saña, and Pacasmayo rented lands, not only to their own subjects but also to the subjects of other *curacas*. The *curaca* Don Francisco of Jayanca, for example, rented land to subjects of his counterpart in Túcume, as well as to other lords. He said that he had

> ciertas chacaras y pedaços de tierras y rroças en que les senbrava y cogia maiz y trigo y otras legunbres en el d[ic]ho rrepartimiento las quales d[ic]has tierras heran suyas propias . . . y como tales suyas las labraua senbraua y arrendaua a los yndios de tucume y de otros rrepartimientos (AGI/J461, 1525).

Irrigation water was, as suggested above, also subject to such "rental" agreements. Theoretically, rights to land depended ultimately on the delegated authority of the Inca. Water rights on the coast, though also ultimately dependent on the Inca, were more immediately dependent on the lord that controlled the headwaters of the river or canal that ran through the coast to the sea. Augusto D. León Barandiarán in a book entitled *Mitos, leyendas y tradiciones lambayecanas* states that the *curaca* of Jayanca "bought" the ravine (*quebrada*) of Canchachalá and the water it channeled toward the coast from the lord of Penachí with "gifts" or "payments" of salt, chile peppers, and cloth before the Spanish conquest (1938? 141).[20] The manuscript from which his account was probably copied adds that these payments continued until the visit of Dr. Cuenca in 1566 (ACMS/ 1654–1765, 7–7v). De la Gama reports much the same relationship.

> El dicho valle de Jajanca es grande y muy poblado e de muchos maizales e conico (sic) y en tiempo de verano hay necesidad de agúa, e porque hay poca en el dicho valle tiénese noticia de xpianes e indios que Caratache, cacique de [don Lorenco de] Vlloa [the encomendero] de los Guanbos, viene por su tierra y nace en ellas el río del agua conque se riega Jayanca e que les estrecha el agua cuando quiere este cacique e no la deja venir sin rescate (Espinoza 1975:271).

Again, implied in the statement is the fact that subjects of a coastal lord worked land to grow pepper, corn, and cotton, and later weaved the cotton into cloth, to supply the highland lord his "*rescate*" (ransom). This example clearly establishes that a *curaca* received "tribute" from subjects of another in return for specific resource use and that the practice antedated the arrival of the Spanish.[21]

The practice of allowing "foreigners" or non-subjects to use land and water benefited both parties. One *curaca* or *principal* and his subjects got the use of resources they might not ordinarily control and the proprietary lord received part of the produce from the incoming users as rent.

This custom of working a portion of land in recognition of the suzerainty of a granting lord explains how a preconquest *curaca* of Jayanca could have his subjects working two days' distance away on land of Túcume in Guambos; i.e., how populations subject to one lord worked land in the jurisdiction of another. The principal could be extended to explain the existence of colonies described by Murra and others.

The published work of several scholars supports this type of relationship. Jürgen Golte suggests that highlanders migrated on a temporary basis to warm, low-lying valleys on the eastern flanks of the Andes where "allí trabajaban en las chacras pertenecientes a los pobladores de los valles, y recibían en cambio la mitad de la cosecha" (Golte 1968, as cited by Rostworowski 1977:186). A similar situation obtained in Ecuador, where the Pimampiro allowed "*indios extranjeros*" to work their coca land in return for part of the harvest. These foreigners were described as *feligreses*, implying visiting status, dependency or, subordination. This may be another example of a form of rental, "share cropping," Andean style (Rostworowski 1977:186).

Rostworowski reports in her interesting article on prehispanic coca plantations, mentioned above, that those of Quivi paid tribute in coca, corn, and other products to the lord of Collique. This suggests a rental agreement. Force might have been resorted to in cases where the labor was not forthcoming (1977:177–80).

The "share cropping" principle also could explain how subjects of the *curaca* of Lima possessed lands dispersed in the territories of neighboring *curacazgos* and vice versa (Rostworowski 1978:54–55); and how Cock could find references to boundaries of the lands of the Collaguas and yet find them living "a una relativa distancia del área que ellos declaran controlar, e insertas en tierras pertenecientes a otras cabeceras o pueblos" (Cock 1976:115).

The argument presented here negates, however, Cock's suggestion that "dentro de un territorio se hallen otros territorios pertenecientes a otros grupos humanos distintos y donde cada uno de estos grupos intrusos reconocen el territorio como propio y de su exclusivo dominio . . ." (115). The apparent contradiction may be explained by the definition of the term "belong(ed)." Indians claimed lands and waters "belonged" to them, even when paying tribute to another (recall the data on Chum and Colloççi above). Both "renters" (subjects) and "lords" claimed ownership. Both were correct, if we recall the distinction between *dominio directo* and *dominio útil.*

Spanish law recognized two aspects of ownership. *Dominio directo* gave the owner absolute control over the land, including the right to "sell" or "rent" the "use" of the land for a number of years or, in the sixteenth and seventeenth centuries, for a specified number of lives. Thus, an estate owner, for example, could "sell" the *dominio útil* or use of his estate to another for a specific number of years or the life of the renter and one or more heirs, while retaining for himself and his heirs the *dominio directo.* At the end of the rental period or upon the death of the last holder of the *dominio útil* specified in the original contract, the use reverted to the owner of the *dominio directo.* Ecclesiastical institutions, Indian communities, and individuals used this arrangement when they did not want to administer the property themselves. Unfortunately, too often in some cases, and especially when the owner of the *dominio directo* was an Indian community, the Spanish renter of the usufruct stopped paying rent after a number of years and the owner of the *dominio directo*, e.g., an Indian community, proved powerless to collect. Over time, some communities lost track of the original conditions of the "sale" and what began as usufruct became, in time, and, in effect, *dominio directo* (Ramírez 1975, especially chapter 7). Cock may have taken the Indians' statements that the land "belonged" to them too literally, without realizing the distinction.

This distinction between *dominio directo* and *dominio útil* was apparently inherent in the "resource sharing" in pre-conquest times (Dillehay 1979). At the level of empire, the Inca, at least in theory, alienated the *dominio útil* to the *curacas,* while retaining the *dominio directo.* For the use of the resources his subjects provided him labor. The same was true of the *curaca,* who sublet the resources to lesser lords and their subjects and the subjects of other lords, in return for tribute in the form of labor services, sometimes on specific pieces of land, physically manifested by the goods they produced. Apparently, the users kept possession, sometimes over several generations, as long as the "tribute" or "rent" was forthcoming (Santillán 1950:70–72).

This mechanism may also have been used by fishermen. The records of the visit of Dr. Cuenca show that scribes wrote petitions at the behest of Indian fishermen so that they could go to fish elsewhere "podían ir a pescar a otra tierra" (AGI/J458, 1298–98v). More than two centuries later, in 1812, fishermen from Mansiche (near Trujillo) fished from or off the beach of Monsefú, near modern Chiclayo. The fishermen of Monsefú, "como dueños de aquellos mares," exacted one *peso* each from the Indians of Mansiche for the "d[e]r[ech]o de piso."[22] Could this be a late colonial manifestation of resource sharing whose origins antedate 1532 (ART/I, AG, 21–III–1815)?

Conclusions

The lord's practice of renting lands both to members of his own community and to others suggests that a *señorío* defined as the relationship between ruler and subordinates did not necessarily have to correspond to the territorial jurisdiction of a lord as established for administrative purposes by the Inca. Thus, in trying to define a *curacazgo,* it is important to distinguish its "social frontiers," defined by allegiance of subjects to a lord, and its territorial base. Emically, the *curacazgo* was people. Over time and etically, the *curacazgo* became identified with a given land area. Because of the possibility of "renting" land from other lords, we can picture a basic incongruence between the lands occupied by a lord's people and his own territorial domain. Many lords had subjects living on another lord's land that still owed the former their primary allegiance. It appears that subjects delivered products to the proprietary lord of the resource in return for use, but did not consider themselves his subjects. The phrase "*territorialidad salpicada*" or "*discontinua,*" used elsewhere in this volume, seems, therefore, misleading, in that it suggests that one lord "owned," rather than used, land in the area of others. What we see are groups of the subjects of one lord scattered, with some using the lands or resources of another. If personal allegiance is the essential characteristic, then, a better phrase might be "*dominio salpicado.*" The use of the phrase "*territorialidad salpicada*" should not be abandoned, but restricted to land and other holdings of a lord that were worked by his own people.

After the Spanish conquest, a *curaca's* jurisdiction was concentrated in a core area by the combined effects of population decline, disarticulation caused by the establishment of the *encomienda*, *reducciones*, and limitations on travel and hospitality, which may explain why some lords lost control over subjects living at a distance (recall Labamy in Guambos in 1540). A careful diachronic reconstruction of these events remains to be done, but is essential to further understanding early Andean society.

The implications of the "share cropping" relationship outlined above suggest areas of further research. The first has to do with the self-sufficiency of a *curacazgo* on the subsistence level. The concept of "share cropping" or "resource sharing" may eventually be found to help explain the highland origin and procurement of large quantities of ore needed by the indigenous metal workers of the coast for luxury good production and consumption. Equally important is the recognition that a commoner, an "indio parque y mitayo," recognized multiple allegiances or obligations. Within his community or ethnic group, he worked for his *principal* and *curaca.* He, or his neighbors, also worked for extracommunity lords, directly or indirectly. Such relationships deserve additional exploration.

Finally, we cannot lose sight of the fact that the coastal *curacazgos* did not exist in a vacuum. They were dependent on the lords of the highlands for water, and, perhaps, in other ways. This suggests that the economy and society of the coast cannot be clearly understood without also studying the situation in the highlands and the contact and interaction between the people of the two regions.

NOTES

1. The analysis will focus on paramount lords or *curacas* (*caciques principales*) and lesser lords (*principales*), above the rank of *mandon* (local boss, overseer). I will identify individuals by their rank and status whenever possible. The generic term "lord(s)" will be reserved for statements that apply to local lords in general.

2. His findings correspond to the *distribución discontinua* of lands and pastures documented by Murra for the Inca empire in general (1980).

3. She also called attention to the same pattern for the central coast in work published in 1978. See especially p. 96.

4. That Cristóbal Ponce de Leon, the visitor, did not tour the entire Conchucos region might be due to the fact that he did not recognize the pattern.

5. For example, Waldemar Espinoza, who uses *tenencia diseminada* (or *salpicada*) to describe the northern highlands in 1979. (1981:96–97, 103). See also Caillavet 1983:17.

6. Understood as the area where the population of an ethnic group is densest. It need not necessarily be a compact, continuous unit of land.

7. The *cacique* of Jayanca in 1540 mentions another group of his subjects under a principal named Apaturruca in Pabur, in present-day Piura, who still served him. Pabur is included on a list of *tambos* dating from 1543, but the Indians who served there are not identified by *encomendero* or origin (BAH/Mata Linares, t. 82, 138v-40).

8. The town of Penachi in 1582 was about 30 leagues north of Saña (ANP/

R, 1. 3. c. 7, 1582, 121v). Brüning places the town east of the town of Motupe, "a falda de la cordillera occidental" (1922–23:III, 4). Santovelico became the site of the modern town of Olmos (León Barandiarán 1938?, 40; and Brüning II, 8). The subjects of Copis were also moved and resettled in the town of Olmos. Originally, the town had been located at a site about one league south of Cascajal and one to two leagues north of Olmos (Brüning II, 13).

9. It is not known whether or not he was referring here to the nine towns of *mitimaes* Sañas living in Cajamarca. Five of the nine towns are known: San Antonio de Cajamarca, San Andrés de Llapa, San Miguel de Catamos (Catamux), San Juan de Pingomarca, and Challaques (Charaques). The residents of these villages still served the coastal *curaca* with cloth as late as the 1560s (AGI/J458, 1749 and 1830; J460, 377v, and 385–85v; and J462, 1860v). Although they were described as *mitimaes* by the Spanish, they seem to be different from the coastal *mitimaes* mentioned in the 1540 visit to Cajamarca who were in the highlands to serve the Inca at the *tambos* (Espinoza 1967). My hunch is that the Spanish used the term *mitimaes* indiscriminantly to apply to Indians living at a distance from their home base, as the chroniclers suggest when they translate the term as "foreigner" (Poma de Ayala 1980:[172]).

10. Cuenca thought all the subjects of one lord should live under his close supervision. He ordered, therefore, that all Indians return to their birthplace (ART/CoJ, 29–III–1558).

11. This is also the case in the central Andes. See Rostworowski 1977:33–34.

12. Supporting this are several petitions from lords enumerating by name the various pieces of their lands (See, for example, AGI/J461, 1515–15v). One lord states he had eleven separate pieces (AGI/J461, 1556).

13. In reality, effective control and use probably never was taken away from the users.

14. In 1566, Dr. Cuenca ordered a stop to the practice of "paying rent" for the use of resources, specifically water and land (Rostworowski 1975:142 for the Ordenanzas of Dr. Cuenca).

15. Irrigation water, Indians told early Spaniards, "belonged" to the *curacas,* too. Several explained to Dr. Cuenca that if they opened a ditch and cleaned and maintained the canal, the products harvested from lands irrigated with the water, and by extension, the land itself, were theirs (AGI/J461, 1395v). See also Netherly 1984; and Rostworowski 1977:82 for the Chillón and 1978:174 for Canta).

16. It follows that the reverse is also true. Without payment in the form of labor service, the subjects of one lord could not use the lands of another. For example, see Rostworowski 1978:58.

17. Both Indians stated that because they lived on an "*arenal*" they did not have good lands nearby. They had to plant on lands far from their homes (AGI/J458, 1801–01v).

18. Lords had lands that were "propios distintos y separado(s) al principalato" (ANP/DI, 1. 6, c. 122, 1649, 28v). See also AGI/J461, 1525.

19. It is not known who initiated contact: the lord looking for labor or

the lord seeking resources. Colonial sources indicate that the *curaca* had to request the labor of his own subjects. Manuscripts suggest that there was growing competition for subjects among the lords. They may have used certain resources as an incentive to persuade subjects of one lord to shift allegiance and work for them. Alternatively, one lord might have sought out access to resources, promising labor in exchange (see note 17). See also, in this volume, Murra's discussion of the changing allegiance of Indians who lived detached at a great distance from their core community for long periods of time.

20. A copy of the original document from which León Barandiarán probably copied the account, almost verbatim, exists in the private archives of the late don Augusto Castillo Muro Sime, giving the "legend" a basis in fact. Archivo Castillo Muro Sime (ACMS), 1654–1765, especially 7–7v. The same story appears in the proceedings of a court case in the ANP/RA, 1. 27, c. 95, 1610, 141 and Brüning, 1922–23, Facsiculo III, 59.

21. Could not the "rescates y trueques" between the Canteños and Colli, described by Rostworowski, also be explained by this mechanism? (1977: 26–27). Jürgen Golte also provides linguistic evidence for this type of relationship. In a discussion, subtitled "Arimsa o trabajo al partir," he defines several Quechua terms that refer to "el que siembra en tierra ajena"; "dar a sembrar o dejar sembrar"; and "sembrar para sí en tierras ajenas" (1976: 493). See also p. 494 on terms referring to "intercambio de trabajo por comida."

22. Indian fishermen from Mansiche and Huanchaco (near Trujillo) protested the payment, claiming that they had always traveled along the coast without hindrance (*embarase*) and that the sea was *comun*. We know that this was not true before 1566 when Dr. Cuenca upheld the right of Indians to claim specific beaches as their own (AGI/J461, 1528v–29) and, thus probably, the right to "rent" them. Nevertheless, the Spanish authorities supported the Trujillanos and informed the fishermen of Monsefú to stop collecting the duties (ART/I, AG, 21–III–1815).

MANUSCRIPT ABBREVIATIONS

AGI	Archivo General de las Indias	
	J	Justicia
	AL	Audiencia de Lima
ANCR	Archivo Notarial Carlos Rivadeneira	
ANP	Archivo Nacional del Perú	
	RA	Real Audiencia
	DI	Derecho Indígena
ART	Archivo Regional de Trujillo	
	CoJ	Corregimiento Juez de Comisión
	CoR	Corregimiento Residencia
	CoC	Corregimiento Compulsa

	I, AG	Intendencia, Asuntos de Gobierno
	IC	Intendencia Compulsa
BAH		Biblioteca de la Real Academia de Historia
BNP		Biblioteca Nacional del Perú
CVU		Colección Vargas Ugarte
OCI		Oficina de Comunidades Indígenas, Lima

REFERENCES CITED

Brüning, Enrique
1922–23 Estudios Monográficos del Departamento de Lambayeque, Chiclayo.

Caillavet, Chantal
1983 Toponimia histórica, arqueológia y formas prehispánicas de agricultura en la región de Otavalo-Ecuador. Bulletin de l'Institut Français d' Etudes Andines 12(3–4):1–21.

Cock C., Guillermo
1976 Los kurakas de los Collaguas: Poder político y poder económico. Historia y cultura 10:95–118.

Cook, Noble David
1976 La visita de los Conchucos por Cristóbal Ponce de León, 1543. Historia y cultura 10:23–45.

Dillehay, Tom
1979 Pre-hispanic Resource Sharing in the Central Andes. Science 204: 24–31.

Espinoza Soriano, Waldemar
1967 El primer informe etnológico sobre Cajamarca (1540). Revista Peruana de Cultura 11–12:1–37.
1975 El valle de Jayanca y el Reino de los Mochica siglos XV y XVI. Bulletin de l'Institut Français d'Etudes Andines 4 (3–4):243–74.
1981 El fundamento territorial del ayllu serrano. Siglos XV y XVI. Etnohistoria y antropología andina. Amalia Castelli et al., comps., pp. 93–130. Lima.

Golte, Jürgen
1976 El trabajo y la distribución de bienes en el runa simi del siglo XVI. Atti del XL Congresso Internazionale degli Americanisti (1972), Genova, 1976, 489–505.

Jiménez de la Espada, Marcos, ed.
1881 Relaciones geográficas de Indias. 4 vols. Madrid: Editorial Atlas.

León Barandiarán, Augusto D.
1938? Mitos, leyendas y tradiciones lambayecanas. n.p. [Lima?], n.d. [1938?]

Loredo, Rafael
1958 Los repartos. Lima.

Martínez, Gabriel

1981 Espacio Lupaqa: Algunas hipótesis de trabajo. Etnohistoria y antropología andina. Amalia Castelli et al., comps., pp. 263–80. Lima.

Murúa, Fray Martín de

1946 Historia del origen y genealogía real de los reyes Incas del Perú [1590], Madrid.

Murra, John V.

[1972] 1975 El control vertical de un máximo de pisos ecológicos en la economía de las sociedades andinas. Formaciones económicas y políticas del mundo Andino. pp. 59–115. Lima.

1980 Derechos a las tierras en el Tawantinsuyu. Revista de la Universidad Complutense (Madrid) 28(117):273–87.

Netherly, Patricia J.

1984 The Management of Late Andean Irrigation Systems on the North Coast of Peru. American Antiquity 49(2):227–54.

Poma de Ayala, Felipe Guamán

1980 Nueva Corónica y Buen Gobierno. México: Siglo Veintiuno.

Ramírez [-Horton], Susan E.

1978 Chérrepe en 1572: Un análisis de la visita general del Virrey Francisco de Toledo. Historia y cultura 11:79–121.

1981 La organización económica de la costa norte: Un análisis preliminar del período prehispánico tardío. Etnohistoria y antropología andina. Amalia Castelli et al., comps., pp. 281–97. Lima.

1985 Provincial Patriarchs: Land Tenure and the Economics of Power in Colonial Peru. Albuquerque: University of New Mexico Press.

Rowe, John H.

1948 The Kingdom of Chimor. Acta Americana 6 (1–2):26–59.

Rostworowski de Diez Canseco, María

1961 Curacas y sucesiones: Costa Norte. Lima: Libreria Imp. Minerva.

1975 Algunos comentarios hechos a las Ordenanzas del doctor Cuenca. Historia y cultura 9:119–54.

1977 Etnía y sociedad. Lima: Instituto de Estudios Peruanos.

1978 Señoríos indígenas de Lima y Canta. Lima: Instituto de Estudios Peruanos.

Santillán, Fernando de Abad

1950 Relación del orígen, descendencia, política y gobierno de los Incas. *In* Tres relaciones peruanas. Asunción: Editorial Guarania.

19

Coast-Highland Interrelationships and Ethnic Groups in Northern Peru (500 B.C.–A.D.1980)

Richard P. Schaedel

What follows is an overview of "state of the art" summation of the development of ethnic groups and their interrelations in Northern Peru within the contextual framework of the ecological zonation and possible climatological modifications of that zonation from the Late Formative to the present. The first part deals with the period of the emerging ethnic groups (*etnías*), which *a grosso modo* corresponds to the so-called Late Formative period (beginning at 500 B.C.), follows with a conjectural reconstruction of ethnic groups "in place" by Early Intermediate and continues to the period between the Middle Horizon and Spanish contact when merging and subordination of ethnic groups became a significant dynamic.

The actual genesis of the *etnías* from their hypothesized roots in the beginnings of sedentarism, going back at least to 3,000 B.C., is not well enough documented to be treated within the theoretical frameworks that inform the subject matter of this symposium. The operational definition of the *etnía* that I use is: a supra-community aggregation with a range of societal complexity that corresponds to the *señorío* (Chiefdom) level polities, having the cultural particularities that lead to their recognition as distinct from others by state administrators of the Inca and Spanish viceroyalty and therefore as significant basic subdivisions in their respective administrative hierarchies.

Above the "cellular" *etnía* there is an ethnic aggregate, which in English might be termed "people," and which may or may not correspond to what Murra (1972) terms *unidades multi-etnicas*, used in the ecological complementarity model. It is not possible at this "state of the art" to consistently identify the emergence of this kind of entity from the archaeological data, although it roughly seems to correspond to the maximum end of the aggregation-and-disaggregation of chiefdoms (*señoríos*) that one can roughly describe for the North Coast between 500 B.C. and A.D. 750. Unfortunately some archaeologists have prematurely labeled such maximal aggregations as "states," a nomenclature which would foreclose the possibility of including them within a discussion of ethnic groups interrelated on the principles of ecological complementarity (Murra 1981: 41). For the purposes of this presentation, I shall refer to such large entities as "*macro-etnias*," and I understand them to be of a scale of socio-economic complexity comparable to Murra's multi-ethnic Lupaca.

In this overview we shall use the combined information from archaeology, linguistics, and history/ethnohistory to reconstruct a hypothetical parnorama of ethnic diversity and the interaction between North Coast and Highland peoples through time.

500 B.C.–A.D. *750: The Etnías Reach Maturity*

From Late Formative times to the advent of the Middle Horizon the archaeological picture is very incomplete, when we consider the total cultivable area that was being reduced to a pattern of food-producing procurement systems during this time span. It ranges from the reasonably well-documented territoriality of the Moche *macro-etnía* (Leche to Nepeña valleys along the coast up to ca. 1,000 m above sea level), to practically no information on any adjacent cis-Andean zones in the Pacific watershed behind each of the valleys. Very weak documentation exists for the Callejón de Huaylas and Huamachuco with *terra incognita* for the Highland between Cabana and Huamachuco; reasonably good recent data on the Cajamarca-Pacopampa North Highland sector, and very weak data for the Far North Coast and Highlands. To obtain a picture of the hypothetical ethnic diversity and coast/highland interrelationships for this period of ethnic emergence, one must summarize from this patchwork quilt of archaeological evidence. The following problematical construct emerges:

In Late Formative times littoral-agricultural ethnic groups such as the Gallinazó in the Virú Valley (Bennett 1950) occupied gradually the domains of the valley from sea level to 1,000 meters with a kind of supra-community polity by 200 B.C. The cultural characteristics of these archaeological cultures reflect a few technological commonalities that suggested to Bennett (1948) the possibility of referring to the Late Formative cultures as participating in the "Negative Horizon." Gallinazo-like sites have been found in coastal valleys from Tumbez to the Santa (Doering 1957; Izumi and Terada 1966). They all seem to have practiced a littoral-agricultural exploitation of niches (what Onuki [1983; in this volume] calls maritime *yunga*) and apparently had their nucleus in the valley plain in the B.C. period, shifting to the valley neck in some valleys by the beginning of Early Intermediate.[1]

There is a strong likelihood that *etnías* of comparable scale occupied the *chaupiyunga* above and behind these coastal groups and probably extending up to the Pacific watershed, but the evidence for these presumed autonomous emerging *etnías* is only based upon sporadic surface reconnaissance of the ecological niche-cluster in the upper Santa, Virú, Moche, Chicama, Jequetepeque, and Zaña valleys together with scarce "intrusive" finds of sherds, and floral and faunal remains in coastal sites of specimens indigenous to higher climes.[2]

The delimiting of the emerging highland *etnías* in the cluster of vertically adjacent niches in the intermontane basins has been recently undertaken by the Japanese missions, the reports of which present us with a picture of the aggregation of the pastoralists with the agriculturalists already by Late Formative times (M. Shimada 1982; Terada and Onuki 1982). We assume from this bi-ethnic conjuncture that they developed some kind of intra-ethnic division of labor for the later periods probably not unlikc what the fishermen and the coastal cultivators must have had (Julien 1980). For neither highland nor coastal *etnía* of Late Formative or Early Intermediate times do we have sufficient cultural data to indicate the nature of the ethnic subdivision. The very fact that *etnías* such as the Cajamarca and Moche folk were subdivided into sub-ethnic groups corresponding to different ecological niches is a datum that comes from the ethnohistorical research of Rostworowski de Diez Canseco (1975) and the interpretation of the archaeological material by the Japanese mission to validate an early manifestation of this datum in Cajamarca represents one of the first attempts by archaeologists of the Andes to cope with ethnic components.

Although we have only a very proximate model for postulating an emerging *macro-etnía* for Cajamarca by Middle Horizon that might have encompassed the Cajabamba area, we have somewhat more evidence for a *macro-etnía* in Huamachuco, encompassing Santiago de Chuco (McCown 1945; Pineda, n.d.; Schaedel 1952; Terada and Onuki 1982; Thatcher 1975). For the area from the headwaters of the Tablachaca to the southern end of the Callejón de Huaylas, which corresponds to the distribution of Recuay ceramics and stone sculpture, a highly conjectural guess is that there are two emerging *macro-etnías* for what has been labeled archaeologically Recuay or Huaylas.

In the case of Huamachuco it is likely that from the Formative through at least the Early Intermediate periods, there were cis-Andean autonomous *etnías* occupying the *chaupiyunga* to the headwaters of the

Chicama, Moche, and Virú valleys located between the Huamachuco *etnía* and the Moche (Topic and Topic 1982a, 1982b, 1983, personal communication; Zaki 1978; Krzanowski 1977; Krzanowski and Szeminski 1978; and others). In the Recuay archaeological area immediately to the south, there are indications that this same "buffer zone" for autonomous cis-Andean *etnías* was confined to smaller "pockets" at the headwaters of the Nepeña and Casma, which—if they allowed for the formation of small autonomous *etnías* in the earliest periods—by Late Formative times, had been joined to the nuclear area of the Northern Callejón de Huaylas (which we might designate Pashash) constituted by the large "pocket" of the Tablachaca tributary of the Santa. Another branch of Recuay-like culture with a higher pastoral component constituted the Southern Callejón de Huaylas *macro-etnía* (which we could designate Huaylas) with its nucleus in the upper southern Santa Valley. In both cases, the territoriality and ecological niche range of the *macro-etnías,* especially in the eastern slopes of the Cordillera Blanca remains to be established.[3] (See Fig. 191.)

My conjecture at this point is of two large *señoríos*: one at the northern end of the Callejón de Huaylas with nuclear settlements in the Pacific watershed and without much reliance on the *puna* niche; and a second at the southern end of the Callejón de Huaylas with considerable reliance on the *puna* niche (Smith 1978). Both *señoríos* would have an extension of their territorialities on the eastern slopes of the Cordillera Blanca. The indications from archaeological evidence on the North and Central Coast regions are that both *macro-etnías* had expanding relationships with coastal cultures. They seemed to have had relationships of mutual co-existence with each other and with what appear to have been relatively autonomous cis-Andean *etnías* in such pockets as Huambo and Aija in the extreme southern margin of Northern Peru (Schaedel 1952).

Summing up the data on multiple niche exploitation for highland *etnías*, scattered and inadequate as they are, we would tend to affirm Onuki's generalization (Onuki in this volume) for the Cajamarca *etnía* as obtaining for the Huamachuco *etnía;* namely that *puna*, *quechua*, and highland (i.e., eastern slopes) *yunga* niches were simultaneously exploited from highland nuclei, but that this limited ecological complementarity did not include the maritime *chaupiyungas*, or maritime *yunga*. When we examine the case for the hypothesized *macro-etnías* of Pashash and Huaylas, however, the picture is one of a much feebler autonomous maritime *yunga* cultural presence in the lower and upper Nepeña and Casma (and conceivably one could extend this to the southern bank of the Santa). The inability of the

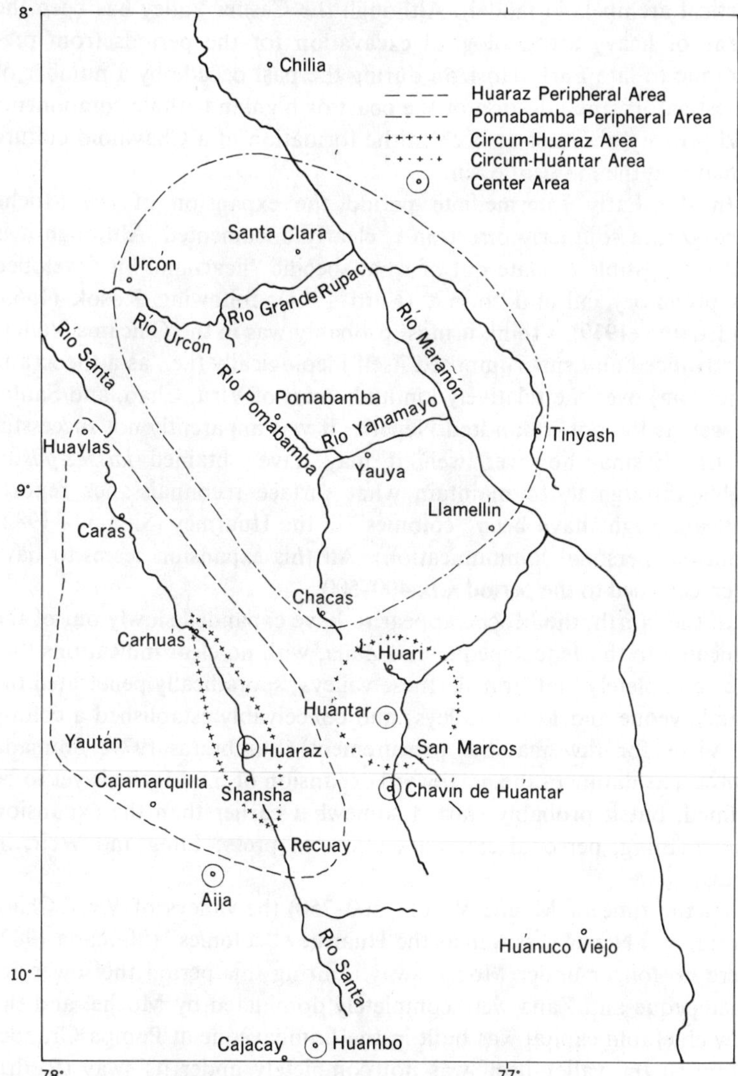

Fig. 19.1 Stone Sculpture Areas of the North Highlands. (After American Geographic Society 1:1000000 map)

archaeologists to reconstruct a coherent sequence between the Early Horizon, and the Early Intermediate (in the Nepeña; Proulx 1973) and the Middle Horizon (in the Casma; Collier 1962; Fung 1977) may reflect inflexibility in their growth models to detect the presence of highland "colonies" in these valleys (assuming they were to use a vertical archipelago model). Although the Casma Valley has been the scene of heavy archaeological excavation for the periods from preceramic to late Early Horizon during the past decade by a number of investigators, the question of the coast or highland ethnic components and priority of either or both in the formation of a Chavinoid culture remains at the moment open.

In the Early Intermediate period the expansion of the Moche *señorío* in a southerly direction is clearly documented. Although it is not yet possible to state out of what specific "heartland" it developed its predatory cultural format (Ford 1974), following Kosok (1965) and Larco (1939), I think it most probably was in the Chicama Valley. It advanced and super-imposed itself ideologically (i.e., as a theocratic chiefdom) over the relatively kindred *etnías* of Virú, Chao, and Santa, as well as the not-so-kindred Nepeña. It was apparently not successful in the Casma, however well it may have obtained *laissez-passer* rights through it, to maintain what surface reconnaissance reports indicate might have been "colonies" in the Huarmey (Shimada 1982; Bonavia, personal communication). All this expansion seems to have been confined to the period A.D. 400–500.

In the North, the Moche appear to have expanded slowly out of the Chicama to the Jequetepeque and Zaña, with no clear indications that they completely "integrated" these valleys; sporadically penetrated the Lambayeque and Leche valleys; and conceivably established a colony in Vicús for raw material procurement (Lumbreras 1979; Shimada 1982). The dating of the northward expansion of the Moche is yet to be refined, but it probably started somewhat earlier than the expansion south (Eling, personal communication, in press; Eling and Weir, in press).

By the time of Moche V (A.D. 500–750) the valleys of Virú, Chao, Santa, and Nepeña, as well as the Huarmey "colonies" (Shimada 1982) were no longer under Moche sway. During this period the lower Jequetepeque and Zaña were completely dominated by Moche, and the new chiefdom capital was built in the Lambayeque at Pampa Grande, although the valley itself was not completely under its sway (Rodriguez 1967; Schaedel 1951, n.d. a; Shimada 1978, 1982, n.d.). One can hypothesize the coexistence in the valley of one or more *micro-etnías* of the Gallinazo type or smaller, occupying significant parts of the valley plain in both the Lambayeque and Leche.

The Far North Coast (between Olmos and Tumbez) was the hearth of one or more *etnías* whose presence in Formative and Early Intermediate times is only barely outlined. Their hinterland neighbors are even less defined. Almost twenty years after Lothrop's (1948) summary article on the archaeology of the Far North Coast, we are not much better off (Lanning 1963) in suggesting that the region was occupied by Late Formative times by a maritime-agricultural-littoral society—more dispersed, but otherwise not unlike the Gallinazo with a minimum threshold of socio-political organization, in which Moche "colonies" were interspersed. We can do no more than speculate on the number and territoriality of the *etnías* in the cis-Andean area and the inter-montane habitats north of Cajamarca (Gaceta 1982). Fung (1975) provides a minimal basis for a possible ethnic bond in Formative times between Pacopampa (the area of the protohistoric Huambos) and Piura (the protohistoric Tallanes).

Summary (Coast and Highland 500 B.C.–A.D. *750)*

Let us examine the patchwork quilt of ethnic relations before the Middle Horizon in terms of the ecological complementarity model. In the area of Moche influence, the picture is one of three types of autonomous chiefdoms: the littoral-agricultural; the cis-Andean agro-pastoral;[4] and the inter-montane agro-pastoral. They seem to have been in relatively peaceful co-existence. That there was more than a seasonal extra-ethnic system of exchange seems unlikely. In terms of the movement of products (and we are mostly talking about raw materials) the process seems to have been manipulated by the highlanders.

The actual incidences of processed highland products on the coast are extremely scarce (the Recuay textile in a Gallinazo grave is a typical example [Bennett 1939:Fig. 15a: 57, 72–74]) and consist mostly of pottery. Processed coastal material in highland contexts to my knowledge have not been found. The representation of highland motives during this period occurs only in the Cerro Culebra site in the lower Chillón (Stumer 1954:228). Conversely, what Kroeber called the realistic, life-like sculptured head tenons found at Marca Huamachuco and Cabana (Kroeber 1950; Schaedel 1952) are the only examples of the diffusion of coastal (in this case Moche) motives on highland architecturally associated artifacts. In both instances it would appear that the "exchange" has to do with elements of a belief system of an alien group that was found congenial rather than the spread of a total corpus of beliefs.

The only sector where there exists the possibility of demonstrating an archipelago, encompassing Highland (including *puna* niches), cis-Andean, and coastal macro-niches is in the area between the Nepeña and Huarmey valleys with their corresponding hinterlands, perhaps including the eastern slope pockets of the Cordillera Blanca.[5] So far, confirmatory evidence is sparse and equivocal.

The Middle Horizon

The position of relatively peaceful extra-ethnic exchange proposed for the period 500 B.C.–A.D. 750 changes abruptly with the southern group of north coast valleys at about A.D. 500 when these valleys became part of a new system of land exploitation, reflected in the archaeological documentation by field systems and the restructuring of the earlier contour canal systems, and also represented by the massive shift in public building types from ceremonial mound clusters to secular, administrative structures. The inspiration for this shift can be identified as exogenous—not only in the lack of appropriate antecedent forms for the secular constructions, but in what appears to be a sudden ideological change in which the iconography of finely made artifacts is drastically altered by designs, motifs, and color combinations that have their antecedents in the Huari (and ultimately Tiahuanacoid) styles of the southern highlands as well as Recuay. However, together with settlement pattern evidence, data from tracing the complex skein of Huari iconography through the filters of Pachacamac, Chimu-Capac, and other Central Coast "nodes" of the Huari hegemony (Menzel 1969, 1979; Stumer 1956) that affected the southern valley shift from A.D. 500–750, indicates movement into these valleys of a combination of influences whose ultimate source is the immediate and South Highlands.

That this movement was not strictly consensual (i.e., mercantile, military, or ideological) is obvious not only from the shift in settlement pattern, but also in land exploitation techniques. I have suggested elsewhere (Schaedel 1966a, 1966b, 1978) that this represents a state-sponsored takeover, much as the Inca conquest did with, perhaps, the "new lands" technique being applied in the valleys to extract a state surplus going elsewhere (Schaedel, n.d.a, n.d.b).

In the northern valleys, this 250-year time span was dedicated to the consolidation of the Jequetepeque and Zaña valleys under the Moche multi-valley chiefdom with a new capital near its northern boundaries in Pampa Grande. After 750, in the valleys from Moche through Zaña, a similar pattern can be established to that for the southern valleys in terms of changes in settlement pattern and land exploitation techniques. Here, however, the iconographic fossil indicators are more cryptic, since the "filters" for Huari or Tiahuanaco-derived iconography have not only been augmented by "Middle Horizon" polities between the Casma and the Moche, but both Recuay and particularly Cajamarca appear as vectors of Huari influence, leading to the hypothesis that these valleys were finally overrun by a Huari-Recuay-Cajamarca confederation that had its proximal base in the Cajamarca region (Schaedel; n.d.c).[6]

In the Lambayeque and Leche valleys, the evidence is less clear that any forceful highland invasion took place. Shimada's interpretation (1982, 1983, in this volume; Shimada et al. 1981) of the Leche-Cajarmarca presence makes it likely that a restructuring of previous chiefdom-type relationships took place with a greater participation of the highland *etnías*. However long or short-lived the period of highland inspired dominance of the several North Coast valleys lasted, the balance of coastal autonomy in all of them was restored by 1300, preceded by the appearance of the first truly contiguous territorial coastal states with their capitals in Purgatorio (Kosok 1959; Shimada 1983, and in this volume) and Chan Chan.

Late Intermediate and Late Horizon (1200–1530)

We move now into the Late Intermediate period when much of the ethnohistoric data can be said to be relevant.[7] In terms of artifact distribution, the evidence of highland influence on the coast is much reduced from that of the Middle Horizon. Although some scant evidence of coastal influence in the highlands has been noted for the Middle Horizon (Shimada 1982) even this trickle has been hardly detected for the subsequent periods (Krzanowski 1977) except for undocumented cases of Chimu pottery in private collections from Cajamarca.[8] In all justice it must be remarked that except for Marca Huamachuco, there is no really major site for the North Highlands which has been excavated covering this period.

What appears to have happened with the growth of the Chimu state on the coast is that it interceded the type of exchange that might have been established during the late Middle Horizon. Shimada (1982, 1983, and in this volume) refers to a fairly good documentation for the Leche area in interaction with Cajamarca *etnías* probably based upon both raw material and product exchange. A preliminary interpretation of the combined architectural and surface collections evidence for post-Moche occupation of the North Coast valleys from Lambayeque to Casma induces me to propose that some such similar pattern of coast-highland exchange characterized most of the region between 1000–1200 (the late Middle Horizon); and that this pattern was largely interceded by the Chimu expansion out of the Moche Valley between 1250 and 1475.

The exchange pattern under Chimu state control is alluded to in one cloudy reference in Calancha (1638:Book III, Chap. II) which refers to the annual enfranchisement of coastal *rescatistas* for the procurement of desired highland products. That Chimu state policy tried to control, or at least canalize what were probably highland inspired and manned trading patterns with coastal partners or entrepots at the village and supra-village level, is the interpretation that we would also give to remains of a series of "Maginot" walls crossing the upper parts of the valleys, most obvious in the Chicama (Watson 1980) and Jequetepeque.

Another type of late prehistoric coast-highland interrelationship was first pointed out by Brüning (1922) who documented the existence of small highland *etnía* water rights to sources from which coastal *etnías* were dependent, between the *señoríos* of Penachi and Jayanca. Netherly (1977) drew attention to this case over fifty years later, and Rostworowski de Diez Canseco (1976, 1981, in this volume; Ramírez, in this volume) has recently discovered several other cases where cis-Andean highland *etnías* and coastal *etnías* had relationships of "exchange' 'of water rights for "tribute" that were not interdicted by the coastal *etnía's* incorporation into the Chimu state.

Incidentally, these references to *señoríos* (or *etnías*) like Jayanca, Pacora, etc., of the type Netherly (1977) calls "local-level lords," (or "lordships") refer to territorial units during the Late Intermediate period which the archaeologists have had difficulty in disaggregating from the Chimu state (some progress in this direction may be anticipated in the work recently completed by Donnan in Chotuna, the "capital" of the Lambayeque "lordship"). Hence we would have to say that the ethnic label Chimu represents some kind of *macro-etnía* for archaeological purposes as did Moche when used as an ethnic label for the Early Intermediate period. It is to be understood that all the combined *etnías* shared the commonality of an ecologically homogenous heartland.

There is no clearcut indication that the Incas relied upon these traditional "lordship" distinctions in balkanizing the Kingdom of Chimor. We do not yet know precisely how it was subdivided into Inca provinces (Ramirez, in this volume). Based upon eyewitness accounts there seems to be a basis for hypothesizing seven provinces south of Olmos: Motupe, Jayanca, Túcume, Lambayeque, Cinto, and Collique (Netherly 1984; Ramirez, in this volume). Brüning (1918) showed there was an archaeological basis for the last two settlements. For the lower south bank of the Lambayeque River and the Zaña Valley, there were probably no less than two (Rostworowski 1961). The Jequetepeque probably constituted one with its capital on the north bank. Chicama, Moche, and Virú apparently were a single province. South of the Virú, there are no indications of the Inca provincializing yardsticks. From Olmos north, the eyewitness accounts are unclear, but with the possible exception of Pohechos, there seems to have been only one province for the Piura area and one for Tumbez.

Moving from the eyewitness accounts to the sixteenth century ethnohistoric sources on North Coast domains we are obliged to add yet another filter to our interpretative lens, namely the vision of Colonial administrators regarding indigenous jurisdictional rights. The evidence of *encomienda* grants (Appendix)—a copy of one of which John Murra sent to me recently, is of this order.[9] In this document Chimu heartland territories are combined with parts of the northern Callejón de Huaylas, conceivably referring to a pre-existent territoriality relation between the ethnic Chimu and highland counterparts—in Conchucos—that I presume Murra would interpret as highland "colonies" in a prospective archipelago model. I have not yet seen enough *encomienda* documents to be able to evaluate their own internal consistencies and reliability in accepting as fact the inferred ethnic information upon which they are based.

While this document represents the only example of coastal claims to highland territoriality in the late prehispanic periods, much of the ethnohistoric data refers to highland *etnías,* particularly between Huamachuco and Cajamarca with land rights in close proximity to or frankly well within what would be ecologically coastal domains. As Netherly (1977) pointed out, some of these have been recently reactivated, thanks to the opportunities offered by the Agrarian Reform.

I interpret this presumed extension of highland territoriality into what was considered the coastal ecological area as a post-Middle Horizon development (Rostworowski, Ramirez, and Shimada in this volume) in which the Cajamarca and possibly Huamachuco *macro-etnías* absorbed or incorporated the cis-Andean *etnías* in the upper Moche, Chicama, Jequepeteque, and possibly Zaña valleys. This did not occur further north.[10]

For the highland areas north and south of Cajamarca the ethnic territorialities remain to be defined from all the lines of evidence. Espinoza Soriano has been publishing documents covering some of this region which require consolidation and verification in the field (1962, 1969–70, 1970, 1973a, 1973b, 1974a, 1974b, 1977, 1978a, 1978b). They should then be checked with the eyewitness accounts of the Inca provinces and *tambo* lists to provide some viable conjectural model with which future archaeological work in the Far North Highlands can be integrated. From the references to the Huambos *etnía* in this symposium we have an illustration of this problem (Ramirez, in this volume; Rostworowski, in this volume).

The Colonial and Republican Periods

As one moves from the sixteenth century documentation into later periods, it is more difficult to follow the destinies of specific *etnías,* but one can glean data to indicate movements of coast and highland peoples. Sixteenth century information on the Santa Valley, for example, indicates that the coastal part of the valley was almost completely depopulated and that the work force was drawn from highland *etnías* (Schaedel 1981). Miniscule information on the Nepeña indicates that it had a basically coastal population with a coastal *cacique* in the late sixteenth century, but that the Casma was very lightly populated.

The valleys north of the Zaña all seem to have experienced an otherwise "typical" coastal population decline like the Nepeña; some more, some less—with little evidence of highland migration into them (Schaedel 1981). Chepen, for example, that was later to become a reception area for sierra migrants, by the mid-eighteenth century was almost depopulated (Gonzalez n.d.). The far northern valleys (north of Olmos) may well have suffered less of a population decline (as the valleys north of Chicama to Motupe experienced less population decline than those further south), but there is still a lack of studies to show this (Cook 1982). Our preliminary conclusion would have to be that between the sixteenth and the end of the eighteenth century no permanent migratory trends from coast to sierra or vice versa took place except for the Casma and Santa. This does not mean that the traditional routes of exchange between the two zones were not maintained.

Rodriguez Suy Suy (1973), on the basis of a comprehensive questionnaire survey, covering the entire northern region, including the eastern slopes of the Andes, tried to reconstruct the traditional routes of exchange between the coast, highland, and eastern slopes to be able to establish points of juncture in prehispanic times. Although this path network reflects a wide range of connections, it neither supports nor denies the pattern of vertical or ecological complementarity as opposed to the model of sierra-born traffic to coastal entrepots that we have suggested was the typical pattern for non-state exchanges.

Late nineteenth century sources indicate a slow but steady increment of highland migration along the entire stretch of North Coast valleys, although much of this was accomplished by the system of *enganche* and corresponded to the commercialization of the sugar-*haciendas* on the North Coast. Data from recent (post-1940) ethnography on the coast (Gillin 1947; Holmberg 1950; Ghersi 1961; Sabogal 1967, 1976) supports a picture of substantially augmented post-1950 migration (in this case voluntary migratory infiltration) from the Cajamarca, Huamachuco, and Huaylas *etnías* to the valleys from Chicama to Chao. My own ethnographic survey data from 1975 indicates that this pattern can be extended to the Leche in the north. Muelle's (personal communication) brief study of the villa de Santa indicated most of the valley population was ethnically Huaylas derived. Millones (personal communication), in his 1975–76 studies in Casma found that it had almost entirely lost its coastal population. Scattered ethnographic data (assembled by Rodriguez Suy Suy and myself) from the Jequetepeque and Moche indicate a regular pattern of small highland groups from the Cajamarca (mostly cis-Andean) region coming to the coast to collect *cal* from seashells and perhaps salted fish in exchange for pottery and services (e.g., rice harvest). This is similar to the situation described by Masuda (in this volume) for the south where *cochayuyo* was the product collected.[11]

These scattered ethnographic references to migrant highland populations in coastal regions add little to "beefing up" a panorama of what remains of the time-of-conquest highland *etnías*. Except for Stein's (1961) monograph on Hualcan, we are almost entirely lacking in North Highland ethnography. What information we have can only serve to block out recent trends, which may reflect a migratory vs. an exchange movement of highlanders to the coast. Some of this may reflect a process similar to the apparent massive highland movement to the coast in the Middle Horizon.

The Evidence from Linguistics

Linguistic data are still sparse, uneven, and not thoroughly analyzed for the North (Rostworowski in this volume). With these provisos we introduce it to indicate how it supports the notion of relatively fixed *etnías*, exchanging mainly by means of highland based traders or caravans. The presence of the Culli language in the cis-Andean sector of the valleys between the Chicama and the Santa, with possibly some speakers in the inter-montane region (Rivet 1949; Loukotka 1968;

Tovar 1961), argues for relatively long-term ethnic autonomy for the cis-Andean *etnías*, since it is bounded in the highlands both to the north and south by Quechua speech communities (Fig. 19.2). If ultimately related to Quechua, the likelihood is that separation was as early or more early than Quechua from Aymara, bringing its period of presumed diversion from an Ur-Quechua back into the preceramic. It appears even less related to Muchik or the other coastal languages.

Other linguistic data are very weak.[12] For the coastal area south of Virú we are not certain what language was spoken, except for Toribio Mogrovejo's ([1593]1920) brief reference that Muchik was spoken as far south as Huarmey. Probably Quechua was spoken in the entire inter-montane area, but other languages such as Hibito and Cholon may have been spoken on the eastern slopes.

Muchik, while seemingly spoken in the coastal parts of all valleys between Virú and Motupe, had a series of islands or enclaves in the cis-Andean, intermontane valleys, and to the east. Carrera ([1644]1939) who gave this datum, attributed this dispersion to Inca-sponsored *mitimaes*—but we do not have any basis for confirming that this was the case. The enclaves have all disappeared—although a cis-Andean one was still functioning in the Temoche-Cachen region in the eighteenth century. The languages north of Muchik are as badly known as Culli. One can simply point to the consensus of drastically independent sources that the southern end of the Sechura desert marked the linguistic frontier between Muchik and the three "dialects" (Sechura, Catacaos, and Colan) usually grouped as "Tallán" spoken from Olmos north (Rabinowitz 1980). This linguistic division would seem to support a broad macro-ethnic division, already detected in the archaeology (Lothrop 1948:66) between the North and the Far North Coast *etnías*. It suggests greater heterogeneity at the micro-level for the macro-group that came to be labeled "Tallánes" in the occasional references in the chroniclers.

Summary of Evidence on Coast-Highland Relations

Summing up the various kinds of evidence for the several periods, our overview supports Onuki's proposition on the long stability of highland, multiple-niche exploitation in the sierra and a maritime self-sufficient group of *etnías* on the coast. We would add that there were autonomous cis-Andean *etnías* between the stable coast and highland *etnías* that in some regions lost their autonomy after the Early Intermediate Period, usually to the highland neighbor. Through-

Fig. 19.2 Linguistic Map of the Ancient Diocese of Trujillio, Peru. (taken from Rivet 1949)

out most of the 2,000-year time span we are reviewing, mutually agreed upon inter-ethnic exchange mechanisms, mobility for which was presumably provided by the highlanders, articulated the product exchange. When coastal *etnías* tried to maximize their productivity, they apparently blocked or constrained traditional highland access to coastal niches. The repercussions of this limitation may have contributed to the causes for subsequent highland population movement (a more massive presence) in the coastal zones that is one of the characteristics of Middle Horizon dynamics. In later epochs, the Chimu appear to have controlled the traditional flow of community-level trade in the Chimu heartland by (1) keeping highlanders out by walling off upper parts of the valleys, and (2) awarding state franchising priviledges to *rescatistas* from coastal *etnías*. Other arrangements could have been operative between component *señoríos* of Chimor, both to the north and south of the Chimu heartland. These arrangements seem to support the type of "tribute for water rights" exchange agreements between component and autonomous groups in separate highland territorialities as Rostworowski (1976, in this volume; Ramirez, in this volume) suggests.

Coast-Highland Relations: The Cognitive Dimension

Finally we come to analyze what I would consider to be the cognitive dimension of coast-highland relationships. The perceptions of how the coastal people regard themselves and their relationships with the highlands and highlanders and vice versa is essential to a full discussion of the theme of this symposium.

While much of the ethnographic research carried out under the inspiration of Murra in the highlands (Cesar Fonseca's [1966, 1972] research in Huánuco, Olivia Harris' [1978a, 1978b, in this volume] work in Bolivia) has given us indications of a not-totally articulate "cognitive" formulation of the principles of ecological complementarity as perceived by highlanders that practice it, we have no corresponding attempts from ethnographers of the North Coastal or Highland Andes to get at perceptions of man/environment or ecological relationships. The closest approximation to cognitive anthropology on the coast is Sharon's (1978) work with the *curandero* Eduardo Calderon. It is unfortunate for our purposes that Eduardo himself is an enculturated Mochero, or an acculturated Santiagueño (from Santiago de Chuco), whom the Mocheros would reject as ethnically alike, however congenial they find him as a *forastero*. In any case the few observations that Eduardo directed to our theme are too tangental to utilize in the present instance.

An effective way at getting at the cognitive dimension would be by having coastal and highland spokesmen express it in their own words. I remember discussing the issues of this symposium with Antonio Rodriguez Suy Suy, a native of Moche, in November 1982, when I brought out the fact that Murra was one of the few, if perhaps the only person, who had cited his paper on the ecological hinterland of Chimu (Rodriguez 1969) and the importance Murra gave to it for the principle of ecological complementarity. From the subsequent conversation of how his paper might be interpreted, I can only convey some vaguely recollected impressions. In general, Antonio made the point that the coastal people recognized a kind of peaceful co-existence with highlanders, that they appreciated their dynamism and "n" motivation. This Antonio had occasion to personally verify in his observation of recent highland migrants' rehabilitation of humid lands which the Mocheros themselves were too lazy to concern themselves with. He said that coastal people *may* go to the eastern slopes, more or less as on expeditions of *turismo*, but that the norm was to await the unscheduled visits of the highlanders who would bring products which the *costeños* might find exchangeable. The coastal people consider the highlanders to have the least favored ecological niches (although not explicitly part of Antonio's formulation, there is evidence from the testimony of the *curandero* Eduardo and a few scattered informants that useful herbs were among the products that could only be obtained in highland niches, and that these were supplied regularly to the markets in Trujillo, Chiclayo, and other coastal towns).

Antonio demonstrated a much closer ethnic identity to the people of the Far North Coast, particularly those in Vicús and Nariguala, a region he did not get to know until he was over fifty years old, that was much closer than the bond with any *serrano* group. Had there been any cognitive awareness of a pattern of ecological complementarity, even of the type that engendered the hostility and endogamy that Tomoeda (in this volume) and Harris (in this volume) refer to, one would expect to find among the *costeños* an awareness or sense of the significance of the highland resources in which they might have an interest.

His stereotype of the *serrano* was positive in crediting the highlanders with a kind of native flair for entrepreneurship and aggressiveness, which the *costeño* lacked—and negative, in attributing to them a lack of refinement and sense of propriety, as well as a lack of regard for the more *dolce vita* values, summed up in Holmberg's (1950) characterization of the Viruñeros with the felicitous phrase, *Fiesta y Siesta.*

When one adds to this general cognitive impression the cultural and structural difference of a phenomenological order, which can be said to be derived from ecological differences between coast and highlands, such as different technologies for *chicha* brewing; different dietary preferences (taste for maritime avifauna, edible snail preferences, guinea pig *qua* food preparation); different wild resource procurement systems; and differences in other basic technologies such as spinning and field preparation, one feels safe in concluding that we are dealing with people who have been in proximity for millenia with fluctuating patterns of mutual accommodation, but with rather sharply distinct cultural traditions that belie a shared pattern of past ecological complementarity.

NOTES

1. The important conclusion of the Virú Valley project that the lower valley was for the first time "unified," in Kosok's sense of the word, is an archaeological indicator that a high degree of cultural homogeneity was attained, representing the birth of the Virú or Guañape *señorío* or *etnía*. The pre-Gallinazo sedentary cultures (Puerto Morrin and Guañape) seem to have reflected a higher degree of community autonomy and a period of small community growth and shifting affiliation in which the supra-community hegemonies were probably short-lived and may have involved alliances across ecological frontiers. Brennan (1982) attempts to reconstruct such extensive units in a highly speculative way for the Puerto Morrin-Salinar period. Wilson (1981, 1982), in interpreting settlement distribution in the Santa, interprets this Salinar to Gallinazo Late Formative development as intra-valley community clusters in belligerent competition for valley hegemony, although his evidence for lower valley settlement is either weak or ignored.

The weakness of complete settlement pattern evidence for the period 500 B.C.–A.D. 500 in all valleys except Virú, makes reconstruction of the community aggregation process subject to only the wildest conjectures.

In dealing with this phase the procedure of designating "interaction spheres" used by archaeologists for the earlier time periods is to be recommended where widely separated cultures are shown to share technologies and occasionally symbols of each others' belief systems, but the question of *how* these transfers take place should be left open and political hegemony should certainly *not* be implied.

2. Unfortunately, no transect studies of Northern Peru (possibly with the exception of Tello's report on the Casma; Tello 1956) have been undertaken to those foreseen in Matos' Junín project for Central Peru. North Coast valley studies have generally had their "cut-off" point at lower than 1,000 m altitude (Shimada 1982:185–87). Sierra studies usually do not encompass much territory in the Pacific watershed. Even though Wilson's reconnaissance of the Santa goes fairly high, it ignores the role of such significant Pacific watershed pockets as the Tablachaco. The likelihood that these *etnías* (which are recognized in the ethnohistoric literature as small but relatively autonomous in Late Pre-Incaic Periods) emerged during Early Intermediate times in North and Central Peru was indicated to me as a result of my survey of stone sculpture distribution in the Andes (Schaedel 1952). Small centers such as Huambo and Aija and isolates like Cajacay in the near North Highlands seem to reflect the presence of shrines of highland *etnías* participating in a regional interaction sphere of shared belief systems but retaining a high

degree of cultural (and in this case) political activity. Zaki (1978) found and excavated such a center at Azangay in the Upper Moche, and the Polish mission in the upper Chicama are in the process of defining later time and space parameters of another of these ethnic groups (Krzanowski 1977; Krzanowski and Szeminski 1978).

On the Central coast, Dillehay's (1979) work on the Chillón has shown considerable multi-ethnic variation from *chaupiyungas* to the Pacific watershed, although the archaeological manifestations from Early to Late Intermediate and the subsequent bounding of the *chaupiyunga etnías* requires further research.

In my survey of Andean stone sculpture (Schaedel 1952) I was obliged to document the reported finds of stone sculpture in areas that had not been previously reconnoitered archaeologically and I am surprised to say not many have been reconnoitered since. Combining my earlier tabulation of sites in the Cordillera Negra and Pacific watershed from which stone sculpture has been reported with work done since, I can demonstrate the presence of either isolates or small centers in the upper watershed sections of all rivers from the Pativilca north to the Jequetepeque (Mejia Xesspe [1940]) reported upon two sites in the upper Casma which I overlooked), and in the reconnaissance of 1975 I found examples of sculpture in the Chicama watershed near Coina. In the *chaupiyunga* area, the sites of Yautan in the Casma, Cochipampa in the Nepeña, and Burro Corral in the Huarmey with lintel described by Bennett (1948) are all the monumental stone sculpture so far reported. Cerro Sechin remains the only coastal site with monumental stone sculpture.

The above distribution of stone sculpture on the Pacific watershed can be taken as gross evidence for the existence of an as yet unstudied but regular pattern of inhabited pockets of cultivable land in the area between *chaupiyungas* and the Pacific watershed. The dating of these sculptures ranges from late Early Horizon at the earliest to a terminal Middle Horizon date. The majority of pieces seem to be local styles dating to the Early Intermediate Period and can be interpreted as substantiating the existence of what appear to be early autonomous *etnías* in this "buffer zone."

3. There is virtually no information, either linguistic, ethnohistorical, or archaeological on the eastern slopes of the Cordillera Blanca except for Chavín de Huántar. In my stone sculpture survey (Fig. 19.1) I divided this region into a Huántar center, a circum-Huántar area, and a northern Pomebamba peripheral area to more or less reflect the pattern of stone sculpture and what little there was known of major site distribution in this region. Because of more information on the Huántar and circum-Huántar section, I hypothesize that this pocket of the Puccha tributary to the Marañon may be linked with the proposed southern *macro-etnía* of Recuay (or Huaylas). Rodriguez Suy Suy's (1973) study of old transverse routes shows a Recuay-Chavín road connecting the two. His second transverse route connects Pomebamba with Yungay, while his third connects Sihuas and Huallanca. It would be premature to propose that these latter correspond to the Northern Pashash *macro-etnía* in some form of highland verticality pattern. They

could be equally well autonomous. In the accounts of Cieza and Garcilasco, this region on the eastern slopes seems to correspond to an ethnic group called Piscobamba, while the Pashash *macro-etnía* seems to be referred to in protohistoric accounts as the Conchucos, and the southern group as either Huaraz or Huaylas. As will be seen later, it would appear that the Northern group were Culli-speaking, and the southern group spoke Quechua in protohistoric times, but there is no indication of what the people on the eastern slopes of the Cordillera Blanca spoke. Although Rowe (1946) lists a Huacrachico province on the eastern tributaries of the Marañon as a possible Inca province, and although there are ruins of some magnitude along the entire stretch between Tinyash and Chillia which might correspond to this possible *etnía*, a single *macro-etnía* can only be postulated as a hypothesis. Presumably it was autonomous until the Inca conquest like its neighbor to the northeast, Chachapoyas. It is interesting to note that in the eighteenth century, in the adjoining Huallaga watershed area, Hibito and Cholon (two so far unrelated languages) were recorded by Martinez Compañon (Rivet 1949: Schaedel and Garrido 1953).

4. The probability that there were at least three *etnías* which had mutually unintelligible languages in protohistoric times, suggests that more detailed archaeological research in the Far North can discern a pattern of regional cultures within which Moche "colonies" were interspersed. By Late Intermediate times, the evidence from private collections of ceramics and some site identifications indicate that these *etnías* were incorporated into the Chimu Kingdom, and there is some indication that some supra-community hegemonies from the Lambayeque Valley may have incorpoarted them somewhat earlier. The few protohistoric accounts and sporadic references throughout the Colonial period confirm the linguistic diversity first posited by Salinas de Loyola. Other early Spanish reports group the inhabitants between Olmos and Tumbes into a kind of *macro-etnía* to which the term Tallán is given.

5. Since we know little of the cis-Andean pattern except from ethnohistory, I hesitate to exclude a pastoral component. Huambos and Azangay sculptures show llama heads. These intermediate *etnías*, in some instances, could have been the means of moving highland produce to the coast.

6. That this effect of a complex, long-range coast and highland relationship (as the Inca chiefdom-state expansion) was not a simple extension of the ecological complementarity principle over a wide area is made clear by the settlement pattern for the Huari state, not only with regard to its installations in its heartland, but throughout the highlands between Huamachuco and Urcos (Isbell and Schreiber 1972). Whether the Huari state was preceded by a phase of extension of ecological complementarity (encompassing, for example, cis-Andean and South Coastal colonies) before its precocious state formation efforts—similar to the Tiahuanaco expansion has yet to be demonstrated. The immediate pre-Huari sequence for the Ayacucho highlands, and cis-Andean and South Coastal *etnías* (poorly understood as they are) might justify this interpretation in the development of nuclear Nawampuquio (Lumbreras 1974).

7. The beginning of the ethnohistoric relevance I date to A.D. 1200, roughly because it correlates with the beginning of the Chimu dynasty (Kosok 1965: 73, Chart II). The Naymlap legend, with which the Lambayeque dynasty can be intercalated, allows one to extend the period of ethnohistoric relevance into the last phase of the Middle Horizon in this particular valley. Rowe (1948) draws more or less the same inference.

8. During his recent survey (summer, 1984) of the western watershed of the North Highlands along the south side of the Jequetepeque River, the region encompassing Cascas, Contumaza, and Guzmango, Paul Jaeckel of Harvard University recovered appreciable quantities of reduced ware ceramics of definite Chimu and possible pre-Chimu coastal styles at several major sites.

9. The *encomienda* reference can be interpreted as simply referring to successive blocks of land, granted in Peru in 1535 on an ad-hoc basis, which was presumably all Pizarro had to go on. Thus, Estete is being awarded the Chimu capital (not necessarily all of it), as Manziz is clearly a reference to Mansiche, the headquarters of the Chimu dynasty in proto-historic times. The *principales* of a certain principal *cacique* named Ispilco of the town of Cavin (which might be a great distance away and even refer to the actual Chavín de Huántar) are then listed as tributaries. The *principales* of a principal *cacique* (Cuycuy with the domain of Naspac) follows. Both the *pueblo* and *cacique* name appear to be Muchik; and we would tend to place them on the coast. The last allocated territory is Conchuco with its principal *cacique*, Poma China. Further on in the document another reference to the *cacique* of Conchucos apears which extends the permit to *rescatar* (which Pizarro had given to Estete's widow for the Chimor *cacique*'s domain) to the Conchucos *cacique*. I see no reason for assuming any particular linkage between the *cacicazgos* of Chimor and Conchucos because they happen to be linked in this *rescate* permit.

The earliest eyewitness references to *etnías* in the Callejón area generally refer to three groups: the Piscobamba to the east, Conchucos in the north, and Huaraz in the south. Huaraz had already been given to another *encomendero* (Varon 1980: 49), as had Huamachuco, the next *etnía* north of Conchucos. It would thus appear that Pizarro was simply allocating a highland area that roughly corresponded to the region between Huamachuco and Huaraz. If this is so, the unidentified Nasapac probably corresponds to a coastal portion to the south of the Chimu capital, probably contiguous with Conchucos. Since Soriano (1941:269) identifies the *cacique principal* of Nepeña in the late sixteenth century as Suy Suy, I suggest this valley (possibly including Casma) as the domain in which Nasapac might have been.

Cavin appears only as a place name in highland areas to the southeast of the Chimu capital. If there were a patterning in the listing of the grants in the document (from what we know of the *encomiendas* granted in the north highlands for Huamachuco and Cajamarca) the grant to Estete would have to be in the region south of Huamachuco. Piscobamba and Conchucos "fit" what the early sources knew as two of the three peoples inhabitating the Callejón. Cavin may refer to an ethnic subdivision south of Piscobamba, where there is a clustering of towns on the Puccha tributary of the Marañon. If this is the picture, then Pizarro was parceling lands from Trujillo south that would have given Estete a block of contiguous lands that included all climes and nothing more.

10. María Rostworowski in this volume refers to the unit of Chondal which has most of the patronyms with *f*, and includes the toponym of Chan Chan. My interpretation of this phenomenon is that this unit was originally a cis-Andean autonomous *señorío* that was incorporated into the Cajarmarca hegemony, and that it was Muchik-speaking but probably different culturally from the maritime *yunga* Muchik-speaking population at least from Early Formative times on.

11. Matsuzawa (1978) referred to llama trains terminating in Casma which had their origin in the villages of the Puccha cluster on the eastern slopes of the Cordillera Blanca. Sr. Julian Aguilar, a native of the Callejón and student in the Institut für Ethnologie, Berlin, confirmed the widespread practice in the Callejón of procuring *cochyayuyo* on the coast, although he could not recall more than informal mechanisms (such as during contracted labor trips to the guano islands) for securing a regular supply.

12. There seems to be no need to recapitulate the erroneous information in Loukotka's (1968) or Mason's (1948) earlier classifications of the Andean languages in what is now northwestern Peru, as most of it has been eliminated in Rivet's map. From Torero's (1972) work with Quechua, it would appear rather likely that the interstices between the distribution of Muchik and Culli were regions with Quechua-speaking communities, at least in post-Middle Horizon times, and the likelihood exists that this band of highland Quechua communities (and probably peoples) extended contiguously from the southern Callejón de Huaylas to Ecuador through what would have been the Inca provinces of Humachuco, Cajamarca, Huambo, Huanuabamba, and Ayabaca (using Rowe's 1946 reconstruction), assuming that even in the Culli-speaking provinces, Quechua was also spoken. This assumption is based upon Quechua toponyms found throughout these regions, as well as the contemporary Quechua-speaking communities in Ferreñafe, Cajamarca, and Incahuasi (the last datum comes from Enrique Brüning's unpublished vocabulary which is being studied by Rosawith Hartmann in Bonn). The only question in the picture of three main language groups in the northern area, as far as the eastern slopes of the Andes are concerned, is the extent of Culli, which in Rivet's (1949) interpretation includes the region in the watersheds of the Chicama, Moche, and Virú valleys, although it might include regions as far to the east as Huaricancha and Manga. This rests on the slender indication in Toribio de Mogrovejo ([1593] 1920) that the language denoted ILINGA is not Inca (as Kubler thought) but a reference to Culli. Torero (1972:103) seemed to accept the likelihood that Culli might even have been spoken as far north as Cajamarca. The first attempt to test the presence of Culli on toponymic grounds was done by Krzanowski and Szeminski (1978) with some slight validation for Rivet's (1949) interpretation.

The clustering of highland sites and adjacent montane *yunga* speech communities given by Carrera ([1644] 1939) in the northern ends of the highland (practically all of the subdivisions of present-day Cajamarca are mentioned as having Muchik communities—Condebamba, Santa Cruz, San Miguel, San Pablo, and Niepos) and the islands in Huancabamba and Frias further north, would argue more for an aboriginal distribution of the speakers in this area than for either of the *mitimae* explanations of Carrera ([1644] 1939). Incidentally, Carrera also observes that the speakers in the *serranias* just mentioned had their own language, which was Quechua, a point that Torero (1972) overlooked in presuming Culli might be spoken further north than Huamachuco. A similar statement on the co-existence of Culli and Quechua on the Pacific watershed of the North Sierra is in Ramos (1955), although Rowe (1946) cites Cieza as stating Huancabamba had its own language.

Languages for the Far North Coast are summarized in Stark (1968) and Rabinowitz (1980). Although they discern a relationship between the three dialects for which word lists exist, neither finds any closer affiliation between them and Muchik than with other languages. It seems inappropriate here to discuss the question of linguistic affiliation of Muchik, since what little investigation has been attempted on the subject (Stark 1968; Campbell 1973) would refer to affiliation at a time period long before our proposed period of emerging *etnías*. I should, however, point out that the rather careful studies of Jijon y Camaaño (1943), attempting to show the existence of a macro-Chibchan family of which Muchik was a part have not been methodically reviewed, nor have the many leads for linguistic affiliation between Muchik and extinct Ecuadorean languages to the north been thoroughly followed up. The type of study that Krzanowski and Szeminski (1978) essayed for Culli/Quechua/Muchik, working with Ecuadorean toponyms, would be helpful. My review of Stark's (1968) essay with Cayapa and Colorado cognates with Muchik cognates indicates greater correspondence than she was able to detect. In short, if linguistic affiliation can be brought to bear on likely roots of different branches of Andean *macro-etnías,* the directions of the affiliation of the Muchik seem to be closer to the Ecuadorean protohistoric groups of the maritime and Pacific watershed than to any of the branches of the Aru-Quechua speakers. The latter seem to have occupied the multiple niche clusters of the Andes which included *puna* country, while the former seem to have a multple niche cluster that does not pass the *paramo*.

REFERENCES CITED

Bennett, Wendell C.

1939 Archaeology of the North Coast of Peru. Anthropological Papers. 37 (1):1–153. American Museum of Natural History, New York.

1948 The Peruvian Co-tradition. *In* A Reappraisal of Peruvian Archaeology. Wendell C. Bennett, assembler. Memoirs of the Society for American Archaeology 4:1–7.

1950 The Gallinazo Group, Viru Valley, Peru. Anthropology 43.

New Haven: Yale University Publications.

Brennan, Curtis T.

1982 Cerro Arena: Origins of the Urban Tradition on the North Peruvian Coast. *Current Anthropology* 23 (3):247–54.

Brüning, Enrique

1918 Provincia de Lambayeque. Contribución arqueológica. Boletín de la Sociedad Geográfica de Lima 33:197–201. Lima.

1922 Estudios Monográficos del Departamento de Lambayeque. Monografía de Jayanca. Chiclayo.

Calancha, Antonio de la

1638 Corónica moralizada del orden de San Agustín en el Perú. Barcelona.

Campbell, Lyle

1973 Distant Genetic Relationship and the Maya-Chipaya Hypothesis. Anthropological Linguistics 15 (3):113–35.

Carrera, Fernando de la

[1644] 1939 Arte de la lengua yunga de los valles del Obispado de Trujillo. Tucumán: Instituto de Antropología, Universidad de Tucumán.

Collier, Donald

1962 Archaeological Investigations in the Casma Valley, Peru. Akten des XXXIV Internationalen Amerikanistenkongresses. 411–17. Vienna.

Cook, Noble

1982 Population Data for Indian Peru: Sixteenth and Seventeenth Centuries. Hispanic American Historical Review 62 (1):73–120.

Dillehay, Tom

1979 Pre-hispanic Resource Sharing in the Central Andes. Science 204:24–31.

Doering, Heinrich

1957 Der Gallinazo-Stil und die Chronologie der altperuanischen Frühkulturen. Bayerische Akademie der Wissenschaften. Jahrgang 1957, Heft 9. Munich.

Eling, Herbert

In press Prehispanic Irrigation Sources and Systems in the Jequetepeque Valley, Northern Peru. *In* Studies in Andean Archaeology. R. Matos and S. Turpin, eds. Institute of Archaeology, UCLA.

Eling, Herbert J., Jr. and Glendon Weir

In press Pollen Evidence for Economic Plant Utilization in Prehispanic Agricultural Fields of the Jequetepeque Valley, Northern Peru. *In* Studies in Andean Archaeology. R. Matos and S. Turpin, eds. Institute of Archaeology, UCLA.

Espinoza Soriano, Waldemar

1962 La incorporación del Curacazgo de Huamachuco al imperio de los Incas. Actas y trabajos del II Congreso Nacional de Historia del Perú 2:117–19. Lima.

1969–70 Los mitmas yungas de Collique in Cajamarca, siglos XV, XVI, y XVII. Revista del Museo Nacional 36:9–52 Lima.

1970 Los mitmas huayacuntus en Cajabamba y Antamarca, siglos XV y XVI. Historia y Cultura 4:77–96. Lima.

1973a Los mitmas huayacuntu en Quito o guarniciones para la represión armada, siglos XV y XVI. Revista del Museo Nacional 41:351–94. Lima.

1973b La pachaca de Puchu en el reino de Cuismancu, siglos 15 y 16. Bulletin de l'Institut Français de Etudes Andines 2 (2):35–71. Lima.

1974a Los señores étnicos de valle de Condembamba y provincia de Cajabamba. Universidad Nacional del Centro del Peru, Huancayo.

1974b El curacazgo de Conchucos. Bulletin de l'Institut Francais de Etudes Andines 3 (1):9–31. Lima.

1977 La poliginia señorial en el reino de Caxamarca, siglo XV y XVI. Revista del Museo Nacional 43:399–466. Lima.

1978a Huaraz; poder, sociedad y economía en los siglos XV y XVI. Lima: Centro de Estudios Rurales Andinos.

1978b La pachaca de Parimarca en el reino de Cajamarca. Historia y Cultura 10:135–180 Lima.

Fonseca, César

1966 La comunidad de Cauri y la quebrada de Chaupiwaranga. Cuadernos de Investigación. Huánuco: Universidad de Huánuco.

1972 Sistemas económicas en las comunidades campesinas del Perú. Ph.D. thesis. Universidad de San Marcos. Lima.

Ford, James

1974 The History of a Peruvian Valley. *Reprinted in* New World Archaeology: Theoretical and Cultural Transformation. E. Zubrow, M. Fritz, and J. Fritz, comp. pp. 164–70. San Francisco: W. H. Freeman and Co.

Fung Pineda, Rosa

1975 Excavaciones en Pacopampa, Cajamarca. Revista del Museo Nacional 41:129–207. Lima.

1977 Exploraciones y excavaciones en el Valle de Sechín, Casma. Revista del Museo Nacional 43:111–55. Lima.

Gaceta Arqueológica Andina

1982 La región norte. *In* Coloquio internacional de arquelogía en homenaje a Carlos Zevallos Menéndez. Suplemento No. 1. Lima.

Ghersi, Humberto

1961 Migración por etapas: el caso del Valle de Virú. Lima: Museo de la Cultura Peruana. Proyecto Peru-Cornell.

Gillin, John

1947 Moche: A Peruvian Coastal Community. Smithsonian Institution. Institute of Social Anthropology, Publication 3.

Gonzalez, Leticia

n.d. Comprobaciones etnohistóricas del panorama socioeconómico en la costa norte durante los siglos XVI-XIX. Ms. submitted for publication in Chimor II, J. Sabogal, ed. Trujillo.

Harris, Olivia

1978a El parentesco y la economía vertical del ayllu Laymi, norte de Potosí. Avances 1:51–64. La Paz.

1978b De l'asymétrie au triangle: transformations symbolique au Nord de Potosí. Annales 33 (5–6):1108–25.

Holmberg, Allan R.

1950 Virú; Remnants of an Exalted People. *In* Patterns for Modern Living: Cultural Patterns. Part 2, Section 9. pp. 367–417. Chicago: The Delphian Society.

Isbell, William and Katharina Schreiber

1972 Was Huari a State? American Antiquity 43:372–89.

Izumi, Seiichi and Kazuo Terada

1966 Andes 3: Excavations at Pechiche and Garbanzal, Tumbes Valley, Peru, 1960. Tokyo: Kadokawa Publishing Co.

Jijón y Camaaño, Jacinto

1974 Las lenguas del sur de centroamérica y el norte y centro del oeste de Sudamérica. *In* El Ecuador Interandino y Occidental 3:390–661. Quito.

Julien, Daniel

1980 Ecological Stability and Maritime Adaptation on the North Coast of Peru. M.A. thesis. Department of Anthropology. University of Texas, Austin.

Kosok, Paul

1959 El valle de Lambayeque. Actas y Trabajos del II Congreso Nacional de Historia del Perú, Epoca prehispánica 1:49–66. Lima.

1965 Life, Land, and Water in Ancient Peru. New York: Long Island University Press.

Kroeber, Alfred L.

1950 A Local Style of Lifelike Sculptured Stone Heads in Ancient Peru. Beiträge zur Gestellungs und Völkerwissenschaft: Festschrift zum achtzigsten Geburtstag von Professor Richard Thurnwald. Berlin.

Krzanowski, Andrzej

1977 Yuraccama, the Settlement Complex in the Alto Chicama Region (Northern Peru). Polish Contributions in New World Archaeology. Krakow: Polish Academy of Sciences.

Krzanowski, Andrzej and Jan Szeminski

1978 La toponimía indígena en la cuenca del río Chicama (Perú). Estudios Latinoamericanos 4:11–51. Ossolineum.

Lanning, E. P.

1963 A Ceramic Sequence for the Piura and Chira Coast, North Peru. University of California Publications in American Archaeology and Ethnology 46(2):135–284. Berkeley.

Larco Hoyle, Rafael

1939 Los Mochicas, Vol. 2. Lima: Editorial Rimac.

Lothrop, Samuel

1948 Parinas Chira Archaeology: A Preliminary Report. *In* A Reappraisal of Peruvian Archaeology. Wendell Bennett, assembler. Memoirs of the Society for American Archaeology, 4:53–85.

Loukotka, Cesimir

1968 Classification of South American Languages. Johannes Wilbert, ed. Latin American Center, UCLA. Vol. 7.

Lumbreras, Luis G.

1974 The Peoples and Cultures of Ancient Peru. B. J. Meggers, transl. Washington, D. C.: Smithsonian Institution Press.

1979 El arte y la vida Vicús. Lima: Banco Popular del Perú.

Mason, J. Alden

1948 The Languages of South American Indians. *In* Handbook of South American Indians, Vol. 6. Julian H. Steward, ed. pp. 157–318. Bureau of American Ethnology, Bulletin 143. Washington, D. C.

Matsuzawa, Tsugio

1978 The Formative Site of Las Haldas, Peru: Architecture, Chronology, and Economy. I. Shimada, transl. and ed. American Antiquity 43:652–73.

McCown, Theodore

1945 Pre-Incaic Huamachuco. University of California Publications in American Archaeology and Ethnology 39(4). Berkeley.

Mejía Xesspe, Toribio

1941 Walun y Chinchawas: Dos nuevos sitios en la Cordillera Negra. Chaski 1:1:18–24. Lima.

Menzel, Dorothy

1969 New Data on the Huari Empire in Middle Horizon Epoch 2A. Ñawpa Pacha 6:47–114.

1977 The Archaeology of Ancient Peru and the Work of Max Uhle. Lowie Museum of Anthropology, University of California, Berkeley.

Mogrovejo, Toribio Alfonso de

[1593] 1920 Diario de la segunda visita pastoral del Arzobispado de los Reyes, don Toribio de Mogrovejo. Publicado por Fray Domingo Angulo, Libro de visitas 1953. Revista del Archivo Nacional del Perú, No. 1: Entrega 1 y 2. Lima.

Murra, John V.

1972 El control vertical de un máximo de pisos ecológicos en la economía de las sociedades andinas. *In* Visita de la Provincia de León de Huánuco. J. V. Murra, ed. 2:429–76. Huánuco: Universidad Nacional Hermilio Valdizán.

1981 The 'Vertical Control' of a Maximum of Ecologic Tiers in the Economies of Andean Societies. D. Chavin Escobar, transl. (1972) and revised by Gabriel Escobar N. Private circulation.

Netherly, Patricia

1977 Local Level Lords on the North Coast of Peru. Ann Arbor: University Microfilms International.

Pineda, José

n.d. Los patrones de asentamiento en el Valle de Condebamba. *In* The Precolumbian Time of Troubles in the Andes. R. P. Schaedel, I. Shimada, and J. Vreeland, eds.

Proulx, Donald A.

1973 Archaeological Investigations in the Nepeña Valley, Peru. Research Report No. 13, Department of Anthropology. University of Massachusetts, Amherst.

Rabinowitz, Joe B.

1980 Pescadora, the Argot of Chimu Fishermen. M.A. thesis. Department of Anthropology, University of Texas, Austin.

Ramos, Josefina

1950 Las lenguas en la region Tallanca. Cuadernos de Estudio 3(8): 11–55. Instituto de Investigaciones Históricas, Lima.

Rivet, Paul

1949 Les langues de l'ancien Diocese de Trujillo. Journal de la Société des Americanistes n.s. 38:3–51.

Rodríguez Suy Suy, V. Antonio

1967 Secuencia cultural en el valle de Lambayeque. Paper presented at the Primer Symposium de Arqueología de Lambayeque, Chiclayo.

1969 Chanchan, cuidad de adobe: Observaciones sobre su base ecológica. *In* The Urbanization Process in America from Its Origins to the Present Day. J. E. Hardoy and R. P. Schaedel, ed. pp. 133–52. Buenos Aires.

1973 Caminos prehispánicos norperuanos: Informe preliminar. Chiquitayap: Boletín del Museo de Sitio Chavimochic, Año 1, No. 1. Article 4. Cooperativo Agraria de Producción Cartavio, Ltda. Trujillo.

Rostworowski de Diez Canseco, María

1961 Curacas y sucesiones, costa norte. Lima: Minerva.

1975 Pescadores, artesanos y mercaderes en el Perú prehispánico. Revista del Museo Nacional 41:311–39. Lima.

1976 El señorío de Changuco-costa norte. Bulletin de l'Institut Français de Etudes Andines 5:97–111. Lima.

1981 Recursos naturales renovables y pesca, siglos XVI y XVII. Lima: Instituto de Estudios Peruanos.

Rowe, John H.

1946 Inca Culture at the Time of the Spanish Conquest. *In* Handbook of South American Indians. J. H. Steward, ed. 2:183–330. Bureau of American Ethnology, Bulletin 143. Washington, D. C.

1948 On Absolute Dating and North Coast Prehistory. *In* A Reappraisal of Peruvian Archaeology. Wendell C. Bennett, ed. Memoirs of the Society for American Archaeology 4:51–52.

Sabogal, José

1967 Las migraciones en Santiago de cao. Anales científicos de la Universidad Agraria, La Molina, Perú 5(1,2):87–117.

1976 Santiago de Cao y el valle de Chicama: Cinco ponencias inéditas. Centro de Investigaciones Socio-Económicas, Lima.

Schaedel, Richard P.

1951 Major Population and Ceremonial Centers in Northern Peru. Proceedings of the 29th International Congress of Americanists 2:232–43. Chicago.

1952 An Analysis of Andean Stone Sculpture. Ph.D. thesis. Department of Anthropology, Yale University, New Haven.

1966a Incipient Urbanization and Secularization in Tiahuanacoid Peru. American Antiquity 31:338–44.

1966b Urban Growth and Ekistics on the Peruvian Coast. Proceedings of the 36th International Congress of Americanists 2:531–39. Seville.

1978 The City and the Origin of the State in America. *In* Urbanization in the Americas from its Beginnings to the Present Day. R. P. Schaedel, J. Hardoy, and Kinzer, eds. Mouton, The Hague.

1981 Late Incaic and Early Spanish Changes in Land Use—Their Effect on Dry Land: The Peruvian Coast. Ibero-amerikanisches Archiv 7 (3):309–19. Berlin.

n.d.a The Transition from Chiefdom to State in Northern Peru. Paper presented at the International Congress of Anthropological and Ethnological Sciences, Amsterdam, 1982.

n.d.b The Prehistory of the Water Control/Social Control Interface. Paper presented for the Homenaje a Angel Palerm.

n.d.c Permanent and Transitory Diagnostics of the Middle Horizon in Central Andes. *In* The Pre-Columbian Time of Troubles in the Andes. R. P. Schaedel, I. Shimada, and J. Vreeland, eds.

Schaedel, Richard P. and José Euloglo Garrido

1953 El Obispo don Baltazar Jaime Martínez Compañon y la etnología del norte del Perú a fines del siglo XVIII. Revista del Museo Nacional 12:71–103. Lima.

Sharon, Douglas

1978 Wizard of the Four Winds: A Shaman's Story. New York: The Free Press.

Shimada, Izumi

1978 Economy of a Prehistoric Urban Context: Commodity and Labor Flow at Moche V Pampa Grande. American Antiquity 43:569–92.

1982 Horizontal Archipelago and Coast-Highland Interaction in North Peru: Archaeological Models. *In* El Hombre y Su Ambiente en los Andes Centrales. Luis Millones and Hiroyasu Tomoeda, eds. pp. 137–210. Senri Ethnological Studies 10. National Museum of Ethnology. Senri.

1983 The Formation of the Middle Sicán Polity: The Highland Connection and Revitalization Movement. Paper presented at the 48th

Annual Meeting of the Society for American Archaeology, Pittsburgh.

n.d. Integration and Segregation of Urbanism and Ceremonialism on the North Coast during the Middle Horizon. *In* The Pre-Columbian Time of Troubles in the Andes. R. P. Schaedel, I. Shimada, and J. Vreeland, eds.

Shimada, Izumi, et. al.

1981 The Batán Grande-La Leche Archaeological Project: The First Two Seasons. Journal of Field Archaeology 8:405–46.

Shimada, Melody

1982 Zooarchaeology of Huacaloma: Behavioral and Cultural Implications. *In* Excavations at Huacaloma in the Cajamarca Valley, Peru, 1979. Kazuo Terada and Yoshio Onuki, eds. pp. 303–36: University of Tokyo Press, Tokyo.

Smith, John W., Jr.

1978 The Recuay Culture: A Reconstruction Based on Artistic Motifs. Ann Arbor: University Microfilms International.

Soriano Infante, Agusto

1941 Monografía de Ancash: Nepeña (Provincia de Santa). Revista del Museo Nacional 10(2):263–77. Lima.

Stark, Louisa R.

1968 Mayan Affinities with Yunga of Peru. Ann Arbor: University Microfilms International.

Stein, William W.

1961 Hualcan: Life in the Highlands of Peru. Ithaca: Cornell University Press.

Stumer, Louis M.

1954 The Chillon Valley of Peru: Excavation and Reconnaissance, 1952–53 (part 2). Archaeology 7:4:220–28.

1956 Development of Peruvian Coastal Tiahuanacoid Styles. American Antiquity 22:59–69.

Tello, Julio C.

1956 Arqueología del Valle de Casma: Culturas: Chavín, Santa, o Huaylas Yunga y Sub-Chimú. Lima: Editorial San Marcos.

Terada, Kazuo and Yoshio Onuki, eds.

1982 Excavations at Huacaloma in the Cajamarca Valley, Peru, 1979. Tokyo: University of Tokyo Press.

Thatcher, John

1975 Early Intermediate Period and Middle Horizon IB Ceramics Assemblages of Huamachuco, North Highlands, Peru. Ñawpa Pacha 10–12. Berkeley.

Topic, Theresa Lange and John R. Topic

1982a Prehistoric Fortification Systems of Northern Peru: Preliminary Report on the Final Season. January-December 1980. Privately circulated report.

1982b The Archaeological Investigation of Andean Militarism: Some

Cautionary Observations. Paper for the Origins of the Andean State Symposium. Annual Meeting of the American Anthropological Association, Washington, D. C.

1983 Informe Sobre Investigaciones Arqueológicas Realizadas por el Proyecto Arquelógico Huamachuco. Department of Anthropology, Trent University, Canada.

Torero, Alfredo

1972 Linguística y Historia de los Andes del Perú y Bolivia. *In* El Reto del Multilingüismo en el Perú. Alberto Escobar, ed. pp. 47–106. Lima: Instituto de Estudios Peruanos.

Tovar, Antonio

1961 Catalogo de las lenguas de América del Sur. Buenos Aires.

Varon Gabai, Rafael

1980 Curacas y encomenderos: Acomodamiento nativo en Huaraz, Siglos XVI-XVII. Lima: P. L. Villanueva.

Watson, Richard

1980 Feeding an Empire: Essays on Late Prehistoric Food Production in the Arid North Coast of Peru. M.A thesis. Department of Anthropology, University of Texas, Austin.

Wilson, David J.

1981 Research abstract on the Santa Valley Settlement Pattern Study. Willay 6:6. Princeton.

1982 Patterns of Warfare in the Early Prehispanic Periods of the Lower Santa Valley: Conflict and the Origin of Complex Society. ms.

Zaki, Andrzej

1978 Ayangay: Polskie Odkrycia Archeologiczne w. Peru. Polski Uniwersytet na Obczyźnie. Zeszyty Naukowe Wydzialu Humanistycznego. London.

APPENDIX

Guayllo 5–iii–1535

Francisco Pizarro. . . . vos el capitan Martin Estete . . . deposyten bos en el valle de Chimo los yndios del pueblo Manziz con la persona del cacique principal del dicho valle que se llama Sachas Guaman e de los principales del q se llaman Yspilco señor del pueblo Cabin

e de otro que se llama Çuyçuy señor del pueblo Nasapac e los yndios de los pueblos Piscobamba con la persona principal del que se llama Bilchacayco

y del pueblo Conchuco con la persona principal del dicho pueblo que se llama Poma China. . . .

5–viii–1535

Francisco Pizarro dixo al cacique de la provincia de Chimo q dixo que se llama don Martin y en nombre de yndios Suchu Guaman q el dicho Martin Estete tiene en encomienda que ya sabia como el lo avia dicho que se desenterase vn casa [¿casu?] de ydolos que estava junto al mar

que los yndios lo nombraban y llamavan la guaca de Chimo Guam que Blas de Atencia abia descubierto andando a caçar

y que su [¿onse?] todo el oro y plata y otras cosas que alli hallase lo tomase para si y por qual se lo dixo el lo avia desterrado y avia sacado della muncha cantidad de oro y plata y otra cierta cantidad de oro lo qual el dicho Martin Estete la mostro y dixo al dicho cacique puesto que el dicho Blas de Atencia que le avia dicho que lo que asi hallase . . . lo tomase todo para si. . . .

27–xi–1536. . . . Maria de Escobar . . . muger que fuy del capitan Martin Este difunto clausula del testamento que hizo el dicho capitan . . . heredera de todos sus bienes. . . . [REPRODUCE documento de 12–vii–1435, firmado por FP en el Cuzco]:

doy licencia a vos el capitan Martin Estete my theniente del valle du Trujillo para que podays rescatar con el cacique Chimo y con sus caciques principales e yndios que teneys depositads

e con el cacique Conchuco y sus principales e yndios

todo el oro y plata q los dichos caciques principales e yndios os quysiere dar de su voluntad con tanto que hagays el dichos rescate ante veedor nombrado por los oficiales de SM e que no le deys armas e que hecho el dicho rescate trayays el dicho oro y plata a manifestar a la caxa real de la fundicion de la ciudad de Los Reyes. . . .

(AGI Justica 1065)

V

Retrospective and Prospective Views

The final section of the book is primarily concerned with critical assessment of achievements and charting productive avenues of future research. Also included here is an "outsider's" perspective on Andean exchange, a view from Amazonia by Kimura.

Morris's paper has the twofold aim of elaborating how some of the principles of ecological complementarity can be seen functioning in *Tawantinsuyu*, and suggesting some of the developmental properties that seem inherent in a system for managing resources in complementary contexts. The latter forms a basis for new research directions that may provide more systematic explanations for the origin and growth of states like *Tawantinsuyu.*

Kimura examines Andean exchange from the perspective of alliance theory and Amazonian ethnography. Widespread endogamy is seen as one of varied Andean social institutions that reinforce internal cohesion of self-sufficient ethnic groups. This and other observations underscore the insufficient attention given to social and ideological dimensions of ecological complementarity in this symposium, an opinion echoed by Schaedel in his comments.

The final two contributions by Schaedel and Salomon are based on the original versions of the conference papers and discussion during the conference. Subsequent revisions made by various participants benefited from their constructive criticism.

20

From Principles of Ecological Complementarity to the Organization and Administration of Tawantinsuyu

Craig Morris

Like other early states, the vast Inca empire has largely eluded our understanding because of lack of reliable information on the one hand and lack of appropriate interpretative models on the other. The Spanish sources are incomplete and highly colored by the interests and biases of sixteenth-century Europe. The early observers simply were not equipped to understand the civilization they were destroying. Our other primary source of data on the Inca, archaeology, has only recently begun to be seriously used to answer substantive questions.

The matter of adequate models is related to generally poor data on early complex societies. While the Inca case is perhaps worse than most, as a class of societies early states did not survive in the pure form long enough to receive the scientific scrutiny of trained ethnographic observations. As a result most of the models we use draw heavily on ideas and principles related to modern nation states, to tribal societies, and to general ecology. They have also usually been viewed from the implicit perspective of one form or another of unilineal evolution—as transitional phenomena on their way eventually to something rather like modern states with market economies. While this perspective may not necessarily be incorrect in the long run, as a research strategy it tends, in my view, to lead us astray in the questions we ask of our fragmentary data on the Inca.

The time is overdue for a theoretical approach that looks at the Inca and the rise of Andean complex societies in terms of the Andean data themselves and such still modest and fragmentary models as we can derive from them. Emerging evidence is beginning to make possible a more complete or at least balanced, view of Andean prehistory. At the same time, at least partial models are being formulated that are based more directly in the Andean data. In this paper I would first like to briefly emphasize some of what I consider the most pertinent features of the Inca state and its administration, and then look at these in terms of some of the ideas on the political organization and utilization of diverse ecological zones proposed by John Murra (1972, 1976) and used extensively in the study of smaller scale Andean polities known from both the ethnohistoric and ethnographic records. The second part of the paper looks, in a tentative and loosely structured way, at some of the developmental implications suggested by the sixteenth century situation. The intent is not explicitly processual, but rather to search for directions from which more systematic explanations of the origins and growth of Andean complex societies might come.

The Study of Inca Organizational Structure

It is becoming increasingly apparent that the Inca empire was not just a huge domain formed through gradual expansion by conquest, with a uniform general policy to turn each newly conquered territory into a replica of those conquered before it in order to create a relatively homogeneous state. The limited evidence to date does indeed suggest that some kind of grand master plan was in place by the time of Pizarro, but that it was a plan that attempted to deliberately order and manage the ecological and cultural diversity the empire encountered, rather than to reduce it to some easy administrative common denominators. In fact, the brilliance of the Inca achievement seems to lie in its ability to accept, use, and perhaps even foster variability.

We cannot say at this point how completely the area had been subjected to state planning. Our impression is that many areas were basically unincorporated, but we do not know enough about Inca planning itself at this point to be certain that a strategy of minimal interference was not in fact deliberate in many areas. No complex scheme of empire organization could have been realized in detail in the scant century allowed the Inca. We are dealing with an empire still in formation. The limitations on the power and influence of the Cuzco rulers would have made the exact implementation of any master plan impossible. But at the same time we can see the advantage in an overall strategy that sets out the nature of the various parts of the state and their interrelationships with each other. If one is going to try to administer a far-flung state encompassing considerable cultural and environmental heterogeneity, the task is made simpler by having a structure that rationalizes the roles of the various component parts.

We do not have sufficient evidence to begin to describe the overall structure and organization of Tawantinsuyu. The purpose here is to underline such evidence as we have of genuinely large-scale planning and organization. If investigators are persuaded of the necessity of broadening their areas of research in keeping with the cultural and political extent of complex societies, we should be able to unravel many of the principles the Inca attempted to implement in their creation of empire. But I cannot stress too strongly the tentative nature of the present enterprise. There has been no opportunity to pursue these problems in the written sources; the record of archaeological contexts on which most of the suggestions are based is, of course, still meager.

1. Perhaps the most evident approach is to look at the *quechua* terms the Inca used to refer to their domain. How did they conceive of it? It is best to leave this to the ethnohistorians and linguists who are more qualified than I to undertake it. The term Tawantinsuyu is obviously indicative of the importance of the matter, and the often seemingly competing systems of dual, tripartite, and decimal principles all deserve detailed study. The study of territoriality from a perspective of state organization cannot ultimately be divorced from other aspects of the study of spatial structure.

2. A second kind of data pertinent to the question of planning on an empire-wide basis is the physical structure that linked it together. The system of roads, way-stations, administrative centers, and supply depots is legendary. John Hyslop's (1984) recent study of the road system reveals both its complexity and enormous extent. He calculates that at least 23,000 kilometers of roads can be charted, and that the figure may eventually rise to 40,000 kilometers when evidence is complete. Many of the roads in use during Inca times, of course, had been constructed earlier.

Obviously the roads and the logistics centers along them were part of a communications and logistics network that facilitated the movement of people and goods from one part of the empire to another. But the preoccupation with roads seems to have been more than a concern with efficient communication and movement. There is a level of formality that suggests somehow that linkage itself was important, that the roads and associated centers built by the state were a way of imposing a structure on the empire—a critical part of its very definition. Centers which in one way or another mirrored or imitated certain facets of Cuzco were placed in various parts of the provinces. Buildings recognizably like buildings in the Cuzco heartland, sometimes equipped with pottery in the style of Cuzco, identified these centers with the state. They were rather like miniature state islands scattered over a landscape originally controlled (and still largely administered) by other polities. The roads linked them together and the combination of state centers, the roads, and the capital itself in a sense constituted a separate

Inca domain, spatially discontinuous and intrusive into a series of other local domains. It interacted with them, was superior to them, and exacted its economic price. But there was no real attempt at cultural (Rowe 1982), political, or economic homogeneity. What was attempted was rather a careful orchestration of hundreds of parts, to maintain a coordinated and balanced diversity.

3. An additional category of evidence will come from the study of the nature and variability of the centers that, in combination, produced the overall plan. These studies, necessarily for the most part archaeological, must include analyses of form and layout as well as activities.

To call for a systematic study of settlement variation in an empire covering many thousands of square kilometers is obviously a tall order and something that will be achieved cumulatively by combining the results of many investigators. There are already some modest beginnings. Aveni (personal communication) and his colleagues have investigated patterns related to astronomical phenomena. Hyslop (personal communication) has pointed to an emerging pattern of orientations for certain areas. Zuidema (1982) has suggested that several sites in the Cuzco area are located on relatively straight lines stretching out hundreds of kilometers from the capital. My own studies of the organization of space at Huanuco Pampa (Morris, in press) have shown that large individual centers incorporated quite detailed and complex planning. Although the exact nature of such planning is very difficult to decipher, some of the same organizational principles observed in the *ceque* in Cuzco appear to be involved. Indeed, at the most general level, some of the same structural principles almost certainly governed the Inca conception of Tawantinsuyu itself.

Cursory examination of a dozen or so Inca installations with substantial standing architecture suggest that common elements occurred. These common elements include both functional units such as storage facilities, elite residences and religious structures, and more abstract structural principles such as spatial divisions reflecting dualism, tripartition, or quadripartition. In spite of these evident common elements, I have seen no two Inca centers that are even closely similar in their details. More thorough investigation will tell us if the variations themselves are patterned. I expect that they are, but the nature of the patterning may be very difficult to discover.

4. A final category of evidence for planning on a large scale is, even in our present state of knowledge, more secure. These are the *mitmaq* settlements moved long distances by the Cuzco rulers. *Mitmaq* populations are documented in many parts of the Tawantinsuyu. By far the most spectacular case is that documented by Wachtel (1982) for the

warm lands of Cochabamba. During the rule of Huayna Capac, 14,000 *mitima* from several different places were brought in, some on a permanent basis and some in temporary labor service, to grow maize for the army. Wachtel suggests that such large-scale shifts of population for economic purposes was a late development, contrasting with earlier use of *mitima* primarily for military and security purposes. Patrick Carmichael and I have conducted an archaeological study of the much smaller groups of *mitima* in the Huallaga Valley. These groups, assigned by Inka Yupanqui, predecessor of Huayna Capac, were clearly population shifts on another scale. They had the stated business of guarding "forts" in the montaña and preventing the rebellion of the Chupaychu. The lands they tilled were not adequate to supply significant quantities of maize to the state. Nevertheless there are some archaeological suggestions of administrative functions, and these too were part of a pattern of population movements that made Tawantinsuyu a patchwork of political and ethnic diversity manipulated by the ruling elite to a degree that is still, for us, difficult to comprehend.

Toward the Administration of Large-Scale Diversity

I turn now to a second major aspect of the Inca state. How were the varied and spatially discontinuous parts of the realm held together? How were the relationships handled between the state, anchored physically in its sets of settlements and its roads, and the various polities into which it intruded and hoped to rule? We are certainly quite far from a full understanding of the mechanisms of Inca administration. There was an army and elements of force and the threat of force were involved. There was also a bureaucracy armed with the *khipu* to aid record keeping and communication; without some such system the coordination of the great complexity of lands, peoples, and resources would have been out of the question. However, the salient feature of Inca control I believe was the amplification of many of the principles of Andean reciprocity from the village level, as Murra (1960, 1980) pointed out long ago (Morris 1982; Pease 1982). It was gifts, such as cloth and the sharing of food and of drink, that set the tone of relationships between leaders and led. Principles of reciprocity provided the labor to till the leader's fields and invoked the obligations of the leader to express his generosity with feasts and gifts that defined and solidified the community as well as reinforcing his own power.

The single most important result of our studies at Huanuco Pampa has been the indication that feasts and ceremonies were the focal point of that center's activities. In terms of both the architectural elaboration and the quantity of space devoted to it, public ritual was predominant. The primary reason for most of the people present at Huanuco Pampa, whether temporarily or permanently, seems to have been either to participate in the city's ceremonial life or to provide services to it. Many, if not most, of the resources delivered from the hinterland and held in the storehouses were used to support the rites and ceremonies of reciprocal administration. Its manufacturing activities were invested in producing cloth and beer, also to fuel the machinery of political ceremony (Morris 1974, 1978) by providing the most valuable products by which generosity and hospitality were measured.

Huanuco Pampa was for the most part a consumer center in terms of economic activities. Primary production was located elsewhere, in other parts of the overall system. Rather than being an economic city it was a political one. Reduced to its simplest terms it was a place where goods could be accumulated and turned into power.

Tawantinsuyu and the Developmental Aspects of Ecological Complementarity

It is evident from the observations made earlier about the emphasis on coordination of large territories with varied peoples and resources that there is much in the Inca approach to empire that is related to the model of "vertical ecological complementarity" outlined by Murra in the 1960s. The *mitmaq* institution and the practice of establishing rather artificial state administrative centers as Inca or imperial "urban islands" are particularly reminiscent of the "archipelago model"; although the scale is much larger and there are several elements here not present in the smaller societies for which the model was first elaborated.

Murra, of course, recognized the link between Inca institutions and the archipelago model. He also noted the critical point that the principles of complementarity at the level of the Inca state had transcended ecology. They were no longer limited to geography and subsistence (Murra 1972). The details of how the principles of complementarity were elaborated and related to the full range of Inca institutions and achievements requires much thought and analysis. Politics, religion, technology, and art are all involved. We really need the complete ethnography of the Andes at the eve of the Spanish conquest that we will never have.

Of course the Inca can really be understood only as a late point in a long cultural process. Sound explanations of institutions depend ultimately on relatively full developmental histories. Some of the *visitas* indicate that the archipelago was reality in many areas in immediately pre-Inca times. Archaeologists have begun to search for archipelagos in terms of ceramic styles in parts of the Andes. But years, if not decades, of work lie ahead of us to really verify systems of ecological complementarity and work out the histories of their development. Extremely thorough contextual archaeology is required to determine the character of relationships between zones, and this must be combined with full ecological and resource assessments. In most of the Andes we still do not even have a detailed chronology on which to anchor these kinds of studies.

Thus not being able yet to comment significantly on the actual development of archipelago forms and their role in the history of Andean civilization, I will look instead at some of the implications of the model that I believe deserve exploring as we seek new data. While we can have little more than hypotheses at this point, the model and its variants have considerable potential for archaeologists, derived as they are from Andean evidence independent of archaeology and dealing with broad areas and multiple ecological zones.

This is not the first time an archaeologist has explored the developmental implications of the model of Andean ecological complementarity. Murra himself alluded to it as a possible explanation for the style horizons and called on archaeologists to investigate the matter. The most systematic consideration from a theoretical point of view has been that of Ana María Lorandi (1980).

It would be misleading to attempt to set up the points I want to make as a logically integrated model. I simply stress a few of the implications that deserve further exploration.

1. First is the point Lorandi stressed in her paper and which Murra has also alluded to. A political unit that is territorially discontinuous and had apparently been formed by a nuclear area or settlement establishing a colony in a territory outside itself could be expected to engender more tension and conflict than a spatially continuous polity. Conflict, of course, has long been recognized in anthropology as a major source of change and frequently of socio-political growth.

The potential for conflict would be especially marked if the discontinuous polity stretched across territory controlled by another polity, or if lands in an area wanted by one group were already occupied or used by another. Also certain kinds of resources, salt for example, tend to be restricted to relatively small areas that were somehow shared or divided by several groups. These "multi-ethnic" islands would seem to present special tensions and administrative problems.

Our data on archipelago systems come either from the Tawantinsuyu-Colonial transition or from the modern republics. There is thus an umbrella of large political hegemony which is very different than would have been the case in a formative situation. There is no shortage of indication of conflict in the archaeological record from quite early times, but the context of the conflict cannot be determined with sufficient precision to be of much help here. We need to get as close as possible to the kind of detail that will allow us to gauge what Murra (1976: 142) has called a "tense but real coexistence."

2. In addition to the administrative needs that may result from conflict and its management, several students of early states (e.g., Adams 1966) have stressed the administrative requirements of diversified ecologies and economies as possible causal factors in the emergence of centralized authority. In this case the complications of coordinating relationships and movements between the islands of the dispersed polities are compounding factors.

We might even suggest that the island arrangement could lead not just to a tendency toward overall centralization, but also to hierarchies of administrative authority, since detached groups would not be subject to constant monitoring from the nucleus. There would thus be a tendency for the growth of a system capable of coordinating groups that were dispersed and to a certain extent responsible for their own day-to-day operation—a kind of closely coordinated indirect rule. If groups were added to an archipelago by conquest or alliances, as I suspect they must have sometimes been as the scale of complementarity systems grew, skills in administering multi-ethnic polities would be gained. By the time of Tawantinsuyu this coordination of ethnic as well as ecological complexities was extreme, as peoples could not only be moved thousands of kilometers, but parts of a polity could be detached *in situ* and assigned to a neighboring polity. The *visita* of Inigo Ortiz for the Huanuco area hints that certain settlements were taken from the Yacha and added to the Chupaychu (Murra 1967). Archaeology was able to confirm that this was in fact the case (Thompson 1967).

The complexity of archipelago systems are of course compounded in conquest state situations where several separate systems are brought under the umbrella of a larger one, creating a system of overlapping tiers of units. At the same time that the scale is large, the overall polity is also highly fragmented along social, political, ethnic, and economic lines. State cities such as Huanuco Pampa were like outliers to the Cuzco nucleus that, in turn, became state political and administrative nuclei for the regions they served. But at the same time they were rather like marginal multi-ethnic outliers to each of the various groups they helped to incorporate into the state. For the most part the incorporated groups retained their economic and social integrity, simply assigning some of their members, either permanently or temporarily, to these new "urban" outliers. We can see in such a system the potential for participation in multiple polities and the relative ease with which alignments could be shifted.

It is hard for us to conceive how all of this rapidly changing complexity could have worked, even briefly. As I have already indicated, I feel that an elaborate formal plan had been constructed as a guide to the placement of the various units for Tawantinsuyu, and there was a sophisticated calendar to coordinate scheduling. That feasts, drinking bouts, religion, and the trappings of elaborated reciprocities evidently played such a dominant role in Huanuco Pampa surprised me, with my expectations of a more military and bureaucratic form of administration. We simply do not think of these kinds of administrative mechanisms playing prominent roles in large and complex states. The ceremonies could, of course, have been a kind of front covering a large, stodgy bureaucracy behind the scenes. But some of the reason for the continuing effectiveness of such mechanisms may lie in the rapidity in which they can be built up in part by simply shifting around some of the blocks in existing units. It may also be that such theater state-like devices are more effective than rigid bureaucracies in managing the fragmented kinds of units we have seen here, which can be shifted and even be physically transported with some ease.

3. A further developmental problem that deserves exploration is the relationship between systems of ecological complementarity and systems of political economics in which labor is the central factor. One may argue about the extent to which the Inca state might have levied tribute in kind, but I remain convinced that in theory tribute obligations were levied in terms of labor except in certain parts of the empire, such as the far north, where it may have gone against local custom (and where archipelago systems were probably absent). I have mentioned previously (Morris 1981) that in a system where human energy is the main source of revenue it is important to be able to move people around so that labor can be effectively utilized for a variety of tasks. I don't presume to suggest cause and effect in either direction, but further exploration of this relationship, so central to the archipelago model, might help us understand both the dizzying population movements the Andean peoples were capable of and the persistence of a reciprocally managed labor based system for the mobilization of state revenues, at a scale where a commodity based system might seem more rational and efficient.

4. As a final point on the developmental aspects of Andean ecological complementarity I look quickly at the potential role of manufactures. In political growth the changes that take place in non-subsistence goods are especially interesting. New classes of goods emerge in relation to status and power; values are transformed as patterns of demand are altered in relation to emerging needs for prestige.

As we study the development of Andean society we will need to monitor especially closely the production, distribution, and consumption of special value goods. Fortunately this is precisely the kind of study archaeology can attempt realistically through studies of artifact distributions, production facilities, and their contexts, as Shimada's paper in this volume shows. In relation to ecological complementarity the primary questions relate to access to raw materials, although other matters are pertinent because of their relationship to reciprocity and redistribution.

Cloth, the most valued of Andean commodities, is a case in point. Most zones had easy access to either cotton or wool. However, wool was almost certainly more valuable in prestige terms because of its much superior ability to take dyes. If the distribution of wool producing camelids even approached that of modern times, the *puna* regions would have had a near monopoly on what was probably the Andes' most important single product. There are suggestions that camelids may not have been so restricted in pre-Columbian times, but nevertheless they were probably much less common in warm valleys and on the coast and were the basis of the *puna*'s vast wealth. Source, production, and distribution studies on cloth are much more difficult than for many other commodities, but they are particularly pressing.

The place of precious metals in the Andean scheme of values is somewhat unclear, but they were obviously important. Here the studies of the management of sources, production, and distribution are already beginning, as they are for ceramics. Goods such as *mullu* (*Spondylus*) and feathers seem to have fit rather differently into the system in Inca times since they came from its periphery and may not have been acquired through the usual revenue measures. Coca leaf and maize were also special products; because of their ritual uses they played unusual and probably changing roles in developing patterns of ecological complementarity.

5. I have made no attempt to tie the observations made above to the actual archaeological evidence; the intent has been primarily to raise questions. Shimada, Mujica, Schaedel, and Onuki in this volume have been more cognizant of the existing evidence. Those papers demonstrate the interest in principles of ecological complementarity for

interpreting the data from the early time periods. As Shimada's paper, in particular, shows, a special and thorough kind of archaeological documentation is required if we are to deal with such issues effectively.

Perhaps the most compelling argument for considerable historical depth of archipelago principles is that the population movements incorporated so importantly into the grand spatial patterns of Inca times would probably not have been accepted by an Andean populace not already familiar with similar practices. Movements of people on the scale documented by Wachtel for the maize fields of Cochabamba and on various scales elsewhere could not have been invented and imposed overnight by what was, after all, a relatively small and, at the beginning, not especially powerful group. A considerable level of consent is implied and therein a familiarity with doing things far from home, even permanently moving—in other words a special concept of one's relationship to the land.

While some of the analysis quickly summarized in the first part of this paper seems to find a loose analogy in Geertz's (1980) study of nineteenth century Bali or Wheatley's (1971) study of the Chinese city, we should not let the rituals of power that were such a vital force in Tawantinsuyu detract us from the economic realities that supported it and allowed it to expand. Political power could not expand without the goods that in a sense bought it. The Inca were able to secure their revenues in part by depriving local leaders of "surplus" production that previously had been at their disposal. They were essentially political goods that had been moved up the scale a notch or two. Another part came from the alienation of community lands. A third part came from what Murra (1980) has called "new lands." These were lands that had been brought into production by the state. In some cases labor had been reorganized to make cultivation more efficient; in others the land itself had been transformed by terracing and irrigation to increase productivity. In a sense these state practices can be seen as exploitative, but they were also creative. We will probably never have comparative figures, but between Inca and pre-Inca times it is likely that production of both subsistence and non-subsistence goods was increased and their use made more effective through storage. While we certainly no longer believe Tawantinsuyu to have been the welfare state some once thought, the state was probably still able to provide for its elite without compromising the subsistence base of most of the people it incorporated. Luxury goods were obviously redistributed differently among the elites, but I would guess that the total quantity of elite goods was at least as great, if not substantially greater.

Thus while many of these presumed increases were the result of increasing state control over human energy, others were the result of the creation of new lands and resources. Both of these are logical continuations of Andean tradition, and the latter is an expression of an ideal which seems basic to the model of Andean ecological complementarity: when a resource is needed an effort is made to acquire land in an area where it can be produced. This is an idea that is imperialistic almost by definition, "una visión totalizadora," to use Lorandi's words (1980). We can argue, however, that some of the Inca conquests were made through advances in technology and organization.

Another change probably inherent in archipelago systems is the tendency to sever ties with kin and community as the scale of the system expands (Murra 1976). As people were moved increasing distances their ties with what had been their home nucleus was undoubtedly altered. The ties and related reciprocities were replaced by fictious ties and reciprocities invented by the state. It was in the creation of these fictive ties and the enactment of the reciprocal rites that made them seem real that the mechanisms akin to a "theater-state" functioned.

As we continue to use and test the model of Andean ecological complementarity in our attempt to describe and explain the Andean trajectory to territorially extensive polities, we will have to be concerned with developing and using plausible archaeological methodologies, as I have indicated above. It will also be necessary to continue to expand and clarify the archipelago model itself. In particular, political, economic, and ideological dynamics need further exposition. It is these dimensions that push the principles of complementarity beyond the ecological that we must cope with in order to deal with the growth of large-scale socio-political systems.

It is already clear that this Andean trajectory differed substantially from one region to another as it led to increasingly grandiose attempts to incorporate people, resources, and activities under increasingly large organizational umbrellas. Political solutions were sought to problems that in other parts of the world were more frequently solved through trade and barter. The still meager archaeological data in hand suggest that the growth in scale was quite rapid, but achievements of large polities were somewhat cyclical and unstable.

As studies proceed we also need to incorporate more systematically work on the ideology and symbolism that helped define the changing patterns the Andean peoples put on their universe. The patterns are too big and complex to understand in economic terms alone. At the same time the more cognitive studies of religion and ritual cannot be very helpful if isolated from the economic and political activities they helped coordinate.

We are obviously only at the threshold of beginning to understand the long developmental process that ended, prematurely, with Tawantinsuyu. But some of the tools for the investigation are beginning to become available. The model of Andean ecological complementarity is one of those tools. If we are interested in answering questions such as why Andean political units seem to have expanded faster and grown larger than in many other parts of the world, that model with its emphasis on inherently political means of resource management and exchange is of considerable explanatory importance.

REFERENCES CITED

Adams, Robert McC.

1966 The Evolution of Urban Society. Chicago: Aldine Press

Geertz, Clifford

1980 Negara: The Theater State in Nineteenth Century Bali. Princeton: Princeton University Press.

Hyslop, John

1984 The Inka Road System. New York and San Francisco: Academic Press.

Lorandi, Ana María

1980 Arqueología y Economía: Hacia una visión Totalizadora del Mundo Andino. Obra del Centenario 2: 27–50. La Plata, Argentina: Museo de La Plata.

Morris, Craig

1974 Non-Agricultural Production in the Inka Economy: An Institutional Analysis. *In* Reconstructing Complex Societies. Charlotte Moore, ed. pp. 49–60. Cambridge, Massachussetts: American School of Oriental Research.

1978 Maize Beer in the Economics, Politics, and Religion of the Inca State. *In* The Role of Fermented Food Beverages in Nutrition. Clifford Gastineau et al., eds.

1981 Tecnología y Organización Inca del Almacenamiento de Víveres en la Sierra. *In* Runakunap Kawsayninkupaq Rurusqankunaqa. Heather Lechtman and Ana María Soldi, eds. Vol. 1, pp. 327–75. Mexico: Universidad Nacional Autónoma de México.

1982 The Infrastructure of Inka Control in the Peruvian Central Highlands. *In* The Inka and Aztec States 1400–1800: Anthropology and History. George A. Collier, Renato I. Rosaldo, and John D. Wirth, eds. pp. 153–71. New York: Academic Press.

In press Architecture and the Structure of Space at Huanuco Pampa. *In* Tecnología urbanismo, Arquitectura de los Incas. Graziano Gasparini and Louise Margulies, eds. Caracas: EDIVA.

Murra, John V.

1960 Rite and Crop in the Inca State. *In* Culture in History. Stanley Diamond, ed. pp. 393–407. New York: Columbia University Press.

1967 La Visita de los Chupacho como Fuente Etnológica. *In* Iñigo Ortiz de Zúñiga, Visita de la Provincia de Leon de Huánuco en 1562. Tomo 1. Edición a cargo de J. V. Murra, pp. 383–406. Huánuco: Universidad Nacional Hermilio Valdizán.

1972 El Control Vertical de un Máximo de Pisos Ecológicos en La Economía de las Sociedades Andinas. *In* Iñigo Ortiz de Zúñiga, Visita de la Provincia de León de Huánuco en 1562. Tomo 2. Edición a cargo de J. V. Murra, pp. 429–68. Huánuco: Universidad Nacional Hermilio Valdizán.

1976 Los Limites y las Limitaciones del Archipiélago Vertical en los Andes. Antofagasta: Anales de la Universidad del Norte 10: 141–46.

[1956] 1980 The Economic Organization of the Inca State. Supplement No. 1 to Research in Economic Anthropology. Greenwich, Connecticut: JAI Press.

Pease, Franklin

1982 The Formation of Tawantinsuyu: Mechanisms of Colonization and Relationships with Ethnic Groups. *In* The Inca and Aztec States 1400–1800: Anthropology and History. George A. Collier, Renato I. Rosaldo, and John D. Wirth, eds. pp. 173–98. New York: Academic Press.

Rowe, John H.

1982 Inca Policies and Institutions Relating to the Cultural Unification of the Empire. *In* The Inca and Aztec States 1400–1800: Anthropology and History. George A. Collier, Renato I. Rosaldo, and John D. Wirth, eds. pp. 93–118. New York: Academic Press.

Thompson, Donald E.

1967 Investigaciones Arqueológicas en las Aldeas Chupachu de Ichu y Auquimarca. *In* Iñigo Ortiz de Zúñiga, Visita de la Provincia de León de Huánuco en 1562, Tomo I. Edición a cargo de J. V. Murra, pp. 359–62. Huánuco: Universidad Nacional Hermilio Valdizán.

Wachtel, Nathan

1982 The Mitimas of the Cochabamba Valley: The Colonization Policy of Huayna Capac. *In* The Inca and Aztec States 1400–1800: Anthropology and History. George A. Collier, Renato I. Rosaldo, and John D. Wirth, eds. pp. 199–235. New York: Academic Press.

Wheatley, Paul

1971 The Pivot of the Four Quarters. Chicago: Aldine Press.

Zuidema, R. Tom

1982 Bureaucracy and Systematic Knowledge in Andean Civilization. *In* The Inca and Aztec States 1400–1800: Anthropology and History. George A. Collier, Renato I. Rosaldo, and John D. Wirth, eds. pp. 419–58. New York: Academic Press.

21

Andean Exchange: A View from Amazonia

Hideo Kimura

Introduction

Many theories, both specific and general, on exchange have been advanced by both anthropologists and sociologists, notably Mauss (1966), Lévi-Strauss (1967), Homans (1961), Blau (1964), and Barth (1966). Our basic ideas on the subject typically come from Mauss's classic work, *Essai sur le don*; however, in this paper I adopt the Lévi-Straussian "alliance" theory perspective on exchange. The term exchange as used here thus carries essentially the same significance as Lévi-Straussian "communication." This perspective allows us to analyze a wide range of social transactions, e.g., donation, verbal and non-verbal communication, marriage, feasting, or even violence. The focus of this paper, however, is analysis of economic transactions and marriages for which we have sufficient ethnographic data from both Amazonia and the Andes.

In speaking of exchange, we are concerned with the kind of social action in which "the participants . . . do not behave as members of the same corporate group but rather as representatives of different and—for the purpose of the action—opposed social groups" (Schwimmer 1973:3). In any social system, the levels of social units can be analytically separated: the individual, the nuclear family, the extended family, the descent group, the tribe, and so on, and corresponding to each level, we might find a particular kind of opposition and exchange.

When we employ alliance theory to analyze social transactions, the corporate group cannot be defined by its internal descent principles. Rather, as clearly demonstrated by Dumont (1966), the opposed groups must be defined by the alliance. It follows that we must analyze the structure of interdependent relationships among corporate groups.

In this paper, my attention is directed to a social unit that can be tentatively called "community." Clearly, Amazonia or the Andes, in regard to their respective ecological and socio-cultural characteristics, is not a homogenous or unified whole. Naturally there are numerous differences in both exchange systems and community structures. However, for the sake of our broad comparison that may highlight differences and similarities in these adjoining areas, Amazonia and the Andes are treated as ideal types constituting useful analytical units.

Amazonia

The first case to be examined is an Amazonian tribe known as Ese Exa which inhabits the northwestern lowlands of Bolivia and was the primary subject of my first ethnographic fieldwork. The present-day Ese Exa is a fairly acculturated tribe that left its homeland more than fifty years ago, and has had frequent contact with local Bolivians and Christian missionaries. Their community structure has been transformed to the point that we cannot reconstruct with precision their original social structure before their contact with the Whites. However, some original features are still recognizable in the present community structure.

The Ese Exa classify themselves into three groups: *Bawaxa*, *Sonene*, and *Madidi*. My fieldwork was conducted among the last group, which is composed of three sub-groups: *Natawa*, *Nawo'o*, and *Ekexati*. The names of the three principal groups correspond to the names of the rivers known in Bolivia and Peru as Río Tambopata, Río Heath, and Río Madidi, respectively. *Natawa* and *Nawo'o* are the names of tributaries of Río Madidi. *Ekexati*, on the other hand, signifies "the mouth of the river." The Ese Exa are river people occupying areas along or near the rivers. For example, those who live along Río Tambopata are called *Bawaxa kuiñaxi*, meaning inhabitants of Río Tambopata. The above major groups and sub-groups are geographically separated, localized units.

Seven Ese Exa villages are scattered along Río Beni in modern Bolivia; one is *Sonene kuiñaxi* and the other six are of *Madidi kuiñaxi*. The village composition of all the Madidi villages is a mixture of subgroups, but the present-day Ese Exa, especially the younger generation, are not conscious of sub-group divisions. Most of the subgroups are merged into one general group, *kueiai kuiñaxi*, inhabitants of the Big River—Río Beni—where they now live.

The Ese Exa assert that strong ties exist between father and child (patrifiliation) in the sense that the father's sperm creates the embryo, his sperm nourishes the fetus by successive copulations and also, the father's soul staff contained in the sperm is transferred to the fetus. The mother is regarded as just a receptacle for the fetus. Nevertheless, this notion does not provide a basis for forming any descent groups (patrilineal) larger than the extended family due to several limiting factors. First, although one's soul is transmitted from his or her father, it can be mixed with other souls by physical contact with others. Dwellers of the same house or community possess some soul staffs in common because their souls can be mixed together by contact. Second, the Ese Exa's genealogical knowledge is poor; they can trace their genealogical relations only to the second ascending generation. Third, the Ese Exa can distinguish "relatives" from "non-relatives" by the *we'e/we'epoxiama* division. These divisions are not groups but ego-centered categories. In the *we'epoxiama* are included FF (Father's Father), MF (Mother's Father), FM, MM, F, FB, FZ, M, MZ, B (Brother), Z (Sister), FBS, FBD, MZS, MZD, S (Son), D (Daughter), BS, BD, SS, SD, DS, DD, and in the *we'e* MB, MBS, MBD, FZS, FZD, ZS, ZD, inlaws, and strangers. This genealogical principle is applied to near kinsmen, but for others whose genealogical relations are not known, they can apply other principles like common residence or relative age to determine the appropriate term. Most typically, if two people born in the same community now live together in another community they are *we'epoxiama* to each other despite the fact that they may be *we'e* genealogically. As I have shown elsewhere (Kimura 1983), this *we'epoxiama/we'e* division is the major determinant of Ese Exa relationship terminology; and it apparently contains no patrilineal principle. To categorize other people, there are determinants like personal friendship, adoption, and relative age. The major internal division, *we'epoxima/we'e*, which also divides marriageable and non-marriageable, is not fixed by one principle but very situationally determined, picking up one principle from others.

Post-marital residence is uxorilocal; the man can marry his *we'e* woman in the same village or can wander among other Ese Exa villages to find a wife, much like the Campa of Peru (Varese 1973), and settle in the house where his wife and father-in-law live. He who does not stay in his home village also may escape and move into another community, looking for some relationship with inhabitants of the community where he wants to settle or take refuge. Diachronically, the Ese Exa communities may have changed form and composition continuously; their members moving in and out, and sometimes the community even splitting in two or three. The internal boundary is not diachronically well-defined.

Nevertheless, the concept of community is firmly fixed in the minds of the Ese Exa and is synchronically a real entity. It is said that in old times they had a system of communal cultivation of agricultural fields, hunting, and fishing under the direction of a village leader, *emeshimese*, who these days does not have such authority and power. Although the community in reality continues to change its form, the ideal of the community is always the same and communities confront each other as social units.

I believe that these characteristics of Ese Exa social structure may be present in many other Amazonian societies. It is clear that kinship ties and communal ideology are stronger among less acculturated tribes. In addition, among these tribes the kinship bond may not be extended to other communities. There may even exist some descent groups or "lineages" in the community, in reality no more than small-scale sibling groups. The community identity is always changing because of the frequent movement of its members (Rivière 1969; Chagnon 1983; Biocca 1969; Maybury-Lewis 1974). And, as in the Alto Xingu societies of Brazil, tribal identity is situationally fixed, sometimes based on kinship ties, sometimes on residence, sometimes on affinal bonds (Cardoso de Oliveira 1976:10–11).

An ideology of dividing things and people into two exists among many Amazonian tribes, but the external principles on which groups' actions are based vary; that is, the ideology of duality exemplified in decisions is based sometimes on descent-based exogamous moieties, sometimes on ceremonial moieties, and other times on non-kinship-based political factions. In short, among Amazonian tribes, though the boundary and the membership of the community are quite vague, the community which may exist only as a category is thought to be a real entity.

Amazonia, as a whole, is not ecologically homogeneous as once thought (Moran 1981; Hames and Vickers 1983). In regions such as the Venezuelan-Brazilian border, some indigenous groups participate in an exchange system based on the varied products of ecological differences (Ramos 1980). However, areas where indigenous groups make exchanges among themselves are more or less ecologically homogenous; typically they have the same or similar flora, fauna, cultivated plants, and raw materials with which they manufacture various artifacts that are available most anywhere within the area. Thus, before contact with Whites, most such groups or communities did not have special material objects to exchange with others.

From an ecological or economic point of view, the Amazonian

communities can be seen as self-sufficient. They can subsist on their own products; there appears to be no necessity to exchange material goods in the Amazonian world. Perhaps the only objects of exchange necessary to the Amazonians are marriage partners for reproduction, partly to avoid excessive inbreeding.

But in reality, systems of tribal and inter-tribal exchange exist in many regions. Because these groups have no "true" need to exchange material goods, they must create a demand. The exchange system of the Alto Xingu area of Brazil and among the Yanomamö of the Venezuela-Brazilian border exemplifies some characteristic features of Amazonian exchange. A wealth of information has been accumulated about the exchange system of the Alto Xingu area (Oberg 1953; Murphy and Quain 1955; Basso 1973; Gregor 1977). Gregor (1977) believed that most of the important product monopolies of the Xingu Indians seem to have some basis in ecological variation. But he thinks as follows:

> The tribal specialities unsupported by variation in natural resources are difficult to explain. Deposits of reasonably good clay, for example, exist in a number of areas outside the Waura's territory, and yet only Waura women make ceramic pots. Since these pots are important in subsistence as well as in measuring wealth, it would be very much to the advantage of the Mehinaku women if they are ceramists. The villagers offer several explanations of why they do not make clay pots. The most significant is that making pots is "properly" an activity of Waura women; if a Mehinaku woman tried to make pots, everyone would ridicule her bad workmanship. In addition, if the village women were to make pots it would break the Waura monopoly; and maintaining the tribal interdependence is in itself perceived a virtue. A Kuyaparei puts it: "They have things that are beautiful, and we have things that they like. And so we trade, and that is good. (Gregor 1977:310–11)

The same kind of phenomenon occurs among the Yanomamö. Chagnon, although he may not agree with my theoretical stand points, reports as follows:

> The third significant trade feature is the peculiar specialization in the production of trade items. Each village has one or more special products that it provides to its allies. These include such items as dogs, hallucinogenic drugs (both cultivated and collected), arrow points, arrow shafts, bows, cotton yarn, cotton and vine hammocks, baskets of several varieties, clay pots, and, in the case of the contacted villages, steel tools, fishhooks, fishline, and aluminum pots.

> This specialization in production cannot be explained in terms of the distribution of natural resources. Each village is, economically speaking, capable of self-sufficiency. (The steel tools and other products from civilization constitute the major exceptions.) The explanation for the specialization must be sought, rather, in the sociological aspects of alliance formation. (Chagnon 1983:149)

In these two systems, the exchange or donation of goods becomes compulsory when a trade partnership is established. In addition, visiting, feasting, and finally marriage accompany trade. As Chagnon asserts, the specialization or monopoly of trade goods, and the compulsory nature of exchange, must not be understood by way of ecological conditions but rather by taking into account social factors. Chagnon continues further:

> Alliances between villages may stabilize at any one of three points: sporadic reciprocal trading, mutual feasting, or reciprocal women exchange. These are cumulative levels in the sense that the third phase implies the first two: allies that exchange women also feast and trade with each other. Likewise, allies that merely feast together also trade, but do not exchange women. (Chagnon 1983:150)

Chagnon analyzes the problem of violence and war as an aspect of alliance. From our point of view, the Yanamamö may be seen to have a system of controlled exchange of violence. They do not usually leave others uncontacted. In other words, if nearby groups are not allies bound by peaceful exchange like trade, feasting, and exchange of women, the Yanomamö establish with them a relationship of violence.

Although we do not have detailed data about inter-community relationships among the Ese Exa, according to oral tradition, the situation was the same among them. They say that before contact with the Whites, many battles occurred between groups or sub-groups of the Ese Exa. The motives of the battle were primarily vengeance for sorcery. And the Ese Exa were notorious among local Bolivians as 'fierce savages' or 'barbarians.' These days, there are no serious conflicts or fights among the Ese Exa communities, but even the present Ese Exa still have no confidence in other communities and sometimes, though not publicly, accuse other communities of sorcery.

With respect to the direct relationship between trade partnership and marriage alliance, we can add other examples. Among the Pemon of Venezuela, trade partnership is sought through kinship ties and marriage alliances (Thomas 1972). Among the Ese Exa, this type of relationship appears in the system of *epeexi* (friend of partner). Each Ese Exa seeks his *epeexi* from his *we'e*, and in many instances these partners exchange their sisters as wives. They exchange material goods and co-operate with each other in work which requires several male adults, and when one man visits another community his *epeexi* offers him lodging, food, or other services. This *epeexi* partnership is symbolically represented on the Ese Exa religious level. In their religious thought, one supernatural being, *edosikiana*, plays a very important role. This being is thought to be a "master of wild animals" who controls game animals, like *Vai-mahsë* who occupies an important position in the Desana symbolism (Reichel-Dolmatoff 1968). As a representative of nature, *edosikiana* regulates the reciprocal relationship between the animal world and the human world. The Ese Exa are afraid of this *edosikiana* as a forest demon which attacks hunters in the forest and devours them but, at the same time, in their mythology this demon appears as the culture hero who brought the first cultural objects into the human world. Moreover, *edosikiana* sits beside and assists the shaman, *eyamikekua*, pointing out the causes of diseases, almost all of which are due to sorcery. This *edosikian-eyamikekua* relationship is thought to be that of *epeexi*; that is, a particular *edosikiana* which is the assistant of one *eyamikekua* is this *eyamikekua's epeexi*. The *edosikiana* is a symbol of nature which has an ambiguous character, harmful or benevolent to humans according to the situation, while the *eyamikekua* is a symbol of culture or society. In the social realm, too, *we'e* can be his allies or enemies, and *epeexi* is the one who is selected as an ally from among enemies. Thus, socially and symbolically, this *epeexi* relationship represents the reciprocal relationship between the inner-world (*we'epoxiama*, human world) and the outer-world (*we'e*, natural world).

In Amazonia, reciprocal exchange of labor and distribution of products are made at the inter-community level. Here, the exchanging units are individuals, families, or groups of siblings. This kind of exchange necessitates the cooperation of village members to maintain an indispensable subsistence economy. At the inter-community level, however, exchange is not necessary or inevitable, but rather artificial from a purely economic point of view. The reciprocal nature of Amazonian exchange is not economic but social; that is, each Amazonian community can be economically independent and socially closed and indifferent to the other. Amazonian communities, in reality, do contact other communities and maintain social relations with them through various mechanisms: attacking each other, exchanging marriage partners, or even by creating artificial economic scarcity by refraining from producing some material goods. Thus, Amazonian peoples seem to introduce "artificial" diversity into their homogeneous world by way of trade sustained by consciously established monopolies, feasting, maintenance of linguistic differences, marriage alliances, and warfare. This diversity may serve to maintain the distinctive identities of social units.

Andes

One of the most frustrating and intriguing problems for the student of Andean social anthropology is how to define the *ayllu*. *Ayllu* can be a kin-based category, but is also used to denote local community (Isbell 1978; Sato 1980:237–38). Naturally, there are regional differences in the use of the term and it has been used with varied connotations during Colonial as well as Republican periods. However, what seems important to me is the fact that in the Andean world, the opposition of *ayllu* against non-*ayllu* has the primary social importance. This observation forms a crucial part of Skar's definition of *ayllu*:

> The last clause of the definition, stating that an *ayllu* group is always conceived of as in opposition to something is included to indicate that the group is exclusive, thus carrying the connotation of *we*, the insiders, against *they*, the outsiders. In village fiestas this opposition is often ritually expressed, but its importance may best be seen in the process of political mobilization, since juxtaposition of groups is an essential element in political conflicts. (Skar 1982:171)

Isbell (1978) reports that the village of Chuschi is divided into two barrios—Hanay and Uray. These barrios are localized, but according to H. Tomoeda (1983, personal communication), during the fiesta of a certain Andean community the participants are divided into two groups, each of which represents Hanay and Uray. The criteria for recruitment of members is not observable. Here we see the dualism which exists in the minds of Andean people expressed in the localized barrio, and it may be expressed in the division of people at a particular moment, such as in the case of Tinku. The most significant point is the existence of dualism which can divide a land, people, or universe. Thus, as in the case of *ayllu*, for the Andean people, the rigid rules of determining membership of a moiety are not so important and the actual recruitment of members seems situational.

It is difficult to determine the boundary and meaning of community or *comunidad* in an Andean context. It can pose serious theoretical problems. Let us start our analysis first considering a community as a geographically separated local village; for example, Amarete where 374 households representing 1,454 inhabitants cluster (INE 1976). Generally, the Andean community is autonomous and closed. Social mobility appears limited, and if some members move to other regions, in the case of immigrants to the cities, the immigrants do not lose their identities as members of the community but maintain contact with their home village. This relationship is reflected in the fact that a great quantity of commodities is sent to villagers in the city from their home community. In the case of Amarete, many adult males are away from home working in the gold mines of the Yungas area, but continually move back and forth between the two areas.

Post-marital residence is neo-local, but newly married couples stay in their home communities because of endogamy rules. In addition to this pervasive village endogamy (Isbell 1978:132; Bolton 1980:343), Burchard (1980) reports local exogamy and regional endogamy. In the latter cases, community members may move to other communities within the region, continuing to retain property and membership in their home villages.

Logically, the ecological diversity of the Andes would be expected to result in varied modes of production. It is known that Andean people have long sought to establish self-sufficient economies, utilizing as wide a range of resources as possible through such mechanisms as "el control vertical de un máximo de pisos ecológicos" (Murra 1975: 60). As Brush (1977:8) observes, "the exploitation of the varied Andean environment rests on the demarcation of different production zones which are determined according to altitude and climate." Thus, it follows that a self-sufficient Andean community practicing vertical control has no need to trade material goods with other social units.

Yet in the Andean region there are many areas where this type of self-sufficient economy cannot be established or is not "convenient" for the villagers. Here we can consider the situation of the *pastores* of the *puna* zone who need to exchange their products with *agricultores* of the *suni* and *quichua* zones. The *pastores* offer animals for transport, meat, alpaca wool, and sometimes *cochayuyo* or coca to the *agricultores* in exchange for agricultural products such as maize and potato. Thus we see economic complementarity between the *pastores* and *agricultores* (Yamamoto in this volume).

From the Amazonian point of view, the exchange of material goods almost naturally accompanies the exchange of marriage partners, because the marriage alliance can ensure the stability of a material exchange partnership. In the Andes, this is not the case. In principle, as Tomoeda and Fujii (in this volume) argue, the marriage alliance does not occur between *pastores* and *agricultores*. This conclusion requires further verification.

According to French philosopher René Girard (1972), when exchange occurs between two different units, this exchange "undifferentiates" these two units. In this regard, the rejection of marriage alliance between the *pastores* and *agricultores* may be seen as the rejection of undifferentiation. We can assume that as material exchange is inevitable, they do not need to make their relationship stronger or that the *agricultores* do not want to assimilate themselves with the *pastores*, but rather maintain their status differences.

Following the above examination of the Andean characteristics of material exchange and marriage alliance, we now consider the problem raised by Olivia Harris:

> The Laymis—Aymara-speakers—today number roughly 8,000 souls, of whom about two-thirds live in the highland *suni* (between approximately 3,800 and 5,000 meters) and the other third in the temperate *likina* (2,000 to 3,500 meters). In both zones households have a broad subsistence base including a variety of both indigenous and Old World crops and livestock. In the *suni* llamas and sheep are reared, and the staple is a rich variety of tubers, together with some beans, wheat, and barley; in the *likina* the main crops are maize and squashes, with some wheat, beans, and certain breeds of potato and *quinoa* that prosper in the warm climate. Goats and some sheep are reared. These two "tiers" of Laymi territory are separated by a journey of several days, which can take as long as two weeks with laden llamas. (Harris 1982:72; also in this volume)

The above two groups of Laymis are geographically separated and settled in two ecologically different zones. Contrary to our generalization regarding the relationship between *pastores* and *agricultores*, "they [the Laymis] are almost entirely endogamous, and many marriages take place between the two zones, thus binding together through kinship ties" (Harris 1976:168). Harris further states:

> The Laymis are numerous enough for endogamy to be possible, even with marriage rules that forbid a union with anyone to whom a kin link can be traced. These rules have the effect both of spreading links

> very widely within the group, and of guaranteeing the common kinship by which they retain their collective identity over time, divided as they are across such a wide area by many intervening, sometime hostile, groups (1982: 75).

In other words, the two groups of the Laymis which reside in two different ecological zones and make material exchange between themselves form an alliance with each other through marriage, in contrast to our previous conclusion about the *pastores-agricultores* linkage. The Laymis regard themselves as a single group. The discrepancy noted here points to the importance of further study of the conditions under which the different social units involved in the material exchange and marriage alliance are formed. I suspect community ideology or group identity and the distinction between "we" and "they", as well as the historical pecularities of the populations involved, are keys to our understanding.

Concluding Remarks: Amazonia and Andes

Comparing the exchange systems of Amazonia and the Andes, we can say that the two regions have established their exchange systems in totally opposite directions. Broadly speaking, Amazonian societies started from ecological homogeneity and sought diversity by means of exchange, whereas Andean societies started from ecological diversity and sought homogeneity or units by a different type of exchange. In Amazonia, the diversity is artificial or socially based, attained only by conscious alteration of some material elements in the naturally homogeneous whole. On the other hand, the Andes are characterized by environmental diversity and extremes.

It may be seen that the social units engaged in material exchange and marriage alliances are analytically separated ideal types, or concepts for analytical purposes. At first we treated the geographically separated, localized community as the social unit involved in exchange. As I stated earlier, the unit of exchange cannot be defined outside of the context of exchange. In other words, the exchange defines the boundaries of the social units; any internal social principle, such as that of descent, which has no direct relationship with the exchange, cannot define the social units engaged in the exchange.

As Leach (1961) pointed out, many rights and obligations are involved in marriage and it serves different functions in different social systems. In "diversity-seeking" Amazonia, marriage alliance functions as a bond between artificially diversified exchange units, and it can help establish the boundaries and identities of the units. In contrast, in the "homogeneity-seeking" Andes, the marriage alliance serves little or no function in linking social units. The rejection of marriage alliance serves to establish the boundaries of a given social unit. The economically self-sufficient social unit may make its boundaries more solid by endogamy, and in regions where material exchange exists between *pastores* and *agricultores*, endogamy prevents assimilation of the two. In Amarete we observed that the *agricultor del valle* sometimes seeks his *compadre* in his exchange partners who are *pastores de puna*. This *compadrazo* might serve functions similar to those of marriage alliance in Amazonia. This is a possibility that requires further analysis.

We have thus far touched upon some limited aspects of Andean and Amazonian exchange that were treated here for the sake of our broad comparison as ideal types, at times ignoring more specific regional variation. We are aware that our work is far from the analysis of *phènoménes sociaux totaux* as urged by Marcel Mauss (1966: 147). For better understanding of Andean, as well as Amazonian exchange systems, we have to pursue the analysis of the remaining aspects of this broadly conceived view of exchange in those two areas.

REFERENCES CITED

Barth, Fredrik

1966 Models of Social Organization. London: Royal Anthropological Institute Occasional Paper 23.

Basso, Ellen B.

1973 The Kalapalo Indians of Central Brazil. New York: Holt, Rinehart, and Winston.

Biocca, Ettore

1969 Yanoáma. London: George Allen and Unwin.

Blau, Peter

1964 Exchange and Power in Social Life. New York: Wiley.

Bolton, Ralph

1980 El parentesco matrimonial Qolla. *In* Parentesco y matrimonio de los Andes. Mayer and Bolton, eds. pp. 327–61. Lima: Pontificia Universidad Católica del Perú.

Brush, Stephen B.

1977 Mountain, Field, and Family: The Economy and Human Ecology of an Andean Valley. Philadelphia: University of Pennsylvania Press.

Burchard, Roderik R.

1980 Exogamía como estrategia de acceso a recursos interzonales: un caso en los Andes centrales del Perú. *In* Parentesco y matrimonio de los Andes. Enrique Mayer and Ralph Bolton, eds. pp. 593–616. Lima: Pontificia Universidad Católica del Perú. 593–616.

Cardoso de Oliveira, Roberto
1976 Identidade, Etnia e Estructura Social. São Paulo: Livraria Pioneira.

Chagnon, Napoleon
1983 Yanomamö: The Fierce People (3rd. ed). New York: Holt, Rinehart, and Winston.

Dumont, L.
1966 Descent or Intermarriage. Southwestern Journal of Anthropology 22:231–50.

Girard, René
1972 La violence et le sacré. Paris: Editiones Bernard Grasset.

Gregor, Thomas
1977 Mehinaku: The Drama of Daily Life in a Brazilian Indian Village. Chicago: University of Chicago Press.

Hames, Raymond B. and William T. Vickers
1983 Adaptive Responses of Native Amazonians. London: Academic Press.

Harris, Olivia
1976 Kinship and the Vertical Economy of the Laymi Ayllu, Norte de Potosí. Actes du XLIIe Congrès International des Américanistes, Paris. Vol. 4, pp. 165–77.
1982 Labour and Produce in an Ethnic Economy, Northern Potosí Bolivia. *In* Ecology and Exchange in the Andes. David Lehman, ed. pp. 70–98. Cambridge: Cambridge University Press.

Homans, George C.
1961 Social Behavior: Its Elementary Form. London: Routledge and Kegan Paul.

Instituto Nacional de Estadística (INE)
1976 Resumen Censo Nacional de Población y Vivienda. La Paz.

Isbell, Billie Jean
1978 To Defend Ourselves: Ecology and Ritual in an Andean Village. Austin: University of Texas Press.

Kimura, Hideo
1983 Ese Exa Relationship Terminology. Shakai Jinruigaku Nenpo 9: 53–81.

Leach, Edmund R.
1961 Polyandry, Inheritance, and the Definition of Marriage: With Particular Reference to Sinhalese Customary Law. *In* Rethinking Anthropology. Leach, ed. pp. 105–13. London: The Athlone Press.

Lévi-Strauss, Claude
1967 Les structure élémentaire de la parenté (2nd. ed.). The Hague: Mouton.

Mauss, Marcel

1966 Essai sur le don. *In* Sociologie et Anthropologie. Mauss, ed. pp. 145–279. Paris: Presses Universitaries de France.

Maybury-Lewis, David

1974 Akwẽ-Shavante Society. New York: Oxford University Press.

Moran, Emilio F.

1981 Developing the Amazon: The Social and Ecological Consequences of Government-directed Colonization along Brazil's Transamazon Highway. Bloomington: Indiana University Press.

Murphy, Robert F., and Buell Quain

1955 The Trumaí Indians of Central Brazil. Seattle: University of Washington Press.

Murra, John V.

1975 El control vertical de un máximo de pisos ecológicos en la economía de las sociedades andians. *In* Formaciones económicas y políticas del mundo andino. Murra, ed. pp. 59–115. Lima: Instituto de Estudios Peruanos.

Oberg, Kalervo

1953 Indian Tribes of Northern Mato Grosso. Washington D. C.: Smithsonian Institution.

Ramos, Alcida Rita

1980 Hierarquia e Simbiose: Relações intertribais no Brasil. São Paulo: HUCITEC.

Reichel-Dolmatoff, Gerardo

1968 Desana—Simbolismo de los Indios Tukano del Vaupes. Bogotá: Universidad de los Andes.

Riviere, Peter

1969 Marriage among the Trio. Oxford: Oxford University Press.

Sato, Nobuyuki

1980 Native Concept of Ayllu and Qata/a'acun (siblings-in-law): A Study of Family, Kinship and Ayllu. Bulletin of National Museum of Ethnology 5:190–239. Senri.

Schwimmer, Erik

1973 Exchange in the Social Structure of the Orokaiva: Traditional and Emergent Ideologies in Northern District of Papua. New York: St. Martin's Press.

Skar, Harold O.

1982 The Warm Valley People: Duality and Land Reform among the Quechua Indians of Highland Peru. Oslo: Universitetsforlaget.

Thomas, David J.

1972 The Indigenous Trade System of Southeast Estado Bolivar, Venezuela. Antropológica 33:3–37.

Varese, Stefano

1973 La sal de los Cerros. Lima: Retablo de Papel.

22

Discussion: An Interdisciplinary Perspective on Andean Ecological Complementarity

Richard P. Schaedel

My commentary, rather than being formally structured, will adhere to one of the characteristics of the ethnic groups, which practice verticality—it will be leap frog-like (Salpicado).

The first point I would like to stress has to do with an issue that somehow did not get joined in this symposium: the kind of nexus that exists between what Shimada called non-subsistence exchange and the supra-community level at which this exchange would be affected. This "non-subsistence exchange" mechanism was also one on which Morris wanted to focus. Actually most of the papers dealt with the community and not the supra-community level, and when the supra-community level was discussed, as in the presentations by Shimada and Onuki, there was ambiguity whether this level was that of a chiefdom, a state, or one intermediate between the two (as yet undefined).

In thc discussion following the presentation by Mujica, a debate ensued in which the issue was raised that I would like to emphasize, namely: is the type of exchange of products beyond those of subsistence conducted on the basis of essentially participatory reciprocity at the time of the first aggregation of communities (according to the ecological complementarity model) that produces a redistributive economy diagnostic of chiefdoms? If this were not the case, would this first aggregation of communities already represent the formation of the state, in which the redistribution is controlled by an elite apart and freed from the constraints of the masses, and consequently one that monopolizes the exchange of these so-called luxury products? As I understand Murra's model of the multi-ethnic entities, however great or small their scale, they represent, if not a pre-state level, a non-state level, since the redistributive system functions without coercive control. It is only with the formation of Tahuantinsuyu, the Inca state, that this coercive force can be detected; and with its appearance, pressures are imposed upon the redistributive economies of the formerly autonomous chiefdoms that threatened the survival of the system. Mujica's position is that Tiahuanaco and probably even Pukara represented the state level of community aggregation. If this were to be accepted, it would weaken the appeal of, and indeed the power of, the ecological complementarity model as a theory that explicates the maximization of the resources of the archipelago. It would imply that the pattern was coercively imposed by the nuclear communities of the altiplano either on their own colonies (formed by displaced exiles) or on alien ethnic groups already resident in other ecological floors.

The second point I should like to stress has to do with the connotation of the word "control" in defining and applying the model of ecological complementarity in this symposium. For some native Spanish speakers in the symposium (e.g. Mayer and Elias) one can easily extrapolate that "control" connotes political control, whatever the context in which it is employed. My own use of the word, and I believe Murra's use of the word in "El Control Vertical de un Máximo de Pisos Ecológicos" (1972) carries no such connotation, and would make the "type" of control rest with the adjective that modifies it. (To make my meaning more clear, let me state that I can visualize a situation in which an ethnic group exercises economic control over an ecological floor without exercising political control over the region to which it has access. If this were not so, the phrase "political control" would be redundant. I am not sure whether to native Spanish speakers this may not actually be the case). My question now is: when the phrase "control of ecological floors" is employed, are we speaking of a system whereby this control can be shared, or does the phrase necessarily imply a political control of the specified territoriality? My observation, should the answer to the question be "control implies political control," is similar to the one I just made regarding the precocious formulation of state hegemony model to supra-community aggregation; i.e., if the "control" exercised over the other ecological floor be from the first instant political, the problem of explaining access to the resources would be relegated to a model of hegemony and not to any principle of reciprocity, or what Dillehay (1979) termed "resource sharing" (in referring to the process in pre-Incaic Chillón area.)

This problem is not germane to the ethnographic papers that have been presented; since, when regarded in a diachronic perspective, they describe the process of the retention of the ecological complementarity principle at the supra-household level or its dissolution under impingement from the market or actually what we should call community disaggregation. In these cases one can perceive the phenomenon of the redistributive economy, but when one changes the level of analysis to the supra-community linkages, one or another model of the state political control intervenes, and these (as Murra demonstrated in the case of Tahuantinsuyu) tend to contravene the principles regulating ecological complementarity.

In this case of Tahuantinsuyu, the principles regulating the state economy, which implies a real political control over the surpluses of the chiefdoms (or if you prefer—"lordships") converted into provinces as well as the establishment and exploitation of ecological floors belonging to the state itself, clearly threaten maintenance of the principles of ecological complementarity. In a paper (Schaedel n.d.) written a few years ago, I argued that prior to the formation of Tahuantinsuyu the first attempt to "extend" the principle of ecological complementarity beyond the chiefdom level, was by the so-called Huari state c. A.D. 700. In the case of the Huari supra-chiefdom hegemony, the evidence for the emergence of state institutions, including coercive force, is overwhelming. It is equally clear both from archaeological and ethnohistoric evidence that this state was short-lived in the highlands, and previously autonomous confederated chiefdoms soon regained their pre-existing domains which were exploited under the ecological complementarity principles. Mujica's model of the Tiahuanaco supra-chiefdom hegemony exemplifies a similar formulation. My own interpretation is that Mujica's model conforms much more closely to a non-state extension of the principle of ecological complementarity, in which the tissue bonding the over-arching supra-chiefdom "hegemony" rested not upon coercive force, but on a more fragile (if longer lasting) network of shared ideological beliefs and practices.

This brings me to the third point that I wanted to stress in summarizing the pros and cons of this symposium, namely the ideological dimension of "ecological complementarity." As Murra clearly states in his presentation, ecological complementarity is not simply "a series of mechanisms active in Andean agriculture" but is an "Andean ideal." At another point he refers to it as "a major human achievement" which can have "future possibilities" by which we take him to mean that it is more than a major paleotechnology that can be resuscitated, but rather a kind of mystique with its ideological and symbolic dimensions. Nevertheless, in virtually all of the papers given, with a few exceptions—those of María Rostworowski, Hiroyasu Tomoeda, and Olivia Harris—emphasis was almost exclusively on economic and to a lesser extent the controversial political dimensions. I feel certain that if we had dedicated specific attention to the ideological dimension of ecological complementarity we should have been able to clarify why the "mechanisms" would run the risk of being extinguished by being subordinated to a state economy or mode of production. Without doubt the economic mechanisms we have been analyzing (as one or another manifestation of the principles of ecological complementarity) had their rationale and ideological justification (something akin to R. Rappaport's [1971] "sacred propositions") which sustained the implementation and even "encoded" the functioning of the complicated land use mechanism. Apparently the Incas grasped the significance of the underlying ideology when they reformulated their state ideology as "reciprocity writ large." To me, it is theoretically imperative to arrive at least at an approximation of the knowledge of the ideological superstructure which reinforced the economic/ecological mechanism in order to be able to diachronically clarify two major trends in Andean history: (1) how did the system evolve to the supra-community level and (2) how has it been able to survive four centuries of destructive attack and impingement.

It is my understanding that at the 1976 symposium in Paris to which Murra referred, at which the name for the model of verticality was changed to "ecological complementarity," several papers dealt with aspects of what I call its ideological dimension, under the rubric of "symbolic practices." A whole symposium of the International Congress of Americanists in Paris, dedicated to Andean symbolism, in 1976 indicates the burgeoning research on the ideological dimension from ethnographers, ethnohistorians, and even archaeologists. The very plethora of hypothetical constructs and the rather achronic manner in which they are applied to a reconstruction of the cosmovision, epistemology, or world view of Andean people makes it difficult if not impossible to evaluate the real progress that has been made. Hence I am apprehensive that my suggestion may be tantamount to "opening up a can of worms" and would propose that the ideological dimension be introduced only with the caveat that the spatial and temporal parameters be relevant to the data.

An illustration of this at this symposium was Rostworowski's valuable insight on the spread or absence of ecological complementarity in the north highlands by her reference to the Huari/Llacuaz dichotomous concept. There are other ideological constructs, such as the metaphor of the human body, encompassing three ecological floors, which Bastien (1978) elicited from the Collahuaya that seems to show a very close epistemiological "fit" with the principles of ecological complementarity, and which he has shown to be surviving in ritual, even though the actual spatial arrangements have been destroyed by the state-imposed land partitioning of the late fifties.

The ideological dimension is not only important to fully comprehend the significance of ecological complementarity to Andean people, but even more important in advancing our ability to cast the concept further back in time, beyond the proto-historic and para-historic domains of ethnohistory to the telehistoric and antehistoric domains of archaeology. The commendable effort, for example, in this symposium by Olivia Harris to relate verbal symbols of complementary spaces to the visual symbols extrapolated from textiles by Cerceda is a necessary first step in undertaking what must be a careful seriation of visual imagery from the protohistoric to the antehistoric Tiahuanaco iconography.

To make this difficult transposition from verbal to visual symbols upon which the reconstruction of the millennium-long continuities (and discontinuities) of Andean cognitive maps depends, we need not only the input of the ethnographers and ethnohistorians specializing in meaning systems, but more in-depth studies from Quechua and Aymara linguistics to elucidate nuances of meaning imbedded in the linguistic behavior and conventions that all too often escape even the best translations. Hopefully, future symposia, dealing with broad macro ecological/economic themes of the Andes will be planned with appropriate attention to the ongoing research on Andean cognition.

(Translation by Freda Wolf de Romero)

REFERENCES CITED

Bastien, Joseph W.
1978 Mountain of the Condor. The American Ethnological Society. Monograph no. 64. New York: West Publishing Company.

Dillehay, Tom
1979 Pre-hispanic Resource Sharing in the Central Andes. Science 204:24–31.

Murra, John V.
1972 El Control Vertical de un Máximo de Pisos Ecológicos en la Economía de las Sociedades Andinas. *In* Visita de la Provincia de León de Huánuco, vol. 2, Murra J. V., ed. pp. 429–76. Huánuco: Universidad Nacional Hermilio Valdizán.

Rappaport, Roy A.
1971 Ritual, Sanctity, and Cybernetics. American Anthropologist 73: 59–76.

Schaedel, Richard P.
n.d. The Prehistory of the Water Control/Social Control Interface. Manuscript in press. Homenaje a Angel Palerm. Universidad Iberoamericana, México.

23

The Dynamic Potential of the Complementarity Concept

Frank Salomon

Introduction

The point of departure for studying Andean systems of ecological complementarity is a single axiom: For geographical reasons, the Andean peoples must achieve the levels of consumption defined by their cultures as adequate through the articulation of complementary productive zones at varied altitudes and distances. In formulating the concept of the "vertical archipelago" in 1972, John Murra drew attention to a lasting Andean preference concerning the satisfaction of the complementary imperative; namely, a preference for direct access to multiple zones and an avoidance of systems resting on indirect access via specialization and external exchange. During the next decade many ethnohistorians, archaeologists, and ethnologists carried out a search for additional cases which might shed light on the distribution of "vertical" systems over space and time, and also on the social institutions which managed ecological diversity. The harvest was impressive, and it made possible important advances.

In the first place, the effort brought to light evidence about previously unsuspected apparatuses of ecological complementation, discovered in different parts of the Andes. It became possible to contrast the "archipelago" with other answers to the ecological imperative. Comparison among these alternatives promises to be an important clue for interpreting differences within the Andean orbit. As a step toward interpreting such findings, the following pages offer a functional typology of the diverse mechanisms of complementation. They are treated with special reference to the themes of the present meeting, under the heading of "Multifarious Complementarity."

In the second place, recent studies begin to inform thinking about complementarity with a diachronic dimension. The archaeological perspective suggests an eventual transition away from the focus on productive structures seen as stable systems, and toward a focus on their role in the historic evolution of the Andean peoples. Despite the incipient state of such work—or perhaps just because of it—it seems opportune to seek in recent data the dynamic factors which have conditioned the historical trajectory of Andean societies. This aspect will be outlined under the heading of "Changing Complementarity."

Finally, there remain to be noted some persisting questions which have not been treated at this meeting nor in other recent contributions, and which have implications affecting the future of complementarity studies. These questions, both theoretical and empirical, will be discussed under the heading of "Reexamining Complementarity."

Multifarious Complementarity

In principle, the arrangements which serve to pass goods from one social unit to another are numerous. Colin Renfrew, in the diagram which Shimada has reproduced on p. 382 of this volume (Renfrew 1975: 41–43) classifies them into ten basic types: "direct access," "home base reciprocity," "boundary reciprocity," "down-the-line exchange," "central place redistribution," "central place market exchange," "freelance or middleman trading," "emissary trading," "colonial enclave procurement," and "port-of-trade operation." When one considers the possibility that exchange between a given pair of units could be carried out through varied combinations and permutations of these types, it becomes obvious that the number of possible institutional arrangements is enormous.

But in practice the variety of exchange systems that connect Andean complementary zones is not infinite. Studies of the last decade, including those presented here, have shown the past or present existence of many modes of interzonal articulation, some similar to Murra's "archipelago" and others different. But, taken together, they do not illustrate all the possible permutations of Renfrew's "modes." Instead they fall into a few patterns or institutionalized relationships which repeat themselves in diverse parts and periods of the Andean panorama.

Fig. 23.1 offers a systematic comparison of institutions which articulate Andean complementarity as described in recent work. They are compared according to the following norms:

1. Each term inside a box refers to one pattern of behavior which serves a collectivity to procure access to varied productive zones or

their products. These are called "mechanisms" of complementarity.

2. The diagram was put together by induction, comparing documented cases, and not by deduction as in Renfrew's scheme. Accordingly it does not contain hypothetical cases nor does it pretend to exhaust the logical dimensions of the problem.

3. Mechanisms of articulation are named according to the terminology in relevant literature, with preference for the "ethno" terminology or local lexicon where it is mentioned, and, where it is not, for the colonial or modern hispanic term which appears most commonly in descriptions.

4. The horizontal axis of the diagram represents the greater or lesser degree of centralized control or state management implicit in the mechanism documented. The left column lists institutionalized mechanisms involving decentralized "reciprocal" exchanges, without the intervention of political authority as a condition of exchanging. The right column lists mechanisms requiring the centralization or central direction of exchange, via redistribution, supervision of markets, etc.

5. The vertical axis of the diagram expresses the greater or lesser number of exterior contacts that a group must contract in order to practice the given mechanism. By "number of external contacts" the number of collectivities placed in contact is meant and not the number of instances of contact. The intent is to express in terms of social contact the "autonomy/heteronomy" contrast, and to suggest as well the information-bearing properties of the mechanism (Zeidler 1977–78).

6. The diagram only reflects relations described as stable and legal, contracted (more or less) by agreement among parties. This is not to deny in principle the importance of access through robbery or warfare. These phenomena are grouped, however, with the conflictual processes dealt with under the heading "Changing Complementarity."

7. The rubric "modes" signals the kinds of exchange (in Renfrew's classification) most probably implicit in the mechanisms that each box contains. The point is double: first, to aid archaeologists in the search for distributional patterns that might be identified with given mechanisms; and second, to underline the likelihood that the mechanisms used in concrete instances do not correspond to abstract types but are instead complex artifacts responding to multiple cultural and environmental demands.

The following paragraphs sketch the articulating systems contained in the eight boxes and offer examples.

1. Mechanisms which achieve *direct access to multiple resources without central control* form a widely distributed and internally diverse class. Nonetheless they may be defined by the fact that, in principle,

each productive unit (usually the domestic unit) enjoys rights to use resources in multiple zones and disposes of their products without the mediation of redistributing authorities. The variation within this class is attributable largely to differences in norms of residence. North-Andean prehistoric "microverticality" (Oberem 1976) presupposes a single residence, but in modern "compressed archipelago" systems (Brush 1977; Vallée 1972; Webster 1971; Fonseca and Mayer 1978) one often finds that each domestic unit has various dwellings. The same trait appears in the system of "double domicile" described here by Harris. Even transhumance and the "gyratory" system model (Núñez and Dillehay 1979) might belong in this box insofar as they serve to diversify ecological reach. Such practices are relevant not only as the archipelago's possible precursors (Mujica, Onuki, and Schaedel, in this volume), but also as parts of its modern successor-systems. Such, at least, seems to be its role in the case of the *qochayuyeros* or seaweed gatherers described by Masuda (in this volume).

2. Mechanisms which achieve *direct access to multiple resources through central control* include the "vertical archipelagos" described by Murra in 1972. Later Rostworowski contrasted to them a model of "horizontality"; that is, of political control of multiple coastal valleys or their parts by the lords of polities whose specialists include fishers, irrigation farmers, artisans, and merchants (Rostworowski 1977; Netherly 1977; Shimada 1982). For present purposes the spatial distribution of resources is less important than their mode of control. In both cases one gets the sense of a state whose power depends on its capacity to widen the gamut of controlled resources and channel the distribution of the products. It is through the linkage to politics that, in the Andes, direct access reaches its unusually vast development.

3. Mechanisms which achieve *access to multiple resources through dyadic relations* between collectivities imply a less direct control. When this type of articulation takes place *in the absence of centralized administrators*, or even when there exist authorities at the *kuraka* level which, however, lack control over the full range of interzonal exchanges, such a system works mostly through acts of reciprocity among productive units belonging to the respective poles of the dyad. The phenomenon of societies constituted by a *huari* sector (agriculturists, associated in ideology with the primordial, the earthly, and the pacific) opposed to a *llacuaz* sector (pastoralists, associated in ideology with innovation, the celestial, and with warfare) demonstrates dyadism with clarity (Duviols 1973). Tomoeda and Fujii (in this volume) call attention to one interesting facet of the relation between modern farmers and herders: despite their permanent interdependency, they

prefer not to express interdependency through matrimonial alliance. It appears as though they felt a need to reinforce continually the opposition between parts, to avoid a fusion which would eventually damage the functionality of specialization. New data offered by María Rostworowski in this volume suggest that complementary organization through *hermanación* (Torero 1974:107) or pairing of herding and farming collectivities was much more widely distributed through Andean space and time than had been suspected.

4. Mechanisms which achieve *access to multiple resources through the centralized regulation of a dyadic relationship* imply, as does the *huari-llacuaz* phenomenon, the constituting of a multi-ecological whole by the interaction of two groups and not by the diversification of one. New data bring to mind the "symbiosis" adumbrated by Condarco (1970–71). The Cajamarca-Sicán case presented by Shimada (in this volume; 1982) raises important questions for future studies; for example, concerning the means of arranging diplomatic and dynastic relations between groups whose supplies and sovereignty appear mutually hostage.

5. Mechanisms which achieve *access to multiple resources through multiple alliances with producer groups* are, like direct access mechanisms, markedly diverse. In dealing with *non-centralized* variants one can recognize as a common trait the establishment of numerous ties of reciprocal exchange, ceremonially elaborated, between each productive unit and its counterparts in other productive zones. The diversity arises mostly with regard to the kinds of activity that pass goods between units. In systems which depend on the producers themselves to carry the goods, it is generally the *puna* collectivities which organize transport caravans. They depend on their "acquaintances" in each productive zone to carry out—always with displays of mutual sentiment—the necessary exchanges. Systems of this sort have been widely documented in the southern Andes (Tomoeda and Yamamoto, in this volume; Flores 1977; Custred 1974; Browman 1974; Casaverde 1977). In other cases, however, transport is not the producer's job but that of a specialist who dedicates himself or herself to cultivating "acquaintances" in varied productive zones and to working as an independent mediator. The *wasaq'epi* peddlers described by Flores display some of this character. (See also Flores and Nájar Vizcarra 1976 on a similar personage, the *likina*, and Ortiz de Zuñiga [1562] 1972:102 for a possible prehispanic precursor.)

6. Mechanisms which achieve *access to multiple resources through multiple alliances* also occur *with centralized authority*. Such instances of "administered trade" generally imply the presence of a specialized

corporate group that undertakes long-distance trade with subsidies and protection from a political lord. This group in turn repays its sponsor by according privileged access to exotic prestige goods, the luxuries that serve as "rewards" in redistributive politics. In prehispanic Ecuador such status traders were called *mindaláes* (Salomon 1980:164–72). Their role appears similar to that of the "merchant Indians" whom Rostworowski has studied for Chincha and the north coast of Peru (1977; Ramírez-Horton 1982; Pease and Shimada, in this volume). In some cases the specialists lived outside their home communities in reserved enclaves. Although not much is known about them, some of the advanced or frontier outposts of the Inca empire may have served a related function (Cieza [1553] 1962:159).

7. Mechanisms which achieve *access to multiple resources through open barter* are those which allow exchange without regard to the presence or absence of a prior social or ceremonial bond. Today open barter or cash sale *without centralization* is the technique used by many artisans and craft-goods middlemen such as the Otavalan textile merchants who circulate long distances from their base in northern Ecuador. Shamans and traditional curers, in both the southern Andes (Bastien 1978:9) and the far north (Taussig 1980) also enjoy occasions to trade goods and services with households beyond their networks of "acquaintance."

8. Mechanisms which achieve *access to multiple resources through open barter* take on a centralized character when the act of exchange must take place in a place reserved for the purpose, and must be *supervised by the political authority* or treaty authority which sponsors the trading place. In the case of a single political authority there arises what early Spanish observers called by the Nahuatl word *tiangez*, or "native market"; the record from Quito documents the existence of *tiangueces* with special clarity (Hartmann 1971). The modern system of the "extended archipelago" (Brush 1977:13–66; Gade 1975) shows some resemblance to this mechanism. So too does market management by colonial native lords. Their practice, examined by Franklin Pease and Susan Ramírez (this volume), served in part to restore interzonal ties damaged by colonial interventions. In the case of a central place for trade belonging to no single authority but functioning by treaty authority among several, a port-of-trade model fits well. In 1569 a Spanish explorer reported that one existed at Ciscala, probably in modern Esmeraldas Province, Ecuador (Carranza [1569] 1965:89). Mujica's contribution suggests that Tiwanaku may have taken part in a "multi-ethnic center" classifiable, perhaps, as a port-of-trade.

The mechanisms or interzonal articulation presented in this typology have been gathered from diverse Andean societies, belonging to distant periods and regions. It is unlikely that the whole gamut ever existed in a single society; to a large extent they are functional alternatives. But it is just as improbable that any Andean society availed itself of any one to the permanent exclusion of the rest. Everything we have learned in the last decade strengthens the suspicion that Andean societies, seen synchronically, combined and combine various mechanisms to form a flexible, versatile, perhaps even redundant system of complementation, capable of guaranteeing access to multiple resources even during disturbances. Such a combination of mechanisms is here called an "apparatus of complementation." Seen in diachrony, it is likely that Andean societies constantly change their respective apparatuses.

By focusing, then, not on the productive zones themselves but on the links that connect them, one can frame a research agenda in terms of three broad questions.

First: What factors explain the choice of a given combination of mechanisms by a given collectivity? On this score the present meeting offered appreciable advances. The contributions taken together, and the literature that precedes them, suggest macro-regional constellations, large patterns of complementing behavior which seem to have typified certain parts of the Andean orbit in certain periods.

For example the south of Peru shows with growing clarity a class of systems depending on centrally controlled direct access. Julien's paper on guano exploitation, and Hidalgo's on tribute in kind, underline the durability of the tendency, even under severely distorting colonial conditions. To what factors should we attribute it? In an east-west ecological transect of the region what stands out is the contrast between the immense Titicaca high plain, which nourishes large numbers of camelids and large populations of herders, and the scarcely populated desert south coast. On the Amazonian side the forest invites swidden horticulture but a lack of wide floodplains limits the density at which cultivation can be practiced. The concentration of population on the heights seemingly gave a potential advantage to any highland group interested in lengthening its "vertical" reach. If the development of "archipelagos" really was limited to areas where a dense highland population bordered on smaller populations at lower altitudes, then it should be possible to retrodict some areas prone to display highland-based "archipelago" development, and also to submit other known "archipelago" regions (e.g., Huanuco) to appropriate tests of the correlation.

Similarly the contributions of Shimada, Schaedel, Rostworowski, and

Ramírez allow a hypothesis about the complementary organizations of north coastal Peru. The exact formulation must rest with specialists in the region, but its theme might be the predominance of dyadic and multiple-alliance formations. Did large, centralized interactive dyads such as Sicán have antecedents or successor fragments in the form of noncentralized *huari-llacuaz* systems? Dyadic systems might be intelligible in terms of the relative balance between population sizes at high altitudes and those in the coastal river oases. The test may be found in other cases where units of about equal political scale and demographic weight faced each other from potentially complementay resource bases.

And what of the other Andean regions? In the ecuatorial north, ethnohistory is beginning to paint a very different picture. Multiple alliance systems and systems of open barter predominate (Carrera Colin 1981; Salomon 1980). In the highlands and the adjacent *montaña*, pre-Incaic polities seem to have achieved a modest degree of centralization on population bases that were likewise modest. More imposing chiefdoms probably existed on the coast than in the highlands but none achieved imperial scale. In these circumstances, highland lords apparently found little opportunity to exert direct control of distant resources. They sought advantage in other means of channeling goods from uncontrolled territory, chiefly through more or less centralized barter systems and especially through "administered trade" resembling that of Aztec Mesoamerica.

Second: What factors explain the greater or lesser degree of centralized control found within a given apparatus? Under what circumstances does the importance of central control grow or shrink? In the end, can we root a hypothesis about the formation and dissolution of Andean states and empires in the functional properties of such systems (Lorandi 1980)?

Here we encounter problems hardly manageable with the data at hand. Nonetheless it may be worthwhile to sketch in broad strokes a few possible avenues. On one hand, it should be feasible to clear up the factors involved in centralization or decentralization along any horizontal line of Fig. 23.1 (that is, for any one type of mechanism). In a recent paper Charles Hastings (1982) offered an example of such reasoning by asking why some direct-access systems have generated states and others have not. His example was Junín in the Late Intermediate period. According to Hastings, decentralized direct access systems do not in themselves tend to generate states, except when they satisfy one of two conditions: "(1) the confinement of individual cultural groups to narrow vertical ranges with less ecological diversity, and (2) rapid and highly concentrated population increases within exceptionally productive localities" (1982:1). Hastings's negative (i.e., stateless) case might be set alongside the data and inferences presented by Mujica or Onuki, where we glimpse increases in social complexity.

On the other hand, we are in need of systematic ideas about the relation between complementarity and Andean imperialism. If we imagine Tawantinsuyu as the political expression of a system of interzonal exchanges managed by an expansive elite, as Golte, among others, has suggested (1968), it becomes necessary to think also about the institutional means which allowed the Incas to coordinate numerous and widely divergent regional systems. Presumably not all mechanisms of complementation are equally compatible with all others. According to Craig Morris, Inca institutions reflected chiefly the need to coordinate, and not to transform, the subject economies: ". . . there was no real attempt at cultural . . . political or economic homogeneity. What was attempted was rather a careful orchestration of hundreds of parts" (p. 480 this volume). Managing institutional heterogeneity therefore becomes an important function for Andean imperialism. The evidence for the continued vitality of non-Inca complementary systems under Inca rule is ever clearer. But this evidence clashes with other data, equally cogent, concerning Inca manipulation and gradual modification of systems far from the Inca norm (Salomon 1978). In "orchestrating" diverse formations, did the Incas formulate some rule determining what features were to be left intact and which were to be transformed? Or do we face a purely *ad hoc* agglomeration, created without a rule defining the complementarity among complementarities?

Third: What factors explain the greater or lesser degree of autonomy demanded by various apparatuses? As Kimura notes, direct access systems, whether centralized or not, try to eliminate external dependencies, while multiple alliance systems and open barter systems multiply dependencies while diminishing the importance of each single tie. What accounts for the contrast represented on the vertical axis of Fig. 23.1? One facet of the question has been formulated in connection with a discussion which, unfortunately, was not considered at these sessions, namely, the debate on the ontogenesis of "vertical archipelago" formations.

At first glance, the preference for direct access in many collectivities seems anomalous, since its disadvantages are considerable. Craig Morris points out the inherently conflictive properties of a system which makes it impossible to consolidate contiguous territories; in each system isolated parcels, long perimeters, and access routes must be defended. The inherently high "overhead" costs of the "archipelago"

Increasing centralized control →

Increase in number of political units in contact ↓

	Decentralized (reciprocity)	Centralized (redistribution)
Direct Access	1. "microverticalidad", "transhumancia", "compressed archipelago", "doble domicilio" Modes: direct access	2. "Archipiélago vertical", "horizontalidad" Modes: direct access, central place redistribution
Dyadic (inter) Dependence	3. "Huari-llacuaz", "hermanación" Modes: Home base reciprocity, boundary reciprocity	4. "interactive dyad" Modes: down-the-line exchange, emissary trading
Multiple Alliance Exchange	5. "caravaneering", "liquira", "wasa q'epi" Modes: home base reciprocity, freelance (middle-man) trading	6. "mindaláes", "status traders", "yndios mercaderes", enclaves de rescate Modes: emissary trading, colonial enclave
Open Barter	7. "rescates y grangerías", "trueque", household expeditionary trading Modes: home base reciprocity, boundary reciprocity, down-the-line trading	8. "tianguez", "port-of-trade", "extended archipelago" Modes: central place market exchange, port-of-trade

Fig. 23.1 Diagram of Institutions of Andean Complementarity.
Note: "Modes" refers to the classification "Modes of Trade and Their Spatial Implications" by Colin Renfrew (1975:41–3).

(transport, communication, warehousing) have also been noted. If some peoples reject interdependency and accept these costs, they must perceive a balance of benefits. Several authors have tried to define this perceived advantage. The ideas proposed are too complex to explore here, save to signal a few hypotheses. Golte (1980) and Camino (1982) adduce the importance of productive diversity to maximize the value of available worker-hours; Guillet (1981) mentions the increased security obtained by distributing risks among many niches; Dillehay (1979) suggests that exploitation of shared multiethnic "islands" offered some safety against armed conflict; Orlove (1977) holds that productive zones form a synergistic whole insofar as the products of some can in themselves be applied to increase the productivity of others. Many authors have commented on the discrepancy between high and low lands with respect to potential for intensification, a difference which allegedly tempts highland peoples to appropriate parts of lower-lying valleys.

But even having taken these arguments into account, we are left halfway through the problem. In accepting the arguments of Orlove, Guillet, etc., or any combination of them, we also accept the obligation to explain why we find Andean cases of peoples who did *not* opt for self-sufficiency. We hardly need more *ad hoc* explanations of the utility of "archipelagos," but we do need general ideas about direct access and its alternatives that take into account the ecological, demographic, and geographic diversity amid which Andean peoples have developed their strategies.

Changing Complementarity

Slowly but decidedly we are approaching a diachronic understanding of complementarity. By widening our view to examine diverse alternatives, and by deepening the archaeological record, we become increasingly aware that by "complementarity" we should not understand a permanent essence of Andean societies, but a collective project continually renewed through processes of adjustment, mobilization, innovation, and conflict. Systems earlier imagined on the plane of synchrony as durable adaptations begin to appear as phases or emergents within long historic transitions.

Mujica, for example, holds that among the groups based in the Lake Titicaca basin prehistory witnessed repeated metamorphoses of complementing institutions. These changes, he suggests, resulted neither from alterations in the natural environment nor from technological innovations, but from changes in the political and demographic profiles of the region. The idea takes us a step beyond those of Carl Troll ([1931] 1958); complementarity appears not just as a response to the natural setting, but to the natural setting as inhabited and transformed by culture. The multizonal order becomes a historical product, and as such, susceptible to analysis in terms not only of intergroup relations but also in terms of cultural postulates generated by groups in the course of their struggle to persist.

Seen in panorama, over long intervals and wide spaces, the relation between highlands and Amazonia also becomes a theater of change. Onuki calls attention to the forest-dwellers role (so far insufficiently explored) in defining multizonal adaptations. What factors influenced organization across the long *puna-suni-quechua-yunga* transect? "Cultural reasons"—that is, the crucial symbolic importance of jungle products—impelled highlanders to seek direct access or exchange ties, but the bilateral logic of relations, which presumably determined the event, remains to be worked out.

The northern landscape likewise looks increasingly like a scene of successive transformations. Rostworowski detects in Late Horizon human geography the traces of two earlier demographic tides: a *yunka* expansion into the heights, leaving behind distinctively named social sectors, and a northward movement on the part of *llacuaz* herders later enclaved among Cajamarcan peoples. Can the Cajamarcan peoples involved with Sicán then be considered "monoethnic" components of a larger dyad? Only on the plane of synchrony, and only in a special sense. From a diachronic point of view, it is possible that "communities" should be conceptualized as temporary associations of units whose presence results from processes and adaptive movements which transcend the organizational scheme of a given moment.

In thinking of such problems we avoid thinking of societies as sets of mechanically equilibrated parts and instead see them as conjunctions of forces whose internal and external tensions give rise to innovation. If we want to advance toward dynamic models, able to explain not only the functioning but the transformation of complementary apparatuses, it will be necessary to isolate axes of conflict and openings to innovation that are characteristic of complementary organization. The following points are offered by way of examples only, to stimulate further hypotheses.

The effects of scale as such. Apparently many Andean systems tend to expand. Murra has expressed since 1956 the suspicion that expansion toward distant resource zones in and of itself has distorting or disintegrating effects on original base institutions. A like theme is observable in Morris's findings where he characterizes the very effort to expand multi-ecological control as a force destructive of decentralized direct access systems: "... several students of early states ... have stressed the administrative requirements of diversified ecologies and economies as possible causal factors in the emergence of centralized authority (p. 484 this volume)."

The autarchy/interdependence dynamic. The management of direct access systems, whose conscious purpose is economic autarchy, may bring with it as a paradoxical consequence new collective commitments to interdependence or even to heteronomy. In the example studied by Enrique Mayer, the collectivity which intends to improve its control over a given resource finds itself constrained to rely on help from non-members. Later, these become entitled participants in a system no longer so "monoethnic." It is hard to imagine how a large multiple-resource system could have been erected in prehispanic times without incurring similar paradoxes; not only because labor needs weigh in the balance, but also because of the likelihood that without "outside" participation the project becomes indefensible. For such reasons it is possible that even the most clearly-defined "archipelago" would entail (unless its outliers used uninhabited land) ties of some sort with multiple allies or partners.

The superimposition of successive systems. In ethnohistoric sources, informants usually set forth the formal organization of their communities as it was defined for administrative purposes at a given moment. But the formal organization of a community—even in places heavily regulated by empires—is not the mere organizational chart of contemporary political order. Almost always, the units named in native administrative schemes had also formed parts of earlier systems. Inca plans were usually clever rearrangements of extant units and even the heavy-handed Toledan Spanish intervention more often reshuffled native units than liquidated them. At the least, the formal organization of a given historic moment usually contains within it the image of earlier orders in the form of terminology, ritualized relations, etc. This can be seen in the Cajamarca study of Rostworowski.

But more interesting still is the possibility that such formations, even when overlapped by later organizations, continued to exercise a latent or potential influence in their own right. When the official organizational scheme suffers disruption, old and submerged strata of organization sometimes serve not only as matrices for ideological reformulation, but also as practical axes of social reorganization. For example, in Ecuador between 1533 and 1560 the collapse of the governance imposed by Cuzco, and the absence of a well-consolidated Spanish replacement, allowed the remobilization of native formations which had earlier remained visible only as bureaucratic categories in Inca schemes.

Internal tensions and countertendencies in complementary systems. No differentiated system of economic organization can be equally advantageous for all its participants. Given any differences of interest among its members, it is highly likely that a complementary structure would contain within itself potential elements of conflict, and also that these would give rise to counter-tendencies superficially incompatible with the overt norm. One might ask, for example, whether the origin of institutions like the *wasa q'epi* or Andean peddler, found with some regularity within systems described over all as apparatuses of direct access and supposedly inhospitable to trade economy, should necessarily be attributed to the diffusion of capitalism. Perhaps not, because the inconveniences implicit in direct access systems—for example, problems in obtaining products from distant niches on short notice—might give incentive for some participants to innovate outside the dominant framework. Such institutions can acquire importance of their own in complementary organization and eventually contribute to its transformation.

The role of conflict among rival collectivities. Despite having a lot of data about Andean warfare, we really know little about the relation between war and multizonal organization. Various writers have suggested that the discrepancy between coastal valleys with ample productive potential, and relatively unproductive highland valleys, has in various eras of prehistory provoked a tendency for highlanders to develop direct access in its simples terms—armed aggression (Torero 1974:98–140)—while the relative opulence of the warm lands favored other mechanisms. But it seems just as possible that warfare might be motivated by the quest for specific goods of crucial importance, and not by the weight of calories in bulk. In any case evidences of coastal militarism are not lacking.

Theoretically it is plausible that mobilizing a complementary system to compete with a neighbor would give it a new form. Military pressures may have favored the transformation of decentralized systems toward more centralized mechanisms within each type; presumably under military pressure central authority has advantages in guaranteeing the conduct of barter or guarding the sites of direct access. It is also possible—and in the ecuatorial case, probable—that the net effect of endemic warfare and the lack of state hegemony was the development of complementary systems lacking direct access. Periods and regions of endemic warfare may favor the development of status trader organizations, bartering enclaves, and ports-of-trade. These are forms of exchange which allow procurement in zones out of political control; such is the case seen in Aztec evidence, and within Tawantinsuyu as well, if one may infer from passages about Inca attempts to penetrate Amazonia through caravans disguised as "merchants" (Oberem 1971: 45).

Reexamining Complementarity

Research has thrown considerable light on "verticality" and its alternatives, at least in regard to its typology and distribution from the Late Intermediate period onward. More remote antecedents are beginning to come to light (Mujica, Onuki, Schaedel, and Shimada in this volume), as well as modifications under colonial pressures. In cases like those studied by Julien and Hidalgo, we begin to read between the lines of the colonial record parts of the "Andean history" proposed by Pease (1978). It is becoming possible to advance from the "comparative anatomy" of such systems to their "physiology"—their functioning within given societies—and to their "evolution" under varied environmental constraints. But before doing so we should take into account the continued existence of some underlying questions that have not been fully treated in the discussion so far.

In part, they are methodological and empirical questions. In formulating the question of "ecological complementarity" we have used the word "ecology" in a colloquial sense, since in reality little analysis of biotic interrelations has been undertaken nor much use made of the ecosystemic perspective. So far, the literature concerns economic and cultural geography rather than ecology. Advances achieved by Paul Baker and his associates (1976) have still not been integrated into ethnohistory, archaeology, or ethnology. Alan Craig's effort to relate the concept of "ecological floor" with large-scale satellite observations presages eventual improvement in the relationship between natural sciences and ethnoscientific methods. It is not too soon to think of applications to prehistory, nor need we postpone the discussion of possible ecological frameworks which could focus, not on the "adapted" and equilibrated ecosystem but on dynamic processes leading to adaptation (Knapp 1983).

But questions proper to the human sciences are also pending. In the first place, the theoretical standing of terms like "vertical archipelago," "interactive dyad," etc., have not been clarified. Different authors use them in dissimilar senses. For example, Murra originally defined complementarity as an "*ideal compartido*" ([1972] 1975:60); that is, as a mental model consciously used by the population studied. But the idea has undergone many mutations. In the work of Shimada (1982:139) and other archaeologists, it seems to have been recast as a model proper to anthropological thought. Its properties as a system of functional relations are described without reference to the criteria of the actors (Cohen 1973:39–42). It thus comes to figure as a "model of," not a "model for," Andean adaptation. Such examples could be multiplied throughout the length of an immense bibliography.

It is not in itself undesirable that different researchers use the complementarity concept in differing ways according to their theoretical preferences, provided that they do so with clarity. The problem is that appropriate proofs for each formulation have rarely been defined or demanded. To test a "model for," a normative, conscious construct, testimony about Andean thought is in order, and not just reports of behavior that can be attributed indirectly and speculatively to an alleged preference. To test a "model of," that is, an exterior rendering of observed behavior, it is not appropriate to describe behavior in terms which derive from the thought of the actors and which may or may not be accurate categorizations of their practice. For example, in describing testing a "model of" a productive regimen, it is appropriate to classify the lands, etc., according to a non-"ethno" terminology, seeking only the highest possible degree of biological precision, leaving for a later stage the comparison between "etically" observed behavior and the mental models of the actors. The use of "emic" and "etic" models of complementarity in unjustified combinations sometimes gives inquiry a shade of circularity: Andean culture, we postulate, uses a model x; we record the behavior of Andean actors using model x terminologically; conclusion, model x governs behavior. Without rigor in formulating the problem, the opportunity to capture the dialectic between Andean thought and adaptive practice is easily lost. The very popularity of complementarity models has itself proven a cause of such lost opportunities.

To recover this dialectic it is necessary to broaden the cultural framework of the complementarity theme. On the "etic" side we need to continue improving descriptions of systems and behavior. The authenticity of description could be improved by modifying the hand-me-down opposition between "ecology" (nature) and "agricultural system" (culture) and recognizing that the agricultural system we encounter is not "in" the ecological system; it is an ecological problem in its own right (Enrique Mayer, personal communication). But on the "emic" side even more efforts are needed. It is absurd to suppose that because the theme concerns material life one can bypass the symbolic and cultural dimension. The adaptive achievement we call complementarity may be susceptible to a rendering based on familiar sciences, but the fact remains that it was constructed using mental paradigms evolved independently from ours. So far very little has been done to interpret its genesis within local culture. Not even Pulgar Vidal's pioneering but outdated ethno-ecological classification has been adequately replaced. Structuralist research covers ethnoterminology but usually only on the religious side, with little attention to thinking about biotic processes and their management. Studies of Andean economic practice do often contain ethnoterminologies, but there rarely emerges any account of local economic reasoning in its original terms. With few exceptions we have scarcely begun to address the anthropological question *par excellence*: How has Andean humanity understood, and through its understanding inhabited, the reality surrounding it?

Progress toward this end is being made from at least two directions: on one hand, studies of the mental organization of "humanized" space in its general terms—that is, the plans Andean actors use in orienting their efforts to inhabit the earth—and on the other, studies of the mental organization of productive life (ethno-technology). Examples of the former appear in studies by Harris and by Tomoeda on the conceptual organization of productive agenda, and examples of the latter in work by Brush (1980) and Earls (1979) on the cultural processes whose results are "adapted" regimens. But almost everything is still to be done.

The authentic description of Andean complementarity must arise from a complementarity inherent in our science: the meeting between ecological thought and the interpretation of symbolic systems. Capturing the interplay between biosystem and system of cultural meanings—always problematic, never easy or axiomatic—will lead to an anthropological synthesis in the full sense of the word.

REFERENCES CITED

Baker, Paul T., and Michael A. Little, eds.

1976 Man in the Andes: A Multidisciplinary Study of High-Altitude Quechua. Stroudsburg, Pennsylvania: Dowden, Hutchinson, and Ross.

Bastien, Joseph

1978 Mountain of the Condor: Metaphor and Ritual in an Andean Ayllu. American Ethnological Society Monograph Series, No. 64. New York: West Publishing Co.

Browman, David
1974 Pastoral Nomadism in the Andes. Current Anthropology 15 (2): 188–96.

Brush, Stephen B.
1977 Mountain, Field, and Family: The Economy and Human Ecology of an Andean Valley. Philadelphia: University of Pennsylvania Press.
1980 The Environment and Native Andean Agriculture. America Indígena 40 (1): 161–72.

Camino D. C., Alejandro
1982 Tiempo y Espacio en la Estrategia de Subsistencia Andina: Un Caso en las Vertientes Orientales Sud-Peruanos. *In* El Hombre y Su Ambiente en los Andes Centrales. Luís Millones and Hiroyasu Tomoeda, eds. pp. 11–38. Senri Ethnological Studies, No. 10. Senri: National Museum of Ethnology.

Carranza, Martín de
[1569] 1965 Relación de las provincias de las Esmeraldas que fue a pacificar el capitán Andrés Contero. *In* Relaciones Geográficas de Indias. Marcos Jiménez de la Espada, ed. T. 3 pp. 87–90. Biblioteca de Autores Españoles, T. CLXXXV. Madrid: Ediciones Atlas.

Carrera Colin, Juan
1981 Apuntes para una Investigación Etnohistórica de los Cacicazgos del Corregimiento de Latacunga S.S. XVI–XVII. Cultura, Revista del Banco Central 11:219–80. Quito. Ecuador.

Casaverde R., Juvenal
1977 El Trueque en la Economía Pastoril. *In* Pastores de Puna, Uywamichiq Punarunakuna. Jorge Flores Ochoa, ed. pp. 171–92. Lima: Instituto de Estudios Peruanos.

Cieza de León, Pedro
[1533] 1962 La Crónica del Perú. Primera Parte. Buenos Aires: Ediciones Espasa-Calpe S. A.

Cohen, Ronald
1973 Generalization in Cultural Anthropology. *In* Handbook of Method in Cultural and Social Anthropology. Raoul Naroll, ed. pp. 31–50. New York. Columbia University Press.

Condarco Morales, Ramiro
1970–71 El Escenario Andino y el Hombre. La Paz: Imprenta y Librería Renovación.

Custred, Glynn
1974 Llameros y Comercio Interregional. *In* Reciprocidad e Intercambio en los Andes Peruanos. Giorgio Alberti and Enrique Mayer, eds. pp. 252–89. Lima: Instituto de Estudios Peruanos.

Dillehay, Tom D.
1979 Pre-Hispanic Resource Sharing in the Central Andes. Science 204:24–31.

Duviols, Pierre

1973 Huari y Llacuaz, Agricultores y Pastores, un Dualismo Prehispánico de Oposición y Complementaridad. Revista del Museo Nacional 39:153–91. Lima.

Earls, John
1979 Astronomía y Ecología: La Sincronización Alimenticia del Maíz. Allpanchis Phuturinqa 13:117–35. Cuzco.

Flores Ochoa, Jorge A.
1977 Pastoreo, Tejido, e Intercambio. *In* Pastores de Puna, Uywamichiq Punarunakuna. Jorge A. Flores Ochoa, ed. pp. 133–54. Lima: Instituto de Estudios Peruanos.

Flores Ochoa, Jorge A., and Yémira Najar Vizcarra
1976 El Likira, Intermediario Ambulante en la Cordillera de Canchis. Antropología Andina 1–2:125–34. Cuzco.

Fonseca, César, and Enrique Mayer
1978 Sistemas Agrarios y Ecología en la Cuenca del Río Cañete. Debates en Antropología 2:25–51. Lima.

Gade, Daniel
1975 Plants, Man, and the Land in the Vilcanota Valley of Peru. The Hague: W. Junk B. V.

Golte, Jürgen
1968 Algunas Consideraciones Acerca de la Producción y Distribución de la Coca en el Estado Inca. *In* Proceedings of the 38th International Congress of Americanists. Vol. 2, pp. 471–68.
1980 La Racionalidad del Sistema Andino. Lima: Instituto de Estudios Peruanos.

Guillet, David
1981 The Cultural Ecology of Mountains. ms.

Hartman, Roswith
1971 Mercados y Ferias Prehispánicos en el Area Andina. Boletín de la Academia Nacional de Historia 54 (118):214–35. Quito, Ecuador.

Hastings, Charles
1982 Implications of Andean verticality in the evolution of political complexity: A view from the margins. Paper presented at annual meeting of the American Anthropoligical Association, Washington, D.C., 1982.

Knapp, Gregory
1983 Soil, Slope, and Water in the Equatorial Andes: A Study of Prehistoric Agricultural Adaptation. Ph.D. dissertation. Department of Geography, University of Wisconsin, Madison.

Lorandi, Ana María
1980 Arqueología y Etnohistoria: Hacia una Visión Totalizadora del Mundo Andino. Obra del Centenario, Vol. 2, pp. 27–50. La Plata, Argentina: Museo de La Plata.

Murra, John V.
[1972] 1975 El Control Vertical de Un Máximo de Pisos Ecológicos en la Economía de las Sociedades Andinas. *In* Formaciones Económi-

cas y Políticas del Mundo Andino. John V. Murra, ed. pp. 59–115. Lima: Instituto de Estudios Peruanos.

Netherly, Patricia
1977 Local Level Lords on the North Coast of Peru. Ph.D. dissertation. Department of Anthropology, Cornell University, Ithaca, N.Y.

Nuñez, Lautaro, and Tom D. Dillehay
1979 Mobilidad Giratoria, Armonía Social, y Desarrollo en los Andes Meridionales: Padrones de Tráfico e Interacción Económica. Antofagasta: Universidad del Norte.

Oberem, Udo
1971 Los Quijos: Historia de la Transculturación de un Grupo Indígena en el Oriente Ecuatoriano 1538–1956. Memorias del Departamento de Antropología y Etnología de América, No. 1. Madrid: Facultad de Filosofía y Letras, Universidad de Madrid.
1976 El Acceso a Recursos Naturales de Diferentes Ecologías en la Sierra Ecuatoriana: Siglo XVI. *In* Proceedings of the 42nd International Congress of Americanists. Vol. 4, pp. 51–64. Paris: Musée de l'Homme/Société des Américanistes de Paris.

Orlove, Benjamin
1977 Integration through Production: The Use of Zonation in Espinar. American Ethnologist 4 (1):84–101.

Ortiz de Zúñiga, Iñigo
[1562] 1967–1972 Visita de la Provincia de León de Huánuco en 1562. John V. Murra, ed. Huánuco: Universidad Nacional Hermilio Valdizán.

Pease G.Y., Franklin
1978 Introduccion. *In* Del Tawantinsuyu a la historia del Peru. pp. 23–30. Lima: Instituto de Estudios Peruanos.

Ramírez-Horton, Susan
1982 Retainers of the Lords or Merchants: A Case of Mistaken Identity? *In* El Hombre y Su Ambiente en los Andes Centrales. Luis Millones and Hiroyasu Tomoeda, eds. pp. 123–36. Senri Ethnological Studies, No. 10. Senri: National Museum of Ethnology.

Rostworowski de Diez Canseco, María
1977 Pescadores artesanos, y mercaderes costeños en el Perú prehispánico. *In* Etnia y sociedad. Costa peruana prehispánica. pp. 211–64. Lima: Instituto de Estudios Peruanos.

Renfrew, Colin
1975 Trade as Action at a Distance: Questions of Integration and Communication. *In* Ancient Civilizations and Trade. Jeremy Sabloff and C. C. Lamberg-Karlovsky, eds. pp. 38–63. Albuquerque: University of New Mexico Press.

Salomon, Frank
1978 Systèmes politiques verticaux aux marches de l'empire Inca. Annales Economies, Sociétés, Civilisations 33 (5–6): 967–89.

1980 Los Señores Etnicos de Quito en la Epoca de los Incas. Serie Pendoneros, No. 10. Otavalo, Ecuador: Instituto Otavaleño de Antropología.

Shimada, Izumi

1982 Horizontal Archipelago and Coast-Highland Interaction in North Peru: Archaeological Models. *In* El Hombre y su Ambiente en los Andes Centrales. Luís Millones and Hiroyasu Tomoeda, eds. pp. 137–210. Senri Ethnological Studies, No. 10. Senri: National Museum of Ethnology.

Taussig, Michael

1980 Folk Healing and the Structure of Conquest in the Southwest Colombian Andes. Journal of Latin American Lore 6 (2):217–78.

Torero, Alfredo

1974 El Quechua y la Historia Social Andina. Lima: Universidad Richardo Palma.

Troll, Carl

1958 [1931] Los culturas superiores andinas y el medio geográfico. Carlos Nicholson, trans. Lima: Instituto de Geografica, Universidad Nacional Mayor de San Marcos.

Vallée, Lionel

1972 Cycle Ecologique et Cycle Rituel: Le Cas d'un Village Andin. Revue Canadienne de Sociologie et Anthropologie 9 (3):238–54.

Webster, Steven

1971 An Indigenous Quechua Community in Exploitation of Multiple Ecological Zones. Proceedings of the 39th International Congress of Americanists. Vol. 3, pp. 174–82. Lima: Instituto de Estudios Peruanos.

Zeidler, James

1977–78 Primitive Exchange, Prehistoric Trade, and the Problem of a Mesoamerican-South American Connection. Journal of the Steward Anthropological Society 9 (1–2):7–40. Urbana, Illinois.

Glossary

ají Hot peppers.

altiplano Extensive high plateau of the South-Central Andes. Ecologically this plateau encompasses the **suni** and **puna** zones.

arroba Unit of weight about 25 pounds or 11.5 kg.

audiencia Advisory and judicial body in Spanish America under the Council of the Indies and the Crown in Spain. It served as the appellate court for the area under its jurisdiction. The **audiencia** of Lima was presided over by the viceroy resident in the city.

ayllu Corporate descent group with collective ownership of resources, including lands and theoretical endogamy (marrying within the **ayllu**). Its members enjoy a relationship of mutual aid or reciprocity and, although they may be dispersed, retain their social linkage and rights to communal resources. Within the Inca decimal system, the term may also be used to designate a unit of 100 tributaries.

batán A heavy, stable anvil (usually of stone) used in conjunction with a rocking stone called a *chunga* to crush various substances.

cabecera Nucleus or principal political seat of a particular region.

cabildo Town council.

cacique Spanish term for the indigenous regional leader; often used as a synonym for **curaca** (see also **principal**).

campesinos Peasants.

capac Chief.

ceja de la montaña Lower reaches of the eastern slopes of the Andes, characterized by abundant rain, rugged terrain, and dense vegetation.

ceque Ray or line. The set of 41 **ceques** radiating out of the center of Cuzco is believed by some scholars to have been the organizational basis (spatially, temporally, and hierarchically) for the complex superimposed cycles of Inca rituals with important social and political significance.

chácra (chácara, cakra) Agricultural field.

chala Region covered by sand and clouds; Pacific coast region; in Pulgar Vidal's classification of the "Ocho Regiones Naturales," **chala** corresponds to the coastal region of 0 to 500 m above sea level.

chaquira Stone, shell, or metal beads.

chaquitaclla Footplow.

charqui (ch'arki) Dried (jerked) llama meat. The English word, jerky is a bastardized form of **charqui**.

chasqui (chaski) Runner who carried messages along the Inca roads.

chaupi Quechua word signifying mid-point or intermediary position (see also **taypi**).

chicha Fermented drink made of maize or other crops, such as peanuts.

chullpa Circular or rectangular burial tower.

chuño (ch'uño) Freeze-dried potato; dried by alternating nocturnal frost and diurnal sun; preserves for several years.

cis-Andean "On this side" of the Andes; in this volume, the term is used from the point of view of the Pacific; thus, the western slopes of the Andes.

cochayuyo (qochayuyu) Quechua word for aquatic plants; in this volume the term designates edible seaweeds.

comuneros Joint-holders of lands, usually local **ayllu** members.

compadre Godfather, benefactor.

cordillera Mountain chain.

corregimiento A major administrative subdivision within the area under the jurisdiction of an **audiencia**.

costeños Indigenous coastal inhabitants.

cumbi (qompi) Fine, multicolor textile.

curaca (kuraka) Regional ethnic leader whose office is inherited. Spanish writers often describe him as the **cacique principal**. Within the idealized Inca decimal administration system, **kuracas** seem to refer to local leaders in charge of a decimal rank ranging from the **hunu** (10,000 tributaries) down to the *pisqa* **pachaka** (unit of 500 tributaries).

curacazgo (kurakazgo) Polity controlled by a **curaca (kuraka)**.

curandero Curer; medicine man.

cuy Guinea pig.

ecotone Conspicuous environmental change.

encomienda Grant giving the labor of specific Indian communities to a Spaniard in return for protection and Christian religious instruction. Spaniards who received the grant are known as *encomenderos* and had the right only to levy labor tribute and no property rights over the land of the Indians under their authority. Unlike the Inca, *encomenderos* usually did not provide food for Indian workers. Abuse of this system was quite common.

etnía (etnia) Ethnic group.

faenas Obligatory work projects.

fanega Grain measure, equivalent to about 1.5 bushels.

fiesta Festivity, feast, festival.

forasteros Outlanders; Indians who work and/or reside in areas distant from their home, often severing their social ties with their **ayllus** to escape the **mit'a** and other Colonial taxations.

garúa Dense winter fog of the Pacific coast (see also **loma**).

guaranga (huaranga, waranqa) Unit of 1000 tributaries in the idealized Inca decimal administration system.

hacienda Landed property, estate, plantation.

huaca (wak'a) Idol or place of worship; a sacred object.

hunu Unit of 10,000 tributaries within the idealized Inca decimal administrative system.

indios de visitación Tribute payers.

jalca (jalka) See **suni**.

likina "Valley lands" in Aymara (typically 2000 to 3500 m elevation).

llaqtaruna Also known as *chacareru*; agriculturalists.

loma Strictly speaking, the term designates coastal vegetation dominated by *Tilandsia* and other xerophytic plants supported by the moisture that condenses from the dense winter fog **(garúa)**. In this volume, a distinction between "herbaceous and shrubby" or "chaparral" type **loma** and *Tilandsia* type **loma** is made.

maizal Maize field.

mandón Indigenous official, local boss, or overseer of a small group of Indians.

mercaderes Traders; in this volume the appropriateness of this Spanish term is debated.

mindaláes Long-distance traders of late prehispanic Ecuador who received the subsidy and protection of a political leader in return for privileged access to exotic prestige items.

mit'a Rotational, periodic labor service levied upon able-bodied individuals by the Inca state for the army, maintenance or building of roads and temples, or other ends. The Spanish colonial program of forced labor called **mita** was assessed in the same way as the Inca **mit'a**. (see **repartimiento**).

mitayos Men engaged in **mit'a**.

mitimas Men not residing in their place of ethnic origin; most commonly the term refers to those who were loyal and transplanted to a new location by the Inca state for military, economic, and/or political ends. In respect to the late prehistoric polities in the South-Central Andes, the term refers to colonists sent by these polities to grow crops, such as maize, at lower elevations.

mitmaq Institution of state-directed population transplantation.

montaña Although literally meaning "mountain," the term designates the sparsely occupied eastern slopes of the Andes.

mullu Large seashell, such as the spiny oyster, called *Spondylus*.

nevados Snow-capped mountains.

pachacas (pachakas) Unit of 100 tributaries in the Inca decimal system.

padrón A list of tributaries.

páramo Upper reaches of the North and North-Central Andean highlands characterized by tall grassland. **Páramo** differs from the **puna** in that the grasses of the former are more luxurious because of greater rainfall and lower elevation of the Andean range.

parcialidad Literally, a part of a whole; a Spanish term describing an indigenous sociopolitical unit typically organized along an economic activity (e.g., agriculturalists, fishermen) that formed a part (usually moiety) of a larger sociopolitical unit.

pisos ecológicos Ecological tiers.

principal Local indigenous leader. Some authors make a distinction between **cacique principal** and **principal**. In such cases, the former refers to the paramount regional leader.

pueblo Settlement; village or town.

puna High altitude (typically ca. 4000–4800 m above sea level) tundra-like short-grassland which suffers from frequent frosts.

punaruna Also known as *uywamichic*; herders (usually of llamas and alpacas) of the **puna**.

qocha Regularly laid out (concentric or linear) ridged-agricultural fields found in the **altiplano** (over 3850 m above sea level). **Qocha** cultivation is based on rainfall.

quebrada Ravine or side valley.

quechua (quichua, qeshwa, kichwa) "Land of temperate climate"; folk-recognized environmental zone typically ca. 2300–3500 m above sea level. The term is now used to designate a language widespread in the Central Andes and its speakers.

quintal Quintal; 100 pounds.

quinua A high protein content Andean grain grown at high altitude. Its small white seeds are cooked like lentils.

quipu (khipu) Sophisticated recording device based on decimal and hierarchical organization of information encoded in the patterned distribution of knots on strings.

rancho Hamlet, small cluster of buildings, ranch site, or station.

real Spanish colonial monetary unit; if used as an adjective, it means "royal."

reducción Re-settlement of indigenous populations in a few nucleated villages; used to designate both the polity and the towns themselves.

repartimiento Literally "allotment" or "distribution"; coercive, official allotment of Indian laborers among jobs and Spanish employers. In the Central Andes, labor **repartimiento** was known as **mit'a**. In labor **repartimiento**, a Spanish employer (rancher, farmer, miner, etc.) in need of laborers, upon approval of the local colonial political authority, was entitled to receive a given number of Indian workers for a designated period and for particular tasks. Indians were apportioned from a labor pool consisting of a certain portion of the able-bodied males of each community. The workers were liable to this labor draft in rotation. This system was often abused.

revisita Re-inspection tour (see **visita**).

salares Natural shallow depressions or basins in arid regions characterized by saline deposits formed by evaporation.

sayas Moieties; dual divisions.

segunda persona Lieutenant or second in command of an indigenous polity.

señorío Ethnic polity.

serranos Indigenous highland inhabitants.

sierra Highlands.

sinchi "Strong man"; chief.

suni "High" places, typically about 3500 to 4000 m above sea level (e.g., around Lake Titicaca). In the northern Peruvian highlands, this zone is known as **jalca** or **jalka**.

Tahuantinsuyu (Tawantinsuyu) "Land of the Four Quarters"; the Inca name for its empire.

tambo (tampu) Resting place or "inn" found along Inca roads maintained by the local population under Inca supervision.

tasa Colonial tribute.

taypi Aymara word for intermediary position or center line (see also **chaupi**).

topos (tupos) Amount of land needed by a household to subsist relative to the productivity of the land and capacity of the cultivators who had the rights of usufruct.

valle Valley; often referring to an area traversed by a major waterway (a natural "river" or large canal).

visita Administrative survey utilized by the Spanish royal government for conducting inquiries into the operation of colonial affairs. Inspectors were sent to gather information about the political, judicial, economic, and demographic status of a region. Inquiries were based on detailed questionnaires supplemented by direct observations. The **visitas** circumvented the slow, tedious procedures of organized government in securing necessary information and implementing corrective measures.

wanu Bird droppings from the coast and offshore islands used as agricultural fertilizer to supply needed nitrogen and phosphorus. The word *guano* is an hispanization of the Quechua word **wanu**.

yanaconas Select men who were personal retainers to Inca officials and **kurakas**, performing a wide range of "honorable" services, including highly responsible political as well as mundane domestic duties. During the Spanish colonial era, the institution of **yanacona** became a euphemism for something akin to long-term servitude.

yunga Warm lowlands or valley land with typical elevation of about 500 to 2300 m. This zone is characterized by year-round warmth and sunlight.

Index